Issues In Canadian Economics

edited by

Lawrence H. Officer
Michigan State University

and

Lawrence B. Smith
University of Toronto

McGraw-Hill Ryerson Limited

Toronto   Montreal   New York   London   Sydney
Johannesburg   Mexico   Panama   Düsseldorf
Singapore   São Paulo   Kuala Lumpur   New Delhi

Issues in Canadian Economics

ISBN 0-07-077447-1 (Soft cover)

ISBN 0-07-077448-X (Hard cover)

Library of Congress Catalog Number 73-21373

1234567890 AP-74 3210987654

Printed and bound in Canada.

Table of Contents

Introduction

Economic issues have become increasingly important in our daily lives as technology becomes ever more complex and all aspects of our lives more interdependent. One can scarcely skim the front pages of our daily press without encountering some important economic issue — workers go on strike, unemployment increases, prices rise, taxes go up, fears of an energy shortage mount, pollution worsens, foreign ownership threatens Canadian independence, and so on. In an attempt to provide a better understanding of the Canadian economy, how it functions and what its major problems are, we invited leading Canadian economists to express their views in their areas of expertise. They provided us with 29 original articles that cover in an easily understandable way the historical and theoretical issues of their fields of specialization, the recent Canadian experience, and proposals for better government policy.

These essays indicate a number of recurring themes. Perhaps the most dominant one is that the Canadian economy is no longer a "free-enterprise economy" in the sense that economic issues are resolved by the free interplay of producers and consumers. Rather, government intervention has become pervasive in all facets of Canadian economic life — ranging from the establishment of the Canada Development Corporation to provide capital for new Canadian industry and to "buy back" foreign-owned industry, to direct assistance to house-buyers and apartment-renters through subsidized mortgages and other techniques; from the establishment of immigration regulations and adult-retraining programs, to the operation of medical-insurance programs; from the regulation of transportation, communication, and other public-utility rates, to the provision of tax incentives to encourage the location and expansion of industry in designated areas; from an influence over interest rates, to the redistribution of income. The complexity of modern society has made government involvement inevitable. The question is no longer should there be government intervention, but rather "how much", "in what form", and "how can it be made more efficient and responsive to the wishes of the public."

A substantial number of the essays in this volume indicate, unfortunately, that government intervention, while potentially desirable, has often been a retarding or disruptive influence on the Canadian economy. Too many government policies have been short-sighted, politically rather than economically motivated, and introduced as expedients to cope with an immediate problem rather than providing a solution over the long term. For example, with an upcoming election the government may try to cope with inflation by instituting price controls, at the cost of potential shortages and rationing of commodities at a future date.

Good policy performance requires an understanding not only of the workings of individual sectors in the economy but also of how the over-all economy operates and how the individual sectors interrelate. Thus, for

v

example, government regulation of agricultural exports not only directly affects the farmer, but also the processors of the farmer's product, the suppliers of farm machinery and implements, the Canadian consumer (by influencing retail food prices), and ultimately all Canadian industry and consumption (by affecting the exchange rate and hence the prices of Canadian goods abroad and foreign goods in Canada). Another example is the use of government subsidies to hold down railway rates. This policy ultimately means higher taxes or a larger government budgetary deficit, the latter leading to more inflation. It also means income redistributed in favour of the individuals using railways or predominantly consuming goods shipped by rail, and away from individuals using other modes of transportation or consuming goods shipped by other means.

A prerequisite for better policy performance is enhanced economic knowledge, both on the part of government officials and on the part of the public. This volume of contributed essays is presented in the hope that it will lead to greater public understanding of economic issues and improved government policy performance.

I. Stabilization Policy

1. Trade-Offs in Stabilization Policy

Lawrence H. Officer
Michigan State University

and

Lawrence B. Smith
University of Toronto

During the last three decades, governments have become increasingly aware of the need for their intervention to stabilize the economy from excesses of both unemployment and inflation. Indeed, today governments assume as one of their major responsibilities the maintenance of a smoothly running economy which neither operates considerably below its output potential, as this would inflict large-scale unemployment on the working force, nor involves excessive inflation, as this would erode the purchasing power of the population's income and savings. The government seeks to guide the economy in reaching and maintaining full employment, a reasonable level of price stability, and a sustainable rate of economic growth. Unfortunately, the simultaneous attainment of these objectives is difficult if not impossible, and the policy-maker is forced to make a variety of compromises and trade-offs. To try to reach its objectives, the government can use monetary, fiscal, and exchange-rate policies, which are the basic instruments (or tools) of stabilization policy.

This paper describes the objectives and compromises available to the Canadian policy-maker, and illustrates the operation of stabilization policy by examining the recent Canadian stabilization experience.

I. Objectives of Macro-Economic Policy

A general consensus seems to exist that the primary objectives of Canadian macro-economic policy should be to promote (1) a high and stable level of employment ("full employment"), (2) a reasonably stable or slowly rising level of prices ("price stability"), (3) a high rate of economic growth, and (4) a sound balance-of-payments position ("external balance").[1] However, conflicts and interrelationships exist between these objectives, which impede the simultaneous pursuit of these policy goals. Because of these conflicts, the emphasis placed on the pursuit of an individual objective varies with the existing economic climate and the shifting political philosophy of society. In periods of high unemployment and moderate inflation, the price-stability objective often gives way to employment considerations; while in periods of low unemployment and rapid inflation, the price-stability objective tends to dominate. In periods in which international financial relations are troublesome, international priorities often dominate domestic considerations; while in periods of international calm, domestic considerations usually hold sway. In this section we discuss the rationale for individual policy objectives, and in the next we consider the interrelationships and conflicts among them.

• *Full employment:* the goal of full employment is supported for a variety of reasons. First, unemployment implies a loss of real output. This means that the amount of goods and services available for consumption, investment, government expenditure, and exports will be less than otherwise and that the nation's standard of living will be lower both in the present and, because of reduced investment, in the future. Second, on a humanitarian basis, higher employment levels remove the material and psychological distress that unemployment often brings to the individual or household affected. From the standpoint of policy-makers who are also politicans and desire a satisfied electorate, these personal considerations may weigh even more heavily than the opportunity loss of output. Third, the full-employment objective does not mean literally zero unemployment, i.e., that everyone of working age should be employed. It implies only that all employable persons seeking work are able to find employment within a reasonable period of time.

• *Price stability:* unlike the objective of full employment, which is universally supported, the objective of price stability is sometimes questioned by those who argue that the cost of inflation is minimal. After all, they claim, in the case of a moderate inflation where prices rise by, say, 3 or 4 percent a year (called "creeping inflation"), the effects are predominantly *distributional* in nature. Families living off relatively fixed incomes — such as pensioners, those living on investment income, and salaried workers — find a steady deterioration in their standard of living as price increases outpace income increases. On the other hand, families of wage-earners generally experience a gain, as their wage-rate increases exceed the price rise.[2] Moreover, to some extent the hardships from this type of inflation are often exaggerated, as people experience what may be called "price illusion." As consumers, we recognize the higher costs of our expen-

[1] In addition, such secondary objectives as an equitable income distribution between regions and economic classes, a decent home for every Canadian, satisfactory access to medical facilities for all Canadians, reduced foreign investment in Canada, and maintenance of the environment have been advanced as further goals of macro-economic policy. These issues are discussed elsewhere in the volume.

[2] For a careful study of the distributional effects of inflation on various economic groups in Canada, see R. Blauer, "Fixed Income and Asset Groups in Canada," in N. Swan and D. Wilton, eds., *Inflation and the Canadian Experience: Proceedings of a Conference* (Kingston, Ontario: Industrial Relations Centre, Queen's University, 1971), pp. 127–148.

ditures without realizing that some of these costs have been compensated for by our rising money incomes.

However, uncompensated redistributional effects often incur more than minimal costs for society. This is clearly seen in the redistribution of income from low-income pensioners to middle- or upper-middle-income wage earners. It may also occur as inflation redistributes income away from the private sector in favour of the public sector (government), as a result of the progressive income tax causing taxpayers to pay a higher proportion of their income in tax.[3] In this case, inflation redistributes income in favour of those using a high degree of public goods and services and away from those using a high degree of private goods and services.[4]

Moreover, the effects even of a moderate inflation are more than just distributional. Because inflation does not proceed uniformly through all sectors of the economy, inflation causes a redistribution of investment capital toward those sectors most likely to experience inflation. This leads to a less efficient allocation of resources if the higher inflation in these sectors arises from non-competitive factors such as inappropriate land zoning or increased monopolization. If marginal productivity in the government sector is less than in the private sector, the income redistribution away from the private in favour of the government sector similarly reduces over-all productivity in the economy.

Another important disadvantage of a moderate inflation is the possibility that it will generate unemployment. If a substantial proportion of an industry's cost increases is thought to be reversible, as might be the case with costs arising from bottlenecks in production or distribution, from less-efficient additional staff or higher wage rates for overtime work, or from high interest rates which are expected to decline, then investment expenditures may be postponed until these reductions occur.[5] Even if base wage rates are expected to increase in the future, the reversible cost reductions could considerably outweigh these wage increases, justifying a postponement of expenditures. This possibility increases if past investment was undertaken in anticipation of future cost increases, since some excess capacity is also likely to exist in this situation.

Finally, the possibility must be raised that a moderate inflation might degenerate into a run-away inflation (called "hyperinflation") if the public expects ever-accelerating inflation and therefore seeks to exchange money for goods at any price. This action fosters even greater inflation, as previ-

---

[3] Evidence of this redistribution is seen from the fact that federal government revenue declined from 16.9 percent of gross national product (GNP) in 1957 to 15.9 percent in 1963, when the average annual rate of increase in the implicit price index (that which converts current-dollar GNP to inflation-free or constant-dollar GNP) was only 1.3 percent; while federal government revenue rose from 16.1 percent of GNP in 1966 to 18.7 percent in 1972, when the average annual rate of increase in the implicit price index was 4.0 percent.

[4] The tying of personal income-tax exemptions, graduated income-tax brackets, and old-age pensions to the rate of inflation somewhat reduces this redistribution, but does not eliminate it.

[5] This employment effect arises if the future rate of inflation cannot be perfectly anticipated and hence is not completely built into interest-rate and wage structures and compensated for in expenditure patterns. If, on the other hand, the future rate of inflation can be perfectly anticipated, it will be reflected in the interest rate, in wage settlements, and in expenditure patterns —and this type of unemployment need not occur; nor would an expected *higher* rate of inflation generate short-run *gains* in output and employment. For an elaboration of this point, see the paper by Thomas J. Courchene in this volume.

ous expectations are reinforced; and, unless checked, the process can culminate in a destruction of the domestic payments system and the production and distribution networks. In effect, the economy could be destroyed.[6]

• *Economic growth:* a high rate of economic growth, defined as the growth in *per capita real* output (i.e., gross national product [GNP] corrected for price changes and divided by population) is held by many observers to be a major goal of policy, since this means an increased amount of goods and services available for society and an improvement in the standard of living of the population. A high growth rate also facilitates the attainment of a variety of other policy goals in the housing, medical-service, foreign-ownership, income-distribution, and environmental areas. Although some occasionally oppose economic growth on the grounds of environmental damage,[7] their opposition is often more semantic than real. If an appropriate price were placed on environmental damage so that real output were measured *net of environmental damage,* the views could be reconciled. The only serious debate would be the price to place on environmental damage and depletion of scarce resources relative to other goods and services, since virtually everyone would favour an increase in this revised measure of output.

• *External balance:* the external-balance objective is interwoven with the exchange-rate system of the country. Under a pegged (fixed) exchange rate (the Canadian situation from 1962 to 1970), the balance of payments, which summarizes a country's transactions with the rest of the world, indicates its external position. A balance-of-payments deficit means that the country spent more foreign exchange (on imports of goods and services, gifts and aid to foreigners, and financial investments abroad) than it received (from exports of goods and services, gifts and aid received, and foreign financial investments in the country). If accompanied by a deficit in goods and services (imports exceeding exports), this implies lower domestic output and employment than would be the case if this account were in a balanced or surplus position; for while exports involve spending on the country's own production, imports represent spending on foreign rather than domestic output. A balance-of-payments deficit also involves an outflow of currency from the domestic banking system, i.e., a reduction in the money supply — another deflationary force on the economy. Finally, it means that the country is losing foreign-exchange reserves (predominantly gold and U.S. dollars), which might be needed to finance any future deficits in the balance of payments. Because a country must maintain some minimum level of reserves for emergency expenditures (for example, to purchase food from abroad in the event of a major domestic crop failure), a persistent deficit cannot be allowed to continue; hence a country must be concerned with a deficit in its balance of payments.

On the other hand, a balance-of-payments surplus also has its costs.

---

[6] Typically, such disastrous consequences cannot occur unless the government helps the process along by an irresponsible monetary policy, expanding the money supply at ever-increasing rates. The classic example would be Germany after World War I.

[7] See, for example, D.H. Meadows *et al., The Limits to Growth* (New York: Universe Books, 1972).

First, a balance-of-payments surplus is usually inflationary, as it implies an increase in the money supply *via* an inflow of currency into the banking system from abroad. Moreover, if accompanied by a surplus in goods and services (exports exceeding imports), the demand for domestic production is higher than it would be otherwise. Second, a balance-of-payments surplus means that a country is giving up command over goods and services today in order to have a claim against output in the rest of the world in the future. Beyond some point, the cost of losing current output will exceed the benefit to be gained from command over future output. Third, if the surplus arises from direct foreign investment into the country (the Canadian case in the 1960s), then in exchange for accumulating future purchasing power (additional foreign-exchange reserves), the country is giving up command of its industries and resources, since by definition such investment involves foreign control of domestic industry. In this situation the direct-investment inflow could be eliminated with no immediate cost to the economy by terminating the balance-of-payments surplus. Therefore, under a fixed exchange-rate regime, both deficits and surpluses can be undesirable, and it is generally appropriate to seek equilibrium in the balance of payments.

If a country has a floating (also called fluctuating or flexible) exchange rate (the Canadian case in 1950–61 and from 1970 onward), the movement of the exchange rate becomes the indicator of the external-balance situation, as the balance of payments is always in equilibrium (neither a deficit nor a surplus). A depreciating exchange rate (fall in the exchange value of the country's currency) indicates that the country is seeking more foreign exchange (for imports of goods and services, gifts and aid to foreigners, and financial investments abroad) than the rest of the world wishes to supply (from spending on the country's goods and services, on gifts and aid to the country, and on financial investment in the country), while an appreciating exchange rate (increase in the value of the currency) implies the opposite.

Depreciation increases the domestic-currency price of the country's imports of goods and services and decreases the foreign-currency price of its exports. This improvement in the competitive position of the country's industry increases its exports and decreases its imports of goods and services, thus expanding its output and employment. However, the increased import costs together with the enhanced demand for the country's production accentuate any inflationary tendencies in the country. Correspondingly, while an appreciating exchange rate decreases output and employment by worsening the country's international competitiveness, it combats inflation by reducing the domestic price of imports and reducing the demand for the country's output. This discussion suggests that an appreciating or depreciating exchange rate may be more appropriate than a stable exchange rate, *providing* the variation in the exchange rate is in the appropriate direction. If it were to go in the inappropriate direction, the costs associated with the variation would be considerable.

II. Trade-Offs of Policy Objectives

1. Inflation–unemployment trade-off

Unemployment and inflation are not mutually exclusive. Unemployment and inflation typically exist simultaneously in Canada (as in other economies). Moreover, there is a tendency for higher rates of inflation to be associated with lower rates of unemployment, giving rise to the concept of a trade-off between the objectives of full employment and price stability.[8] However, even in the absence of an unemployment–inflation trade-off, positive rates of unemployment and inflation are likely to exist because of the structure and institutional framework of our society.

• *Positive rate of inflation:* on the inflation side, quality changes in products are constantly occurring for which adjustments in official price indices are not made, or are made only with a lag, and this gives an upward bias to our measures of inflation. Apart from this "apparent" inflation, true price increases are built into the economy as labour leaders continually seek wage increases in excess of the expected rate of inflation, to increase the real return for their members and to retain their leadership position. Since these increases are likely to be in excess of productivity increases, at least in some sectors, unit labour costs (the ratio of the wage rate to a unit of output) will rise and higher prices will follow. *Via* the demonstration effect, unions in slow-growth productivity sectors will seek wage increases equal to those received by workers in sectors with faster productivity gains, causing non-inflationary wage settlements in one sector to be inflationary in the slow-growth sector. Moreover, since contracts are negotiated for lengthy periods, often two to three years, provision for future wage increases is made in one period to become effective in another. This causes inflationary pressures to persist considerably into the future even in the face of falling demand. These contracts also typically provide for "escalator clauses" in which increases in the cost of living are automatically translated into higher wages, thereby maintaining the upward pressure on prices.[9]

Furthermore, with the high concentration of market power in the hands of large corporations and unions, wage settlements made with one company are likely to set the pattern throughout the industry. This means that all firms in the industry will face the same cost increases and thus need not fear a decline in their share of the domestic market by granting wage increases. If there is a relatively inelastic demand for the domesti-

[8] This trade-off is sometimes called the "Phillips curve," after the economist who is generally credited with the first statistical estimation of the relationship between the rate of inflation and the unemployment rate. See A.W. Phillips, "The Relation Between Unemployment and the Rate of Change of Money Wage Rates in the United Kingdom, 1861–1957," *Economica*, New Series, XXV, No. 100 (November 1958), pp. 283–299. However, some fourteen years after Phillips' article appeared, it was discovered that Irving Fisher had performed a study along similar lines that was first published in 1926. See Irving Fisher, "A Statistical Relation Between Unemployment and Price Changes," *Journal of Political Economy*, Vol. 81, No. 2, Part I (March/April 1973), pp. 496–502.
[9] For an elaboration of this view and a somewhat different explanation of the persistence of inflation in Canada, see Prices and Incomes Commission, *Summary Report: Inflation, Unemployment and Incomes Policy* (Ottawa: Information Canada, 1972), pp. 13–22.

cally produced product (fostered by the oligopolistic industry structure and reinforced by tariff protection — phenomena applicable to many Canadian manufacturing industries), firms will have little reason to risk the possibility of labour unrest and a prolonged strike with resultant loss of profits. Hence they will accept wage settlements higher than they would in a more competitive environment, knowing they can pass the higher wage rates on to the consumer in the form of higher prices. The concentration of market power is thus responsible for a persistent positive rate of inflation regardless of the unemployment rate, and an increase in the concentration of market power would be responsible for an increase in the rate of inflation.

Another explanation for a positive rate of inflation independent of the amount of unemployment focuses upon sectoral differences in demand and downward rigidity in wage rates. If demand increases in some sectors while correspondingly decreasing in other sectors, total demand and hence employment may remain unchanged while prices rise. The increased demand in the former sectors can be expected to generate price inflation, while the reduced demand in the latter sectors, in the face of downward rigidity in wages, will likely leave prices unaffected. Consequently, such shifting of demand can generate a positive rate of inflation without affecting the level of aggregate employment. A variant of this which is prevalent in an "open" economy, i.e., one greatly dependent on international trade (the Canadian situation), occurs when the price of imports increases. To the extent that imported goods are used as inputs in production, costs will rise and inflation will develop, independent of the unemployment rate. If these imports are consumer goods, then the cost of living will rise automatically, and in addition foster inflation *via* escalator clauses and enhanced union demands for higher wages to offset the increased cost of living. Similarly, if there is an increase in the demand for Canadian exports (say, agricultural products), this could trigger a wage–price spiral because of the consequent reduced supply and increased price of these goods in Canada.

• *Positive rate of unemployment:* a positive rate of unemployment will exist regardless of the rate of inflation, because literal full employment in which the entire labour force is employed is virtually impossible. In a free and evolving society, the matching of job vacancies and available workers happens neither instantaneously nor precisely, but involves numerous delays and imperfections. Unless the economy has large numbers of vacancies in all occupational classifications and geographic locations, unemployment will arise as people search for new jobs. With many people eligible for unemployment insurance while seeking new jobs, there is a reduced disincentive to leave a job and a significant persistent level of unemployment seems inevitable.[10] The unemployment arising from job-search frictions is further aggravated in Canada by seasonal factors which reduce activity in a variety of sectors, such as agriculture, fishing, and construction, during the winter. Unemployment will also exist because the labour force includes young people looking for their first job, immigrants seeking their initial employment in Canada, and many workers whose

[10] Statistics indicate that approximately 6 percent of all existing jobs are turned over each month. See Prices and Incomes Commission, *op. cit.*, p. 26.

labour-force participation is weak or variable and who are seeking only part-time or temporary work. Finally, in economies experiencing rapid technological change, "structural unemployment" often develops as people, though willing to work, lack the necessary training and ability required for modern industry. Consequently, significant positive rates of unemployment will exist regardless of the state of inflation.

• *Short-run trade-off:* although positive rates of unemployment and inflation are likely to co-exist at all times, there are reasons to believe that in the short run higher rates of inflation will be associated with lower rates of unemployment. As the economy moves toward full employment, demand for the economy's output increases relative to supply and upward pressure is exerted on prices. At the same time the cost of production increases, exerting further inflationary pressure. Cost increases arise from the bidding up of factor prices as producers compete for factors of production, from the hiring of additional employees at a given salary or wage who are less efficient than their previously hired and trained counterparts, from the payment of higher wages for overtime, from higher interest rates as the demand for funds increases, and from bottlenecks that arise in production and distribution as the full capacity of the economy is approached.

An interesting dynamic element reinforces this relationship in the short run. As increasing economic activity accelerates the rate of inflation, expectations of future high or accelerating rates of inflation are developed, and this often leads to the moving forward of investment and spending plans, temporarily increasing demand and employment as people strive to beat the future price increases.[11] To some extent this process is self-limiting, because it satisfies some future consumption demands in the present and because it generates excess capacity as investment takes place before it is actually required. Nevertheless, in the short run, these expectations generate further inflation by increasing aggregate demand and causing lower levels of unemployment to be associated with higher rates of inflation.

• *Long-run trade-off:* in the long run the trade-off between inflation and unemployment is likely to be less pronounced. First, to the extent that inflationary expectations shift forward future demand, this demand will be satisfied and will dissipate, leading to a higher level of unemployment with the high rate of inflation. Second, to the extent that inflationary expectations become incorporated into wage settlements, so that wage contracts approximate the expected future rate of inflation plus expected productivity increases, higher current rates of inflation will generate expectations of higher future rates of inflation and hence higher wage settlements. These settlements will have the effect of bringing about the very inflation that was anticipated, and this process is largely independent of the level of unemployment.[12] Thus, over time, the trade-off between

---

[11] For a statement on the role of expectations in inflation, see L. Rasminsky, "Interest Rates and Inflation," a statement before the House of Commons Standing Committee on Finance, Trade and Economic Affairs, July 3, 1969. At the time Mr. Rasminsky was Governor of the Bank of Canada.

[12] For a summary of this position, see David Laidler, "The Phillips Curve, Expectations and Incomes Policy," in H.G. Johnson and A.R. Nobay, eds., *The Current Inflation* (London: Macmillan, 1971), pp. 75–98.

unemployment and inflation is not so clear, since a given rate of unemployment can co-exist with a multitude of rates of inflation. This discussion suggests that the short-run (SR) and long-run (LR) trade-offs[13] would compare as shown in Figure 1.

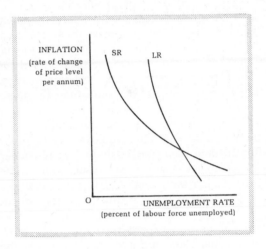

Figure 1

2. Stabilization—growth trade-off

Along with the stabilization of employment and the rate of inflation, economic growth is an objective of macro-economic policy. Unemployment involves income forgone and thereby an opportunity loss as well in savings, and investment, thus retarding the growth in the productive capacity of the economy. In this respect, low unemployment and rapid growth are complementary, and there is no trade-off between the goals of full employment and economic growth.

The relationship between inflation and growth is controversial. Some distinguished economists have argued that there is a trade-off between price stability and economic growth. Their position is that moderate inflation is conducive to growth, indeed, that it is inherent in the growth process.[14] For example, innovators desiring to apply improved techniques in the production process must bid up the prices of labour and capital in order to attract these factors of production. Analogously, increased govern-

---

[13] For further theoretical discussion of the inflation—unemployment trade-off, see S.F. Kaliski, "Is the Phillips Curve Still With Us?" in Swan and Wilton, op. cit., pp. 9–18, and the references cited therein. For investigations of the trade-off in the Canadian case, see Ronald G. Bodkin et al., Price Stability and High Employment: The Options for Canadian Economic Policy, an Econometric Study, Economic Council of Canada (Ottawa: Queen's Printer, 1967) and S.F. Kaliski, The Trade-Off between Inflation and Unemployment: Some Explorations of the Recent Evidence for Canada, Economic Council of Canada (Ottawa: Information Canada, 1972).

[14] See Joseph A. Schumpeter, Business Cycles (New York: McGraw-Hill Book Company, 1939) and Sumner H. Slichter, "Thinking Ahead on the Side of Inflation," Harvard Business Review (September–October 1957), pp. 15–22.

ment spending, especially on investment goods, generally contributes to an increase in productive capacity and is often facilitated by a monetary expansion which can be inflationary. However, most economists see inflation and growth as competitive°rather than complementary, (1) because of the danger that creeping inflation might develop into hyperinflation, (2) because inflation may cause a postponement of investment projects when a large portion of the higher costs are considered to be reversible (i.e., when it is thought that these costs may come down in the future), and (3) because in an open economy with a fixed exchange rate, domestic inflation greater than that abroad may destroy or seriously handicap the country's competitive position. If one accepts these arguments, then the objectives of price stability and economic growth are compatible and there is no trade-off between them.

Consequently, there is a strong likelihood that anything which promotes general economic stability (high employment and low inflation) will also foster economic growth. Furthermore, the policies designed primarily to foster economic growth usually would be not demand oriented (as is stabilization policy), but rather supply oriented (such as developing educational and training institutions, improving transportation and communications facilities, etc.). It follows that stabilization policy as such need not be aimed directly at the goal of economic growth. However, the *allocation* (as distinct from the over-all levels) of government expenditures and taxation should pay attention to this objective.

3. Stabilization–external-balance trade-off[15]

The relationship between external balance and unemployment and price movements is clear. As a country moves along its unemployment–inflation trade-off curve to points of lower unemployment and higher inflation (a movement from right to left along the SR curve in Figure 1), its imports of goods and services increase and its exports decrease. The reason is two-fold. First, the greater the rate of inflation in a country relative to that in the rest of the world, the less competitive are its domestically produced goods, both at home and abroad. Second, the higher income associated with lower unemployment involves an increase in the demand for goods and services, which both increases the amount of imports and decreases the amount of domestically produced output available for export.

Now, with a *fixed* exchange rate, the balance of payments would

[15] This trade-off is particularly important for Canada because of the openness of the Canadian economy in general and its relationship with the United States in particular. In the 1960s, for example, Canada imported goods and services amounting to approximately 25 percent of its GNP, with almost 70 percent of these imports coming from the United States. During this period Canada exported approximately 23 percent of its GNP, with 60 percent of these exports going to the United States. In contrast, the United States (a relatively closed economy) has exports and imports each equaling about 5 percent of GNP.

In addition to the openness in product markets, Canadian capital markets are closely integrated with world markets. Between 1962 and 1969, for example, more than 40 percent of all net new security issues by Canadian entities (excluding Canada Savings Bonds) were payable in foreign currency, with 85 percent of these payable in U.S. funds.

deteriorate under these circumstances: there would be an increased deficit or reduced surplus due to the reduced exports and increased imports. This implies an enhanced supply of goods and services available to the domestic economy, and thus a moderation in the rate of inflation. However, the decreased exports and increased imports also involve a reduction in output and employment.[16] Therefore the balance-of-payments "leakage" moderates the movement along the unemployment–inflation trade-off, and this holds true for a movement in either direction.

What difference would a *floating* exchange rate make in this situation? This exchange-rate system always equilibrates the balance of payments, causing the incipient deficit to be eliminated *via* depreciation of the country's currency. Exports and imports would reverse their respective directions of movement, exports now rising and imports falling. Although the higher rate of inflation would not be moderated, neither would the output and employment increase be mitigated. Thus a floating exchange rate reduces the balance-of-payments leakage and permits the economy to move easily along its unemployment–inflation trade-off curve.

The above analysis implicitly assumes that the right-to-left movement along the trade-off curve is domestic in origin, i.e., that the increased output is due to stabilization policy stimulating the economy or perhaps to autonomous expansion in consumption and/or investment expenditure. In such situations, a floating exchange rate amplifies the impact of such domestic disturbances. With a floating rate, rising domestic inflation causes the exchange rate to depreciate, thereby reinforcing the inflation; while rising unemployment causes the exchange rate to appreciate (as imports are reduced), thereby accentuating the domestic unemployment. Thus movements along the trade-off curve due to domestic disturbances are enhanced with a floating exchange rate as compared with a fixed exchange rate. This has the very important implication that the impact of stabilization policy — whether this policy is appropriate or perverse — is greater under a floating than a fixed exchange rate.

Now suppose that there is a foreign rather than a domestic disturbance on the economy. For example, assume that the United States (Canada's major trading partner) were to experience a sharp expansion in economic activity and rising prices. Rising U.S. income and prices would increase the demand for Canadian exports, while the increased U.S. prices would lead to a reduction in Canadian imports. If Canada were on a *fixed* exchange rate, its balance of payments would improve (reduced deficit or enhanced surplus). While output and employment would increase, inflation in Canada would be exacerbated. Alternatively, under a *floating* exchange rate, the incipient balance-of-payments surplus would be eliminated by an appreciating Canadian dollar, which would reverse the respective directions of movement of exports and imports (exports now falling, imports rising). This effect would moderate the worsened Canadian inflation caused by external forces. Furthermore, the rising value of the Canadian dollar in terms of the U.S. dollar would offset the increased U.S.-dollar

---

[16] There is also a drain in foreign-exchange reserves, which could necessitate corrective government policies which would also moderate the inflation and increase unemployment.

price of goods imported from the United States, leaving Canadian prices relatively unaffected. On the other hand, the reversal in Canadian imports and exports would mean that employment and output gains would be inhibited.

Similarly, an economic contraction or depression in the United States would spread to Canada under a fixed exchange rate but have relatively little effect on Canadian output and employment under a floating rate. Thus a fixed exchange rate allows both economic expansion and economic depression in Canada's trading partners to be transmitted to Canada, while a floating exchange rate largely insulates Canada from both of these influences.

Movements along a country's unemployment–inflation trade-off curve initiated by *foreign* disturbances are thus facilitated by a fixed exchange rate and checked by a floating rate, while movements initiated by *domestic* disturbances are facilitated by a floating exchange rate and checked by a fixed rate.

III. Operation of Stabilization Policy

1. Stages in policy-making

Rational operation of stabilization policy involves a four-stage process. First, the policy-maker must list his "target variables," that is, those variables the values of which he will attempt to influence, and assign ideal values to them. While the generally recognized target variables of stabilization policy are the employment level, the rate of inflation, the balance of payments, and the rate of economic growth, we have argued that the growth variable may be omitted from this list. Under a floating exchange rate, the balance of payments also disappears as a target variable. The policy objectives or policy targets (ideal values of the target variables) thus reduce to full employment and price stability under a floating exchange-rate system, and to full employment, price stability, and balance-of-payments equilibrium (or perhaps a small surplus — to increase the country's holdings of foreign-exchange reserves) under a fixed-rate system.

The second stage in policy-making is to delineate the "feasibility frontier," that is, the set of attainable values of the target variables. With a floating exchange rate, the feasibility frontier is simply the unemployment–inflation trade-off curve. Under a fixed rate, the magnitude of the balance-of-payments deficit or surplus must be attached to each point on this curve. The policy-maker must endeavour to find out not only the shape of the curve (its slope at various points) but also its location, both of which can change over time.

The third step is to select the desired point on the feasibility frontier. In general, the ideal values of all target variables do not converge to a single point on the frontier. For example, full employment and price stability cannot be achieved together (indeed, neither goal can be achieved fully even alone), as the unemployment–inflation trade-off relationship does not pass through the origin (Figure 1). The policy-maker must weigh the relative costs of increased unemployment versus increased inflation, as discussed in section I, in determining the optimum feasible combination.

Under a fixed exchange rate, his choice is further constrained by the fact that continued reductions in unemployment carry with them a reduced balance-of-payments surplus and then an ever-increasing deficit.

The fourth step is to use the tools of stabilization policy to attain the selected values of the target variables. These policy tools are monetary policy, fiscal policy, and exchange-rate policy. If it has been decided to increase employment, an expansionary (or "easy") monetary and fiscal policy may be pursued — increasing the rate of increase in the money supply, reducing taxes, and increasing government expenditure. If the policy-maker desires to curb inflation, contractionary ("tight" or "restrictive") monetary and fiscal policies ("monetary and fiscal restraint") are in order — decreasing the rate of expansion in the money supply, increasing taxes, and reducing government expenditure. If the country is running a balance-of-payments deficit (possible only under a fixed exchange-rate system), it can eliminate the deficit either by tight monetary and fiscal policies or by currency depreciation (devaluation), that is, re-pegging the exchange rate at a lower value for the country's currency. Depreciation would also have the effect of expanding output and inflation; so the government might check this effect *via* contractionary monetary industrial-organization and international-trade policies.

Of course, sensible policy-making aims also at *improving* the feasibility frontier, for example, moving inward the unemployment–inflation trade-off relationship (SR in Figure 1). Some claim that wage and price controls would accomplish this objective. It is clear to us, however, that the resulting loss or mitigation of the price mechanism in resource allocation would actually worsen the trade-off (move the SR curve outward) if the controls were maintained for any length of time. Effective policies to improve the feasibility frontier are long-run in nature and operate by changing either expectations or the institutional structure of the economy. For example, expectations of reduced inflation — generated by a *believable* threat of restrictive policy because of a history of good stabilization-policy performance — would lead to a lower rate of inflation at any given rate of unemployment.

Techniques to improve the unemployment–inflation trade-off by changing the economic structure are generally not classified as stabilization policy. For example, better job-vacancy and unemployment information would reduce the average job-search time, and more job-retraining programs would reduce the amount of structural unemployment, thereby reducing the unemployment rate at any rate of inflation. Here the vehicle for improving the trade-off is manpower policy. Another policy would be

---

[17] For further discussion of the tools of stabilization policy with special reference to the Canadian institutional context, see Lawrence H. Officer and Lawrence B. Smith, "Stabilization Policy in the Postwar Period," in Officer and Smith, eds., *Canadian Economic Problems and Policies* (Toronto: McGraw-Hill Company of Canada, 1970), pp. 21–25.

the reduction or elimination of tariffs and other trade restrictions.[18] This action would provide additional import competition that would reduce the market power of monopolistic or oligopolistic firms and thus move the (SR) trade-off curve inward, as indicated in our discussion of the "positive rate of inflation" in section II. This would be an application of industrial-organization and international-trade policies.

2. Hazards in policy-making

Each step in the operation of stabilization policy carries with it hazards that can mar the over-all policy performance. In step 1, the policy-maker might omit a variable that is properly classified as a target of policy. In step 2, he might not perceive the true feasibility frontier, and thus select inconsistent values of the target variables. In step 3, the policy-maker might overestimate the costs of deviating from the ideal value of one target variable and underestimate the costs of deviating from the ideal value of another, and thus select an inappropriate — even if consistent — point on the feasibility frontier. Finally, in step 4, the use of policy tools might be inappropriate (in the wrong direction), insufficient (of low intensity, even though in the right direction), or inconsistent (one policy tool operated in an expansionary, another in a contractionary direction). These problems are heightened by the fact that in reality there is not merely one policy-maker but several. In Canada, the Prime Minister, the Minister of Finance, and the Governor of the Bank of Canada, together with their advisors, are all involved in stabilization-policy-making, and thus the danger of conflict in the selection of policy targets and lack of co-ordination in the application of policy tools is increased.

IV. Highlights of Canadian Stabilization Policy: 1958–1973

In order to appreciate the problems of stabilization policy, it is instructive to examine the operation of these policies in their actual setting. We will proceed to describe Canadian stabilization policy in the fifteen-year time period, 1958–73, by focusing upon six major episodes:

1. the recession of 1958–61,
2. the demise of the floating exchange rate in 1962,
3. the economic recovery of 1962–65,
4. the inflation of 1966–70,
5. the managed exchange rate of 1970–72, and
6. the continuing inflation in 1972–73.

Since these episodes are arranged in chronological order, they also

[18] An exception to this policy arises when distortions occur through actions originating in the economy of a major trading partner. For example, the introduction of price controls by a trading partner (such as the freeze on meat prices in the United States in 1973), which creates shortages in that economy, might necessitate the imposition of export controls (such as Canada's imposition of controls on meat exports in the summer of 1973) to prevent a major export drain leading to domestic shortages and severe price rises in Canada. In this situation, the imposition of restrictions on international trade is said to be justified on "second-best" grounds. A similar justification could be made for Canadian export restrictions on oil during the anti-U.S. Arab oil embargo that followed the 1973 Middle East War.

provide a continuous view of stabilization policy throughout this period.[19]

1. The recession of 1958–61

In the period 1958–61, the Canadian economy was in an unusually depressed state. Unemployment averaged 7 percent, or one out of every fourteen people seeking work, in 1958, 1960, and 1961, and growth in real GNP (inflation-free GNP) was virtually non-existent. In spite of this, the government and the Bank of Canada pursued restrictive debt-management and monetary policies which generated a sharp rise in interest rates and contributed substantially to the recession.

Debt management is a technique of fiscal policy that involves altering the term structure of the public debt (the amounts of bonds outstanding at various terms to maturity). Early in 1958 the federal government became concerned that the money it had borrowed during the Second World War through the issuance of "Victory Bonds" would soon have to be repaid. Since repayment of government debt is usually accomplished by the government borrowing new funds to pay off old loans, the concern was how to borrow sufficient funds to pay off these maturing bonds.[20] Rather than wait for these Victory Bonds to become payable, the government tried to induce bond-holders to convert their Victory Bonds into new, long-term securities. The government offered a variety of inducements, including a higher coupon interest rate and the acceptance at par of Victory Bonds selling at a substantial discount.

As a result of these efforts, this "Conversion Loan" was highly successful, as 90 percent of the eligible Victory Bonds were converted in the two-month period July 15 to September 15, 1958. However, the success of this conversion operation, which almost doubled the average maturity of the public holdings of government securities (from 8 to 15 years), had numerous undesirable effects for a period of high unemployment.

First, the substantial lengthening of the term to maturity of the government debt significantly reduced the liquidity of the public, thereby reducing their willingness to undertake major expenditures. Second, the high coupon rates and conversion of discounted bonds at par sharply increased interest rates during a period of high and rising unemployment. Third, the large increase in the money supply that accompanied the Conversion Loan, as the Bank of Canada tried to maintain bond prices and support the conversion operation, led the Bank to become preoccupied with the dangers of inflation and to introduce a very restrictive monetary policy, which further raised interest rates.[21]

---

[19] Canadian stabilization policy in the earlier postwar period, 1946–58, is surveyed in Officer and Smith, *op. cit.*, pp. 26–34. The basic sources of information on stabilization policy in Canada are the *Annual Reports* of the Bank of Canada, the *Budget Speeches* of the Minister of Finance, the *Annual Reviews* of the Economic Council of Canada, and the *Economic Review* of the Minister of Finance. Macroeconomic statistics are found in the *Bank of Canada Review* and Statistics Canada's *National Accounts, Income and Expenditure* and *The Canadian Balance of International Payments.*

[20] Victory Bonds outstanding at the end of 1958 accounted for 59 percent of all federal-government direct and guaranteed securities (excluding treasury bills).

[21] The impact of these policies can be seen from the fact that the yield spread between Government-of-Canada and U.S.-government long-term securities in 1959 was almost double that existing prior to the Conversion Loan.

Throughout 1959 and most of 1960, the monetary restraint was vigorously pursued. The Governor of the Bank continued to be preoccupied with the dangers of inflation, was concerned that imports exceeded exports of goods and services, and seemed unmindful of the high unemployment rate. Unfortunately, these priorities were quite wrong. Economic statistics at the time clearly showed that the danger to the economy was a severe recession, not inflation, while the floating exchange rate operating at the time guaranteed equilibrium in the *over-all* balance of payments (gifts and financial investment as well as goods and services). Moreover, the tight monetary policy had a perverse effect on imports and exports, as the high interest rates increased foreign financial investment in Canada, thus increasing the demand for Canadian dollars (to carry out this investment) and appreciating the exchange rate (increasing the value of the Canadian dollar), thereby reducing the competitiveness of Canadian industry, reducing exports and increasing imports.

Further compounding the economic problems of the country, the government did not pursue an active expansionary fiscal policy. Although the government ran actual deficits (expenditures exceeding tax revenues), they were passive in nature, reflecting the effect of the recession itself rather than any positive steps to combat it.[22] Thus at the beginning of the 1960s, Canada had a restrictive monetary policy and an inactive fiscal policy in the face of high unemployment and a depressed economy. A more inappropriate application of stabilization policy would be hard to find.

2.   The demise of the floating exchange rate in 1962

With the Canadian economy depressed relative to its trading partners in the late 1950s and early 1960s, one could not expect Canada's floating exchange rate autonomously to mitigate this recession. True, a depreciating exchange rate would have increased the competitiveness of Canadian industry, increasing exports, reducing imports, and thereby increasing GNP. But during a recession of domestic origin, the exchange rate tends to move in the opposite direction, appreciating, as discussed in section II. A depreciation in the exchange rate would have occurred only if Canada had vigorously pursued an expansionary stabilization policy. However, the Canadian policy-makers applied inappropriate stabilization policies, which far from causing the exchange rate to depreciate, made it tend to appreciate. The Bank of Canada's restrictive monetary policy kept the exchange value of the Canadian dollar at a high level by inducing financial investments into Canada. The high exchange rate, by inhibiting exports and enhancing the substitution of imports for domestically produced goods, worsened the Canadian recession.

The correct policy response would have been to stimulate the economy by shifting to expansionary monetary and fiscal policies. This action would

[22] See H. Scott Gordon, "A Twenty Year Perspective: Some Reflections on the Keynesian Revolution in Canada," in *Canadian Economic Policy since the War* (Montreal: Canadian Trade Committee of the Private Planning Association of Canada, 1966), pp. 40–41.

have increased output and employment both directly and indirectly (by currency depreciation). For example, an easier monetary policy would have reduced domestic interest rates and moderated foreign investment in Canada. This would have depreciated the exchange rate and increased output as a result of both the depreciation of the exchange rate and the stimulating domestic effects of lower interest rates.

Instead of pursuing an expansionary fiscal policy, the Minister of Finance attempted to lower the exchange rate by another route. In March 1960 he sought to discourage foreign investment in Canada initiated by Canadian borrowers by remarking that:

> . . . those who undertake commitments in terms of United States dollars or other external currencies expose themselves to the risk of having to repay at a time when the exchange rate for the Canadian dollar may be quite different from what it is today.[23]

In the face of continuing monetary restraint, this comment had little effect. The exchange value of the Canadian dollar fell only slightly; so on December 20, 1960 the government took substantial action. It attempted to discourage foreign investment in Canada by increasing taxes imposed on the earnings of these investments, i.e., on interest and dividends paid to non-residents. While these increased taxes on income transferred abroad had some retarding effect on the capital inflow, they did not bring about a pronounced reduction in the exchange value of the Canadian dollar. Therefore the government decided to intervene directly in the foreign-exchange market, and in June 1961 the Minister of Finance declared:

> No one can say today what the appropriate level of our exchange rate would be when our balance of payments is in a position better suited to our present economic circumstances. But the rate will certainly be lower than it has been of late . . . It will be government policy to facilitate such a movement. Accordingly the exchange fund will be prepared, as and when necessary, to add substantial amounts to its holdings of United States dollars through purchases in the exchange market.[24]

In effect, the Minister was announcing a switch in the floating exchange-rate system from a *freely* fluctuating rate or "clean float," in which the government permits the exchange rate to find its equilibrium level on the basis of private demand and supply of foreign exchange, to a *managed* fluctuating rate or "dirty float," in which the government would sell Canadian dollars for U.S. dollars, thus adding to the supply of Canadian dollars in the foreign-exchange market and reducing the exchange value of the Canadian dollar. Concurrently, monetary policy was co-ordinated with exchange-rate policy and loosened considerably, as indicated by a sharp decline in interest rates, and these steps set up an economic expansion.

---

[23] Minister of Finance, *Budget Speech,* March 31, 1960, p. 8.
[24] Minister of Finance, *Budget Speech,* June 20, 1961, pp. 12–13. The Exchange Fund is the account in which the government carries out its foreign-exchange operations (buying or selling Canadian dollars for U.S. dollars).

Initially, the desired result in the foreign-exchange market was obtained, as the value of the Canadian dollar fell by about 5 percent (from $1.00 Can. = $1.01 U.S. to $1.00 Can. = $.96 U.S.). Interestingly, although the government declared that it would manage the exchange value of the Canadian dollar downward to a new level and hold it there, the main reasons for this fall in the Canadian dollar were the Minister's announcement itself (the market anticipating the government's action — a so-called "announcement effect") and the decline in interest rates, rather than direct government intervention in the foreign-exchange market.

From July to October 1961, the government did intervene in the market, buying up U.S. dollars to hold down the value of the Canadian dollar. However, by October the new exchange-rate policy had so weakened confidence in the Canadian dollar that private participants in the foreign-exchange market feared that the exchange rate would fall still further and they sold Canadian for U.S. dollars, causing the exchange rate to fall even further than the government had desired. By February 1962, the government was actually *defending*, not suppressing, the exchange value of the Canadian dollar, as it now sold U.S. dollars for Canadian dollars, trying to stem the fall in the exchange rate. By April the private outflow of Canadian dollars reached flood proportions, causing the government's holdings of foreign-exchange reserves (gold and U.S. dollars) to decline so rapidly that continuance of the "dirty float" became impossible.

The government now had two principal alternatives. It could return to a "clean float" by withdrawing its support from the Canadian dollar and allowing the exchange rate to find its own level, or it could institute a fixed exchange rate by pegging the dollar at a somewhat lower level and, if necessary, intervening in the foreign-exchange market to support the pegged value. Fearful of a further and excessive depreciation if the exchange rate were set free, the government chose the latter course. On May 2, 1962 the Canadian dollar was pegged at 92.5 cents in terms of the U.S. dollar ($1.00 Can. = $.925 U.S.). Thus the Canadian floating exchange rate that had begun in 1950 came to an inglorious end. One should note that its demise was brought about not because of deficiencies in the floating exchange-rate system itself, but because of ignorance of how this system operates, because of inappropriate monetary and inadequate fiscal policies in the 1958–60 period, and because of an unwise attempt to manage the exchange rate in 1961–62. Although the floating exchange rate provided greater latitude for stabilization policy, the inappropriate and unco-ordinated operation of this policy brought about the destruction of the floating-rate system.[25]

The depreciation and repegging of the Canadian dollar did not completely end the exchange crisis, as speculation continued against the dollar.

[25] For more elaborate discussions of Canada's experience with a floating exchange rate in the 1950–62 period, see Richard E. Caves and Grant L. Reuber, *Capital Transfers and Economic Policy: Canada 1951–1962* (Cambridge, Mass.: Harvard University Press, 1970); Lawrence H. Officer, *An Econometric Model of Canada under the Fluctuating Exchange Rate* (Cambridge, Mass.: Harvard University Press, 1968); and Paul Wonnacott, *The Canadian Dollar 1948–1962* (Toronto: University of Toronto Press, 1965).

However, the Bank of Canada and Department of Finance took decisive and co-ordinated action in June 1962 to restore international confidence in the Canadian dollar by reducing government expenditures, tightening monetary policy, imposing temporary tariff surcharges on imports, and obtaining standby international loans of foreign exchange. As a result of these concerted monetary, fiscal, and tariff measures, the exchange crisis was soon over.

3. The economic recovery of 1962–65

The economic expansion which began in the middle of 1961 intensified in early 1962 and continued at an encouraging pace into the middle of 1965. During this period real GNP grew at an average annual rate of 6.3 percent, unemployment declined from 7.6 percent in early 1961 to 4 percent in late 1964, and the consumer price index rose at an average annual rate of only 1.8 percent.

This highly satisfactory expansion was reinforced by co-ordinated and enlightened policy. Fiscal policy was mildly expansionary during this period,[26] and the Bank of Canada followed an expansionary policy almost throughout the period. Together with the stimulating effects of the currency depreciation of 1962, these policies contributed to the orderly economic expansion.

4. The inflation of 1966–70[27]

The economic expansion which began in 1961 continued virtually without interruption until the last quarter of 1969. Between 1961 and 1969, real GNP increased by 57 percent, and unemployment averaged only 4.1 percent in 1965–68. In view of these gains, it would have been astonishing if some distortions and excesses had not arisen, and these appeared in the form of a progressively worsening inflation. Consumer prices, which rose at an average annual rate of only 1.7 percent in 1961–65, increased at an average annual rate of 4.1 percent in 1966–69.

In the spring of 1965, the Bank of Canada became concerned with the emerging problem of inflation and tightened its monetary policy. During the period from mid-1965 to mid-1970, the Bank placed top priority on combatting inflation, although partial policy reversals occurred in mid-1966 and mid-1968. However, this generally restrictive monetary policy was frustrated by special aspects of Canada's international monetary arrangements and by a completely inappropriate fiscal policy.[28]

In July 1963, the United States introduced an "Interest Equalization

---

[26] This and future references to fiscal policy are based upon estimates of the full-employment budget deficit or surplus (that which would occur if the economy were operating at full employment) supplied by the Department of the Treasury and Economics, Province of Ontario. For a slightly different calculation of the full-employment budget, see *Report of the Royal Commission on Taxation*, Volume 2 (Ottawa: Queen's Printer, 1966), pp. 69–79.

[27] This and the following section are based upon James Pesando and Lawrence B. Smith, "Monetary Policy in Canada," in Karel Holbik, ed., *Monetary Policy in Twelve Industrial Countries* (Boston: Federal Reserve Bank of Boston, 1973), pp. 70–116.

[28] For a slightly different interpretation of monetary policy during this period, see Thomas J. Courchene, "Recent Canadian Monetary Policy," *Journal of Money, Credit and Banking*, III, No. 1 (February 1971), pp. 35–56.

Tax," designed to reduce foreign borrowing in the United States by increasing the cost to foreigners of raising funds in the U.S. capital market. To avoid impediments to the free flow of funds between Canada and the United States, Canada immediately sought and was granted an exemption from this legislation, on the understanding that it would not permit its foreign-exchange reserves to rise above the then existing level. This ceiling imposed on its foreign-exchange reserves meant that Canada now had a two-directional balance-of-payments constraint. It could permit neither a balance-of-payments surplus, which would increase its foreign-exchange reserves, nor any prolonged balance-of-payments deficit, which would substantially deplete its reserve holdings. Because of the generally well-behaved nature of the country's economic growth, this reserve ceiling did not impose a severe hardship for most of the 1963–65 period. However, in order to obtain a partial exemption from a new set of U.S. balance-of-payments controls, Canada agreed in December 1965 to lower the reserve ceiling and to reduce its reserve holdings to this new ceiling by the end of 1966, thus tightening the balance-of-payments constraint.

Although the Bank of Canada desired to pursue a restrictive monetary policy in the second half of 1965 and in 1966, the reserve ceiling inhibited the degree to which it could pursue this policy. A tighter monetary policy in Canada than in the United States would increase Canadian relative to U.S. interest rates. This would attract additional financial investment into Canada and thus increase Canada's foreign-exchange reserves in violation of the reserve ceiling. Fortunately, U.S. monetary policy was also restrictive during this period, permitting a corresponding degree of tightness in Canadian policy. Nevertheless, as a result of the reserve ceiling, the Canadian money supply was expanded at a much faster rate than the Bank would have wished.

The inability of the Bank to pursue as tight a monetary policy as it would have liked was particularly unfortunate in view of the inappropriate policy stance taken in fiscal policy. The 1965 budget, probably following the U.S. lead, provided for a reduction in federal taxes. The rationale for this fiscal stimulation is hard to find, coming at a time of very low unemployment (3.6 percent), a fast rate of growth (real GNP rose 7.5 percent from mid-1965 to mid-1966), and increasing inflationary pressures. Monetary and fiscal policy were thus unco-ordinated and this, together with the constraint of the reserve ceiling, substantially impaired if not voided the restraining influences of monetary policy.

In mid-1966, in response to preliminary evidence that the rate of growth of the economy was slowing down, the Bank of Canada shifted to a policy of monetary ease. This monetary policy continued into the first half of 1967 and coincided with a fiscal policy that was neutral or perhaps slightly stimulating. By mid-1967 it became clear that the anticipated slowdown in the economy was not arising and that inflationary pressures were mounting further. Consequently, the Bank once again moved to try to restrain an overheating economy.

The story of 1967 and 1968 is a repeat of the previous two years. Monetary policy was considerably limited in its effectiveness by the reserve ceiling in 1967 and by the lack of co-ordination with fiscal policy (which continued its essentially neutral stance). The middle of 1968 saw fears of an economic slowdown reappear as the unemployment rate crept to 5 percent, and monetary policy again turned expansionary. As before, the anticipated slowdown failed to materialize and the Bank once again turned to a tight monetary policy in the face of continuing inflation.

Monetary restraint continued into 1969 and became increasingly effective, as the United States agreed to the removal of the ceiling on Canadian foreign-exchange reserves and fiscal policy was finally brought into play. In 1969 the budgetary surplus was increased significantly, and fiscal and monetary policy were finally co-ordinated in an effort to combat inflation. Unfortunately, co-ordinated restraint, which was called for in previous years, was now inappropriate, as the economic slowdown finally appeared. Although the rate of inflation continued unabated, the unemployment rate rose dramatically and exceeded 6 percent by mid-1970.

From this discussion it is clear that stabilization policy failed to control inflation during the last half of the 1960s for a variety of reasons. First, monetary and fiscal policy were unco-ordinated, if not pulling in opposite directions, for most of the period. Fiscal policy was approximately neutral from 1966 to 1968 and did not become contractionary until 1969. This lack of fiscal restraint forced the Bank of Canada to assume the primary responsibility for combatting inflation. Second, the combination of a fixed exchange rate and a foreign-exchange reserve ceiling constrained the Bank in its pursuit of monetary restraint by limiting the degree to which domestic interest rates could rise.

Third, the direction of monetary policy was inappropriate on several occasions. The expansionary policies of mid-1966 and mid-1968 appear in retrospect to have been a mistake, since they were predicated on expectations which failed to materialize. Furthermore, the continuing policy reversals created uncertainty in the minds of the public and also enhanced inflationary expectations, since the Bank seemed to jump into an excessive monetary expansion at the first sight of success for its restraining policies. Thus, the economic community came to anticipate that an all-out attack on inflation was unlikely.

Fourth, Canada's inflationary problem by no means originated solely from domestic causes but was part of an international phenomenon, although the Canadian inflation experience was generally worse than that of the United States during this period. An attempt to reduce the Canadian rate of inflation below that of the United States was likely to meet with serious difficulties under the combination of a fixed exchange rate and a reserve ceiling. In retrospect, we suggest that the Canadian dollar should have been permitted to float when the reserve ceiling constrained Canadian monetary policy.[29] The likely appreciation of the Canadian dollar and greater flexibility in monetary policy might have slowed the inflation before inflationary expectations became entrenched.

5. The managed exchange rate of 1970–72

Despite a relatively high rate of domestic inflation, the Canadian bal-

[29] A similar view has been expressed by Robert A. Mundell, "Discussion," in *Canadian–United States Financial Relationships*, The Federal Reserve Bank of Boston Conference Series, No. 6 (September 1971), p. 45.

ance of payments achieved a substantial surplus in 1970 in response to a strong world demand for Canadian exports. The surplus was reinforced by large-scale foreign investment in Canada in response to the high interest rates which accompanied Canada's very restrictive monetary policy. Speculators, sensing a repegging of the Canadian dollar at a higher level (to remove the balance-of-payments surplus), accentuated the upward pressure on the Canadian dollar by buying up Canadian dollars for U.S. dollars. Thereupon the government felt it could no longer hold the exchange rate fixed, and rather than appreciate the currency, the exchange rate was allowed to float on May 31, 1970.

The floating of the exchange rate during a period of high and rising unemployment and strong inflation introduced a new set of problems for Canada's policy-makers. Since the freed exchange rate quickly appreciated, it provided a temporary respite for the inflation Canada was experiencing, as the Canadian-dollar price of imports fell. However, the reduction in the Canadian-dollar price of imports and the increase in the foreign-currency price of Canadian exports caused by the appreciation reduced the demand for Canadian output and further aggravated the high level of unemployment.

Under these circumstances, monetary policy became very expansionary, attempting to reduce unemployment by stimulating aggregate demand directly through lower interest rates and indirectly through restraining the appreciation in the Canadian dollar. Fiscal policy, on the other hand, seemed to be primarily concerned with inflation and remained very restrictive. The appreciating exchange rate, monetary ease, and fiscal restraint were reflected at the end of 1970 in a high and rising unemployment rate of 6.4 percent and a temporarily reduced rate of inflation.

The highly unsatisfactory unemployment picture attracted increased attention from policy-makers in 1971 and 1972, and the thrust of monetary policy continued to be expansionary. Fiscal policy remained restrictive, although somewhat less so than previously. The main responsibility for achieving the primary domestic objective of reduced unemployment was once again left to monetary policy. In spite of a highly expansionary monetary policy, the unemployment rate remained at the high level of 6.4 percent throughout 1971 and rose to 6.7 percent in the latter half of 1972. After the deflationary effects of the currency appreciation wore off, the rate of inflation again accelerated and averaged 5 percent in both 1971 and 1972.

As previously mentioned, the appreciating Canadian dollar exacerbated the unemployment situation. Although the Canadian dollar was ostensibly free to float at the end of May 1970, this freedom was far from complete, as the government undertook a "dirty" rather than "clean" float. Because of the undesirable employment effects of a rising exchange rate, stabilization policy was aimed at restraining the appreciation in the exchange rate. Not only was monetary policy excessively expansionary in an attempt to retard this upward movement, but direct government intervention in the foreign-exchange market occurred, in the buying up of U.S. dollars, and Canada's foreign-exchange reserves rose by an incredible 17 percent in 1971, even excluding the impact of an increase in the U.S.-dollar value of Canada's gold reserves and the Canadian allocation of

Special Drawing Rights (a new kind of reserves). Despite these policies, unemployment persisted and inflation accelerated.

The 1970-72 period thus provides another illustration of the dangers of an unco-ordinated stabilization policy and the impact of international considerations on an open economy. If the Canadian balance of payments were not so vigorous (that is, if there were not such a strong tendency toward currency appreciation) and if fiscal policy had been more expansionary during this period, monetary policy could have been more restrained and the rate of growth of the money supply could have been maintained within reasonable limits, rather than allowed to reach the incredible rate of 15.4 percent per annum in 1971–72. Given the state of the U.S. economy, exceptionally low unemployment and a very moderate inflation were objectives beyond the reach of the Canadian economy. However, had monetary, fiscal, and exchange-rate policies been judiciously selected and co-ordinated, the Canadian stabilization experience could have been vastly improved.

6.   The continuing inflation in 1972–73

From late 1972 to mid-1973, Canada went through a period of accelerating inflation and falling unemployment. As in many previous periods, this pattern corresponded to the U.S. experience and was to a large extent a result of U.S. conditions. However, the inflation rate no doubt was exacerbated by the extremely high rate of growth of the money supply in the previous two years. At the same time, the inflation in Canada was fed by an unusual set of causes emanating from the agricultural sector, inappropriate U.S. price controls, and an ineffective Canadian policy stance (continuation of an overly expansive monetary policy). An illustration of this was the sharp increase in U.S. demand for Canadian agricultural products in the summer of 1973 when shortages were created in the United States as a result of a price freeze and an advance announcement of the removal of the freeze on meat. The rise in U.S. demand exerted tremendous pressure on Canadian prices, and this was not reduced until the Canadian government belatedly imposed export controls on these agricultural products.

Although Canadian policy could not have prevented rising domestic inflation in the face of world-wide pressures, a slower rate of growth of the money supply and faster imposition of export controls to offset distortions introduced by U.S. price controls would have led to a vastly improved employment–price performance.

7.   Conclusion

This survey indicates that two important themes keep recurring throughout the experience of Canadian stabilization policy: that international considerations are of overwhelming importance in the formulation and implementation of policy (under both fixed and floating exchange-rate systems), and that co-ordination in monetary, fiscal, and exchange-rate policy is required if stabilization attempts are to be successful.

2. Stagflation: The Canadian Experience *

Grant L. Reuber with Ronald G. Bodkin

University of Western Ontario

"Stagflation" here is defined as the simultaneous existence of unemployment and inflation. More precisely, it is characterized by a rapid rise in prices in combination with high and rising levels of unemployment. The causes and cures of this phenómenon are the subject of much controversy. However, on two points at least there seems to be widespread agreement. First, the problem of reconciling full employment with stable prices is common to all industrial countries and is by no means unique to Canada. Second, despite the ambitious claims of some commentators, no one anywhere has yet come up with a satisfactory answer to this policy dilemma, now recognized as one of the foremost issues facing many governments.

In part the differences of view about policy reflect different estimates of the relative costs and benefits of rising prices versus unemployment, as well as underlying preferences. And in part these different viewpoints reflect a difference of view about the circumstances found in the country and about the empirical relationships that determine how the economy works. A host of issues arise along both of these avenues. Rather than attempt a comprehensive review of these issues, this article touches on two areas: (1) the chief factors that have given rise to stagflation in Canada, and (2) the main policy options that face the country and some of the implications of each.

I. Principal Factors Accounting for Stagflation

1. Exceptionally rapid increases in the labour force combined with labour-market imperfections

The Canadian labour force has grown at an unprecedented rate since

* An edited version of a brief presented to the Standing Senate Committee on National Finance, May 20, 1971.

1965 and will continue to grow very rapidly throughout the 1970s.[1] The present rate of growth far exceeds the recent and projected growth rates in the labour forces of other industrialized countries. This rapid growth rate in Canada is mainly the lagged consequence of the large postwar baby boom, but it has also been influenced by rising female participation in the labour force, as well as by positive net immigration. Looked at from the standpoint of job creation rather than from the standpoint of absorbing available labour supply, the Canadian economy has performed with a success that is unprecedented, at least since immediately after World War II, and that exceeds by a substantial margin the performance of the U.S. and European economies.

A rapid increase in labour supply is to be welcomed on a variety of grounds, including the possibility which it opens up for more rapid increases in output because of the large increments in this fundamentally important productive resource. Moreover, with perfectly functioning labour markets, little or no difficulty would arise in absorbing exceptionally large increases in labour supplies. Indeed, in a well-functioning labour market, increasing labour supplies are likely to make market adjustments easier since the increments in labour supply will tend to be absorbed into growing sectors of the economy, thereby reducing the need to reallocate labour from slow-growing to fast-growing sectors in a dynamic economy. The difficulties of absorbing a rapidly growing labour force arise for the most part because labour markets are far from perfect. Among the many imperfections that are evident are various regional occupational immobilities; inadequate information about job opportunities; restrictions on entry into various employments because of trade unions, professional and governmental barriers and regulations; labour-pricing arrangements such as wage-parity and minimum-wage laws; non-portable pension-plan arrangements; fiscal incentives to substitute capital for labour; seniority arrangements to protect the interests of older, established workers; social-welfare and other measures that undermine labour mobility and work incentives.

Such imperfections become particularly serious, especially in the short run, when the labour force grows at the rapid pace now experienced in Canada. Moreover, the effects of these imperfections are further exacerbated when aggregate demand is dampened in order to cope with inflationary pressures. Given the rapid increase in labour supplies in Canada, the anti-inflationary policies that have been followed, and the imperfections found in the Canadian labour market — which may well be greater than in most other countries because of the geographic dispersion of the labour force and the importance of regional and seasonal factors — it is hardly surprising that unemployment levels in Canada have generally been higher since the 1950s than in Western Europe and the United States, where the labour force has grown more slowly and where labour markets are more homogeneous.

2. External price changes

As is widely recognized, external price and wage changes, especially

---

[1] See Economic Council of Canada, Fourth Annual Review: The Canadian Economy from the 1960's to the 1970's (Ottawa: Queen's Printer, 1967), p. 72.

those in the United States, have a fundamental influence on price and wage changes in this country. This influence arises directly through our heavy volume of foreign trade, as well as through the ease with which productive factors move between Canada and the United States. This external influence also arises indirectly through at least two channels: the first is through institutional links between businesses and trade unions in Canada and the United States; the second is through the influence of events in the United States on expectations in Canada about future trends in prices, wages, and ouput.

Throughout recent history, Canadian price changes have moved closely in line with international prices — particularly U.S. prices. Barring truly extraordinary measures entailing substantial readjustments and economic costs, all our history indicates that it is unrealistic to believe that Canadian prices over any period of time can be expected to follow a path that differs significantly from that of price changes in the United States and other foreign countries.

3. Poor market performance in product markets

With the appearance of substantial excess capacity in the economy, one would expect prices to decline gradually in response to competition. However, one finds little evidence of such reductions. Indeed, many prices have consistently continued to increase. While this phenomenon partly reflects the effect of foreign price changes, it possibly also reflects the exercise of market power in some cases. Had producers had less market power, prices might have been more sensitive to the increased competitive pressure entailed by greater slack in the economy.

The effects of market power in Canada, in both factor and product markets, are not only found in upward pressure on prices but may be even more important because of the downward rigidity in prices arising from this power. As a consequence of this downward rigidity, the resource and output reallocations required in a dynamic economy tend to raise prices as expanding industries outbid stagnant and declining industries where prices tend to remain unchanged. Although too much can be made of this phenomenon, which was first emphasized by Charles Schultze,[2] the evidence available suggests that it has been of some significance in Canada.[3]

4. Rapid growth in the size of the public sector

From 1965 to 1969 total government (all levels) revenues as a percentage of GNP increased from about 30.5 percent to 36.5 percent and total government expenditures (including both purchases of goods and services and transfer payments; i.e., unilateral payments, such as subsidies) in-

---

[2] Charles L. Schultze, "Recent Inflation in the United States," Study Paper No. 1, prepared for the Joint Economic Committee of the United States Congress, *Study of Employment, Growth, and Price Levels* (Washington: U.S. Government Printing Office, 1959).
[3] See Thomas J. Courchene, "An Analysis of the Price-Inventory Nexus with Empirical Application to the Canadian Manufacturing Sector," *International Economic Review*, X (October 1969), pp. 359–62.

creased from 30 percent to over 33.5 percent.[4] Not only were these ratios substantially larger than at any time since World War II, but, more important, the rates of increase — 20 and 12 percent in four years — were very large by historical standards and standards in most other countries. Moreover, the projections prepared by the Economic Council suggest that further increases in these ratios can be expected.[5]

A rapid increase in the public sector is inflationary in that it increases the marginal propensity to consume: first, because the first expenditure round through the government sector omits the bite that would be absorbed by savings in the private sector and second, because such expenditures may redistribute spending from groups with a higher propensity to save to those with a lower propensity to save. Moreover, a growing public sector may lead to a reallocation of resources from sectors where productivity growth is relatively rapid to the public sector, where historically productivity growth has been very slow. Given small and gradual changes in the size of the public sector, demand–management policies can adapt and compensate for these factors. This is also true with a large and rapidly growing public sector, but it is likely to be much more difficult operationally, given the various factors constraining these other policies and the uncertainties about their effects. In other words, adjusting to and compensating for a large and rapidly moving element is likely to be more difficult and in practice less successful than adjusting to and compensating for a small and slowly changing element.

Another inflationary factor in the rapid growth of the public sector has been the lack of co-ordination between the demand and supply aspects of the policy. Thus the introduction of Medicare, which greatly expanded the demand for medical services of all kinds by offering medical care to everyone at greatly reduced private cost, failed to make adequate provision for a corresponding increase in the supply of medical services. The predictable result has been a large increase in the relative prices of medical services. Many other types of policies, such as those designed to support declining industries, to fund pollution control, to subsidize technology, housing, and other types of investment, have had a similar inflationary bias.

A further factor to be recognized in this context is that with a progressive tax system, rising prices tend to generate an ever-growing public sector. This could be offset, of course, by tax reductions. Such reductions are rare, however. In situations of rising revenues and a backlog of unfilled demands for public services, recent governments have generally given priority to expenditure increases over tax reductions.

5. Exchange depreciation, an undervalued exchange rate, and the failure to adopt a free rate sooner

Early in the 1960s, Canada depreciated the exchange rate by about 11 percent at a time when there was significant excess capacity in the

---

[4] *The National Finances: 1970-71* (Toronto: Canadian Tax Foundation, 1970), pp. 9 and 13.
[5] Economic Council of Canada, *Sixth Annual Review: Perspectives 1975* (Ottawa: Queen's Printer, 1969), ch. 3.

economy. As this excess capacity disappeared and a high level of aggregate demand developed in subsequent years, the full inflationary impact of this devaluation was gradually transmitted throughout the economy. Moreover, the new exchange rate undervalued the Canadian dollar in terms of foreign currency, as evidenced by the continuing improvement throughout this period in the current-account balance (exports minus imports of goods and services) and the large increase in Canada's reserves of gold and U.S. dollars. This undervaluation further added to the inflationary demand pressures on the economy from 1963 onward. It probably was a mistake for Canada to adopt a fixed rate in 1962 and it may have been a mistake not to have returned to a floating rate before 1970. Had we adopted a floating rate sooner, it is likely that we would have experienced less price inflation than we have and that our problems would now be somewhat less than they are.

6. Monetary–fiscal policies

Over the period 1963 to 1968, the federal government can scarcely be said to have followed very active monetary and fiscal policies to combat inflation, as argued in greater detail elsewhere.[6] On the fiscal side, a surplus of $625 million gradually became a deficit of $256 million in 1967 and $165 million in 1968. A substantial surplus in 1969 was followed in 1970 by a small deficit. Other Canadian governments have had large and growing surpluses, reflecting their particular revenue and expenditure patterns and especially the revenues generated by the Canada and Quebec pension plans. Although these surpluses have not reflected active anti-inflationary policies on the part of provincial and municipal governments, these surpluses have nonetheless served to dampen inflationary pressures.

Turning to the money supply, one finds not only a very rapid increase during the period since 1965 but also wide fluctuations in the rate of increase, ranging from over 20 percent per year in mid-1968 to a net reduction in the third quarter of 1969. During the period of rapidly rising prices from 1965 to 1969, the money supply increased almost 55 percent compared with a 19 percent increase in real output. Thus $2.87 of new money was created per $1.00 of additional real output. In 1969 the increase in the money supply matched the increase in real output, but in 1970 — when inflation had become a major preoccupation — the rate of change in the money supply again accelerated (10.0 versus 5.6 percent).

From 1969 to 1971, as the unemployment rate rose from about 4.5 percent to almost 7 percent, both monetary and fiscal policy were much tighter than from 1965 to 1968, when unemployment was generally well below 5 percent.

This picture scarcely conforms with prevailing conventional notions of appropriate monetary and fiscal policy. During much of this period one might have expected changes in the money supply at least not to exceed significantly the changes in real output. And, on the fiscal side, one would

---

[6] Grant L. Reuber, "Incomes Policy: Canada's Experiment with Organized Voluntarism to Curb Price Inflation," Research Report 7003, University of Western Ontario, pp. 3–11.

have expected to find large and growing federal surpluses deliberately designed to reduce inflationary pressure. Thus, the indictment of conventional monetary and fiscal policy can hardly be that it was tried and didn't work. Indeed, during much of this period these conventional levers appear to have been moved in the wrong direction; and to the extent that they were effective, the policies followed tended to enhance the upward pressure on prices rather than decrease them.

No attempt will be made here to review the various factors that contributed to this situation.[7] In part, it reflected political pressures, in part a series of events beyond the control of the authorities, and in part inadequate analysis and understanding, within the government as well as without, of the unfolding economic scene and the degree to which the policies being followed were inconsistent with the requirements of stabilization policy. From the standpoint of policy, the important point is not to establish with the benefit of hindsight that policy during this period might have been better, but rather to ascertain what lessons might be learnt from this period to improve future policy.

II. Policy Options for Coping with Stagflation

Given the continuing growth in labour supplies, continuing growth in the public sector, and an inflationary world environment, it seems likely that within the framework of current policies there will be a continuing tendency for labour supplies to exceed labour demand and for Canadian prices to continue to rise over the next few years. What options are open to try at least to ameliorate these conditions?

1. Labour–market policies

First and foremost, it is important that every effort be made to improve the performance of labour markets through a series of policies that make these markets more competitive and permit the absorption of increasing labour supplies more easily than at present. This issue has been much discussed over the years[8] and has been frequently emphasized by the Economic Council. Although some marginal measures have been adopted, this country has yet to adopt comprehensive labour-market policies which are fully integrated with welfare and other types of policy and which will greatly improve the performance of labour markets. Without covering all the possibilities in detail, it is evident that measures are needed to reduce the control over labour supplies exercised by trade unions and professional organizations; to increase occupational and regional mobility through training programs, better information and job-placement services, financial assistance for moving and so forth, together with measures to increase the portability of pension and other benefits; to reduce the disincentives arising from social-welfare measures to move and

---

[7] See *ibid.* for a more detailed discussion of these factors.
[8] Robert A. Gordon puts heavy stress on such "manpower policy" as a means of making the goals of full employment and stable prices more compatible. See *The Goal of Full Employment* (New York: Wiley, 1967).

accept employment in another locality; to reduce present fiscal incentives to substitute capital for labour; to reduce the incidence of artificial wage levels through wage-parity arrangements and minimum-wage laws. We fully recognize that implementing such changes means challenging a variety of vested interests and sacred cows. Substantial progress along these lines will call for not only technical skill but also political courage of a very high order. On the other hand, failure to take substantial steps in this direction will imply unnecessarily high political and social as well as economic costs associated with unnecessarily high levels of unemployment.

2. Competition policy

Policies to improve the efficiency of labour markets need to be accompanied by policies to increase competition and improve efficiency in product markets. In this connection, we should especially like to emphasize the importance in Canada of reducing barriers to foreign trade as a means of checking price increases and reducing market power. In addition to reducing and eliminating tariffs and quotas generally, special attention might be given to liberalizing export restraint agreements, government procurement policies, aid-tying policies, and tariff and quota restrictions against low-cost imports from less-developed countries. Particular attention might also be given to tariff reductions in areas where past investigations under the Combines Investigation Act have indicated substantial elements of market power: e.g., dental supplies, matches, rubber goods, fine papers, paperboard, zinc oxide, sugar, and drugs.[9]

Such policies, as in the case of labour-market policies, mean challenging various vested interests which can be expected to mount strong resistance. Nevertheless, to the extent that this resistance can be overcome, the result will be better-functioning, more competitive markets tending to produce more stable price levels.

3. Closer co-ordination of public policy outside the realm of monetary–fiscal policy with the objectives of stabilization policy, and increased efficiency in the public sector

Although monetary and fiscal policy are directly concerned with stabilization policy, it is apparent that many other areas of government policy have an important impact on prices and unemployment. It is also evident that government policies in these other areas frequently are poorly co-ordinated with the objectives of stabilization policy, and in many instances have an adverse influence on the effectiveness of stabilization policy.

This problem arises primarily in four areas. The first concerns income-support policies, particularly in connection with food and agricultural prices. Price-support policies are particularly inconsistent with the desire to stabilize the over-all level of prices. Canada, fortunately, has relied

---

[9] See Grant L. Reuber, brief presented to the Special Joint Committee of the Senate and House of Commons on Consumer Credit (Prices), February 9, 1967, Table II.

mainly on a deficiency-payments approach (subsidies to farmers without price-setting by the government) rather than a price-support approach (government pegging of prices at levels higher than the free market by means of government purchases and stockpiling of the product involved). Nevertheless, even a deficiency-payments approach tends to hold up prices, since it is normally linked to restrictions on imports.

A second range of policies is concerned with fostering development in particular areas (e.g., research and development) or regions. Such policies have sometimes been planned and implemented with little or no attention having been given to their impact on national employment and price levels. It is not obvious, for example, that policies which subsidize technical innovations that lead to the substitution of capital for labour are in the national interest when the country has widespread unemployment. Nor is it obvious that regional-development policies that subsidize sub-optimal allocations of labour and capital from a national viewpoint are in the best interest of increasing employment, raising incomes, and slowing down the rate of increase of the price level. This is not to say by any means that all such development programs are inconsistent with the aims of stabilization policy. In many cases, they may in fact strongly reinforce stabilization policy. It is evident, however, that this is not always the case and that there is considerable scope for closer co-ordination of development policies with stabilization goals.

A third area is in the field of social-welfare programs, where again one can find examples of a lack of co-ordination with the aims of stabilization policy. The empirical evidence we have suggests, for example, that government transfer payments and unemployment-insurance benefits inhibit labour mobility.[10] Difficulties of a different kind arise when policies such as Medicare are introduced, which greatly increase the demand for services but make no provision for a corresponding increase in the supply of services, as mentioned earlier.

The fourth area relates to the need to improve efficiency in the public sector, including not only government departments but also government-related agencies, such as educational and health institutions. Total employment in government and government-related agencies now accounts for about one-eighth of the civilian labour force. Although it is very difficult to measure productivity in the public sector, it seems to be generally conceded that productivity growth in the public sector, as in other service sectors, has been very slow and has been a drag on the over-all growth in productivity in the country. Upward pressure on prices has arisen as wage demands have outstripped productivity gains. Given the size and growth of the public sector and its apparent low rate of productivity growth, steps to improve efficiency in the government sector are of major importance in attempting to bolster over-all productivity.

In order to advance the principle of greater co-ordination of government policy, we suggest that consideration might be given to three specific

---

[10] See Thomas J. Courchene, "Interprovincial Migration and Economic Adjustment," *Canadian Journal of Economics*, III (November 1970), pp. 550–76; also, Thomas J. Courchene, "Unemployment Insurance in Canada: Some Implications of the Present System and an Evaluation of the White Paper Proposals," Research Report 7025, University of Western Ontario.

steps: (1) a review by the Bank of Canada and the Department of Finance of existing income, development, and welfare programs to determine their implications for stabilization and to consider how these programs might be amended to make them more fully consistent with the goals of stabilization policy; (2) an extension of the functions and capabilities of the Treasury Board to foster greater policy co-ordination within the federal government and to ensure that appropriate priority is placed on stabilization and other objectives by individual operating departments; and (3) adoption of the principle that all departmental proposals in the future should be accompanied by a careful assessment of the implications of the proposal for national and regional employment and price levels in both the short and the long term.

Co-ordination within the federal government is, of course, only part of the problem of co-ordinating public policy in this country. The other part relates to co-ordinating policy among different levels of government. This is a long-standing, widely recognized problem to which almost everyone pays lip-service, in which some progress has been made, but much more remains to be done. About all one can recommend is that everyone concerned keep soldiering on.

4. Exchange-rate policy

We endorse a floating exchange rate for Canada, given the desirability for Canada to retain some freedom to follow somewhat independent monetary and fiscal policies. In saying this, we do not claim that a floating rate will make it feasible to have a price–employment experience that is totally or even largely independent of developments abroad. The claim is rather that the free rate makes it feasible to gain somewhat greater freedom in the short run and to make adjustments to changing circumstances more smoothly.

5. General monetary–fiscal policy

All the policy options so far considered attempt to improve the trade-off relationship between price stability and full employment in the sense of making it feasible to operate the economy at lower levels of unemployment with less price inflation. Changes in monetary and fiscal policy attempt to regulate the level of economic activity. As such, they determine at what point on the short-run trade-off curve the economy finds itself; but by the manner in which they are employed, monetary and fiscal policy may also affect the position of the curve itself. This may be illustrated with the aid of Figure 1. The policies discussed earlier are concerned with moving the trade-off curve closer to the origin, O, say, from aa' to bb'. Depending on the stance adopted by monetary–fiscal policy, the economy in the short run may, in principle, be regulated to operate at point 1 or at point 2, the latter implying more unemployment and less price inflation than the former. In addition, the way in which policy is exercised may itself tend to move the curve closer to the axis, improving the trade-off relationship, or away from the axis, making things worse.

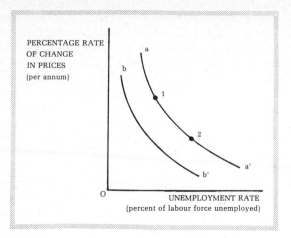

Figure 1

More stable and predictable monetary–fiscal policies that are geared to longer-term prospects and potentials may tend to improve the trade-off relationship. This does not mean that we endorse proposals to adopt automatic and rigid rules about increases in the money supply or changes in fiscal policy, nor that we believe immediate circumstances can safely be ignored. There is, however, some danger of becoming too mesmerized by the immediate situation, and that by frantically adjusting in response to the changing current situation things may turn out worse than if policy were less influenced by immediate prospects and more influenced by longer-term prospects and the potential of the economy. Looking over the period from 1965 to 1971, one may argue that the large swings in fiscal and monetary policy themselves tended to be destabilizing. Had policy been confined to a more limited range linked to longer-term employment and output prospects and potentials, the trade-off relation might now be better.

Aside from the stability of monetary and fiscal policy, there is the question of where to aim on the trade-off curve. Given the openness of the Canadian economy to external price developments, especially in the United States, it seems evident that any attempt to achieve significantly greater price stability in Canada than in the United States and elsewhere over any extended period of time is likely to entail very high levels of unemployment, even if various policies are adopted to improve the trade-off relationship. The question then is one of preferences and weighing the *relative* costs of these high levels of unemployment against the benefits of marginally greater price stability. Although economists have been intrigued by the problem of assessing the *relative* economic costs and benefits of price inflation and unemployment, the fact remains that the *relative* economic costs and benefits of price inflation and unemployment remain highly uncertain and that the *relative* social and political costs and benefits are even more uncertain. As a consequence, there is a considerable diversity of opinion. It is our view that when unemployment exceeds a rate of 4 to 4.5 percent of the labour force, the economic, social, and political costs of unemployment outweigh the benefits resulting from the marginal gains likely to be achieved in greater price stability in this country. On the other hand, historical experience suggests that when unemployment falls below 4 percent in Canada, strong inflationary pressures develop that make it costly as well as impractical to maintain unemployment at these low levels — especially when the attempt to do so is usually followed by a swing in unemployment to levels well above 5 percent, as belated efforts are made to offset the pressures that have built up. Accordingly, we would argue that the authorities should set their eyes firmly on a target of about 4 percent averaged out over two to three years. When unemployment is tending to fall below this level, restrictive measures should be applied even if prices are slow to reflect developing inflationary pressures; and when unemployment exceeds this level, expansionist policies should be adopted even though prices may be rising at rates comparable to those experienced in the late 1960s.

6. Selective fiscal policies

Historically, selective fiscal policies have usually taken the form of imposing or reducing taxes and other financial restrictions on various sectors which are assumed to be in the van of inflationary or deflationary pressures: e.g., sales and excise taxes on consumer durables, changes in house-mortgage regulations, consumer-credit regulations and margin requirements, changes in depreciation allowances, and so forth. Such regulations were used frequently during the 1940s and 1950s but lost favour during the 1960s. This seems to have happened mainly because serious doubts developed about the effectiveness of these policies and their effects on the distribution of income and wealth, and also because anticipations began to develop in the minds of the public, based on experience, which tended to accelerate precisely the changes that some of these measures were designed to reduce.

It is possible that we now have too great an aversion to the use of such measures and to the development of new types of special fiscal measures of this kind. Among the latter are such possibilities as income-tax holidays for a month or more, or double taxation for a comparable period. On balance, we believe that it probably would be helpful to provide the authorities with stand-by authority to invoke and revoke certain types of special fiscal measures of this kind.

In advocating stand-by fiscal powers to be exercised within a limited range on a discretionary basis, we are endorsing the view that on balance a well-run discretionary monetary–fiscal policy is likely to outperform a policy based on automatic rules. Moreover, this suggestion, together with our earlier recommendation for more stable and predictable monetary–fiscal policies, rather implies an argument for greater flexibility in fiscal policy and less variability in monetary policy than we have had during the past decade. It implies furthermore that such flexibility as is provided in both fiscal and monetary policy will be geared to longer-term prospects and potentials and not exclusively to the immediate situation.

7. Direct controls

All the options so far discussed are conventional in the sense that they are market-oriented. The main alternative to such measures is non-market measures that attempt to exercise direct control on prices paid in product and factor markets. Proposals based on direct controls take a variety of forms and differ greatly in the range of product and factor markets to be encompassed by such controls. For example, in the United States under "Phase 1" of President Nixon's "New Economic Policy" (Aug.–Nov. 1971), they took the form of a freeze on virtually all prices and wages in the economy, with only a few specified exceptions. Under "Phase 2" (Nov. 1971–Jan. 1973), a Price Commission and Pay Board established binding guidelines for price and wage increases, with permission required for exemption from the controls in individual cases. While these policies did result in reducing the U.S. rate of inflation, they did so only temporarily. The resurgence of inflation after "Phase 2" indicated that the controls had suppressed rather than eliminated the problem. In any event, the United States is a closed economy, one in which there is a minimum of influence of foreign on domestic prices. We seriously question the usefulness of direct controls in an open economy such as Canada, except perhaps on a short-term basis to meet a particular emergency such as a major war. Given what we see as a long-run problem of reconciling full employment with more stable prices, we doubt the effectiveness of such controls in achieving their objective. Furthermore, such controls in our view would mean substituting one set of policy problems for another and possibly more difficult set of policy problems. In addition, as matters stand constitutionally, it would not be feasible for the federal government to impose such controls in many areas exhibiting large price and wage increases; and we can discern no disposition on the part of provincial governments to collaborate in implementing price and wage controls.

Assuming that the constitutional obstacle could be surmounted — and that is a very big assumption — direct controls on prices and wages in our view could be justified only in industries where for political or economic reasons it proved impossible to develop reasonably competitive markets. On this basis, the case for direct controls is reduced to the classical case for regulating prices in so-called "natural" monopolies, such as public utilities — perhaps extended to what we might call "natural oligopolies." In general, the regulation of natural monopoly attempts to achieve the level of output and prices that would be justified by market-efficiency criteria rather than by monopoly criteria. But there is no suggestion even in these cases of regulating prices simply to hold prices down irrespective of economic efficiency. We would venture the judgement that there probably is limited scope in Canada for direct controls to improve economic efficiency successfully — given the openness of the economy, the competition that already exists, and the possibilities of opening up markets to greater competition.

8. Voluntary incomes policy

We believe that voluntary incomes policies such as those developed by the Prices and Incomes Commission in this country and by corresponding agencies in other countries at best are ineffective and may even be harmful from the standpoint of stabilization policy as well as other objectives of policy.[11] Such policies, in effect, attempt to levy a voluntary tax which is used to subsidize prices. Not only does this lead to gross inequities, but also it is likely to be highly ineffective. If such taxes are to be levied, they should be universal and mandatory and it may be questioned whether the proceeds should be employed to subsidize the price of the product to the taxpayer. Moreover, such measures are naive in implying that anyone in a responsible position in either business or the trade unions would voluntarily accept them, knowing full well the influence of international prices and other influences on Canadian wages and prices, as well as the high probability that many other sectors of the economy will not accept them.[12] Furthermore, such measures, by creating the mirage that something is being done, may forestall more useful policies from being implemented and may indeed generate expectations that enhance rather than alleviate the difficulties facing the economy. Finally, by pursuing incomes policy through a vigorous public-relations job, the Prices and Incomes Commission, far from ameliorating the adverse effects of inflation by having the public correctly anticipate it, may have enhanced these effects by temporarily misleading the public into incorrectly anticipating more stable prices than were justified by underlying economic conditions. If one accepts David C. Smith's review of incomes policies,[13] it is difficult to be sanguine about the prospects for incomes policies in this country.

[11] The Prices and Incomes Commission was established in 1969 and terminated in 1972. For a detailed discussion of its policies, see Reuber, "Incomes Policy," op. cit.

[12] Leo Durocher used to say, "Nice guys finish last!" The existence of voluntary incomes policies would appear to guarantee this outcome, as only the angels will accept the invitation to become the sacrificial lambs on the altar of price-level stability. If intervention is decided upon, a law with mandatory provisions would seem, in our view, far more acceptable.

[13] Incomes Policies — Some Foreign Experiences and their Relevance for Canada, Economic Council of Canada (Ottawa: Queen's Printer, 1966).

3. Stabilization Policy: A Monetarist Interpretation

Thomas J. Courchene *

University of Western Ontario

Virtually all introductory texts in economics inform students of the quantity-theory relationship,[1] namely

$$MV \equiv PQ \qquad \ldots \quad (1)$$

where M = the money supply;

  V = the income velocity of money, i.e., the number of times an average dollar is spent during a given period, say, a year;

  P = the price level, normally conceived as a weighted average of the prices of all goods and services, with the weights determined by the proportion of total output represented by the particular good or service;

  Q = real output or income.

Equation (1) is written as an identity rather than an equality. This reflects the fact that, in its crudest form, the quantity equation embodied little or no analytical content, since V was *defined* as PQ/M. In order to convert (1) into an economic theory, the following assumptions are usually employed:

  a) M is determined exogenously by the monetary authorities (i.e., the central bank);

  b) Q is the *full-employment* level of output, which is determined in the *real* sector of the economy and is independent of monetary variables, such as M;

* I wish to thank G. L. Reuber, Ken Avio, Gérard Gaudet, Joel Fried, Peter Howitt, and Russ Boyer for comments on an earlier version of this paper. Responsibility for the views expressed in the present version rests entirely with the author.

[1] For example, see P. A. Samuelson and A. Scott, *Economics*, 3rd Canadian ed. (Toronto: McGraw-Hill Canada, 1971), pp. 345–351. The quantity-theory tradition originated very early in the history of economic ideas. It was well developed in the writings of David Hume (middle 1700s), and Schumpeter links its origin with Jean Bodin in 1568. See J.A. Schumpeter, *History of Economic Analysis* (New York: Oxford University Press, 1954), p. 311.

c) V is a *numerical constant,* determined, say, by payment periods in the economy and by the degree of sophistication of the monetary sector, including the prevailing technology for clearing monetary transactions.

With these assumptions, (1) now becomes the familiar "transactions" version of the quantity theory:

$$M\overline{V} = P\overline{Q} \qquad \qquad ... \quad (2)$$

where the "bars" above V and Q indicate that these variables are fixed outside the monetary sector. Hence, if the authorities engineer an increase in the money supply of, say, 10 percent, the theory suggests that prices should increase by 10 percent. In short, the quantity theory as embodied in (2) is a theory of the price level or, if you will, a theory of *money income,* remembering that real income, Q, is assumed to be given.

The essence of equation (2) can also be expressed as a "cash-balance" equation, normally referred to as the "Cambridge equation,"[2] i.e.,

$$M = k \, P\overline{Q} \qquad \qquad ... \quad (3)$$

where k = 1/V and is the (assumed constant) proportion of money income that the private sector holds in the form of money or "cash balances." The right-hand side of equation (3) represents the *demand* for nominal (or current-dollar) balances and M represents the supply. Again, changes in M lead to equivalently proportional changes in P.

With the advent of the Keynes' *General Theory* (1936), the quantity theory fell upon hard times. Specifically, not only did Keynes maintain (correctly) that velocity was not a numerical constant but also that, at least for periods like the depression-ridden 1930s, changes in M could well be offset entirely by changes in velocity. In terms of equation (2), an increase in M need not affect prices at all, because V would adjust in an offsetting manner. For the next two decades the quantity theory remained dormant. Indeed, so did monetary policy for that matter. Keynesian theory suggested that monetary policy influenced the real sector via changes in interest rates — an increase in money would lead to a fall in interest rates, which would stimulate investment and, via the investment multiplier, would increase income. The potential instability in velocity (or in the demand for money) implied that increases in money might not lead to decreases in interest rates. Combined with the studies which appeared in the *Oxford Economic Papers* in the late 1930s purporting to demonstrate that interest rates were not important determinants of investment, this led to the downplaying of the role of monetary policy both absolutely and in relation to fiscal policy.

However, championed by the University of Chicago's Milton Friedman, the quantity theory made a resurgence in the mid-1950s. The principal driving force behind this resurgence was Friedman's classic "Restatement" of the quantity theory.[3] Again, most introductory texts alert the reader to

---

[2] The "transactions" approach to the quantity theory, as represented by the formulation in equation (2), is, in more recent times, normally associated with Irving Fisher. The "cash-balance" interpretation in equation (3) was popularized by a group of Cambridge University economists and has come to be known as the "Cambridge equation".

[3] M. Friedman, "The Quantity Theory of Money — A Restatement," in M. Friedman, ed., *Studies in the Quantity Theory of Money* (Chicago: University of Chicago Press, 1956), ch. I.

this "modern" quantity theory. Indeed, as this modern quantity-theory approach (now more frequently referred to as the *monetarist* approach) gathered momentum, more and more attention was directed toward its underlying thoeretical basis as well as its policy implications, even at the introductory level. Nonetheless, it is our impression that a full treatment of the monetarist position is generally lacking and the reader comes away with an inadequate impression of the monetary approach, especially as it relates to the implications for policy.

The purpose of this paper is to present in a simple but comprehensive manner the *assumptions underlying, concepts embodied in, and implications deriving from the monetarist position*, especially as they relate to stabilization policy. In order to demonstrate the extent to which the monetary approach can generate policy prescriptions different from those "traditionally" accepted, we shall couch the stabilization implications in terms of the familiar "Phillips Curve." Section I outlines the monetarist model under the assumption that the economy is "closed." Section II extends the monetarist model to an open economy, such as Canada's, dealing first with a fixed-exchange-rate regime and later with flexible rates. In Section III we interpret recent Canadian policy in light of the monetarist approach. Throughout the analysis the words "monetarist approach," "monetarism," "monetary model," and "quantity theory" are used interchangeably.

I.   Monetarism in a Closed Economy

For convenience we shall organize the discussion of monetarism by parading in point form the various assumptions underlying the model.

1. Crucial to the monetary approach is the distinction between monetary magnitudes and real magnitudes. Hence, it is important to distinguish between real (or constant-dollar) GNP and nominal (or current-dollar) GNP. Likewise, one must differentiate between *real* rates of interest and *money* rates of interest. The real rate of interest is that which would prevail if the rate of inflation were zero. The money rate of interest must, in addition, reflect the expected rate of inflation; i.e., the money rate equals the real rate plus the expected rate of inflation.[4] However, *the most important distinction is between nominal money balances and real money balances* or, equivalently, between the nominal quantity of money and the real quantity of money. The nominal quantity of money is expressed in whatever units are used to designate money. In Canada this is, of course, dollars. Assuming that money is defined to be currency outside banks plus the public's holdings of bank deposits, the nominal quantity of money at the end of 1972 was approximately $42 billion.[5]

---

[4] The nominal interest rate can be viewed as the opportunity cost (forgone-earnings cost) of holding money. For example, with a real rate of 4% per annum and an expected rate of inflation of 3%, the "full" cost of holding cash is 7% — 4% which could be earned (in real terms) if the money was invested and another 3% due to the erosion of the purchasing power of money over the year if inflation is proceeding at 3%. Ideally, interest rates on bonds should reflect expected inflation and, hence, are proxies for the money rate of interest.

[5] For comparison purposes, we note that Canadian GNP for 1972 was approximately $105 billion. In terms of the *income velocity* of money, this corresponds to a value of V in the neighbourhood of 2.5. There are, of course, alternative ways to define money. A narrower definition would consist of currency plus only demand deposits at chartered banks. For 1972 this averaged about $13 billion, corresponding to an income velocity of about 8.0.

The *real* quantity of money is probably best conceived in terms of the *volume* (rather than current-dollar value) of goods and services that money will purchase. However, there is no unique way to express this real quantity of money. The most common method is to express it in terms of a standard basket or bundle of goods and services. Implicitly, this is what is done when the real quantity of money is calculated by dividing the nominal quantity of money by a price index, such as the consumer price index. Since the consumer price index is calculated as a weighted average of various goods-and-services prices, this implies that the "standard basket" is composed of these same commodities and services. Notationally, the real quantity of money calculated in this manner is normally expressed as M/P, where M is the nominal quantity of money and P is the price index. There are other ways in which the real quantity of money could be expressed, such as, for example, the *number of weeks* of GNP to which it is equal.[6]

Although in official statistics P is generally a price index (thus a dimensionless or pure number), in theoretical work P can be taken to be the *absolute* price level (number of dollars per bundle of goods and services). The *reciprocal* of the absolute price level (i.e., unity divided by the price level) represents the "goods-and-services" price of money (as distinct from the money price of a particular good or service).[7] As the absolute price level rises, its reciprocal falls. Thus an increase in the absolute price level represents a fall in the price of money or, equivalently, a fall in its purchasing power.

2. "The quantity theory of money takes for granted that what ultimately matters to holders of money is the real quantity rather than the nominal quantity they hold and that there is a fairly definite real quantity of money that people wish to hold under any given circumstances".[8] In more conventional terms, the quantity theory assumes that there exists a *stable demand function for real money balances* and, further, that the arguments in this function are relatively few in number. Countless empirical studies have "tested" the stability of the demand-for-money function and found that it is indeed very stable. For our purposes, we shall simply assume that the demand for real balances is positively related to the level of real income and negatively related to the money rate of interest, i.e., the demand for real balances will increase if real income increases, other things remaining unchanged, and it will fall if the money rate of interest increases, again keeping other things unchanged. The rationale for the negative relationship with interest rates is that as interest rates rise, the opportunity cost of holding real balances increases and, hence, fewer real balances will be held. The rationale for a positive relation between real balances and real income is that as real income rises, people will desire to hold larger real balances for transactions purposes or as a temporary

[6] Many of the sentences in this paragraph are based on M. Friedman, "A Theoretical Framework for Monetary Analysis," *Journal of Political Economy*, Vol. 78, No. 2 (March/April 1970), p. 194.

[7] Suppose wine costs $2 a bottle. This is the money price of wine — and the "wine price of money" is ½ bottle per dollar. In the case of the price level, of course, we are dealing with not just one commodity but a bundle or standard basket of goods and services.

[8] Friedman, "A Theoretical Framework for Monetary Analysis," p. 194.

store of purchasing power.[9] Therefore, while the demand for money may vary, it will vary in a predictable and quantifiable manner.

3.   Closely related to the postulate that a stable demand function for money exists is the proposition that *the public can and does obtain its desired level of real money balances.*

4. Furthermore, the supply of *nominal* money balances *(in a closed economy)* [10] is a policy-determined variable, i.e., it is under the control of the central bank. Moreover, changes in these nominal balances often tend to be substantial, abrupt, and largely independent of the factors that determine the demand for real money balances.

We have argued under points 3 and 4 that *the monetary authorities determine the nominal money supply while the public determines the real money supply.* It is precisely *via* the actions of the public in converting this exogenous nominal stock into the desired real stock that money has its impact on the economy. Specifically, suppose that the nominal quantity of money in relation to the absolute price level corresponds to a real quantity which is *larger* than that which the public desires to hold. Individuals will attempt to spend these "excess" money balances. Clearly, they cannot succeed in diminishing the *nominal* supply — the existing money stock must be held by someone. But, in the process of attempting to do so, they will increase the volume of nominal expenditures, which in turn will lead either to a bidding up of prices or to an increase in output. In either case, the discrepancy between the actual level of real balances and the desired level of real balances will tend to be eliminated, even though there has been no change in the level of nominal balances. In short, the public by its actions in attempting to dispose of excess money balances brings into equality the actual and desired real money balances "by either a *reduction in the real quantity available to hold through price rises* or an *increase in the real quantity desired through output increases*".[11]

5. This suggests that an excess supply of nominal balances is as likely as not to generate increased output as increased prices. For the short run this may well be true, especially if the exogenous increase in nominal balances represents an abrupt shift from past changes in, or rates of growth of, nominal balances. However, over any medium-run period such a proposition is *unacceptable* to the monetary position, at least as I interpret the thrust of the theory. Individual economic units are assumed to be rational in their decision-making, and *rationality implies making decisions in terms of the real value of economic variables.* Money illusion (i.e., acting on the *nominal* value of variables) may be an acceptable description of economic behaviour over a short-term cycle, but "it makes no theoretical sense as an assumption about behaviour in the face of a sustained unidirectional trend

---

[9] In terms of our earlier notation, we might express the demand for real balances as $k(i)Q$, where Q is real output as before, and $k(i)$ is the proportion of real output that the public desires to hold in the form of real balances. The parenthesized i (with i denoting interest rates) is meant to indicate that the proportion k will depend on the rate of interest. Specifically, the larger i is, the smaller will be the value of k.

[10] Later we will present the monetarist position for an open economy.

[11] Friedman, "A Theoretical Framework for Monetary Analysis," p. 195 (italics added).

in the level of prices".[12] In short, individuals should and do incorporate expectations relating to price changes into their decision-making, i.e., they act in response to real rather than nominal variables. What this implies is that a sustained increase in the rate of growth of nominal money balances (e.g., from 4 percent per annum to 8 percent) may initially have a sizeable impact on the growth rate of real output. But as the rate of inflation increases, the expectation of further price increases will become incorporated into the public's decision making, and in the intermediate term (say, 3 years) the principal effect of a sustained 4 percent increase in the growth rate of nominal balances will be a 4 percent increase in the inflation rate with little change in the growth rate of real output.

While on the subject of expectations, it seems appropriate to focus on the manner in which the monetarist approach deals with the relationship between rates of change of nominal balances and interest rates. The nominal interest rate (essentially the market interest rate) is, as we have mentioned above, assumed to equal the real interest rate (the real rate of return to investment) *plus* the expected rate of inflation. From a position of zero inflationary expectations (where nominal and real rates are equal), rapid increases in money balances *via* central-bank purchases of bonds from the public will, in the short term, lead to an excess demand for bonds, rising bond prices and, therefore, falling nominal interest rates.[13] However, as these nominal-balance increases lead to price increases and generate inflationary expectations, nominal interest rates will tend to rise to incorporate these inflationary expectations so that the longer-run relationship between increases in the rates of monetary expansion and nominal interest is *positive*, not negative. With across-the-board inflationary expectations of 4 percent and with real rates also 4 percent, rational behaviour requires that nominal rates be in the neighbourhood of 8 percent.

This proposition that the public can, and to a substantial degree does, alter its behaviour to reflect changes in real rather than nominal variables leads to a further tenet of monetarism, or perhaps more correctly to a generalization of proposition 5.

6. *Changes in nominal policy instruments have their main impact on nominal variables*. Thus the principal impact of, say, a sustained increase in the rate of growth of nominal money balances will be a corresponding rise in the rate of inflation rather than in real output (i.e., a rise in nominal income rather than in real income) and a rise in nominal interest rates rather than in real interest rates. Nominal policy variables have little impact on real variables such as employment and real output, especially in the longer run, and vice versa. From these observations follows Friedman's familiar dictum: "Inflation is always and everywhere a monetary phenomenon".[14]

7. Finally, monetarists assert that "substantial changes in nominal

[12] H. G. Johnson, *Inflation and the Monetarist Controversy* (Amsterdam: North-Holland Publishing Company, 1972), p. 54.
[13] The reader is reminded that there is an inverse relationship between bond prices and bond interest rates. For example, consider a bond selling for $100 and paying a yearly coupon interest of $7. Now let the demand for bonds rise such that the price of this bond is pushed up to $105. The effective interest rate simultaneously has fallen — from 7/100 to 7/105.
[14] M. Friedman, *An Economist's Protest* (Glen Ridge, New Jersey: Thomas Horton and Company, 1972), p. 29 (reprinted from *Newsweek*, September 28, 1970).

income are almost invariably the result of changes in the nominal supply of money".[15] In short, the monetary authorities by their actions can cause major swings in private-sector nominal income, which in turn can generate cyclical swings in real income. As a result, monetarists often prescribe relatively constant money-supply growth rates as the appropriate central-bank policy. In part, this follows from their belief that money interacts with the economy with a long and variable lag. But more importantly, it follows from the knowledge that too often in the past erratic growth rates in monetary aggregates have generated private-sector instability. Hence, predetermined growth rates within certain limits (say, between 2 and 6 per-cent per annum for the money supply) would encourage stability in the private sector.

Monetarism and the Phillips curve

Public policy in the last decade or so has been influenced to a very substantial degree by what has come to be known as the *Phillips curve* or the trade-off between the rate of unemployment and the rate of inflation, represented by curve CC in Figure 1. Essentially, the Phillips curve suggests that an economy cannot get *both* less inflation and less unemployment. Given the institutional structure of markets as well as the state of tech-nology, less inflation can be purchased only at the expense of greater un-employment, i.e., the economy is constrained to move along CC.

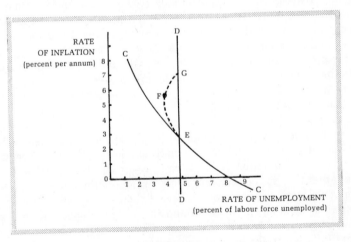

Figure 1

From the analysis above, it should be obvious that the concept of a Phillips curve does not rest well at all with the monetarist school. Basically this is because the Phillips curve purports to express a relationship between a *monetary variable* (the rate of inflation) and a *real variable* (the level of unemployment). In any sort of medium or long term, when expectations re-

15 Friedman, "A Theoretical Framework for Monetary Analysis," p. 195.

lating to inflation rates are fully incorporated in the public's behaviour, *any level of inflation* is consistent with a given unemployment rate. Hence the monetarists view the "Phillips curve" essentially as a *vertical line*, such as DD in Figure 1, at what they refer to as the "natural" rate of unemployment. In turn, this natural unemployment rate depends upon the real structure of the economy (things like growth rates in the labour force, labour-management institutional relationships, seasonality of industry, job-market information, etc.) and is largely independent of changes in nominal policy variables.

In the short run, monetarists are willing to concede that something akin to a Phillips curve can be generated. Assume that the economy is at point E. Now assume that the rate of growth of the money supply jumps 4 percentage points. The immediate result will be an excess of nominal money balances that individuals will attempt to spend for goods, services, bonds, equities, and the like, as in points 4 and 5 above. It is likely that prices and wages will not fully adjust immediately, so that some increase in real output will result, i.e., the economy will move along a curve like EF in Figure 1.

Investment will also be encouraged if bond rates fail to anticipate correctly the future inflation, because the *ex post* cost of borrowing will be below the real rate of interest. However, as businesses and individuals begin to anticipate inflation correctly and incorporate it into their decision making, the "trade-off" will appear as FG. The system will eventually come to rest at point G, with the same rate of unemployment as at E but with the inflation rate 4 percent higher. Curve EFG represents the dynamics of how the economy gets from point E to point G. The long-run Phillips curve is vertical. *Any level of inflation is consistent with the natural rate of unemployment.*

Perhaps this interpretation of the Phillips curve as being vertical is a bit extreme. For example, the natural rate of unemployment could be an interval or band (say, between 4.5 and 5.5 percent for Canada) rather than a fixed number. Furthermore, recent work on the related concepts of information and transactions costs that is accepted by most monetarists would point in the direction of a very steeply sloped rather than a vertical curve in the long run. Another important question is how long it takes before the private sector incorporates inflationary expectations in its decision making. If it involves a time period of a decade or longer, then perhaps EF or CC would be a meaningful concept. I believe, however, that it is increasingly the case that money illusion is on the wane and that the public is adjusting ever more quickly to inflation, so much so that even for short-run monetary-policy purposes the authorities are well advised to view DD (or a vertical band centred around DD) rather than CC as the likely relationship between unemployment and inflation.

II. Monetarism in an Open Economy

1. Fixed exchange rates

The monetarist position outlined above assumes that the economy is closed. We now alter this assumption and deal with a *small, open economy on fixed exchange rates.* Indeed, we shall present a very extreme case — the country is so small and so open that it is a "price-taker," and international capital is assumed to be sufficiently mobile that the country has to accept the world interest rate as well. In other words, price* levels are determined by the monetary policies of the rest of the world and are regarded as a *parameter* for our small, open economy. Real income in our model economy is again assumed to be independent of monetary magnitudes and determined by factor endowments, technology, tastes, etc., both at home and abroad. As in point 3 above, the public determines the real demand for money.

With real money balances determined by the private economy and with prices determined in world markets, this implies that the *nominal quantity of money (M) is automatically determined by the economic system and is not under the control of the country's central bank.* This is very different from the closed-economy model, where M was fixed exogenously by the monetary authorities and the public determined the real stock of balances by setting the price level. In our stylized open economy, prices are *already given* and by setting the desired stock of real balances the public determines M, the nominal stock. If the central bank does not provide this desired level of nominal balances, *the difference will flow in via the balance of payments.*

Consider a situation where the central bank creates a quantity of M which is larger than that which the public wishes to hold. In its attempts to spend these excess money balances, prices of goods, securities, and bonds will tend to be bid up. As a result of domestic prices tending to rise above world levels, exports will fall, imports will rise, and, most important in the short run, capital will flow out because domestic citizens will buy the lower-priced, higher-interest-bearing foreign bonds and foreigners will divert their money away from domestic bonds. In short, our small, open economy will incur a balance-of-payments *deficit,* thereby losing international reserves and decreasing the domestic money supply. *This process will continue until the domestic level of M is reduced to the level desired by the public.*

Note that a balance-of-payments deficit implies that nominal money balances are flowing out of the private sector. To see this, consider a situation where Canadians are importing in value terms more goods and services than they are exporting. In order to pay for this excess of imports over exports, Canadians would be *net* purchasers of foreign exchange from the government's Exchange Fund Account (or indirectly from the Exchange Fund *via* the chartered banks). This implies that on balance Canadians are writing cheques on their bank accounts to buy the foreign exchange, which in turn will end up in the hands of the foreign exporters. Hence the money supply is decreased by this process, since money is transferred from the public to the government. If the government wishes, it can offset this decrease in money by conducting an appropriate open-market purchase of bonds, thus increasing bank reserves and thence the money supply. This process of insulating the domestic money supply from balance-of-payments deficits or surpluses is known as *sterilization.* In the previous example, if the government opts to sterilize the impact on the money supply of the balance-of-payments deficit (by conducting open-market purchases of bonds), the original disequilibrium will still exist. That is, there will still be an excess supply of money and the balance-of-payments deficits will continue. In theory, the government could continue a sterilization policy as long as it had foreign exchange or gold to cover the resulting balance-of-payments deficits. In practice, however, the ability of a country like Canada under fixed exchange rates to sterilize deficits is very limited. Speculators will very quickly realize that Canada is attempting to run its monetary policy counter to that of the "world" and will move funds out of the country (in anticipation of a devaluation of the Canadian currency whereupon they would repatriate the funds and pocket the profits). In order to prevent these potentially massive speculative outflows and the accompanying devaluation of the dollar, Canadian monetary policy must supply the nominal quantity of money to ensure that domestic prices and interest rates remain consistent with world levels, i.e., it must acquiesce to the desires of the public with respect to M.[16]

What role does this leave for independent monetary policy in our stylized economy? Not much. To see this, it is convenient to view the central-bank balance sheet as composed of high-powered money or, equivalently, the monetary base (i.e., bank reserves plus currency) on the liability side and of international reserves (gold plus foreign exchange) and domestic assets (essentially government bills and bonds) on the asset side. In short, we wish to consolidate the central-bank operations with the government's foreign-exchange operations.[17] The thrust of the above analysis suggests that the private sector controls high-powered money.[18] All that

---

[16] The speed of this acquiescence depends on such factors as the degree of capital mobility. If capital is perfectly mobile (i.e., the slightest change in domestic relative to foreign interest rates will trigger massive capital flows), then the monetary-authority response must be immediate.

[17] For example, the balance sheet for the combined Bank of Canada and Exchange Fund as of December 31, 1969 might be presented as follows:

Assets		Liabilities	
($ billions)		($ billions)	
Foreign Exchange and Gold	3.34	High-Powered Money	4.98
Domestic Bonds	1.64		

where the figure for domestic bonds is calculated as the difference between high-powered money and the $3.34 billion of foreign exchange. (The latter two values are taken from International Financial Statistics (December 1970), p. 71.) Obviously, this calculation is somewhat superficial, since there are some other assets and liabilities that are ignored. It is quite possible for "domestic bonds" to be negative; i.e., the value of gold plus foreign exchange could exceed high-powered money, implying that Canada has enough international reserves to "buy back" all the government-bond holdings of the Bank of Canada, and then some. Indeed, for periods in 1971 the domestic-bond holdings were approximately zero. It is interesting to note that the International Monetary Fund does present such a consolidation for each country in its monthly publication International Financial Statistics. However, nowhere in the Bank of Canada publications does a consolidation appear. I believe that the failure to present such a consolidation serves to divert attention away from the critical interaction between Bank of Canada operations and the balance of payments, as outlined in the text above.

[18] This assumes a constant ratio between the money supply and high-powered money — an assumption that distorts reality to some degree. See T.J. Courchene and A.K. Kelly, "Money Supply and Money Demand: An Econometric Analysis for Canada," Journal of Money, Credit and Banking, Vol. III, No. 2, Part I (May 1971), pp. 219–244.

the central bank can do is decide the *composition* of this given amount of high-powered money between international reserves and domestic assets. If the monetary authorities insist on purchasing domestic assets in order to increase M beyond the desired level, this will be offset by losses of gold and foreign exchange which will return M to the desired level. Hence, international reserves serve as the adjustment mechanism to guarantee the desired level of M.

• *Implications for the Phillips curve:* The Phillips curve for our model economy is very different from that for the closed economy above. Small, open economies with international capital markets *must accept the world's inflation rate.*[19] In the immediate run, the central bank might be able to run the domestic economy "tighter" than the world by keeping the money supply below the equilibrium level. But it is only a matter of time before the resulting international-reserve inflows become too large to sterilize and the country is forced either to increase the domestic money supply (and therefore, prices) back to the world equilibrium level or else to appreciate its exchange rate. The combination of a "natural" rate of unemployment and the world inflation rate implies that the Phillips relationship is a *point,* at least in the longer run. But granting that the natural unemployment rate may be a range of unemployment levels and that real variables can be influenced by monetary variables in the short run, it might be more appropriate to describe the Phillips curve as a *very horizontal line* in the inflation–unemployment graph. Hence, for a closed economy the Phillips curve is basically vertical, especially over the longer run, while in an open economy under fixed exchange rates the Phillips curve is basically horizontal.[20] In order to generate better price performance under fixed exchange rates, a *large* increase of unemployment must be accepted. And this better price performance will be only a temporary one.

Again we have focused on an extreme example. To the extent that a country has some "monopoly" power in the world, i.e., to the extent that it is capable of influencing world price levels, the scope for some independence in domestic monetary policy broadens. However, as far as Canada

---

[19] One must be careful in defining what is meant by accepting the world inflation rate. If all commodities and services were traded internationally and there were no transportation costs, tariffs, and the like, absolute price levels would everywhere be identical. Even in such a hypothetical world, individual country price indices would not be equal unless the weights attached to each commodity and service were also identical across countries, i.e., consumers must have identical tastes in order for price indices to be identical. Reality is such, however, that these assumptions are inappropriate. Countries have different proportions of their total output which are traded internationally, so that it is quite possible for prices of non-traded goods and services to diverge across countries. Indeed, some countries' over-all inflation rates can appear to be considerably different from the world rate because of varying proportions of traded goods and differing price-index weights. What is meant by saying that countries have to accept the world inflation rate is that their own rates of inflation must be such as to guarantee that traded-goods prices are in conformity with world prices of these goods.

[20] If the policy authorities did not attempt to alter the inflation–unemployment trade-off, the appropriate curve would be a narrow, relatively horizontal line in the natural-rate-of-unemployment range. However, by attempting to affect the inflation–unemployment trade-off under fixed rates, the curve that will be traced out will be a very horizontal one, i.e., it is quite possible to generate significant increases in unemployment by trying to produce Canadian rates of inflation below the world level. See section III for a recent policy example.

is concerned, under fixed rates the assumption of anything other than that the short-run Phillips curve is very horizontal is, in my view, untenable.

2. Flexible exchange rates

Flexible exchange rates effectively "close" an open economy in the sense that the nominal money supply again becomes an exogenous or central-bank-controlled variable. Hence, a country can pursue its own policies with respect to domestic prices. Indeed, the closed-economy monetarist model is basically the relevant one for a country with flexible exchange rates. Nonetheless, some important differences do remain between a truly closed economy (e.g., the world) and an open economy with flexible exchange rates. For example, if the flexible-rate economy is small and most of the rest of the world is on fixed rates — a situation in which Canada has frequently found herself — *world inflation rates still exert a significant influence on its domestic policy.* Specifically, from the point of view of the numeraire currency (the key currency and reserve currency — in practice, the U.S. dollar), Canadian prices must still increase at the same rate as world prices. Under fixed rates, all of this price increase had to come from domestic inflation. Under flexible rates, our prototype economy has the option of choosing how much of the world inflation rate will come from internal sources (domestic inflation) and how much will come *via* exchange-rate appreciation — the two must sum to the world inflation rate. Therefore if the world inflation rate is 5 percent and our model economy sets nominal balances so as to engineer a 3 percent domestic inflation rate, the exchange rate will appreciate by 2 percent.[21] If the policy authorities generate a 6 percent domestic inflation, the exchange rate will depreciate by 1 percent, and so on. *The role, then, for the central bank under flexible rates is, by its policy toward nominal money expansion, to allocate the world inflation rate between domestic inflation and exchange-rate changes.* It *cannot* attempt to set inconsistent rates for domestic inflation and exchange-rate changes. Once it decides on one, the international economic system determines the other.

We began our discussion of the monetarist model by emphasizing the distinction between nominal or monetary variables and real variables. From the analysis of open economies, it should be obvious that monetarists view *the over-all balance of payments* (for fixed exchange rates) and the *exchange rate* (for flexible rates) as *monetary variables.* This is not to deny the important repercussions that changes in productivity, market structure, or technology can have on the balance of payments and exchange rates. But for policy purposes, *changes in international reserves under fixed rates are really a substitute for domestically generated changes in the nominal money supply.* And under flexible rates, *changes in the exchange rate are a substitute for changes in absolute price levels* (i.e., rates of domestic inflation). An excess supply of real money balances will, under fixed rates, lead to an over-all balance-of-payments deficit and a corresponding outflow of these excess balances. Under flexible rates, it

---

[21] Again this relationship may not hold in the short run, but it will hold over a period of two or three years.

will lead to domestic price increases (and hence a reduction of these balances to the desired level) and a corresponding exchange-rate depreciation.

We can illustrate this by means of intercountry comparisons of interest rates under both regimes. Assume that real interest rates are identical across countries under both fixed and flexible rates. For fixed rates, the money or nominal interest rates will also be equal across countries because each country will have approximately the same rate of inflation. However, for flexible rates, nominal rates of interest need not be equal across countries. Nations with higher rates of inflation will have higher nominal rates of interest. For example, the United States may have the following interest-rate configuration: real rate 3%, inflation rate 4%, nominal rate 7%. Canada could have a 3% real rate, 6% inflation rate, and a 9% nominal rate. But then one should observe that Canada's exchange rate would be depreciating at 2% per year. *Corrected for exchange-rate changes, nominal interest rates will also be equal under flexible-exchange-rate regimes.*

III. Monetarism and Selected Canadian Policy Experience

Pursuant to the Bretton Woods' agreement establishing the International Monetary Fund (IMF), Canada and most other countries established initial par values (fixed exchange rates) for their currencies on December 18, 1946. The Canadian dollar was fixed at 100 U.S. cents (i.e., at par with the U.S. dollar). On September 19, 1949 Canada following Britain in devaluing with respect to the U.S. dollar and set the value of the Canadian dollar at 90 U.S. cents. From September 30, 1950 to May 1, 1962 Canada was on a floating exchange rate. On May 2, 1962 the Canadian dollar was again assigned a par value, this time equaling 92.5 U.S. cents. Finally, on June 1, 1970 Canada returned to a floating exchange rate.

The purpose of this section is to focus briefly on certain facets of Canadian policy experience under both fixed rates and flexible rates. No attempt is made to chart the course of monetary policy during these different exchange-rate regimes.[22] Rather, two or three selected policy episodes are examined in order to relate the monetarist approach to actual policy actions.

1. Fixed exchange rates

We have argued above that the monetary authorities of small, open economies such as Canada have to gear domestic monetary policy to maintaining the par value of their currencies. Some degree of maneuverability does exist because countries can allow their stocks of gold and foreign exchange to accumulate or run down in order to absorb short-term balance-of-payments surpluses or deficits. Even this limited degree of policy freedom was denied Canada between 1963 and 1968, because Canada agreed to place a limit on the level of its international reserves ($2.6 billion

---

[22] For a blow-by-blow account of monetary policy during much of the early part of this period, the reader is referred to P. Wonnacott, *The Canadian Dollar 1948-1962* (Toronto: University of Toronto Press, 1965).

U.S.) in return for an exemption from the Interest Equalization Tax imposed by the United States in 1963. Hence, not only was there a fixed price of the Canadian dollar in terms of U.S. dollars, but there was as well an upper limit on the quantity of U.S. dollars that Canada could hold.[23] And since this reserve ceiling was effective for much of the 1963–1968 period (i.e., Canada's reserves were often near the ceiling level), Canadian monetary policy was effectively emasculated. The large variations in rate of money-supply growth that occurred over the period are best interpreted as dictated by the requirements of maintaining exchange-rate parity and avoiding international-reserve accumulation beyond the agreed limit. Indeed, in terms of monetary independence, the Bank of Canada may as well have been the 13th Federal Reserve Bank. This interpretation is precisely what our above analysis would suggest.

However, with the increase in the U.S. rate of inflation in 1968 and 1969, the Canadian government moved boldly in the direction of charting an independent course for Canada as far as prices were concerned. In its position paper *Policies for Price Stability*,[24] Ottawa recommended the formation of the Prices and Incomes Commission and later established it. Underlying this policy action was the belief that the Phillips curve for Canada looked something like CC in Figure 1. Specifically, Canada hoped it would be possible to (a) move downward along the Phillips curve and achieve a considerably lower rate of inflation at the expense of somewhat greater unemployment, and (b) shift the entire Phillips curve toward the origin so that the over-all result would be less inflation with not much effect on unemployment at all. Interestingly enough, the Bank of Canada lent its support to this policy.[25]

While there is little doubt that by changing the institutional structure of the Canadian economy, especially as it relates to all aspects of the labour market, Canada may indeed be able to shift the Phillips curve toward the origin (and hence achieve a "better" trade-off between inflation and unemployment), there is also little doubt that a program of voluntary restraint, as advocated by the Prices and Incomes Commission, was not the appropriate vehicle for such a change. More importantly for our purposes, the entire operation was based on the faulty premise that Canada could chart a course independent of the world economy with respect to the rate of inflation. From the above analysis, the monetarist approach would suggest that this was flouting the basic economic laws underlying the fixed-exchange-rate system, i.e., the Phillips curve is essentially a horizontal line at the world inflation rate for a small, open economy with a fixed exchange rate. I believe that the events which occurred confirm the monetarist position. To these we now turn.[26]

---

[23] Virtually all of Canada's foreign exchange in this period consisted of U.S. dollars or U.S.-dollar assets.

[24] Government of Canada (Ottawa: Queen's Printer, 1968).

[25] For example, see the Bank of Canada, *Annual Report 1967*, p. 8.

[26] For a more detailed description and evaluation of monetary policy over the 1965–1970 period, see T.J. Courchene, "Recent Canadian Monetary Policy," *Journal of Money, Credit and Banking*, III, No. 1 (February 1971), pp. 35–56; reprinted in J.P. Cairns, H.H. Binhammer, and R. Boadway, eds., *Canadian Banking and Monetary Policy* (Toronto: McGraw-Hill Ryerson Limited, 1972), pp. 204–225, and in *Canadian Perspectives in Economics* (Toronto: Collier-Macmillan Canada Limited, 1972).

Monetary policy in Canada became very tight during the latter half of 1969 and the first half of 1970. Indeed, the Canadian money supply (as defined by the IMF) in February 1970 was 11 percent *lower* than it was in February 1969.[27] No other industrialized nation exhibited a negative growth rate in money over this period. The idea behind such a stringent monetary policy was to suppress aggregate demand and in this manner to curtail the rate of inflation. The problem was that the Canadian authorities failed to appreciate the interrelationship between the Canadian economy and the world economic community. Not only did this policy generate an excess demand for money within Canada, but as well an excess demand for money in Canada relative to the rest of the world. Predictably, from the above analysis, reserves began to flow into Canada.[28] Rather than allow these reserve inflows to increase the money supply and satisfy the public's desire for greater nominal money balances, Canada engaged in a vigorous policy of sterilizing these inflows of international reserves. This served only to worsen the disequilibrium. From a level of just under $3 billion (U.S.) in September 1969, Canada's international reserves rose to $3.1 billion by year end, $3.6 billion in March 1970, $3.8 billion in April, and $4.1 billion in May.

Despite the fact that the government and the Bank of Canada engaged in some highly interesting emergency measures to deal with the ever-increasing inflows of foreign exchange,[29] it became obvious that Canada had only two options open to her: (a) allow the inflows to increase the domestic money supply in order to remove the monetary disequilibrium, or (b) allow the exchange rate to appreciate, either by revaluing the dollar or by setting it free on the world's currency market. Option (a) would have represented the antithesis of the whole thrust of Canadian policy at that time. Accordingly, on May 31, 1970, the government announced that the Canadian dollar would no longer have a par value and that its price would be determined by forces of supply and demand in the world's currency markets.

The moral of the story is simply that a small, open economy cannot chart an independent monetary course in a fixed-exchange-rate world. That the Canadian dollar is floating may well be a desirable thing. But it does not detract from the fact that the Canadian authorities had a very inadequate understanding of the economic laws underlying the fixed-exchange-rate regime.

Interestingly enough, Canadian officials pointed with pride to the fact that for the year or so following the floating of the Canadian dollar (and its eventual appreciation with respect to the U.S. dollar), Canada had one of the most enviable price performances in the western world. Indeed, it was even strongly hinted that this was largely due to efforts of the Prices and Incomes Commission. However, the main reason why Canada's inflation rate was less than that of her trading partners was that the Canadian dollar *appreciated* approximately 7 percent. As we stated in the analysis above, exchange-rate appreciation is a substitute for do-

[27] *International Financial Statistics*, December 1970, p. 34.
[28] By this time the ceiling on international reserves had been lifted.
[29] See Courchene, *op. cit.*, p. 50.

mestic inflation. Taking account of the 7 percent appreciation, Canada's price behaviour since 1969 has not been appreciably different from that of the United States.

On the *unemployment* side, however, things did not fare so well. The principal result of the period of excessive monetary tightness was an *increase in the unemployment rate from 2.9 percent in 1969 to 4.4 percent in 1970.*[30] The Canadian Phillips curve under fixed exchange rates turned out to be far more horizontal (at the world inflation rate) than the policy authorities had anticipated.

2. Flexible exchange rates

Much has been written on Canada's experience with flexible rates during the 1950–1962 period. We wish only to highlight one incident. In 1959 the Bank of Canada began to run monetary policy very tight both in absolute terms and relative to the United States. The result was that interest rates increased substantially (the average treasury-bill rate went from 2.29 percent in 1958 to 4.81 in 1959) and the exchange rate appreciated. This was clearly inappropriate policy in the light of the fact that the economy was in need of expansionary and not contractionary policy at the time. Unemployment rates hit an annual average high of 7.2 percent in 1961.

Under flexible rates a country is able to chart its own course, whereas under fixed rates a country must keep in step with the economic policy of the world. Flexible rates are a clear advantage if a country is able to generate better economic policies than the rest of the world. But the lesson from Canada's 1959–1961 experience is that under flexible rates a country also has to live with its monetary-policy errors.

Consider now the more recent period of flexible rates. From June 1970, when the Canadian dollar was unpegged, until mid-1973 the money supply grew at annual rates in the neighbourhood of 15–20 percent. Indeed, the growth rates for 1971 and 1972 were both higher than any recorded in the previous decade.[31] This is somewhat surprising. In 1969–1970, when Canada really had no ability to chart an independent monetary course, she nevertheless attempted to restrict the growth of monetary aggregates in order to achieve better price performance. In 1970–1973, under flexible rates, when Canada did have the ability to influence the domestic inflation rate, monetary policy appeared to be geared to maintaining parity with the U.S. dollar, i.e., to "fixing" the flexible rate.

As stated in section II, subsection 2 of this paper, the central bank can, by its policies toward the rate of increase in nominal balances, allocate the world inflation rate between domestic inflation and exchange-rate changes. By generating lower rates of monetary expansion in 1970–1973, Canada could have achieved a lower inflation rate and a correspondingly higher value for the Canadian dollar. It appeared that the Bank of Canada was fully aware of this,[32] but opted instead to attempt to keep the Cana-

---

[30] *Bank of Canada Review* (June 1973), Table 55.
[31] *Bank of Canada Review* (June 1973), Table 1.
[32] See the statement by former Senior Deputy Governor J.R. Beattie, "Monetary Policy," *Bank of Canada Review*, December 1971, pp. 21–25.

dian dollar in line with the U.S. dollar. Hence the large growth rates in the money supply and the accompanying high domestic inflation rates.

What does the monetarist have to say about wage and price controls? To argue for controls to suppress inflation is to fail to understand the very nature of the problem. The driving force behind inflation in a flexible-rate economy, such as Canada, is a tremendous growth rate in nominal money balances. Controls, per se, do nothing to attack the basic cause of inflation. Rising prices are not the cause of inflation; they only measure the degree of inflation. Price controls do not remove the underlying inflationary pressure. Rather, they prevent it from being recorded. Unless rapid rates of money-supply growth are severely curtailed, a country such as Canada has to learn to live with inflation.

On this point, Friedman suggests that an economy characterized by very rapid monetary expansion is very much like a steam-heating furnace running at full blast.[33] Closing the radiator in one room results in the other rooms being even more overheated. Closing all radiators builds up pressure in the boiler and increases the danger that it will explode. A system of selective price controls will not eradicate the inflationary pressure. It will only divert it elsewhere. Clearly, the appropriate solution is to attempt to remove not the symptoms of the disease (i.e., rising prices) but rather the cause (i.e., excessive monetary expansion).

[33] M. Friedman, *Dollars and Deficits* (Englewood Cliffs: Prentice-Hall, 1968), p. 100.

II. International Influences On the Canadian Economy

1. Canadian Trade Patterns And Commercial Policy

Thomas L. Powrie and Bruce W. Wilkinson

University of Alberta

The first section of this essay briefly defines "commercial policy" and discusses its goals. The second and third sections describe the pattern of Canada's international trade and some of the commercial policies that have affected the pattern. The fourth and last section comments on possible Canadian commercial policies for the future.[1]

I. Goals of Commercial Policy

International trade is a means, not an end. A national government will encourage or hinder trade between its residents and outsiders as it believes such transactions will help or harm its own objectives.

The policies a government uses to encourage or hinder foreign trade are called commercial policies. Tariffs against imports are the best known of such policies, but there is a wide range of others, such as quotas (quantitative limitations) on exports or on imports, government credit on export sales, special trade treaties with other governments, and promotional activities by commercial attachés in consulates and embassies.

Commercial policies may be used to pursue various national objectives, including political or military ones. For example, a government may prohibit exports by its citizens to an unfriendly country in the hope of harming it, or it may enter into trade treaties designed to assist a friendly government that needs help. Canada's livelihood, however, is too heavily reliant on international trade for us to feel free to use commercial policies

---

[1] For more extensive discussion of Canadian trade and trade policy, see B.W. Wilkinson, *Canada's International Trade: An Analysis of Recent Trends and Patterns* (Montreal: Canadian Trade Committee, 1968), and H.E. English, B.W. Wilkinson, and H. C. Eastman, *Canada in a Wider Economic Community* (Toronto: Private Planning Association of Canada and University of Toronto Press, 1972).

for other than economic goals. Our commercial policies are almost entirely, and this esay about them is entirely, concerned with economic objectives.

Even the merely economic objectives are diverse. Commercial policy alone cannot achieve any of them, but it can contribute toward the achievement of some of them, including these:

— a high and rising standard of living
— full employment
— a viable balance of payments

The principle of comparative advantage is concerned with the first of these three goals. It tells us that if each country specializes in those products that it can produce at the lowest opportunity cost relative to other countries, and trades its surpluses for those of other countries, then all countries can enjoy a higher standard of living. Among countries as among individuals, specialization and exchange can lead to higher real incomes for all. This principle is of great practical importance; it is one of the basic reasons for the major efforts that have been made since World War II to reduce tariffs in world trade, and it is one of the basic reasons for the formation of the European Common Market. The commercial policy indicated by the principle of comparative advantage is in general a gradual removal of all tariffs and other impediments to international trade.

There is an open question in the principle of comparative advantage: How does a particular country come to have a comparative advantage in one range of products instead of in another? In part, the answer is given by nature. For example, Canada's rich endowment of natural resources obviously tends to give her a comparative advantage in forest and mineral products. But in part the answer is shaped by the government and people of the country itself. Switzerland's comparative advantage in the production of fine watches was created not by nature but by the Swiss. In order to use international trade as a support for a high and rising standard of living, a country must not only make use of its present comparative advantage but must also choose and develop its comparative advantage for the future. The creation of comparative advantage for the future may require the protection, by tariffs or otherwise, of industries which are presently at a comparative disadvantage but which we wish to get started because there is reason to believe they will develop to advantage in the future. This is the "infant-industry argument" for protection in commercial policy.

Our second goal is full employment. Commercial policy may also be used toward this goal, to create or protect jobs. The policy may be to increase exports and thus to create new jobs in export industries; this requires the willingness of other countries to accept these exports and the possible displacement of their own production and employment in those lines of production; some mutual agreement is often necessary, involving greater exports in both directions — in which case there may not be much net increase in employment. Alternatively, commercial policy may be protectionist, seeking to protect or create domestic jobs by restrictions against imports of competing products. Protectionist commercial policy does not require the direct co-operation of other countries, but it can lead to retaliation on their part against the exports of the protectionist. At the extreme, such retaliation and counter-retaliation is known as a trade war, and benefits no country's employment but reduces the standard of living of all.

Third, commercial policy may be used to correct balance-of-payments problems. If the residents of a country cannot earn (or borrow) enough foreign currency to pay for their purchases (or investments) in foreign countries, that country has a balance-of-payments deficit. One way to correct such a deficit is to use tariffs and other restrictions to limit spending on imports, and to use subsidies to encourage exports to earn more foreign currency. Canada has not suffered any such shortage of foreign currency in recent years; in fact, we have had surpluses. In the past we have relied heavily on new inflows of foreign capital, i.e., new net borrowing, each year to provide part of the foreign currency spent on imports. If we had reduced our reliance on foreign investment, we would have had to close the resulting foreign-currency gap by exporting more and importing less. Commercial policies might have helped toward this end, provided other nations did not retaliate.

Thus, with only three economic goals considered, we find situations that seem to require freer trade and others that seem to require more protection. It is obvious that commercial policy cannot achieve all goals by itself; it cannot go in all directions at once. Fortunately, governments do have other policy tools, including monetary policy, taxation, subsidies, exchange-rate policy, and so on; the pursuit of several objectives requires the use of several tools.

One can easily think of other economic goals that commercial policy might help to achieve. For example, special assistance to the exports of a depressed region might improve the regional distribution of income within a country. Or removal of tariffs against imports might help to restrain price inflation. But we will not try to expand the subsequent discussion beyond the three economic goals listed above.

We turn now to a survey of the structure of Canadian trade and of past and current Canadian commercial policies.

II.   Recent Canadian Trade Patterns

The composition of Canadian merchandise exports and imports is shown in section A of Table 1. Canada has always tended to export foods and raw materials and to import manufactured goods. This is easily explained in terms of comparative advantage, given the country's rich endowment of agricultural land, forests, and minerals.

Agricultural products have long been a mainstay of Canadian exports, although their share has been diminishing. They are an unstable source of exports, partly because of the variability of wheat sales. Canadian wheat exports are sold by the Wheat Board, a government agency established to try to protect farmers from some of the instability of the world market for wheat. This instability was apparent in the 1960s. World surpluses accumulated, and Canada lost large sales because the Wheat Board was reluctant to enter into price competition with other exporters. More aggressive salesmanship, combined with greatly increased world demand, resulted in increased wheat sales after 1969 and a record level in 1972. One moral is that no exports can be taken for granted; there is always a competing supplier willing to replace them.

Canada also imports agricultural products, including many tropical or sub-tropical items such as coffee and bananas.

Forest products and raw or partly processed metals and minerals are the other mainstays of our exports. Among the most important individual

Table 1: *Current Receipts and Current Payments by Canadians In International Transactions, 1972*

	Current Receipts from exports of goods and services and from transfers		Current Payments for imports of goods and services and for transfers		Balance (receipts minus payments)
	million dollars	% of total	million dollars	% of total	million dollars
A. Merchandise					
Agricultural products	2662	10.5	1593	6.1	1069
Forest products	3594	14.2	352	1.4	3242
Energy	1738	6.9	1087	4.2	651
Metals and other crude & semi-processed materials	4082	16.1	2668	10.3	1414
Motor vehicles and parts[a]	4682	18.5	4987	19.2	−305
Other highly manu-factured goods	2742	10.8	8049	81.1	−5307
Adjustments[b]	437	1.7	−185	−0.7	622
Total merchandise	19937	78.7	18551	71.6	1386
B. Services (Non-Merchandise)					
Travel	1226	4.8	1456	5.6	−230
Interest and dividends	616	2.4	1553	6.0	−937
Freight and shipping	1260	5.0	1297	5.0	−37
Other	1433	5.7	2425	9.4	−992
Total services	4535	17.9	6731	26.0	−2196
C. Transfers[c]					
Total transfers	858	3.4	632	2.4	226
Total	25330	100.0	25914	100.0	−584
D. Net retained earnings[d]	?		?		−1000
Total including net retained earnings (rounded)	?		?		−1600

Footnotes and source of Table 1 on next page.

a These items show a deficit balance for Canada, in spite of U.S. concern about Canada's surplus under the automotive agreement. The explanation is partly that the item also includes trade with overseas countries, and partly that there are large discrepancies between U.S. and Canadian statistics. The discrepancies are being corrected, and will require rather large revisions to both countries' trade statistics in this and in other categories.
b The "adjustments" to merchandise exports and imports reflect a change in definitions between different parts of the Table.
c "Transfers" include personal, institutional, and government gifts and certain taxes on international income flows.
d "Interest and dividends" paid out do not include an additional amount, between one and two billion dollars, of retained net earnings of foreign-owned firms in Canada, nor do receipts on this account include the much smaller amount of retained net earnings of Canadian-owned firms in foreign countries. While these retained earnings are not a part of official statistics on international transactions, they are of major importance in contributing to the growth of foreign ownership in Canada and should not be overlooked. Data for 1972 are not available; the figure given above is a very conservative personal estimate.

Source: Compiled from Statistics Canada, *Summary of Exports, Summary of Imports*, and *The Canadian Balance of International Payments*.

products are woodpulp, newsprint, softwood lumber, and copper, nickel, lead, zinc, and aluminum. By the early 1970s the most rapidly growing part of these exports — indeed of all exports — was energy, which includes coal, electricity, natural gas, uranium, and, largest of all, crude oil. Both exports and imports of crude oil are large. Imported oil supplies the Atlantic and Quebec markets (the rest of the Canadian market is reserved by government regulation for Canadian oil), while exports of Prairie oil to the inland United States have grown very rapidly in response to shortages there.

The most dramatic change in Canada's foreign trade in the 1960s was the result of the automobile pact signed between the United States and Canada early in 1965.[2] This pact enabled the North American automobile companies to ship vehicles and parts across the border without paying tariffs. (No overseas company meets the eligibility conditions of the agreement.) Thus the companies could rationalize their production between the two nations. For example, a plant in Canada, instead of producing any number of different car models, can now produce a single model and export a large proportion of its output to the United States, while other models are imported from the United States. To take advantage of the cost-savings thus permitted, the auto companies have increased both their exports and imports tremendously. But, partly because Canadian plants were assigned some of the more popular car models, exports have outstripped imports in recent years. As a result, the U.S. government has sought changes in the auto pact on the grounds that it has damaged the U.S. balance of payments and employment in the U.S. auto industry. Canada has argued that the imbalance is likely to disappear by itself.

Other highly manufactured goods (apart from automobiles and parts) are traditionally imports, not exports, for Canada; as Table 1 indicates, they are by far the largest component of our imports. They include an immense variety of items, from toys and clothing to office equipment and electric generators. Our traditional reliance on foreign producers for many

[2] For a full study of the pact, see C.E. Beigie, *The Canada–U.S. Automotive Agreement: An Evaluation* (Montreal and Washington: Canadian–American Committee, 1970).

of these items reflects a comparative disadvantage in these industries, which variously require one or more of inexpensive labour, or highly skilled labour, or advanced technology, or aggressive salesmanship, or the economies of very large-scale production. Inexpensive labour is something the less-developed countries have much more of than Canada, and it is a source of comparative advantage for them that Canada does not wish to replicate. But the other four items listed are sources of exports that can support high wages, and they are items that are partly a function of government and industry policies. Such Canadian deficiencies as may exist in these areas can be partly corrected if we so choose. This point is discussed later in the paper.

Meanwhile, we should observe that exports of these other manufactured goods grew in the 1960s and early 1970s roughly in step with the general trend of world trade in them. Growing maturity and sophistication of Canadian industry, and efforts toward export promotion by the federal government, have helped. An important stimulus came from the devaluation of the Canadian dollar in 1961–62; this improved the price-competitiveness of Canadian products in foreign markets. (The rise in our dollar after mid-1970 was unwelcome to exporters because of its adverse effects on them.) The Canada–U.S. defence-production-sharing agreement gave Canada an export surplus on defence contracts over the 1960s. Under this agreement Canadian producers can bid on defence contracts offered by the American government without the hindrance of tariffs. Canada has the option of imposing a 10 percent duty on imports. (This option has been exercised for orders of less than $250,000.) Most of Canada's surplus here accumulated during the 1968–69 American build-up in Vietnam.

In addition to merchandise exports and imports (called "visible" trade), there is non-merchandise (often called "invisible") trade. These transactions involve trade in services rather than goods, and are shown in section B of Table 1. They include travel expenditure, transportation charges, payments of interest and dividends arising from foreign investments, and various other items such as consultants' fees, patent leases, or movie rentals. Canadian earnings from merchandise exports have been greater than expenditures on merchandise imports in all years since 1960, but this surplus has been more than exhausted by the invisible transactions. There is a large deficit on interest and dividends, which reflects the build-up over past decades of foreign investments in Canada. And "other" service payments also reflect foreign ownership, in the form of payments for various consulting and other services provided by parent companies to their subsidiaries in Canada. In addition, as indicated in section D of the table, there are net profits of foreign-owned companies that are not paid out as interest and dividends but are ploughed back into the growth of the companies as retained earnings. These retained earnings are of major importance in contributing to the growth of foreign ownership in Canada.

Together with transfer payments (flows such as foreign aid, for which no payment is received — shown as section C in Table 1), merchandise and non-merchandise trade constitute the "current account" of the balance of payments. The combined total of transactions in merchandise, services, and transfer payments typically yields a Canadian current-account deficit.

For example, Table 1 shows that in 1972 this deficit was $584 million, or some $1600 million, if retained earnings were also counted. Such deficits reflect continued new net borrowing by Canadians from other countries, that is, continued growth of foreign investment in Canada, as would appear in the "capital account" of the balance of payments. If we as a nation ever decide to reduce our reliance on foreign capital, one necessary (but not sufficient) step will be achievement of at least a balance between current receipts and current payments on foreign transactions. Note that because of the very large deficit on interest and dividends and retained earnings, arising from past investments, an over-all balance requires an equally large net surplus on all other current transactions.

So far this survey of Canada's international trade has described the kinds of goods and services traded. Now we look at the directions of this trade. Canada conducts a larger proportion of its trade with a single country than does any other nation in the world. Canada's reliance upon the United States as a trading partner is greater even than that of any member of the European Common Market (except possibly Belgium) upon all the other members combined. About 70 percent of our merchandise trade is with the United States. Geographic nearness is part of the explanation. Government policies in recent years have also worked to increase our reliance on trade with the United States. Of these policies, the auto pact and the defence-production-sharing agreement have already been mentioned, and one should also mention the establishment in 1944 of free trade with the United States in agricultural machinery. (The United States removed its tariffs on those products in 1913, but Canada did not reciprocate until 1944.) The massive amount of U.S. direct investment in Canada also contributes to closer trading ties, since foreign-owned firms tend to trade with their foreign parents.

Canada's second largest trading partner is now the expanded European Common Market, including the United Kingdom. We conduct about 12 percent of our merchandise trade with that area. Japan, at about 5 percent, is the third largest trading partner, and a rapidly growing one, because Japanese initiative is overcoming a depressing Canadian lack of awareness of that market. Both of these overseas markets are mainly interested in our raw-materials exports, in exchange for their highly manufactured goods. Only the United States is a good customer for exports other than our raw materials; of Canada's exports of sophisticated manufactured goods, 85 to 90 percent go to the United States.

III.   Traditional Canadian Commercial Policy

Today Canada has one of the highest tariff structures to be found among the wealthy nations.[3] In 1879, Sir John A. Macdonald launched a new policy of higher protective tariffs for Canadian industry; the policy has been retained, with variations, ever since. The main objective was to encourage the development of a large and diversified manufacturing

---

[3] For an analysis of the structure of the Canadian tariff, see J.R. Melvin and B.W. Wilkinson, *Effective Protection in the Canadian Economy*, Economic Council of Canada (Ottawa: Queen's Printer, 1968).

sector in the Canadian economy. Successive governments have generally believed that Canada needs more industrialization; the main argument has always been that extraction of raw materials for export does not provide enough jobs for a growing population and that the many additional jobs provided by processing and manufacturing are also needed. It was and is recognized that protection of relatively high-cost domestic industry means that Canadian consumers are worse off than if they had tariff-free access to the less-expensive foreign products. (The cost to Canadian consumers is the cost that the principle of comparative advantage explains will result from tariffs.) But there has always been the hope that this sacrifice would be temporary, and that in time many Canadian manufactures would become competitive in world markets. In other words, a long-term objective, or at least hope, has been that the protective tariff would help to bring about a change in Canada's comparative advantage, toward manufacturing. Tariffs have been used to start infant industries in the hope that they would grow up.

How well has the tariff worked? Its prime objective, to foster manufacturing industry in Canada, has been achieved. Canada is a fairly advanced industrial country; the portion of our labour force employed in manufacturing is about as high as in any industrial country; the economy produces an immense range of manufactured goods including highly sophisticated ones. The economy has been able to absorb more labour as a result; we have had more immigration and less emigration, and our population is greater than it would have been without the tariff.[4]

However, the hope that Canadian manufacturing would outgrow the need for protection continues to be disappointed. There are some impressive exceptions, such as parts of the steel industry, but over-all, Canadian manufacturing industries operate at per unit costs that are about one-third higher than those of comparable American industries.

Another feature of the tariff-induced industrialization of Canada is the high degree of foreign ownership and control involved. Sixty percent of all Canadian manufacturing is done by firms owned by foreigners. In a great many cases, a U.S. or other foreign company that would have exported to Canada from its home plants if there had been no Canadian tariffs, found it profitable because of the tariff to establish a producing subsidiary inside Canada. The tariff alone did not cause foreign investment, of course; it created investment opportunities, of which foreign firms were often the ones to take advantage. However, the result all too often was an excessive number of firms establishing plants, each one either too small or too unspecialized to be efficient by world standards. In retrospect one can argue that there should have been restrictions on foreign investment to limit the number of plants.

As we approach the one-hundredth anniversary of Macdonald's tariff policy, we should not only accept the gains it has achieved but also consider how to cope with the problems it leaves unsolved. It has given us industrialization and faster population growth, albeit at some cost to

---

[4] J.H. Dales, *The Protective Tariff in Canada's Development* (Toronto: University of Toronto Press, 1966), concludes, *inter alia*, that the tariff has increased the population and lowered *per capita* income.

per capita incomes. But the problem of high costs in manufacturing remains, as do the problems associated with a heavy degree of foreign ownership and control of Canadian industry.

IV. Alternatives for Canadian Commercial Policy

Before we consider alternatives for Canadian commercial policy in the future, it is helpful to look at the world trade situation and the concerns and likely behaviour of the countries with whom we trade. Some of the main characteristics of world trade of interest to Canada are the need of the less developed countries to industrialize, the desire of the European Common Market to protect its domestic agriculture, the rapid growth of trade in manufactured products among industrialized countries, and the emergence of a persistent balance-of-payments problem in the United States.

The desire to industrialize is not unique to Canada; every nation seeks to process its own raw materials rather than export them in crude form, or, if it is importing materials, to import them in as crude a state as possible for domestic processing. This desire is most urgent in the underdeveloped countries. One of their most important resources is large amounts of unskilled labour. This labour is low-priced, so they obviously can specialize in products that require large amounts of it.

Such products include textiles, clothing, leather goods, toys, and components for electrical equipment such as television sets or radios. Currently, multinational corporations that produce these types of products are shifting their production to developing nations such as Taiwan, Korea, or Singapore, and shipping the output back to the parent countries, to the dismay of workers affected in the parent countries, particularly in the United States.

Many nations have highly protectionist agricultural policies. The European Common Market (ECM) countries and Japan are the chief offenders in this regard, from Canada's point of view. (The original ECM nations were France, Germany, Italy, Belgium, Netherlands, and Luxemburg; the later members, Britain, Ireland, and Denmark, were required to adopt the Market's protectionist agricultural policies.) The Common Market imposes very high tariffs (some over 100 percent) against imports of agricultural products, and uses the proceeds from their tariffs to subsidize agricultural exports. Canada and other outsiders thus suffer doubly, first from reduced sales to Europe and second from subsidized competition in third markets.

The most rapidly growing component of world trade is trade in highly manufactured products among the industrially advanced nations. Production for export in this sector of world markets requires, among other things, advanced technology, in the form of new products or improved products or improved methods of production. Comparative advantage in this sector thus depends heavily on research and innovation. The United States, Japan, Germany, France, Britain, and Sweden are some of the leaders in applied research and development of new technology. In those nations, expenditure on research and development as a percentage of the gross national product greatly exceeds that in Canada.

Of all developments on the world trading scene, the most important for Canada is the growing strength of protectionist views in the United States. After World War II, successive U.S. administrations took the initiative in leading the world toward freer trade. But by the early 1970s, the United States had to cope with a worsening balance-of-trade position (while trying to sustain capital outflows for new investments in other countries) and with domestic unemployment, both of which strengthened the case of those Americans who argue that tariffs and other forms of protection are desirable. Concern in the United States over its balance-of-payments deficit is aggravated by forecasts that that country will be increasingly short of raw materials, especially crude oil and other forms of energy, and will have to spend rapidly increasing amounts for imports of these items. Next to Japan, the United States sees Canada as the country most responsible for its balance-of-payments deficit, as it has experienced large deficits on merchandise trade with Canada. Washington has requested that Ottawa undertake measures to reduce this merchandise imbalance. However, Canada needs a large surplus on merchandise account in order to cover its large deficit on non-merchandise items, unless it is to continue to finance the deficit by continued inflows of foreign capital and the selling of Canadian assets.

What should Canadian commercial policies be for the future?

In assessing some of the possibilities, we must keep in mind that unemployment in Canada remains high and promises to continue to be a problem for some years to come. This means that employment effects will have to be given more than usual weight in judging possible changes in commercial policy. For example, however desirable from the consumers' point of view, it would not be timely to relax restrictions on imports of, say, textiles, clothing, or furniture until there is assurance of alternative jobs for the Canadian workers who would be displaced by these imports.

Over the longer run, given time for employment problems to be overcome, it would be inconsistent with our objective of a high standard of living to deny Canadian consumers free access to the inexpensive manufactured goods of low-wage countries. Many mass-produced, standardized, quality items of this kind can be produced in Canada only at wage rates lower than Canadian workers need to accept or at selling prices higher than Canadian consumers should be expected to pay. Canadian tariff policy has never been based on much analysis of which industries might be true infant industries with prospects of becoming competitive in world markets. There has been a tendency to protect all areas of manufacturing; we should become more discriminating in our protection, in spite of the technical and political difficulties, and gradually remove protection from those industries that have no hope of ever becoming competitive with imports.

Are there any manufacturing industries in which Canada is or can become competitive in world markets? Such industries must be able to pay high and rising wages at the same time as their selling prices meet world competition. One set of such industries is those that need highly skilled labour, or have a product that is newer or better than that available elsewhere. Swedish furniture, American computers, and Canadian snowmobiles and high-fashion clothing from Montreal are examples that contain one or both of these characteristics. Tariff protection itself is perhaps not too helpful for such industries; it provides protection from foreign competition for industries copying foreign products, but these products are not copies but originals. The role of commercial policy in fostering these industries is to negotiate free access for their products into foreign markets, that is, to bargain down foreign tariffs presumably with reciprocal offers. We probably need to join more vigorously in the game of government aid to industrial research to create new and better products, and this involves among other things a recognition and acceptance of the fact that some projects are bound to cost a lot of public money and then fail. Risk-taking is required, and risk means possible success, possible failure.

Another set of such industries is those in which long production runs yield important economies of scale. This set (household appliances, fine papers, chemicals, automobiles, and numerous other items that are not necessarily new or different) has been discussed a great deal in Canada.[5] It is in these industries that a major improvement in productivity seems possible, if only the plants involved could produce much larger volumes of a much smaller variety of styles, models, sizes, or the like, and thereby avoid the cost of frequent down-time for changeover. How could commercial policy achieve this result? A frequently heard suggestion is free trade with the United States,[6] so that Canadian plants would face a total market large enough to absorb much larger volumes of a smaller variety of models, etc., while Canadian consumers would not lose diversity of choice because they would have free access to the whole variety of North American production. Given its current preoccupation with balance-of-trade and other pressing questions, it is unlikely that the United States would even consider such a scheme at present on terms that could be acceptable to Canada. In any event, a Canada–U.S. free-trade arrangement would lead to a still greater integration of the two national economies through the mechanisms of the international corporation, and correspondingly greater concentration of economic decision making and research and development in these companies' head offices, most of which are in the United States. There would be controversy in Canada about that. Free trade with the United States, then, is for the longer run, if ever.

Again, where short production runs are the problem, another way of overcoming it is a government-imposed rationalization of the Canadian industries involved. This means a reduction in the number of competing firms in each industry, through encouragement or requirement of mergers; and a reduction of the range or variety of product types produced by individual plants. The Canadian market is large enough to give full economies of scale to one or a few producers of almost any product. And as efficiency is achieved, tariff bargaining with other nations could be conducted both to

---

[5] For example, H.E. English, *Industrial Structure and Canada's International Competitive Position* (Montreal: Canadian Trade Committee, 1964); D.J. Daly, B. A. Keys, and E. J. Spence, *Scale and Specialization in Canadian Manufacturing,* Economic Council of Canada (Ottawa: Queen's Printer, 1968); and H.C. Eastman and S. Stykolt, *The Tariff and Competition in Canada* (Toronto: Macmillan Company of Canada, 1967).
[6] For example, Paul Wonnacott and R.J. Wonnacott, *U.S.–Canadian Free Trade: The Potential Impact on the Canadian Economy* (Montreal: Canadian–American Committee, 1968).

assist in developing diverse foreign markets for the Canadian products and to admit foreign products more freely into Canada. The freeing of imports would be a necessary part of the plan, both to restore to Canadian consumers the wide range of choice of products that would be lost through domestic mergers, and to help contain by means of import competition the monopoly power of the new Canadian giant firms. Anti-combines policy would continue to be necessary also for the latter purpose, if only to prevent collusion between domestic firms and suppliers of potentially competing imports. Imposition of mergers on Canadian subsidiaries of U.S. parent companies might place the parent companies in the position of having to break U.S. antitrust laws, a problem that should be resolved in part in discussions between the two governments. But Canada, of course, as a sovereign state has the right to make decisions affecting corporations within its own boundaries.

Wholesale mergers in Canada may seem an unrealistic suggestion. Steps may have to be gradual and undramatic. "Mergers where necessary, but not necessarily mergers", is an important and feasible strategy that would have useful long-term results. We can support multilateral tariff reductions in international negotiations. Such support involves our willingness to remove, gradually but firmly, protection from our hopeless industries. We can continue to expand government efforts as a catalyst in making smaller Canadian manufacturing firms aware of and known by the international market place. Where firms are owned and controlled abroad, we may need to ensure that they do not rely unduly on foreign suppliers of machinery, parts, or other needs to the neglect of competitive Canadian suppliers, and that they are not excluded from export markets in which they could compete by the policies of the foreign parent or government.

Finally, there are those exports that we achieve relatively effortlessly, the exports of raw materials that our endowments of natural resources enable us to produce at high wages and sell at acceptable prices. They are still the core of our exports; still the basis of most of our comparative advantage in world trade, however much we may hope to develop a comparative advantage in other activities; still the first level of support for our high standard of living. Why not rely mainly on them to make a living in the world? What is wrong with being "hewers of wood and drawers of water," and being very well paid for it? One thing that is wrong is that natural resources, even Canada's, are exhaustible, and that their extraction by itself does not create very many high-wage jobs. Pick-and-shovel extraction would create a great many jobs, but at wage rates inconsistent with the objective of a high standard of living. High-wage-rate exploitation of natural resources is extremely capital-intensive, not labour-intensive. In order to provide high-wage employment for the rapidly growing Canadian labour force entirely on the basis of natural-resource extraction, the rate of extraction would have to be so fast as to be alarming in terms of rates of exhaustion of our natural resources.

Therefore we must continue to strive for man-made comparative advantage in processing and sophisticated manufacturing. The export of the produce of our farms, forests, and mines provides current income only, part of which must be invested in the development of future comparative advantage. Commercial policies and other policies affecting natural resources must be held to this goal. There is a major respect in which current policies may fail to harmonize with this goal. Canada is under strong pressure from the raw-materials-hungry United States, and from development-hungry provinces, and from profit-hungry corporations, to increase exports of energy and other raw materials to the United States. Such exports would increase our merchandise-trade surplus with the United States, and thus increase the pressure on us (both market pressure through a rise in the value of the Canadian dollar and political pressure through increased concern in Washington over our surplus which is their deficit) to import more and export less of manufactured goods from and to the United States. Obviously we should seek the best possible returns from our exports of raw materials (returns net of foreign-company profits), but we need to be very restrained about the quantities exported, not only where conservation is a concern but also where materials exports might actually displace manufactured exports and thereby possibly increase unemployment in this country.

All of the foregoing discussion of alternatives has been concerned with the objectives of a high standard of living and of full employment, both now and in the future. As for the objective of a "viable" balance of payments, it is first of all high time for Canadian authorities to adopt a more meaningful word than "viability" to describe what is wanted. It is time to end our reliance on new additions to foreign investment in Canada. Our objective for the balance of payments then must be a surplus on merchandise trade and other current transactions at least sufficient to pay for all of the annual net payments of interest and dividends to foreigners, and additionally large enough to offset the growth of foreign investments through domestic retained earnings. This objective does give possible comfort to those companies and provinces who rely on exports of natural resources, for the following reason.

We argued that it is against the national interest to permit rapid growth of such exports, because such exports would have to displace manufactured exports if we were to have balanced trade. But if our goal is to cease reliance on net inflows of capital and reduce our net international indebtedness, we need a large trade surplus. Raw-materials exports can then displace foreign capital inflows and financial capital outflows, rather than displacing manufactured exports. And we will be able to build up productive investments both in Canada and abroad, to yield growing returns for Canadians as our non-renewable resources are depleted.

2. International Capital Flows And Domestic Stabilization Policies

Ronald A. Shearer

University of British Columbia

The international-economics sections of introductory textbooks are concerned primarily with international trade in goods and services, its determinants, and its implications for economic welfare at home and abroad. Equal attention is not devoted to international capital flows, their determinants and consequences, even though international capital flows have become one of the main preoccupations of those responsible for the formulation and implementation of economic policies.

In this essay, we review the nature and the recent history of Canada's international capital flows, and explore, on a theoretical level, the implications of capital flows for domestic stabilization policies. A companion essay by A.E. Safarian explores one of the contentious results of Canada's capital imports, foreign ownership and control of Canadian industries.

I. The Nature of International Capital Flows

The economics of international capital flows can be discussed on two very different levels: "real" and "financial".

1. Real aspects

On the real level, we conceptualize international capital flows as international transfers of a productive resource, capital. What is of interest is the *net* capital flow, which is necessarily equal to the deficit (capital inflow) or surplus (capital outflow) in the current account of the balance of international payments.[1] It is in this sense that there is a *real* transfer. A country

[1] This should be a familiar proposition to any student of the principles of economics, either from the study of international economics or from the study of national-income accounting. See, for example, P.A. Samuelson and A.D. Scott, *Economics*, 3rd Canadian ed. (Toronto: McGraw-Hill Canada, 1971), pp. 237, 785–800.

69

with a net capital inflow (capital import) is receiving goods and services from the rest of the world which are not offset by exports of goods and services to the rest of the world. The opposite holds true for a capital outflow (capital export).

A net capital outflow is an alternative use of domestic savings. They are invested abroad rather than at home. A net capital inflow, similarly, is a substitute for domestic savings. It permits additions to the capital stock employed (but not necessarily owned) in Canada without the necessity of offsetting additional domestic savings. Capital imports can thus add to the productive potential of the Canadian economy, permitting more income to be generated in Canada. However, they also create a foreign claim to a share of Canadian income, which will show up in the future as a continuing flow of interest and dividend payments to non-residents.

Will the economic welfare of *residents* of Canada be improved as a result of the inflow of capital and the associated outflow of income? The analysis of this question is quite complex. We know from elementary economic theory that an addition to the capital stock should increase the marginal product and hence the income of other factors of production, such as labour and land. But is this all there is to the matter? Can we assume competitive conditions in our analysis? Are there economies of scale to be taken into account? What will happen to the distribution of income in Canada? Will Canadian labour benefit, or will immigration be induced? Who collects the additional rents to land? Canadians? Non-residents? Will there be important side-effects on the level of technology employed in Canada? On managerial skills? On Canada's social and political life?

These are obviously very fundamental issues about the long-run effects of international capital flows which should be the centre of attention in theoretical and empirical research if we are to formulate rational public policy toward foreign investment in Canada. By contrast, the issues which arise on the financial level, with which we are concerned here, may appear somewhat superficial.

2. Financial aspects

On the financial level, we are concerned with financial decisions and financial adjustments which are only a preliminary to the real transfers which affect economic growth and economic welfare in the long run. Generally, the problems considered are short-run and transitory. They are, nonetheless, important. We will show that domestic financial policies implemented for totally different reasons (e.g., to restrain inflationary pressures) can create financial inducements for international capital flows — and the resulting capital flows may make it difficult, and perhaps impossible, to continue the domestic policies. Under some conditions, domestic macro-economic policies can become the slave of speculative flights of capital. These are clearly matters of considerable consequence for the day-to-day management of the economy.

On the financial level, we conceptualize international capital flows as international transactions in financial assets and liabilities. These assets and liabilities can take a wide variety of forms, ranging from equity in corporations and unincorporated businesses, through bonds, treasury bills, short-term commercial paper, and bank deposits, to gold and money itself. Perhaps we can call them all "securities" for short (although we must remember that we are including bank deposits and money as "securities").

In some cases, the securities will be newly issued when they cross the national boundary. In other cases, they will have been issued long ago, and held in someone's asset portfolio, here or abroad, in the meantime. The *purchaser* may be an individual, corporation, institution, or government; the *seller* may be an individual, corporation, institution, or government; and the *security* may be a claim on an individual, corporation, institution, or government (and it may be a claim on a third party, not necessarily on the seller). The important point is that a transaction which changes the foreign-asset or foreign-indebtedness position of residents of Canada occurs between *residents* of Canada and *residents* of other countries. Thus, Canadian purchases of any kind of security from non-residents involve a *capital outflow*. The securities may be claims on foreign corporations or governments (and hence their purchase increases Canada's international assets), or they may be claims on Canadian corporations or governments (and hence their purchase reduces Canada's international liabilities). Similarly, foreign purchases of securities from Canadian residents involve a *capital inflow*. The securities may be claims on Canadian corporations or governments (and hence their sale to non-residents adds to Canada's international liabilities), or they may be claims on foreign corporations or governments (and hence their sale to non-residents reduces Canada's international assets).

3. Types of capital flows

Considered in terms of the financial decisions involved, international capital flows can be classified as direct investments, portfolio investments, other capital movements, and changes in official international reserves.

• *Direct investment* is associated with the ownership and effective control of a business enterprise. Direct-investment inflows to Canada involve the transfer of funds, in any form, from foreign owners to their Canadian firms. Direct-investment inflows are mainly used to finance the capital expenditures of foreign-controlled firms in Canada, but they may also be used to finance the take-over of existing Canadian firms, or to refinance existing foreign-controlled firms (e.g., by retiring Canadian debts or Canadian equity). Canadians also make direct investments abroad, although such capital outflows have generally been small relative to direct-investment inflows.

• *Portfolio investment*, in contrast, involves the purchase of securities simply for the financial returns (interest, dividends, or capital gains) which can be expected, without any intention or possibility of managing the enterprise. The purchase of institutional or government bonds is always portfolio investment. The purchase of corporate securities, whether stocks or bonds, by anyone except the controlling owners of the firm is also portfolio investment. The behaviour of capital flows involving very short-term securities is significantly different from that of longer-term portfolio investments. Accordingly, it is sometimes helpful to consider separately short-term capital flows, including transactions in short-term money-market instruments (treasury bills, commercial paper, finance-company paper) and Canadian investments in foreign-currency bank deposits.

• *Other capital movements* is an omnibus category including a variety of items which do not fit easily into other categories, such as governmental loans (which presumably reflect political considerations rather than market forces) and foreign-currency bank loans to Canadian residents. It also includes a residual balancing item, which is required to make the balance-of-payments accounts balance, and which is assumed to reflect undetected short-term capital flows. It is important to remember, however, that the balancing item also reflects all of the errors in measuring all of the other accounts in the balance of payments.

• *Official international reserves* (also called foreign-exchange reserves) are governmental holdings of gold, foreign exchange, and claims on international institutions which can be used as "international money" to settle deficits in Canada's international payments. Like an increase in private holdings of foreign securities, an increase in official reserves is a capital outflow. A decrease in international reserves is a capital inflow.

II. Canada's International Capital Flows: The Record, 1950–1972

Over the period 1950-1972 as a whole, Canada was a net importer of capital on a large scale.[2] However, the magnitude of the net capital imports fluctuated widely, and from the late 1950s there was a pronounced downward trend, including two years (1970 and 1971) of large-scale net capital exports.[3]

That part of the capital flows accounted for by changes in official foreign-exchange reserves may be distinguished from that part accounted for by private capital transactions.[4] Aside from 1950, there was only one occasion on which changes in official reserves were a major factor in capital flows. The large-scale capital exports of 1970 and 1971 were associated with substantial increases in official reserves.[5] Private capital flows showed more "normal" behaviour in these years.

In contrast to net capital flows, foreign direct investment in Canada over this period had an upward trend, which is somewhat more pro-

---

[2] For the actual balance-of-payments statistics underlying the description provided in this section, see Statistics Canada, *The Canadian Balance of International Payments, 1965–70* (Ottawa: 1972) and *The Canadian Balance of International Payments: A Compendium of Statistics from 1946 to 1965* (Ottawa: 1967).

[3] It can be argued that the downward trend is somewhat exaggerated. Part of the profits of foreign-controlled firms is reinvested in the enterprise rather than paid out as dividends to foreign owners. Since these are foreign-owned funds, their reinvestment in the firm is the equivalent of a capital import. Many economists would argue that the balance-of-payments statistics should be adjusted to reflect this. Reinvested profits should show up in the current account as implicit dividend payments, and in the capital account as direct-investment inflows. If this were done, the current-account deficit and the net capital inflow would appear larger. The downward trend would still exist, but it would be less pronounced.

[4] Although we have used the word "private," one should remember that "other capital movements" includes government loans and the balancing item.

[5] Remember, an increase in official reserves is a capital *outflow*; a decrease is an *inflow*.

nounced if the reinvestment of profits by foreign-controlled firms is taken into account. Direct investment also showed significant fluctuations which roughly paralleled fluctuations in gross business capital expenditures in Canada (although capital expenditures had a stronger upward trend, such that direct investment became less important as a source of finance for business capital formation). As noted earlier, Canadian direct-investment flows abroad were relatively small.

While there was a steadily increasing outflow of capital to retire outstanding Canadian securities in the hands of non-residents, the behaviour of long-term portfolio investment was dominated by new issues of Canadian securities. These were primarily long-term bonds, issued by provincial and municipal governments and corporations, denominated in U.S. dollars, and sold in the United States. New issues of securities showed a similar pattern to direct-investment inflows, with a stronger upward trend (even if allowance is made for retirements) and much more pronounced fluctuations. Trade in outstanding securities did not assume any importance until the mid-1960s, when heavy purchases of U.S. stocks, particularly by mutual funds, produced a sizeable capital outflow for a few years.

While never negligible, short-term capital flows assumed major importance in the balance of international payments only in the late 1960s. Earlier, annual flows were relatively small and were dominated by "other" capital movements, which include the net effects of all errors in measuring all international transactions. Over time, there was a growing volume of transactions in short-term money-market paper, but the dramatic change in short-term capital flows was in foreign-currency bank deposits of Canadian residents, most of which are with Canadian banks.

Canadian banks have aggressively cultivated the foreign-currency deposit business since the early 1960s.[6] They now provide an efficient link between Canadian investors and world money markets, accepting funds on deposit which are converted to U.S. dollars and used primarily for short-term investments in U.S. dollar assets in the United States and Europe.[7] The Canadian banks are important participants in what has come to be called the Euro-dollar market: a market, centered in the major financial centres of Europe, in which the stock in trade is U.S. dollars.

• *Summary:* over the whole period, the dominant components of Canada's international capital flows were foreign direct investment in Canada and new issues of Canadian securities abroad. Both showed significant, and related, fluctuations and upward trends. However, from time to time other components had a decisive impact on Canada's net international capital flows. Of particular note is the increased volatility and, on balance,

[6] The foreign-currency business of Canadian banks is discussed more fully in D. Bond and R. Shearer, *The Economics of the Canadian Financial System: Theory, Policy and Institutions* (Toronto: Prentice-Hall, 1972), pp. 180–181, 199–202;; and R. Shearer, "The Foreign Currency Business of Canadian Chartered Banks", *Canadian Journal of Economics and Political Science*, Vol. 31 (August 1965), pp. 328–357.

[7] The bank-balances series published in the balance-of-payments statistics exaggerates the capital flows generated through the banks because it neglects changes in foreign-currency loans to Canadians. These are included in "other" capital movements. This presentation of the statistics has been critized. See R. Shearer, "A Critical Note on Two Sectors of the Financial Flow Accounts", *Canadian Journal of Economics*, Vol. 5 (November 1972), pp. 549–553.

the net outflow of short-term capital since the mid-1960s, especially as a result of Canadian investments in foreign-currency bank deposits. Coupled with major increase in official foreign-exchange reserves in 1970 and 1971, these short-term outflows turned the upward trend in direct investment and net issues into a downward trend in net capital inflows.

What explains the behaviour of international capital flows?

III. Theory of International Capital Flows

1. Portfolio investment

International portfolio investments involve two complementary decisions. Someone must decide to take foreign securities into an asset portfolio, and someone must decide to sell securities. He may be selling securities presently held in his asset portfolio ("outstanding securities") or he may want to borrow funds, issuing new securities ("new issues"). It is these decisions which, in the first instance, a theory of international capital flows must explain.

A great many diverse factors may enter into particular decisions. In a general sense, however, there are three basic elements. To the potential purchaser, they are the funds available to be invested, relative yield, and risk. To the potential borrower, they are the funds required, probably for capital expenditures, relative yield, and risk.

Obviously, a potential purchaser of foreign securities must have funds to invest. These funds may be provided by current savings, but the purchaser may also consider selling securities which he presently holds in order to purchase foreign securities. As long as he has this option, the funds potentially available are not limited to his present current savings, but include his whole portfolio of assets. He may also borrow to purchase foreign securities.

But given that he has funds available, there must be some incentive to purchase a foreign security rather than a domestic one. That incentive is provided by the yield which can be expected from the foreign security, whether in the form of interest, dividends, or capital gains. If we can take interest rates as roughly representative of the yields to be obtained on securities, then, other things being equal, higher interest rates in Canada than in the rest of the world will induce non-residents to purchase Canadian securities. Higher interest rates in Canada will induce capital inflows.

Similarly, for a Canadian firm or government to borrow abroad, it must have a "need" for the funds, perhaps an investment opportunity the returns from which will more than cover the cost of borrowing; and, other things being equal, it must find the foreign borrowing less expensive (in terms of interest which must be paid) than domestic borrowing. Relatively higher interest rates in Canada will induce borrowing abroad and hence capital inflows.

One of the effects of international capital flows induced by interest-rate differentials should be, other things being equal, the equalization of interest rates internationally. Borrowing is shifted from countries with high interest rates to countries with low interest rates, putting downward pressure on the high rates and upward pressure on the low ones.

But what are the "other things" which must be equal? Among the most important is *risk*. Three types of risk might be noted: risk of default, risk of capital loss from a rise in interest rates, and foreign-exchange risk.

The first two types of risk are familiar, and occur in domestic as well as international investments. Institutions and businesses may fail, rendering their bonds or stocks worthless. Even governments, particularly provincial and local governments, may be unable to meet their debts on occasion. Fluctuations in the market price of securities, even when there is no real risk of default, are a common occurrence. Among other things, they are closely associated with changes in the level of interest rates. As interest rates rise, bond prices (and in principle also stock prices) fall. As is well known, a rise in interest rates will have a greater effect on prices of long-term bonds than short-term bonds, which may lead some investors to prefer short-term bonds over long-term bonds ("liquidity preference"). These considerations are not unique to international investment decisions. However, they do mean that in international comparisons of interest rates we must compare rates on securities of comparable quality (risk of default) and comparable term to maturity (risk of capital loss).

What is unique in international investments is the foreign-exchange risk. A foreign-exchange risk arises because the currencies of two nations are involved in any international investment transaction, and the market rate of exchange between these currencies (the foreign-exchange rate) may change during the term of the contract. An American holding a bond denominated in Canadian dollars will incur a loss if the Canadian dollar falls in the foreign-exchange market. On the other hand, he stands to gain if the Canadian dollar rises.[8]

The existence of foreign-exchange risk means that we cannot expect international equalization of interest rates to occur. Investors may require a premium over domestic interest rates to be willing to assume the foreign-exchange risk.[9] International differentials may persist without inducing capital flows. The presence of foreign-exchange risk may also reduce the sensitivity of international capital flows to changes in interest rates. Even though Canadian interest rates are high, foreigners may be reluctant to

---

[8] It is worth noting that most bonds sold by Canadian governments and corporations to non-residents are denominated in U.S. dollars. This means that the Canadian issuer of the bonds bears the foreign-exchange risk, not the American purchaser. If the American dollar rises in the foreign-exchange market, the Canadian borrower must make larger interest payments. Of course, if the American dollar falls relative to the Canadian dollar, the cost of foreign borrowing also falls.

[9] On very short-term securities, it is possible to "hedge" the foreign-exchange risk, using a forward-exchange contract. This is a contract under which the bank agrees to purchase foreign exchange in a specified amount, on a specified date in the future, at a specified price. Such a contract will remove any uncertainty about the exchange rate at which the proceeds of a foreign investment will be converted into the domestic currency. But it also means that the rate of return on the investment depends on the cost of the forward contract, which in turn depends on demand for and supply of such contracts. The whole subject of forward-exchange contracts is somewhat complex, more suitable for treatment at an advanced level. The important point is that short-term capital flows may depend as much on the forward exchange rate as on interest-rate differentials, and hence may show significantly different behaviour from long-term capital flows.

take more Canadian securities into their portfolios, depending, among other things, on the relative size of their present holdings of such securities.

Finally, further to complicate the matter, the same conditions which create foreign-exchange risk also create opportunities for speculative gains. We have noted that unexpected changes in the exchange rate can cause severe losses, and that concern over such losses may deter international capital flows. Correctly anticipated changes in the exchange rate can yield substantial profits. Speculation on such changes will induce international capital flows. If the Canadian dollar is expected to fall in the foreign-exchange market, speculative capital will flow out of Canada. If the Canadian dollar is expected to appreciate, speculative capital will flow in.

From time to time, speculation appears to be the dominant factor determining the magnitude and direction of international capital flows. Indeed, the period of greatest turmoil in foreign-exchange markets, 1967–1972, was also a period of great volatility in portfolio-capital flows.

2. Direct investment

In the case of direct investment, the borrower and the lender are, in a sense, the same party. A foreign parent firm must decide how the capital expenditures of Canadian subsidiary firms are to be financed — through transfers from the parent firm (direct investment) or through borrowing in Canada. The incentive to direct investment is the profits expected on capital expenditures. However, relatively low interest rates in Canada may induce firms to borrow in Canada to finance the expenditures, marginally reducing the inflow of direct-investment funds. High interest rates in Canada, by contrast, should have a marginal effect inducing direct investment.

3. Empirical evidence

Theoretical considerations thus suggest that both portfolio and direct investment should respond positively to the level of capital expenditures in Canada, and negatively to the level of interest rates in Canada. There have been several important statistical studies in recent years which have attempted to verify these theoretical speculations.[10] We cannot summarize those studies here. However, for our purposes it is important to note that the link between interest rates and portfolio investment is now rather well established. There is much less clear evidence on the sensitivity of direct investment to interest rates. However, one study does provide some support for this argument.[11]

---

[10] For example, L.H. Officer, *An Econometric Model of Canada under the Fluctuating Exchange Rate* (Cambridge: Harvard University Press, 1968); R.E. Caves and G.L. Reuber, *Capital Transfers and Economic Policy: Canada, 1951–1962* (Cambridge: Harvard University Press, 1971); R.E. Caves and G.L. Reuber, *Canadian Economic Policy and the Impact of International Capital Flows* (Toronto: University of Toronto Press, 1969); J.F. Helliwell, et al., *The Structure of RDX2*, (Ottawa: Bank of Canada, 1971).

[11] Helliwell, et al., *The Structure of RDX2*, Part 1, pp. 203–208.

IV. International Capital Flows and Domestic Financial Policies

The effects of domestic financial policies on international capital flows should be obvious from what has been said. Other things being equal, any domestic policy which tends to raise interest rates — a restrictive monetary policy, or an expansionary fiscal policy with a fixed money supply — will tend to attract capital inflows and retard capital outflows. Canadian corporations and governments will be induced to borrow abroad, and Canadian investors will be deterred from investing abroad. The opposite will be true of any domestic policy which tends to reduce interest rates. Capital outflows will be encouraged, and capital inflows reduced.

The implications of the impact of domestic policy on international capital flows for the effectiveness of the domestic policies depends on the nature of foreign-exchange-rate policy.

1. Flexible exchange rate

One possible regime is a flexible exchange rate. In principle, such a policy was followed by Canada in the years 1950–1962 and 1970 to the present. Under such a regime, the exchange rate is supposed to be free to find its own level in the marketplace, depending on the balance of pressures of supply and demand.

With a flexible exchange rate, domestic financial policies will have an indirect effect on demand and supply in the foreign-exchange market, and hence on the foreign-exchange rate (the number of Canadian dollars required to purchase one U.S. dollar). We have seen that a restrictive monetary policy will tend to induce international capital inflows. This will add to the supply of foreign exchange (U.S. dollars) offered for sale in the foreign-exchange market, and depress the price of foreign exchange (the price of the U.S. dollar in terms of Canadian dollars). Through the same mechanism, an easy-money policy, tending to lower interest rates, will increase the foreign-exchange rate.

The change in the foreign-exchange rate should reinforce the domestic effects of monetary policy. A restrictive monetary policy, designed to restrain aggregate demand in Canada, will depress the foreign-exchange rate. This will make foreign goods appear less expensive to Canadian purchasers, and hence will stimulate imports as substitutes for domestic production. Similarly, Canadian goods will appear more expensive to foreign customers, and this will tend to retard exports. The combination of increased imports and reduced exports will reduce aggregate demand for domestic production, and this reduced demand was the purpose of the restrictive monetary policy. Through this mechanism, international capital flows and a flexible exchange rate can reinforce domestic monetary policy.

It should be noted, however, that if the higher interest rates were a result of an expansionary fiscal policy, the flexible exchange rate would tend to frustrate the objectives of domestic policy. Any direct expansion in aggregate demand through fiscal measures would be partly offset by the expansion in imports and reduction in exports.

The analysis can be applied in reverse for an expansionary monetary policy.

The important point of this discussion is that in a regime of flexible exchange rates and highly interest-sensitive international capital flows, any change in domestic financial policy will have repercussions on the exchange rate, and through the exchange rate on international trade and economic activity. A flexible exchange rate helps to adjust the balance of trade (exports minus imports of goods) to produce the desired net capital flow. Domestic policies must be formulated with this linkage in mind.

2.   Fixed exchange rate

If the exchange rate is fixed, the reinforcement or frustration of domestic policies as a result of changes in the exchange rate will not occur, of course. However, the government is left with the problem of coping with shifts in the balance of supply and demand pressures in the foreign-exchange market.

If the government is to peg the exchange rate without elaborate controls over international transactions, it must act as a residual buyer or seller of foreign exchange. It must stand ready to purchase foreign exchange if there is excess supply, and to sell if there is excess demand. This is the function of foreign-exchange reserves.

This means that a restrictive monetary policy may force the government to increase its foreign-exchange reserves, and hence to export capital to offset private imports of capital. International capital inflows will add to supply pressures in the foreign exchange market, which the government will have to absorb if the foreign-exchange rate is to remain fixed. The opposite will be true of an expansionary monetary policy. An expansionary monetary policy can lead to a drain of official international reserves.

The government cannot be indifferent to changes in foreign-exchange reserves. An increase in reserves must be financed. Somehow, the government must find the Canadian dollars with which to purchase the foreign exchange. The government must force the taxpayer to invest in foreign exchange (thus providing an offsetting capital outflow), or it must relax the domestic policy which initiated the capital inflow.

A decline in foreign-exchange reserves poses even more severe constraints on the government. A continuing drain will eventually exhaust reserves. Then what? Obviously, faced with a drain of reserves, the government would be forced to relax the domestic policies which elicited the capital outflow.

The lesson is simple. With a fixed exchange rate and highly sensitive international capital flows, domestic financial policy cannot be pursued without due regard to its balance-of-payments repercussions.

Indeed, the situation may be even more severe. Balance-of-payments pressures may develop which, quite independently, force a change in domestic financial policies. A given, fixed, exchange rate can become inappropriate in light of changes in prices, costs, trade flows, etc. Even though the rate is nominally fixed, speculation may develop that it must be changed — speculation that will be reinforced if there are substantial changes in official holdings of international reserves. Speculative capital flows will aggravate these changes in reserves. Thus, speculation on de-valuation of a country's currency will induce a capital flight (outflow), further reducing reserves; and speculation on appreciation will induce a capital inflow, further increasing reserves. If the speculative pressures are severe, domestic policies may have to change to offset these pressures, unless the exchange rate is adjusted. If the decision is taken to maintain the exchange rate, domestic policy will become a slave of international capital flows.

V. Conclusions

We have barely scratched the surface of the analysis of international capital flows. But perhaps we have made the point that such capital flows have powerful implications for what can and cannot be accomplished with domestic monetary and fiscal policies. Much depends on the exchange-rate system. With a flexible exchange rate, changes in the exchange rate will help adapt imports and exports of goods to achieve the "real capital trans-fer" (i.e., the change in the balance of trade) which is the counterpart of the financial capital flows elicited by domestic financial policies. The change in the exchange rate and trade flows will have repercussions on domestic economic activity as well. With a fixed exchange rate, the govern-ment, through changes in official reserves, has to offset all or part of the private capital flows elicited by its domestic policies. Only if it is successful in doing this can it avoid either changing the exchange rate or modifying domestic policies. Since there are clear limits to changes in exchange reserves — in either direction — there are limits to the independence of domestic policy.

Canada has been a laboratory for the study of international capital flows under fixed and flexible exchange rates. On two occasions, in 1950 and 1970, Canada was forced to adopt a floating exchange rate in order to cope with accelerating increases in foreign-exchange reserves. On several other occasions, including 1961-62, 1963, and 1968, the government was forced to adjust domestic policies to cope with severe speculative pressures against the Canadian dollar. There is a rich literature on these matters which merits further study.[12]

---

[12] In addition to the items cited in footnote 10, reference might be made to: P. Wonnacott, *The Canadian Dollar, 1948–1962* (Toronto: University of Toronto Press, 1965); R.M. Dunn, Jr., *Canada's Experience with Fixed and Flexible Ex-change Rates in a North American Capital Market* (Montreal: Private Planning Association of Canada, 1971); and the *Annual Reports* of the Governor of the Bank of Canada.

3. Issues Raised
By Foreign Direct Investment in Canada

A. E. Safarian

University of Toronto

This article considers some basic economic and political issues raised by the emergence and growth of foreign-owned firms in the host country (the country in which investment takes place), with particular reference to the Canadian experience. The concern is with foreign *direct* investment in Canada (stocks, bonds, and other assets owned by non-residents in Canadian enterprises in which the voting stock is *controlled* by non-residents). This is to be distinguished from *portfolio* investment (foreign holdings of bonds and stocks which do not carry with them foreign control of Canadian enterprises).

A brief look at the data is in order before the consequences are considered. Canada accounts for 29 percent of all United States direct investment abroad. Almost 80 percent of all foreign direct investment in Canada is from the United States. In 1969, between 24 and 29 percent of all business assets in Canada were in firms whose voting stock was controlled abroad. Foreign direct investment is highly concentrated in manufacturing, petroleum and gas, and other mining and smelting industries, where foreign control of capital amounted in 1967 to 57, 74, and 65 percent respectively (or 45, 60, and 56 percent respectively for the United States alone). Foreign-controlled firms are much better represented among the larger firms; of the 556 corporations in Canadian non-financial industries in 1969 with assets of $25 million or more, fully 298 were foreign-controlled.[1]

What are the problems with foreign direct investment in Canada? There is concern that the economic benefits traditionally associated with such investment are accompanied by high economic costs, both as conventionally defined and otherwise. There is even greater concern that whether

[1] See Statistics Canada, *Canada's International Investment Position 1926 to 1967*, and Corporation and Labour Unions Returns Act, *Report for 1969*.

or not economic progress in a narrow sense is involved, foreign direct investment poses a threat to political sovereignty or to the exercise of political power, and to cultural distinctiveness. This is particularly the concern in the case of the large American firms so prevalent in Canada, a concern which is sometimes indistinguishable from the fuller range of questions in the relations between Canada and the United States. Lastly, there is growing frustration at the inability to mount effective policies to modify perceived problems, given the differing views on their importance and the highly regional nature of the country and of its government.

I. Economic Benefits and Costs

The expansion of domestic production in a country at full employment is determined broadly by increases in the supplies of the agents of production, and by increases in productivity arising both from the improved quality and more efficient use of these agents and also from economies of scale. Foreign direct investment contributes to these sources of expansion to the extent that it supplies capital, makes available a range of technology, or provides access to markets and entrepreneurship which are otherwise not available, or are available only at greater over-all net costs. These potential gains from increased capital stock and improved technology may appear as one or more of higher real wage rates or employment, or be reflected in lower prices or better quality of output. An important benefit is the tax payments to various governments from the higher level of output, since double-taxation agreements between countries allow the host country to tax such firms without losing the investments.

It will be clear that whether these gains are realized for the host country and how they are realized depend on a number of assumptions with respect to public policy. In particular, how far can competition in the system be relied on to ensure that the impact of new entry to an industry *via* new products and processes does spill over from the firm, increasing general productivity or lowering prices rather than being captured solely by the firm? If competition cannot ensure that these potential benefits are realized, can tax and other policies ensure this? It is difficult to tax international firms effectively because of (1) the problems of determining "transfer prices" for unique services within the firm (e.g., between the U.S. parent company and its Canadian subsidiary) where there is no market price or equivalent, and (2) the opportunities in such firms for shifting taxable income so as to minimize taxes internationally over time.

One major question, then, is the nature and extent of the benefits which occur through the spill-overs from the firm, and whether they can be achieved at less cost in other ways. It has been suggested that two of these — benefits from manpower training and uncaptured productivity spill-overs — may be important possibilities. The gains can come from the movement to domestic firms by executives and others trained in the foreign firm at the latter's cost, from education of suppliers in production and quality control and of customers in better use of products, and in numerous other ways.

The costs that offset these benefits are quite direct in some cases, such as payments abroad for interest, dividends, and business services.

Despite considerable shortcomings of both theory and measurement in this area, some useful measures have been attempted of the over-all net economic impact of portfolio and/or direct investment in Canada. One approach indicated that, under the full-employment conditions prevailing in 1950–1956, net foreign investment (both portfolio and direct) contributed from 8 to 20 percent of the growth in per capita real income in that period.[2] A second study estimated that if only domestic capital were used in production, the gross domestic product (produced in Canada) would be 16.5 percent lower. Gross national income (received by Canadians) would be only 3 percent lower, since interest and dividend payments to foreigners would fall.[3] Both studies necessarily make important assumptions which greatly affect their conclusions.

There are further effects, both positive and negative, which have been claimed for direct investment. The list of negative effects is long. What all lists of negative effects have in common is a view that important decisions about Canadian-based facilities, made in the context of the international firm and heavily influenced or determined abroad, lead to less than the maximum efficient development of the subsidiary. This outcome is attributed to various forces, such as poor information or lack of interest by the parent's officers, private or public pressures on them to favour facilities at home at the expense of the subsidiary, or limiting of the subsidiary's initiatives by the habit of dependence on decisions abroad. Thus the host country's development is geared away from manufactured exports and research toward reliance on imports and technology from abroad.

The view that foreign direct investment per se yields a pattern of industrial development which is inimical to certain kinds of growth is particularly strongly held in Canada. Paradoxically, this view appears to co-exist with a number of careful empirical studies which largely refute it. In the typical case, other things being constant, the performance of foreign-owned firms in these respects in Canada appears to be as good (or bad) as that of their resident-owned counterparts. This is the case for exports, where performance of foreign-owned firms has been found to be similar to that of resident-owned firms, whether one considers all such firms, larger ones only, or only those in manufacturing. The Canadian research performance of foreign-owned firms is at least as good as that of resident-owned firms, whether judged as a percentage of sales, or by the degree of sophistication. Again, while both positive and negative effects appear when the relation of foreign ownership to industrial concentration and merger activity is examined, the most general conclusion which appears possible is that the extent of foreign ownership has not clearly increased or decreased the degree of competition looked at in these

[2] Rudolph G. Penner, "The Benefits of Foreign Investment in Canada, 1950–1956," Canadian Journal of Economics and Political Science, May 1966, pp. 172–83. The estimate deducts Canadian investment abroad; the contribution of gross inflows alone would be greater.
[3] Philip A. Neher, "Capital Movement, Foreign Ownership and Dependence on Foreign Investment in Canada and British Columbia;" and John Helliwell and Jillian Broadbent, "How Much Does Foreign Capital Matter?" both in B.C. Studies, Department of Economics, University of British Columbia, Vancouver, Spring 1972, 13, pp. 31–42.

ways. This conclusion is stronger for firms owned in the United States, incidentally, than for firms owned overseas. General empirical tests do suggest, however, that foreign-owned firms have a higher share of imports in purchases, despite evidence of substantial substitution of domestic purchases for imports over time.[4]

The performance of foreign-owned firms in Canada, while it may not be as bad as some fear, is nevertheless not as good as many might have expected from the assumed advantages in access to foreign research, financing, and marketing. Why is performance typically not better than in the Canadian-owned counterparts where they exist, and why is the performance of both sets of firms so often worse than the best-practice techniques in the United States and elsewhere over long periods? The large and long-standing gap in productivity between Canadian and United States manufacturing generally, and the direct comparisons of subsidiaries with parents, raise questions of this kind. It has been established by aggregative and industry studies that the large foreign-owned manufacturing sector and its domestic counterpart both suffer from too many firms, too many products, and too-short production runs. It is fairly convincingly established that the most important ultimate determinants of this inefficient industrial structure have been Canadian and foreign protection against trade, a lack of effective competition (partly because of tariffs and a weak anti-combines policy), and badly devised government industrial policies on research and other matters.[5] Industrial policy may well have dissipated part of the potential gain from both foreign and domestic investment in an inefficient and fragmented structure of industry. Indeed, until recent years, much of what passed for industrial strategy in Canada consisted simply of inducing firms to invest in Canada (rather than import goods) *via* a high tariff wall. In recent years, this has been combined with substantial tax concessions as well, by both federal and provincial governments, partly to induce firms to locate in certain regions or to undertake more research activity. To the extent that such policies do not succeed, not only is the specific policy goal unrealized, but much of the potential benefit from direct investment is lost both by way of tax loss and inefficient industry.

The main responsibility for this state of affairs should be borne by the complex of policies historically used to speed industrial development in this country. Even so, certain opportunities exist for potentially profitable intervention in the initial investment or subsequent operations by such firms. A firm with many international affiliations by investment,

---

[4] For exports, imports, and research, see A.E. Safarian, *Foreign Ownership of Canadian Industry* (Toronto: McGraw-Hill Canada, 1966), ch. 9; for exports and imports, see B.W. Wilkinson, *Canada's International Trade* (Montreal: Canadian Trade Committee, 1968); for research, see N.H. Lithwick, *Canada's Science Policy and the Economy* (Toronto: Methuen Publications, 1969), chs. 4 and 5; for concentration, see G. Rosenbluth, "The Relation Between Foreign Control and Concentration in Canadian Industry," *Canadian Journal of Economics*, February 1970, 3, pp. 14–38.

[5] For studies in this area, see H.C. Eastman and S. Stykolt, *The Tariff and Competition in Canada* (Toronto: The Macmillan Company of Canada, 1967); H.E. English, *Industrial Structure in Canada's International Competitive Position* (Montreal: Canadian Trade Committee, 1964); Economic Council of Canada, *Scale and Specialization of Canada's Manufacturing Industry* (Ottawa: Queen's Printer, 1968); and A.E. Safarian, *op. cit.*, ch. 7.

trade, or otherwise — regardless of nationality of ownership — has more opportunities for such matters as tax shifting and sourcing of supplies, whether it uses these opportunities or not. Foreign subsidiaries may certainly have advantages, but it does not follow in any particular case or industry that they necessarily benefit the host country, or benefit it as much as is feasible with a more intelligent use of policies to capture more "spill-overs" and/or taxes. While my presumption would be that there is generally more competition with foreign firms than without, in principle the presence of foreign firms can either increase or decrease the degree of monopoly or competition.

All of this raises questions perhaps more fundamental than whether foreign direct investment is likely to create net economic gains. The first question is whether these net gains can be maximized, or better, optimized. One set of answers exists in improving the set of government policies which determine the social gains of corporate policies generally, without regard to nationality of ownership My earlier comments suggest that much remains to be done in Canada in this regard. Second, even if the gains exist, they might be derived with less cost by alternative forms of access to foreign technology. There is a range of ways in which a project can be undertaken — licensing, joint ventures, purchase of management services, protection for domestic firms whether private or public, direct investment of various types, or state purchase of technology for distribution to all without charge. These have quite different economic costs and benefits, as well as different political and social consequences. The presumption in some of the literature is that the direct-investment "package" of capital, of production and distribution techniques, and of management skills is most often indivisible. However, it is not yet possible to say, from a social rather than private viewpoint, how far this is so and in what industrial situations, with given objectives, is a split of the package least costly.

Third, there is the question of technique, that is, the extent to which general tax and other policies or specific policies directed at particular industries or even firms should be used, whether the object is to improve the economic setting for all firms, or to try to distinguish between them on the basis of ownership. In both cases, the mood in the government and, to some extent, other circles seems to favour attempting direct case-by-case intervention through a screening agency or similar institution, rather than formulating general or market-oriented policies. Either the latter is mistrusted or the former is regarded as yielding more predictable outcomes; apparently it is assumed that present knowledge and skills justify some confidence in the welfare effects. The direct case-by-case approach also increases bureaucratic costs and powers.[6]

Perhaps even more fundamentally, it has been suggested that a high degree of dependence on imported techniques has created an environment in which entrepreneurial effort is dampened permanently. One example is the "truncation" argument, which provides the framework for a recent

---

[6] For a defence of the direct approach and a discussion of policy approaches generally, see Government of Canada, *Foreign Direct Investment in Canada* (Ottawa: Information Canada, 1972).

government study of foreign investment in Canada. This argument maintains that direct investment leads to many important activities being performed in the parent firm or country, with the result that significant gaps occur in Canada's domestic capacities in these respects. How far have managerial, technical, distributive, and financial capabilities been "stunted" because of easy access to supplies of these abroad, mainly through subsidiaries? If one accepts that a certain mass of such activity on an integrated basis is necessary either to give autonomous capacity to exploit innovation privately, or to implement policy in this area publicly, the case is made for the creation of more capacity in this area.[7]

Some doubts must be expressed, however, about the relevance of this argument to Canada. First, it is not obvious that it is supported by the evidence directly bearing on it. The frequent assertion that foreign firms monopolize markets or stifle domestic entrepreneurs has not yet been rigorously tested by the counter-hypothesis that there are external benefits from such direct investment — training of managers who then move outside the subsidiary, the education and financing of suppliers, the stimulus from competition, and so on. It may be noted that an aggregative test of whether foreign direct investment merely substituted for domestic capital without adding to capital stock in Canada turned out negatively.[8]

Second, this proposition fails to take into account the ways in which extended protection itself inhibits the development of entrepreneurial skills by removing competition, restricting market horizons, and leading to an inefficient structure of industry. The "truncation" argument fails to test the counter-hypothesis that the continuing reliance on imported inputs associated with foreign direct investment is due not to the presence of such investment but to the policies (including protection) which foster inefficient industrial development and which also entice to Canada excessive direct investment in some industries. A more promising approach would be trying to achieve more efficient organization of industry through more liberal foreign-trade policy, a far more efficient use of competition policy, and more effective government tax-and-subsidy and regulatory policies. An associated approach is to tackle directly the many market and societal imperfections which continue to make it difficult to mobilize entrepreneurial capital for many purposes. The hindrance to effective national financial markets because of differences in provincial securities regulations is a case in point. The historic official restrictions on merchant-banking roles, or even on non-controlling equity participation, for many major financial institutions must have formed a formidable barrier to entrepreneurship through much of the history of this country. Finally, under-investment in those educational skills which are closely related to economic growth could still be improved; the granting of four doctorates

[7] *Ibid.* See also Kari Levitt, *Silent Surrender: The Multinational Corporation in Canada* (Toronto: The Macmillan Company of Canada, 1970), where the argument is extended to the possible effects of economic dependence on the capacity for political decisions as well.

[8] For the period 1951–1962 as a whole, every $1.00 of new direct investment from abroad was associated with $2.00 of additional domestic investment — a figure falling to $1.50 in recession and rising to $3.00 in boom. See Richard E. Caves and Grant L. Reuber, *Capital Transfers and Economic Policy: Canada, 1951–1962* (Cambridge: Harvard University Press, 1971), ch. 4.

in business administration in 1970–71 in all of Canada is hardly a warrant that we are taking seriously the need for research on our distinctive business problems. The linguistic and social barriers to managerial roles for significant portions of the population are being corrected, but the pace is still slow. Some of the changes needed involve minor tax or expenditure changes; others require fundamental attitudinal changes. These changes are worth taking on their own merit and they lead to an approach which yields more self-reliant expansion while maximizing rather than sacrificing the gains possible from foreign investment. They also have the major effect that they do not sacrifice the interests of those parts of the country or population whose real incomes are still deplorably low.

II. Primary Resources

In principle, it is not clear why primary resources should be treated differently from manufacturing insofar as direct investment is concerned. A general theory of direct investment, for example, should be capable of explaining both phenomena. In practice, there are sufficient differences of degree to warrant separate treatment of primary resources as a sub-category of a more general phenomenon. One difference is that the benefits external to the firm are often smaller in manpower training and productivity effects, because, for example, the subsidiary may be capital-intensive or may buy little in domestic markets. A second point is that the profits of foreign subsidiaries in primary resources often include substantial rents which the government should collect for maximum benefit, and can collect without adverse supply effects.[9]

It is very uncertain what the rents are, however, until the resources have been discovered, the technical problems of production solved, the transport and other infrastructures built, and financing and markets provided. Any bargain struck before all of this has been successfully undertaken quickly obsolesces afterwards, and generates pressures to capture more of the rents, to secure more processing, and so on.[10] A second difficulty is that the bargaining power of governments in such circumstances varies widely by resource, depending on the ease of access to the resource in other countries, the degree of collusion among firms, and the co-operation (if any) among governments controlling the major resources. In Canada, the situation is complicated still further by the competition between provinces to attract resource development through various concessions, compounded by the fact that some provinces have relatively few development alternatives. The outcome is an even further reduction in the net gain from such investment to the host country.

One possible alternative is for governments to set leases and other aspects of contracts as short and as flexible as possible, thus permitting

---

[9] See R.E. Caves, "International Corporations: The Industrial Economics of Foreign Investment," *Economica,* February 1971, pp. 1–27. The discussion here focuses on the case where a primary-resource firm is integrated with a parent abroad, rather than with a manufacturing subsidiary in Canada.

[10] See Raymond Vernon, *Sovereignty at Bay: The Multinational Spread of U.S. Enterprises* (New York: Basic Books, 1971), ch. 2. This chapter also reviews the extensive literature on attempts to control foreign investment in primary resources.

re-negotiation more easily, but with variations by type of resource reflecting problems of exploration, the degree of bargaining power in each case with regard to concessions, and the effects on the economy generally. It is even more important to recognize that Canada's comparative advantage in some types of resource development cannot be realized more fully without greater and continued freedom of access for processed products to foreign markets.

The substantial presence of many large foreign-controlled corporations in Canada should not obscure the fact that what is involved in these issues, and in issues such as environmental control or tax subsidization, is more a matter of government policy and control of the large corporation in resource development than of domestic versus foreign ownership. It is not at all clear why resident-owned firms in primary-resource development should be exempted from such questions. There is a presumption for more regulation in the primary-resource field than elsewhere, for reasons noted above. Whether domestic ownership as such is necessary depends on how far foreign ownership limits the possibilities for effective regulation, as well as on the kinds of questions on economic benefits and costs raised earlier.

III. Some Political and Social Issues

The economic consequences of foreign direct investment in host countries do not, by themselves, explain the reaction to such investment. When an economist moves to such issues as national independence, he is on slippery ground, not only because they do not lend themselves readily to his customary approaches, but also because other social scientists have failed to give those questions the systematic attention they deserve. Nevertheless, venture we must or evade the issue most often and most fervently raised about foreign direct investment.

A major relevant question is the ways and the extent to which foreign direct investment affects the ease with which a state can implement its policies and how far any losses here can be said to cancel out any net economic gains. The question is not strictly amenable to a cost-benefit approach; for people differ widely on both the meaning and the value they will put on independence in the sense just noted. In particular, they differ on which aspects of it should be regarded as absolutes which cannot be traded off whatever the gain in other respects.

One useful, although sometimes blurred, distinction is between those aspects of direct investment which are largely or wholly related to the actions of firms in pursuit of their own objectives, and those which are largely or wholly related to the state in the pursuit of its objectives through direct pressures on firms.

Does the nation state have something to fear, in terms of its capacity to mount programs, from foreign direct investment as such? The answer must surely be that it does in some directions, but there are important offsets. A multinational firm by definition involves some assets, including important head-office assets, which are located outside the borders of the host country. The multinational firm allocates these and other resources, over time, among its affiliates, within the important constraints of law, economic circumstances, and the organizational settings of such firms. If one poses this situation against a firm whose entire assets are located in the host country, or the great bulk of whose assets and head-office facilities are so located, then clearly there is more *potential* control for a government in the operations of such domestic firms. This is particularly true for the range of administrative policies in which corporations are subject to that blend of persuasion and coercion which often appears necessary, at least to government bureaucrats, to implement duly passed laws. The point involved goes beyond this type of situation. For example, the opportunities for tax minimization through transfer pricing among differing tax jurisdictions are greater for multinational firms. If multinational firms continue to spread, and if governments cannot singly or together implement their policies except at great cost, then there is clearly a loss of sovereignty — and that is true even if one agrees that there is some gain to the national and international community in other respects.

Stating the issue in this way raises important qualifications and questions. It is clear that there are different kinds of international businesses with different degrees of integration with the host and home countries. It is not clear whether foreign firms are less responsive in practice to government policies, or more likely to escape laws. The studies of *economic* performance of subsidiaries in high-income host countries, as noted earlier, do not lend support to such views on any generalized basis, whatever specific cases may show to the contrary. Nor is there much point in discussing actual or potential political costs without looking at actual or potential benefits. Too often the assumption is made that economic integration merely limits or complicates the exercise of some forms of policy. There are both opportunities and constraints in practice, with the opportunities arising in part from the larger and enriched economic base which is available to support initiatives in both domestic and foreign policy. If only constraints were involved in foreign direct investment, or if foreign direct investment was fairly easily matched by alternative forms, then governments would long since have acted to restrict it severely. The fact is that we know rather too little to comment in a general way on the effects of the spread of multinationals on a host country's capacity to implement policies. There is no general study of the probable degree of harmonization of national policies which the spread of multinational firms will require. Nor is there any major empirical study on such important specific topics as the effects of transfer-pricing practices on tax revenues.

One can distinguish in principle the effects on independence of the spread of direct-investment firms as such from the attempt by the government of the home country to exercise sovereignty over subsidiaries in the host country. There have been a series of situations in the past 15 years where United States law has been interpreted as extending to American-owned subsidiaries in Canada and elsewhere. These include regulations under the United States Trading with the Enemy Act which, by threatening to levy penalties on the parent, prohibited all trade by such subsidiaries abroad with North Korea, North Vietnam, Cuba, and China. Canadian law included no such general prohibition, although strategic goods were not exported to them. Exemptions could be secured from this prohibition on a case-by-case basis, but little is known about how this worked in practice. There have been similar problems in the area of United States antitrust law, which has on occasion been interpreted to apply to subsidiaries abroad because of their effects on United States trade.

In each of these cases there is a United States as well as a Canadian interest. On occasion also, the effect of the United States policy may even be beneficial to Canada economically, as with some antitrust decisions. Nevertheless, there is a serious problem of erosion of sovereignty for a host country if it fails to assert the principle that its laws, regulations, and policies take precedence over foreign ones insofar as its residents are concerned.

It will be noted that the problem arises not because of foreign direct investment as such, but because of the unilateral extension of law abroad through the international firm, which then finds itself caught between two sovereigns with different laws or policies. It is a problem of inter-governmental relations, and the optimal solution involves inter-governmental negotiation and agreement. The Canadian government in particular is well placed to launch such proposals, and there are some precedents in international or bilateral law which might be helpful. The field of competition policy might be a good place to start. Meanwhile, few issues are as likely as this one to jeopardize the future of direct investment, at least in Canada; for these types of issues dramatically confirm the view that the presence of such firms directly limits sovereignty and serves as a vehicle for imposing the values and policies of foreign governments on host countries.[11]

A phenomenon as widespread as multinational corporations inevitably becomes bound up with both the question of the social and political consequences of large corporations and the larger range of issues in the field of Canada–United States relations. When one state is much more powerful than the other and is a major world power as well, terms such as interdependence are often likely to take on a one-sided meaning; one state has more of it than the other, and more than it wants on occasion. Here we are at the heart of the Canadian dilemma — the ties through investment, trade, communications, military alliances, population transfer, and in many other ways to the powerful and restless giant to the south. I do not have a handy panacea to deal with the complications of this relationship, which will always challenge our ingenuity. I would suggest that when certain larger issues are linked closely to foreign direct investment, there is likely to be considerable mis-specification. One example is the attempt to link foreign firms to the production of what some regard as socially undesirable commodities, or to private wants at the expense of public-sector spending. No one would deny that such corporations transmit or create certain kinds of wants, but so do many other processes which involve no foreign direct investment. Another example is the view that

---

[11] For an analysis of this issue, see the Report of the Task Force on the Structure of Canadian Industry, *Foreign Ownership and the Structure of Canadian Industry* (Ottawa: Privy Council Office, 1968).

such firms may be incompatible with a high degree of planning, and of course, with state ownership, both of which would tend to integrate a firm more fully within a country rather than to integrate an industry internationally. Direct-investment firms appear to co-exist with varying degrees of planning, but let us grant the point that direct investment as now generally conceived is certainly more compatible with a capitalist than a socialist orientation to enterprise. This leaves a prior question, however; for the difficulty of controlling such firms in a more highly planned society cannot be treated as both necessary and sufficient evidence of the undesirability of such firms, or of the desirability of more direct planning. We are not even in a position yet to know how far it is possible to deal with the problems created by such firms simply by more active and effective use of present instruments of policy, applied either nationally or internationally.

An important consequence of foreign direct investment is its uneven effect on private groups within the host country. This may help to explain some types of policy responses to direct investment, particularly those which prevent its competitive effects and perhaps those which attempt to secure some of the economic rents for domestic investors.

The most convincing general long-term result of more direct investment is that the real wage rate will rise, given the addition of capital and the improvement and spread of technology. Given some degree of competition with domestic owners or other subsidiaries, the benefit will come in part through lower prices and improved products. Domestic owners of capital and suppliers of technology (i.e., high-skill labour) may gain to the extent that they are complementary to foreign-owned firms and to the extent that capital formation and national income have risen. But domestic owners of capital and suppliers of technology may lose if they are competitive with foreign-owned firms, since the presence of the latter can require them to face higher wage rates, lower market prices, or a reduced share of the market. Where these competitive effects are not the likely ones, but entry to an industry is barred for a time, potential domestic entrants lose in other ways. Moreover, foreign subsidiaries are likely to cause further resentment among local capital owners because of their evident dislike of minority share issues (new stock offered to those who do not have a controlling interest in the enterprise), i.e., their unwillingness to share the rents and profits which are returns on their knowledge and market power. The effects on the demand for senior personnel are less clear. Foreign investment increases the scope for employing such persons directly and in some cases in the affiliates abroad, and supplies managerial and technical training which may subsequently spill over into the economy. What is also evident in the host country is that a significant percentage of the most senior positions in the subsidiary are filled by nationals of the parent company.[12]

All of this produces significant group differences in views on the effects of direct investment, and on policy proposals which might curb

---

[12] See A.E. Safarian, *The Performance of Foreign-Owned Firms in Canada* (Montreal: Canadian–American Committee, 1969), ch. 2.

such investment. Significant regional differences also occur for similar reasons. The low-income regions, such as most of the Maritimes, eastern Quebec, and northern Ontario, are unable to compete with the more developed parts of the country for capital and technology. Since they have fewer alternative sources of jobs and tax revenue than other parts of Canada, they tend to view with suspicion any measures which might further reduce their access to these. There are also a considerable number of persons in eastern and western Canada, and not only in Quebec, who appear to be almost neutral in their attitudes to direct investment from Ontario and direct investment from abroad.

A policy which reduces the inflow of foreign capital and technology — and does nothing to substitute for it — may well shift income away from labour and to domestic owners of capital and professionals. Restrictive policies might also tend to widen the already wide and persistent regional income differentials in Canada. These effects on personal and regional income distribution can be offset in principle by tax and transfer policies. Whether they could be fully offset in practice is a complicated question. The other critical assumption is that nothing is done to substitute for the capital or technology to which access is restricted, or to compensate for any other losses such as marketing connections. Of course, some substitutes would be found abroad or created at home, with benefits and costs which are unclear as noted earlier.

While it is desirable to find or develop substitutes which appear less costly in economic and political terms for some types of direct investment, some questions about the political process by which decisions of this kind are made raise doubts that this will be the most probable path for policy. There are other and perhaps easier ways to reconcile group differences so as to yield agreed policies, especially in a setting where some become convinced that national survival itself is at stake. Breton and others have suggested a theory of the economics of nationalism which helps explain how group differences are reconciled to yield agreed policies in circumstances such as those described here.[13] In essence, nationalism is regarded as a collective consumption good which yields both general and particular benefits. The general benefits accrue to all of those who derive psychic income from investment in nationalism. The particular benefits accrue to those who benefit directly by higher real income or better jobs (as well as by psychic income) from policies of economic nationalism. The particular beneficiaries, as already noted, tend to be in the higher-income groups. The political process involves persuading those who lose economic income or jobs to accept the policies because their psychic income is increased. Most major policies will have some differential impact on groups, of course. Policies in an area as divisive as this one should give close attention to the effects on the policy objective of levelling economic incomes and opportunities for Canadians. That issue, in my

[13] Albert Breton, "The Economics of Nationalism," *Journal of Political Economy*, August 1964, 72, pp. 376–86. See also Harry G. Johnson, "A Theoretical Model of Economic Nationalism in New and Developing States," *Political Science Quarterly*, June 1965, 80, pp. 169–185.

view, has had far more to do with the survival of the country historically than any issues raised by foreign direct investment.[14]

Moreover, national feeling and national self-interest ought to serve better ends than this particular form of protection for special groups; and national investment and regulation can yield higher real income and satisfaction where social and private costs or returns diverge. And that is true for both domestic and foreign corporations in Canada. One of the heavier costs of economic nationalism is the way in which it diverts public attention from such issues, focusing it on multinational corporations and encouraging policies which will have little or even negative effects on the more important issues.

IV. Conclusions

From the viewpoint of the host country, a large multinational presence in the corporate area brings both benefits and costs, either actual or potential. There are likely to be net economic benefits, the size of which depends on how well domestic policy options are exercised in tax policy, competition, or regulation. Some other forms of access to international technology may be less expensive economically, and will certainly create less political tension. It is difficult to know the types of industries and situations where this is likely to be the case, given present knowledge of the consequences of splitting the package of inputs which come over time with direct investment, and the various possible mechanisms for international transfer of such inputs. The quality of the domestic policy and private entrepreneurial response is the other critical determinant of an outcome where less or little direct investment is specified. Indeed, it is suggested that many of the problems allegedly associated with multinational corporations are not, in fact, due to them. The term has become a catch-all for the problems of control of the large corporation, the failures of domestic policies in correcting abuses of the market system, and a protest against a particular life-style. Canadian policy is an object lesson in this respect, both for the inefficiency and excessive foreign direct investment which Canada's industrial policies have encouraged, and for the failure to encourage a stronger capacity to undertake efficient ventures or to transmit knowledge from abroad in other ways.

It is inevitable, and in some cases desirable, that host countries will attempt to improve the net gain from direct investment, in part by developing techniques to offset the bargaining power which such firms have because of location in several nation states. Some countries will have a

---

[14] Other elites are involved. Government officials may believe that administrative control of business activity is more difficult to maintain with foreign direct investment in the country. Those who promote a competing ideology understandably oppose the extension of the largest and often most successful examples of capitalism to their country. The issue becomes even more complicated when important elements of the media, whether for reasons of the psychic income of nationalism or because of competition, or both, determine that they have a direct stake in the outcome. The debate on this subject in Canada is not uninfluenced by the fact that the national broadcasting system, and both the daily newspaper with the largest circulation and the magazine with the second largest, warmly support economic as well as cultural nationalism.

high degree of public planning for other reasons, extended also to any direct-investment firms. In other countries, I am doubtful that detailed administrative controls are either justified by the evidence of damage or likely to give clear improvements in national welfare, given the problems of operating such controls and the state of knowledge of the subject. If I am correct in my view that the economic literature suggests such firms are highly responsive over time to economic stimuli, and that the influence of ownership as such is far less important than relative prices as determined by comparative advantage and by economic policy, then there are ways to influence such firms' policies far short of direct controls.

This takes us to my final point. If one assumes that the host and home country can both gain from direct investment in the case of high-income countries, then independent policy approaches to the distribution of these gains are not likely to maximize the combined outcome. The same is likely to be true of independent policy approaches to limit some of the disadvantages which accompany direct investment. Indeed, it is not difficult to see situations today across boundaries where unrestricted competition for direct investment or unco-ordinated regulation of it are diminishing the combined social return which might be expected from it. In this article, I have restricted myself largely to a national framework. Ultimately, domestic policy in this and other respects depends on the extent to which one considers that an international setting for trade and investment and the resulting improvement of international resource allocation is also most likely to be conducive to the national interest. One does not have to accept the view of the unconditional supporters of direct investment, who regard it as nothing less than the basis for a new political world order, to suggest that binational or multinational policy approaches to some of the opportunities and constraints posed by such investment would be in the national interest. This is the case particularly if one believes that only a few of the criticisms of such firms amount to mountains of evidence, that some of the evidence consists of foothills capable of being ascended by governments, and that all too many of the alleged shortcomings amount to nothing more than molehills.

III. Economics
In the Political Process

1. Consumerism and Consumer Protection

David E. Bond *

Statistics Canada

The development and promulgation of government policies and pro-grams is inextricably bound to the working of the Canadian body politic. While one individual or a group of individuals may advance an idea, there is a substantial amount of consultation and discussion between con-cept and implementation. The people and/or institutions involved are usually consulted and given an opportunity to advance arguments relevant to the proposed concept. Depending upon the scope and importance of the proposal, these submissions can range from a few to many hundreds (as in the case of tax legislation and the proposed revision of the Com-petition Act in the early 1970s). On particularly sensitive issues, of which tax reform is again an example, substantial efforts may be made to or-ganize public opinion in favour of one position or another. After all the submissions have been made and the pros and cons of each position weighed, the elected officials of government make the final decision. This is as it should be in a democratic society, provided that all concerned are able to participate in the deliberative process.

For consumers there is a difference between being afforded the chance to comment on policy proposals and being able to mount the necessary effort. Both the resources which consumer groups can bring to bear on a problem and the access which the groups or individual consumers have to the centres of power are modest compared with those of other groups such as business, agriculture, and labour unions. These organized pressure groups not only have substantial financial and technical resources that can be marshalled to advocate their particular point of view; but more

*The opinions contained in this article are my own and are not in any way to be construed as reflecting the opinion of the Public Service of Canada or Statistics Canada.

important, they usually can command a hearing of their viewpoint by those at the very apex of the decision-making apparatus. If the presidents of major Canadian industries wished to advocate their companies' positions, it is conceivable that they (together with appropriate counsel) would fly to Ottawa and ask, and indeed, expect, to be received by a Minister or senior officials of a department or departments. Yet, if the individual citizen were to undertake the same activities, his travel and legal costs would not be tax-deductible and an appointment with a Minister or senior government officials would be almost impossible to obtain.

Many reasons can be advanced for this apparent discrimination. For example, if the Minister were to see each and every citizen who wished to talk with him or her, little time would be left for other activities; that is, priorities have to be assigned. This is true enough, but the fact remains that governments act upon what they perceive to be the demands of the body politic. What demands governments perceive, in turn, depends on who has the ability and the opportunity to present reasoned arguments that governments will hear. Consumers at present lack that facility and, therefore, may be considered under-represented in the political process at all levels of government.

Just why have consumers not organized into an effective voice with an impact comparable to that of other special-interest groups? After all, each one of us is a consumer and should, therefore, be concerned with improvements in consumer welfare. The paradox is that while each of us has a direct and continuing interest in advancing consumer welfare, little is accomplished.

I. Why the Consumer Voice Is Weak

Perhaps one of the keys to the explanation for the lack of an effective consumer voice lies in the fact that *while each of us is a consumer, he is a consumer second* to being a labourer, manager, dentist, lawyer, civil servant, teacher, etc. Seldom, if ever, does anyone consider himself a consumer first. Herein lies the problem: there is no primary, consistent, and long-run self-identification with a coherent group known as consumers. This lack of central identification in turn serves to hinder greatly the organization of consumers into a group aiming to achieve increases in consumer welfare.

In the case of a union, for example, the objectives of higher wages, greater fringe benefits, and stability of employment are well recognized and supported by the members. Disagreement may exist about the methods to be used in achieving these goals, that is, about the use of strikes, arbitration, political activity, or whatever. What is true of a union can be universally applied to any group which has some easily identifiable central purpose and also some degree of collective-decision mechanism for determining the method by which the goals are to be attained.

Equally important, if the group achieves its goals, of a new contract, increased protection, or favourable tax treatment, for example, the benefits are primarily (though not exclusively) visited or conferred upon the group which agitated for the action. True, there may be some externalities.

A substantial wage increase for firemen will usually bring a similar increase for policemen. The granting of tax relief in one industry will make a similar concession in another industry easier to obtain. But for most of these groups, *the direct benefits obtained by collective action far outweigh externalities which may flow to other groups or individuals from the action.*

Consider, on the other hand, the case of a group of consumers or even an individual consumer anxious to achieve some new consumer legislation or to punish the butcher who habitually weighs his thumb along with a steak. Should a group or an individual succeed in getting a new law passed or getting the butcher to refrain from weighing his thumb, the group or the individual benefits. But all the other consumers who are subject to the law or who are customers of the offending butcher also benefit. *The externalities are extensive and usually, though not always, the direct benefit to an individual is far less than the effort required to correct the injustice.*

As if this existence of extensive and indeed overriding externalities were not enough, the *process of identifying common consumer goals* is further complicated by two factors. First, each of us is a consumer second. For example, a reduction in or the complete removal of tariffs would mean a substantial reduction in prices for all consumers. The reduction or removal of tariffs should, therefore, be a consumer goal. But for the consumer who is a worker, shareholder, or manager of a protected industry faced with extinction by foreign competition, the benefits of lower consumer prices may be offset by financial loss or unemployment. When choices are put into that context, the preference for increasing consumer welfare must take second place. Lower prices are of little benefit when income and wealth are reduced to zero.

Second, individual patterns of consumption are a reflection of personal choice: what we consume, how we consume, and when we consume is a demonstration of personal freedom. But here again there are externalities. One person's consumption — for example, a preference for driving to work rather than using public transportation — may well affect the consumption pattern of someone else, in the form of air pollution or in the diversion of government expenditures away from the construction of parks or sewage systems toward the building and expansion of expressways. These interpersonal overlaps make the establishment of common consumer goals very difficult, if not impossible.

The consumer problem is compounded by an inequity in the tax system which provides a form of support to certain parties which is not available to the individual consumer or even to consumers collectively. Should a particular firm or industry wish to lobby for or against some policy, the costs of such action are considered to be legitimate costs of business. Yet, should the individual consumer attempt to charge as "business" costs the legal or other expenses involved, say, in intercession before a regulatory tribunal, his claim would be disallowed by the Department of National Revenue. In an admittedly narrow interpretation of this fact, one could say that *the state "subsidizes" the business voice without providing equitable treatment to the consumer.* And this advantage is well utilized to mount effective, persistent, and highly sophisticated campaigns on matters of vital interest to particular groups. Without an active consumer voice that may counsel action different from that desired by organized vested-interest groups, the impact of the latter groups may be far greater than their true importance in the body politic, or in the general economic and social fabric of the nation. In this sense, *the voice that governments hear may be articulate and effective, but not truly reflective of what some call the "silent majority" and what may be called the "socially disenfranchised."*

The piecemeal nature of the impact of other organized groups' efforts also tends to work against organized consumer reaction. If consumer welfare were reduced significantly in one discrete move, reaction might be swift and vocal; but, as in the case of wood rot in a boat hull, gradual erosion is seldom noticed before substantial damage is done. There is no clandestine conspiracy to defraud the consumer, to make him or her exist for the system rather than vice versa. Rather, an over-all frame of mind, which is attacked in Reich's *Greening of America,*[1] for example, works against the consumer. The concern of critics such as Reich, Mumford, and Illich is with the quality of life *together* with the usual economic goals of output and efficiency.

II. Is It Important?

The lack of an effective voice retards development of new policies and programs beneficial to the consumer. In the day-to-day actions of governments, on a thousand fronts, the failure to consider the consumer viewpoint results in a constant infringement of consumer welfare. While a tariff on chocolate means little to each of us individually, collectively it can cost us substantial amounts annually. And what is true in the case of the chocolate bar is true in a multitude of different actions involving expenditures, transfer payments, taxation, etc.

Why should this inability of the consumer individually or collectively to articulate his interests and opinions be of concern to anyone? On a very lofty plain, it can be argued that this distortion in voices means that we are still far short of the goal of effective and equitable participatory democracy. On a somewhat more pragmatic level, it could be held that this distortion of the flow of information to the government leads to a misallocation of resources which might not exist if consumers were better organized. The fact that *any* consumer legislation exists reflects in part basic social progress; but it also proves that, given sufficient cause, consumers can frequently, if only temporarily, unite to achieve some very specific and narrow goal. If more complete information as to price, contents, or performance of products were available, the consumer would be able to make more rational or informed choices in the market. Without such information, the rates of return on certain economic activities are inflated and the equilibrium of the economy is distorted away from what it would be if the consumer were better informed, or at least placed on a more equal footing when "the rules of the game are determined", i.e., when government policy and legislation are formulated.

[1] Charles A. Reich, *The Greening of America* (New York: Random House, 1970).

If such a distortion in the allocation of resources and services is in fact occurring, it may explain, in part, the evidence of increased alienation and discontent with the "system" as it now exists. Evidence of this alienation can be found not only in the existence of social dropouts, but also in increased agitation among the rank-and-file members of labour unions, the rising tide of mail to Box 99 (the consumer-complaint office of the federal government), and the increased sensitivity of the corporate sector to consumer complaints.

If we are indeed engaged in the process of reorienting society from its excessive concentration on the growth of output toward the acceptance of additional goals such as improving the quality of life and increasing social justice, the success of such a policy will depend, to a large extent, on redressing the imbalance of voices raised, perceived, and considered. After all, the essence of these goals is really to advance consumer welfare not only with regard to products and services in the private sector, but also in the public sector.

When placed in this wider social perspective, many policies may be subject to significant revaluation and change. If a strong and reasoned consumer attitude were interjected into society, the process of reorientation would be greatly aided. The aim here is not to force the acceptance of the consumer viewpoint, but rather to focus attention on it so that it will at least be considered when policy decisions are made.[2]

III. Alternatives for Filling the Participation Void

1. The traditional way

The obvious need for consumers to have some input into government policy formulation was perceived long ago, and indeed the history of consumer political activity in the countries of the North Atlantic community is long-standing. Organized consumer participation dates back to the late 19th century in Sweden and to the 1940s in Canada. The Consumers' Association of Canada is the primary organized body of consumers in the nation and is affiliated with similar groups in the United States, the United Kingdom, and elsewhere.

These groups, at the beginning, primarily tried to provide more information so that consumers could make more rational choices in their purchases. Thus, for example, the U.S. Consumers' Union until very recently concentrated almost entirely upon the question of product testing, with only moderate effort devoted to effecting changes in government policy.

In most cases, the political activity, if any, of these organizations was founded primarily on the idea that reason is the obvious motivating force for the improvement of consumer legislation. The reasonableness of the argument and the large number of supporters would, the organization believed, encourage the government to enact legislation. The prime example of this kind of activity is the bacon-packaging law, which requires

---

[2] For further discussion of various aspects of consumerism, see David A. Aaker and George S. Day, eds., *Consumerism: Search for the Consumer Interest* (New York: Free Press, 1971) and Mark V. Nadel, *The Politics of Consumer Protection* (New York: Bobbs-Merrill, 1971).

that one full strip of the bacon be clearly visible. The intention here is to prevent the packaging from giving the consumer a false impression about the actual meatiness of the product. These traditional types of activities by consumer groups, both in North America and Europe, have in recent times been subjected to severe criticism.

2. The new consumer activist

Beginning in the middle of the 1960s, primarily in the United States, an increased political awareness arose on the part of individuals whose middle- and upper-middle-income backgrounds suggest that they would be anything but political activists. These groups, epitomized by Ralph Nader, became increasingly concerned about the apparent inability of the consumer to participate with any degree of fairness in the marketplace. This concern mainly centred on the inability of existing regulatory authorities in the United States to protect the interests of the consumer. These regulatory agencies were, in a sense, "captured" by the industries that they were supposed to supervise in the public interest.

The participatory-democracy activities of civil-rights leaders, such as Martin Luther King and similar individuals in the North American political context, seemed to be ideally suited for dealing with consumer problems. Nader perceived that the combination of a desired improvement in consumer welfare and the use of these new political tools could result in significant gains. All this coincided with some particularly "hot" issues which were sure to rouse strong public opinion. The rising toll of auto deaths, a concern for the environment, and a basic feeling of alienation on the part of many members of society collided with the almost erotic love affair of North Americans with their cars. The atmosphere thus created suggested that the automobile was an excellent issue to bring about the political radicalization of the consumer movement.

Nader used charges of inept management and poor engineering in the construction of automobiles to rouse substantial support against what had been considered an almost invulnerable power: the General Motors Corporation.[3] Then, all at once, a host of new issues sprang up in the United States. Besides tackling the issue of automobile-safety legislation, Nader latched on to a strong demand for stricter meat inspection, playing on the fear of a health hazard. In addition, there was concern about the environment and a new degree of activism on the part of younger members of the legal profession who wanted to see the law used by *all* people within the body politic, not just the rich.[4] As a consequence of this political

---

[3] See Ralph Nader, *Unsafe at Any Speed: The Designed-in Dangers of the American Automobile* (New York: Grossman, 1965).

[4] Among the studies by "Nader's Raiders" are: Mark J. Green, *The Closed Enterprise System: Ralph Nader's Study Group Report on Antitrust Enforcement* (New York: Grossman, 1972); Ralph Nader, Peter J. Petkas, and Kate Blackwell, eds., *Whistle Blowing: The Report of the Conference on Professional Responsibility* (New York: Grossman, 1972); *Old Age: The Last Segregation: Ralph Nader's Study Group Report on Nursing Homes* (New York: Grossman, 1971); *Vanishing Air: The Ralph Nader Study Group Report on Air Pollution* (New York: Grossman, 1970); David Zwick and Marcy Benstock, *Water Wasteland: Ralph Nader's Study Group Report on Water Pollution* (New York: Grossman, 1971).

activism in the consumer movement, a substantial number of alternative methods for strengthening the consumer's voice were suggested. It is worth our while to consider a few of these methods and their implications for the workings of the economy.

IV. The Activists' Approach

1. Boycotts

Perhaps the best examples of the political radicalization of the consumer movement in North America were the strong efforts to establish boycotts of various kinds of products, from grapes to cheese, from drugs to automobiles. The boycott and its impact had been clearly demonstrated by Martin Luther King's attempt to integrate the buses in Birmingham, Alabama by persuading the black community to boycott the downtown merchants. If the heart of Dixie could be laid low, Dominion Stores or Loblaw would be pushovers. In the spring and summer of 1968, housewives in Canada tried to organize a boycott of supermarkets in an effort to force them to lower their prices, and the same thing was tried again in 1973 as the price of meat started to rise sharply.

The boycott procedure can be quite effective *provided that it receives almost total support.* The customer in this case does have the upper hand, but the trick is to make sure that everyone participates and that discipline is maintained until the impact is really felt. King was able to win the cooperation of the black community in Birmingham. However, the task of getting all consumers in the United States and Canada to boycott meat not just for a week, but for a longer period, is extremely difficult (the demand curve does not shift to the left). Consider, for example, that you might want to have the neighbours over for a barbecue in the backyard, and that serving barbecued peanut burgers is not quite the same as serving thick, juicy steaks. The North American public has long been conditioned to believe that only meat can provide the vitamins and protein necessary for maintaining health; besides, meat has become a symbol of success.

The number of chinks in the boycott of a product is in direct proportion to the universality of the product's use. For example, it is unlikely that a boycott of oil products, started in order to stop the practice of price fixing by oil companies, would be successful. The automobile is part of the North American way of life, and it is highly doubtful that public transportation could be expanded to meet the needs of the entire population. Automobile-owning Canadians would not willingly give up the use of their vehicles for a period of, say, a month or four months so as to avoid gasoline consumption. Those who heat their homes with oil would be equally reluctant to join such a boycott.

2. The big-brother approach

A second approach to strengthening the consumer's voice has been advanced in Canada. It calls for the establishment of a consumer advocate. This individual is often visualized as arguing on behalf of the consumer before various regulatory tribunals such as the Canadian Transport Commission (CTC), which regulates the rates for rail and air fares and federally chartered phone companies.

The need for such public advocacy of the consumer's welfare is clearly demonstrated in a series of articles that were written for the Canadian Consumer Council.[5] Consider the following example. The Bell Telephone Company, which is subject to supervision by the CTC, petitions for a rate increase. You, as an individual subscriber faced with, say, a doubling of your telephone bill, desire to oppose such an action. Theoretically, under the participatory democracy in which we live, you should be able to go and argue the case on its merits and allow the Commission to decide whether or not the rate increase will be allowed.

However, should you proceed along these lines, you would be faced with innumerable roadblocks. First, the CTC conducts all its activities on the basis of court procedure, and thus there is a series of long-established traditions about cross-examination and the ability of witnesses to provide evidence in support of their contentions. For example, the telephone company may, in support of its plea, produce three or four thousand pages of highly technical evidence about both the accounting side and the economic and scientific implications of a rate increase. It would take a rare individual to be able to interpret all this. Moreover, you would be provided with only part of the information and not given total access to the company's books on corporate strategy. Second, if you wished to participate, it would be advisable to have a legal counsel at your side and that involves expense. As the meetings are usually held in Ottawa, if you were living in Chicoutimi, for instance, you would pay a substantial amount for transportation and accommodation alone. Finally, in the case of any legal proceeding, one of the instruments that is essential to your application is a transcript of the proceedings of the hearing. In the hearings of Bell Canada in the spring of 1972, the cost of a complete set of transcript was over $1,700. The staff at the Canadian Consumer Council in the summer of 1972 estimated that the minimum cost of intervention by a private citizen in the case of a rate hearing before the CTC would come to about $8,000.

Faced with such costs of participation (entry), it is not hard to explain why the public is rarely heard by these commissions. Given the externalities associated with a successful objection, the reason for non-participation becomes even clearer.

To overcome these barriers, the establishment of a federally subsidized official, known as the consumer advocate, has been proposed. This official would have legal standing to represent the consumer and would argue the consumer's case before these commissions.

Supporters of this method of solving the consumer problem are really in a sense trying to use the law to effect a substantial social change. Consumer-advocate legislation proposed within the U.S. government was vetoed in the fall of 1972 by President Nixon. At the present time, no such legislation has been proposed by the Canadian government, although in 1973 the Minister of Consumer and Corporate Affairs gave a special grant

[5] E. Belobaba et al., On the Question of Consumer Advocacy (Ottawa: Canadian Consumer Council, 1973).

to the Consumers' Association of Canada to allow it to mount a substantial counter-effort to the Bell rate-increase application for 1973.

3. Greater information

In many instances, consumers have asked for more information to help them make more rational choices. In the United Kingdom and in some countries in Europe (Sweden and Denmark), attached to each consumer article is a tag which gives basic information. For example, in the case of a refrigerator the tag would give the cubic capacity, the cost of cooling one quart or litre of water one degree or of making one pound or kilogram of ice, and other information which would be standard for all refrigerators and thus provide facts that would facilitate product comparison. With more information, the consumer is better able to match his own personal interests and preferences with the goods available and thereby maximize his welfare. "Tell-tag" schemes of this nature have been proposed in Canada, but there has been strong resistance from manufacturers. As might be expected, this is particularly true in industries in which the basic products are similar and extensive advertising has been used to differentiate products in an effort to gain monopoly rents. Perhaps the best example of this is the "white" appliances, i.e., stoves, refrigerators, and washing machines. As yet, the government (federal or provincial) has shown little inclination to go into this "tell-tag" operation, arguing that it is extremely costly and not very effective.

A variant of the tell-tag information is known as "unit pricing," in which the price of the product must be listed not only as the price for the total product, e.g., 14 oz. of saltines or 32½ oz. of detergent, but also as the basic unit price, that is, the price per ounce, pound, quart, or litre. This basic price information facilitates comparison shopping, which is otherwise difficult when there are a multitude of different package sizes and shapes. The consumer-packaging industry in Canada has strongly resisted any attempt to legislate unit pricing, but in several states in the United States, notably Massachusetts and Rhode Island, unit pricing is now required by law. However, it does not seem to have brought about any repercussions in the marketplace. Indeed, the primary beneficiaries of unit pricing have been those middle-class individuals who have suddenly become price-conscious because consumer-consciousness has become rather chic.

4. Cutting back advertising

In attempting to deal with the consumer problem, many people have interpreted the consumer's inability to effect change as partly a function of the fact that he is outweighed by the substantial funds spent on conditioning him to think in certain ways. It has been proposed that if a company is found fraudulent in its advertising, it should initiate corrective ads, saying that it has "sinned" in the past. For example, if a particular product is supposed to wax your floor and leave it shiny and bright for six months, and if in fact it does not perform as promised, then a public-service group, at the company's expense, should be able to publicize the deception.

The arguments both for and against advertising are extensive and have filled numerous pages. But the idea of corrective advertising to restore the balance of power in the marketplace between the consumer and the producer is of continuing interest to consumers.

5. Power to the people

A final approach, which is gaining increasing support from some members of the legal profession, can be put under the rubric of "power to the people." The idea here is to use the courts to enforce the consumer's rights in the marketplace and to strengthen government further by the rule of law. This is an extremely complicated question relating to the legal status an individual has in dealing in the marketplace and particularly in affecting government activity.

One thrust of this kind of thinking relates to the demand for an omnibus act that would be analogous to the Environmental Protection Act in the United States. Among other provisions of the Environmental Protection Act is a clause which requires that the government show, if asked to in court, that the impact of any given government policy on the environment has been carefully evaluated. If, in the course of events, it is shown that the government did not consider the impact on the environment, any individual has the right to go to the courts and enjoin the government from carrying out the policy until the impact on the environment is considered. This technique was used, for example, in assessing the Trans-Alaska Pipeline in the early 1970s.

If such an act were to be passed in Canada with reference to consumer protection, it could forestall many policies which would be detrimental to the consumer's welfare, or, at least, it would force consideration of the consumer's viewpoint. It has been suggested that such an act would give the consumer the dominant voice, but that is not its purpose. Rather, its aim is to provide a method to ensure that the consumer's point of view is considered before any policy is undertaken. The probability of such a general administrative act being enacted in Canada, is, at the present time, rather remote. But legislation of this kind is gaining increasing favour among the younger members of the legal profession in Canada and is of general interest to the federal Law Reform Commission. The principal opponents of this kind of legislation argue that the result would be a substantial increase in the burden on the courts and a constant increase in expenses for both industry and the government. Naturally, most of these costs, they rightly argue, would be passed on to the consumer, in the form of taxes and/or increased prices.

It is this final point which is of crucial importance to the consumer. What needs to be ascertained and what is very difficult to quantify, especially where externalities are so important, is just how much the consumer is willing to pay for increased voice in the setting of government policy. As with any public good, the natural tendency of the individual is to say: "Let someone else pay for it, and I will gain the benefits." But some decision has to be made to "tax" the general public for its general welfare.

V. Conclusion

The effort to increase the welfare of the consumer involves a critical application of distribution theory and the theory of micro-economics. In the period subsequent to the Keynesian Revolution, the major emphasis in economics has been on macro-economics. Now as we face the questions of redistribution of income and social status and an increased awareness of human civilities and quality of life, the emphasis on micro-economics and the contribution it can make to solving these problems will become increasingly important. The future wave, to paraphrase the bard, lies "not in the system, but in its parts."

2. Modeling the Behaviour of Exchequers

Albert Breton

University of Toronto

I. Exchequers as Bureaucratic Institutions

In this paper, I would like to examine one aspect of the behaviour of Exchequers — a name I use to denote institutions that in some countries are known as the Department of Finance, in others as the Treasury, in others as the Department of Economics or Department of Economic Affairs, and in others still as Exchequer Courts — and to provide a hypothesis to explain that behaviour. These institutions are also called the "fiscal authorities," because they are responsible for fiscal policy, as distinct from the "monetary authorities" (the central bank), responsible for monetary policy. It is important to stress that I limit myself to one aspect and one aspect only of the behaviour of these institutions and that as a consequence the hypothesis provided might have to be altered — though, I am confident, not rejected — when other activities of Exchequers are ultimately modeled.

The study and analysis of institutions and of their behaviour, which historically was an important part of economic analysis, has since the turn of the century claimed a smaller and smaller proportion of the attention and talent of economists, so much so that it is fair to say that now a number of economists believe that perfect markets are the only institutions that are worthy of study and relevant to an understanding of economic activity. They, however, are a passing breed.

Indeed, in very recent years a growing number of economists have been returning to the analysis of institutions in an effort to understand a larger part of economic processes. Among the institutions now being studied as institutions are corporations, labour unions, non-profit corporations, governments, bureaucracies, federal structures, laws (for example, the first amendment to the U.S. Constitution: why should freedom of expression, an activity that can impose grave harm on others, be constitutionally protected?), and many others. At the present time, the work in this area is being conducted at many different levels of abstraction and lacks consistency; but until much more is known, a general theory of institutions is bound to be a failure.

This effort is best seen as a contribution to the analysis of the behaviour of bureaucracies. There are currently three or four different theories of bureaucracy,[1] not, I must add, totally inconsistent with each other, but certainly very difficult and perhaps impossible to reconcile elegantly with each other. The best hope of progress in such circumstances is to examine new bodies of data and new facts and to try to interpret them with the help of one hypothesis or another. If such exercises are conducted in a spirit of non-controversy and non-partisanship, our knowledge of bureaucracies will certainly be improved.

II.   Actual vs. Forecasted Revenue

The particular aspect of the behaviour of Exchequers on which I wish to focus my attention can be described by the following stylized fact[2]: the actual measured revenues of governments in period t_1 are often in excess of those that were forecasted in t_0.[3] The fact to be explained is the excess of actual over forecasted revenue. This phenomenon, which has characterized the Canadian Department of Finance for at least the last twenty years, is not a feature that is peculiar to that department, although, as we will see, some forces may and do exist in some contexts to prevent an actual excess from being realized. Let me put this point differently. If the institutional context or environment in which the Department of Finance operates were repeated in other countries, all would show an excess of actual over forecasted revenues; however, since that context is not everywhere the same, and in some instances is very different, the excess is in some instances not observable.

Before proceeding with the analysis, we must note that this paper is not concerned with the fact that the Department of Finance sometimes *plans* a budgetary surplus when aggregate demand is deficient or, more seldom, *plans* a deficit when excess demand exists. That is a different, though no less important, problem. Here we are solely preoccupied with the excess of actual receipts over the amount forecasted, although it is

---

[1] C.N. Parkinson, "Parkinson's Law or the Rising Pyramid," in *Parkinson's Law and Other studies in Administration* (Houghton Miffin, 1957); G. Tullock, "The Rand-Parkinson Effect", *Papers on Non-Market Decision-Making*, III (Fall 1967); W.A. Niskanen, Jr., *Bureaucracy and Representative Government* (Aldine-Atherton, 1971); A. Breton and R.S. Wintrobe, "A Theory of Public Bureaus" (mimeo, September 1972).

[2] A stylized fact is one which has been sheared of all "deviations" on the assumption that these are exceptions not representative of the central tendency which the fact or facts are presumed to represent. The constancy of relative shares of factors of production in GNP — for which the expression was invented — is a stylized fact. It is presumed in this case that the variations that we observe in relative shares are accidental and irrelevant and should not be allowed to detract from the presumed central phenomenon.

[3] See W.I. Gillespie, "The Federal Budget as Plan, 1968–1972", *Canadian Tax Journal* (Jan.–Feb. 1973), pp. 64–84.

recognized that this excess has direct and significant implications for over-all budgetary deficits and surpluses: it means that deficits are always smaller and surpluses larger than announced.

III.   An Example from Insurance

To gain additional understanding of the nature of the problem, it may be useful to look at hypothetical examples and, if only briefly, to ponder their significance. Consider an enterprise in the business of selling protection against fire hazards. Imagine that at a given point in time the management of that company underestimates its revenues, that is, charges a price for insurance (or premiums) that does not "correctly" reflect the probability of damages from fire. There is, to put it differently, a probability density function of damages by fire for any relevant market area,[4] and a company can use the probability density function to determine the price of insurance. If we neglect administrative costs and other similar charges — what is termed the loading factor in insurance vocabulary — and if we observe a company charging a higher price for insurance than is dictated by the true probability of damages, we have to assume that this company uses a probability density function different from the true one in setting its rates. If it does this at all systematically, and if at each period we compare the forecast of its revenues with its actual revenues and observe that the latter are systematically underestimated, we are entitled to assume that the company knowingly underestimates its revenues and that it does this for one or more specific reasons.

Before we look at these reasons, it is well to observe that, given the market demand curve for insurance-protection against fire, the freedom that an insurance company has of using a systematically biased density function in determining its rates is a function of the degree of competition in the market. Indeed, if competition existed in the market, the excess of the upward-biased over the true premiums would attract new entrants which would force the premiums down.

Thus we need a monopoly to achieve our result. But we need more, since there is no reason to believe that a monopolist would find it advantageous to contrive his accounting practices in such a way as to produce a systematic underestimation of his revenues. What incentive, therefore, could a monopolist have to lead others to believe that his revenues will be lower than he himself knows they will be? It is not my purpose in discussing this example to provide a complete explanation of the behaviour of such a monopolist, but simply to illustrate the nature of the problem facing us in trying to understand the behaviour of Exchequers.

Suppose that our monopolist was regulated by a public body and that the regulator relied on the probability density function provided by the insurance company to set the limits on the price of insurance; this would provide an incentive for using a biased probability density function and, human nature being what it is, there seems to be no reason to believe it would not be used.

---

[4] This function relates the dollar amount of loss from fire to the probability of this amount of loss occurring.

IV. Why Exchequers Underestimate Revenues

Before examining some of the incentives that Exchequers may have to underestimate their revenues, it is well to note that some Exchequers are in a position of virtual monopoly, as is the Canadian Department of Finance, while others are in effect in a more competitive position, like the U.S. Office of Management and Budget. Indeed, in the United States that Office is in effect "balanced-off" by the Federal Reserve Bank, which is independent of the Office, by the Council of Economic Advisors, and by the Treasury, while in Canada the central bank is not independent of the Department of Finance and, still traumatized by the memory of the "Coyne" Affair," does not dare take issue with the Department.[5] Also, the Economic Council of Canada is not an integral part of the government and, in any case, it is prevented by its terms of reference from engaging in short-term forecasting.

One should not, therefore, expect the systematic underestimation of revenues characteristic of the monopolistic Canadian Department of Finance to be observed in the United States. In all cases, before investigation of the incentive that may lead to underestimation, care should be taken to establish the nature of the environment in which the governmental body operates.

Given that the Department of Finance in the Canadian government is in a monopoly position in that no competing organism can effectively challenge its revenue forecasts, we are provided with the polar case of an institution that, it must be assumed, knowingly underestimates its revenues. We are therefore justified in trying to unravel the mixture of incentives and motives which lead to that behaviour.

The hypothesis put forward in this paper is that the underestimation of revenues by Exchequers is the most efficient way of minimizing the risk of confrontation with other departments of government, while at the same time providing the Exchequer with an instrument — a form of internal patronage — whereby it can maintain some control and exercise some power over these departments. To clarify the hypothesis, let me state it in more formal terms. I assume that the objective function that Exchequer bureaucrats maximize is an expected-utility function which, in this paper, I take to be defined solely in terms of one variable, namely, power.[6] To simplify, I restrict the number of possible uncertain states of the world in which power is used to two: one in which the level of general economic activity is high and another in which it is low.[7]

---

[5] In 1961 Mr. J.E. Coyne, Governor of the Bank of Canada, was in effect fired from his post in the face of a lack of co-ordination of monetary with fiscal policy and a highly inappropriate monetary policy pursued by the Bank in the 1958–61 period. See the essay by Officer and Smith in this volume.

[6] An intuitive notion of power is sufficient for my purposes. The best way to think of power is to think of it in the same way that economists think of wealth. Indeed, the problems of defining power are in many ways similar to those of defining wealth. Like wealth, power is a stock which can be augmented or depreciated; it is difficult to imagine what it could be in a timeless world and, as a consequence, it would appear to be intimately related, like wealth, to uncertainty and hence to contingent states of the world.

[7] Thus the Exchequer maximizes its expected-utility function (expected power), $p.H + (1-p).L$, where H is its amount of power when economic activity is high, L is this amount when economic activity is low, p is the probability of a high level of economic activity, and $(1-p)$ the probability of a low level.

Now, suppose that the Exchequer forecasts a flow of revenue on the assumption that the level of activity will be high, but it turns out to be low. What would the consequences be? Clearly, revenues will be less than forecasted and the Exchequer will either have to borrow (from the public at home or abroad, or from the central bank), or it will have to ask some or all operating departments for reductions in expenditures, or both. If the Exchequer decides to ask for expenditure reductions, it would have to confront some or all departments and it could possibly be defeated in its demands. Such defeats with all the consequences that would follow — including the demotion of some bureaucrats — are to be avoided as much as possible. Furthermore, even if it is not defeated, the Exchequer will necessarily use up some of its power.

It should be noted, however, that if the pattern of requiring reductions in expenditures as well as the magnitude of the reductions became predictable — not an easy thing to achieve — the operating departments would adjust their behaviour and would, at the beginning of each period, request appropriations which would in effect be funds to pay for expenditure reductions. Once that equilibrium pattern was achieved, the risk of confrontation would be zero and, consequently, the Exchequer would not seek to avoid an overestimation of revenues.

But if Exchequers seek to avoid confrontation with operating departments, why do they not borrow the funds that are necessary to cover the difference between forecasted and actual expenditures? The answer is that Exchequers do borrow, but that they seek to avoid borrowing whenever possible. Why? To answer this question, we must address ourselves to a difficult problem about which there is much misunderstanding.

We must begin by distinguishing between borrowing from the public and borrowing from the central bank. Exchequers seek to minimize the amount borrowed from the public, simply to maintain their credit-worthiness or, to put it differently, so as not to use up all their borrowing capacity. This is what one would expect a risk-averter to do and this is what risk-averse Exchequers do.

But why do Exchequers not like to borrow from the central bank? After all, their credit-worthiness there is infinite. It has sometimes been asserted that Exchequers do not borrow from their central bank because they have a preference for price stability and are indifferent about the level of unemployment. Since borrowing from the central bank would increase the supply of money and push real interest rates downward, in inflationary periods it would lead to more upward pressure on prices, and in non-inflationary periods to increased use of resources. Given the assumed preference pattern, Exchequers can be expected to avoid borrowing from the central bank as much as possible.

That line of analysis, however, is not convincing. Indeed, it is more consistent with available evidence to assume that Exchequers have a strong positive preference for inflation as long as the public does not develop "correct" expectations about the rate of price increase. Exchequers are large net borrowers, and the greater the rate of inflation and the more biased the public's expectations about that rate of inflation, the less the real cost of carrying the outstanding debt becomes. Only if the public held "correct" expectations about the rate of inflation, would Exchequers develop neutral or negative preferences about inflation.[8]

Many of the activities of Exchequers can be understood only if they are seen as ways of leading the public to develop "incorrect" expectations about the rate of inflation. The reluctance to borrow and to be seen borrowing from the central bank is one of these. There are many others, which would distract us too much to examine here.

To avoid confrontation with other departments and to avoid having to borrow more than a "reasonable" amount, Exchequers assume that the state of the world in which they operate is one characterized by a low level of economic activity and, as a consequence, they seek to underestimate revenues.

This course of action is seen as the optimal one for risk-averse, power-maximizing bureaucrats, not only because it reduces the risks described above, but also because the excess funds (the positive difference between actual and forecasted receipts) can be used as patronage money in the dealings of the Exchequer with operating departments.

The distribution of patronage is almost totally inseparable from the exercise of power, so much so that efforts to eliminate patronage — usually proposed and favoured by those who have no power — only succeed in transforming the form that patronage takes. In the case of the relationship between Exchequers and other departments of government, patronage can take many forms. For example, part of the excess funds can be made available to all departments, but only after some departments have been told of their existence and, as a consequence, have been able to prepare the formulation of programs to absorb these funds. Or patronage can take the form of proposals for expenditure, originating in the Exchequer, that clearly favour one department over another. It is interesting to note in this connection that Exchequers, even when they recommend that taxes be cut to deal with the excess funds resulting from their underestimation of revenues, rarely go the full way and recommend that the tax reduction eliminate the excess completely; indeed, they usually come up with a package of tax cuts and expenditure increases, the latter not usually tailored in a way that would lead an outsider to deny with certainty the existence of internal patronage.

V. Areas of Reform

The question that inevitably arises at the end of an exercise such as this one is that of whether the underestimation of revenues which is a characteristic tendency of Exchequers can be overcome or whether we are stuck with it. The answer has already been hinted at in an earlier part of the paper. In this section, I would like to make the answer explicit by pointing to three possible areas of reform.

The first, to which allusion has already been made, would consist in reducing the incidence of underestimation by reducing or even destroying

---

[8] It should be noted that many of the activities of Exchequers bring them into contact with people in the private sector who are also net borrowers and hence have the same views as Exchequers about inflation.

the monopoly position of Exchequers. This is most easily done by creating alternative sources of forecasting, of monitoring the behaviour of the economy in the short run, and of advice, and by giving an operational and effective voice to these alternative sources in administering the economic affairs of the country. It should be understood that such a remedy is more easily formulated than effected, since Exchequers can be expected to fight with all their power against such an eventuality. In a significant way, one can say that the viciousness of the fight that an Exchequer would put up is a measure of the gain that would accrue to a country from de-monopolization. Canadians have not reflected enough on the reasons why President Truman created the Council of Economic Advisors. It is true, of course, that the Canadian form of government is very different from the American, but we should not let references to "cabinet government" act as conservative smoke screens to maintain a harmful *status quo*.

The second reform which is implied in the above analysis is that the management of the national debt and the administration of the government's finances should not be part of the business of Exchequers. In the Canadian context, this means that everything that has to do with debt financing of the Canadian government should be removed from the control of the Department of Finance. Debt management and fiscal management should be structurally separated, and the structure should be devised in such a way as to avoid collusion between these management branches. If the two were separate, the temptation to manage fiscal affairs in the interest of "orderly" debt administration would be largely eliminated and the incentive to underestimate revenues systematically would be reduced.

The third and last reform suggested by the foregoing analysis would consist in altering budgetary practices by requiring the Treasury Board to formulate alternative budgets for alternative expected states of the world. Thus the budget would be formulated for possible over- as well as underestimation of revenues. This would eliminate internal patronage, since it would remove the disposition of excess funds from the discretion of the Exchequer.

Since the third reform is probably the most difficult and most costly to implement, and since it is not necessary to implement all three reforms to achieve the desired result, I suggest that we should strive to apply the first two. That both of these should be implemented follows from the fact that de-monopolization is unlikely to be completely achieved and collusion between the fiscal and debt-management units is likely to exist to some degree, whatever precautions are taken. If the de-monopolization of the Exchequer and the separation of fiscal and debt management were implemented, the systematic underestimation of revenues which characterizes a number of economies to-day would disappear. Economies would be much more efficiently managed.

VI. Summary

In this short paper, I have addressed myself to the question of the systematic underestimation of revenues which characterizes the fiscal management of some countries and, in particular, that of Canada. I have

IV. Natural Resources

1. The Resource - Industry Problem

Gunter Schramm

University of Michigan

Natural resources have traditionally provided the foundation for Canada's economic development and growth. Furs and fisheries; later agriculture, forestry, and mining; and later still hydropower, oil, and natural gas have been the major stimulants for the settlement of the country. The surpluses created from their exploitation have provided the basic means for industrialization and modern urban development. While today the industrial and service sectors of the economy provide the bulk of the employment opportunities, natural resources, their exploitation, processing, and export still form a major component of gross national product. In 1971, for example, merchandise exports accounted for almost 20 percent of GNP (more than in any other large industrialized nation), and some 62 percent of these exports were accounted for by processed or unprocessed raw materials. Economic issues affecting Canada's natural-resources industries, therefore, are of major importance for the well-being of the country.

When we talk about natural resources, we can differentiate between two categories: those that are "renewable," such as water, air, forestry, agriculture, and fisheries, and those that are fixed, or "depletable", such as minerals, coal, oil, and natural gas. Both groups have distinct characteristics that require a differentiated treatment in economic analysis. In this paper, we will be concerned only with "depletable" resources, and among those mainly with non-energy resources. Energy (e.g., oil, natural gas, and coal, to some extent) is dealt with in the paper by Professor Waverman.

The central question which will be addressed here is: what is the present and probable future contribution of the extractive industry to Canada's economic well-being and what type of public policy is likely to enhance or diminish this role?

In order to answer this question, we will first address the problem

116

of depletion and ultimate resource exhaustion in a macro-sense. This is an issue of considerable public controversy at present, and one that could have a major impact on governmental policies with respect to present and future exploitation rates. We will then analyze the aggregate impact of the non-fuel mineral industry on the Canadian economy. Finally, we will look briefly at the rationale of some of the governmental subsidy policies vis-à-vis the extractive industry, asking ourselves whether it makes sense to subsidize the extractive industry through tax incentives or other means for the sake of more rapid economic development in general, or the relief of economic distress in certain regions of the country in particular.

I. Resource Depletion: How Serious a Threat?

Canada is blessed with an abundance of mineral resources. It is the world's largest producer of nickel, zinc, silver, and asbestos, and among the three-to-five largest producers of potash, copper, lead, and iron ore. Much of this output is exported. In 1971, mineral exports accounted for 31 percent of total Canadian exports.[1] However, mineral deposits, by definition, are fixed. Exploitation results in depletion and ultimate exhaustion of the existing stock.

In recent years, much has been written about the finiteness of the earth and its resources. Boulding[2] has spoken of the "spaceship earth" and Forrester, Meadows, and others[3] have used computer models to "prove" the imminence of resource exhaustion and the ensuing economic and social catastrophe. This view of impending disaster brought about by resource depletion is not new. It was at the heart of Malthus' view of the world, a view that was supported by Ricardo, albeit modified by the latter's assumption of a gradual decline in resource quality.[4] It was also a view that motivated many of the supporters of the conservation movement around the turn of this century. If it proves to be correct — and the finite size of our globe would seemingly tend to support it — then a national-resource policy which allows massive exports of these precious and increasingly valuable resources appears to be short-sighted indeed. Export restrictions would appear to be called for, if the interests of future generations of Canadians are to be safeguarded. In part, such a policy is being followed now. In 1972, the National Energy Board denied the application for additional gas exports to the United States on the grounds that existing reserves had to be retained for future Canadian use.

At this point, we may ask ourselves why economic market forces by

---

[1] However, this is partially offset by mineral imports, which accounted for 16 percent of total imports in the same year. Major imports are coal and crude oil (to Eastern Canada) and bauxite and alumina for Canada's large aluminum-smelter industry.

[2] Kenneth E. Boulding, "The Economics of the Coming Spaceship Earth," in Henry Jarrett, ed., Environmental Quality in a Growing Economy (Baltimore: Johns Hopkins, 1966), pp. 3–14.

[3] See, for example, D.H. Meadows et al., The Limits to Growth (New York: Universe Books, 1972).

[4] For a detailed discussion of the views of Malthus and Ricardo, see Harold J. Barnett and Chandler Morse, Scarcity and Growth: The Economics of Natural Resource Availability (Baltimore: Johns Hopkins, 1962).

themselves would not bring about an optimal inter-temporal allocation of these resources. After all, economic theory tells us that increasing scarcity in the future should be reflected in rising prices. Any rational decision about production now versus production in the future must account for the present-value equivalent of the forgone future profit resulting from future production.[5] But if future prices are going to be higher because of increasing scarcity, it may pay the owner of a finite mineral resource to reduce production now and shift it into the more profitable future. However, while these effects may have some modifying influence on present output decisions of private mining operators, these decisions may be far from optimal from a social point of view. The reason for this is that private and public rates of discount may differ rather substantially. Mining firms usually operate at average rates of return of 12 to 20 percent or even more. These rates are generally higher than those of other industries or the economy in general, in part because of the higher risk elements involved in mining. But while the risk of any one individual mining venture might be high, a fact which accounts for the high cost of risk capital in the industry, for the economy as a whole these risks average out because some operations will have higher than expected rates of return while others may fail. In evaluating the social worth of mining ventures, therefore, the government should apply a riskless rate of discount, while the individual operator will use a rate that includes the risk premium. This difference in rates can have a significant effect on temporal production decisions.

Assume that the discount rate applied by a mine operator is 12 percent,[6] while the riskless rate used by the government is 6 percent. If future prices are expected to remain constant, postponing production into the future will reduce the present-value equivalent for the mine operator by 12 percent for each year's delay, but only by 6 percent per annum for society as a whole. This has the effect that the present value of future income falls much more rapidly for the mine operator and that his production decisions will be tilted much more toward the present than might be optimal from a social point of view. Suppose, alternatively, that expected increasing future scarcity of the mineral is reflected by an expected annual price increase of 7 percent. For the mine operator, this has the effect that the present value of delayed production will fall much more slowly (i.e., by approximately 5 percent per annum). However, it will still fall, and, everything else being equal, he will still prefer to produce now rather than later. From society's point of view, however, producing now entails a net loss, since waiting for the future actually increases the present-

---

[5] Scott, who succinctly clarified this point, called this forgone future profit the "user cost" of present production. See Anthony T. Scott, "The Mine Under Conditions of Certainty," in Mason Gaffney, ed., Extractive Resources and Taxation (Madison: University of Wisconsin Press, 1967), pp. 25-62.
  The present-value equivalent is obtained by discounting future profit to the equivalent present value by means of an appropriate discount rate.
[6] The discount rate can be thought of as the forgone earning opportunity of utilizing a scarce resource in its next-best alternative use. In this case, the 12-percent rate implies that the mining firm could earn a 12-percent return per annum on any revenue that it might get today instead of one year from now.

value equivalent of the mineral by approximately one percent *per annum*.[7] Such divergences between private and social evaluations of mineral-exploitation strategies may sometimes lead to government regulations directly designed to slow down output. Alberta's pro-rationing system of oil and gas production provides a good example.

A second and frequently even more important reason for a divergence between private and social evaluations of benefits from delayed production is that a government will and should include the future net benefits from forward-linkage (i.e., secondary-producer) effects into its evaluation, while the individual mining firm will not (unless it is a vertically integrated firm that also owns processing and fabricating facilities, and then it will do so only to the extent of its own profit considerations). While it might be argued that these secondary producers (i.e., the smelters, processors, rolling mills, chemical factories, or fabricators) could buy minerals at the future higher world market price in order to keep producing, this might not be feasible if local mineral supplies are exhausted and freight costs from more distant sources or from abroad are high. This is frequently the case.[8]

For both reasons, therefore, private decisions with respect to the temporal allocation of production cannot necessarily be relied upon to be optimal from a social point of view. This divergence between public and private evaluations of future resource values is at the heart of such policies as Canada's former prohibition of long-term exports of hydro-power and Mexico's restriction of sulphur exports. Neither policy was successful, however, since in neither case did the projected future scarcity materialize.[9]

Let us now return to the more general question of threatening resource exhaustion. If one surveys statistics of present mineral production rates together with estimates of future growth rates in demand and compares them with known mineral reserves, the picture appears disquieting enough.[10] Presently known global reserves for most minerals are likely to be exhausted within a few decades if rates of consumption keep rising at expected rates. Given such low reserve–output ratios, we would expect a continuous and significant rise in the prices of these commodities relative to other goods and services.

However, such a price rise has not materialized. This becomes apparent if one examines long-term relative price trends for the various groups of extractive resources, measuring these trends as prices of ex-

---

[7] The implication appears to be that for society the present-value equivalent is maximized by an indefinite delay in exploitation. However, the government would not postpone production indefinitely; for the increase in value would ultimately reach a point at which the demand for the mineral in question would fall to zero. This issue is discussed at length in Orris C. Herfindahl, "Depletion and Economic Theory," in Gaffney, *op. cit.*, pp. 63–90.

[8] See Gunter Schramm, "The Effects of Low Cost Hydropower on Industrial Location," *Canadian Journal of Economics*, II, No. 2 (May 1969), pp. 210-229.

[9] For a discussion of these two cases of misguided public resource-conservation decisions, see Schramm, "The Effects of Low Cost Hydropower," and Miguel S. Wionsek, "Foreign-Owned Export-Oriented Enclave in a Rapidly Industrializing Economy: Sulphur Mining in Mexico," in Raymond F. Mikesell, ed., *Foreign Investment in the Petroleum and Mineral Industries* (Baltimore: Johns Hopkins, 1971), pp. 264–311.

[10] See, for example, Meadows et al., *op. cit.*, pp. 56–60.

tractive products relative to non-extractive products (since a measurement of change in absolute money costs per unit would be meaningless because of inflation).[11] Only in forestry and possibly in fishing is there a relative upward price trend from 1870 to 1960. In agriculture, minerals, and all extractive resources combined (the four product groups cited), the trend is approximately horizontal. Indeed, in the case of minerals it is slightly downward sloping, which would imply decreasing rather than increasing scarcity.

More recently, one can consider Canadian market prices for lead and copper deflated by the Canadian wholesale price index for the decade 1960–70. These two commodities have a relatively low reserve–output ratio. Nevertheless, what we find is that prices for these two metals, despite wide year-to-year fluctuations, did not increase in real terms at all but decreased slightly, at least in the case of lead.[12] Why did the market not react to the seeming future scarcity?

There are several reasons for this. The first is that not all existing reserves of minerals are known at present. Finding new ore and mineral bodies is a costly process. It usually does not pay a mining company to incur heavy exploration expenses in proving the existence of reserves that would not be extracted until far in the future. While this fact alone would suffice to explain the unresponsiveness of world market prices, there are more fundamental forces at work that have prevented so far, and are likely to prevent far into the future, the development of true mineral-resource scarcities.

These forces can be summarized under the twin-heading of substitutability and technological change. The two are closely related. When we try to evaluate reserve–output ratios, we have to realize that the estimated mineral reserves refer only to those known concentrations and deposits that appear to be economically recoverable, given presently known mining methods and market prices for the mineral in question. The definition of "reserves," hence, is not a physical one but an economic one. If we look instead at the actual physical stock of minerals and assume that these were uniformly distributed throughout, we would find in a cubic mile of rock a billion tons of aluminum, 625 million tons of iron, 260 million tons of magnesium, and over 12 million tons of manganese. These metals are all relatively abundant in the earth's crust. Toward the other end of the scale, a cubic mile of rock would yield over one million tons of zinc, 650,000 tons of copper, 185,000 tons of lead, and some 60 tons of gold.[13] However, these minerals are not uniformly distributed. Instead, as a result of geological processes that occurred over many millions of years, concentrations of many of these materials have been formed which contain percentages far higher than those found in the crust on average. Copper concentrations in some ores may be 1000 times, and lead concentrations up to 3000 times, greater than those found in average rock. Unfortunately, these concentra-

[11] See Barnett and Morse, op. cit., p. 210.
[12] See Department of Energy, Mines and Resources, The Canadian Mineral Industry in 1970 (Ottawa, 1971), pp. 44 and 55.
[13] From James F. McDivitt, Minerals and Men (Baltimore: Johns Hopkins, 1965), p. 11.

tions are unevenly distributed and hard to find. While our mineral industries have concentrated their efforts on finding and exploiting such deposits,[14] utilization of average rock strata would not be beyond present technology.[15] It simply would be far too expensive compared to the alternative of finding and utilizing high-grade deposits. In terms of purely physical adequacy, therefore, we can hardly speak of resource scarcity, but rather of abundance for the infinite future, since the limit to availability of mineral supplies becomes the earth itself, with constant recovery and recycling the ultimate answer.

Mineral scarcity, depletion, and exhaustion, therefore, can be defined only in economic terms. And here the combined effects of substitution and technological change have continuously allowed us to increase the known and economically usable range of resources. Let us first look at the substitution effect. As any one resource gets scarcer, its relative price increases. Increasing price becomes a signal to mineral producers as well as users to look for suitable substitutes. With increased prices, the producer can afford to incur higher production costs by mining lower-grade or more-difficult-to-recover deposits. For most minerals, lowering the economically recoverable grade of ore means a geometric increase in the quantity of known deposits. For example, a one-percent decline in grade increases lead resources by 25 percent and copper resources by more than 100 percent.[16] The user, on the other hand, faced with higher costs for a given resource, will look closely at potential substitutes. A dramatic example of such substitution effects is provided by the changing utilization patterns of timber resources. In the 19th century's frontier society, timber was frequently only an unwanted by-product of agricultural land development. Because it was cheap, it was used in large quantities even for such unlikely uses as steam-engine frames and road surfaces. But as available timber resources declined relative to population and demand increases, the price of timber began to rise, quadrupling between 1870 and 1950. This increase triggered off substitution by other inputs, such as iron and steel in shipbuilding and machinery, or concrete, brick, and masonry in construction. More recently, aluminum, plastics, fiberglass, and glass have replaced forestry products in many uses, such as packaging, for example. As a result, in the United States consumption of timber products on a *per capita* basis fell to almost one-half its 1900 level by 1954, and remained constant in absolute terms.[17]

Similar substitution effects can be observed between metals, minerals, and man-made materials. A good example is copper. During periods of

[14] However, there are notable exceptions. Since World War I, most of the nitrogen used for fertilizers and other chemicals has been extracted from air, and most of the magnesium produced in the world today comes from sea water.
[15] In fact, some scientists have suggested that the utilization of common rock will ultimately provide all the necessary raw materials for a highly advanced civilization. While this would require prodigious amounts of energy, this energy could be supplied from atomic breeder reactors fueled by the uranium that is recovered from the rock. Such a future world is discussed in Harrison Brown, *The Challenge of Man's Future* (New York: Viking Press, 1954).
[16] See David B. Brooks, "The Lead-Zinc Anomaly," *SME Transactions* (Society of Mining Engineers, June 1967), p. 5.
[17] See Nathan Rosenberg, "Innovative Responses to Materials Shortages," *American Economic Review*, LXIII, No. 2 (May 1973), pp. 111–118.

high demand, such as the two World Wars, the Korean War, and the massive U.S. involvement in Vietnam in the mid-1960s, copper prices rose prodigiously, frequently to multiples of previously prevailing price levels.[18] As a result, major user groups systematically turned their attention to the development and utilization of substitutes. Frequently, these substitutes permanently replaced copper in a given use. The best-known example of such permanent substitution is in electric overhead conductors. Prior to World War I, most were made out of copper wire. Since then aluminum, first thought to be a poor substitute because of its lower conductivity, has totally replaced copper. Whenever copper prices get out of line, galvanized-steel water pipes and, lately, plastic PVC piping replace copper piping in home construction, just as insulated copper wiring can be, and frequently has been replaced by aluminum or magnesium-core wiring.

Such substitutions, however, would frequently not have been possible without technological change and, in fact, it is technological change that has brought about and continues to bring about the extension and enlargement of our usable-resources base. Technological change has produced new substitute inputs or raised the productivity of old ones. While the pervasiveness of these changes defies attempts at simple classification, some of the major effects include the following:

1) *Development of improved techniques for finding mineral resources:* Examples are aerial and satellite surveys, improved seismic techniques, use of helicopters instead of ground vehicles, and further refinements of statistical correlation analysis used to evaluate geological data.

2) *Raising the productivity of the mining and mineral-recovery process itself:* For example, average output per man-hour in Canadian mining increased by almost 400 percent between 1947 and 1968.[19] This dramatic increase in productivity was the result of the development of much more sophisticated machinery and mining technology. In many cases, open-pit mining operations have replaced more conventional shaft and tunnel operations. The developments of huge excavators that can scoop up several thousand tons of material per hour, together with material-handling and mineral-beneficiating equipment of similar capacity, have reduced costs per ton of material so much that today, for example, copper deposits with a grade of as low as 0.4 to 0.6 percent can be profitably mined, while 40 or 50 years ago the cut-off grade was 2 percent or more. British Columbia's rapidly growing copper-mining industry, which was practically nonexistent in the early 1950s but now produces over 15 percent of Canada's output (Canada is the world's fifth largest producer), would not have come into being without these technological developments.

3) *Development of new mineral-processing techniques:* An outstanding example of such development is the U.S. iron-ore deposits around Lake Superior. These huge deposits, together with the immense reserves of high-grade coking coal from Pennsylvania and West Virginia and the cheap water-transportation network of the Great Lakes, have provided the

---

[18] For a fascinating analysis of the development of the world copper industry, see Orris C. Herfindahl, *Copper Costs and Prices, 1870–1957* (Baltimore: Johns Hopkins, 1959).
[19] John Dawson, *Productivity Change in Canadian Mining Industries* (Ottawa: Economic Council of Canada, 1971), p. 8.

foundation for the U.S. steel industry, until recently the world's largest. However, the high-grade ore deposits originally utilized started to give out shortly after World War II, and the U.S. industry became more and more dependent on imports, largely from Labrador. By the late 1950s, however, a new process was developed that allowed the utilization and enrichment of low-grade, hard-taconite and jasper ores, of which there are huge deposits in Minnesota and Wisconsin. While the combination of mining and beneficiation is more expensive per ton than the production of traditional ore, savings were possible in the subsequent phases of shipping and steel production, so that over-all raw-material plus processing costs per ton of steel produced actually declined. Today beneficiating plants for similar, low-grade ores have been built in Labrador in preference to the use of standard ores, although huge deposits of the latter still wait for exploitation.

4) *Raising output per unit of resource:* For example, modern coal-fired power plants now use less than 0.9 pounds of coal per kilowatt-hour, while their predecessors at the turn of the century used seven pounds. Aluminum smelters, built in the early post-World-War-II period, typically use about 20,000 kwh of electricity per ton of metal, while recent smelters make do with about 14,000 kwh.

5) *Development of totally new materials, such as synthetic fibres, plastics, etc.:* Wood shingles for houses have been largely replaced by asphalt shingles, while wood siding of frame-houses first yielded to aluminum and later to plastic siding with superior wear characteristics.

6) *Development of technologies for the recovery and recycling of scrap or waste-materials:* The trend for the recovery of waste material is accelerating. In many mineral-processing industries, recovery and recycling already provide a large percentage of the raw-material base. Examples are steel production, with a total scrap and recovered steel-slag share of about 45 percent in the early 1960s,[20] and aluminum smelting, for which scrap recovery in the United States probably amounted to 12–15 percent of total consumption in recent years, while projections for 1980 and beyond forecast a recovery rate of 15–25 percent of total world consumption.[21] In the United States, old scrap (i.e., scrap recovered after use) accounts for approximately 5 percent of zinc production (most zinc uses are non-recoverable), over 25 percent of copper, and approximately 40 percent of lead consumption.[22]

A particularly strong stimulus for the recovery and recycling of by-products comes from our efforts to clean up the environment. Perhaps the most outstanding example is provided by sulphur, a base chemical used in large quantities for fertilizer production and many chemical feedstocks and industrial processes.[23] Until after World War II, world sulphur production and trade was dominated by a group of four U.S. companies which

[20] McDivitt, *op. cit.*, p. 76.
[21] Sterling Brubaker, *Trends in the World Aluminum Industry* (Baltimore: Johns Hopkins, 1967), pp. 75–77.
[22] McDivitt, *op. cit.*, p. 76.
[23] All data quoted in this and the following paragraph are from *The Canadian Mineral Industry in 1970* and Jared E. Hazleton, *The Economics of the Sulphur Industry* (Baltimore: Johns Hopkins, 1970).

recovered elemental sulphur from salt-dome formations in Southern Texas and Louisiana. Their operations were so profitable that even during the depression of the 1930s after-tax rates of return never fell below 12–20 percent on invested capital, while ranging as high as 50 percent and more in recurring periods of high demand. By the mid-1950s Mexican sulphur mines entered the market. In the ensuing price war, the U.S. producers lost much ground and their profits fell to less than 10 percent in the early 1960s, while their Mexican, U.S.-owned competitors still earned 20 percent and more. At that point in time the Mexican government, afraid of ultimate exhaustion of its sulphur deposits, imposed export controls, declared large unexploited sulphur-bearing areas as national reserves, and ultimately bought out the privately owned mines.

In the meantime, however, the large western Canadian natural-gas deposits had been discovered. By the late 1950s they were connected to distant markets by the West Coast Transmission and the Trans-Canada pipelines. Many of the Canadian deposits are "sour," i.e., they contain up to 30 or 40 percent hydrogen sulphides. Sulphur recovery methods from sour natural gas were developed in Arkansas in the late 1940s. In 1950 the only sulphur recovered from gas was produced in the United States and amounted to 142,000 tons, compared to 5.2 million tons of native, i.e., mined, sulphur. By 1965 U.S. sulphur mine production was 6.1 million tons and Mexican mine production, non-existent in 1950, was 1.5 million tons, while recovered sulphur production in the United States was 1.2, in France 1.5, and in Canada 1.8 million tons. In the meantime, the patterns of world sulphur production changed even more drastically. In 1960 the United States accounted for 46, Mexico for 31, and France for about 19 percent of world exports. In 1969 Canada, until 1960 a net importer, had become the world's largest exporter, accounting for almost 30 percent, followed by Poland, the United States, Mexico, and France, in that order. (It is noteworthy that 50 percent of Canada's exports go to the United States, formerly the world's largest exporter.) By the mid-1960s, sulphur was still in short supply and f.o.b. Alberta prices reached $37 per ton. By 1970, however, surpluses had mounted because of the very large increases in production, and Alberta prices dropped to $7.88 per ton. Because of the large increases in natural-gas production throughout the world, surpluses are piling up. Canadian production alone is expected to increase to about 10 million tons by 1975, and unsold Canadian stockpiles, amounting to 3 million tons by the end of 1970, may reach 50 million tons by 1980. As one authoritative source analyzes the situation:

> Sulphur can no longer be considered as a commodity likely to be in short supply. . . . The present world oversupply is unlikely to ease in the foreseeable future as output from a multitude of "involuntary" sources, many related to pollution abatement measures, will continue to increase far beyond market demands.[24]

What, then, can we conclude about the likelihood of increasing resource scarcities in the future? From all the evidence at hand, it appears

---

[24] *The Canadian Mineral Industry in 1970*, p. 104.

that any true, long-term, and unavoidable resource exhaustion is a long way off and is not likely to occur, provided, of course, that net population increase can be stopped in the not too distant future. Technological change in mineral recovery, processing, and consumption, improvements in factor substitutability, development of new processes and new materials, and increasing waste- and by-product recovery all combine to stave off the threat of an ultimate exhaustion of most vital resources into the indefinite future. Meadows and his collaborators predicted resource exhaustion in the foreseeable future because they assumed that presently observed increases in demand would continue indefinitely, while at the same time they assumed that total available resources are fixed at levels three times higher than presently known "reserves." What we have seen, however, is that the concept of "reserves" is a rather flexible one, determined at any given time solely by technological and economic, not by physical-availability considerations. As new technologies develop, therefore, materials and deposits that cannot be economically utilized now will become the "reserves" of tomorrow. For government decision-makers this means that any policy which attempts to restrict output or exports of any single resource on a permanent basis because of the fear of long-term resource exhaustion is likely to be self-defeating and costly in terms of forgone economic benefits.[25]

II.   The Economic Impact of the Mineral Industry[26]

Since World War II, Canada's mineral industry has consistently grown at a more rapid rate than the economy as a whole. In 1971 it employed 265,000 workers (nearly 4 percent of the labour force) and produced goods valued at $6 billion (slightly more than 6 percent of GNP). Its gross fixed capital formation was $2.4 billion (14 percent of total business investment). The industry also accounted for 31 percent of Canada's exports, which made it by far the largest single source of foreign-exchange earnings. By almost every measure, therefore, the mineral industry plays a significant role in the development of Canada's economy.

While the above data are impressive by themselves, they are only a measure of the direct, or primary impact of the industry. In order to assess the over-all impact, we have to trace in addition the forward and backward linkages that connect it with domestic suppliers of input factors, on the one hand, and domestic users of its output on the other.

One type of backward linkage is represented by the purchases of the mineral industry from other sectors of the economy. These purchases create additional income and employment in these sectors. The other type consists of the consumption components of final demand that are a

---

[25] This does not mean that export controls, market allocations, and other restrictive means may not be appropriate policy instruments for dealing with temporary demand-and-supply imbalances. These will occur from time to time as they have in the past, and some of them may persist for quite a few years before new resource developments or technological adjustments alleviate the shortage.

[26] The statistical data and their evaluations in this section are based largely on John E. Stahl, "Aggregate Impacts of the Mineral Industry on the Canadian Economy," paper presented at the *Seventh Annual Meeting of the Canadian Economics Association,* Kingston, Ontario, June 3, 1973.

result of the industry's payment of wages, salaries, profits, dividends, royalties, rents, etc. Forward linkages are the result of mineral outputs that move into further processing stages within Canada. Ore that might leave the mine in the form of concentrate may be shipped to a Canadian smelter, while the refined metal from the smelter in turn might be shipped to rolling mills, then to fabricators or consumer-goods manufactures, etc. All these subsequent stages of processing and manufacturing represent forward linkages. Their magnitude can be measured by counting the total "value added" (i.e., the wages, profits, rents, etc.) in the subsequent processing stages.

A number of conceptual and analytical difficulties beset the accounting procedure, however, While some of the forward linkages can unambiguously be assigned to the primary extractive-resource activity, others sometimes cannot. For example, the metal smelters at Trail, British Columbia; Thompson, Manitoba; or Sudbury, Ontario undoubtedly would not have come into being in the absence of the rich ore deposits in their vicinity. Hence their value added can be accounted for as a derived forward linkage of the primary mining activity. However, this does not necessarily hold for any subsequent processing stage. Atlas Steel of Ontario, for example, has long been a major producer of stainless steel. Nickel, as produced in Sudbury or Thompson, is an important ingredient of stainless steel, and Atlas undoubtedly satisfies all of its requirements from Canadian smelters. However, if Canada had not been a major nickel producer, Atlas Steel presumably would still be a major producer of stainless steel but it would satisfy its nickel requirements from imports instead. Similarly, as we have seen above, sulphur is a major industrial raw material, with Canada by now being one of the world's largest producers. Many industrial processes, from fertilizers to iron and steel or rubber production, depend on sulphur. However, prior to the commencement of large-scale Canadian sulphur production in the early 1960s, these domestic Canadian requirements were largely supplied from imports. The existence of Canada's tire, iron and steel, or fertilizer industry is not dependent on Canadian sulphur production and, hence, cannot be counted as a derived activity, or forward linkage. Nevertheless, if as a result of the very low prices of Canadian sulphur some large new fertilizer plants will be established in Canada that would not have been built in the absence of domestic sulphur production, then the value added of these plants definitely would represent a derived activity.

Even activities based on large-scale mineral imports can sometimes be accounted for as a forward linkage of Canadian mineral production. The Consolidated Mining and Smelting Company (Cominco), with its smelter and processing facilities at Trail and Kimberley, was originally just a mining and metal-smelter complex. However, because of large-scale mineral by-products recovery from its base activities, the company developed also into a major fertilizer producer. One important group of fertilizers is based on the use of phosphates. Cominco did not have a Canadian source for phosphate rock. Phosphate rocks are abundant in adjacent Montana, however. So Cominco began to import phosphate rock from there and developed into a major phosphate-fertilizer producer as well. In this case, it could be argued that phosphate-fertilizer production would not have been established at Trail and Kimberley in the absence of the primary lead-zinc-silver mining operations of Cominco. Hence, these phosphate-fertilizer production facilities might be looked upon as a forward linkage of the original unrelated metal-mining activity.[27]

The magnitudes of true linkage effects, therefore, are usually rather difficult to establish. In most situations, they can be evaluated only on the basis of detailed, individual case studies. Macro-approaches that utilize regional or national statistical data (such as that of Stahl, quoted below) can do no more than provide some rough approximations of the probable net impact of a given industry on the national economy as a whole. They cannot truly answer the question, for example, whether the activities identified as forward linkages would or would not exist in the absence of the primary activity, but can only trace the observed flows of goods and services between the various sectors of the economy.

Stahl's results show that the mineral industry's backward linkages are relatively low while its forward linkages are relatively high compared to other industries.[28] However, its combined output effects are relatively low compared to other industries. For example, the total induced effects of an additional dollar's worth of output of the metal-mining industry are $2.70, while they are as high as $4.71 for the fabricated structural-metal industry. In fact, metal mining has the lowest over-all impact on income of all the industrial groupings examined. On the other hand,

> One dollar worth of ore generates $2.70 in combined impacts and if that ore moves to the smelting and refining stage it would mean an output of $2.20 worth of refined metal with an output impact of $9.40. As an input to the primary metal industry, the refined metal will produce $6.20 of primary metal having an impact on the economy of $30.30. Thus by exporting at the ore stage rather than at the primary metal stage the economy foregoes an output impact of $39.70 from the refined $1.00 of ore or concentrate.[29]

Hence, if the goal is the creation of additional job opportunities and income for Canadians, it would appear to be more desirable to restrict the exports at the raw-material or concentrate stage in order to encourage further processing within Canada. Such policies have often been pursued. Examples are Canada's prohibition of long-term exports of electric energy between the end of World War I and the mid-1960s,[30] British Columbia's restriction on log exports and its more recent law that requires all provincial copper mines to ship a certain percentage of their production to a B.C. copper smelter, if such a smelter is built. In a similar vein, in the summer of 1973 the federal government announced massive tax incentives

[27] On the other hand, another independent Canadian phosphate-fertilizer producer, which also uses Montana rock, has established itself at Medicine Hat, Alberta. Therefore it could equally well be argued that Cominco's phosphate production capacity would have been established somewhere in Western Canada in any event, in which case the linkage argument no longer holds.

[28] Stahl, op. cit., pp. 6–8.

[29] Stahl, op. cit., p. 11.

[30] For a discussion of the inimical effects of this policy, now abandoned, see Schramm, "The Effects of Low Cost Hydropower."

to those industries that would enlarge secondary processing and manufacturing operations of Canadian raw materials. However, such policies are effective only if markets are also available for the processed materials. Given the combined effects of frequently higher transportation costs for finished materials,[31] higher foreign import duties on processed rather than unprocessed mineral products, and the availability of competitive, unprocessed minerals from other countries, such policies are frequently ineffective and, in terms of the over-all employment and income goals, even counter-productive. For example, it would surely be totally unrealistic for Canada to attempt to restrict Labrador iron-ore exports in the hope that this would stimulate Canadian steel exports, or to restrict exports of Canadian-produced aluminum ingots in the hope of increasing fabricated metal exports instead. In most of these cases, existing foreign markets for our primary or semi-processed minerals would simply disappear and be taken over by our foreign competitors, as soon as these could develop the necessary capacity to substitute for the Canadian supplies.

III. Taxes and Subsidies

It has long been an article of faith in Canada that the mineral industry serves as a major vehicle for the economic development of the country. This belief accounts, at least in part, for the favourable treatment that the industry has traditionally received from the federal government and, to a lesser degree, from the various provincial governments. This preferred treatment has taken the form of special tax incentives and/or direct or indirect subsidies.

At the federal level, some of the better known of the direct-subsidy programs are the Emergency Gold Mining Assistance Act and the Coal Production Assistance Act.[32] More recent ones are those granted under the heading of Regional Economic Expansion, such as the massive aid to the Cape Breton coal-mining industry. Most of these programs are in the nature of "rescue operations," i.e., they represent government attempts to keep alive some existing mineral operations that would fail and close down in the absence of such assistance. Whether such aid should be granted or not depends largely on an assessment of the alternative employment opportunities for the labour and capital resources (which include infra-structure investments, private housing, etc.) serving the failing mineral industry. If no immediate alternative use exists for these human and man-made resources, their social opportunity costs are zero. In such a case, the subsidy program may well represent the economically most efficient alternative for employing those otherwise idle resources.[33] How-

---

[31] Unprocessed minerals in concentrate form can usually be shipped in bulk carriers by rail or ships at rates per contained ton of pure metal that are significantly lower than the shipping costs for the refined metal itself. For a discussion of these factors, see Brubaker, *op. cit.*

[32] For a detailed summary of the various federal and provincial mining laws and regulations, see E.C. Hodgson, *Digest of Canadian Mineral Laws*, Mineral Resources Division, Department of Energy, Mines and Resources, Mineral Report No. 13 (Ottawa, 1967).

[33] For a detailed discussion of the evaluation of the opportunity costs of unemployed resources, see Robert H. Haveman and John V. Krutilla, *Unemployment, Idle Capacity and the Evaluation of Public Expenditures* (Baltimore: Johns Hopkins, 1968).

ever, the longer the time span during which such assistance is granted, the more likely it is that alternative, non-subsidized employment might have become available in the absence of the subsidy program (which keeps the resources tied to the non-viable mineral operation without the need to look for alternatives). Hence, while short- or medium-term subsidies may well be defensible, longer-term programs usually are not. When we note, for example, that the Emergency Gold Mining Assistance Act has been continuously in force since 1948, the question arises whether such a policy really makes sense, either in national-income or income-distribution terms.

Indirect subsidies are usually provided in the form of government expenditures for infrastructure developments, such as the building of roads, railroads, ports, etc., or in the form of research and exploration activities undertaken by governmental agencies. Such expenditures are generally directed toward the goal of mineral-industry expansion and development. In specific cases, the economic justification of such governmental assistance can be readily ascertained. For example, if the building of a special road is a necessary precondition for the establishment of a new mine, and if the discounted flow of the mine's tax payments is greater than the total present-value costs of the road, then the direct governmental benefits outweigh the costs. This means that even in a narrow governmental-accounting sense the road-building project is efficient. The situation is somewhat less certain if direct payments do not outweigh the costs, but the mining operation is evaluated instead in terms of the true net value-added income that it creates for all of its beneficiaries. The major problem that arises is not the need to ascertain the value added from the mine, which is relatively easy, but — and this is not easy at all — to ascertain and deduct the value added that would have been created within the jurisdiction of the subsidizing government if the resources utilized for the development and operation of the mine had been used in their best alternative use instead. On occasion, no such alternative may exist. In such a case (which probably is rare), the actual net value added is equal to that of the mine; in more normal situations, however, there will be some, and perhaps even some very significant forgone opportunity costs, and the real net addition to society's value added from the proposed mine will be correspondingly less. It also could be negative, of course.[34]

The most significant and also most controversial subsidy programs for the mineral industry are those of special tax incentives. Most of these measures are granted by the federal government. They consist basically of (a) immediate write-off provisions for most exploration and development expenses, (b) three-year income-tax holidays for new mines (now being phased out), and (c) depletion allowances that allow a mining company to deduct a substantial proportion of its before-tax income as so-called depletion. Taken together, these incentives have the result that effective income-tax rates are substantially lower for the mineral industry than for other industries. As a matter of fact, many large firms with an active expansion program (particularly those in the oil and gas-producing sector)

---

[34] For an accounting framework that allows the evaluation of the net addition to or diminution of national or regional income resulting from direct or indirect subsidies, see Gunter Schramm, "The Design of a Resource Allocation Function," *Canadian Journal of Economics*, V, No. 4 (November 1972), pp. 515–530.

have paid little or no corporate income taxes for many years. This seeming inequity has been attacked by many economists on the grounds of equity as well as economic inefficiency in resource allocation. Defenders of these special tax incentives, on the other hand, have claimed that they are no more than a just and necessary compensation for the combination of high risks and high capital intensity of mineral operations. From the government's point of view, the rationale for these incentives is usually explained in terms of (a) the need to provide a sufficient supply of domestically produced minerals for the economy and (b) the beneficial expansionary economic effect of such incentives on the over-all level of economic activity.

In the Canadian context, neither argument necessarily holds. These issues are analyzed with the help of the two diagrams shown in Figure 1.

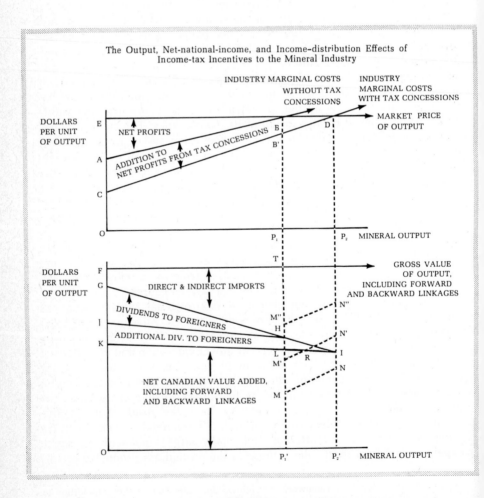

The Output, Net-national-income, and Income–distribution Effects of Income-tax Incentives to the Mineral Industry

Figure 1

The upper one indicates the likely response of the industry to the introduction of income-tax concessions. Without them, output will be OP_1, since at B the marginal costs of the last unit produced are just equal to the market price, here assumed to be constant for simplicity. Income-tax concessions lower the industry's cost curve from AB to CB'D. Over time, the industry can be expected to increase output to OP_2 in response. One of the immediate consequences is that an income transfer takes place from the government to the mining industry. This income transfer is represented by the area CABB'. To the extent that these funds are needed to pay for given government expenditures, the other taxpayers of the nation now have to pay higher taxes in this amount, although some or, in unusual circumstances, even all of these tax losses could be recuperated by the tax revenues created from the expansion of the mining industry and its forward and backward linkages resulting from its increased output P_1P_2.

The lower diagram analyzes the question whether the income-tax concessions are "efficient" in an aggregative national-income-accounting sense. Here OF measures the total dollar value of a unit of ouput, including all forward and backward linkages within the Canadian economy. This value also has been assumed to be constant for all ranges of output, in order to simplify the exposition. From this gross value, two components have to be deducted to arrive at net Canadian value added; one consists of the value of direct and indirect imports, indicated by GFTH, and the other of dividend payments to foreigners, represented by the area JGH. $OJHP_1'$ then represents the net Canadian value added resulting from the mining industry's activities before tax concessions.

After the introduction of tax concessions, this value added will increase by an amount equal to area $P_1'LIP_2'$. However, this is only the most immediate, direct effect. The increased profits of the already existing operations, shown in the upper diagram by CABB' will also lead to increased dividends to foreigners, indicated in the lower diagram by KJHL. This amount must be deducted from the newly created value added, $P_1'LIP_2'$. Furthermore, at least some of the capital and labour resources utilized in bringing about the output increase from P_1 to P_2 would have been employed elsewhere in the economy. Three possible cases of such opportunity costs are shown. The first is given by area $P_1'MNP_2'$. As long as this area, plus area KJHL, the additional dividend payments to foreigners, is smaller than the total addition to value added, as given by $P_1'LIP_2'$, the tax concessions can be claimed to be "efficient" in an aggregative national-income-accounting sense. However, this is no longer true if the opportunity costs are represented by area $P_1'M'N'P_2'$. Here, beyond point R, the marginal opportunity costs alone (not even counting the increased dividends to foreigners) are greater than the gains in value added; and if the forgone opportunity costs are as high as indicated by the area $P_1'M''N''P_2'$, there is no question whatsoever that the tax concessions are inefficient even though the apparent direct and indirect gain in value added, as given by area $P_1'LIP_2'$, appears positive and impressive.

Unfortunately, the question whether the true net value added created by Canada's tax concessions is positive or not is a question that has yet to be answered. However, even if it is found that the true net value added, minus all direct and indirect opportunity costs and minus increased foreign dividends, is positive, the implications for income distribution may be such that tax concessions are judged to be unacceptable policy tools for bringing about otherwise desired increases in national income. This, at any rate, was the opinion of the well-known Carter Report of the Royal Commission on Taxation. Whether or not this is true is a value judgment that an economist, qua economist, cannot answer.

IV.   Implications for Policy

There is no question that Canada's extractive industry has played a major role in the economic development of the country. It has helped to open up previously inaccessible areas, has provided substantial employment opportunities, and has contributed in a major way to the formation of capital that in turn has been essential for financing Canada's economic growth. It can safely be said that without its mineral industry, Canada would not have reached the high level of economic development that it enjoys today.

Nevertheless, the transformation of Canada from a basic raw-material supplier to a modern, diversified industrial nation during this century has inevitably reduced the importance of the mineral industry relative to other sectors of the economy, even though it has kept growing at substantial rates in absolute terms. Today, its major contributions are as a supplier of raw materials to domestic industries, a major source of foreign-exchange earnings (amounting to approximately one-third of total exports), and as the major source of income and employment in specific, mineral-rich regions of the country which have few, if any, other sources of income. Furthermore, mineral shipments account for a major share of the revenues of Canadian railroads and the St. Lawrence Seaway. Without this revenue, many of Canada's vital transportation routes could not be maintained and the shipping costs of other goods would have to increase substantially, impeding the competitive position of all other industries at home and abroad. On the other hand, the extractive industry now makes only a modest contribution to over-all employment (somewhat less than 4 percent in recent years), and its forward and backward linkages to other sectors of the economy are low. Its capital/labour ratio is high and apt to grow higher; hence its relative contribution to employment objectives will diminish even further.

These changes in the role and characteristics of the industry have significant policy implications. Traditionally, mineral development was looked upon as a key to further economic development of the country. As a result, the mineral sector obtained substantial subsidies, both in the form of direct government aid (such as geological surveys, infra-structure investments, loans, and financial grants or subsidies) and in the form of substantial tax relief. Today the question is whether these forms of special aid should be continued, redirected, or even reinforced, given the changed role that mineral exploitation plays in the context of Canada's present and future economy.

The major policy issues are the following. First, should present mineral production, and particularly mineral exports, be reduced to protect the country from the threat of increasing future scarcities? Second, should policy measures be adapted (or reinforced) that will bring about increased processing of domestic mineral production within Canada? And, third, should the industry be subsidized for the purposes of increasing employment in general, fostering the opening-up of underdeveloped frontier areas, or alleviating regional income disparities?

Despite many vocal claims to the contrary, the threat of imminent resource exhaustion appears to be grossly overstated and must be rejected. The over-all availability of a few minerals might diminish. This would result in significant relative price increases. However, the combined possibilities of utilization of lower-grade deposits, technological changes in production, recycling, and substitution by other materials are such that serious economic disruptions on a global scale are not likely to occur. Policies aimed at preserving known, economically attractive mineral deposits for "future generations," therefore, should be rejected.

Policies aimed at inducing additional processing in Canada appear attractive because of the potential increase in domestic value added. Such policies can basically take two forms. One would be to prevent or reduce exports of raw or semi-processed materials, while the other would consist of subsidies or other incentives to stimulate further domestic processing. Direct export restrictions should generally be rejected, since there is usually no guarantee that this would result in additional domestic processing. If it does not, it simply means that present production, income, and employment in the mineral sector will be reduced. Incentives are more attractive, because they do not have a potentially negative effect on mineral output. However, unless they are quite massive, their effectiveness might be limited because of the combined effects of usually higher transportation costs to, and higher import duties for, processed materials in foreign markets. They have the added disadvantage (as do all general subsidies to any one industrial sector) that they result in windfall gains for those domestic processing operations that would have come into being even in their absence. Mineral-processing operations (such as smelting and refining) are highly capital-intensive. This means that their effect on employment levels will be rather modest per unit of subsidy. Since additional employment and higher labour-force income are usually cited as the major objectives of such policies, the question which must be asked is whether this governmental aid should not be granted rather to other types of economic activities that are characterized by a significantly higher labour/capital ratio.

Many of the present direct and indirect subsidies to the mineral industry are justified on grounds of employment effects. The wisdom of such policies must be questioned because of the low labour/capital ratio prevailing in the industry. Similar subsidies granted to other sectors of the economy are likely to have a considerably higher pay-off in terms of new jobs created. However, such subsidies, if they are provided in the form of special income-tax relief, might be justifiable on the ground that their opportunity cost, in terms of forgone tax payments by alternative activities, is low or non-existent, if such alternative activities would not come into being in the absence of the special tax concession to the mineral industry. Nevertheless, it must also be recognized that the activities of the mineral industry make substantial demands on public expenditures for infra-structure facilities, which then have to be paid from taxes raised in the rest of the economy. Furthermore, the favourable income-tax treatment of the mineral industry by the federal government has led, in some cases, to a significant indirect revenue transfer from the federal to provincial governments. The latter, as owners of the mineral rights, are frequently able to increase mineral leasing and royalty rates as a result of these federal policies. (This is particularly true in the case of Alberta's oil and gas industry.)

"Canada's future lies in the North" has long been a firmly held part of Canadian folklore. Since minerals provide almost the only potential base for any type of economic activity there, subsidies to northern mineral operations are often justified on grounds of "essential" economic development in these frontier areas. However, there does not seem to be any inherent value in "developing" those empty stretches of the country for the sake of development alone. Life in the north is generally arduous, costly, and unpleasant. It seems to make little sense to subsidize it, unless it can be shown that such subsidies will produce spill-over effects on other present or future activities in these areas or elsewhere which will more than compensate for the initial losses incurred.

Similar considerations apply to those subsidies which are granted for the sake of alleviating regional income disparities. If they are designed to provide temporary relief in the form of "rescue operations" to *existing* mineral operations, either because the latter face a temporary market slump (as in the case of the uranium industry), or because alternative employment opportunities are not readily available, they may well be justified, provided they do not continue indefinitely (as in the case of the assistance to the gold-mining industry in the period after World War II). Subsidies to *new* mining operations, however, are usually inefficient, because of the low employment effect per unit of investment. Alternative policies, such as resettlement of the economically depressed population, may prove to be much less costly.

In general, it may be concluded that special industry-wide subsidies or tax relief are warranted only to the extent that they do not place additional burdens on other sectors of the economy, while specific aid to specific operations may well be in the best interests of the country or the specific region, as the case may be. Detailed benefit-cost studies in terms of social objectives should precede any decision for providing such relief or aid.

2. Energy in Canada : A Question of Rents*

Leonard Waverman

University of Toronto

> "Corn is not high because a rent
> is paid but rent is paid because
> corn is high."
>
> David Ricardo

Every few years a specific topic seems to become the vogue among journalists and other trend-setters. Recently, much attention has been devoted in the press to the so-called "energy crisis". Learned newspaper reporters, geophysicists, environmentalists, and others, short of anyone who really knows a great deal about the topic, have tried to impress the public with visions of doom, catastrophe, or at least rising prices in energy. In a number of accounts, Canadians have been warned to conserve their stock of energy, not to sell it to anyone at any price or we will soon run out.[1] An impressively naive computer model of the world has been used to suggest not only that we will run out of most resources in 100 years, but that there is little that we can do about it.[2]

In this paper, let us attempt to use evidence instead of conjecture, reason in place of rhetoric, and economics in place of historical fantasy to examine the role of energy in the Canadian economy and possible developments.

I. Trends in Energy Consumption

Table 1 gives the changing percentage distribution of Canadian energy

---

*This paper was written prior to the Arab oil embargo that followed the 1973 Middle East War.

[1] For example, see J. Tuzo Wilson, as quoted in *The Globe and Mail*, Toronto, October 17, 1972, and September 4, 1973.

[2] D.H. Meadows, *et al.*, *The Limits to Growth* (New York: Universe Books, 1972).

consumption since 1900. Wood, which was a major source of energy in 1900, is insignificant today. Natural gas was not discovered until the late 1920s, and it was not brought east out of Alberta until 1959. It now represents nearly 25 percent of total Canadian energy consumption. Petroleum, which represented about 1 percent of Canadian energy consumption at the turn of the century, satisfies over half the demand today.

Table 1: Canadian Energy Consumption

(percentage distribution by year[a])

	Wood	Coal	Petroleum	Natural Gas	Water Power
1900	39	56	1	—	4
1910	26	70	2	—	2
1920	16	75	7	—	2
1926	16	68	10	2	4
1930	16	62	15	2	5
1935	16	56	17	2	9
1940	13	56	20	3	8
1945	12	57	21	2	8
1950	8	48	32	3	9
1955	5	33	46	5	11
1960	4	18	53	12	13
1965	2	16	53	18	11
1970	1	13	53	24	10

[a]Total for the year may not sum to 100 due to rounding.

Source: Various publications, National Energy Board, Ottawa.

Therefore, anyone contemplating energy in 1900 would have discussed the important role of wood and coal. Very likely, there were then soothsayers who saw the diminution of the forests and the depletion of coal reserves as leading to an energy crisis. Yet wood and coal were not displaced as leading forms because their stocks were depleted. For example, today in terms of energy equivalent, coal reserves in Canada are some 600 times those of oil and gas. Instead of depletion, obsolescence occurred. New sources of energy — petroleum and, later, natural gas — were discovered. These new sources proved superior, i.e., the same energy value represented by wood or coal could be produced far more cheaply by petroleum or natural gas. Today we see the phenomenon of rising prices of oil and gas making coal once more a potentially important source of energy.

Can we today merely count existing stocks of oil and gas and then suggest that there is an energy crisis because these stocks are only 20 or 30 years' present consumption? If we are to learn from the past and use economic tools, the answer is that this view of a crisis is naive. New forms of energy are already near the final stage of development. Nuclear reactors, although far more costly than predicted in the early 1960s, are expected to produce half the Canadian electricity supply in the 1990s.[3] Fast-breeder nuclear reactors, if development plans are correct, will be in service in the year 2000. These breeder reactors produce their own fuel, thus ensuring no dependence on outside resources. Solar energy, the use of photo-electric cells to store the daily rays that fall on the earth, is another possible source. Coal gasification, the use of coal to make natural gas, is near final development. These are but three known techniques. While we are uncertain as to what new techniques will be discovered, who among us would suggest with certainty that none will be found?

We have looked at Canadian energy consumption. Given the 1971 production levels (of which half is exported), there remain in Canada proven oil reserves equal to 12 years' production, natural gas reserves of 25 years' production, and coal for almost 1,000 years.[4] The trends in discoveries in the early 1970s have not been encouraging. There was an absolute reduction in all reserves in 1970 and 1971 and a low rate of discoveries of oil in 1969, 1970, and 1971, and of natural gas in 1970. However, it is impossible merely on three years' evidence to suggest that all oil and gas reserves in Canada have been found. The figures on reserves given above do not include non-conventional reserves, such as oil found not in pools but in the Athabaska tar sands in Alberta. Tar sands are literally oil-soaked sands. Until recent years, production from these tar sands was uneconomic. However, with improved production techniques and rising prices for oil, oil production from some surface portions of the Athabaska tar sands is becoming economically viable. For example, in 1972 the Canadian Petroleum Association stated that the proven reserves — reserves within economic reach at existing prices — of the existing production plant on the Athabaska tar sands were 6 billion barrels, or 15 years' existing total Canadian oil production.[5] The ultimate recoverable potential oil reserves of these tar sands are 300 billion barrels, the largest single reserve of oil known in the world.[6] The proportion actually produced over time will depend on technological advances and the price of crude oil. The energy-reserve estimates used above do not include potential reserves off the east coast of Canada. Some oil and gas have been found there, it is uncertain in what quantity, but the potential is high. Most important, the discussion thus far has not considered the oil and gas reserves of the north slope — the Mackenzie-Delta region near Alaska and the Arctic Islands deposits. No firm estimate of reserves in the Mackenzie-Delta region is available. However, conjecture has it that 30 trillion cubic feet of natural-gas reserves have been found, equal to 15 years' present production.[7] Identical volumes may well be found in the Arctic Islands.

[3] See J. Bell, "Canadian Electricity Supply to 2000", National Energy Board, mimeo., 1973.
[4] Canadian Petroleum Association (and American Petroleum Association), *Reserves of Crude Oil, Natural Gas Liquids and Natural Gas in the U.S. and Canada*, December 31, 1971, Vol. 26, May 1972, Washington, D.C.
[5] *Ibid.*
[6] *The Globe and Mail*, Toronto, August 22, 1973, p. 13.
[7] Various reports in the media have cited gas sales by companies operating in the Mackenzie-Delta area, e.g., *The Globe and Mail*, Toronto, September 4, 1973.

II. Demand and Supply, Facts and Economics

What we have implicitly begun discussing is the supply response to changes in price, or the supply schedule of energy. At higher and higher prices, more energy will be available. The process is as follows. With an increase in price, existing known reserves which were uneconomic to produce at the old price are tapped, thus increasing supply. The Athabaska tar sands are an excellent example. Moreover, an increase in price increases the incentives of producers to explore for energy deposits. Although exploration is a risky venture, we do have good evidence that price increases call forth increased exploration activity which on average produces new reserves.[8] There is, of course, a time lag in this process. Even tapping known reserves presently not worth producing would require expansion of pipelines, producing plants, etc. The lag between exploration and production is even longer, say five to seven years. In the following analysis, let us neglect this time dimension.

In the three parts of Figure 1, we depict an industry equilibrium (C), and two firms (A and B). Assuming perfectly competitive conditions, equilibrium is where demand (DD) equals supply (SS) at a price of P_0 and a quantity produced of Q_0. Diagram B shows an existing oil field which at the present price is just covering its long-run average cost (LAC includes a normal rate of return). Diagram A shows a field which cannot produce to break-even at the existing price. Assume demand increases (Americans need our oil) to D_1D_1 in diagram C, and that the price rises to P_1. Assume, for simplicity, that the supply schedule can be moved along instantaneously. (This could easily be changed to discuss short-run and long-run movements, but that would just confuse the main issue.) At the new price of P_1, a field A can now come into production just earning a normal rate of return, producing quantity OQ_A. But in field B, where production is increased to OQ_B, excess profits are now being earned (in amount abcd). These profits are the rents to the scarce factor, which in this case is low-cost oil land. These rents will not be competed away in the long run unless they induce more production of B-type fields.

The rising supply schedule in competition denotes rents. At a price of P_0, total rents of area EP_0F are being earned by the oil industry (diagram C). Remember that these rents are determined by the price; they do not determine the price. Rents can be earned only because less-accessible or higher-cost fields are needed at the margin to meet demand. If all fields were equally low-cost or equally accessible to markets, then the supply schedule would be perfectly horizontal. This is unlikely to be true for energy reserves. The issue of rents is at the heart of much of the present controversy over the price of energy.

This discussion of rents has assumed perfect competition. There are few economists who would characterize the energy industry as perfectly competitive. Four major firms account for over 80 percent of the refined oil

---

[8] Erickson and Spann estimate a supply elasticity of 2.4. See E.W. Erickson and Robert M. Spann, "Supply Response in a Regulated Industry: The Case of Natural Gas", Bell Journal of Economics and Management Science, Vol. 2, No. 1 (Spring '71), pp. 94–121.

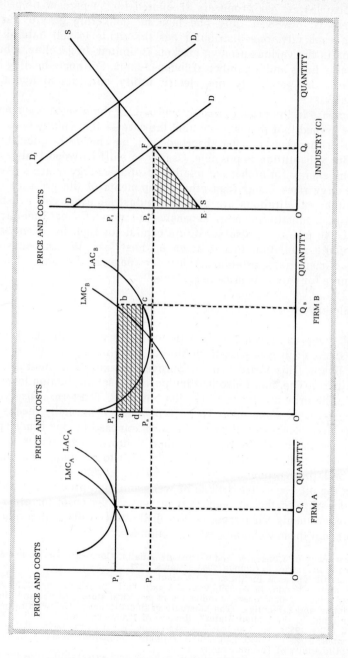

Figure 1

production in Canada.[9] Natural-gas production is not as concentrated. In 1971, the five largest gas producers accounted for 39 percent of production.[10] There is, however, only one pipeline delivering gas to Eastern Canada. In each city, one distributor has the rights to sell natural gas. Competition in the various product markets is limited. In gasoline, a buyer faces six large firms and a number of independents. For home heating fuel, a buyer faces one gas utility, one electric utility, and four or five major fuel-oil dealers.

An increase in the price of energy will reduce the quantity demanded. Some have argued that this is not in fact the case — that energy is so vital that all price increases will be absorbed with no change in quantity demanded. But substitution is possible. Users can shift between fuels as the price of one energy form changes relative to other energy sources. As the price of energy rises faster than other components of the gross national product, other substitutions are possible. Industrial users can substitute capital for fuel, substituting more expensive but more efficient fuel-burning equipment. All users can also substitute capital for fuel, for example, by installing more insulation to cut down on heat loss. We can substitute more fuel-efficient transportation services for our present automobiles. The demand curve for energy is price responsive.[11]

III. Regulation

Regulation was first imposed on the oil and gas industry back in the 1930s. In 1938, a bill was passed in Alberta establishing the Alberta Conservation Board. This board had to approve the exports of hydrocarbons outside Alberta. The board also had the power to set production levels for all wells in the province for conservation purposes. The term conservation means all things to some men. To an economist, it normally means preventing technological diseconomies, the costs imposed by one firm's operations on a second firm.[12] Picture a number of firms, each owning acreage above a common oil pool. Each firm would wish to maximize the number of wells and their production rates, so as to prevent other firms from producing the oil. Excessive drilling of wells and high production rates reduce the pressure in the oil pool, thus increasing the costs for other producers. Governments thus regulate the drilling of wells and production rates to prevent these technological diseconomies.[13]

[9] Department of Consumer and Corporate Affairs, Concentration in the Manufacturing Industries in Canada, 1965, Ottawa, 1971.
[10] Stanford Research Institute, The Market Price for Natural Gas from Sources in Western Canada, 1972–1990, Vol. 1, Menlo Park, June 1972, pp. 222–223.
[11] This price responsiveness is indicated by empirical studies of demand. See J.B. Vermetten and J. Plantiga, "The Elasticity of Substitution of Gas with Respect to Other Fuels in the United States", Review of Economics and Statistics, XXXV, No. 2 (May 1953), pp. 140–143; K.P. Anderson, Rand Corp. memo R-719, NSF, December 1972; L. Waverman and P. Halpern, "Industrial Demand for Natural Gas", University of Toronto, mimeo, 1973.
[12] Pollution is another example of such technological externalities. See the paper by Dewees in this volume.
[13] Other policies are possible besides regulation-taxation or compulsory unitization (forcing all the operators in a single pool to submit a joint drilling program). See L. Waverman, Natural Gas and National Policy: A Linear Programming Model of North American Natural Gas Flows (Toronto: University of Toronto Press, 1973), chs. 1 and 2.

Once an agency whose operations require data on each well and the power to set quotas has been established, it is all too easy to change the objective from minimizing waste (through preventing increases in cost) to maximizing profits.

In 1950, excess capacity appeared in Alberta oil fields. As Hanson stated: ". . . the production potential increasingly outstripped the quantity that could be marketed."[14] Oil companies suggested that the Alberta government, which had the ability to set quotas to maintain conservation practices, could establish quotas so as to prevent excess production which would tend to decrease the price and thus producers' profits. George Stigler has suggested that when one sees an industry being regulated, one sees industry members who have captured society's interest and are using it to maximize profits.[15] Conservation may have been introduced not with the specific altruistic goal of maximizing consumer welfare, but simply to extend the area of rents earned by producers.

Early in the 1950s, the Alberta government decided to implement an exportable-surplus policy for hydrocarbon exports. Producers had to be able to prove that there was an adequate supply within the Alberta borders of 25 to 30 years' production in order to meet domestic Alberta demand. In 1953, the federal government announced its desire to use an exportable-surplus policy for the entire Canadian gas industry. Imports of oil were allowed into Quebec and the Maritimes but not the rest of Canada. Gas exports were limited to reserves in excess of estimates of 30 years' Canadian requirements: ". . . the policy of the government of Canada is to refuse permits for moving natural gas by pipeline across an international boundary until such time as we are convinced that there can be no economic use, present or future, for that natural gas in Canada."[16]

In the late 1950s, the American government through its agency, the Federal Power Commission, reduced imports of Canadian energy into the American market. Canadian natural-gas imports are allowed freely into the United States. Prior to 1973, all oil imports into the United States came under a quota. Canada was, however, much favoured over all other producing nations. Canadian oil did not come under the usual American oil quota, but was limited by discussions between American and Canadian officials. Until 1973, these voluntary quotas were lower than what Canadians were willing to sell. A sharp increase in American imports of oil in the spring of 1973 caused Canadian officials to limit our oil exports for fear of creating supply shortages in Canada. Since all export-oil pipelines were operating at full capacity when this policy was announced, it is not clear whether these temporary limits on exports were more than a clever political move. It is up to the National Energy Board to decide whether permanent export controls are needed for oil as well as gas.

Canada exported half of its production of oil and gas to the United States in 1971. This production, however, amounted to only 22 percent of American energy imports in that year, and that is only 6 percent of

---

[14] E.J. Hanson, *Dynamic Decade* (Toronto: McClelland & Stewart, 1958), p. 203.
[15] G.J. Stigler, "The Theory of Economic Regulation", *Bell Journal of Economics and Management Science*, Vol. 2, No. 1 (Spring '71), pp. 3–21.
[16] C.D. Howe before the House of Commons, March 13, 1953; quoted in W. Kilbourn, *Pipeline* (Toronto: Clarke, Irwin, 1970), pp. 35–36.

American energy consumption. Canada is thus a minor element in the American energy market.

Given the nature and volume of our reserves and the policies of the Canadian government, it is likely that we will remain a minor element in the American energy picture. But if the world price of oil rises sufficiently to make most of the Athabaska tar sands economically viable, then Canadian production will become a large part of American consumption. Notwithstanding this possibility, let us examine our possible role when we are the minor actor in the play. In the case of oil, it was largely because of American oil quotas on other countries that we exported as much as we did to the United States. With the American government allowing quota-free imports from every part of the world (this policy change took place in 1973), it is unlikely that Canadian oil producers will sell as much as they did before in the American market. Canadian oil is relatively costly to produce compared with Middle Eastern oil.

As long as we are a minor element in the American oil picture and a high-cost producer to boot, there is little possibility of getting higher prices for our oil other than what the general trend is in oil prices. The trend in oil prices is upward. The generally rising oil prices in the world are thought by some experts to reflect the growing power of OPEC (the Organization of Petroleum Exporting Countries) rather than any real physical shortage of oil.[17] OPEC is a cartel of the major oil producers in the western world, outside North America and Europe. Through increased taxes, these countries have been able to drive up the price of oil and earn higher royalties. The price of Western Canadian crude appears to be increasing along with the world price.[18] However, it is Western Canadian producers who are largely profiting from these price increases, not Canadian governments. The province of Alberta presently levies approximately a 20-percent royalty and reserve tax on all receipts from oil and gas sales. The effective corporate-profit tax rate on these producers is likely under 14 percent, since producers of depletable reserves (energy) are able to deduct a depletion allowance (33 percent of the net value of production) before calculating income taxes.[19]

IV. Specific Topics

There are many energy issues which are topical today in Canada. Let us single out three of these for detailed discussion — the question of whether or not to export, the efficiency and equity of a two-price system (one price for exports and a lower price for domestic sales), and proposed northern pipelines.

1. Exports

The arguments of those who question the value of exporting energy run along these lines. Energy is scarce and depletable. Canada has finite

---

[17] See M.A. Adelman, *The World Petroleum Market* (Baltimore: Johns Hopkins, 1973).
[18] *Oilweek*, May 1973.
[19] Statistics Canada, *Taxation Statistics*, 1970.

reserves which some day will be needed to meet domestic demands. Exporting the scarce resources is giving away our heritage and places a real burden on future generations.[20]

All resources are scarce. If they were not, they would be free. Because of the scarcity, we must allocate resources efficiently, i.e., to maximize social benefit.

It is clear that foreign demand represents a shift in the demand schedule, and with a rising supply schedule increases the price. If foreign demand did not exist, the price would be lower and less would be produced. The benefits of energy production to Canadians are the sum of consumers surplus (the area under the demand curve and above the price) and producers surplus (the area below the price and above the supply curve, i.e., rents). With exports, the sum of producers and consumers surplus in Canada is higher than without exporting. Opponents of exports will argue that with exports, consumers surplus is lower (a higher price must lower consumers surplus), and producers surplus is higher. These opponents will then argue that producers are largely foreigners and, therefore, allowing exports reduces the welfare of domestic Canadians and improves the welfare of foreigners. This is a simplistic argument, which assumes falsely that foreign corporations remove their entire revenue or their entire profits from Canada and provide no benefits to the Canadian economy. To refuse to recognize producers surplus or rents as a relevant addition to national income is to discriminate against this income source. It is equivalent to suggesting that the wages of blue-eyed people should not be included in GNP because we all know that blue-eyed people provide no real contribution to the economy.

If there are some real costs to foreigners' investments, let us enact laws to eliminate those costs. If Canadians do not feel that they are receiving the proper division of the rents from natural resources, then Parliament should enact laws to divide these rents according to the agreed-upon value system. To subvert the price system and reduce GNP by eliminating exports is a very costly means of reducing the outflow of rents. If a greater share of the pie is desired, let us be honest and at the same time maximize our gains by the best means available — the tax system. Adjusting prices will lead only to social waste and inefficiency. Let us turn to a case in point, the proposed two-price system for natural gas.

2. The two-price system

A number of individuals, including some economists, have suggested that energy, specifically natural gas, be sold at a higher price in foreign markets and at a lower price in domestic markets.[21] Make the foreigner pay a high price for our natural gas and keep the price low to the Canadian consumer. Energy prices are rising rapidly, possibly due to inept American policy. Why should the Canadian consumer be hurt because Americans cannot properly handle their affairs?

---

[20] See M. Moore, "Problems of Optimal Management of Arctic Oil and Gas," mimeo, University of British Columbia, 1973.
[21] Ibid.

These arguments, although superficially appealing, contain a number of misconceptions. Indeed, they are quite representative of the views held generally in society in the Mercantalist period before Adam Smith.

The view of the two-price system could be attacked on purely philosophical grounds. Why are only energy prices to be kept low to the Canadian consumer? Why not wheat, shirts, or cars? Why is energy singled out for such attention? If we don't like the fact that energy prices are being determined in international markets, does it bother us that the prices of wheat, gold, silver, zinc, and even the Canadian dollar, are determined by foreign demand? Are we suggesting that the price of every commodity be determined solely by Canadians? It is obvious that the two-price system is on very shaky philosophical grounds. The economic justifications for a two-price system are equally unappealing. There are three major economic issues involved: opportunity cost, the inefficiency of indirect subsidies, and inequitable income redistribution.

The opportunity cost of a unit of energy sold to a Canadian under a two-price system is the alternative value which could be received in foreign markets. If gas sells for one dollar a unit in Canada and two dollars in the United States, the opportunity cost is two dollars. Lowering the price to Canadians by one dollar per unit is equivalent to subsidizing Canadian consumers of natural gas by one dollar per unit. This, however, is a hidden or internal subsidy. Internal subsidies are inefficient, i.e., they involve a reduction in GNP. It can be shown that eliminating the internal subsidy results in greater income, which can then, with the appropriate income-redistribution scheme, be directed toward desirable individuals or firms.[22]

The best case, then, is for the revenue from the sale of energy to be maximized by charging everyone the appropriate (the opportunity-cost) price. If then it is thought desirable to subsidize specific groups, this can be done with an explicit subsidy. Not only is this explicit subsidy preferable because society knows what the costs are; but, as was indicated above, there is more income available to society as a whole.

A number of readers at this point may mutter to themselves that if the revenue of producers is maximized, little flows to the Canadian public. At least, they will argue, a two-price system, whatever its efficiency drawbacks, gets money to the right pockets. But if rents accrue in an undue amount to producers and foreigners, why do we not simply improve that allocative mechanism we use to redistribute income generally — the tax system? Is the government too weak to increase royalties, increase taxes, or cut depletion allowances — the proper measures to capture rents?[23] If there is weakness in the tax system, improve the tax system; do not create distortions in the economy through prices. As was mentioned earlier, the real issue behind much of the discussion we see today is how to generate a greater share of the rental value of Canadian energy revenues. The proposals for limiting exports or instituting two-price systems for energy supplies emanate from an analysis of inept government regulation and

---

[22] L. Waverman, "The Natural in Natural Monopoly: The F.C.C. and Regulation of Intercity Telecommunications", in R. Noll and A. Phillips, eds., *Antitrust Policies and Regulated Industries* (Baltimore: Johns Hopkins, 1973).
[23] The Royal Commission on Taxation (Carter Commission) suggested the removal of depletion allowances, but the suggestion was not adopted.

taxation in the past. The individuals behind these proposals feel that these direct government measures cannot be changed. Therefore indirect means of tapping rents are suggested. Indirect means of capturing rents may, however, be inequitable.

In the above paragraph, a statement was made that a two-price system has the one major benefit of getting dollars into the right pockets, the pockets we as a nation would like to see subsidized. This is probably a false statement. Keeping gas prices low to Canadians benefits only a few and, likely, the wealthier segments of society.

The major industrial users of natural gas are: paper and allied products, primary metals, non-metallic mineral products, chemicals and chemical products, transportation equipment, and the food and beverage industry.[24] In keeping the price of energy below its opportunity-cost value, these industries are being subsidized. It is very difficult to determine the incidence (ultimate receipt) of a subsidy to a corporation. It can be passed on to consumers or shareholders. Three of these six industries export nearly 50 percent of their production (paper, chemicals, and transportation equipment).[25] Of these six industries, five have at least 40 percent of their assets controlled by foreigners and three have over half controlled by foreigners.[26] If we are keeping the price of natural gas within Canada low to prevent profits from flowing to foreign-owned gas and oil corporations, it is quite possible that the industries that benefit will pass on part of their savings to foreign shareholders or foreign customers.

Who are the residential consumers who are subsidized by a two-price system? These consumers are largely in urban areas of Ontario, not, obviously, the lowest-income region of the country. Within urban Ontario, residential gas consumers are largely in new developments and apartments, and represent the high-income end of the high-income urban dwellers. A two-price system redistributes income toward the higher-income households. Is this the kind of subsidy we desire?

The incidence of a subsidy to the transportation industry is the most difficult to measure. Since transportation is largely an intermediate service, a study would require flowing transport inputs through industries to ultimate consumers and shareholders. For simplicity, assume that the subsidy accrues entirely to domestic Canadians.

How much is the subsidy? In 1970, nearly 1.2 trillion BTUs (British thermal units are the measure of heat value) of natural gas were consumed in Canada.[27] Assume that this gas is available at a price of 20 cents per million BTUs lower than opportunity costs. This would have amounted to a subsidy of some $240 million. Assume that instead of asking for a two-price system, a group of MPs in the House of Commons put forth a bill to subsidize a group of higher-income residential consumers, foreign shareholders, and the transportation industry for $240 million a year for an indefinite period of years. This measure would stand no hope of adoption.

The two-price system is being discussed because of fears that govern-

[24] Source: Statistics Canada, *Energy Statistics*, 1970.
[25] This is based on data from Statistics Canada, *Import and Export Statistics*.
[26] Data are from *Corporations and Labour Returns Act*, 1970.
[27] Source: Statistics Canada, *Energy Statistics*, 1970.

ments will not act to increase tax revenue from the sale of energy. The constitutional fights between Alberta, where most of these low-cost reserves exist, and the federal government are just beginning. Alberta wishes to maximize the revenue, no matter where energy is sold, domestically or in the United States. At the same time, Alberta wishes to increase exploration activity and manufacturing. Consumers in Ontario are horrified by Alberta's attempts to increase the price of natural gas by 10¢ per MCF (thousand cubic feet, equal to a million BTUs) to gain 1.7¢ to the province (Alberta's royalty rate is 16.6 percent), thus yielding producers additional profits of 8.3¢ per MCF.

A preferable policy for Canadian consumers would be a *production tax* of 3.5¢ per MCF, half going to Alberta, half to the Canadian government. Taxes on energy production would siphon off all new rents (profits to B-type fields in Figure 1) to governments, and would not subsidize Canadian consumers to consume energy at values below its opportunity cost. It is doubtful, however, whether such a tax could be agreed upon federally and provincially.

A tax on energy exports would increase the price to Americans, and the government would capture all additional rents on foreign sales. However, the price in Canada would then be below the opportunity cost of these reserves. Canadians as a whole would be better off to reduce domestic consumption and increase exports, thus increasing GNP. Accompanying an export tax with an equivalent domestic sales tax would leave the price of energy equal in domestic and export markets. An export tax would, however, be instituted federally; sales taxes would be the responsibility of provinces. It is difficult to see how such co-ordination could be achieved. Without special transfers to Alberta, that province would see little of the tax revenue from this type of scheme.

Given the conflicting desires of the western provinces, which have energy reserves, and the eastern consuming provinces, and in view of the constitutional division of taxing powers, it is difficult to see how a consistent policy can be worked out which will be in the best interests of all Canadians.

3. Northern pipelines

The final topic to be discussed is the question of the construction and financing of a northern natural-gas pipeline.

Large volumes of natural gas have been discovered in the Mackenzie Delta–Prudhoe Bay area on the Alaska–Canada border and in the Arctic Islands. A company, Canadian Gas Arctic Ltd., has put forward a proposal to construct a pipeline from the Mackenzie-Delta area to carry both Canadian and American gas to markets in North America. A number of Canadians have expressed concern that the project and the sale of gas will damage the Canadian economy.[28] On what economic grounds do these arguments rest and what are their merits?

The initial question is, of course, whether Canada should tap its

---

[28] See, for example, M. Moore, *op. cit.*, and J. Helliwell, "More on the National Economic Effects of Arctic Energy Developments", mimeo, 1973.

northern energy reserves now and export part of this production, or maintain the reserves in the ground for future use. This question is not unrelated to the previous discussion on the question of the two-price system. Should we export part of the oil reserves now for an immediate return, or wait? There are high costs to waiting — the interest cost on the billions of dollars already sunk in northern exploration and development, the forgone opportunity costs of selling the gas, the possibility that the reserves will be obsolete in fifteen years. The last of these is not a completely idle speculation. Remember the importance of coal in 1900 and its subsequent decline, even though coal reserves are great.[29]

Since the holders of Arctic reserves are at least as well acquainted with possible future energy prices as academic economists, the sale of these reserves, at present, must yield producers the maximum revenues. The other view is that producers do not have as much knowledge as outsiders to the industry, or are irrational. Each of these views is naive. A conscious policy by the Canadian government to forestall present development of these reserves must recognize that it likely reduces revenues, raises costs, and increases risks.

If it is decided to proceed with the project, a number of other issues will have to be solved — ownership of the pipeline, financing it, and, once again, maximizing the Canadian public's share of rents.

The question of the ownership of the pipeline itself is largely irrelevant in analyzing the possible economic impact of the pipeline. Its discussion tends to obscure the real issues. Ownership is likely immaterial, because the pipeline is a *regulated* common carrier — its path, method of construction, and the prices it can charge are all controlled by the federal government, as are, for example, the prices and policies of most existing telecommunications firms. Moreover, as common carriers, the pipelines must carry at reasonable prices the gas which any producer wishes to ship. To own such a project which the government already controls in every aspect is redundant.

Two points which could be important in the ownership question are financing and the division of rents. If ownership changes the possible means of financing the pipeline, then ownership has real impact. For example, if foreigners are prepared to own and build the line, but do not care to invest in bonds, then forcing Canadian ownership will likely increase financing costs. Government concern with the Canadian content of construction is irrational, since rules on the minimum Canadian content can be imposed regardless of ownership. Moreover, the ultimate degree of domestic ownership is uncertain even if the entire equity in the line were Canadian at the beginning. Since shares can be traded on stock markets, how is resale to foreigners to be prevented?

Many people feel that the financing of the projects may have a number of deleterious side effects on the Canadian economy. These effects on the economy will, however, be independent of the manner in which financing is arranged. Because of the magnitude of the investments and the open

---

[29] I have calculated that north-slope gas is slightly lower in cost than natural gas brought to the east coast of the United States liquified in tankers. See L. Waverman, "The Impact of North Slope Gas on the Natural Gas Industry of North America", mimeo.

nature of the Canadian economy, construction, whether financed here or abroad, will have similar impacts.[30]

The project will be in the order of $5 billion. Ignoring interest costs, present values, and the very important issue of cash flows when the lines are operating, assume that the projects will add $1.5 billion in investment annually in the three-year period 1975–1978. Total private investment, including residential construction, without these projects is expected to run at an annual rate of $20 billion in the period. The effects will depend on a number of characteristics of the economy and the investment: (1) the import content of the pipeline projects, (2) mobility of international capital, (3) whether the exchange rate is fixed or floating, and (4) compensating government policies. The important areas of the economy where an impact may be felt are: (a) balance of payments, (b) exchange rate, (c) interest rates, (d) inflation, and (e) unemployment.

The import content is vital. If the import content is equal to the percentage of financing outside the country, then little pressure will be placed on the Canadian dollar. Assume that this will not be the case, that import content will be 20 percent and that foreigners will provide 80 percent of the required funds. As investors wish to purchase the pipeline bonds in amounts greater than the import content of the pipeline, the demand for Canadian dollars increases. If the Canadian dollar is freely floating, as it is now, this increased pressure on the Canadian dollar will tend to increase the value of the Canadian dollar in terms of the American dollar. One study indicates a likely appreciation in the range of 3 percent.[31] As the value of the dollar increases, the price of Canadian exports rises and the price of foreign imports in Canada falls. The decrease in exports and rise in imports is necessary to achieve the real transfer of purchasing power. Note that if the import content were 80 percent, the same as outside financing, no gap would have to be induced between imports and exports.

If the Canadian dollar is fixed in terms of the American dollar, increased foreign demand for Canadian dollars cannot raise the price of the Canadian dollar. The Canadian government must provide the dollars with the appropriate monetary policy, by buying bonds to increase the domestic money supply, for example. The construction of the pipeline increases economic activity in Canada. To bid away resources from alternative uses, the construction will raise prices in Canada generally. An increase in the price level will increase imports (which are now cheaper) and decrease exports until sufficient resources are freed to transfer resources to the pipeline industry.

Now, assume that the Canadian government allows no foreign financing of the pipeline. To finance the pipeline in a world of flexible exchange rates, the government (company) issues bonds. To bid away financial dollars from other investment areas within Canada, interest rates rise. Assuming that the world interest rate is not affected by flows of capital within Canada (we're small fish in a big pond — the assumption of inter-

---

[30] Part of this argument follows L. Waverman, "Transportation and Communications in the Seventies", Toronto Stock Exchange *Annual Review*, 1973, and M.I. Gordon, *The Toronto Star*, May 1973.

[31] Helliwell, *op. cit.*

national capital mobility), the interest-rate rise in Canada induces foreign capital flows until interest rates fall back. These capital inflows raise the value of the Canadian dollar, discouraging exports and encouraging imports. Since this foreign capital cannot flow into the pipeline project, it moves into other sectors of the economy.

Under fixed exchange rates, the domestic financing of capital to construct the pipelines must increase interest rates and induce capital inflows. Without the benefit of exchange-rate movements creating offsetting changes in exports and imports, one would expect higher capital inflows under fixed exchange rates.

While the example of 100-percent domestic financing will not be borne out in reality, a lesson can be learned. For a country like Canada, which is small and has a large proportion of its economy in international trade, the question of where a large-scale project is financed is largely irrelevant in terms of the final volume of foreign-capital flows. Whether we like this or not, it is a fact we must accept. If constraints are placed on foreign investment in the pipeline, then induced foreign capital flows are likely to occur in other sectors of the economy.

The pipeline itself will not generate great profits (it will be regulated to earn, say, 8 percent). The discussion of the lack of benefits to Canadians rests on the expected division of rents from the sale of Arctic gas. To reiterate the central theme of this paper: if it is rents Canadians are worried about, tax them. Let us not refuse to export northern gas if the only issue is the small share of profits accruing to Canadians — tax the producers. Since these reserves are in federal hands, the question of taxation is relatively easy. Remember, however, the Ricardo case. The introduction of Arctic gas, increasing the price of all gas, raises the rental value of reserves in Alberta and British Columbia. It is for these additional rents that all the fights will occur.

3. Agriculture in the Canadian Economy

W. J. Craddock and Errol T. Lewis

University of Manitoba

An historical feature of agriculture has been its interrelationship with other sectors of the economy. Today, the relationship of the agricultural sector with the rest of the economy is still one of its distinguishing features; however, in direct contrast with years gone by, agriculture has become much more dependent on other sectors in the multi-dimensional, multi-dependent industrial complex of the national economy. At the same time, the value of agricultural production has increased by leaps and bounds. Also, the value of the services involved in marketing farm products — including manufacturing, transport, buying, selling, processing, packaging, storage, distribution, wholesaling and retailing — has increased significantly. It is now much greater than the value of those products as they leave the farms. Generally, for all products of the farm, the cost of marketing exceeds the farm-gate value of the product.

I. Market Structure

Some idea of the role of the agricultural industry in the Canadian economy may be gleaned by looking at the monetary value of some of the indicators of its scope and dimensions. The production side of Canadian agriculture reveals a total farm-land area of 170 million acres with a farm population of about 1.5 million people on about 366,000 farms. Taxes paid were approximately $200 million in 1971. The 1971 Census reveals an expenditure of about $3,910 million on farm machinery and equipment and $131 million on fertilizer. In the processing and marketing sector, sales from firms processing farm products were about $5,000 million. On the consumption side, approximately $13,000 million worth of food, tobacco, and alcoholic beverages were consumed by Canadians. In addition, the

Canada Department of Agriculture has an annual budget in excess of $200 million.[1]

Whereas the above figures reflect the magnitude of the impact of the agricultural sector on the Canadian economy, monetary values are not true indicators of the economic relationships. More important may be the institutional and organizational framework of the relationships. What then is involved in market structure, or what constitutes the structure? Market structure consists of: (1) the marketing facilities including assembly, transport, processing, and retailing; (2) market services such as grading, credit, and farmer information; (3) the make-up of the economic environment, such as whether the economic sectors consist of many or few firms, large or small firms; (4) how prices are generated; and (5) the manner in which farm products are directed into final use.

The Canadian agricultural sector does not function in vacuo; it is part of the entire social, cultural, political, and technological complex. Differences within parts of the system must be expected, since there are differences between the regional resource endowments. These differences are to be found in the production, performance, prospects, and outlook in all the market components. To this may be added the fact that Canada, being an open economy, is subject to all the effects of market forces throughout the trading world.

The structure of the farming complex in Canadian agriculture is affected by those forces of the supply–demand relationship affecting any theoretically perfectly-competitive market system. There are always forces within and without the system which interact to generate change of either a rapid or gradual nature. Such changes as increased or declining consumption of farm products result in problems of adjustment and resource allocation for the entire industry.

The structure of Canadian agriculture may be viewed as a dichotomy of physical and institutional components. Under the physical aspect are resource endowments, regional patterns of agriculture, and land use. From the institutional point of view, we find such factors as government participation, agribusiness, and farm organizations. As should be obvious, it is virtually impossible to separate the two branches; for there is a very strong interplay. In this paper the emphasis is on the institutional (market) structure.[2]

The dominant components of the Canadian agricultural industry are the many individual farms, the various agribusiness firms, the very many consumers, and the ever-present government. The government, both federal and provincial, provides a link for relationships among the other components and also plays a dominant role in the inter-group behaviour. Agribusiness firms provide services to the farming community, and farmers in turn supply produce to firms. Agribusiness firms are an integral part of the agricultural sector; for they are involved in all aspects of assembly, transport, processing, selling, and storage of farm products.

The Canada Department of Agriculture provides employment for

---

[1] *Canada Year Book, 1972* (Ottawa: Information Canada, 1972).
[2] A good general introduction to agricultural economics is David Metcalf, *The Economics of Agriculture* (Baltimore: Penguin Books Inc., 1969).

approximately 12,000 full-time employees, including some 2,000 professional scientists. The government administers 200 institutions, including 27 experimental farms, 13 research stations, and 8 research institutes. Complementing this, the Rural Development Branch in the Department of Forestry and Rural Development administers central research under the Agricultural and Rural Development Act (ARDA) and jointly participates in programs with provincial governments to the combined extent of about $40 million annually.[3]

Several other central-government agencies are integrated components of the agricultural structure, including the Fund for Rural Economic Development (FRED), the Canadian Wheat Board, the Farm Credit Corporation, the Canadian Dairy Commission, the Canadian Livestock Feed Board, the Canadian Grain Commission, and the Veterans' Land Act Administration.

From a regional or provincial viewpoint, there are ten well-administered and well-equipped provincial departments of agriculture, six universities actively involved in agricultural research, and several other semiprofessional institutes.

II. The Government Component

It has been noted that the government constitutes a vital component of the agricultural industry in Canada. Certain questions arise about this fact. What should be the role of government in such a complex industry, in which struggles for advantage can be anticipated and in which the farmers operate as perfectly competitive producers? What should be the limits of government involvement in important issues? Should the government seek full control over the industry? Some answers to the above may be gleaned throughout this paper. Intuitively, it could be expected that the answers to such questions will depend on whether the involved groups are farmers or consumers, agriculturally related, or what have you.

In Canada both the federal and the provincial governments are very much involved in agriculture, and their influences, broadly speaking, revolve around the ultimate authority to decide and/or give directives and guidelines with reference to national and/or provincial objectives and policies. Government retains the power for the legislation and implementation of programs; it can distribute and allocate money to agriculture generally and, in the case of the federal government, also to the provinces for distribution. The overpowering influence of government control in agriculture of necessity brings with it several philosophies with regard to the role it should play.

Undoubtedly, some interest groups are against the dominant involvement and influence of government while others support the evolved degree of involvement. It is also to be expected that a third group would prefer complete control of the industry by government. As to whether or not government's involvement has been a success, the same sort of division of opinions is to be expected. Some may note that rural poverty has existed

[3] See *Canada Year Book, 1972;* and Report of the Federal Task Force on Agriculture, *Canadian Agriculture in the Seventies* (Ottawa: Queen's Printer, 1969).

for decades and will continue to be a haunting indictment of society. Yet programs and policies have been initiated to combat it with no apparent impact.

Among the programs started, as they were warranted by the economic climate, was the Prairie Farm Assistance Act, 1939, which provided for direct money payments to farmers in low crop-yield areas. The main purpose of this program was to assist farmers to overcome crop failures. Another was the Feed Grains Assistance Regulation, the main purpose of which was to assist in the movement of western feed grains to eastern Canada. Many more programs have been initiated, including the Small Farms Development Program of 1971. The granting of this form of assistance reflects government concern about the farm population's leaving agriculture, as well as the apparent crystallization of the tendency toward large-scale farming.

Some critics of government contend that the government has not been orderly in dealing with agriculture, but, as with so many other government policies, the government reacts to crises as they develop. The case of the Small Farms Development Program may be quoted as an example. This program was the result of the government's reaction to the crisis of dwindling farm population brought about by the pressures of economic forces and the consequent tendency toward bigness. It may be said that such a program, if it is to be initiated and successful, should be the culmination of research, planning, and programming, and would represent a more or less natural stage in the planning and organization of agriculture. Otherwise, any approach of this nature lacks direction, is haphazard and inefficient, and invariably leads to conflicts of policies and programs, and more importantly, to conflicts among the eventual goals. The Report of the Federal Task Force on Agriculture notes that:

... the basic conflict in Canadian agricultural policy has been an implicit cheap food policy and an explicit small farm maintenance· policy. The developmental policies of research, extension, subsidized credit, settlement expansion and resource development, actually contribute to and constitute the so-called 'implicit' cheap food policy. The provisions of various acts favoring small farms, such as the Homestead provisions, Agricultural Stabilization Act, P.F.A.A., credit ceilings and cash grants, are evidence of the existence of an explicit small farm maintenance policy. Not only have the two policies been pursued simultaneously in Canada but are in direct conflict with each other. This is the heart of the basic conflict in agricultural policy, a cheap food policy together with a small farm maintenance policy.[4]

Governmental jurisdiction has become so complex that it prohibits description or assessment. Both federal and provincial government ministries and departments, as well as agencies involved in agriculture, are many and diffused. Federal–provincial cohesiveness in policies and programs is

---

[4] Report of the Federal Task Force on Agriculture, *op. cit.*, p. 273. Reproduced by permission of Information Canada.

shadowed by poor authoritative structure for the co-ordination, integration, and organization of activities.[5]

III. The Agribusiness Component

There are essentially nine major industries providing agriculture with its requirements of factor inputs; the most important of these industries are machinery and power, chemicals, petrochemicals, finance, and transportation. A look at the output component reveals that the food, alcoholic beverage, and tobacco industries are the main domestic markets in the processing–distributing sector for agricultural products. Generally, the degree of efficiency in agribusiness is considered to be reasonably satisfactory and improving. Increased efficiency could result only from the availability of new and more modern plants and equipment accompanied by better planning. A serious obstacle to improved planning of inputs and outputs in the agricultural system is the low level of integration among the segments.

The competitiveness of the market structure of agriculture is in agreement with the philosophy of some economists.[6] But both internal pressures on the industry due to technological developments and external pressures emanating from the market for farm produce have forced a change toward highly integrated organizations. Horizontal and vertical integration are part of the market structure for farm products and cause divergences from the perfectly competitive model. When firms develop to a large size in a given industry or market sector, the result is referred to as horizontal integration. This growth may result from the increased size of a particular firm or from the amalgamation of several firms into one. Such growth gives control to the firm with a resultant reduction of the competitive spirit.

On the other hand, vertical integration arises when there is a form of direct control at any stage in the system as a substitute for market exchange.

It violates one of the tenets of traditional agriculture: namely, that each proprietor conduct his affairs with his suppliers and his outlets — sometimes called the agri-business sector — by means of buying and selling of products. Vertical integration as a sharply different system could change the make-up of agriculture substantially.[7]

Vertical integration in agriculture is usually considered from the farmers' point of view, in terms of the producers who integrate with agribusiness either individually or as a co-operative. Farmers integrate for the benefit of superior technical knowledge, credit facilities, and marketing. However, vertical integration should also be approached from the agri-

[5] For a description and assessment of government agricultural policy in Canada, see W.M. Drummond et al., A Review of Agricultural Policy in Canada (Agricultural Economics Research Council of Canada, 1966); S.W. Garland and S.C. Hudson, Government Involvement in Agriculture (Ottawa: Queen's Printer, 1969); and Report of the Federal Task Force on Agriculture, op. cit.
[6] See, for example, Frank H. Knight, Freedom and Reform (New York: Harper and Brothers, 1947), p. 330.
[7] Harold F. Breimyer, Individual Freedom and the Economic Organization of Agriculture (Urbana: University of Illinois Press, 1965), p. 100.

business point of view. Agribusiness firms may find it useful to integrate if there are profits to be made, as for example, by the processing firms entering the production phase if they find it difficult to obtain an even supply of produce of uniform or desirable quality, or by entering the marketing phase if the firms are convinced of the need for a guaranteed market for their products and services.

IV. Farmer Organizations

In Canada there are some 10,000 farmer organizations. There are the active ones which operate at the national, provincial, and local levels. In addition, the larger organizations have branches throughout the country. Apart from co-operatives, marketing boards, and breeders' associations, there are many local bodies, such as horticultural societies, whose memberships consist of large numbers of farmers. Farmer organizations generally have the following characteristics:

1. There is no deterrent against farmers joining more than one organization, and farmers may be members of organizations whose views and goals are opposed to each other.

2. There is no barrier to entry into the industry, unless the restrictive system of quotas is operative.

3. There are two types of organization. One is of a voluntary nature and involves direct membership, as in co-operatives and farmers' unions; the other involves compulsory participation.

As there are large numbers of these organizations, it can probably be concluded that there are far too many of them. The vastness of the numbers precludes a united stance by the organizations in their relationships with government and other sectors of the industry. If farmers were able to form one body instead of the present type of structure, a more efficient and effective form of organization would result. Yet one may doubt that the individual organizations will do this, since each (and especially marketing boards) would have to give up some autonomy. There may be the alternative of continuing the type of structure currently existing and having a National Farmers' Union, which would result from a merging of all the presently constituted farmer organizations and would have over-all responsibility for the betterment of the farmers' economic position. To be effective in negotiations, farmers need a national body truly representative of the agricultural producers.

V. Marketing Boards

The creation of marketing boards was the result of the perfectly competitive market structure in agriculture. Producers of farm products often become disenchanted with the prices and incomes they receive, and thereby seek market power. Prices for farm products are determined by the supply and demand conditions existing in the market. To the farmers there was an apparent imperfect relationship; for, contrary to the dictates of perfect competition, there were very many producers (farmers) but a small number of intermediaries (agribusiness firms).

To render some form of protection against market imperfection, co-operatives were formed. But co-operatives have been basically unable to bargain with agribusiness firms for all producers or to control the supply of commodities reaching the market. Eventually, producer-controlled marketing boards were established. These boards, numbering in excess of 100, are provincially organized and are much involved in the sales of farm produce.

In considering marketing boards, two issues become of far-reaching import — namely, the types of programs and their effectiveness, and the format and composition of the board. Broadly speaking, the goals of all marketing boards are identical, although the vehicles for attaining these objectives travel differing routes. Regardless of the paths taken, the central goal of a marketing board is the increase of net income for each of its members.

The programs used by marketing boards are varied, but the most common include product promotion, improvement of the institutions for marketing, two-price systems, quota allotments, and collective bargaining. Promotion of products is usually executed by embarking on advertising campaigns, including displays and exhibitions. Improvements in marketing institutions are those aspects such as exist in the hog industry, whereby the utilization of teletype installations has enhanced the ability to establish prices and to rationalize the marketing of hogs. There have been improvements in the transportation of fluid milk and in the assembling, storage, and forward delivery of grain. Each type of endeavour has benefited the producers of farm products.

The operation of a two-price system results when the producer (seller) could obtain different prices in different markets for his produce — in particular, a higher price at home than abroad, supported by restrictions on competing imports. This is an example of what is called "discriminating monopoly." While this policy results in a greater revenue than normal, it is discriminatory in favour of foreign buyers (consumers) against Canadian consumers. The Canadian Wheat Board is an example where a board has central licensing (selling) privileges over imports of wheat and coarse grains. The desirability of this privilege, when a two-price system is operative and when other boards are not given the same privilege, may be questioned. There are no import restrictions for vegetables or soybeans, for example.

Collective bargaining is sometimes practised by marketing boards in cases such as dealing with buyers for minimum prices. Thus in Ontario, for example, there is a minimum price for processing-vegetables, which is a result of this type of negotiation; processing companies enter into contracts with producers to grow a certain number of acres of a crop. The risk of producing vegetables in the absence of a contract is high, and negotiations through collective bargaining can render stability to production, quality of product, and income. Collective bargaining may result in reduced efficiency, since the only entry of new entrepreneurs (farmers) into the industry would be by obtaining a contract from a processor. In this way, the allocation of resources and/or locational activities of producers is determined by processors. It is also possible that boards may demand prices high enough to make the production phase so profitable that processors enter this stage of the industry. Ultimately, however, the bargaining strength of boards depends on how much control they hold not only over the supply of the given commodity, but also over the supply of substitutes.

Marketing boards have also utilized input and sale quotas, on the grounds that if the last few percentage points of output are eliminated, incomes would rise. Any quota system is subject to erosion unless proper constraints are established for the initial allocation, transfer, and expansion of quotas. Quotas may be given out on the basis of production in a specific period in the past, on the basis of current production capacity, or on the basis of auctions.

A major problem in this whole aspect of marketing boards involves the movement of produce interprovincially. Often, provincial marketing boards have had administrative problems with each other due to the under-cutting of one province by the other through changes in provincial production and prices. A classic case is the recent situation where one province seized "illegal" eggs which entered from another province. This may be an example of the need for the establishment of marketing boards or commissions with a national flavor.

A vital missing element in the structure of agriculture is the absence of national marketing boards (the exception being the Canadian Wheat Board). These boards would deal with interprovincial difficulties resulting from the failure of provincial boards to agree on a common policy or to control the movement of products into, or away from, any given province. The policies of national marketing boards, of necessity, would depend on the authority vested in them by both the provincial and federal levels of government. Such bodies would try to act in the best interests of Canadian agriculture without creating unnecessary interprovincial or provincial–federal frictions. To be wholly effective, any such agency would have to create an effective, cordial relationship with agribusiness concerns, marketing co-operatives, and provincial boards and agencies.

VI. Farm Credit and Capital Requirements

The rapid development in technology over the past quarter of a century has transformed Canadian agriculture from a low capital-oriented industry to one that is highly capital-demanding. Correspondingly, credit institutions have increased in number and changed in form. Credit is made available to Canadian farmers through many agencies, chief among which are those of the federal government: the Farm Credit Corporation, which provides long-term mortgage loans (as of March 31, 1971, 69,050 loans totalling $1,202,546,986 were outstanding); the Veterans' Land Act Administration; the Farm Improvements Loan Act; the Prairie Grain Advance Payments Act; and the Industrial Development Bank. Also deeply involved in providing credit to farmers are provincial governments, commercial banks, credit unions, trust and loan companies, supply houses, insurance companies, finance companies, and individuals.

The sufficiency of the credit-capital complex and all of its problems and administrations are a function of the trend in farm structure. If the basic producing structure is to move toward amalgamation, integration, or a corporation-type system, the credit structure as obtained in the non-agricultural sector should suffice. If the structure for the future is to continue along the traditional family-farm arrangement, the credit structure must have engrained into it special provisions for dealing with the credit and capital requirements of the family farm.

Some idea of the capital structure of Canadian agriculture can be obtained by looking at the capital involvement of large and small units. In 1971, only about 7 percent of all commercial farms (those farms which had a value of products sold of over $2,500) had invested capital of $120,000 or more, and approximately 66 percent of all commercial farms had invested $55,000 or less. There appears to be a significant correlation between capital investment and value of products sold, and it is estimated that the upper 33 percent of commercial farmers (in terms of sales income) produced about 66 percent of the value of products sold by all commercial farmers.[8]

There is a wide difference in capital investment and income among Canadian farmers, and this poses no easy problem for credit policies of a national character. The variation in the capital structure from a provincial viewpoint is very noticeable. Alberta has an average investment for commercial farms of about $76,000, compared with $29,000 for Prince Edward Island.[9]

It is worth re-emphasizing that credit policies should have specific conditions for dealing with the problems of the family farm. The rate of increase of capital requirements for farming has forced many owner-manager-operators and their families to curtail current consumption in order to ensure sufficient savings to purchase and operate the family farm. The traditional attitude of independence is still strong for many farmers, and as a result they are strongly motivated toward a debt-free status at retirement.

VII.   The Low-Income Component

Without going into the conceptualization of what constitutes a low income or into how it is measured, it is safe to say that low incomes and small farms show a strong correlation. The small-farm sector in Canadian agriculture, where a small farm is one reporting less than $5,000 gross sales annually, takes in about 55 percent of all farms. This includes about 47 percent of the farms in the western provinces, over 50 percent of the farms in Quebec, about 45 percent of all farms in Ontario, and about 80 percent of all farms in the Atlantic Provinces. These farms have gross expenses of about 60 to 70 percent of gross sales, leaving something less than $2,000 in net income per farm.

Low income is probably the most vital problem of the agricultural sector. In 1966 almost 238,000 farms had less than $3,000 in farm income, corresponding to 55.2 percent of all farms. For 1971 the corresponding

---

[8] These figures have been estimated from 1971 Census data.
[9] Figures are those estimated by the Federal Task Force. See Report of the Federal Task Force on Agriculture, op. cit.

figure was 170,000 farms, or 46.5 percent of all farms.[10] Even many farms having more than $5,000 gross sales are near or below the poverty line. Many small-scale farmers are able to survive by earning income cff the farm. However, not all low-income farmers have this opportunity.

If these farm families are to achieve a satisfactory level of existence, programs such as ARDA and FRED must be continued with much more purpose. Even so, a large portion of the low-income farm group is outside of welfare and ARDA-type programs. Special public policies may be necessary to meet the requirements of this sector of the farming public. It was with such thoughts in mind that the Small Farms Development Program was initiated in 1971.

VIII.   International Aspects of Canadian Agriculture

Perhaps the most relevant and highly significant aspects of Canadian agriculture relate to the export of agricultural products. In this regard, the national (domestic and trade) agricultural policies of other countries are extremely important. There has been a growing tendency throughout the world to adopt price-support and protectionist measures, all of which have adverse effects on trade. The adoption of price-support programs has developed agricultural surpluses, which are directed to third markets through the implementation of export subsidies. Canada's accessibility to markets is eroded because of the determination of these countries to attain self-sufficiency. The formation of trading blocs causes new preferential-tariff alignments, all of which work to the disadvantage of Canadian exports.

The Common Agricultural Policy (CAP) of the European Economic Community (EEC) involves price supports (discussed in the next section), export subsidies, and the meticulous control of imports. It provides for free trade among the member countries of the Community, variable import levies to raise prices of imports, and subsidies to stimulate exports by reducing their prices abroad. The increased production within the EEC, brought about mainly by the high support prices, has reduced demand for Canadian farm products by the countries of the EEC, as well as by those third-country markets where the EEC subsidizes exports heavily (e.g., barley exports to Japan).

The restrictions on imports by the EEC will continue to cause a reduction in Canadian exports, especially in the case of wheat. The EEC policy (CAP) also involves an increase in the taxes on vegetable oils, increased production of rapeseed, and free entry of oilseeds from African countries. These will all work to reduce oilseeds exports to the EEC. In 1973 Britain became a member of the EEC, and British membership undoubtedly will be very disadvantageous to Canadian exports.

Even prior to Britain's entry into the EEC, imports were being replaced by increased domestic production, as a matter of deliberate government policy. The need for this step was claimed to be the saving of foreign exchange and the protection of British farmers. British agricultural output had been stimulated by government assistance, such as guaranteed prices

[10] These figures have been estimated from 1971 Census data.

in the form of deficiency payments (discussed in the next section). This technique worked to ensure that the British consumers possessed the advantage of purchasing at or near the world prices. As mentioned before, Britain is now a member of the EEC and must abide by the procedures of the CAP.

The United States is a large importer of food products, especially those produced in this country, but also of tropical products. U.S. agricultural policy is discussed in the next section.

Canadian exports are competitive with those of the United States, which is the largest exporter of agricultural products. If Canada is to continue to keep pace with, and to be competitive with the United States in the world market, there must be continued efforts to attain a higher degree of efficiency in production, distribution, and marketing.

Japan's market is of vital importance to Canadian exports. Japan imported some $200 million of agricultural products from Canada in 1972. Of this total, wheat and wheat products accounted for over $100 million. Japan is Canada's main export market for rapeseed and flaxseed. Canada's exports to Japan could be more than what they are, were it not for Japan's policy of dividing the market among the major suppliers.

As Japan grows and develops and becomes less self-sufficient in wheat, barley, rapeseed, and flax, Canada can expect to expand these exports. Also, as the Japanese population continues to alter its dietary habits, Canada should continue to export larger quantities of meat and meat products. In 1973, the great demand for meat by Japan and its high domestic price (about $14.00 per pound) caused suppliers to ship large amounts of meat (beef) there, and contributed to short supply and high prices in Canada.

Canada may be able to generate outlets for farm products in the developing countries of the world. Even though aid from developed countries is working toward agricultural self-sufficiency for the developing countries, it is unlikely that this goal can be achieved in the near future. Canada's aid to such countries may be in the form of food products as well as educational and promotional work involving her farm products.

Restrictions on imports are not playing a very significant role at the present time, because of a world-wide shortage of farm products and the increased demand by the importing nations. Canada's exports of agricultural products, particularly grains, to these countries have been substantial during this period of abnormally high prices for agricultural output.

IX. Price Stabilization

It has long been the experience that a single free-market price for farm products, when there are rapid changes in the agriculture sector, produces unsatisfactory prices and unstable incomes for farmers. Several devices have been proposed and used in an attempt to alleviate these conditions. Some of these are:

1. Gift or relief payments made to those farmers who could demonstrate their need.

2. Programs designed to benefit farmers by causing an increase in

the demand for farm products or permitting a reduction in the costs of production.

3. Supply-management programs (marketing-board programs) designed to reduce the amount of farm output and to generate a price rise — use of marketing (delivery) quotas and acreage allotments.

4. Price supports.

5. Direct payments or deficiency payments.

• *Gifts and reliefs:* farmers and farmers' organizations are not enthusiastic about this form of support. The lower-income sector can obtain assistance through programs such as ARDA and FRED. Farm lobbying groups share the belief that the solution to the problem is not relief and support, but rather one of complete farm adjustment.

• *Demand expansion:* several vehicles are available. Use can be made of direct distribution of excess products acquired by the government to needy persons; examples are the food-stamp program in the United States in the 1960s, the expansion of foreign demand through the selling of farm products for foreign currency, and the use of subsidies. The use of sales-promotion and market-discrimination techniques is also available. One form of market-discrimination program has been the two-price plan. This is based on the theory that if the markets for a product can be separated and a limited quantity sold in that market where the demand is less elastic (less responsive to price), then total revenue from a specified output will be increased. An example is export-dumping, which involves the separation of domestic and foreign markets by price discrimination, the establishment of a higher domestic than foreign price, the limitation of quantity available on the domestic market, and the selling of the remainder at the price it can command in the foreign market.

• *Supply management:* acreage allotments and marketing quotas may be associated with supply management. Land-retirement programs may also be used. A special aspect of supply management in Canada involves the Canadian Wheat Board, which plays a vital role in the marketing of grain. The Wheat Board possesses complete control over the manner in which wheat, oats, and barley are marketed and the prices at which they are sold. While flax, rapeseed, and rye are not marketed through the Canadian Wheat Board, it does control their movement through the marketing and distribution systems. By controlling the amount of grain that farmers can sell individually, the Board indirectly controls crop production.

• *Price supports:* one principle on which the use of price supports is rationalized is that the prices farmers get for their products rise less than the prices they pay. To attain "parity" of farm and non-farm prices would require, therefore, that farm prices be supported. But attempts to support prices at an arbitrary level have resulted in overproduction and high costs to governments. The excess supply (resulting from the guaranteed price which is higher than what the farmers would get in the free market) purchased by the government must be stored, dumped on the foreign market, or destroyed. The end result of price supports is increased prices, with consumers paying more and buying less, while the government's tax receipts are used to bolster farm incomes.

This form of assistance is used in Canada for butter and some other products. Prior to 1965, this was the method practised in the United States through support programs at prices above world prices, which led to a vast accumulation of stocks and to the use of export subsidies and the export of farm products as foreign aid, and efforts to restrict production by means of acreage-retirement, acreage-allotment, and acreage-diversion programs. The excess output acquired by the government was sold at world prices. The American consumers met a large part of the cost of this program. In 1965 the level of price supports was significantly reduced, so that prices were supported at or near world levels, and farmers who co-operated in reducing production were provided with a per-bushel payment above the guaranteed price-support level.[11]

The Common Agricultural Policy (CAP) of the EEC involves variable import levies on grain imported from non-member countries, government sales and purchases at intervention prices (slightly above and below the target price), export subsidies, and a denaturing premium for wheat.[12] The import levy is a variable tariff that is adjusted to maintain uniformity between the import price and the target price. Grain is bought by the EEC authority to maintain the target price, a price which will provide producers with a reasonable return. Such purchased grains are withdrawn from the market and must be held until such a time that their sale will not depress the market (target) price, which is held higher than the world price. Export subsidies are used to make the higher-priced products from within the EEC competitive in the world market.[13]

In Canada, the Canadian Wheat Board establishes initial prices for the basic grades of wheat, oats, and barley at the beginning of the crop year. The Board sets the initial prices for other grades in relationship with those set for the basic grades. The Board buys all wheat, oats, and barley delivered by farmers and pays on the basis of the initial prices less handling charges. While the initial prices are in the nature of support prices, they are set at a relatively low level, so that typically the realized (market) price exceeds the initial price, and subsequent payments are made to farmers on the basis of the difference between the realized price and the initial price. All farmers receive the same price (return per bushel) each year for the same grade of crop. The adoption by Canada of similar types of programs as used in the EEC and prior to 1973 in the United States — price supports set at above rather than below expected world market prices, export subsidies, etc. — would be relatively more costly for Canada, since agricultural exports make up a much larger portion of our GNP.

- *Deficiency payments:* this form of price support guarantees the

---

[11] For discussion and evaluation of traditional U.S. agricultural policy, see Vernon W. Ruttan, *et al.*, eds., *Agricultural Policy in an Affluent Society* (New York: W.W. Norton & Company, 1969); and Charles L. Schultze, *The Distribution of Farm Subsidies* (Washington, D.C.: The Brookings Institution, 1971).

[12] The denaturing premium for wheat is used to encourage the use of wheat for feed by rendering the wheat unfit for human consumption, thus reducing the price of wheat to a price comparable with barley.

[13] For further description of the CAP, see Mordechai E. Kreinin, *International Economics: A Policy Approach* (New York: Harcourt Brace Jovanovich, 1971), pp. 303–305.

farmer a price, but instead of storage or dumping, the output is brought to the market and sold for current consumption at whatever price it can clear. Payments are then made directly to farmers to make up the difference between market-clearing and guaranteed price. This was the British policy prior to the adoption of the CAP consequent upon joining the EEC. The system was adopted by the United States in 1973, when target prices were set below world prices and direct payments were to be made to farmers only if market prices fell below target prices. In Canada, the deficiency-payments technique is used to support the prices of sugar beets, potatoes, and eggs.

Both price supports and deficiency payments benefit producers, but a deficiency-payment system costs the Treasury more than a price-support plan. However, deficiency payments are considered economically more efficient than price supports; for in the former, prices are determined in the market-place by the supply–demand interaction. It therefore permits consumers to have a larger supply of food at a cheaper price and allows the government to avoid buying and selling farm products.

The major disadvantage of deficiency payments is that they do not really solve the problem of low farm incomes. Rather, they may reduce farm income by decreasing the out-migration of farmers from the industry. They may direct other factor inputs to agriculture, despite low productivity and returns, instead of shifting them to enterprises where their productivity is higher.

X. The Problems of Canadian Agriculture

The problems of Canadian agriculture are really no different from those of other developed countries, such as the United States and West Germany. Paramount among these are low incomes, rigidities inhibiting resource transfer and adjustment, over-production, unstable and uncertain prices, the existence and prevalence of small and non-viable farms, increasing regional disparities, the cost-price squeeze, slow market growth, declining farm share of national income, and the ineffectiveness of government policies and programs.

To some degree, the foregoing problems are related to a lack of effective formulation and implementation of policies and programs, together with or accompanied by an inadequate organizational structure to ensure cohesiveness and co-operation among the several parts for the betterment of the entire agricultural sector.

The problems which confront agriculture are seen differently by different groups. From the farmers' viewpoint, the major problems are low farm incomes, uncertainty of agricultural direction in the future, unstable prices and income, high and increasing cost of credit, uncertainty of wheat export sales, and the unavailability of farm labour.

To the agribusiness sector, market availability is of major concern. To them, such problems as marketing-board regulations, lack of competition, talk of price fixing, and inefficiency are disconcerting.

From the viewpoint of government policy-makers, the problem in the agricultural sector traditionally has revolved around low incomes for farmers. In an attempt to alleviate this problem, programs involving price supports and subsidies for agricultural products were introduced. These programs exert pressures on government finances and are today unpopular, given the relatively high cost of food for the consumer. Thus politicians are placed in the difficult position of opposing high and rising food prices to combat inflation and at the same time supporting the principle of, and programs for, higher farm incomes.

It is no coincidence that the main problems of Canadian agriculture are embodied in low farm incomes. Apart from its own undesirability, low farm incomes generate problems involving basic resource endowments and allocative disbursements of resources between the varying sectors and regions of the economy. The question of labour mobility, including training of the labour force and location of emplyment, is persistent and disturbing. The competitiveness of farm products is a problem too; for the questions of the degree of subsidization and barriers to entry of foreign products are involved.

Low incomes in Canadian agriculture force a look at the sufficiency and administration of government programs. The problem of low income is not a situation unique to Canadian agriculture; rather it is a haunting reality in all agricultural countries. The problem is unique to agriculture by reason of the very nature of agricultural production and supply. It takes only a cursory look at the supply and demand situation for the sector to divulge some factors that contribute to the problem. The industry is generally dominated by the participation of large numbers of producers and the inability of an individual producer to affect market prices — a characteristic which economic theory postulates as giving rise to perfect competition and eventually to optimum social welfare.

In a general context, Canadian agriculture (until the abnormally high prices beginning in 1972) was going through a period of declining farm income while the income of the nation as a whole was increasing rapidly. Traditionally, the major problem in agriculture has been one of surplus and income. The production of food had been increasing much faster than could be utilized by the increased population and national product. Export demand for many commodities was decreasing. Low farm incomes were considered the offshoot of a rapidly growing economy foisting a cost-price squeeze upon farmers.

In the past, as peoples' income increased, the percentage spent on food decreased. This trend was expected to continue in the future as national income continued to grow and the expenditure on non-farm products increased. With increases in incomes and GNP, there had been no increased premium on farm products. Prices had been kept comparatively low, primarily because people bid up the prices of non-farm products. The consequence of this behaviour was that farmers paid higher prices for their factor inputs (especially for machinery).

Over time, it has been taking a much smaller proportion of the labour force to produce food requirements for the entire population. Agriculture has been able to do that by providing the farm worker with more efficient, productive, and expensive equipment. This has resulted in increased output per worker. If we assume improved technology and the consequent increased output per worker, we could postulate that given constancy of farm product prices, output in the industry would increase in direct relationship with improved knowledge. A disparity could then be expected to exist in farmers' abilities to utilize the new advancements. Those farmers who are unable to keep up in terms of the above will lose ground. At the same time, it should be noted that the nature of agriculture supply (large number of producers, lengthy production period) means that decreased prices would cause only small or negligible effects on output.

The climatic environment in which agriculture is practised brings with it the possibility of crop failures due to hail storms, floods, etc., resulting in a very high degree of uncertainty in incomes and, most importantly, an intolerably high degree of output instability.

The major components of any economic sector are supply and demand. Some of the problems confronting the supply aspect of Canadian agriculture were mentioned above. But the demand for the output of the industry plays no small part in alleviating or contributing to the problems. Again, until the recent situation of abnormally high agricultural prices, the cost–price squeeze was all-important. Canadian consumers preferred more resources to be expended in producing non-farm products, as a result of higher incomes and rapid advancement in technology. Fewer resources should have been devoted to producing farm products. All this was indicated by the price that was bid for farm products in the marketplace. It is fair to say that apparently Canadian consumers were telling the producers that too much food was being produced. Resources should have been shifted out of agriculture.

Producers had not heeded this; for, as mentioned above, output has far outstripped demand. There has been some involvement by the government in terms of price supports; but unless the basic nature of the resource adjustment is understood, such programs may prove ineffective. At this juncture, two aspects of the demand for agricultural products are re-emphasized:

1. An increase in income normally generates a less than proportionate increase in per capita demand for agricultural products. On the other hand, an increase in population tends to give rise to a proportionate increase in demand.

2. Canadian exports encounter domestic protection in some foreign markets and third-country export subsidies in others. This type and amount of competition is significant, as approximately 25 to 30 percent of Canada's farm output is exported. It is of interest to note that because the exports of the agricultural sector in Canada are a greater percentage of the GNP than their counterpart in the United States, there would be a proportionately greater cost of export subsidies in Canada.

Since each producer operates on the belief that his output decision does not affect the price of the product, the net result of all farmers' decisions is the production of a total output which does not maximize individual returns. Consequently, producers are forced to seek out good advice in supply management. Generally speaking, on a national level, per capita net income in agriculture has been low relative to that obtained in non-farm employment. This has contributed to a reduction in the Canadian farm labour force to the tune of some 50 percent since the end of the Second World War.

In the past, the supply of farm products exceeded the domestic demand, forcing a major portion of output to be sold in strongly protected markets or in competition with subsidized exports. Because of poor alternatives, no alternatives, or because they prefer low farm incomes to other economic, social, and psychological problems which accompany migration from farms, many farmers stay on.

The dependence of agricultural output on the weather leads to crop failures in one year and excessive production in another, resulting in price fluctuations. Problems in foreign countries such as may lead to reductions or increases in Canadian exports also result in similar price variations. Concomitant with fluctuating and uncertain prices are income variability and instability.

XI. The Family Farm

The establishment of the family farm has been invaluable in the settlement and development not only of rural areas but also of urban communities. To some, the family-farm unit has been a very efficient form of agricultural development; as the entrepreneur and his family normally dedicate themselves unselfishly in production and in the utilization of their scarce resources — land, labour, capital, and management — they generate a high level of efficiency.

The rise in technological innovations, instability of income, unstable prices, increasing costs of factor inputs, together with increasing and better off-farm opportunities, all are working against the persistence of the family farm unit. The present economic environment of inflation necessitates a continuing expansion and improvement in skills and management if above-marginal incomes are to be attained. The small farm unit, in many cases, lacks the "economies of scale" (declining per-unit costs as output increases) required to obtain credit and to expand to meet the ever-challenging demands for economic viability.

In a vain attempt to maintain viability or because of a lack of any alternative, many small-farm operators who are unable to keep pace with modern technological development and management skills fall farther and farther behind and inevitably leave agriculture. To keep a farm viable eventually generates a farm of such size and complexity as to strain the resources of the individual. This leads to excessive borrowing, unplanned for and over-expensive machinery, and a host of other problems.

It is believed that the family farm as a unit of agricultural production will persist in Canadian agriculture. To do so, there must be changes in line with new developments. Yet to believe that the unit does not face the threat of extinction would be irrational. Wherever events point to the disassembly of the family unit, they may be traced to the economic forces and the individual actions of the operators.

What the family farmer is confronted with is a changing requirement for success in agriculture. Unlike in the past, where determination (hard work), small amounts of capital, and "good intentions" were sufficient conditions to achieve success, nowadays they are necessary but not sufficient. It is sometimes construed that the family-farm unit was really a form of recluse away from the real pressures of urban existence, where low levels of education and on-the-job farming experience prevailed. Today, the demands of technology and management, and the complexity of farming operations necessitate advanced knowledge. In the 1971 Census, over 60 percent of farm operators had only attained at the most a grade-9 level of education and only one in 250 possessed a university degree.[14] There is a definite class differentiation among farmers, on the one hand the higher echelons and on the other the poverty-stricken. The difference between the two is a result of differences in education and experience.

The agricultural sector is one of the most highly competitive sectors of the Canadian economy and still has much influence. The existence of many small producers internally and the competitiveness of foreign producers brings home the tremendous importance and relevance of the bargaining ability of the producers and/or their representatives. Possession of political influence and the important contribution of the sector to the gross economy stand agriculture in good stead.

XII. A New Situation

Traditionally the problems of agriculture have been low and unstable prices, excess output, and low and uncertain incomes. Beginning in 1972, prosperity came to the farm sector of the agricultural industry unlike anything heretofore seen. Prices of many agricultural products soared far beyond their highest levels in recent history. The cause appears to have been a unique combination of reduced supplies and unprecedented expansion in demand.

The situation seems to have been triggered by poor crops in Russia in 1972, coupled with an almost complete cessation of fishing for anchovies off the coast of Peru beginning in the fall of 1972 and continuing through much of 1973. The importance of the Peruvian fish catch to world protein supplies was never fully appreciated until this development. Further complicating the supply of agricultural products were the extremely unfavourable harvest conditions in the United States in the fall of 1972. Significant quantities of corn and soybeans were lost in the field due to excess rainfall, or were harvested in a poor-quality condition with reduced livestock-feeding value and in some cases complete deterioration while in storage. Furthermore, the devaluation of the U.S. dollar meant that North American food supplies were relatively cheap to many foreign buyers. As a result, they could and did bid higher prices for these products.

For many farmers, the new situation of high agricultural prices and apparently unlimited demand means incomes far in excess of aspirations. However, for many others, notably some classes of livestock producers,

[14] *Canada Year Book, 1972.*

the current high prices are a mixed blessing. The relatively high prices for finished livestock is in some cases being offset by the extremely high cost of feed, which is the major input cost for some enterprises. Even for grain producers, the impact of the high prices on income is eroded through input costs, such as machinery, fertilizer, and land rent rising significantly in response to the ability of farmers to pay higher prices. From the viewpoint of some agribusiness firms, however, the price increases either reflect their currently rising costs and/or involve bringing into balance prices which could not be adequately increased during the latter years of the 1960s and early 1970s when the agricultural outlook in much of Canada was severely depressed.

The new situation will have a lasting and profound impact on agriculture in Canada. Many producers will take advantage of the high commodity prices and the resulting buoyant land market to retire from farming. Others will undertake major adjustments in their farming operations; for example, expansion through land purchase or achieving more efficient utilization of existing resources. Some will probaby find themselves in a worse economic position than before the rise in prices because of over-reaction to the high prices.

There is no question that agricultural prices will decline before too long. It is, however, completely uncertain as to whether they will return to their levels of the late 1960s and early 1970s. Whatever happens in terms of market prices, problems will continue to exist in agriculture, and change and adjustments will prevail.

V. Industry and Sectoral Economics

1. The Structure of Canadian Industry

Max D. Stewart

University of Alberta

Canadians face a central economic issue created by a persistent belief that the economic activity of the nation is guided by effectively functioning competitive markets à la Adam Smith. Virile or virulent, as you choose, that notion displays remarkable strength in the face of increasing and nigh on massive evidence to the contrary. At the risk of brief boredom, selected glances at Adam Smith's observations and warnings and a look at the world of oligopoly will prepare us, perhaps, to break new ground in promoting a more efficient and dynamic economy. Our survey of oligopoly (in some instances, near-monopoly) will include, in more or less detail: manufacturing, mining, financial intermediaries, communications, and self-governing occupations. Although that is very far from comprehensive and omits several sectors in the economy that are active candidates for improved performance, its weight is sufficient for this essay.

I. Competition and Adam Smith

The theory of pure competition is elegant in its logic and comforting in its conclusions. *If* the necessary conditions prevail, self-seeking producers and sellers of products and services will be brought by inexorable market forces to offer their goods and services at the lowest costs *and prices* attainable on a continuing basis: private greed transformed by the fierce play of competition into public benefit. No more than that could be achieved by government intervention, and taxpayers would have to pay some costs to no better end. Left to themselves, sellers must accept the market price; they have no room to manoeuvre. There is a defect, however, in that approach: the rare occurrence of pure competition, the crowd of oligopolistic and other imperfect markets, and numerous monopolies are a significant economic reality. There is no guarantee in oligopoly of an ideal outcome. As there is good evidence that competitive markets embrace too little of Canadian economic activity, thus denying a guarantee of efficiency and protection against excess profits, the relevant issue is to create an effective competition policy.

It is well to be warned at the outset that proposals for new economic policies will be opposed. As one economist states:

> The great barrier — and indeed the only barrier of substance — to the adoption of an effective competition policy (or any other social change) is the rejection of realism and relevance. The barrier to changes is the refusal to change a public stance, no matter how untenable it may be. Most people who have held executive positions with large corporations are acutely aware of the creed of the managerial class to which one must give at least lip service if one is to climb the ladder of promotion. Among other things, the creed prescribes that the freedom of the company is sacrosanct. As a consequence, the theorem has been developed that all markets that are free of government regulations operate well; the market system is the attainable optimum in this imperfect world.
>
> This article of faith is applied not just to markets for commodities, services, and securities but also to markets for companies. . . .
>
> Possibly the second most formidable barrier to social change is the disposition to stay with the devil we know rather than the devil we don't know.[1]

So many continue to call upon Adam Smith's arguments in support of curtailing government intervention that it is useful to recall a few of his other remarks, especially his warnings regarding situations not controlled by pure competition.

> Consumption is the sole end and purpose of all production; and the interest of the producer ought to be attended to, only so far as it may be necessary for promoting that of the consumer. The maxim is so perfectly self-evident, that it would be absurd to attempt to prove it. But in the mercantile system, the interest of the consumer is almost constantly sacrificed to that of the producer; and it seems to consider production, and not consumption, as the ultimate end and object of all industry and commerce.[2]
>
> The price of monopoly is upon every occasion the highest which can be got. The natural price, or the price of free competition, on the contrary, is the lowest which can be taken, not upon every occasion indeed, but for any considerable time together. The one is upon every occasion the highest which can be squeezed out of the buyers, or which, it is supposed, they will consent to give: the other

---

[1] Milton Moore, *How Much Price Competition? The Prerequisites of an Effective Canadian Competition Policy* (Montreal: McGill-Queen's University Press, 1970), pp. 10–11.
[2] Adam Smith, *An Inquiry into the Nature and Causes of the Wealth of Nations* (New York: Random House, The Modern Library, 1937), p. 625.

is the lowest which the sellers can commonly afford to take, and at the same time continue their business.[3]

People of the same trade seldom meet together, even for merriment and diversion, but the conversation ends in a conspiracy against the public, or in some contrivance to raise prices. It is impossible indeed to prevent such meetings, by any law which either could be executed, or would be consistent with liberty and justice. But though the law cannot hinder people of the same trade from sometimes assembling together, it ought to do nothing to facilitate such assemblies; much less to render them necessary.[4]

That legal difficulty and the problem posed by it will be discussed later in the essay. A final warning by Adam Smith deals with policy-makers and business advisers. In speaking of the expertise and understanding of merchants and manufacturers, he says:

As their thoughts, however, are commonly exercised rather about the interest of their own particular branch of business, than about that of the society, their judgment, even when given with the greatest candour (which it has not been upon every occasion), is much more to be depended upon with regard to the former of those two objects, than with regard to the latter. . . . The interest of the dealers, however, is always in some respects different from, and even opposite to, that of the public. To widen the market and to narrow the competition, is always the interest of the dealers. To widen the market may frequently be agreeable enough to the interest of the public; but to narrow the competition must always be against it, and can serve only to enable the dealers, by raising their profits above what they naturally would be, to levy, for their own benefit, an absurd tax upon the rest of their fellow-citizens. The proposal of any new law or regulation of commerce which comes from this order [the dealers], ought always to be listened to with great precaution, and ought never to be adopted till after having been long and carefully examined, not only with the most scrupulous, but with the most suspicious attention. It comes from an order of men, whose interest is never exactly the same with that of the public, who have generally an interest to deceive and even to oppress the public, and who accordingly have, upon many occasions, both deceived and oppressed it.[5]

Let it be enough to contend that Adam Smith placed his confidence in the efficacy of competitive markets to achieve benefit to society, because the competitive market forces would produce beneficial results in spite of the personal interests of the marketers themselves.

Once out of the world of pure competition, producers and sellers will seek to manipulate prices and outputs toward the upper profit limit of monopoly. Villainy is not always a prerequisite to obtaining excess

---

[3] *Ibid.*, p. 61.
[4] *Ibid.*, p. 128.
[5] *Ibid.*, p. 250.

profits; recognition of mutual interdependence may suffice. So many elements combine in so many different ways to determine their behaviour that the outcome cannot so far be reliably predicted. Oligopolists may compete; they may collude and approach monopoly results; they may take similar action without collusion. The policy issue is that the purely competitive result is far from assured and rarely occurs. Individual sellers are all too frequently of significance in their markets. Although there is little prospect of determining the precise number of large firms or of all firms in an industry that would constitute the boundary between pure competition and oligopoly, there is nonetheless a range of small numbers of important firms, say up to twenty, that seems to represent a key element of an oligopolistic market structure, an economic environment of few sellers, which affects the behaviour of sellers so that there is no longer assurance of the optimal outcome of pure competition.

II. Market Concentration in Canada

A few remarks of Professor Dorfman[6] will suggest that in the United States oligopoly is pervasive and poses economic problems.

> Practically all the famous companies you can name are, in fact, oligopolists. . . . Instead of attending to their demand and cost curves, oligopolists are preoccupied with market strategy. . . . Oligopoly is an awkward form of market organization from the viewpoint of the participants. . . . They can neither take full advantage of their individual opportunities as atomistic [pure] competitors can, nor coalesce into an efficient, money-making monopoly. . . . oligopoly . . . has many of the drawbacks of monopoly and, in addition, a rigidity and an incitement to wasteful forms of competition that are peculiarly its own. . . . How to live with oligopoly is one of the most challenging current problems of economic policy.

The major components of market structure, the economic environment of firms affecting their behaviour, are:
concentration of market control: whether by ownership concentration (number and relative sizes of firms), interlocking directorships, trade agreements, or group associations;
product differentiation: differences in technical characteristics and in buyer preferences;
condition of entry: the difficulties confronting new rivals vis-à-vis established firms.
A market should be defined so as to comprise all those producing "close" substitutes: products or services, cloth or court contests, agricultural implements or appendectomies. Different brands of gasoline do not pose a definition problem. For example, the retail gasoline market is usually characterized by some price differentials that seem related to some blend of technical differences and brand preferences, but it is still a market of reasonably close substitutes. Geographic dispersion of service stations

---

[6] See Robert Dorfman, *The Price System*, © 1964, pp. 97–103. Reprinted by permission of Prentice-Hall, Inc., Englewood Cliffs, N.J.

may, on the other hand, create so many sub-markets that many outlets may not mean a close approximation to pure competition; there can be a small number of sellers in each sub-market. However, it is generally necessary to use published statistics with their classifications, which are on an industry rather than a product basis. Acceptance of that must be with a recognition that the boundaries may sometimes be quite different from the ideal market boundaries. The relatively large transportation element in many Canadian industries also tends to create many regional markets which are often obscured in national figures.

A few examples of market concentration will raise the competition-policy issue by making it evident that oligopoly is the most widespread market form and that the pure-competition model is too seldom relevant. It is hardly comforting to come to see that the elegance of analysis of pure competition is matched by its rarity of occurrence in Canada. That conclusion can be reached by taking into account only ownership concentration, which will be our first step. The enduring nature of market concentration is reason enough for stressing that element of market structure.

The conditions of ownership concentration in Canadian manufacturing may be seen in Table 1, which brings together results from two recent Canadian government studies and an earlier private investigation. Each industry covered is placed in one of five categories of concentration, according to the number of largest firms or enterprises required to account for 80 percent of shipments, employment, or value added. The first four concentration categories (VERY HIGH, HIGH, FAIRLY HIGH, and FAIRLY LOW) are defined as stated in the table. The fifth concentration category (LOW) embraces those industries where over 60 largest firms are required to account for the 80 percent, and covers the remainder of each entry. Note that the table shows *cumulative* figures. For example, the first 1948 entry shows that 43.0 percent of the manufacturing employment covered (and the coverage is 48.3 percent of the total) was in industries in high-concentration categories (VERY HIGH, HIGH, and FAIRLY HIGH), where 20 or fewer firms accounted for 80 percent of each industry's employment. The inclusion of industries of FAIRLY LOW concentration, where over 20 and up to 60 firms accounted for 80 percent of each industry's employment, brought the figure to 60.5 percent. That means that 39.5 percent (100 minus 60.5) of 1948 manufacturing employment covered by that entry was in LOW-concentration industries, where more than 60 firms were required to account for 80 percent of each industry's employment.

The selection of three different measures in Table 1 — employment, value of shipments, and value added — was dictated by the material found in the studies that are compared. Value of shipments generally means the selling-price value of shipments from manufacturing establishments during a year; that includes the costs of materials produced outside a particular

Table 1: *Concentration in Canadian Manufacturing*

Manufacturing Industries Grouped According to the Number of Largest Firms or Enterprises[a] Accounting for 80 Percent of Value of Shipments, Value Added, or Employment

		Cumulative Percentages by CONCENTRATION CATEGORY (No. of Largest Firms or Enterprises)				
Year	Concentration Measure	VERY HIGH (up to 4)	HIGH (over 4 to 8)	FAIRLY HIGH (over 8 to 20)	FAIRLY LOW (over 20 to 60)	Percentage of Manufacturing Shipments, Employment, or Value Added Covered
1948	Employment	16.0	26.4	43.0	60.5	48.3
	Shipments	16.3	24.7	38.6	59.3	65.6
	Value Added	8.9	21.2	40.9	75.7	34.0
1964	Employment	20.2	35.9	55.3	77.5	43.9
	Shipments	11.9	34.0	55.2	74.7	100.0
	Shipments[b]	16.2	35.9	69.3	82.0	100.0
1965	Shipments	26.5	36.6	58.0	78.6	89.8
	Value Added	14.0	36.6	69.2	85.3	28.0

[a] For 1948 and 1964, a "firm" is taken to be all establishments in a single manufacturing industry operated by one company. For 1965, an "enterprise" is defined as all establishments in a single industry which are under common control, thereby acknowledging intercorporate connections. Firms are used for all industries in 1948 and 1964 and enterprises in 1965. Recognition of intercorporate networks would be expected to reveal higher concentration in some industries.

[b] The national concentration figures shown in the preceding line have been modified to show the estimated effects on concentration, industry by industry, of regional markets (reflecting the geographic dispersion in Canada), exports, imports of substitute commodities, cases of imperfect substitutes being produced in a single "industry," and of close substitutes being produced in different ones. What might be called "effective concentration" tends to be increased by regional markets, by exports reducing the output that is available to Canadian buyers, and by the presence of imperfect substitutes within an industry's output. It tends to be lowered by imports adding to the choices open to Canadian buyers and by close substitutes from other industries. A comparison of these modified concentration percentages with the national ones of the preceding line indicates increased concentration on balance. The regional-market factor is the most important contributor, shifting 16 industries to higher concentration categories out of the 22 in higher categories because of the modifications. Five industries were estimated to be in lower categories, because of imports of close substitutes.

Sources: Max D. Stewart, *Concentration in Canadian Manufacturing and Mining Industries,* Background Study to the *Interim Report on Competition Policy* (Ottawa Economic Council of Canada, 1970), pp. 13, 18, 21, and 51.
　　Director of Investigation and Research, Combines Investigation Act, *Concentration in the Manufacturing Industries of Canada* (Ottawa: Department of Consumer and Corporate Affairs, 1971), pp. 17 and 45.
　　Each of these studies uses results for 1948 found in Gideon Rosenbluth, *Concentration in Canadian Manufacturing Industries,* National Bureau of Economic Research (Princeton: Princeton University Press, 1957).

industry but used in the processes of that industry. There is, in general, a close correspondence of shipments with sales, though changes in inventories and prices could, from time to time, create more divergence. Industry value added measures the value of economic activity carried on within an industry; it includes wages, interest, rent, and profits and excludes the value of purchases from other industries.

The first 1948 entry and the first 1964 entry in Table 1 show an increase in concentration for a comparable set of industries, e.g., from 43.0 percent in the three high-concentration categories to 55.3 percent. The third 1948 entry and the second 1965 entry show a sharper increase in concentration for a comparable set of industries: the percentage in high-concentration categories rising from 40.9 to 69.2. The most comprehensive entries for 1948 (the second) and 1965 (the first) have a lesser degree of comparability but nonetheless reveal increasing concentration, from 38.6 percent in the three high-concentration categories in 1948 to 58.0 percent in 1965. An important factor in deciding to use only some manufacturing industries in those years was to avoid those that seemed to be influenced significantly by the elements involved in the 1964 modifications of the national concentration figures given in that year's second entry (see Table 1, footnote b). Hence the third 1964 entry would seem to afford a more reliable comparison with the second 1948 entry and the first 1965 entry. The fact that the conservative estimating procedure followed tended to restrict the number of industries that fell into the highest-concentration categories in 1964 would suggest that the 1965 increase shown in the VERY HIGH category should be treated with caution. The most reliable comparisons are the first entries of 1948 and 1964 and the last entries of 1948 and 1965. It can thus be noted with some confidence that there has been an increase in concentration between 1948 and the more recent years studied.

If the three high-concentration categories are taken to show oligopolistic markets,[7] considerably more than half and possibly more than two-thirds of manufacturing shipments in the mid-1960s come from oligopolies. In these sectors of high concentration one would expect to find many cases of collusion or "live-and-let-live" conscious parallel action, tending to bring about a kind of joint-monopoly outcome: less competition, higher prices, higher profits, etc. Given that mutually accommodating behaviour can also occur in groups much larger than 20 or 30 firms or enterprises, using the boundary between FAIRLY HIGH and FAIRLY LOW concentration (up to 20 firms accounting for 80 percent of shipments, employment, or value added) to encompass oligopoly may well be conservative. Interlocking directorships can facilitate "people of the same trade assembling together." Trade associations and self-regulating authorities can often minimize price competition and foster cost-increasing forms of rivalry in quite large groups. A few very large firms may exert effective leadership (tacit or overt) over a great many quite small firms in the same industry.

Mining is even more highly concentrated than manufacturing. Of

[7]Milton Moore is convinced "that most industries are oligopolies, including some consisting of well over a score of independent firms" (op. cit., p. 3). Some would find it easy to argue that Manufacturers of Pharmaceuticals and Medicines are a case in point, because of the large number of sub-markets with few producers of specific drugs.

46 minerals, accounting for 96.7 percent of the 1964 value of mineral production, 32 are produced under conditions of VERY HIGH concentration, another 5 are in the HIGH category, and 4 are in the FAIRLY HIGH category. The cumulative percentages of value of production are 35.1 percent with 4 or fewer firms accounting for 80 percent of production, 57.9 percent with 8 or fewer firms, and 66.4 percent with 20 or fewer firms. The greatest contrast with manufacturing is found in the two categories of highest concentration. Additional details on mining concentration are available elsewhere[8] and need not detain us in this exploration.

Because financial institutions mobilize savings and channel them into a variety of uses, the financial intermediaries play an important role "in determining the nature and structure of the economy, the level of industrial efficiency, the rate of economic growth and the degree of domestic control over the national economic environment. . . . The main worry is that Canadian savings are not being transmitted by financial intermediaries to business enterprises for the starting up and expansion of capital stock to the extent that the level of savings in the economy would permit."[9]

As Table 2 shows for some financial sectors, high concentration is also found in this part of the economy. The 1967 Bank Act imposed limitations on interlocking directorates that may be held by chartered-bank directors,[10] placed restrictions on permissible ownership percentages between banks

Table 2: Concentration in Selected Financial Sectors

Sector	Total No. of Firms	Percentage of Assets or Insurance in Force Accounted for by the			Number of Largest Firms Accounting for: 80%	Total Assets or Insurance in Force: (billions)
		4	8	12		
			Largest Firms			
Chartered Banks, Total Assets, October 31, 1972	10	79.0	99.5	100.0	4.1	$ 44.5[a]
Trust Companies, Corporate Assets, year-end, 1971	60[b]	54.2	84.0	93.5	7.4	$ 7.5
Life Insurance Companies, Insurance in force in Canada, excl. Industrial, December 31, 1970	129[c]	34.2	55.0	66.6	19.7	$110.5

See notes for Table 2 on p. 178.

[8] See Max D. Stewart, "Industrial Organization," in L.H. Officer and L.B. Smith, eds., Canadian Economic Problems and Policies (Toronto: McGraw-Hill Canada, 1970), p. 168. That essay also discusses geographic and ownership concentration, interlocking directorships, multi-market companies, and advertising. See also Max D. Stewart, "Concentration in Canadian Mining", chapter 3 in Concentration in Canadian Manufacturing and Mining Industries, Background Study to the Interim Report on Competition Policy (Ottawa: Economic Council of Canada, 1970), pp. 31–41.
    Ownership concentration in mining and some aspects of foreign ownership are surveyed in Hon. Herb Gray, Foreign Direct Investment in Canada (Ottawa: Information Canada, 1972), pp. 224–25.
[9] Gray, op. cit., pp. 91, 113.
[10] See Stewart, "Industrial Organization," pp. 170–72.

a Total Canadian and *net* foreign assets (that is, foreign assets minus foreign liabilities), therefore an understatement of foreign assets.

b Nine firms, though incorporated as trust companies, are private and do not conduct ordinary trust-company business.

c Forty-five firms are classified as Canadian and have 69.4 percent of the life insurance in force in Canada; 14 British and 70 other foreign firms doing business in Canada have placed 5.2 and 25.4 percent, respectively, of the amount in force.
    Life-insurance company assets in Canada amount to roughly 16 to 18 percent of the dollar value of insurance in force. The asset concentration among the Canadian companies is HIGH, the four largest holding 55 percent and the eight largest 80.2 percent in 1969.

Sources: *Bank of Canada Review;* annual statements of banks; Financial Post Survey of Industrials; Reports of the Superintendent of Insurance for Canada: Insurance Companies, 1970; Trust and Loan Companies, 1971; E.P. Neufeld, *The Financial System of Canada* (Toronto: Macmillan of Canada, 1972).

and trust companies, and removed the previous 6-percent ceiling on the bank lending rate. The new restraints would seem to be aimed at preventing the continuation of what might be considered anti-competitive factors. At the same time, there is now presumably a reliance on the social control of competitive market forces instead of an arbitrary and fixed interest-rate limit. As Table 2 clearly indicates, these policy changes were made in an economic setting better characterized as rivalry among oligopolists than as pure competition among the many.

    A few indications of the likelihood of mutually accommodating conduct of a rather pervasive nature can be seen in a few examples of numerous joint enterprises, national and international:

A. Business financing: Two Canadian banks and three Canadian trust companies.
B. Credit-card system: Four Canadian banks.
C. International: Six banks; Canadian, American, Japanese, British, Italian, West German.
D. International: Ten banks; Canadian, American, and eight different Western European countries.
E. International: Seventeen banks; one Canadian, one Japanese, five American, and ten Western European.

The question posed by this phenomenon is not whether competition is or is not too limited or excess profits are or are not obtained, but that *there is not an assurance* that competitive market forces are operating effectively in a vital sector of the economy.

III.   Concentration, Barriers to Entry, and Profits

    "Communications in Canada is a big business — a billion-dollar business, as a matter of fact, in terms of advertising revenue alone."[11] A Senate study has revealed a number of areas of concentration. There are only nine cities with at least two daily newspapers under separate ownership. Two-thirds of the country's daily newspapers and almost half of the private TV stations and radio stations are owned by groups — corporations

11 Hon. Keith Davey, *Mass Media,* Vol. 1, *The Uncertain Mirror,* Report of the Special Senate Committee on Mass Media (Ottawa: Queen's Printer, 1970), p. 15, Reproduced by permission of Information Canada.

which own a significant or controlling interest in media outlets in more than one community. There are also several multi-media owners of substantial size. The cost conditions tend to create natural monopolies; that is, barriers to entry are high. Meaningful financial regulation by public authorities is absent. Leaving aside the detailed financial studies (revealing some TV before-tax returns on equity of over 90 percent and over 30 percent for some daily newspapers), one gains a clear picture of the Senate Committee's assessment from the fact that they quote Ray Thomson's memorable remark that a television broadcasting permit is "like having a licence to print your own money." The Committee goes on to add that "ownership of a daily newspaper often amounts to the same thing, except you don't need a licence."[12] In order to capture the vigour of this analysis and the sparkle of the comments, a final quotation is valuable:

> But *on the average*, media corporations are onto a very good thing indeed. If the brewing industry made profits half this large, and the people knew it, we suspect there would be sit-ins in the beer stores. Most media corporations, fortunately for them, don't have to disclose these earnings. Because their very large profits allow them to pay for expansion and acquisitions out of retained earnings, most continue as private companies. And so we are confronted with a delicious irony: an industry that is supposed to abhor secrets is sitting on one of the best-kept, least discussed secrets, one of the hottest *scoops*, in the entire field of Canadian business — their own balance sheets! . . .
>
> In a few cases, the corporations concerned are making genuine efforts to deliver quality editorial content and quality programming in return for their privileged economic position. But the general pattern, we regret to say, is of newspapers and broadcasting stations that are pulling the maximum out of their communities, and giving back the minimum in return. That is what, in contemporary parlance, is called a rip-off.[13]

Adam Smith would hardly have been surprised. He seemed to have understood that the guardian of the public interest was to be found not in the good nature of sellers but in the harsh mechanism of the competitive market.

Before recommending the use of a newly created weapon of competition policy to confront the fact of oligopoly, we should at least touch upon another sector and another approach: the land of the self-governing professions and occupations. Provincial governments have granted statutory power to license, govern, and control their members to each of some two dozen self-governing bodies. The findings and recommendations of the Ontario Royal Commission Inquiry into Civil Rights[14] will be relied upon to bring out the common concern and the inherent economic conflict be-

---

[12] *Ibid.*, p. 47.
[13] *Ibid.*, p. 63.
[14] Hon. J.C. McRuer, Commissioner, Ontario Royal Commission *Inquiry into Civil Rights*, 1968. Report Number One, Volume 3, Section 4, pp. 1159–1228, concerns self-governing professions and occupations.

tween sellers, no matter how professional, and buyers, no matter how carefully termed patients or clients.

> The granting of self-government . . . can only be justified as a safeguard to the public interest. The power is not conferred to give or reinforce a professional or occupational status. The relevant question is not, "do the practitioners of this occupation desire the power of self-government?", but "is self-government necessary for the protection of the public?" . . .
>
> It is not easy to see why powers of self-government, with all the possible monopolistic attributes, have been extended to some of the bodies covered by the enumerated statutes.[15] . . .
>
> The power of self-government is essentially the power to decide who shall be permitted to earn his living by the pursuit of a particular calling. . . .
>
> The right to control admission to a profession or occupation . . . and to issue licences . . . confers a power to control the number who may be admitted to it, as well as to ensure competence of its members. The power to set educational standards and prescribe training includes the power to exclude persons even though they may qualify to meet reasonable standards.

The Royal Commission makes, among many administrative and procedural ones, an unequivocal recommendation that lay members should be appointed by government to the governing bodies of all self-governing professions and occupations, pointing out that specialist expertise is not necessarily the same thing as the ability to perceive the public interest and to promote its just protection.

A final remark or two of the Commission can give us an illuminating background for a survey of a few recent increases in professional income levels.

> We have made it clear that the power to admit a licensee is not conferred to protect the economic welfare of the profession or occupation . . . What has to be guarded against is the power to license for purposes other than establishing and preserving standards of character, competence and skill. . . . the power . . . has real monopolistic attributes.

Changes in the incomes of individuals are a function of changes in the amounts, types, and prices of services performed. Consider Table 3, in which occupational groups are listed in order of their 1970 average incomes. As well as payments for occupational services, the incomes include interest, dividends, rents, etc. The latter are likely to be higher

---

[15] There are 22 such bodies listed, including architects, chiropodists, lawyers, medical doctors, nurses, pharmacists, public accountants, surveyors, etc.

Table 3: Average Net Income of Taxable Self-employed Professionals from all Sources and Average Income of all Taxable Employees from all Sources

Occupation	1960	1968	1969	1970
Physicians and Surgeons	$16,323	$29,181	$32,338	$34,757
Lawyers and Notaries	14,597	23,597	25,884	26,738
Dentists	12,238	20,164	21,773	22,794
Consulting Engineers and Architects	15,670	22,707	22,612	22,385
Accountants	11,446	17,002	18,038	19,303
Taxable Employees	4,021	5,665	6,047	6,454

Source: *Earnings of Physicians in Canada 1960–1970*, Health Care Series No. 29 (Ottawa: Department of National Health and Welfare), p. 4, Tables 4 and 5. Reproduced by permission of Information Canada.

for those individuals with more wealth, which in part at least depends on past saving (related to past income); this tends to reinforce income differences. Substantial increases in over-all demand for specific services would tend to raise prices to the extent that increases in the supply of those services (more individuals and/or more hours of work and/or more efficient delivery) would fail to keep pace with rising demand. The average income of each professional group, except consulting engineers and architects, rose more rapidly over the decade than that of all employees. The ten-year relative increases in the *numbers* in each profession were in the same rank order as the 1970 average incomes; all were less than the ten-year increase in all employees.

At least three economic issues are raised: Have any of these self-regulating professions maintained unduly high or inappropriate barriers to entry or failed to lower barriers that were already more than necessary for the adequate protection of the public? They do possess the power to impede responses to rising demand for their services.

Have self-determined fee increases been "reasonable"? Without price increases or with lesser ones, there might or might not have been "enough" entrants. Self-regulation confers some control over both supply and price. The usual composition of medical-care insurance commissions sustains any doubts: doctors are in a majority.

Were self-governing bodies active in support of attempts to improve the delivery and quality of services, or neutral, or resistant to efforts to accomplish more efficient delivery systems?

The crucial issue is that these markets give no guarantee of adequacy; the extent of control possessed and exercised by the sellers is unknown, but it is known that none specifically guards the interest of the public. To sum up with the viewpoint of an economist quoted very early in this essay:

> ... the public good takes precedence over the right of the individual to pursue his economic self-interest. Lurking in the background are two primary assumptions. The first is that there is no ground on which an individual can rest a claim to any natural

economic rights or economic privileges; all his economic rights are conferred on the individual by the community, including the right to retain the income earned by participating in the vast, cooperative, communal endeavour that constitutes the economy of a modern industrial state. The second is that political, economic, and social stability cannot be long sustained in a democratic state in which political power is widely diffused unless there is an acceptance by most members of the community of the ethical rule that the welfare of each has equal weight.[16]

IV. Performance Failures, Correcting Policies, and a New Approach

The preceding catalogue of difficulties leads us to consider:
—some performance failures in the Canadian economy
—some correcting policies, existing or officially recommended
—the role of the Canada Development Corporation.
We have not sought knaves nor found heroes. We have seen "victims" of our oligopoly world and now ask for ways to escape from the results.

That Canada's economic prospects are not as bright as we might wish them to be can be seen in Table 4, which shows Canada with the lowest projected gain in productivity among 15 selected industrial nations.[17] Confirmation of this sad forecast is found in another performance comparison of 10 countries (marked with an asterisk in Table 4), which reveals that Canada outperformed only Belgium in terms of numbers of patents taken out in foreign countries (1963), export performance in research-intensive industries (1963-65), and export performance in 50 research-intensive products,[18] all of which are indicators of technological advance and economic-growth potential. Given the oft-quoted argument that oligopolists (and some say especially multinational ones) promote more research and development, it is hard to imagine how little would have been carried out in Canada if previous policies had resulted in a less oligopolistic economy!

Table 4: Projected Productivity Index: 1980 (1970=100)

Japan*	236	Belgium*	150	Sweden*	137
France*	169	Norway	149	United States*	134
Italy*	159	Austria	148	United Kingdom*	133
West Germany*	154	Denmark	144	Switzerland	132
Finland	151	Netherlands*	141	Canada*	130

Source: Government of Ontario, *Report of the Interdepartmental Task Force on Foreign Investment* (Toronto: Department of Treasury and Economics, 1971), p. 19.

16 Moore, *op. cit.*, Preface, xiii–xiv.
17 Although the immediate concern of the Task Force (source of the table) was foreign investment, that might be simply one factor out of many. The indeterminate outcome of a highly oligopolistic economy casts doubt in all corners.
18 Keith Pavitt, "Performance in Technological Innovation in the Industrially Advanced Countries", in Maurice Goldsmith, ed., *Technological Innovation and The Economy* (London: Wiley-Interscience, 1970), p. 95, Table 1.

As it now stands, Canada is high in terms of oligopoly and multinational firms in its economy and low in research-and-development performance. The Canadian case would seem to argue persuasively against any general reliance on research and development being associated with market concentration. The Canadian experience seems to lend support to the idea that a joint monopoly, whether achieved by collusion or simply similar action by fellow oligopolists, is likely to be *less* innovative.

Existing corrective policy relies chiefly upon anti-combines legislation with its criminal-law basis. This has meant strict requirements of proof of guilt and narrow scope for coping with essentially economic problems. The courts have persistently declined to consider the economic effects of business arrangements brought before them. They have determined whether the arrangements have contravened the statute or not, and their judgments have not been influenced by the economic effects. The important service sector has remained outside the Combines Investigation Act. Selective tariff reductions have not been a policy, possibly because broader trade issues would need to be overriding. Although it is difficult to assess the deterrent aspect of a number of convictions arising from specific forms of conduct, it is fairly clear there has been almost no effect on the structure of the Canadian economy from the operation of the law. Continuing and increasing concentration exerts a persistent influence on firms in favour of patterns of conduct which are, to say the least, inimical to the free play of competition.

In advocating a more effective competition policy, the Economic Council of Canada, expressing its aversion to the cumbersome apparatus of government regulation or wholesale public ownership, recommended:[19]

general extension of competition-policy requirements to the service industries, with specific exemption granted only on the grounds that an adequately functioning alternative (*not* self-regulation) is in effect; retention of *per se* prohibition of several anti-competitive practices, which has heretofore been the main thrust of anti-combines lawsuits; establishment, on a civil-law basis, of a Competitive Practices Tribunal with power to approve, disapprove, or modify privately initiated mergers after an economic evaluation, and similarly to assess specialization and export agreements and certain trade practices not under a *per se* ban.

The odds seem high that these changes in approach to the improvement of malfunctioning markets would yield beneficial results. There remains, nonetheless, the nagging question, "is it at all reasonable to expect a significant alteration in the structure of Canadian industry in the foreseeable future?" Tinkering with the precise number of substantial firms in an industry will rarely alter an oligopolistic environment enough to make satisfactory price-output-profit relations an *assured* outcome.

A recently created enterprise may prove to be an effective means of harnessing oligopolies to improve over-all economic performance. The Canada Development Corporation (CDC) was established by Parliament in mid-1971 to "help develop and maintain strong Canadian controlled and

[19] Economic Council of Canada, *Interim Report on Competition Policy* (Ottawa: Queen's Printer, 1969).

managed corporations in the private sector of the economy".[20] Shareholdings in some successful Crown Corporations, such as Eldorado Nuclear Limited (nuclear fuels) and Polysar Limited (synthetic rubbers; prior to 1973 called Polymer Corporation Limited), were transferred to CDC at its inception. The CDC has the power to create businesses, invest in existing businesses, and acquire property. It is anticipated that there will be individual Canadian shareholders in the CDC, as well as the Government of Canada. In effect, it has begun as a state-owned conglomerate.

Although the CDC owes its origin to the increasing concern over foreign domination of key sectors in the economy, it could become an effective instrument for controlling general industry patterns by gaining in selected industries a leadership position, oligopoly style. Without bureaucratic apparatus, mutually interdependent group action could then be led along lines of public benefit toward the competitive norm and away from the monopoly goal. Its operational model seems to be the Italian Industrial Reconstruction Institute (IRI).[21] The productivity rankings on Table 4 should certainly direct our attention more to Japan, France, Italy, and West Germany and less to the United Kingdom and the United States, if we are truly seeking economic models with fine prospects.

IRI is Europe's largest market-disciplined public-enterprise group, employing in 1969 over 300,000 people and having sales of nearly $5 billion. It is a multi-sectoral conglomerate usually in competition with private firms. Many of its companies also have outside shareholders. It owns three of the largest national banks (one-fifth of Italian bank deposits), Alitalia, the main shipping companies, Italian radio and television, most of the nation's telephone and telecommunications systems, Alpha Romeo (manufacturer of sports cars and racing cars of the same name), etc. IRI produces three-fifths of the country's steel and builds over three-quarters of the ships. The IRI group is able to appreciate the inter-sectoral effects of innovation as they occur at operating company level and hence realize more of the innovation potential.

Its philosophy is to develop entrepreneurs rather than bureaucrats as the leaders of its companies. Within an over-all strategic framework, the individual IRI company leaders have wide operational autonomy. They use the yardstick of profits, but with a longer time horizon than would often be acceptable to private firms, and seem generally to maintain a high level of efficiency in a market environment.[22] The key point is that, by means of IRI, "the state as entrepreneur can mobilize the oligopolistic mechanisms concerned in its own and thus the public interest. Moreover, it can do so in a pre-emptive manner and on a continuing basis, rather than on occasion and after the infringement of competition has occurred."[23] Ninety percent of IRI's financial needs since World War II have been secured through the financial market, a more economical scheme than many

---

[20] An Act to Establish the Canada Development Corporation, 19–20 Elizabeth II, C. 49, S. 2.
[21] See Stuart Holland, ed., The State as Entrepreneur: New Dimensions for Public Enterprise: the IRI State Shareholding Formula (London: Weidenfeld and Nicolson, 1972).
[22] Ibid., pp. 47 and 54–55.
[23] Ibid., p. 36.

Canadian subsidy programs. IRI competes successfully with leading national and international companies and secures the maximum economic and social return for a given cost.[24]

The oligopoly issue is more critical in Canada than in Italy, and the Canada Development Corporation has had a more auspicious beginning than IRI's birth to avoid private-banking calamities in Italy in the 1930s. CDC is already creating a chemical-pharmaceutical corporation; this seems to be a route of high promise.[25] If CDC is promoted with government enthusiasm and boldness, instead of the reluctance and timidity that have too often characterized past anti-combines policy, it offers promise of a fresh approach. On the IRI model, it could play a critical role in key sectors, in the very industries that are the most highly concentrated oligopolies. As IRI avoided "nepotism, political placemanship, bureaucracy and corruption", so must and so can CDC, by the same means: capable leaders of integrity. The success of selective CDC participation in several industries will bring successes to the Canadian economy and will be "a tribute to the public spirit and good sense of a limited number of its leading personalities."[26]

---

[24] Ibid., pp. 53–54.
[25] See Edmonton Journal, 3 April 1973, p. 8. The chairman of CDC calls it "an opportunity to bring competitive pressure on the multinational corporations to rationalize their Canadian operations. ... social purpose plus monetary return."
[26] Holland, op. cit., p. 55.

2. Telecommunications And the Regulation of Public Utilities

Carl E. Beigie

C. D. Howe Research Institute

The doctrine of laissez-faire is still deeply imbedded in the minds of most Canadians when they consider the role of government in the economy. It is now universally accepted, of course, that the federal government does have the responsibility of ensuring the proper functioning of the economy at a macro level. The public expects monetary and fiscal policy tools to be used to keep unemployment down, to control inflation, and to maintain a sound international-payments position. These expectations have been difficult to meet, as is evident in the widespread concerns about inflation and unemployment during recent years. Still, there has been great progress during the postwar period in devising and using macroeconomic policy tools to moderate the violent swings in economic performance that were so characteristic of the past.

Government intervention in the *microeconomic* affairs of the nation is quite a different matter. So far as individual decisions and industry actions are concerned, the basic view persists that the government governs best that governs least. If an industry is to be subject to government regulation, that industry must be regarded as having very unique features that would prevent market forces from operating in the national interest. Probably because of the strength with which the free-market philosophy is held, however, the rationale for government intervention at a microeconomic level has not been well-formulated in Canada; few people understand the regulatory process, and most economists treat regulatory issues as a minor part of their training and teaching. It is not surprising, therefore, that government policies for regulating individual parts of the economy are much less refined than those for directing the course of the economy as a whole.

It is unfortunate that government regulation of industry has not received greater attention in Canada. For one thing, regulation is far more

186

common than is generally recognized, and it affects many major sectors of the economy. The focus here will be on regulation of the telecommunications industry in Canada, but regulation is also important in the transportation, banking, and energy sectors, to name just a few. Furthermore, government intervention is increasing in terms of both the number of industries regulated and the degree to which business activities are controlled. In any case, one does not have to go very far into the subject of regulation before realizing that it involves some very important and interesting issues in modern economics.

Telecommunications services constitute a public utility and thus provide an example of the most conventional type of government regulation. Contrary to the traditional view of public utilities as rather dull industries exhibiting little change over time, the telecommunications industry is going through a period of rapid technological change that has made it one of the key sectors in the so-called "post-industrial society." Technological change is affecting the industry to such a degree, in fact, that regulators are having a great deal of difficulty trying to cope with it.

In the following sections we will examine the basic structural features of the Canadian telecommunications industry, the various ways in which governments control the industry, and the key economic issues arising from this control in view of evolutionary developments taking place in the industry. Before turning to this specific task, however, it will be useful to take up the more general topics of the rationale for government regulation and the alternative methods of government control over industry activities.[1]

I.   Why Regulate?

There are essentially two reasons why governments choose to regulate certain industries rather than to allow the behaviour of firms in these industries to be determined by market forces alone. First, the basic economic characteristics of the industry are such that only a few firms can operate efficiently in that industry. In the extreme case, the market can support only one firm, a situation known as "natural monopoly." Second, the output of the industry is an "essential" good or service that government decides must be provided under conditions that are different from those that would occur in unregulated transactions. A combination of both these factors — limited opportunity for competition and designation of the output of the industry as essential — is found in industries conventionally classified as public utilities.

Competition is limited by the size of the market relative to "economies of scale" in the production process. If average costs are falling continually as output increases, at least within the range of output that is likely to be demanded in a given market, prices will drop until just one firm survives in the industry, assuming that there were more than one firm to begin with. Economies of scale are important in all public utilities, but this

---

[1] A good general text in the area is Charles F. Phillips, Jr., *The Economics of Regulation*, revised ed. (Homewood, Illinois: Richard D. Irwin, 1969). Recent developments in the theory of regulation can be found in the *Bell Journal of Economics and Management Science*.

is not the only factor limiting competition in these industries. An additional consideration is that government restricts entry of new firms in order to avoid duplication of facilities under the ground and along streets. Such duplication would cause unnecessary disruptions of city life, would involve wasted resources, and would raise the price of services to customers. Government restricts entry into these industries by requiring licenses to operate or, more frequently, by granting an exclusive franchise to a firm subject to certain constraints on its activities.

Competition, in the sense of numerous sellers with no single firm being able to control price, is the exception rather than the rule in Canadian industry. Automobiles, computers, and gasoline are only a few of the products sold under conditions of imperfect competition, but these industries escape regulation in the conventional sense. A feature that distinguishes public utilities is that everyone expects to be able to get the output of these firms, and at prices that are "reasonable." In practice, this means that public-utility companies must sell their output to all customers who want it at a common price, even though the cost of supplying different customers may vary over a wide range. In other words, regulation usually involves a degree of subsidization of some customers by others.

II. Methods of Regulation

Given that government is going to control a particular industry, there are a number of different approaches that might be adopted. One approach is government ownership, as in the case of provincial hydro companies, municipal water works, Air Canada, Canadian National Railways, and, as we shall see, certain telecommunications firms. The basis for choosing government versus private ownership is rarely discussed intelligently in Canada. It is hard to make a strong case for one over the other on strict economic grounds. The main reason for government ownership in most instances appears to be that government-owned firms follow practices — such as maintaining unremunerative activities — that privately owned firms could not continue without subsidies that might be hard to explain to the public politically. Also, there is the problem of knowing how much subsidization a private company would require. A secondary reason for government ownership is to provide revenue; but this assumes the operation is generating true profits over and above the cost of funds employed. It should be noted that most government-owned utilities in Canada are subject to regulation by public-utility commissioners.

Since competition is severely restricted in most regulated industries, government control of privately owned firms in these industries is designed to prevent the use of this privileged status to extract excessive profits from customers. This objective can be achieved directly through profit controls or indirectly through price controls. In practice, the most common method is to regulate prices with reference to an over-all rate-of-return target, although this target may consist of a range for permissible earnings and may be implicit rather than explicit in the regulatory process.

It should be noted that an alternative to price or profit regulation would be to allow the firm to charge what the traffic will bear and then to tax away all profits over and above the amount judged necessary to cover the firm's investment costs. This approach would be inconsistent with the view that public utilities provide essential services, and there is very little precedent in Canada for differential excess-profits taxes.

Other approaches to the regulation of public utilities include standards for and access to services, terms for interconnection with facilities of other companies, and rules for determining allowable expenses. An approach that is applied very infrequently, and then mainly in the field of broadcasting, involves variations in the terms of entry by a new firm into an industry, depending upon the performance of existing firms relative to government objectives. Another approach to governmental control that could be very effective in certain Canadian industries, selective tariff reductions to increase foreign competition, would be of limited value in the case of public utilities, since opportunities for trade are restricted by the nature of the services. Finally, anti-combines laws and other forms of competition policy could be applied to public utilities, but this would require that existing legislation in Canada be extended to cover services.

III. The Canadian Telecommunications Industry

In order to understand regulatory issues, it is useful to examine a particular regulated industry in some depth. This section will describe the basic organizational features of the Canadian telecommunications industry, the economics of telecommunications, and the process of technological change taking place in the industry.[2] In the next section we will review how the industry is regulated in Canada, and in the final section we will take a brief look at some economic-policy issues in the industry.

Telecommunications is defined simply as the art or science of communicating at a distance. Thus the postal system is, strictly speaking, a form of telecommunication, but conventional usage restricts the term to communication methods employing electrical transmissions. We are talking, therefore, about such services as telephone, telegraph, and broadcasting. Since broadcasting (radio and television) raises a unique set of issues, we will omit it from our discussion.

The Canadian telecommunications industry has historically been divided into telephone and telegraph companies. There are about two thousand telephone systems in Canada, but most of these are small rural co-operatives. In 1970 the fifteen largest telephone systems accounted for $5.865 billion of a total of $5.988 billion recorded as the cost of plant for all systems. Bell Canada dominates the industry, with $3.9 billion in plant

[2] As a result of recent government studies, there is now a wide range of documents dealing with the telecommunications industry in Canada. The Telecommission, a major study program undertaken by the Department of Communications, produced a series of published monographs on virtually all phases of the industry and its role in the nation's future development and a report entitled *Instant World: A Report on Telecommunications in Canada*, which was published in 1971. In March 1973, a position paper on policy issues involving the industry was published by the Minister of Communications, entitled *Proposals for a Communications Policy for Canada*. The relationships between communications and computers have been explored by the Canadian Computer/Communications Task Force, which issued a two-volume report, *Branching Out*, in May 1972. All the documents noted above are available from Information Canada.

in 1970, nearly six times that of British Columbia Telephone, the second largest.

The organizational structure of Canada's telephone industry differs considerably from that of the U.S. industry, where A. T. & T. (American Telephone and Telegraph) affiliates dominate in most regions of the country. Bell Canada, which serves Quebec, Ontario, and Labrador, is a federally chartered, investor-owned company, as is British Columbia Telephone. In Manitoba, Saskatchewan, and Alberta, telephone service is provided mainly by provincial crown corporations. Each of the Maritime provinces is served by a different provincially chartered, investor-owned company, although Bell Canada owns a controlling interest in New Brunswick Telephone and Newfoundland Telephone, and the majority of shares — although it can only vote one thousand of them because of provincial legislation — in Maritime Telephone (serving Nova Scotia), which, in turn, controls Island Telephone (serving Prince Edward Island).

In addition to these systems, there are municipally owned telephone companies in Edmonton and Thunder Bay. Also, Québec-Téléphone, Northern Quebec Telephone, and Northern Telephone (controlled by Bell) are among the larger systems in Canada.

Canada's telephone systems are owned by Canadians, for the most part. Contrary to popular belief, A. T. & T. owns less than 3 percent of Bell Canada's common shares. The major exceptions to Canadian ownership are British Columbia Telephone and Québec-Téléphone, which are owned by General Telephone and Electronics.

The telegraph industry in Canada is dominated by two large transportation conglomerates, Canadian National and Canadian Pacific, with several other small companies serving limited markets. CN-CP Telecommunications shares the bulk of the market, with CN concentrating in the eastern provinces and CP in the western provinces. CN, of course, is a federal crown corporation, and CP is a federally incorporated, investor-owned firm. Their combined gross telecommunications plant and equipment amounted to $435 million in 1970.

Telecommunications services can be divided into two broad classes — switched network (or public message in the case of telegraph) and private line. Switched-network service is what most people are familiar with, since it connects telephones throughout the country — and, indeed, the world. Private-line service provides a continuous telecommunications link between two or more locations. Telephone companies have an effective monopoly in this service in the regions they serve. The only alternatives a customer has to the telephone for communicating over distance are telegrams and letters, which allow no instantaneous response and, in the extreme, travel to the person with whom communication is desired. Telephone and telegraph companies do compete in the private-line market, which basically consists of large users such as government and business, and in the teletypewriter market, which is really a special type of switched-network service.

Telephone companies are responsible for providing all switched-network services within the territories they serve. All local calls and those toll (long-distance) calls originating and terminating within a given territory are therefore carried over facilities owned by a single company, with minor exceptions. When toll calls are made between customers in adjacent territories, the rates charged and the division of revenues received are worked out by the two companies involved. When toll calls are made between companies that do not serve adjacent territories, service is supplied through agreements reached within the Trans-Canada Telephone System (TCTS).

The TCTS has eight full members, including the main telephone company in each province except Prince Edward Island (Bell Canada represents both Quebec and Ontario). This organization is a consortium with no independent legal status. It sets nationwide price schedules for services involving non-adjacent territories and serves as a co-ordinating body for most phases of the industry. It is also responsible for co-ordinating traffic between Canada and foreign destinations. Overseas traffic is carried over facilities owned by the Canadian Overseas Telecommunications Corporation, a federal crown corporation that is an associate member of TCTS. All decisions reached by the TCTS require unanimous approval of the eight full members.

Two aspects of the organizational structure of the Canadian telecommunications industry merit special attention. First, telephone companies have traditionally adopted very restrictive conditions on access to the switched-network system, basing these restrictions on the need to maintain the technical "integrity" of the system. It is difficult for potential entrants into the industry — such as firms wishing to provide mobile phone service — to obtain interconnection privileges. The telephone companies go so far as to prohibit cable-television companies from owning the cables that are carried on the poles and in the conduits of the telephone companies; instead, they have to rent these cables. Also, potential suppliers of specialty phone sets have been impeded from selling these phones by the telephone companies' rules against "foreign attachments" to switched-network services.

Second, vertical integration is an important policy issue in the industry. Bell Canada owns the Northern Electric Company, the dominant supplier of telecommunications equipment in Canada. It has been charged that this ownership link may give rise to excessive prices being charged to Bell on its equipment purchases, that it limits the potential for competition in the telecommunications-equipment industry, and that it enables Bell to extend the scope of its monopoly power. These charges are long-standing and have been the subject of government inquiry over the years, but no action has been taken to modify the Bell-Northern relationship.

Few industries can match the complexity of telecommunications economics. The industry is by nature complex, but additional complicating factors arise from the way firms in the industry behave. A good way to approach the economics of the industry is to consider five characteristics of telecommunications in relation to the traditional treatment of the firm in introductory and intermediate economics texts.

First, it is conventionally assumed that an individual's demand for a firm's product is independent of any other individual's demand for that product. In other words, if a person buys more or less of a product, this will not cause other consumers' demand to shift. In telecommunications the value of switched-network service, which is the dominant source of revenue in the industry, is affected by the total number of parties that take the service and can therefore be reached. Thus, individuals' demand curves are interdependent. One of the complications raised by this interdependence is that a customer might be willing to pay part of another customer's service costs in order to have access to that party over the switched network.

Second, the average-cost curve for a firm is usually drawn with a U shape, indicating that unit costs initially fall but eventually rise with increases in output. In the transmission-trunking phase of telecommunications, which is the key phase in long-distance services, economies of scale are significant, at least at existing traffic levels on most routes in Canada. Economies of scale differ markedly in other phases of the telecommunications process. When economies of scale are present, the efficiency rule of equating price to marginal cost would require the firm to operate at a loss. The reason is that the marginal-cost curve is always below the (falling) average-cost curve. Hence, price equal to marginal cost implies that average cost exceeds price (average revenue).

Third, it is standard practice to treat the firm as a seller of a single product. This approach is appropriate when different products can be standardized into equivalent units of a single product or when separate facilities are used to make each product. In telecommunications, however, the same facilities are used to carry a wide variety of services, ranging from voice messages to television transmissions. Furthermore, firms in the industry increase the multi-product nature of their operations through service differentiation. The problems that are raised by multi-product output from common facilities relate to the determination of an appropriate pricing structure for these products. These problems are especially difficult when economies of scale are also present.

Fourth, most introductory texts treat the "long run" as being a fairly distinct period of time — usually relatively short by implication — during which the firm can adjust all factors of production to changing circumstances. The long run is very long in the telecommunications network. Capital equipment is very durable, on average, and changes in the capital stock are made in relatively small increments each year. Thus technological change must be introduced gradually and subject to the requirement that new equipment be compatible with old equipment unless a completely new service is being introduced.

Fifth, public utilities other than telecommunications are essentially one-way systems — a customer takes gas, water, or electricity from a distributor, but he does not put anything into the system. Telecommunications services involve two-way systems, at least in the case of messages carried over the switched network, since customers send and receive information. As a result, telecommunications companies must enforce standards to protect the system from abuse, and there is a problem in determining whether these standards are legitimate protection mechanisms or merely forms of unfair competition to restrict entry.

Technological change is making the telecommunications industry more complicated, especially from the standpoint of effective government regulation.[3] There are essentially three types of economic issues arising from the technological changes that are affecting telecommunications.

First, technology is changing the basic structure of the industry and altering the basis of competition among firms. It was formerly true that a fairly sharp distinction could be made between telephone and telegraph companies. Now, however, basic facilities, especially in long-distance transmission, have become more flexible in terms of the services they can provide. Therefore, telephone and telegraph companies are increasingly in direct competition with each other and with firms that might wish to enter certain phases of the industry.

Second, customers are placing greater demands on the industry in terms of service requirements. The rapid growth in computerization of the economy, for example, has increased the use of telecommunications for data transmission. One set of questions that is raised by this development is what prices and other terms of service should be established for non-voice use of the network. Another set of questions concerns the extent to which telecommunications firms should be permitted to extend their operations from simply transmitting information to storing information in data banks or modifying information *via* computer services.

Third, technology is affecting the relative cost of providing different telecommunications services. In particular, the cost of providing local service is rising in relation to the cost of long-distance service as a result of advances in transmission technology. Since local service is regarded by regulators as an essential service, however, rate schedules are slow to adjust to changes in relative costs, and certain users of the network have been adversely affected by the fact that the charges they bear have had to finance the subsidization of other users.

IV. Telecommunications Regulation in Canada

The telecommunications industry is a most unconventional industry, but it is regulated as a conventional public utility in Canada. After reviewing who does the regulation, we will discuss briefly how telecommunications firms are regulated and what important aspects of these firms' activities are not regulated.

Federally chartered telecommunications companies are regulated by the Canadian Transport Commission (CTC). This category of firms includes Bell Canada, British Columbia Telephone, and CN-CP Telecommunications. Provincially chartered companies are regulated by public-utilities commissions in the respective provinces, although the government-owned system in Saskatchewan is not regulated in the conventional sense. The only form of national control over the entire industry that now exists in Canada is exercised by the federal Department of Communications. This department must approve the construction of facilities using the airwaves as a transmission medium — e.g., microwave systems — but it has no control over such facilities as wires and cables. The members of the Trans-Canada

---

[3] The role of technology is explored in William M. Capron, ed., *Technological Change in Regulated Industries* (Washington, D.C.: The Brookings Institution, 1971.)

Telephone System are regulated individually, but the TCTS as an entity is not regulated.

The mechanics of regulation vary somewhat among regulatory jurisdictions, but basic procedures are the same. Since Bell Canada is the largest firm in the industry, we will examine how it is regulated by the CTC.

To begin with, Bell Canada's charter places certain restrictions on its activities. The company may not, for example, own a cable-television system. Also, it is obliged by its charter to provide telephone service on demand in the territory it serves, subject to certain limitations, and the charter states that this service must be the "latest improved design in use in the locality at that time." All of Bell Canada's telecommunications services are regulated.

The broad outlines of regulation are as follows. Either Bell Canada or the CTC may initiate a request for a rate hearing. At this hearing, evidence is presented by the company and other interested parties in support of, or in opposition to, changes in the rates charged by the company. The test that is used to determine the issue is whether or not the rates are "reasonable." There are no rigid criteria that can be used to determine reasonableness, but most public-utility rate hearings eventually get around to the question of the return the company is earning on its rate base with existing prices and how much it could be expected to earn if these prices were altered.

Rate-of-return decisions are complicated and involve subjective judgments on the part of the regulator. The basic procedure begins with a deduction of allowable operating expenses from operating revenues. Then a rate base is determined on the basis of either the assets or the liabilities of the company. A rate of return is then calculated by dividing net revenues by the rate base. Finally, an attempt is made to compare this rate of return with the rates of return being earned by comparable companies, comparability being evaluated basically in terms of the risk associated with the companies' activities. If it is determined that the company is, or is likely to be, earning a rate of return that is too low, it is permitted to increase its service charges in a manner approved by the regulator.

One of the complexities of rate hearings, especially in periods of inflation, concerns the valuation of the rate base. Should the firm's capital stock be valued at the original cost of purchasing it or the cost of replacing it? The CTC uses original cost, but methods vary widely in different public-utilities commissions.

In terms of the issues raised by telecommunications regulation in Canada, it is important to note what is not regulated or what is only loosely regulated. There are three broad areas that are especially significant.

First, there is far more attention given to the mechanics of regulation than to the structure of the industry that is being regulated. Very little attention has been paid, for example, to the conditions of entry into various phases of the industry or of expansion in the range of activities that telecommunications firms are permitted to undertake.

Second, prices for services are examined in terms of "value of service" — meaning the worth of the service to the customer — rather than in terms of the cost of providing the service. Value of service is a subjective concept that may result in prices that cause marked inefficiencies in resource allocation.

Third, regulators pay very little attention to such "discretionary" cost items as advertising and research and development (R & D), or to the results produced by these expenditures. Thus it has been charged that waste may be encouraged by a system that transfers unproductive expenditures into higher service costs. It might also be argued that regulators do not pay enough attention to the importance of R & D expenditures in an industry undergoing rapid technological change.

V. Issues in Telecommunications Regulation

Canada has one of the best telecommunications industries in the world, and performance has been getting even better in relation to most other countries. Therefore, the issues raised by current regulatory methods concern potential barriers to a continuation of the superior performance of the past and possible areas of improvement in the future.

Before examining these issues briefly, it should be stressed that public pressures have at least as much impact as regulation on the behaviour of a major telecommunications firm. Economists have been slow to incorporate the fact that major companies do worry a great deal about their "image," when they analyze how firms behave. In fact, experience in the telecommunications industry in Canada indicates that firms are often quicker to resolve issues than regulators are to identify them. This is not to say, however, that the management's concept of the national interest necessarily matches the nation's best interests.

Telecommunications serves the function in advanced industrial countries that railways and roads served in the initial development of these countries. One of the basic issues in Canadian telecommunications is the pace of technological development and the rate at which new developments are made available to the public. This issue is especially important in view of the way in which regulation has lagged in responding to inflation, making it difficult for telecommunications firms to obtain funds for expansion.

A related issue concerns the fact that the cost of new services may delay the spread of these services throughout the economy. In the past, telephone development was maximized by charging very low rates for basic residence service and making up the difference on other services. Is this approach appropriate now in view of the fact that high-cost services may retard such developments as nation-wide data banks and teleprocessing of data, instead of merely transferring income from one group of customers to another as was true in the past?

In terms of the structure of the industry, two primary issues concern the extent of competition in long-distance transmission and the conditions under which telecommunications carriers should be allowed to enter such fields as cable television and computer services. On the first point, we need more information than is now available on economies of scale to make judgments. The second point gets us into the question of whether regulatory procedures can be developed that will ensure that regulated firms do not use their monopoly positions to gain an unfair advantage over competitors in new fields.

It is clear that regulation and other forms of government control over the telecommunications industry are going to have to become far more sophisticated if this control is to respond to the issues that have arisen in this industry. There is a strong case for increasing government participation in and support for technological research in the industry, as research will play an increasingly important role in the evolution of the Canadian economy. It is also worth exploring whether outright government subsidies might not be appropriate for encouraging the use of advanced telecommunications equipment on as wide a scale as possible.

Issues in regulatory procedures are more mechanical, but no less important. Economists in Canada need to devote more attention to these issues, but the essential requirement is to incorporate sound economic analysis in decisions affecting government control of industries in general and of telecommunications in particular.

3. Models, Markets, and Medical Care

Robert G. Evans

University of British Columbia

At first glance, the Canadian medical-services market appears to present the symptoms of a textbook case in market analysis. Rapidly rising prices and costs of care are associated with widespread perceptions by consumers of a "physician shortage" and a steady increase over time in the demand for medical care.[1] Increases in demand are traceable to increases in consumer income and education, changes in technology, and the spread of medical insurance culminating in the 1968 Medicare legislation.[2] Since both demand for and supply of medical services are relatively price-inelastic, at least in the short run, the above set of observations fits neatly into a straightforward demand-and-supply analysis with concrete policy implications for improving the structure of Canada's Medicare program and mitigating the medical-care crisis. The only problem with the analysis is that it is wrong.

It is worth tracing through the standard model, however, since it is important to understand *why* the analysis is wrong. Much of the rather confused debate over what is wrong with the organization of medical care

[1] Data on personal health-care expenditures, medical-care expenditures, and physician distribution and income are prepared annually by province by the Department of National Health and Welfare, Research and Statistics Directorate, and issued irregularly as Research and Statistics Memoranda. Physician distribution and income data are now published annually in the periodic Health Care Series, the most recent being *Earnings of Physicians in Canada, 1960–1970*. The same source prepares but does not publish price data on a provincial basis.

[2] The federal Medical Care Act of 1968 provides a framework within which the federal government will pay (approximately) half the cost of any provincially established medical-insurance plan. To be eligible for such cost sharing, the provincial plan must be universal, comprehensive (federal rules determine "shareable" and "non-shareable" benefits), portable across provinces, and open on "equal terms and conditions" to all provincial residents. "Equal terms" includes both charges for participation and access to physicians. By 1971 all provinces had established such plans.

and how (or whether) it should be restructured is debate over alternative models, or stylizations, of the reality of consumer and supplier behaviour in the medical-care market. Reality is, as usual, too varied and too complex to be adequately analyzed, or even described. Hence it must be abstracted and simplified, represented by a model or theoretical structure which, while deficient in detail, seeks to convey the essential characteristics of the market process. The trouble is that if you get the theory wrong, the conclusions and the policy recommendations may well come out backwards. And this is the problem with the "textbook" analysis of medical care — it suppresses the essential characteristics of the medical market and is thus the wrong theory. In this article, I shall first outline the standard case, then show why and how it breaks down, and finally suggest an alternative model which I believe to be more "realistic." The policy conclusions of this model will stand in obvious contrast to the "textbook case."

I. The Standard Demand/Supply Model

The crucial abstraction of conventional analysis is the separation of consumer and supplier behaviour into demand-side and supply-side, with each side of the market influencing the other only through the price variable. We are thus able to define demand and supply curves, relating quantities demanded and supplied by each market participant to the current market price, holding all other factors constant. It is further assumed that bidding by suppliers and demanders will lead to an equilibrium price where quantity supplied equals quantity demanded. In the case of medical care it is argued on both *a priori* and empirical grounds that the price-elasticity of demand is relatively small, that is, a given percentage change in the price of medical services will lead to a less than equal percentage change in total quantity demanded.[3] The supply curve is similarly believed to be price-inelastic, due to the long time-lags involved in training new physicians and the relatively limited substitution of capital or other personnel for physicians. If this description correctly characterizes the medical market, then an increase in demand (rightward shift in the demand schedule) would lead to relatively large increases in price and cost, and relatively small increases in quantity of output, as shown in Figure 1. As demand increases, because of increases in income and education, population per supplier, age of population, etc., price must be bid up to draw more services from a relatively static group of suppliers, or, alternatively, to choke off the increase in demand. Since neither suppliers nor demanders are very price-sensitive, large changes are necessary to influence their behaviour. As the demand curve shifts from D_1D_1 to D_2D_2, price and quantity rise from P_1q_1 to P_2q_2, and total expenditures escalate rapidly. The same phenomenon is consistent with a rightward-moving sup-

[3] A comprehensive review of demand studies is C. Lloyd, "The Demand for Medical Care: A Selective Review of the Literature," University of Iowa Bureau of Business and Economic Research, Working Paper 71–2, January 1971. More recently, J. Newhouse, C. Phelps, and M. Thompson, "Price and Income Elasticities for Medical Care", Rand Corporation mimeo, 1972, gives reference to other recent studies besides providing additional results.

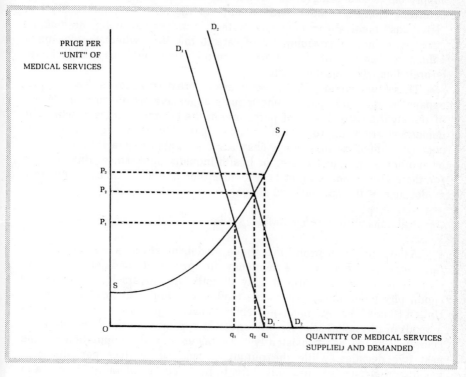

Figure 1

ply curve so long as demand is shifting (due to increases in population and per *capita* demand) faster than supply (due to increases in physician stock and productivity). If a public insurance plan is introduced, consumers effectively pay nothing for care, and if the demand curve was previously D_1D_1, the quantity demanded will now shift to q_3, the zero-price point on that curve. Price will rise to encourage suppliers to increase output. Shortages and rationing (queuing and patient selection) will allocate supply until the price reaches a new equilibrium level (if there is one) at P_3; and physicians will complain of excessive demands on their time while their incomes soar upward. The correspondence between this set of predictions and commonly observed medical-market phenomena makes the model very appealing.[4]

The prescriptions inherent in this model are relatively straightforward.

[4] This model appears in D. North and R. Miller, *The Economics of Public Issues* (New York: Harper and Row, 1971), ch. 9, "The Economics of Medical Care." Furthermore, it underlies most discussions of co-insurance and the welfare burden of medical insurance, particularly M. Pauly, *Medical Care at Public Expense* (New York: Praeger, 1971), and "A Measure of the Welfare Cost of Health Insurance", *Health Services Research*, Winter 1969.

If prices are to be restrained and shortages alleviated, then either supply must expand or demand must contract (or both). This involves training more physicians and/or substitutes for physicians, so as to move out the supply curve and bring prices down and re-introducing various forms of deterrent charges imposed on patients to discourage "unnecessary" or "frivolous" medical-care demand. Note that movement along the demand curve to q_3 implies consumption of care to the point where the consumer values the last unit of care at almost zero — this could reasonably be interpreted as frivolous demand!

These two broad policy themes are of great importance. The supply-expansion approach may be enormously expensive, as physicians are one of the most costly classes of personnel in the economy to train, while the demand-restraint approach amounts to a partial dismantling of the whole concept of medical insurance. They are both urged regularly in one form or another by political figures or health-industry spokesmen. But the case for their effectiveness must be rooted either implicitly or explicitly in a model such as the one outlined above.

II. Problems with the "Textbook" Model

As we begin to probe the above model, however, a number of odd facts emerge. There was a tendency for prices of medical services in Canada prior to Medicare to vary directly, not inversely, with the *per capita* physician stock.[5] The same tendency is apparent in studies in the United States.[6] Yet the inelastic demand curve requires that high prices be a result of physician scarcity. Moreover, it appears that the stock of physicians in Canada has consistently risen faster than the population for the past two decades, while the output of medical services per physician has likewise risen at a dramatic rate, in part because of rapid increases in the stock of capital equipment and personnel at each physician's disposal.[7] In other words, the supply curve in Canada has moved outward at a rate 2 to 3 percent a year faster than the demand curve, if the latter were driven by population alone. Moreover, in spite of increases in life expectancy, the proportion of Canada's population in the aged, high-demand years has not increased significantly in 20 years. Add to this the dramatic drop in birth-rates and the consequent fall in numbers of obstetrical cases and very young children, and it appears that on demographic grounds alone the demand curve may have moved leftward. Of course, unmeasured changes in "tastes" may have led to rightward shifts in spite of this, just as people in high-physician-density provinces may be sicker than in low-

---

[5] R. Evans, *Price Formation in the Market for Physicians' Services in Canada: 1957–69*. A study prepared for the Prices and Incomes Commission (Ottawa: Information Canada, 1973), ch. 3.
[6] See M. Feldstein, "The Rising Price of Physicians' Services", *Review of Economics and Statistics*, May 1970, and J. Newhouse, "A Model of Physician Pricing", *Southern Economic Journal*, October 1970.
[7] Evans, *op. cit.*, chs. 1 and 3.

density ones, but these explanations have a certain *ad hoc* flavour.[8] Moreover, the latter argument says that high prices of physician care in Ontario indicate relatively high demand and a greater "shortage" there; so ideally we should allocate physicians *away* from low-density, low-price provinces like Saskatchewan and New Brunswick to Ontario and British Columbia!

Further puzzles emerge on looking at more detailed data. The "shifts in demand" which are supposed to have driven up prices of medical care are most heavily concentrated among consultations, diagnostic tests, and hospital procedures — activities initiated by physicians. Physician–patient contacts initiated by patients, such as home or office first visits, have risen relatively slowly in the past fifteen years.[9] Where dramatic changes have taken place, as in the substitution of office for home visits, no significant change in relative prices has occurred. Tests of deterrent fees in Saskatchewan suggest that while deterrents may reduce utilization overall, their effect is heavily concentrated on low-income people and that for large groups of high-income people "deterrents" lead to utilization *increases*.[10] Finally, it has been shown that the workload of physicians in different regions of a province all working under a common fee schedule is relatively insensitive to the number of physicians available per head of population. This indicates that physicians may be able to generate enough work to keep themselves busy despite large fluctuations in physician/population ratios.[11]

In summary, the empirical evidence suggests that physicians have a considerable degree of influence over the total volume and the composition of the work they perform, and can thus shift the demand curve right or left at any given level of prices. This influence is, of course, much stronger over physician-initiated classes of procedures and is probably increased by the introduction of universal insurance. Thus when physicians wish to discourage house-calls, for example, they do not simply raise the fee for such calls until demand is restricted. Rather, they refuse to perform this service and call the patient to the office instead. When a deterrent fee in Saskatchewan reduces patient-initiated contacts, the volume of work done for less-price-sensitive upper-income groups expands as physicians move their "demand curves" rightward. In short, physicians control their own demand.

[8] The concept of shifting "tastes" refers to changes in attitudes toward and perceptions of health care. It is also possible that shifts in *private* insurance coverage prior to Medicare might have led to rapid expansion in demand and upward price pressure. Unfortunately for this hypothesis, *per capita* health expenditures by persons insured through non-profit service-benefit plans were less than 5 percent above national average *per capita* expenditures throughout the period 1957–67. (Data drawn from annual reports of Trans-Canada medical plans and personal-health-care-expenditures tabulations of the Department of National Health and Welfare, presented in Evans, *op cit.*, ch. 2.)

[9] Evans, *op. cit.*, ch. 4.

[10] R. Beck, *An Analysis of the Demand for Physicians' Services in Saskatchewan*, unpublished Ph.D. dissertation, Edmonton, 1971.

[11] R. Evans, E. Parish and F. Sully, "Medical Productivity, Scale Effects, and Demand Generation", *Canadian Journal of Economics*, August 1973. This finding is also consistent with an absolute shortage of physicians, each working at full stretch, and turning away patients. If so, why do prices not rise faster? Moreover, if such absolute shortages exist in areas such as Vancouver, with 30 percent more physicians *per capita* than the national average, how can such a shortage ever be met? In any case, there exist data on physician-practice patterns inconsistent with the shortage idea.

The "abstraction" which models the physician market by suppressing physician/patient interaction and focusing only on price has ignored the essential nature of the professional relationship. The patient demanding medical services is subject to ignorance and uncertainty to such a degree that he delegates to the physician the choice of what services to purchase — whether medical, hospital, pharmaceutical, or other health services. The patient is more or less ignorant of his own condition, the capacity of technology to alleviate his condition, and the competence of any given supplier to apply that technology competently. Hence he consults a professional who is to choose on his behalf. This description is, of course, also an abstraction, since many patients are much better informed and cost sensitive than the standard medical model of "doctors' orders" assumes. But it is an abstraction which is closer to the essence of the professional relation than a model in which the patient consults his symptoms and obtains price quotes from the various medical suppliers available, then "places his order" without asking for any substantive information about his condition or cure. And yet it is just such a model of the "informed consumer", adjusting his demand for medical care in response to price signals so as to optimize his own health status subject to budget constraints, which underlies the argument for deterrent fees. Similarly, a "profit-maximizing" physician, telling his patients nothing but his price (since they know everything else) and independently raising or lowering his prices to contract or expand his patient flow, lurks behind the argument that price and cost increases result from shortage and can be curtailed by increasing the supply. If he is implausible, so is the policy recommendation.

III.   An Alternative Model of the Medical Market

In proposing an alternative model, we shift attention from the price of medical services to the incomes of service suppliers — particularly physicians. This is the variable which physicians themselves appear to regard as fundamental to the price-setting process.[12] Physicians' incomes depend on the price of their services, the quantity of work they do, and the expenses of their practice. Since we are interested in the price and quantity of medical services made available, we can disregard the latter factor by assuming that physicians try to run their practices as efficiently as possible, so that expenses of practice are determined by volume of workload. The assumption that physicians can vary their own workload at any given price level implies that price and quantity are independently variable, whereas the "demand-curve" concept constrains the supplier to choose either quantity or price, his choice of a value for one variable determining the value of the other.

If both are variable, then the physician can attain his desired income level by raising either his prices or his workload. The former, however,

---

[12] This is substantiated in the *Task Force Reports on the Cost of Health Services in Canada*, Vol. III, "The Price of Medical Care" (Ottawa: Queen's Printer, 1969), and in D. Gellman, "Medicare, Medical Income Disparities and Fee Schedule Changes: Facts, Fallacies, Problems, and Positions", *Canadian Medical Association Journal*, Sept. 18, 1971, as well as in numerous references in the medical press and private conversation.

will be constrained in Canada by the procedures for revision of fee schedules and the informal pressures brought to bear by provincial insurance agencies. Thus, no one physician can move his prices up beyond his colleagues unless (in certain provinces only) he charges his patients directly; and the rate of adjustment of province-wide fee schedules is slowed by political action.[13] No *economic* restraint prevents physicians as a group from setting prices so as to gain any income target they choose, but in the short run there may be delays in price increases. A similar sort of mechanism appears to work in the United States, as physicians price according to "usual and customary" regional fees, but opportunities for individual discretion are, of course, greater.[14]

In Canada, the individual physician can vary his workload, by rationing services to patients or by directly stimulating demand for certain services. His ability to do this, however, is constrained by the amount of his own time he is willing to work, and how thin he is willing to spread his time across his patients. Physicians differ greatly in their willingness to work extra hours or speed up "patient processing" in order to generate extra incomes.

Thus each physician will adjust his own workload, subject to a given fee schedule, in order to attain his target income. If his target cannot be attained without an unacceptable number of working hours or patients per hour, he will seek upward revisions in the fee schedule. When a "sufficiently large" group of physicians agree that upward revision is necessary, fee schedules are re-drafted. At this point the price revision becomes a political question. The process does not appear to be self-limiting in the absence of political intervention, however, since the target incomes of physicians have risen fast enough to keep their actual incomes rising relative to the Canadian average by 43.4 percent from 1957 to 1970.[15]

If the supply of physicians is increased, such a model predicts that each physician's income and workload will tend to fall. Each physician will respond to this drop by increasing his efforts to generate demand. If he is unable to restore his old output level, he will seek price increases. This is consistent with observations that prices are higher where physician densities are higher and that workloads are lower but not proportionate to differences in density.[16] Thus expanding output of physicians will drive

---

[13] A distinction must be drawn between billing of the patient arising because the provincial agency pays only 85 or 90 percent of the Medical Association fee schedule, and extra billing over and above the fee schedule. Regulations differ, and some changes have occurred since the plans were initiated. In general, physicians may extra-bill above the fee schedule (except in Quebec) and still submit a bill at the schedule rate to the public authority, providing the patient has been notified in advance and (in some provinces) written consent obtained. Alternatively, they may refuse to participate in the provincial plan and bill the patient directly for any amount they choose; the patient may then seek reimbursement from the plan up to the approved rate (again, excepting Quebec). The physician may not, however, split bills, sending, say, 90 percent to the public agency and billing 10 percent to the patient; this Ontario practice of the early years of the plan has been disallowed. "Informed observers" have asserted that over-billing of whatever form is uncommon in Canada, although no data have been collected.

[14] See U. Reinhardt, *An Economic Analysis of Physicians' Practices*, unpublished Ph.D. dissertation, Yale, 1970.

[15] Evans, *Price Formation*, ch. 3.

[16] *Ibid.*

total output, prices, and costs *up,* not down. Similarly, deterrent fees, such as a token charge for each physician visit, will tend to reduce workloads and incomes.[17] Physicians will respond by stimulating new demand (hence the observation that for higher-income groups in Saskatchewan utilization *rose* with deterrent fees) and trying to negotiate higher prices. (Saskatchewan's deterrents coincided with a major fee-schedule revision.) The final result will be less medical care provided at higher prices.

IV. Conclusion

The above treatment has left many important considerations untouched. Is more medical care "needed" or not? Is there really a physician shortage, and how could one measure it? What technical scope is there for the substitution of lower-cost personnel for physicians, and what would this do to the quality of care (if we knew how to measure it)?

The main theme is that the medical market violates two crucial assumptions fundamental to the use of the supply-and-demand market model — the independence of supply and demand, and the adjustment of price in response to market shortages or surpluses. Its behaviour is thus inadequately described by that model, and policy measures based on such a model will be inappropriate and harmful. An alternative model, which appears to be more successful in rationalizing observed behaviour, emphasizes the discretionary power of physicians over demand, and the consequent difficulty of modifying their behaviour through conventional market forces.

This alternative model is offered as a more "realistic" way of abstracting from a complex real world — the choice of a correct model is not a black-and-white problem, since it is possible to construct a number of models each containing some degree of validity. Model-builders are rather like the seven blind men studying an elephant. Nevertheless, the choice of model *is* important — in this case the "conventional" supply/demand model declares that rising medical prices are due to increases in demand and can be corrected by either expansion of supply or re-imposition of point-of-service charges to patients. The alternative model identifies rising prices as due to shifts in physicians' income aspirations and increases in supply, and predicts that expanding physician stock or introducing deterrent charges will escalate the increase. What policy recommendations can one draw from the alternative model?

Medical-care costs in Canada are currently measured (with some modifications) as the product of the stock of fee-practice physicians and the average gross receipts per physician. Since the physician stock is growing relative to the population, and the average physician's gross receipts are growing relative to average community incomes (receipts net of expenses are growing still faster), both factors lead to an increase in expenditure on physician services. To a large extent, increases in physician incomes

---

[17] This assumes that the charge is collected by the physician from the patient without an increase in the physician's total fee. If such a charge were added onto the existing fee structure, a price increase would be combined with the deterrent charge and physicians' incomes would probably rise.

appear to be due to price increases.[18] If the expansion of medical expenditures is to be moderated, the rates of increase of physician stock, or incomes, must be slowed.

If the physician stock is to grow less rapidly, then either real medical services must be expanded less rapidly, or physicians must individually work harder, or substitutes must be trained. The first option is probably fine in theory, since a certain degree of "overdoctoring" is believed to be taking place;[19] but there is no reason to believe that simply reducing the physician stock would selectively eliminate only the "unnecessary" care. The second option is unlikely, if we believe physician hours-of-work studies. Thus we are left with the use of substitutes. There is much evidence that large parts of a physician's practice can in fact be handled by more specialized and less-highly-trained personnel, but under fee-for-service private-practice medicine this substitution takes places only to a very limited extent. The problem of the substitution of personnel turns out to be bound up with that of the organization of medical practice — extensive use of physician substitutes appears to require forms of medical organization which are not reimbursed by fee-for-service and are not practitioner-managed. This is part of the message of the Hastings Report and the Castonguay-Nepveu Commission.[20]

If we look at billings per physician, we find that, here too, present forms of organization of medical practice make moderation of the steady climb in absolute and relative incomes difficult and probably self-defeating. Limitation of fee schedules leads to procedural redefinition and expansion of workload in order to keep incomes rising. The latter method creates side-effects of increased hospital costs and non-monetary costs to the patient. Moreover, under present arrangements provinces can only limit what the insurance plan will pay — medical associations may choose to set fee schedules above this level and advise their members to charge the difference directly to the patient. Scaling-down fee payments to high-income physicians merely reallocates incomes within the medical profession; it does not influence trends over time. Fixed annual pools of funds, such that physicians are reimbursed for a portion of their bills equal to the ratio of the total reimbursement pool to the total volume of bills submitted by all physicians, encourage the same multiplication of procedures[21] as limitations of fees, except that in the short run total *medical* costs may be controlled. Thus consideration of physicians' price and income patterns again leads to the conclusion that private fee-for-

---

[18] "Appear" is emphasized because of the difficulty of measuring output quantity. See Evans, *Price Formation*, ch. 1.

[19] Unnecessary surgery is a widespread problem, particularly tonsillectomy, while the rapid expansion of diagnostic procedures is also frequently criticized.

[20] *The Community Health Centre in Canada*, Report of the Community Health Centre Project (Hastings Report), July 1972, and *Report of the Commission of Inquiry on Health and Social Welfare*, Quebec, 1967.

[21] Procedural multiplication covers several sorts of activities. For example, physicians can speed up patient throughput by short initial visits with frequent recalls. They can bill separately for injections, lab tests, supplies, and materials normally included in a visit charge. They can keep patients in the hospital so they can submit a bill each day they walk past a bed. They can redefine partial examinations as general, raising the fee code, or call in extra surgical assistants or more consultants.

service practice is inherently uncontrollable. Direct intervention by alternative medical-service suppliers, called community health centres or health-maintenance organizations or whatever, seems to be the only way of moderating price increases and encouraging substitution of less expensive forms of personnel.[22]

Once such alternatives exist, one might reintroduce market signals by allowing consumers to choose less or more expensive forms of *medically equivalent* care, and to pay the difference — thus if health centres are cheaper, their users might receive rebates on their health-insurance premiums. The economic incentives would then be applied to healthy consumers choosing among alternatives of which the medical equivalence was independently determined; not to ill patients, lacking information, and dependent on the advice of the supplier. Under such circumstances, the market might have a useful role to play in allowing people to choose (and pay for) the style of medical care they prefer. But the actual content of medical care seems too complex to be communicated to the consumer, and a market mechanism which registers uninformed choices by people in states of diminished rationality seems a less-than-optimal solution to the allocation problem.

---

[22] Evans, *Price Formation*, ch. 5. A similar conclusion was reached by J.Y. Rivard, *La Rémuneration du Corps Medicale*, a study prepared for the Castonguay Commission, Quebec, 1967.

4. Transportation in Canada

James Seldon

University of Manitoba

Transportation is one of those items which most Canadians take for granted — except perhaps while sitting stalled in the midst of a rush-hour traffic jam, or while stranded in an air terminal by a heavy fog, or while anxiously awaiting cargo held up by a rail strike! Then we see how dependent most of us are on a transportation network which can keep people and goods moving. In fact, that network plays a crucial role in the functioning of the Canadian economy. If we could not get workers and materials to jobs, and buyers and sellers and their goods to markets, our economy could never realize the advantages of specialization and trade which economists spend so much time talking about; our standard of living would be lower (however we chose to measure it) because so many of our options would be cut off. One estimate places the aggregate bill for commercial transport alone at some six percent of the Canadian gross national product,[1] but its contribution to the economy is certainly much greater than that.

I. Transportation as a Factor in Canadian Economic Development

Canada's development as a nation has paralleled the development and expansion of a transportation and communications network. When natural waterways provided the only practical means of long-distance travel, settlements remained small and were limited to the shores of major lakes and rivers. With the coming of canals, then railways, a highway system, air service, and oil and natural-gas pipelines, it became

[1] H.L. Purdy, *Transport Competition and Public Policy in Canada* (Vancouver: University of British Columbia Press, 1972), p. 4. For an up-to-date description and discussion of Canadian transportation issues, Purdy provides an excellent starting point.

worthwhile not only to expand the areas of settlement, but also to exploit a wider and wider range of natural resources. Precisely the same process is at work today as new transport technology — containerization, supertankers, jumbo jets, commodity pipelines — changes both what is technically possible and what is economically desirable.

Prior to World War II, it was possible to identify one means or another as the form of transportation most important to the economy. (Actually, since Confederation, it was always the railway; that made identification pretty easy!) Today, depending on how we decide to measure "importance", we get a variety of answers. If we use the total miles of routes, arguing that this measure best indicates the potential usefulness of a transport mode to the economy, we find that roads lead the way. If we use ton-miles of freight carried, measuring the actual pattern of use, railways are in the lead. We could use total trips made, or the dollar value of shipments carried, or total passengers carried, or total passenger-miles of travel, or any of a variety of other measures, each valuable in its own way, but no single one the "right" indicator. Today, we need to look at the entire network of transportation services and to recognize explicitly the interdependence of the various components of that network.

Transport facilities are elements of what economists call "social overhead capital." (Economists like to have fancy names for rather simple concepts, and this is one of them.) That is, transport facilities are part of the foundation upon which economic and social development rests, because they permit specialization and trade to develop on a broad scale. They do not guarantee that development will take place — the completion of a trans-continental rail link by the Canadian Pacific in 1885 did not immediately stimulate development of the West — but they are a first step in the process. Without the rail link, the large-scale settlement of western Canada, which took place in the decades following 1885, would probably have occurred much later.

II. The Search for a Transport Policy

Partly because transport facilities are social overhead capital, and partly because of the technology characteristic of transportation, governments take great interest in the construction and operation of the system. The direct and indirect regional effects of such facilities in channeling growth and development and in redistributing income and wealth provide one reason for their involvement. The massive investment required to build a St. Lawrence Seaway or a Trans-Canada Highway, for example, provides another reason. Yet another is that the very large scale of efficient operation of most transportation modes (compared to the size of the Canadian market for their output) means that normal competitive forces may not be a reliable means of controlling the behaviour of firms in the industry. We will have more to say about this last point shortly.

In what ways, and to what extent, do we wish to have Canadian governments interfere with the workings of the market for transport services? (If we tell them to keep their hands off entirely, they're really not very likely to take our advice!) Which goals are appropriate to pursue through the use of transportation tools? Should freight rates be used as a stimulus to regional development? To bring about income transfers between regions? Should prices of transport services reflect costs of production? If so, short-run or long-run? Or should we permit producers to set their prices at the maximum levels consumers will pay? These are hardly questions to be answered in a few short pages when two postwar Royal Commissions on Transportation each took volumes to attempt to find answers to some of them;[2] but we can hope to get at least some idea of the alternatives open to Canadian policy-makers, and of the reasons why these questions need to be asked at all.

The search for a transport policy for Canada is made considerably more complex by the variety of conflicting governmental jurisdictions and goals. Interprovincial and international carriers and their facilities are generally under federal control and are regulated by the Canadian Transport Commission (CTC). Intraprovincial transport is the responsibility of the provinces. As a general rule, this seems a reasonable enough division of powers, but problems of interpretation and co-ordination arise almost immediately. Highways, which are used for travel both within and between provinces by trucks, buses, and automobiles, are under provincial jurisdiction, so that there is a clear need for co-ordination of often-diverse provincial objectives. Commercial trucking operations are under provincial control within a province, but fall under federal jurisdiction when interprovincial or international travel is involved. (To date, the federal government has confined the exercise of this power to the setting of safety standards for trucking.) Railways and airlines, which are a federal responsibility, have important provincial, regional, and local effects, as hearings of the Transport Commission into route awards and rail-branch line abandonment make clear. Urban streets, roads, and mass-transit facilities are directly planned and instituted by municipal authorities, but are inextricably linked with federal and provincial interests through their funding. Oil and natural-gas pipelines are a federal responsibility, but are regulated by the National Energy Board, and not by the Canadian Transport Commission at all.

As if these difficulties were not enough, there is also the problem — even for a single, omnipotent transport-regulation agency — of choosing a strategy for regulating the behaviour not of a single producer, not even of a single mode of transport, but of a complex and changing network of transportation services. For some purposes, road and rail are close substitutes for each other, and there may be intermodal competition for customers; for other purposes, road and rail complement each other (as with the railways' "piggyback" services); and for still others, the two are entirely independent. Air and automobile travel are sometimes either/or choices (you might travel from Montreal to Toronto by either auto or plane), sometimes joint services (the auto gets you to and from the airport), and sometimes entirely independent (you are unlikely to

---

[2] Logically enough, these are titled Report of the Royal Commission on Transportation (Ottawa: Queen's Printer, 1951), and Report of the Royal Commission on Transportation (Ottawa: Queen's Printer, 1962).

take a plane to the corner grocery store, or to drive your car to Europe). Subways and buses can be substitutes for private automobiles, or they may complement the car through various "park-and-ride" linkages. And so on. The "best" policies, then, are not going to be easy to identify.

III. Without Regulation: A Theoretical Setting

To try to make sense out of a complex problem, and to see what sort of government intervention is desirable, likely to occur, or both, it is useful to imagine what the transport network would look like in an economy where firms were unregulated.

Our starting point is a characteristic common to road, rail, air, water, and pipeline transport: the need for a large expenditure on capital equipment (roadbed, terminals, and so on) before any output can be produced. For such a large investment to be profitable, a firm would require a heavy volume of traffic. Then, since the total Canadian demand for any transport service is limited by the size of the Canadian economy, this means that there would be room for only a few profitable producers, and perhaps for only one.

Further, once installed, capital facilities such as airport runways or seaway locks have few, if any, alternative uses, and thus have no resale value. Once they have been purchased, the expenditure is a "sunk cost" which firms have paid (remember, there is no government in our model to build these facilities out of public funds) whether they subsequently remain in business or cease operations. After the fixed cost has been paid, the extra costs of actually providing output are relatively low. The cost of operating a trucking service, once a roadway and terminals exist, is relatively low; the cost of providing air service, once runways and terminals have been provided, is relatively low; the cost of broadcasting TV signals, once cameras, transmitters, microwave stations, and satellites have been provided, is relatively low.

But this is not the whole story. Not only is the total cost of operations low relative to the heavy fixed cost, but the cost of providing *additional* units of service (or, in technical terms, the marginal cost) is also low, and probably declining, over a wide range of output. Once a train or a plane is travelling from one city to another, for instance, the cost of carrying an extra passenger, or an extra ton of freight, is almost zero, up to the point where the plane is full, or an extra boxcar must be added; and this characteristic, as we shall see, has important consequences for inter-firm competition in the short run.

Making use of these characteristics, we can make some predictions about the way in which the market for transport services would operate if there were no government intervention. Because the average and marginal costs of production (in the short run) tend to be low, and falling, a large scale of operation will be highly desirable for businessmen trying to make maximum profits. Firms, then, will have to compete with one another for the volume of business necessary to make their investments pay off; and if there are too many firms entering the market to begin with, we could expect to see vigorous price competition for customers.

It will be worthwhile for a firm to cut prices in order to expand sales as long as (i) the firm feels it can bid away a sufficient number of competitors' customers to more than offset the revenue it loses due to the lower prices, and (ii) price remains above marginal cost. The trouble with this sort of short-run competition is that because of the high fixed costs, firms which compete in this way will tend to make losses. While they will cover their operating costs, they will not be able to cover the costs of the capital they have purchased. This does not mean that they will immediately close down their operations, of course; but in the long run, as capital wears out it will not be repaired or replaced and firms will drop out of the industry, or will at least cut back on their less-profitable operations.

The CNR, to take one example of this sort of situation in Canada, has long been in a position of making losses because of its heavy fixed debt (incurred for historical reasons) and requires annual subsidies out of tax revenue. This does not mean that the government should necessarily shut down or even cut back the CNR's operations. Because the railway can cover its operating costs, and can even pay off a small part of its fixed debt, the government loses less when the CNR is operating than it would if the CNR went out of business (in which case the government would have to pay off the CNR's debt). There may be other reasons for the government to continue operating the CNR, of course; but even if the CNR were privately owned and operated, it would remain in operation at least until its capital began to deteriorate seriously.

Without regulation, therefore (and assuming that firms' managers are too shortsighted to see these problems coming), we would expect results similar to those of the early years of railways in North America: too many firms initially entering the market, duplication of expensive capital equipment, under-utilization of capital facilities; then intense price competition, losses, bankruptcies, mergers; and finally, an industry with just a few firms (oligopoly) and little or no price competition. In more densely populated regions, where the market is large enough, some competition would probably remain both within and between modes, while in sparsely settled areas there would be either no service provided at all, or the price would be high because of the exercise of monopoly power.

In Canada, vestiges of this sort of destructive competition are found in the railways' complex freight-rate schedules and in the efforts of the government to prevent this sort of price discrimination between regions. Where there are competitive modes, as with rail and water transport of bulk materials in eastern Canada, rail freight rates are considerably lower than rates for the same goods shipped comparable distances in areas such as northern Canada which lack an alternative.

The technical term for an industry in which it is unprofitable for more than one firm to operate (as in this theoretical example) is "natural monopoly." The Canadian transportation picture provides us with numerous examples of this situation if we look at the regional, rather than the national, picture. It would be as undesirable, from the point of view of efficiency, to have numerous railways competing for business, all serving the same points, but each with its own roadbed and track, or to have numerous private toll roads competing for a driver's business, as it would be to have many water, sewer, or telephone companies competing for householders' business.

In short, then, our theoretical model of over-investment, destructive competition, and ultimate rationalization of the industry into regional oligopolies or monopolies gives a simplistic but reasonable picture of what might have happened in the transport industries in the absence of regulation. (An alternative model would suggest that investors are smart enough not to over-invest in the first place, so that regional monopolies and oligopolies would be established almost immediately — the result then is the same; the only difference is in the mechanism which gets us there.)

IV. Postwar Transport Competition

Changes in technology since World War II, particularly those leading to the emergence of commercial trucking as an alternative to rail freight, have led to the contention that increased competition between modes has reduced the need for government interference with the market.[3] While the argument is persuasive, there are two possible difficulties with it.

First, the claim depends upon the assumption that the various modes which are potential alternatives do indeed compete with one another, so that the competitive results follow. The changes in technology have certainly increased the chances of competition, but actual competition may not have increased. The major Canadian railways also operate trucking firms, to take one example, and Canadian Pacific also operates air and water facilities. Just how much competition there is between these modes on a within-firm basis is a matter which needs further study. The changes in technology may simply have carved up the larger market into sub-markets for long-haul, short-haul, bulk shipping, rapid transit, and so on, leaving considerable monopoly power in many of these sub-areas.

Second, the argument assumes that the market will produce socially optimal results so long as competition is present. That is, it assumes that a market which is technically efficient, and in which there are competing firms, will be efficient in its contribution to social welfare. The trouble is that even in a perfectly competitive market, with many small competing firms, we may observe "market failure" — failure due to external effects (on regional development, perhaps) which do not get incorporated into the price paid for the good or service when it is sold in the marketplace. Thus we cannot be sure that just because there is competition, the government ought to adopt a hands-off policy. We will take a closer look at this matter a little later on.

V. Regulatory Alternatives

If we are unwilling to rely on the market to control firms in the transport industries, what policies would we like our regulatory bodies to

---

[3] See, for example, W.J. Stenason, "Transportation Policy", in L.H. Officer and L.B. Smith, eds., *Canadian Economic Problems and Policies* (Toronto: McGraw-Hill Canada, 1970), pp. 210–219.

select? We have three main alternatives, each of which, separately and in combination, has been used in Canada.

First, we might have a government agency regulate the performance of private firms in the industry by specifying requirements for quality, frequency, and price of service. This is the basic role of the Canadian Transport Commission.

Second, we could set up a government agency to provide the transport service directly, either as the sole producer or in competition with private carriers. This has been the typical Canadian approach to urban transit.

Third, we could choose to finance the necessary capital facilities out of public revenues, and to permit those facilities to be used by competing firms, as we do in the case of trucking.

As one example of the use of all three policies at the same time, Air Canada (1) is regulated by the Canadian Transport Commission, (2) is a government-owned corporation in competition with other Canadian and international air carriers, and (3) uses airport facilities such as runways, terminals, and communications equipment financed out of public revenues.

VI. Evaluating the Regulators

Just trying to decipher the complex system of rules and regulations which govern Canadian transport operations is bad enough, let alone trying to explain how these rules came into being, or what their effects are. One look at the railways' rate schedules, for instance, is enough to scare almost anyone away. There are Class Rates, Commodity Rates, Competitive Rates, Fixed Rates, and Agreed Charges. There are rates for full carloads, and for less-than-carload lots; there are special Small Shipment Rates; and special rates for shipping livestock. (Perhaps the railways should consider themselves lucky that Canadians manage to get anything shipped at all.)

What, in the light of this complex setting, can economists say about the role of regulatory bodies such as the Transport Commission, or about the choice between public and private ownership? Unfortunately, not much, and certainly not as much as we might like. By pointing out areas in which the market may fail to do its job properly, we can contribute some useful policy guidelines, but the network is so complicated that that may be about the limit of our practical contribution. With this rather discouraging assessment in mind, let us look at two cases in which we are able to be of help.

1. Option demand — a case of market failure

What if destructive competition does drive all but a small number of firms out of business? Should we be concerned, as long as we restrain the remaining firms from unduly (whatever we may decide that should mean) exploiting consumers? If there are not enough customers on a route to enable the transport firm to break even, should we be worried if that service is not offered? Why should that route not just be abandoned — doesn't the "invisible hand" of competition know best?

The not-so-obvious answer to these questions is that, our fears of monopoly exploitation aside, it might indeed be worthwhile from society's point of view to keep such a service in operation, even at the cost of subsidies out of public funds.

To illustrate, consider a Canadian businessman who prefers to do his travelling by air, rather than by road or rail. What value does he place on being able to make his trip by rail if, as will happen some of the time, his plane is grounded by fog? The answer, as far as the railroads are concerned, is none at all, over and above his fare for the trips he actually makes, since he pays nothing to keep the rails available as a standby service. Even if he would be willing to pay for the option of travel by train, there is no way for the railways to charge him for the service. (A higher fare for the trips he does make will not do the job, since it is a charge for a service he actually *does* buy, rather than a charge which will permit him the *choice* of buying or not buying — and even if he never makes a trip by rail, the existence of that alternative is still of value to him.)

In urban areas, the problem of option demand is illustrated by the value we place on being able to take the bus or the subway should our car refuse to start some cold winter morning. Since we pay no specific price to have this option kept open, the market does not translate our demand into the provision of the service, and we may well have an under-supply of bus, or subway, or taxi services available when we wish to use them. (Have you ever wondered why there never seem to be enough taxis available on cold and rainy days?)

If this sort of problem is judged to be serious, we have a rationale for the support of money-losing services out of public funds, politically unpopular though that course may be, or for a government-run enterprise to supply those services even at a loss. Losses, then, do not necessarily indicate that a service should be discontinued, even in the long run; but we should note that the opposite is also true: just because the local urban-transit system, or Air Canada, or the CNR, manages to break even, we cannot assume that they must be operating in a socially optimal manner.

2. External effects — the market fails again

It was suggested earlier that one of the alternatives open to government was to provide the required capital facilities, and to permit competing firms to use those facilities, as is done with roads, airports, and waterways. This solution raises problems of its own if (as is typical) firms are not charged appropriately for the use of the facilities; but nevertheless, this may be the preferred policy, probably in combination with regulation by the CTC.

The congestion which is typical of urban streets and roads, or of airport facilities, is the predictable outcome of the traditional pricing mechanism for the use of publicly financed capital. For example, on a busy highway the presence of an additional driver forces those on the road to slow down. This "external effect" on other drivers is important because it causes private costs (to the individual driver) to differ from social costs (to all drivers), and results in misallocated resources. Each individual driver makes the decision to use or not to use his automobile on the basis of the benefits he expects from its use and the costs he expects to incur in using it. That is, he obtains the benefits of a trip which may be faster, or more comfortable, or more convenient than it would have been had he taken a bus, and he pays costs in the form of wear and tear on his car, consumption of oil and gasoline, and so on. The trouble is that he imposes costs on other drivers in the form of delays, increased chance of accidents, higher frustration levels, and the like, for which he is not charged, and he thus has a tendency to use the facility beyond the point where the marginal costs to society as a whole equal the marginal benefits to society. (If, by some lucky chance, drivers are altruistic and take into account the inconvenience they impose on others, the situation will be less serious; if they happen to be malevolent in their views of fellow drivers, perhaps we would be safer staying off the roads entirely.)

Similarly, when air carriers are not charged directly for the costs they impose upon others (in the form of noise, pollution, and congestion delays) through their use of scarce runway and terminal facilities, there will be a tendency for greater than socially optimal use of that capital equipment. Thus it is appropriate for the Canadian Transport Commission to resort to non-price rationing through the granting of exclusive air-lanes, flight times, and so on. Public ownership of capital facilities is not enough; other forms of intervention in the market are likely to be needed.

VII.   A Canadian Transportation Policy?

If no clear picture of Canadian transport policy has emerged from this discussion, we should hardly be surprised. There really is no concrete policy to be identified. In Canada the most visible approach to the regulation of commercial transport has been Transport Commission rate regulation, combined with the setting of performance criteria; but there are as many provincial policies (or lacks of policy) as there are provinces, and there really is no consistent national aggregate.

In short, Canadian transport policy is a rather mixed bag of attempts by various levels of government to pursue often-divergent goals. Among those goals have been the following: (i) to prevent destructive competition, (ii) to obtain the advantages of large-scale operation, (iii) to protect consumers from the potential excesses of monopoly power, (iv) to foster national development, both economic and social, and (v) to eliminate regional disparities. Whether we judge the over-all result to be a success or failure depends upon two factors: the desirability of the goals pursued, and the efficacy of the tools employed. Our conclusions are bound to be mixed.

5. Economics of Pollution

Donald N. Dewees

University of Toronto

I. Why Is There an "Environmental Problem"?[1]

It is a fundamental principle of economic theory that the free operation of perfectly competitive markets will lead to an efficient allocation of resources in the absence of externalities. The laws of supply and demand operating in the marketplace will cause prices to rise or fall until at some price the quantity of the resource which is supplied will just equal the quantity which is demanded. If the price of a resource rises, buyers will economize on its use and purchase less of that resource. If the price falls, the resource will be used more extravagantly. When an equilibrium price has been reached, no individual in the economy can be made better off without making some other individual worse off. Scarce resources are thus allocated to their most efficient and productive uses.

The problem with environmental quality is that it is a technological externality not currently included in the market system.[2] Any firm or individual may discharge wastes into the air or water without payment, subject only to existing pollution-control legislation. Polluters need not pay for the harm caused to the community around them or to downstream users

---

[1] An excellent collection of essays on environmental economics is contained in Robert Dorfman and Nancy S. Dorfman, eds., *Economics of the Environment* (New York: W.W. Norton & Co., Inc., 1972).

[2] A technological externality exists when one person's activities have an impact on another that is not transmitted through the price system. If, for example, the air pollution from my smelter kills your apple trees, that pollution represents a technological externality. For analysis of externalities, technological and otherwise, see Francis M. Bator, "The Anatomy of Market Failure", *Quarterly Journal of Economics* 72:3, August 1958, pp. 35–79; J.E. Meade, "External Economies and Diseconomies in a Competitive Situation", *Economic Journal* 62, March 1952, pp. 54–67; and R. Turvey, "On Divergences Between Social Cost and Private Cost", *Economica* 30, August 1963, p. 309.

of air and water because of their pollution. Because this resource is free, it is used more extensively than if a price were paid for its use.

This treatment results in part because centuries ago, when the common-law system of property allocation developed, air and water were considered to be unlimited resources. While local pollution problems existed, there was no thought that the capacity of the air and water to carry off wastes was anything but infinite. Economic growth and population growth, however, have so increased our capacity to generate wastes that these resources are now properly regarded as finite and scarce, as is oil, iron, and timber. Recent serious public concern about environmental quality suggests that reliance on a legal system which assumed abundance will not properly allocate a scarce resource. It cannot produce the degree of environmental quality desired by the public, because the public desire has no means of expression in a market.

Suppose that one firm in a competitive industry decided unilaterally to reduce its pollution emissions as a service to the local community. Pollution control costs money, so it would find its costs higher than before. This would either lower profits, in which case shareholders would be upset and capital for expansion would become unavailable, or it would raise prices, whereupon the firm's market share would be eroded by competitors. In either case, the firm would perform poorly relative to its pre-control performance, and might fail completely. Thus, pollution does not result from corporate malevolence or negligence; it is virtually compelled by the market.

Unsatisfactory environmental quality is a perfectly natural result of the operation of our economic system, or any other economic system without environmental legislation.[3] The only solution to the problem is to recognize the scarcity of environmental resources and to legislate some means of allocating these resources among competing users. Governments must act to specify the rules by which waste may be discharged into the air or water. No one has suggested that we should allocate coal or steel or automobiles by a system of moral strictures and admonitions against excessive use, and it is unreasonable to suggest that such measures should be applied to equally important resources such as air and water quality.

II. How Much Environmental Quality Should We Buy?

It is sometimes suggested that pollution should be eliminated, with absolute prohibitions against any discharge of wastes into the air or water. As a practical matter it is often impossible to achieve zero discharge. We do not have the technology for 100-percent removal of many pollutants from stack gases and discharge water. Total prohibition of emissions would entirely eliminate the production of many goods, necessities as well as luxuries. Even societies with very primitive economies have found it necessary to discharge wastes, as evidenced by piles of

---

[3] Environmental problems in Russia are depressingly similar to ours. See Marshall I. Goldman, "The Convergence of Environmental Disruption," in Dorfman and Dorfman, *op. cit.*, pp. 294–307.

bones in prehistoric caves, and smoke smudges from cooking fires on the ceilings of those caves. Furthermore, some pollutants have a lower threshold level below which they are not perceptible or not harmful, or both. It would be hard to justify expenditures to reduce pollution when it is not harmful, or when it cannot be distinguished from naturally occurring background levels of the pollutant. The question is thus not *whether* to allow pollution but *how much* pollution to allow.

Some recent legislation has required that pollution be controlled as far as is technically feasible. If this is interpreted literally, it means that an existing pollution-control device, even if outrageously expensive, must be used. Such a standard implies that we are prepared to spend unlimited amounts of money to control pollution, even if this diverts resources from other socially desirable activities, such as disease prevention, education, and production of basic necessities such as food and housing. This is also clearly nonsensical. In a society which must satisfy its needs from limited resources, we must decide how to allocate those resources among many competing needs. No single goal, no matter how meritorious, can command unlimited quantities of these resources.

Environmental quality must therefore depend on the cost of providing it and the benefits which are derived from it. Economic theory suggests that a proper rule would be to reduce pollution until the marginal cost of an additional unit of reduction is just equal to the marginal benefit which that unit of reduction will provide. Whatever its theoretical appeal, however, this standard is difficult to apply in practice because benefits of abatement are usually quite difficult to measure and quantify.[4] If we do not know by how much Canadians will benefit from a ten-percent reduction in air pollution through lower medical costs, longer life span, and greater enjoyment of the atmosphere, then we can hardly determine when this marginal benefit is just equal to the marginal cost.

The problem presented here is, fortunately, not unique. We have difficulty measuring the benefits from other public goods, such as education, national defence, and police and fire departments.[5] When analytical methods fail, we can use a trial-and-error procedure of supplying the public good, determining public satisfaction, and then increasing or decreasing the supply depending on whether the public is willing to spend more or less for it.

If we can estimate the benefits of pollution control, we can embark upon a pollution-control program, and gradually improve environmental quality until the public either individually or through its elected representatives determines that further expenditures are not warranted by the improvements they will cause.[6] An important element in this program is

[4] See the discussions in William J. Baumol and Wallace E. Oates, "The Use of Standards and Prices for Protection of the Environment", *Swedish Journal of Economics* 73:1, March 1971, pp. 42–54.

[5] Some aspects of public-goods problems are discussed in Paul A. Samuelson, "The Pure Theory of Public Expenditure", *Review of Economics and Statistics* 36:4, November 1964, pp. 387–89; "Diagrammatic Exposition of a Theory of Public Expenditure", *Review of Economics and Statistics* 37:4, November 1955, pp. 350–356; and "Aspects of Public Expenditure Theories", *Review of Economics and Statistics* 40:4, November 1958, pp. 332–338.

[6] This approach is suggested in, e.g., John H. Dales, *Pollution, Property and Prices* (Toronto: University of Toronto Press, 1968).

the adverb "gradually." If we were to require today that five years hence all sources of pollution must reduce emission by 90 percent, we would run the risk that half-way to that goal rising costs might have outstripped public demand for further improvement. If, on the other hand, we embark upon a program which will be certain to bring significant improvement in environmental quality each year over a substantial period of time, then we can be assured that at least things are getting better, and that we are not going to overshoot the point at which further investment is unjustifiable. By this method we can approach the theoretically desirable goal of equating marginal costs and marginal benefits.

An important distinction must be made between stocks and flows of pollutant. The flow is the hourly or daily emission of pollution into the air or water, while the stock is the total amount in the air or water at any moment of time. Some pollutants are removed rapidly from the environment, as large particles fall from the atmosphere, or carbon monoxide is converted by some plants and bacteria; here there is no accumulation over time, so that a reduction in the emission rate improves environmental quality at once. Other pollutants are conservative and remain in the air for long periods, such as very fine particulates and some gases; some, such as mercury and DDT, move through the environment and food chain contaminating plant and animal life for a long time. Here the harm results not from the daily discharge, but from the stock in the air or water which has built up over a period of years. A reduction in the emission rate will not necessarily reduce the stock; it may only reduce its rate of growth. The long-run equilibrium solution for conservative pollutants may be to eliminate all emissions, while this would rarely be the case for a disappearing pollutant. A less-than-precipitous approach may still be appropriate even for a conservative substance, however, on the ground that if it is truly conservative, one year's production will increase the stock only by a small percentage, and thus the increase in harm from a few years' delay in phasing out the pollutant may cause small incremental damage.

A moderate rate of improvement has other advantages. If pollution control is new to a particular industry, there is every reason to expect that over time, better and less expensive means will be found to achieve a given degree of control. If we require a high degree of control in a short period of time, very high costs will be incurred. If a longer period of time is allowed to reach the same goal, in general, that goal will be achieved at substantially lower cost. Furthermore, short-run economic dislocations caused by the closing of some marginal plants or large-scale investment in other plants can be minimized. The problem, then, is to devise a strategy which will ensure that progress is continually made but which will not impose excessive costs.

Of course, not all pollution-control programs should be gradual. If a toxic metal or other discharge is discovered to present an immediate health hazard, very large expenditures may be justified to reduce its emission as soon as possible, and perhaps eliminate it. Mercury presented such a danger, and its emissions were greatly reduced shortly after the danger led to serious public concern. This is as it should be. But we must distinguish cases of immediate danger from those where the benefits of abatement are of a far less serious magnitude.

III. Should Standards Be Uniform Across the Country?

It is sometimes suggested that pollution-control standards should be uniform across Canada. This is defended on the grounds that if pollution control is important to residents of Toronto or Montreal or Vancouver, it is no less important for residents of Orillia, Fort Francis, and Banff. Two conflicting kinds of equality might be considered. The first is equal pollution control. In practice, this has meant that all sources of a pollutant achieve the same degree of treatment. If pollution-control costs were similar in all areas, this would be equivalent to a single effluent charge to be applied across the country. However, since the density of pollution sources varies from one place to another, uniform abatement would still leave widely varying environmental quality levels.

The second kind of uniformity is uniform environmental-quality standards. These specify that no area should be allowed to have an air-pollution density greater than some specified amount, or water dirtier than some specified amount. Since polluters are more concentrated in some places than others, the currently dirty areas will require much greater abatement than others. We can evaluate these alternatives with reference to the economists' yardstick of attempting to equate marginal benefits of abatement with the associated marginal costs.

Other things being equal, the harm done by a unit of air-pollution density will be proportional to the population exposed to it. Much of the benefits from air-pollution control come from improved health levels, and from aesthetic improvements which will also be experienced on a *per capita* basis. Furthermore, for a given population, it is frequently true that the harm done by pollution increases more than proportionally to the density of that pollution. At low levels, some pollutants are not harmful or not perceptible or both, while at high levels the same pollutant may cause serious illness or death. Thus, marginal benefits will rise as pollution density increases. On the cost side, the costs of improving air quality by a given amount will increase with the number of sources of pollution in an area, because the same percentage abatement must be applied to more firms or individuals.

Let us compare two areas with similar weather conditions and similar proportions of pollution sources and population. If city A has twice the population and pollution of city B, the benefits of pollution control will be higher in A than in B, as will the optimal marginal costs of abatement. Thus, if the concern of people in both cities about pollution is similar, it will be desirable to have a higher degree of pollution abatement in the larger and dirtier city than in the smaller and cleaner one. The resulting air quality may be similar, but the marginal cost and benefit of abatement will be higher in A than in B.[7] This suggests that if these considerations were the dominant ones in specifying pollution-control standards, it would

[7] See Sam Peltzman and T. Nicolaus Tideman, "Local Versus National Pollution Control: Note", *American Economic Review* 62:5, December 1972, pp. 959–963.

be more efficient to have uniform environmental-quality standards than uniform pollution-abatement or effluent-charge standards.

This conclusion need not always hold, however. Tastes are not uniform among all individuals, and some people may live in cleaner areas simply because clean air is more important to them than to others. Here, uniform environmental-quality standards would no longer be appropriate. In addition, the ability of the environment to carry off wastes can vary substantially from one point to another. Thus, some cities may have more sources of pollution but, because of favourable weather conditions, experience lower pollution-density levels in the air or water. In principle, these differences should also be reflected in pollution-control strategies.

There is also the danger that national standards of any kind will tend toward the lowest common denominator and require nothing more than that which can be achieved in the worst areas. Adherence to such national standards would thus forgo the opportunity to do much better in many areas where this can be achieved at a very reasonable cost if it is done with a reasonable program over a sensible period of time.[8]

One defence of uniform emission standards is that they will prevent the creation of pollution havens. If the people of one area are more concerned about jobs than about environmental quality, uniform standards will prevent them from attracting industry from other places by allowing it to avoid pollution-control costs there. Such intervention could only be justified on the grounds that people do not know what is good for them or that irreversible damage may be done to the environment against the interests of future generations. The latter argument may be valid where applicable, but the former is not very palatable in a democratic society. If the decision-making unit includes all persons who will be affected by the pollution, it may be best to let them make their own decision.

It would thus appear that there are numerous reasons for approaches to pollution control that are not uniform nationally. National standards will fail to reflect differences in the assimilative capacity of the environment from one place to another and differences in density of both population and pollution sources. The fear that regions may fail to act because of loss of jobs may be unfounded, at least in the long run, so long as the programs under consideration are carefully devised.

IV. Who Pays for Pollution Control?

A substantial amount of pollution comes from people themselves or from governmental activities. Much of Canada's water pollution originates in domestic sewage, which is controlled, if at all, by expensive sewage-treatment plants. These will, of course, be paid for by city, provincial, or federal taxpayers, depending upon the funding arrangements. If pollution-control devices must be installed on municipal incinerators for solid wastes, these too must be paid for out of the tax dollar.

---

[8] Arguments in favour of a regional approach to water-pollution control may also be found in Allen V. Kneese and Blair T. Bower, *Managing Water Quality: Economics, Technology, Institutions* (Baltimore: Johns Hopkins Press, 1968), pp. 89–94, chapter 10; and Marc J. Roberts, "River Basin Authorities: A National Solution to Water Pollution", *Harvard Law Review* 83:7, May 1970, pp. 1527–1556.

It is sometimes suggested, however, that when industry is the source of pollution, industry rather than consumers should pay for its control. In most cases, this is both infeasible and undesirable. We referred earlier to the principle that environmental resources will be best allocated if they must be paid for, as are all other resources used by private firms. The advantage of this system is that it will provide a means of rationing a scarce resource. But if some industries produce more pollution than others so that their pollution-control expenditures are higher, it is also desirable that this be reflected in the price of their products. A high price for pollution-intensive products will not only pay for the cleanup; it will also discourage use of these products. This is clearly a proper incentive effect if we are seriously concerned about environmental quality. If it were possible for dirty industries to absorb pollution-control costs themselves, this would not achieve the desirable end of reducing the consumption of pollution-related commodities.

Even if it were desirable for industry to pay for the cleanup and not pass this on to its consumers, it is not clear how this might be arranged. If costs go up because of pollution controls and prices are not raised, then the profits of the industry decline, reducing the value of its shares. In the short run the shareholders suffer because of pollution-control costs, and in the long run the industry will find it hard to raise new capital. This will lead to reduction in output or deteriorating performance by the industry. Either of these consequences will have an undesirable impact on consumers of the industry's products. There is thus no way of entirely protecting consumers from the cost impact of pollution controls, and no reason to do so.

It is sometimes suggested that government subsidies be used to ease the cost of pollution control. This may be desirable in the short run to reduce the economic dislocations suffered by marginal firms that would otherwise go out of business rather than incur even modest pollution-control costs. In the long run, however, we have already established the desirability of consumer prices reflecting the use of environmental resources. Government subsidies for pollution control would precisely negate this effect, and are therefore undesirable.[9] Subsidies might be better than no policy at all, but aside from easing transitional burdens, they have no place in a long-run pollution-control program.

V. Choice of Pollution-Control Policies

We have dealt primarily with the question of how much pollution control is desirable. Beyond this, there is the choice among several kinds of policies to achieve a desired improvement in environmental quality. Two popular policies limit pollution quantity by specification of the required percentage of pollution abatement and specification of the total emission permitted to each stock or per unit of product produced. Another policy limits the density of pollution in discharged air or water. Economists generally recommend prices instead of quantity limitations, such as an

[9] See Richard M. Bird and Leonard Waverman, "Some Fiscal Aspects of Controlling Industrial Water Pollution", in D.A.L. Auld, ed., *Economic Thinking and Pollution Problems* (Toronto: University of Toronto Press, 1972), pp. 75–102.

effluent charge per unit of pollution discharged. Several criteria are important in choosing among these policies.

1. Efficiency

Efficiency might include setting marginal costs equal to marginal benefits of abatement, the issue discussed in sections II and III above. We have already noted the problems in applying this concept.

Efficiency has a second meaning for environmental problems. Whatever degree of environmental quality is to be provided, it is desirable to do so at the least possible cost. As between two plans to produce a given air-quality level, the cheaper one must be better. It can be shown that abatement costs will be minimized if all sources of pollution in the area under consideration face the same marginal cost of abatement. If all firms were identical, with identical abatement cost functions, this would imply equal abatement from all firms. In general, however, some firms are large and others small, and the technology for pollution control will vary widely. Thus, a given marginal abatement cost may mean vastly different degrees of abatement among different firms. An effluent charge which imposes a constant price on every gram, pound, or ton of pollution discharged, will cause firms to equate marginal abatement costs to the charge, and thus equalize marginal cost. Therefore the effluent charge is always superior to the uniform standard in cost minimization. This desirable quality is shared by other schemes such as the Dales pollution-rights measures, which would create a market for rights to discharge waste. The market would result in a uniform price to all firms.[10]

2. Technological progress

In fields where pollution control is relatively new, we might expect that substantial improvements in abatement technology would occur over a period of time. It is usually the case that when an incentive to innovate appears, there will be a burst of innovative activity resulting in substantial improvements. Thus, the cost of abatement may depend just as much on a system which encourages technical progress as on one which achieves other goals such as equating marginal abatement costs.

A standard which specifies the maximum amount of pollution to be discharged per firm creates incentives to develop new technology until that standard is met, and to develop increasingly lower-cost technology for meeting the standard. It does not, however, induce development of devices which might exceed the standard. And if technology is relatively new, the standard may have to be set at a sub-optimal level until it can be demonstrated that some higher level can be achieved.

Here again the effluent-charge schemes seem to have an advantage. One can impose an effluent charge at a reasonable level without knowing precisely how much abatement is currently feasible. Firms will then reduce pollution so far as is economical, subject to that charge, and pay for any

[10] See Dales, *op. cit.*

pollution that remains. These payments provide a continual incentive to develop better technology in the future. Thus, the administrative agency requires less information to introduce an effluent-charge scheme than a pollution standard. In cases where it is reasonable to expect technological progress in abatement and where the capabilities of emerging technology are unknown, the effluent charge seems to be superior to other forms of control.

3. Information for regulatory agency

One reason why pollution abatement has moved slowly in many fields is the problem of developing expertise in the government. It is frequently suggested that no action can be taken until the regulatory agency knows what abatement technology is available, what can be developed in the future, and what the impact of abatement on the industry will be. Regulatory processes where an administrative agency sets standards after someone has proven the standards can be met are inherently subject to delay, since the industry to be controlled almost invariably is the best source of information about capabilities of control processes. Shelves are filled with millions of pages of testimony taken in hearings in Ottawa, Washington, and elsewhere to determine whether a particular standard can or cannot be met, and when it might be met. Each page adds to the cost and delay.

Any system which reduces the amount of technological expertise required of the agency will lead to more rapid imposition of control and thereby to greater abatement progress. For the reasons mentioned in section 2 above, the effluent charge will generally require less expertise than emission standards, and therefore will probably lead to more rapid abatement.

VI. Canadian Automobile-Pollution Policy: An Example

The control of automobile emissions provides an interesting illustration of some of the principles enunciated above. Until now, new cars sold in Canada have incorporated the same pollution-control devices as those sold throughout the United States. Regulations which first took effect with 1968-model cars progressively reduced the rate of emissions of hydrocarbons and carbon monoxide from new cars, and beginning in 1973, oxides of nitrogen have also been under some control.[11] U.S. standards adopted in 1971 required that automobiles built in 1975 and 1976 emit 90 percent less of all three pollutants than the average of cars built in 1970. If these standards are met, then new-car emissions will be only five percent of those from a pre-control car.

It appears, however, that the marginal cost of abatement rises very rapidly as auto emissions decline toward zero. The first 50-percent reduction of hydrocarbons and carbon monoxide was achieved at very low cost

[11] The Air Pollution Control Act, 1967, which enables Ontario to regulate automotive emissions, and a corresponding regulation are reprinted in Auld, op. cit., pp. 164–165, 167–174.

once efficient devices were developed. Estimates are that vehicles meeting the 1973 standards cost up to ½¢ per mile, or $50 per year, more for the average owner than an uncontrolled car. Part of this cost comes from higher purchase price and part from increased maintenance and increased fuel consumption. For North American models to meet 1975 standards would probably involve an increase of several hundred dollars in the price of a new car and another significant increase in fuel consumption.[12] In total, the 1975 standards may cost $100 per year for every new car. This produces a total abatement cost curve such as that shown in Figure 1, and a marginal abatement cost curve that is similarly upward sloping. With such steeply rising costs, it is important to consider carefully how much abatement is really necessary.

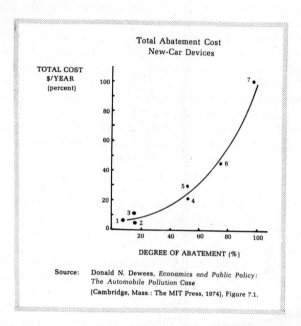

Total Abatement Cost New-Car Devices

Source: Donald N. Dewees, *Economics and Public Policy: The Automobile Pollution Case* (Cambridge, Mass.: The MIT Press, 1974), Figure 7.1.

Figure 1

It also appears that technological progress continues to shift the abatement cost curve downward over time as experience is accumulated in building control devices. When 1968 controls were first imposed, they cost up to $50 per car for installation alone. It appears that those same standards could be met today by modifications of the basic engine which would barely increase production costs.[13] Thus, while the 1975 and 1976 standards now appear either impossible or very expensive to meet, it is reasonable to expect that at some time in the future, meeting them will be feasible and perhaps not enormously expensive. There is, however, no way to predict when this may occur.

[12] In 1973 the U.S. Environmental Protection Agency postponed the original 1975 standards for one year and imposed less stringent interim regulations for 1975. The original 1975 standards continued to be referred to as the 1975 standards, although they were not to be effective until 1976.
[13] See Donald N. Dewees, *Economics and Public Policy: The Automobile Pollution Case* (Cambridge, Mass.: The MIT Press, 1974), ch. 7 and Appendix C.

Finally, we must consider that changes in new-car emission rates are reflected in actual air-quality levels only after a substantial time lag. The average life of a car in North America is ten years, so that although a new car is driven more miles per year than an old one, not more than 15 percent of all vehicle miles in any year are driven by cars which were new in that year. Thus, even if a non-polluting car were suddenly produced, it would be ten years before all pollution were eliminated. This means that whenever a substantial reduction in emission standards is imposed, its full effect will not be felt for a number of years.

The original schedule of U.S. standards described above involves very rapid emission reduction. If at some time in the near future it is determined that air quality has become satisfactory so that no further expenditure on emission control is desirable, we will already have gone too far. At that time, even if no further standards were imposed, air quality would continue to improve for many years. This overshooting of environmental quality involves unnecessary expenditure of money, particularly when abatement costs rise with abatement level and tend to fall over time.

Suppose that instead of following the original U.S. schedule of emission reductions, Canada were to postpone the 1975 and 1976 standards for five years. Hydrocarbons and carbon monoxide in the air would decline during this period, and there would be some reduction in oxides of nitrogen. As air-quality improvement slows down, the new standards would be imposed and once again there would be a long period of improvement.[14] Under such a program, the five-year delay would save Canadians over $2.5 billion in pollution expenditures forgone between 1975 and 1980. Scarce petroleum would be preserved, since part of the cost of auto-emission controls is increased fuel use. Yet air quality would at all times be better than at present.

It has been noted that there is no analytical basis for specifying the proper equilibrium rate of emission from automobiles. Consequently, we cannot determine for certain at what pace the emission-control program should proceed. The above relationships, however, suggest that unless auto emissions are regarded as an immediate and serious danger to Canada and Canadians, it might be more sensible to pursue a policy which would result in continuous and gradual improvements in air quality rather than a much more expensive one which results in precipitous changes in emission rates. The $2.5 billion which might be saved by the suggested alternative timing can profitably be used for emission control in other sectors in the Canadian economy or for other worthy public purposes. It would be unfortunate if that amount of money were spent to purchase changes in air-pollution levels which were not regarded as important by Canadians.

A few other points should also be considered in formulating Canadian automobile-emission policy. The emission rates referred to here and appearing in most public discussions are those based on standard testing procedures developed in the United States. The "cold-start" tests are run

14 *Ibid.*, Figure 7.4.

after the car has been in a room at 68 degrees Fahrenheit for a long period of time. This is appropriate for Southern California but is clearly not representative of typical Canadian conditions, where mean annual temperatures are 45 degrees or less. Since temperature has an important effect on emission rates, it is possible that actual Canadian emissions are far different from those projected from using U.S. figures. At a time when auto-pollution control promises to become a major expenditure, we should develop tests which accurately reflect Canadian emissions, so that choices can sensibly be made among alternative policies. These changes would alter the performance used in cost-effectiveness calculations, shifting the curve in Figure 1.

Finally, it was suggested above that where technology is uncertain or rapidly changing, the rigid standard may not be an effective policy mechanism. This is clear from the problems of the 1975 standards, which were postponed one year, wherein the manufacturers were in continued debate with both Ottawa and Washington as to whether those standards could be met, and if not, whether they should be relaxed, postponed, or otherwise modified. Where, as in the United States, the penalty for failing to meet the standards can be a $10,000 per car fine, there is little flexibility in the enforcement program. If rigid standards are used, they can be made more reasonable by replacing the punitive fine with one which adequately reflects the severity of the problem. If every manufacturer had to pay a few hundred dollars for each car which did not meet a set of standards, and if that fine was proportional to the degree to which emissions exceeded the standard, then we would have something which looks very much like an effluent charge. We could call it a "potential-pollution charge". There would be a continual financial incentive to improve control technology and incorporate it when that was cheaper than paying the fine or charge. There would be no need for continuing review by government agencies of technological progress by the industry, and no need for the industry to argue continually the impossibility of what was requested. The program would then become self-enforcing, and improvements would be automatic.

It is also possible that a single new-car standard may not be appropriate for all of Canada. As some areas have much more serious problems than others, it might be desirable to have two standards. One could represent current emission rates and be required for all cars sold in Canada. A more stringent standard could be applied for cars registered in high-pollution areas. While manufacturers would resist a vast proliferation of standards, meeting two separate standards would probably not be considered an unreasonable burden. The more stringent standard might even be the 1975–76 U.S. standards, or a Canadian equivalent, enforced by a reasonable fine system.

VII. Conclusions

Any time that a scarce and valuable resource is omitted from the market system, we can expect to find problems in its allocation. In the past, the discharge of wastes into the air and water has been entirely outside the economic system, with the predictable results that environmental quality is not consistent with public wishes. This outcome is not even a result of the capitalist system, since pollution problems are frequently as severe in communist and socialist countries as they are in capitalist countries. It should not be surprising that improvements in this situation arise only when governments step in to regulate use of the resource directly or to set up quasi-market mechanisms to do so automatically.

Because government action is necessary, we need some criteria by which to evaluate that action. While it is almost impossible for economists to suggest *how much* environmental quality should be provided, we can say something about *the way* in which it is provided. If pollution-control costs are non-trivial, it appears that programs which differentiate among cities and regions of the country based on population density, density of pollution sources, and the ability of the environment to carry off wastes, are superior to uniform national programs. Any program will be better to the extent that it creates incentives for technological change in pollution-control devices, since this is frequently a very important factor in determining long-run abatement costs. Furthermore, programs which achieve a given degree of abatement at least cost are favoured over those which are more costly. This often implies an advantage for programs involving effluent charges rather than uniform standards, because the former leads to abatement where it is least expensive, promotes technical progress, and minimizes endless hearings on the feasibility of complex abatement technology.

Because the cost of abatement will generally be borne by consumers, they have a direct interest both in selecting a reasonable degree of abatement and in using mechanisms to achieve it which do so at least cost. The public has complained that industry has not developed pollution controls fast enough to save us from serious pollution problems. If this is true, it is our own fault. For in fact, the public and the government have failed to produce the innovations in regulatory mechanisms which would induce the best performance by the private sector. A general understanding of the problems, combined with institutions which create reasonable incentives to better performance, can produce a satisfactory environment without undue financial burden on the public.

VI. Labour and Manpower

1. The Canadian Occupational Wage Structure

Stephen G. Peitchinis

University of Calgary

In theory, differences in pay among occupations will tend toward a level which will reflect the differences in costs incurred in the acquisition of the different occupational qualifications. The costs involved are both the actual expenditures related to the acquisition of the relevant qualifications and the earnings forgone during the period when the qualifications were being acquired.

This postulate is based on the hypothesis that as long as differences in pay among occupations exceed differences in costs, supply will increase in the occupations which have the pay advantage until the appropriate relationship is attained. It is assumed, of course, that there are no barriers to entry into occupations, that cost-pay relationships dominate decisions on occupational choice, and that there are no physiological and other natural constraints on supply of potential candidates for the various occupational classifications.

In the context of such an assumption, pay differences among occupations which involve the same costs can be explained on the basis of barriers to entry — incapacity to bear the actual cost burdens, inability to forgo income, inadequate educational and training facilities necessitating the imposition of quotas, institutional and organizational barriers designed to restrict supply — and natural deficiencies in potential supply.

Reference is warranted also to the fact that the equalizing postulate relates to the long run. At any given point of time, differences would exist which would manifest prevailing market conditions, relative industry profitabilities, employer–employee relations, and other current influences.

Generally, the occupational wage and salary structure manifests three broad market conditions and hence can be divided in three broad groups of wage and salary rates:

—those which are established under *competitive market conditions* and reflect changes in market forces;

—those which are established under *imperfect market conditions* and reflect the market imperfections imposed by interest groups;

—those which demonstrate *exceptional conditions* — extraordinary abilities reflecting extraordinary earnings, or mental and physical disabilities reflecting sub-standard earnings.

I. The Nature and Role of Imperfections

1. Barriers to entry

Imperfect market conditions prevail where there exist obstacles to entry into occupations and employments: quotas, financial obstacles, restrictive regulations relating to qualifications, discrimination on the basis of sex, age, nationality and residence, inadequate or misleading information, and others. Through the manipulation of such artificial barriers, the manipulator exercises effective control over market forces and thereby facilitates monopoly gains by those who gain entrance into the relevant occupations and employments. By implication, the removal of monopoly gains rests with the effective removal of the conditions which facilitate such gains, namely, the restrictive powers that are exercised by the relevant occupational groups.

2. Consumer ignorance

Another imperfection which facilitates excessive income gains is related to consumer ignorance of the nature of service provided by some specialized occupations. When the buyer of a service is relatively ignorant of the nature, quantity, and quality of service that he requires or purchases, he is subject to exploitation not only in terms of the price per unit of service, but also in terms of the quantity and nature of it that he is actually sold. For example, the quantity, quality, and nature of legal, medical, dental, television, car-repair, and other similar services purchased by the average consumer depend largely on the motivations and judgments of those who provide them, rather than on the rational choice of those who purchase them.

The making of rational choices is conditional upon the existence of alternatives and knowledge regarding the nature of services available, their relative qualities, the nature of need, and the quantity of service that will satisfy the need. How many consumers of legal, medical, or car-repair services possess the competence for rational decision-making in the purchase of such services? Friedman and Kuznets state:

> Since he [the layman] can seldom judge directly the quality of the highly specialized services, he must discriminate among professional men on the basis of reputation, personality, and the like. Hence, the market for professional services is dominated by differentiation of product and imperfection of competition. Different practitioners can charge different prices for services that seem simi-

lar, though they may not be so; and each can charge different prices to different customers. Each has customers he will not lose by charging higher prices than his rivals, and each knows that he cannot attract large numbers of new customers by charging lower prices.[1]

3. Monopsony control in labour markets

A different kind of imperfection exists where there is only one buyer of labour services. The quantity of service that he will purchase and the price that he will pay for it will depend largely on his assessment of the effect on the quality of the labour service and of the long-run effect on his monopsony control. The more remote the possibility of the emergence of competition or the reduction in supply of desirable quality of service, the greater would be his freedom to pay prices which are below those prevailing in markets where competition exists.

4. Inadequate information on prevailing pay rates

Another source of imperfection is imperfect knowledge regarding prevailing rates of pay for the same or similar occupational qualifications.[2] Secrecy regarding the actual rates paid enables buyers to pay different rates for the same or similar occupational qualifications and work activities. This is particularly common in enterprises and institutions in which terms and conditions of employment are not set out in collective agreements. The rates of pay are set for each individual at the time of hire, and are likely to reflect the prevailing market conditions for the relevant occupations as well as scores of personal and economic variables that influence the job seeker and the prospective employer in the course of the exploratory contact between them.

5. Education

Reference was made in the introductory comments to the existence of a relationship between rates of pay and the acquisition of occupational qualifications. It was postulated that differences in pay reflect generally the different costs incurred in the acquisition of the education and training required for the efficient performance of the tasks involved in the relevant work processes.

The relationship between education and income from employment is indicated in Table 1: evidently, there exists a close relationship in the aggregate. In the year to which the statistics refer (1960), the employment

---

[1] Milton Friedman and Simon Kuznets, *Income From Independent Professional Practice*, National Bureau of Economic Research, New York, 1945, p. 3.
[2] See George J. Stigler, "Information in the Labor Market," *Journal of Political Economy*, October 1962 (supplement); Armen A. Alchian, "Information Costs, Pricing, and Resource Unemployment," *Western Economic Journal*, June 1969; Albert Rees and George P. Shultz, *Workers and Wages in an Urban Labor Market*, University of Chicago Press, Chicago, Ill., 1970; Dennis R. Maki, *Search Behaviour in Canadian Job Markets*, Economic Council of Canada, Information Canada, Ottawa, 1972.

income of those who held university degrees averaged two-and-a-half times above the income of those who had only elementary education, just over twice above that of those who had one to three years of high school, and 67 percent above the income of those who had four to five years of high school. The implication of this relationship for the wage and salary structure is that in a market economy barriers to educational opportunity, and the resulting inequalities in educational attainment, will become reflected in differences in wages and salaries.

Table 1: Level of Education and Average Annual Income from Employment, Non-farm Labour Force, Canada, 1960

Level of Education	Income
0-8 years Elementary	$ 3,526
1-3 years High School	4,478
4-5 years High School	5,493
Some University	6,130
University Degree	9,188
Total Average	$ 4,602

Source: Economic Council of Canada, *Second Annual Review: Towards Sustained and Balanced Economic Growth*, Queen's Printer, Ottawa, 1965, p. 86. Reproduced by permission of Information Canada.

6. Preferences and abilities

Worker preferences of employers, places of employment, and nature of employment, and employer preferences of workers in terms of sex, age, education, and other characteristics bear on the rates of pay offered and accepted. Also, varying abilities and rates of productivity become reflected in the pay structure.

The differences in pay which reflect worker and employer preferences represent, in fact, preference costs. The employer who prefers a university graduate for work that can be performed with equal efficiency by a high-school graduate will bear the cost burden of his preference, which is the difference between the pay rates prevailing for the two levels of education. Similarly, the worker who demonstrates preference for employment in a relatively small enterprise, institution, or town over larger establishments and cities bears the cost burden of his preference, which is the difference in pay rates between rural and urban employments, between large, capital-intensive and generally more efficient and higher-paying employments, and small, less efficient but less impersonal employments.

7. Labour organizations

There is no doubt that collective action by workers, whether they are engineers or technicians, doctors or orderlies, lawyers or garbage collectors, constitutes an important market imperfection. There is doubt, however, on the extent to which collective action for bargaining purposes influences the rate of increase in the level of wages. It is most important to note that a distinction is made here between collective action for wage-bargaining purposes and collective institutional action in the form of rules and regulations designed to restrict the supply of manpower and/or to control processes of production. Initially we are concerned with the former.

The problem is that we cannot determine how much wage rates would have increased in the absence of collective bargaining. Hence, we cannot say with any degree of accuracy how much of a given increase in wages is attributable to the collective-bargaining process and the actual or potential coercive powers that unions can exercise, and how much is attributable to the prevailing and anticipated market for the labour involved. Indeed, if the market for a certain type of labour is exceptionally "tight" (a large excess of demand over the existing supply at the prevailing wage rate), it is conceivable that employers doing the hiring would be forced to pay higher wages under the dictates of a competitive market than they in fact do under the coercive bargaining with union representatives.

Therefore, although we can identify the various ways in which labour organizations (unions)[3] can raise the wages[4] of their members, we do not really know to what extent collective bargaining has been responsible for the wage increases that have been granted, since we have no way of knowing how much wages would have increased in the absence of collective bargaining. The conventional wisdom is that in the absence of unions, wages would have increased considerably less. Yet it is conceivable that they would have increased more.

The latter proposition suggests the possibility that collective determination may have had an arresting effect on the increase of wages in some instances. For example, there have been occasions in the past twenty-five years when the Canadian economy experienced serious shortages of labour generally, and very serious shortages of specific kinds of labour. It is conceivable that in a competitive labour market, these shortages would have manifested themselves in higher increases in wages than were obtained through the process of collective bargaining.

There is no agreement among economists on the extent to which unions influence the level of wages.[5] It is generally recognized that through the exercise of their considerable organizational powers and the use of legal coercive procedures most unions can extract increases in wages which may not be justifiable on the basis of prevailing economic realities (the actual and potential economic state of the firm) and tradi-

---

[3] By "unions" we mean all labour organizations whose purpose it is to protect and enhance the economic and other interests of their members. In this context, Teachers' Federations, Medical Associations, and Associations of Public Employees are as much trade unions as are the organizations of bricklayers, plumbers, electricians, steelworkers, and labourers.
[4] By "wages" we mean payments for services rendered, regardless of unit of measure used or method of payment — hour, week, month, year, fee per unit of service, commissions, etc.
[5] For references to the economic literature on this topic and a summary of the various views, see Clark Kerr, "The Impacts of Unions on the Level of Wages," in *Wages, Prices, Profits and Productivity*, The American Assembly, Columbia University, 1959, pp. 91–108.

tionally acceptable criteria in wage determination. However, it is also recognized that most employers are able to counteract such "excessive" increases in pay, particularly over the longer run, through adjustments in labour–capital ratios, changes in the mix of produced inputs used, improvements in production and distribution processes, changes in the occupational structure of the manpower used, adjustments in price structures, etc.

The ability of employers to offset excessive increases in wages does not mean, of course, that unions do not influence wages. When a union extracts from a firm more than the firm is able to pay within its existing structure and operational processes, and thereby forces the firm to undertake appropriate adjustments in order to accommodate the excessive increase, the union becomes the casual factor for the increase even though the increase may be accommodated without reductions in payments to the other factor inputs. Assuming the firm would not have undertaken the adjustments in the absence of the union-imposed wage burden, then the adjustments which accommodated the excess burden can be viewed as union-induced, and the higher wages as union-influenced.

Some observers, however, assert that unions cannot raise wages at all. They base their argument on the theoretical premise that in a competitive market, where payments to factors of production are proportionate to their respective productivities, increases in factor payments can come only from increases in productivity. There are three weaknesses in this argument: the first, and major one, is the fact that the introduction of a union in a perfectly competitive market renders the market imperfect. It is theoretically contradictory to consider the influence of a union on wages in a perfectly competitive market. If there is a union, the market cannot be perfectly competitive. The second weakness rests in the assumption that redistribution of factor proportions is not possible. And the third weakness is found in the assumption that an increase in wages cannot precede an increase in productivity.

The third is an important weakness, which bears significantly on the discussion of the influence of unions on wages. When increases in wage rates are negotiated, one of the criteria to which reference is made is productivity. But the reference is to increases in productivity that have taken place over the period of the expired or expiring contract. Considering that the increase in wages that is being negotiated relates to a specified period in the future, reference to past productivity does not provide a rational basis for wage determination. The practice of relating future increases in wages to past increases in productivity is based on, the assumption that the physical structure and operational processes cannot be altered during the life of the labour–management contract. In other words, it is based upon a static model. In reality, most firms function in a dynamic state: technology changes, produced inputs change, the organizational and operational structures change, and continuous changes in knowledge take place.

Many commentators on the influence of unions on wages convey the impression that there is a positive relationship between wage increases and the size and power of unions. If this were true, then the highest increases in wages and the highest wages would be enjoyed by workers who belong to the *largest* unions. The evidence does not support such a proposition. An examination of the ranking of occupational and industrial wages would reveal a positive relationship between wages and *the degree of control that labour organizations have over production processes.*

This aspect of the problem has not been examined adequately. It relates to the influences exerted on wages and salaries through controls over production processes and influences on market forces. The traditional approach to the examination of trade-union influence on wages has been to analyze the effect of pressures on management through strikes, slowdowns, and other collective pressures. No effort is in evidence of a comprehensive examination of the effect on wages and salaries of institutional (organizational) rules and regulations which relate to the supply of manpower, the rate of manpower utilization, and the methods of manpower utilization. Yet it is well known that many occupations command relatively high wages and salaries because their organizations have succeeded in keeping the supply of manpower in their occupation at levels which ensure continuous scarcity.

It can be argued, of course, that continuous scarcity, and the concomitant rise in prices, will result in the emergence of lower-priced complementary and supplementary occupations, designed to perform lower-level functions in the production of some less-expensive substitute services, and in the introduction of greater efficiency in the production processes. An examination of the occupational composition and qualifications of workers performing related services, and of the instruments employed in the relevant production processes, would establish that over time such changes do, in fact, take place. But it would also show significant differences in the nature and degree of changes that are permitted to take place.

The extent to which complementary and supplementary occupations, instruments, and substitute services have been allowed to emerge and become established appears to be related to the degree of control that occupational organizations exercise over the work processes in which their members participate. The more comprehensive and rigid the control, the fewer the changes are likely to be. Consider, for example, the changes introduced over time in the occupational composition of the labour force related to the provision of legal services and judicial processes, and compare them with changes in the occupational composition and processes related to engineering and technical services, architectural services, and health services. Examples of this nature lead to the general conclusion that organizations do influence relative wages and salaries, both over the short run and over the long run, but the influence over the long run is exerted largely through regulations concerning the qualifications of persons authorized to perform given work functions, rather than through strikes and slowdowns.

II. The Wage and Salary Structure

1. Relative differences between high-paid and low-paid

In 1970 differences in earnings from employment ranged between a high of 385 percent above the national average of wages and salaries and a low of 55 percent below the national average of wages and salaries. On the high side stood physicians and surgeons, with average annual net incomes from employment of $31,970, and on the low side stood thread-clippers employed in the clothing industry, with average annual earnings of $3,086. By contrast, the national average of wages and salaries stood at $6,595. Thus, in 1970 the earnings gap between the highest-paid occupation and the lowest paid occupation was 936 percent.[6]

Table 2 contains information on the average annual earnings of a number of high-paid and low-paid occupations, and on the standing of each relative to the national average of wages and salaries. In 1951 the earnings of high-paid occupations exceeded the national average of wages and salaries by up to 225 percent; by 1959 the difference increased to 270 percent; and by 1970 it increased further to 385 percent. By contrast, in 1951 the earnings of low-paid occupations stood below the national average of wages and salaries by as much as 54 percent. Furthermore, their relative position appears to have deteriorated in subsequent years: in 1959 they stood below the national average by as much as 46 percent, and there is no evidence of any relative improvement in 1970.

Table 2: *Average Annual Earnings of High-Paid*
and Low-Paid Occupations, Absolute Amounts and
Relative to National Average Wages and Salaries: 1951, 1959, 1970

Occupation	Average Annual Earnings From Employment			Relative to National Average of Wages and Salaries		
	1951	1959	1970	1951	1959	1970
National Average of Wages & Salaries	$ 2,602	$ 3,820	$ 6,595	100	100	100
1. Medical Doctors & Surgeons*	8,102	14,151	31,970	312	370	485
2. Lawyers*	8,093	12,019	24,609	314	315	373
3. Consulting Engineers*	8,416	12,980	19,637	326	340	298

[6] A distinction is made here between "occupation" and "administrative position." Hence, comparisons are not made with the average salaries of presidents and general managers of corporations and institutions, which exceed substantially the net incomes of physicians and surgeons. For example, in 1968 the average total remuneration of general managers ranged between $26,150 in the Atlantic region and $52,350 in the Pacific region. See H.V. Chapman and Associates Ltd., *Report on Executive Salaries in Canada 1967–68.*

4. Dentists*	5,199	10,038	21,009	202	263	319
5. Accountants*	6,849	9,833	17,251	265	257	262
6. University Teachers (19 universities)	4,797	7,979	14,887	184	209	226
7. Threadclipper (man's clothing)	1,400	1,747	3,086	54	46	47
8. Freezerman (fish products)	1,975	2,708	3,738	77	71	57
9. Press Operator (dry cleaning)	1,387	1,826	3,573	54	48	54
10. Warper & Beamer (woolen industry)	2,576	2,873	4,422	100	75	67
11. Employees of Institutions	1,754	2,211	4,491	68	58	68
12. Junior Clerk (male) — (manufacturing)	2,413	2,699	4,935	94	71	75
13. General Labourer — (manufacturing)	2,493	3,217	5,525	97	84	84

*Net earnings from self-employment.

Sources: Nos. 1–5, from Department of National Revenue, *Taxation Statistics,* Queen's Printer, Ottawa (annual); No. 6, from Statistics Canada, *Salaries and Qualifications of Teachers in Universities and Colleges, 1970–71;* Nos. 7–13 from Department of Labour, *Wage Rates, Salaries and Hours of Labour,* Queen's Printer, Ottawa (annual).

2. Differences in wages between skilled and unskilled wage-earners

The percentage difference in wage rates between skilled and unskilled wage-earners was substantially greater in 1939 than in 1970; in many industries the difference narrowed by more than one half. For example, in 1939 the pay rate of a sheet-metal worker exceeded the rate of the labourer in the sheet-metal-products industry by 105.3 percent; in 1970 the difference between the two was 9 percent. In the railways, the difference between the rate of the shop labourer and the rates of shop mechanics and dispatchers narrowed from 92.7 percent and 180.5 percent, respectively, in 1939, to 42.7 percent and 66.2 percent, respectively, in 1970. In the sawmilling industry in British Columbia, the differential between the labourer's rate and the rate of a sawyer narrowed from 172 percent in 1939 to 44 percent in 1970; and in the pulp and paper industry (newsprint), the differential between the beaterman's rate and the rate of the machine tender narrowed from 196 percent to 54 percent over the same period. In the construction industry in Toronto, the percentage difference between the rate of the labourer and the rates of bricklayers and masons, electricians, and plumbers narrowed from 122 percent in 1939 to 46 percent, 59 percent, and 57.7 percent respectively, in 1970.

Table 3: Occupational Wage Differentials, 1939–1970

(percent of base rate)

Year	Construction[a] Base Rate: Labourer			Railways Base Rate: Shop Labourer			Pulp & Paper— Newsprint Base Rate: Beaterman		Sheet Metal Products Base Rate: Labourer	
	Brick- layers	Carpenters	Painters	Shop Mechanics	Section Foreman (Classified Yard)	Dispatchers	Machine Tenders	Third Hands	Shipper	Sheet Metal Workers
1939	222	200	167	193	156	281	296	188	118	205
1944	180	162	147	160	137	216	259	181	127	171
1950	205	184	158	139	120	182	207	156	108	153
1956	180	166	141	138	121	160	191	147	112	142
1962	156	144	131	136	120	156	160	125	113	145
1966	139	136	119	133	118	176	174	135	118	120
1970	146	139	123	143	121	166	154	122	122	109

[a]Buildings and Structures, City of Toronto.

Source: From hourly rates published in Department of Labour, *Wage Rates, Salaries and Hours of Labour*, Queen's Printer, Ottawa (annual).

Table 3 contains information on the behaviour of wage differentials between skilled and unskilled occupations over the period 1939–1970. The figures (in percentage terms) are the ratios of the straight-time (as distinct from overtime) wage rate of skilled workers to that of unskilled workers (labourers or their equivalent). Account is not taken of bonuses and fringe benefits, nor is consideration given to increases in pay through upgrading of skilled workers. The first of these may not have a serious distorting effect on the differentials, since skilled and unskilled employed by the same firm generally enjoy the same fringe benefits; but the second can be the source of serious distortions, particularly in periods of full employment and when wage and price controls are in effect. At such times the straight-time rates may remain unchanged, which would be reflected in constant differentials, but in fact skilled workers may gain substantial increases in pay through movement up the scale of grades. A study by the Organization on Economic Co-operation and Development provides the following explanation for this process of "wage drift":

> From time to time, drift has been a symptom of excess demand for labour, where employers have competed for labour in the same bargaining area, or have been reluctant to incorporate additional payments into basic rates lest the increases thus granted spread to less scarce groups.[7]

An examination of Table 3 reveals a general and substantial contraction in pay differentials over the period 1939–1970. It is manifested in every industry, and it is particularly pronounced in relation to the rates of unskilled and skilled occupations — more substantial in relation to skilled and unskilled than in relation to unskilled and semi-skilled. The table also reveals that most of the contraction occurred within the 1940-50 decade. Since about 1950 a narrowing trend continues to be in evidence, but the rate is relatively small and there is no evidence of consistency. Indeed, there have been brief periods when differentials widened, but over time the narrowing trend continued. In this context, it is not possible to draw any definite conclusion regarding the future, from the widening in evidence during recent years.

3. Factors accounting for the narrowing of wage differentials based on skill

From a strictly statistical standpoint, the most certain factor contributing to the sharp contraction in differentials during the period 1939–1944 was the Canadian government's wartime wage policy, which provided for (a) equal cents-per-hour increases to all workers, regardless of skill, designed to offset increases in the cost of living, and (b) equal cents-per-hour increases in the basic rates of all workers in individual industries who could demonstrate that their rates were lower than rates paid for comparable work in the same locality. Both provisions had strong levelling effects on wage differentials.

[7] Organization for Economic Co-operation and Development, *Wages and Labour Mobility*, Paris, 1965, p. 22.

The question arises whether economic conditions justified the wage policy in effect during the period, and, by implication, whether the levelling process would have taken place in the absence of the administrative intervention to which it is being attributed. In relation to the cost-of-living increment, both economic and welfare considerations were postulated: low-paid workers have limited opportunity for substitution in their basket of goods; hence, relatively small increases in the cost of living reduce their living standard to subsistence or below subsistence. Therefore, when the state deems it necessary to impose wage controls, welfare considerations dictate the adoption of measures designed to ensure relative stability in the purchasing power of the wage income of those whose opportunity for substitution in consumption is limited.

The granting of equal monetary increments to all categories of workers, regardless of skill, could be justified on the basis of the prevailing economic conditions at the time. First, the demand for unskilled labour was as strong as that for skilled workers. Second, from the standpoint of their effect on prices, it is better to raise the wages of all workers by the same *absolute amount* as that granted to the lowest paid, than by the same *proportion* as that granted to the lowest paid. The latter approach will preserve the differentials, but will raise wage costs substantially more than the former approach.

Furthermore, because skilled workers became relatively scarce, many of them were assigned work-functions which only they could perform, transferring their less difficult functions to the unskilled and semi-skilled workers. Such transfers of functions from highly specialized to less specialized and from the less specialized to non-specialized workers are characteristic of labour markets which experience acute shortages of specialized labour.[8] They manifest themselves in (a) an upgrading of the job functions of the unskilled, (b) a relative decrease in demand for the skilled, and (c) a corresponding decrease in supply of unskilled workers. It is relevant to note that each of these effects provides further economic justification for the reduction in pay differences between the skilled and unskilled.

The attribution to wartime wages policy of a significant role in the narrowing of differentials invites the question: why did the gap continue to narrow when the controls and regulations were no longer in effect? An examination of the economic conditions that prevailed in the period 1944–1949 suggests the continued existence of forces which favoured a continuation of the narrowing process: prices were rising at a higher rate than during the war and the economy was expanding at a very rapid rate, thereby generating an increase in demand for both skilled and unskilled workers.

An important force accounting for narrowing wage differences in the postwar period has been the expansion of industrial unions. Since their memberships were constituted predominantly of semi-skilled and unskilled industrial workers, it should not be surprising that they sought equal

[8] For obvious reasons this is particularly characteristic and widespread in periods of war. Melvin Reder comments on it in "Wage Differentials: Theory and Measurement," in *Aspects of Labour Economics*, National Bureau of Economic Research, New York, 1962, p. 271.

cents-per-hour increases in pay for all workers on whose behalf they negotiated. What is surprising to interested observers is the absence of evidence that employers or skilled workers opposed such a policy. It would appear employers were not concerned about the possible negative effect of narrowing differentials on the supply of skilled workers; while skilled workers demonstrated a degree of silent acceptance which can only be interpreted as admittance on their part that the prewar differentials, for which they were responsible in part, did not represent a fair distribution of the wage bill. It has been suggested that in some industries they exercised a sort of monopoly power and got for themselves shares of the wage bill which exceeded their marginal products.[9] Therefore the apparent lack of opposition to the narrowing process from either employers or skilled workers can be interpreted to add credence to the argument that the wage structure was strongly biased in favour of the skilled. By implication, their silence can be interpreted to constitute an implicit agreement to allow the narrowing process to continue until a more equitable wage structure evolved.[10]

However, by the early 1960s the opposition of craft (i.e., skilled-worker) groups to continuation of the "equal-cents-per-hour" wage policy gathered momentum and threatened to split industrial unions in some instances and multi-union negotiations in others.[11] Craft groups threatened to secede and form independent organizations, unless provision were made for a craft premium on top of the general uniform monetary increases. They argued that their consent over a period of twenty years to press for uniform improvements in wages, benefits, and working conditions was motivated by a desire to assist in the betterment of the economic position of the low-paid unskilled workers. The time had come to establish "more appropriate" wage relationships among occupations.

Claims for the restoration of wage relationships in existence sometime in the past, or for the establishment of different sets of relationships from the prevailing ones, rest on the implicit assumption that labour-market conditions and occupational relationships within processes of production are as they were at the relevant period in the past, or that changes in processes have taken place which are not reflected in the existing sets of wage relationships.

Nevertheless, there is evidence that most industrial unions modified their wage policies to accommodate the demands of their skilled members. Beginning in about 1965, the skilled–unskilled wage gap has manifested signs of relative stability and, in some instances, a slight widening. It is conceivable, of course, that the accommodation of the demands of the skilled is a manifestation of the changed demand–supply situation for skilled and unskilled workers. If the accommodation is politically motivated, that is, if it is the consequence of intra-union conflict, then in the

[9] See Mary Jean Bowman "Human Capital: Concepts and Measures", in Selman Mushkin, ed., The Economics of Higher Education, U.S. Government Printing Office, Washington, D.C., 1962.
[10] Richard A. Lester examines this issue in "Economic Adjustments to Changes in Wage Differentials," in George W. Taylor and Frank C. Pierson, eds., New Concepts in Wage Determination, McGraw-Hill, New York, 1957.
[11] The conflict was particularly forceful within the United Auto Workers Union and between craft and non-craft railway unions which were negotiating jointly.

long run adjustments can be expected to take place in processes and occupational mixes to provide the new sets of wage relationships with economic foundations.

Another development in the postwar period which favoured the continuation of the narrowing process was the demand–supply situation for both skilled and unskilled workers: the supply of skilled immigrants from Western Europe and the British Isles was rising at a rate which at times exceeded the rate of increase in demand; concurrently, many of the unskilled workers who had demonstrated aptitude for skilled functions during the war, were given opportunities to acquire skills in the postwar period, and thousands of them accepted the challenge. The effect of these two developments was to increase the supply of skilled workers and to decrease the supply of unskilled workers. Furthermore, beginning in the mid-1940s, an increasing proportion of young people remained in school longer and attained higher levels of schooling. Longer schooling and the consequent postponement of entrance into the labour market had the effect of reducing the supply of unskilled young workers, while the attainment of higher levels of schooling resulted in an increase in supply of workers with potential for skilled occupations. Other things being equal, the effect on wages of these changes in the actual and potential supply of skilled and unskilled workers would be to raise the wages of the unskilled proportionately more.

The downward transfer of work functions from the skilled to the unskilled, which became necessary during the period of wartime scarcity of skilled manpower, was increasingly facilitated in subsequent periods by generally rising levels of education. The education gap that existed between skilled and unskilled workers began to narrow, and increasing numbers of the unskilled were attaining levels of education which qualified them for low-level skilled positions or for skill-training programs.[12]

Concurrent with the general increase in levels of education attained, there evolved a better understanding of the nature of functions involved in work activities, and a better assessment of the levels of education required for the efficient performance of those functions. For many work activities, the level of general education required for training in the skilled functions differed little from the level possessed by those who performed the unskilled functions. Wilkinson found that in 1961 the education required of machinists, sheet-metal workers, welders, and electricians, respectively, was on the average, only 0.6, 0.4, 0.1, and 0.6 years higher than that required of the labourer.[13]

Generally, employers have tended to demand higher educational qualifications of some employees than could be justified by the nature of work functions performed by them. There are good reasons for doing so: (1) when a general increase in educational requirements for all or some work functions is anticipated, it is quite rational to demand such qualifica-

[12] The effect of on-the-job training on occupational differentials is examined by Jacob Mincer in "On-the-Job Training: Costs, Returns, and Some Implications", *Journal of Political Economy*, October 1962 (supplement).
[13] Bruce W. Wilkinson, *Studies in the Economics of Education*, Occasional Paper No. 4, Economics and Research Branch, Department of Labour, Ottawa, July 1965, p. 118.

tions now; (2) the widespread adoption of seniority rules and internal regulations regarding promotions compels the introduction of hiring policies which take into account the possibility that the individual may become a candidate for automatic elevation to a position of greater responsibility; and (3) when significant technological changes take place continually, there exists considerable uncertainty regarding the nature of change that might be necessary in the educational and skill qualifications of the labour force. The greater this uncertainty, the greater the tendency to demand educational qualifications which would enable the average worker to perform a range of new work functions with the minimum of additional training. It follows that the greater the uncertainty regarding the nature of changes in work functions, the greater would be the tendency to demand more uniform educational qualifications — particularly when the only known common requirement for all work functions is a higher level of general education. This implies a lessening in the heterogeneity of the industrial labour force, which in turn would mean the emergence of characteristics of a more perfect industrial labour market. If this in fact is the trend, then it should follow that there exists an economic justification for the narrowing of relative occupational wage differentials.

2. Implications
Of Manpower and Immigration Policy

Noah M. Meltz *

University of Toronto

With the exception of crisis periods of high unemployment, manpower and immigration policies have concentrated on changing the size and composition of labour supply. In this article we will explore the developments of manpower policy during its various phases since 1960. Section I discusses the theoretical framework for manpower policy. Section II provides the background to the development of manpower policies in the 1960s. Section III discusses manpower and immigration policies from 1960 to 1965, while Section IV does the same for the period 1966 to 1970. Section V outlines the policy situation in the early 1970s. In Section VI the general implications of manpower and immigration policy are explored. This final section proposes a more balanced approach to manpower policy, which operates on labour demand as well as labour supply.

I. The Theoretical Framework for Manpower Policy

The term "manpower" has come into popular usage but it remains a somewhat vague concept subject to differing interpretations. Everyone agrees that manpower policy focuses on the labour market. Differences arise over what public policy should aim to do in the labour market and how it should be done. Before we examine the manpower policies which have been followed in Canada since 1960, we will outline the general working of labour markets in order to indicate the context within which manpower programs operate.

The labour market brings together the demand for labour and the

* The author would like to acknowledge the helpful comments and suggestions on an earlier draft of this article by Professors W.R. Dymond and David Stager.

supply of labour, producing both employment and earnings. In addition, the operation of the labour market usually leaves some people unemployed at any one point in time. Some people will be between jobs, some people will not be suited for available jobs or not prepared to take available jobs, some people may not be aware of available jobs, and there may also not be sufficient labour demand for everyone to be hired.

The supply of labour, which in practice is measured by the labour force, comprises all persons who are either employed or unemployed (without work and actively seeking work). This supply is drawn from the adult population of Canada, both persons born in Canada and those who have come as immigrants. These people enter the labour force with certain education and training, and will in turn acquire both experience in certain kinds of work and further training and perhaps further education. It is important to note that the labour force is continually changing from year to year, not only in total numbers but also in terms of the composition of individuals who make it up. People enter and leave the labour force. Students enter the labour force in huge numbers in the summer and then withdraw in the fall. Other people also enter and leave; some to take seasonal jobs, others to take retraining courses. In addition, a large number of people change their jobs every year and even several times a year. This means that the supply of persons for particular occupations changes frequently.

The demand for labour is a derived demand, meaning that the demand for the goods and services which people purchase for final consumption provides the ultimate source of demand for labour. Employment and wages therefore depend on the demand for goods and services in the economy. By the same token, the prices and output of goods and services will be affected by developments in the labour market. The labour market is closely linked with developments in the final-product market, and manpower-policy considerations have to keep this two-way relationship in mind.

Manpower policies can affect the labour market in a number of ways. Policies can be designed to change the supply of labour to particular occupations and to particular geographical areas through training and apprenticeship programs, licensing requirements, immigration, and information on job and worker availability. Policies to affect labour demand include direct job creation, or indirect job creation through stimulating the economy.[1]

It is important to note that labour markets are interrelated. Developments in one particular market have effects on other markets as well. If the supply of a particular type of labour is increased, some persons with this type of skill may decide to transfer to other occupations in which earnings and non-wage considerations appear to be much more attractive. A training program to increase the supply of a particular kind of labour may unintentionally produce an increase in supply for other occupations, and may or may not alter supply to the intended occupation. By the same token,

---

[1] Some economists designate general economic stimulation as "employment policy" and include under "manpower policy" only selective job-creation programs. Other economists exclude all demand-side policies from the term "manpower policies". In this article we will include all actions on the demand-side under the manpower heading.

a policy to provide employment in a particular occupation for previously unemployed persons could raise wages in the occupation, thereby inducing some persons to leave their current jobs and seek work in the expanding sector. The net effect could be to increase employment in the sector but leave the number of unemployed unchanged or perhaps even higher than it was previously. These examples show how labour markets are interrelated and how programs designed to produce one result could produce another, perhaps opposite, result from that intended.

Not only are labour markets closely related, but they are tied in with the market for final products. Changes in employment permit changes in output, while changes in wage and salary rates affect the cost of production. In 1958 it was discovered that there was a historical relationship between the level of unemployment in an economy and the rate of change in average wages. The lower the level of unemployment, the greater the rate of increase in wage rates, and vice versa. This historical statistical relationship was called the "Phillips curve," after the researcher who first discovered the relationship.[2] Subsequently, a similar inverse relationship was found to exist between the level of unemployment in a country and the annual rate of change in prices. This latter relationship has been called the trade-off curve, implying a policy dilemma between reducing unemployment on the one hand and producing a higher rate of inflation on the other. The theoretical underpinning for the trade-off curve is the Phillips curve and the underpinning for the Phillips curve is the concept that as the level of unemployment is reduced, bottlenecks are encountered in certain labour markets such that demand exceeds supply even though in other labour markets supply may exceed demand. The result is that increases in employment can be made only by raising wages to attract labour to the bottleneck markets, and this increase in wages in turn means an increase in costs of production, which is passed on to consumers in the form of higher prices. It is further assumed that the monetary authorities permit an expansion in the money supply to enable consumers to purchase the same volume of goods at the higher prices, in order to avoid large-scale unemployment and to permit economic growth.

Manpower policy enters the picture as a means of solving the dilemma. If manpower programs can remove some of the labour-market bottlenecks by increasing labour supply in shortage areas (and perhaps at the same time reducing surpluses in other areas), then output and employment can be expanded with less pressure on wages and in turn on prices. Manpower policies would thereby shift the Phillips curve and the trade-off curve to more favourable positions in which there would be a lower wage increase and a lower price increase, respectively, at each level of unemployment. Manpower policy aims to prevent the wage rates of some workers from increasing as fast as they might otherwise have done in certain bottleneck occupations. On the other hand, the workers that transfer into the bottleneck occupations may raise their earnings. Manpower programs therefore contain equity considerations, since they not only affect workers' incomes

[2] A.W. Phillips, "The Relation Between Unemployment and the Rate of Change in Money Wage Rates in the United Kingdom, 1862–1957", Economica, No. 25, November 1958, pp. 283–299.

but can affect incomes of different groups of workers in different ways.

The trade-off relationship contains another important theoretical concept relating to the cause and the cure for unemployment which is in excess of the normal frictional levels. A change in the trade-off relationship as a result of bottlenecks in certain labour markets could be interpreted as a product of a mismatching of available labour supply and labour demand. If the structure of the economy changed as a result of shifts in labour demand and/or labour supply, increases in total demand may not reduce unemployment, but only increase prices. This would occur if there were bottlenecks due to structural changes which prevented labour from moving from surplus to shortage areas. Under this concept, the cause of a particular high level of unemployment could be structural changes and not simply insufficient aggregate demand. The appropriate remedy would depend on the ailment which was diagnosed. If the cause of the high unemployment were insufficient aggregate demand, then the remedy would be to increase aggregate demand. If the cause were structural changes, then the remedy would be to concentrate on correcting the structural imbalances through appropriate manpower programs such as training.

The importance for public policy of the diagnosis of the causes of economic problems can be seen from the foregoing. We now turn to the evolution of manpower policies in Canada as they attempted to deal with changing economic problems.

II. Background Factors to the Development of Manpower Policies in the 1960s

In 1945 the federal government set as an economic goal the maintenance of a high level of employment. For more than a decade after 1945 employment was not a serious concern, because the level of unemployment was very low. The major economic issue in that period was the need to expand production. Immigration has always been an important source of supply of labour. Prior to 1945, the massive inflows of immigrants into Canada were almost entirely offset by equally large outflows of emigrants (not necessarily the same people), most of whom went to the United States. After 1945 the number of persons leaving Canada was far less than the number entering, so that immigrants provided a means to enable the economy to expand rapidly.

In 1955 the Royal Commission on Canada's Economic Prospects was established, and two years later it saw only a rosy economy ahead with no problems of unemployment. It was perhaps a touch of irony that in the same year the Commission reported, the Canadian economy entered a period of prolonged recession with high rates of unemployment and much slower real growth than previously.

In 1958 unemployment averaged 7 percent. Not only was unemployment high, but it was observed that the successive economic slowdowns after 1945 left in their wake higher and higher plateaus of unemployment. In the period 1946 to 1953, unemployment averaged 2.8 percent. From 1953 to 1957 the average was 4.3 percent. From 1958 to 1961 the unemployment rate was a still higher 6.8 percent on average. In addition to this upward creep in the unemployment level, it was observed that marked changes were taking place in the occupational distribution of the labour force. The proportion of white-collar and service workers was steadily increasing, especially professional and clerical workers, while that of primary and manual workers was declining, particularly agricultural labourers. The occupations which were growing were those utilizing persons with higher levels of education, while those which were declining were characterized by low levels of education. The unemployed tended to be those with low educational and skill levels. During this period there was a great deal of discussion about the impact of automation on employment opportunities, particularly opportunities for lower-skilled and less-educated persons. When a prolonged recession began in 1958, many people attributed the slowdown to the effects of automation. Since the unemployed were mainly manual workers, including unskilled labourers, it was argued that they did not have sufficient skills to be able to perform the type of work that was being required as a result of automation. The belief grew that there was a mismatching of labour demand and labour supply and that this was the primary cause of the high levels of unemployment in Canada. Those who propounded this explanation of the cause of unemployment were called "structuralists," because they believed that most of the unemployment arose from changes in the structure of the economy. An opposing school of thought saw the primary cause of unemployment as insufficient aggregate demand. The solution for the latter group was to increase total spending in the economy. The structuralists' solution was to adapt the labour supply to fit the types of labour being demanded, by increasing the amount of technical training provided to workers, particularly to youth — who would be entering the labour force in greater and greater numbers in the years to come.

Other developments in the late 1950s supported those who believed in a need for more training of workers. Studies by the federal Department of Labour revealed a high drop-out rate of males from high school and a lack of vocational preparation. These male youths had unemployment rates 2.5 times the over-all rate. Another factor which aided the argument for more training was the decline in the number of immigrants from the peak inflows during 1956 and 1957. There was a question whether Canada could continue to recruit as many trained persons from abroad as formerly. At the same time as there was increased interest in the technical training of youth, there was also more interest in professional training, including university education. The knowledge that the postwar population bulge was about to reach post-secondary school age meant that policy-makers were forced to consider increasing expenditures for advanced training and education. All of these developments underlay the first large-scale manpower program in Canada, which began in 1960.

III.   Manpower and Immigration Policies, 1960 to 1965

The years 1960 through 1965 can be called the period of the federal government's first attempt at a large-scale manpower program. The major objective of the program was to reduce the high levels of unemployment of manual and primary workers which prevailed at the end of the 1950s, by increasing the levels of skills of youth who were about to enter the labour force and increasing the skills of workers who were already unemployed. In addition, there were programs designed to create employment directly and to facilitate movement from depressed to expanding regions. For the white-collar occupations, the objective was to expand the supplies of professionals through financial encouragement to universities and students. One general theme ran through all of the manpower programs: youths were advised to stay in school so they could earn more money and experience a lower incidence of unemployment.[3]

The major element in the manpower program from 1960 to 1965 was the Technical and Vocational Training Act of 1960. This Act, which was the responsibility of the federal Department of Labour, was a shared-cost program with the provinces, which covered both capital grants for the construction of training institutions and the sharing of the costs of operating the programs. The purpose of TVTA, as the Act became known, was to provide financial assistance for the development and operation of technical and vocational training facilities and programs throughout Canada. The capital building projects were also conceived as a way of reducing unemployment through increased activity in the construction industry. TVTA represented a massive increase in government spending in the manpower area. In the forty years before 1960, the federal contribution to technical training in Canada amounted to $110 million.[4] Between 1960 and 1965, more than $600 million was spent. One third of this sum went for operating expenses devoted mainly to three programs: Program 5 — training of the unemployed; Program 3 — trade and other occupational training; and Program 2 — technician training. By 1965–66, 163,000 people were enrolled in these three programs, and half of these were unemployed persons being retrained. A year later the three programs contained 254,000 persons, of whom 150,000 were in the unemployed category. All of this training had the additional effect of lowering the measured rate of unemployment, since persons taking TVTA programs were considered to be outside the labour force.

The government also introduced direct assistance for job creation through various programs to stimulate winter employment. The two major programs were the Municipal Winter Works Incentive Programs and the Winter House Building Incentive Program. The former was a shared-cost program with the provinces and municipalities. The latter provided a payment of $500 to the owner-builder or the first purchaser of housing substantially built between December and March. Spending on these two programs reached a peak of $60 million in 1964–65 and was $58 million

[3] In 1960–61 the federal Department of Labour initiated a pamphlet, poster, and media campaign to encourage youth to stay in school. Almost one and a half million copies of a pamphlet entitled "Why Bother to Graduate" were distributed in English and French through provincial Departments of Education and the Quebec Department of Youth to all students in grade 8 and in secondary schools. The same quantity of another pamphlet, "Education, Training and Employment," was distributed through the schools to parents. (Annual Report, Canada Department of Labour, 1960–61, p. 50.)

[4] J. Stefan Dupré, David M. Cameron, Graeme McKechnie and Theodore B. Rotenberg, Federalism and Policy Development, The Case of Adult Occupational Training in Ontario (Toronto: University of Toronto Press, 1973), p. 17.

in 1965–66. The impact of these progams on on-site jobs was estimated to be in the hundreds of thousands, even excluding jobs in supporting industries. If one adds the job content of projects spurred by the capital portion of the Technical and Vocational Training Act, the number would be further multiplied .

A final factor in the domestic portion of the manpower program during 1960 to 1965 was the transfer of the National Employment Service (NES) from the control of the Unemployment Insurance Commission (UIC) to the operating part of the federal Department of Labour. Before 1965, the NES, under the jurisdiction of the UIC, reported to Parliament directly through the Minister of Labour. As of 1965, the NES became a part of the Department under the authority of the Deputy Minister.

The contribution of foreign countries to Canada's labour supply in terms of quantity was at a low ebb between 1960 and 1965. Gross immigration has tended to follow the economic cycle in Canada with a lag of about a year or so, and the prolonged recessionary period from 1958 to 1961 showed in the immigration figures.

What were the implications of manpower and immigration policies between 1960 and 1965? If we consider the stated objectives of increasing the supply of technically trained persons, the policies were a success. The number of both youth and adults participating in training programs offering some skills increased greatly, as did the number of apprentices who obtained skills, particularly in the field of motor-vehicle repair and in the construction trades. By 1966, the unemployment rate was down to 3.6 percent. This was the lowest rate in 10 years and was close to the 3-percent interim target for full employment which the Economic Council of Canada had set in its *First Annual Review* in 1964. The almost full-employment situation had ended the earlier debate over structural versus insufficient-demand unemployment. The Economic Council of Canada concluded that "the previous excess levels of unemployment were primarily associated with inadequate levels of total demand."[5]

At the close of the TVTA program, the economy was judged to be healthy and the federal Department of Labour had introduced a full range of manpower programs dealing with upgrading the quality of the supply of labour. Furthermore, it had begun to work on improving the effectiveness with which labour markets operate by introducing the manpower-mobility program in 1965 to enable workers to move from stagnant or economically contracting areas to expanding areas. The Department had also introduced the manpower-consultative service in 1964–65 to assist employers in research and planning in order to minimize the impact of industrial changes. There were only two areas of manpower policy outside the control of the federal Department of Labour: immigration and professional education. The second area was regarded as being under the jurisdiction of the provincial governments. Only immigration had to be added to the Department of Labour to locate all manpower policy in one place. In 1966, manpower programs and immigration were combined in a new department which was to provide a comprehensive manpower policy for Canada. The background

[5] Economic Council of Canada, *Second Annual Review: Towards Sustained and Balanced Economic Growth* (Ottawa: Queen's Printer, 1965), p. 31.

and results of the policies of the Manpower Department are discussed in the next section.

IV. Manpower and Immigration Policies, 1966 to 1970

Just as the manpower programs from 1960 to 1965 were heavily influenced by the economic developments in the two or three preceding years, so were the manpower programs in the second half of the 1960s. From 1962 to 1965, the economy had recovered from the previous recessionary period and had experienced the longest peacetime cyclical expansion in Canadian history. A similar expansion took place in the United States and other industrialized countries. By 1966 Canada had reached virtually full employment without inflationary pressure. In order to maintain stable growth and full employment, the Economic Council suggested the need for increased efficiency and better matching of supply and demand. In fact, the Council asserted: *"The area of greatest need for urgent and effective action is that of manpower and labour market policies."*[6] The purpose of these policies was to shift the trade-off curve between unemployment and inflation. By increasing the mobility of labour and improving the matching of labour supply and labour demand, the economy would be enabled to continue its rate of real growth and high employment would be be maintained. By increasing the supply of labour to bottleneck occupations, pressures for wage increases and subsequently price increases would be reduced. The Economic Council proposed the establishment of a new ministry of manpower services to carry out labour-market policy. On January 1, 1966, the manpower-related branches of the Department of Labour, including the National Employment Service, were transferred to the Department of Citizenship and Immigration, which was soon renamed the Department of Manpower and Immigration.

The new Department undertook several major revisions in previous manpower programs. First, the Technical and Vocational Training Act of 1960 was phased out[7] and, in its place, the Adult Occupational Training Act of 1967 was introduced. Under this Act (referred to as OTA) the federal government drew a sharp line between the education of youth, which was viewed as a provincial responsibility, and the training of adults, which was to be a federal responsibility because of federal concern for economic developments. The OTA program was to deal with adults who were at least one year beyond the school-leaving age and at least one year out of school or in an apprenticeship program. The Manpower Department would purchase space in training courses from both public and private institutions for persons who could improve their employment and earnings prospects by taking training courses. Unfortunately, specific-skill training was limited to a maximum of 52 weeks, and university education was excluded. A further 52 weeks of basic educational upgrading were allowed, for a maxi-

---

[6] *Ibid.*, pp. 178–179 (italics in original).
[7] As part of the phase-out arrangement for TVTA, the federal government continued to pay capital grants to those provinces whose total spending under TVTA had not reached a figure of $480 per capita of the population aged 15 to 19 years. As a result, in 1970–71 there were $170 million in capital grants under the TVTA extension in addition to the $290 million under OTA.

mum of two years of training. Training allowances, which had been introduced under Program 5 of TVTA, were extended to the entire OTA program and the amount of the allowance was increased.

A second change was that the National Employment Service was renamed the Canada Manpower Division, and the offices were retitled Canada Manpower Centres (CMCs). Placement officers became manpower counsellors. More important, the CMCs, through the counsellors, were to select the persons for training and feed information to the Division, which was to purchase training courses. A third innovation was the establishment of a network of manpower economists who would use the manpower counsellors' information, plus other statistical data, to advise the Manpower Division on what training courses to purchase. Fourth, immigration intake, excluding those sponsored or nominated by relatives, was to be integrated with general manpower policy by assigning "points" for entry into Canada. "Point" values were assigned by taking into consideration labour-market conditions in particular occupations and geographical areas as well as the person's general education and training and particular skill.[8] In addition, the vocational-rehabilitation program, the mobility program, as well as the manpower-consultative service were continued. All of these programs together constituted an attempt to develop a comprehensive manpower program, or what Stefan Dupré has termed the "federal Grand Design for Manpower Policy."[9]

During the period 1966 to 1971, the Canadian economy gradually slipped into another recession, with the rate of unemployment almost doubling from 3.6 percent in 1966 to 6.4 percent in 1971. At the same time, the annual rate of increase in prices moved steadily upward each year, with the exception only of 1971.[10] The result was a worsening during this period in the trade-off between unemployment and inflation, as Kaliski has documented.[11] This result is exactly the opposite of what was desired. The objective of manpower policies in the second half of the 1960s was to improve the trade-off; instead, the trade-off deteriorated. How much, if any, of the blame for the worsening economic situation could be placed on manpower policies as opposed to fiscal and monetary policies or developments in other countries, such as the United States?

In retrospect it would appear that more faith was placed in the ability of manpower policies to alter the trade-off situation than was justified, for several reasons. First and foremost, later studies conducted by the Economic Council showed that a substantial portion of price changes in Canada was imported from abroad.[12] Because exports and imports are so

[8] For a discussion of the "point" system and immigration policy in general, see Lawrence H. Officer, "Immigration and Emigration", in L.H. Officer and L.B. Smith, eds., *Canadian Economic Problems and Policies* (Toronto: McGraw-Hill Canada, 1970), pp. 142–156.

[9] Dupré *et al.*, *op. cit.*, pp. 50–53.

[10] The main factors in the slower rate of price increase during 1971 were the small increase in food prices, due partly to a food-price war among supermarkets, and the appreciation of the Canadian dollar.

[11] See S.F. Kaliski, *The Trade-Off Between Inflation and Unemployment: Some Explorations of Recent Evidence for Canada*, Special Study No. 22, prepared for the Economic Council of Canada (Ottawa: Information Canada, 1972).

[12] See Economic Council of Canada, *Third Annual Review: Prices, Productivity and Employment* (Ottawa: Queen's Printer, 1966).

important to the Canadian economy, developments in other countries, particularly the United States, have an important impact on the Canadian economy. The fact that prices in other countries were rising in the late 1960s provided a spur to price increases in Canada independent of Canadian economic policies. Second, the Canadian government decided to reduce the rate of economic growth as a means of increasing the amount of unemployment in the country in order to dampen the rate of price increase. The government appeared to believe that the historical trade-off curve would also operate in the short run and that by increasing unemployment prices could be reduced. There was a brief reduction in the rate of price increase in 1971, but this was primarily the result of decreases in food prices arising from a supermarket price war and of the appreciation of the Canadian dollar.[13] In 1972 prices rose at the rapid rate of 4.8 percent, while unemployment was at a high level of 6.3 percent. A further factor in the trade-off deterioration was the change in unemployment-insurance regulations, which more than doubled the maximum weekly benefits, extended the benefit period, reduced the number of weeks required for eligibility, and extended the coverage to almost all persons in the labour force. These changes may have increased the measured level of unemployment somewhat, perhaps to the order of 0.5 percent or more, and in the process worsened the trade-off position.

If the manpower policies were not able, by themselves, to improve the trade-off position, what impact did the programs have from 1966 to 1970? The Department of Manpower and Immigration has developed a model to measure the benefits and costs of training under its OTA program. The meager results which have been made public show benefits of the program exceeding costs by $3 for every $1 of government expenditure on the program. This is encouraging, but we need to know much more. Since the model has no control group, no allowance is made for developments which would have occurred if the persons had not taken the training programs. Gains in employment due to changes in the economic situation or normal turnover patterns, as well as increases in wages due to inflation and normal productivity gains, are not included. In addition, no account is taken of what are termed "displacement" and "vacuum" effects. Displacement effects occur when the graduate of a training program simply replaces someone else in a job, thus producing no net employment gain. The vacuum effect occurs when the training of a person, particularly in a profession or skill, results in the creation of jobs for persons in related or supporting areas. How would the inclusion of a control group alter the results of the model? We are told that half of those who were unemployed before courses were unemployed after taking the courses. This result by itself can be interpreted in either a favourable or unfavourable light. W. R. Dymond, a former assistant deputy minister in the Manpower Department, has criticized the manpower program as being irrelevant to the whole issue of the trade-off, since the occupations for which persons have been trained were

---

[13] The federal government's Prices and Incomes Commission, which ran from 1969 to 1972, attributed the improvement in price performance "...to a sharp temporary decline in food prices, a substantial appreciation of Canada's exchange rate and the 1970 price restraint program" — *Summary Report: Inflation, Unemployment and Incomes Policy* (Ottawa: Information Canada, 1972), p. 2.

not occupations which generated inflationary pressures, such as construction, health, and education.[14]

V. Manpower and Immigration Policies in the Early 1970s

The slowdown of the Canadian economy, which became particularly marked during 1970, produced another change in manpower policy. The stated emphasis in policy was away from attempts to shift the trade-off curve or support economic growth and was placed instead on aiding disadvantaged persons and disadvantaged regions of the country. This new emphasis was on what are termed "equity" considerations, which include questions of outright poverty and low-income groups and areas.[15] The training program became an important vehicle for maintaining the income of the unemployed as an alternative (and perhaps an addition) to unemployment insurance, and training funds tended to be allocated on the basis of the incidence of unemployment rather than current or anticipated job opportunities. In addition, the government introduced the Local Initiatives Program (LIP) as a means to create some employment, and subsequently in 1972 added winter-construction incentives to its employment program. At the same time, the unemployment-insurance system was changed to provide increased benefits, increased coverage, a shorter period necessary to qualify for benefits, and a longer benefit period. No comprehensive assessment of either of these developments has been conducted. Assessments of the LIP program have tended to paint a mixed picture of its success, indicating that some persons receiving LIP grants may have been drawn into the labour force specifically by the LIP program rather than being unemployed previously. The unemployment-insurance revisions were criticized in the press and in government for raising the unemployment rate.[16] An academic study tends to confirm that the revisions did raise the unemployment rate somewhat.[17]

A final element in the mixed picture of the early 1970s was the change in immigration regulations. The revised regulations in 1967 allowed visitors to Canada to apply for immigrant status. In 1971–72 the number of persons coming to Canada with the intention of applying for immigrant status in-

---

[14] W.R. Dymond, "Canadian Manpower Policy: A Policy in Search of a Problem", in Industrial Relations Research Association Series, *Proceedings of the Twenty-Fifth Anniversary Meeting, Toronto December 28–29, 1972*, edited by Gerald G. Somers (Madison, Wisconsin: 1973).

[15] For a discussion of the various manpower-policy goals, including equity, see Sylvia Ostry and Mahmood Zaidi, *Labour Economics in Canada*, 2nd ed., (Toronto: Macmillan of Canada, 1972), and Economic Council of Canada, *Eighth Annual Review: Design for Decision-Making: An Application to Human Resources Policies* (Ottawa: Information Canada, 1971).

[16] There was a division on the issue among cabinet members and presumably among the civil servants in different departments, particularly between the Department of Manpower and Immigration on the one hand, and the Department of Finance on the other hand. Apparently, the Manpower Department blamed the Finance Department for slowing down the rate of growth of the economy and thereby increasing the rate of unemployment. The Finance Department blamed the Manpower Department, particularly the then Minister, for introducing the revisions in the unemployment-insurance program, which they felt were raising the unemployment rate and at the same time leaving some jobs unfilled.

[17] Christopher Green, "The Impact of Unemployment Insurance on the Unemployment Rate", paper presented at the Seventh Annual Meeting of the Canadian Economics Association, Kingston, Ontario, June 3, 1973.

creased tremendously. In the fall of 1972 this regulation was changed. Tens of thousands of people thus were living in Canada illegally, many of them in unskilled categories and ineligible for immigration to Canada because of insufficient "points." Subsequently, in the summer of 1973, the Manpower and Immigration Minister announced that any person who came to Canada illegally or as a visitor prior to November 30, 1972 could apply for immigrant status under a substantially relaxed "point" system, provided he did so within a limited time period. These persons are likely to be employed in the unskilled jobs which are almost always "short" of labour. Whether we want to increase the supply of unskilled labour to these occupations depends on national objectives in relation to the Canadian labour market. In order to decide on our policy, we must first have a stock-taking of the over-all implications for the labour market of recent changes in labour demand and labour supply.

VI.   General Implications of Manpower and Immigration Policy in Canada

Manpower and immigration policy in Canada has concentrated on altering labour supply in response to various perceived needs. In the period 1960 to 1965, the major thrust of manpower programs in terms of the number of dollars spent was to train youth and unemployed workers so that they could fit the new jobs which the economy was likely to provide in the light of automation and technological change. From 1966 to 1970, the major manpower objective was to train people to fill labour shortages in order to avoid bottleneck pressures which would first raise wages and subsequently prices. In 1971 the objectives were changed again. This time training was to be viewed in the light of equity considerations, which meant in practice providing income to the unemployed even though the prospects of utilizing the skills were uncertain. Also in 1971 a crash program of job creation was introduced through Local Initiative Projects and Winter Construction projects.

With the exception of crisis periods of very high unemployment, manpower policy has been concerned only with altering labour supply. Several comments can be made about this approach. Virtually no information has been made public as to the results of the spending on training programs. We are told how much money is spent and in what general categories, but we do not know what occupations people have been trained for or how successful the program is in terms of the Department of Manpower and Immigration's own benefit–cost model. A knowledge of what areas people have been trained for is an important additional piece of information, which can be used as an independent check on the results of the benefit–cost model. For example, the occupation with the largest number of vacancies in Canada is that of sewing-machine operators.[18] This is a semi-skilled occupation which is relatively low paying. The occupation is persistently "short" of people. During the 1960s, workers were trained under manpower programs for this occupation, yet shortages per-

---

[18] See David Gower, "The Occupational Composition of Job Vacancies", Canadian Statistical Review, Vol. 48, No. 4, April 1973, pp. 4, 118–123.

sisted. In order to assess the effect of training in this occupation, we need to know how many people were trained for this occupation and how long they remained in this trade. The fact that this shortage has persisted in spite of training programs raises some questions about the role of manpower programs in operating almost exclusively on the supply side of the labour market.

After all, there is no reason why manpower policy should be concerned only with the supply side of the labour market. Programs to affect labour demand could be developed in a number of ways in addition to the crisis-oriented winter-works and local-initiatives programs. Policies to create employment tend to be scattered among a number of government departments, including the Department of Regional Economic Expansion. Such programs should be either brought under one administrative roof or at least co-ordinated with programs to alter labour supply. Second, and perhaps even more important, the manpower-policy reaction to a situation of shortage or surplus does not have to be only one of changing labour supply through training. The case of sewing-machine operators referred to earlier suggests some alternatives. Manpower policy could operate on the side of labour demand by advising firms on ways to improve their productivity and profitability, which in turn would enable them to pay higher wages and/or provide more attractive non-wage benefits, which would enable the firms to solve their labour shortages. Policies designed to alter labour demand could be subject to benefit–cost analysis in the same way as training programs, and this would enable policy-makers to have a wider choice of programs to meet a particular situation. The same approach could be taken to the operation of labour markets. Efforts are being made to introduce self-service employment offices as a means of improving the operation of labour markets, and these efforts should be continued. In approaching a particular labour-market problem, manpower authorities should be able to assess the implications of making adjustments in labour demand, labour supply, or the effectiveness of the particular labour market itself.

A final comment concerns the need for an overview on the operation of labour markets in Canada and the effect of manpower programs. To date, no over-all assessment has been undertaken of the impact of changes in labour demand and labour supply on employment, unemployment, and earnings. Research has tended to be piecemeal. What we need is a regular overview of the Canadian labour market which would periodically take stock of the effect of changes in the economy such as flows of persons from the education system and immigration, as well as the impact of training and other manpower programs. Only when such an assessment is undertaken on a regular basis can we fully assess the implications of manpower and immigration policy.

3. Economics
And the Problems of Minorities

Jean-Luc Migué

École Nationale d'Administration Publique, Québec

The purpose of this essay is to provide an overview of the status of economic knowledge on a subject which covers a wide range of issues, but which could be usefully called the problems of minorities. Whether they are differentiated by race, religion, sex, colour, social class, or other personality characteristics, certain groups within nations somehow seem to fare differently relative to others in terms of economic achievement. Can economics throw some light on the factors behind this state of affairs? I will try in this paper to outline the main theses advanced by economists to explain various phenomena associated with minorities. As applied to the Canadian setting, the greater part of our attention will be devoted to the understanding of the problems of three "minority" groups, namely, women, the young, and French Canadians. The economic status of women and the young will be dealt with first. Then two different hypotheses developed to explain the income and employment pattern of French Canadians will be discussed.

I. General Framework

Let us assume to start with that the economy is composed of only two factors of production, labour and capital. All units of labour are assumed to be identical, and so are all units of capital. Classical analysis teaches us that a profit-maximizing producer in competition will adopt a combination of production factors such that unit costs of production will be minimized. Each firm will employ quantities of a given factor, say labour, until its marginal value product is just equal to the wage rate. More concretely, if an additional worker can add $30 per day to the value of the production in a textile firm (this is his marginal value productivity), it will pay the producer to hire him as long as the wage rate is below $30 per day. Symmetrically, if a worker can earn $30 per day in a textile firm, he will not offer his services to another employer offering less than $30.[1] Within the competitive and full-employment conditions specified, this rule applies to all firms in all industries and for both factors of production. In equilibrium, no movement of factors could be accomplished which could increase the money value of production in one firm or industry without reducing that value in another firm or industry by a larger amount.[2] Unit costs are minimized in all firms in all industries. Production effciency is attained.

In this frictionless world, no differences in money wages could be observed that would not be accounted for by differences in marginal value productivity. Retaining our assumption that all units of labour are identical, the wage rate would not differ between men and women, young and adult persons, French Canadians and non-French Canadians, Negroes and whites. Furthermore, the distribution of employment between firms and between industries would reflect the relative supply of these various groups.

II. The Economic Status of Women and the Young

Some data will help in formulating the questions to be addressed in the analysis of women's and youths' working conditions. The relevant facts are shown in Tables 1, 2, and 3. It is first seen from Table 1 that women consistently experience lower rates of unemployment. The differential (column 5) was of the order of 3.0 to 4.5 percentage points in the early 1960s, but it began to shrink in the later 1960s, reaching some 2.0 percentage points by the early 1970s. Second, the unemployment rate of the young is very substantially higher than for the working population as a whole. It also fluctuates much more markedly over the cycle. The spread between the two rates (column 6) widens when total unemployment rises and diminishes when total unemployment declines. Third, the career orientation of women differs strikingly from that of men. Women are underrepresented in positions of responsibility and higher economic status (Table 2). Most importantly, women's earnings stand at some 55 percent of men's (Table 3). When adjustment is made for differences in the number of hours worked per week and for the number of weeks worked per year, the differential is reduced slightly. Such a differential appears to have persisted for a long period of time. It could also be shown that women's earnings do not increase with age at as high a rate as men's earnings. The spread therefore widens with age. It would appear that the "equal pay for equal work" rule does not apply in the real world. How can this state of affairs be explained? It is shown in the following paragraphs that an analysis based on the dynamics of investment in training can be a powerful tool in explaining these conditions.

Training and education can usefully be considered as investment in human capital, i.e., as expenses designed to improve the productivity of

---

[1] It is assumed here that the entire income of workers is in monetary form. In the real world, other working conditions can be taken into account by potential employees and employers.

[2] In more technical terms, this result is equivalent to the equality between the ratio of the marginal products of the two factors in all industries.

Table 1: Unemployment Statistics, by Sex and Age, Canada, 1961–1972
(percent)

		Unemployment rates			Unemployment differentials	
	1	2	3	4	5	6
	Total	Women	Men	Young (14-24 years)	Col. 3–Col. 2	Col. 4–Col. 1
1961	7.1	3.7	8.4	10.9	4.7	3.8
1962	5.9	3.3	6.9	9.4	3.6	3.5
1963	5.5	3.3	6.4	9.2	3.1	3.7
1964	4.7	3.1	5.3	8.0	2.2	3.3
1965	3.9	2.7	4.4	6.5	1.7	2.6
1966	3.6	2.6	4.0	6.0	1.4	2.4
1967	4.1	3.0	4.6	6.8	1.6	2.7
1968	4.8	3.4	5.5	8.2	2.1	3.4
1969	4.7	3.6	5.2	7.9	1.6	3.2
1970	5.9	4.5	6.6	10.4	2.1	4.5
1971	6.4	5.1	7.0	11.4	1.9	5.0
1972	6.3	5.3	6.8	11.1	1.5	4.8

Source: Statistics Canada, The Labour Force.

Table 2: Occupational Distribution of the Labour Force,
by Sex, Canada, 1961

	(percent)	
	Men	Women
All occupations	100.0	100.0
Owners and managerial occupations	10.2	3.3
Professional and technical	7.6	15.4
— Teaching & Nursing	1.3	11.7
— Other professional	6.2	3.6
Clerical occupations	6.9	28.8
Sales occupations	5.6	8.3
Service and recreation	8.5	22.4
Transport, communication, farming, mining and quarrying	23.5	6.4
Skilled workers and semi-skilled (assembly-line) workers	28.8	11.6
Labourers	6.3	1.2
Not Stated	2.6	2.5

Source: Dominion Bureau of Statistics, Census of Canada, 1961, The Labour Force, Occupations by Sex, Bulletin 3.1–3, 1963. Reproduced by permission of Information Canada.

Table 3: Average Earnings of Women as Percent of Men's Earnings,
Selected Occupational Classes, Canada, 1961

All Occupations	Managerial	Professional (except teaching and nursing)	Teaching	Nursing
54.4	48.1	50.9	59.8	79.5

Clerical	Construction	Commerce	Service
68.6	50.1	35.0	36.6

Source: D.B.S., Census of Canada 1961, *The Labour Force, Earnings, Hours and Weeks of Employment of Wage-Earners by Occupations,* Table 21. Reproduced by permission of Information Canada.

those who acquire such training.[3] By analogy with physical capital, it can be assumed that the incentive to expand the amount of human capital acquired by individuals depends on the returns expected. Included in the cost of the investment are the value placed on the time of trainees and also the direct payments to production factors in the education and training industry. The returns consist in the differential earnings accruing to trained persons relative to untrained persons over their working life.[4]

This way of stating the problem has proved to be a powerful instrument capable of explaining a good proportion of the phenomena observed above in relation to women's and young workers' employment and earnings patterns. First, it is easily understood that an increase in the lifespan spent in an activity by a trained person increases the rate of return on a given investment in education. Now, it is known that women spend less time than men in the labour force. Whether this is the result of the socially determined division of labour between home responsibilities and work, or of the voluntary choice of women to place their role at home first, does not change the outcome.[5] Women have less incentive to invest in marketable skills because the duration of their working life is shorter. This may explain why the representation of women declines as students move upward through the stages of the educational system beyond high school.

[3] The framework of the analysis in these pages was first developed by G.S. Becker, *Human Capital: A Theoretical and Empirical Analysis,* National Bureau of Economic Research, Columbia University Press, New York, 1964; see also G.S. Becker, "Investment in Human Capital: A Theoretical Analysis", *Journal of Political Economy,* LXX, No. 5, Part 2, Supplement, October 1962, pp. 9–49.

[4] In algrebaic terms, the rate of return on investment in training is defined as

$$\sum_{j=1}^{m-1} \frac{C_j}{(1+r)^j} = \sum_{j=m}^{n} \frac{Y_j - X_j}{(1+r)^j}$$

where C_i is the cost of training in period j. The investment period is assumed to extend over the first $m - 1$ periods.
Y_j is income in each period in activity Y, requiring training. The duration of the working life after training is completed is assumed to go from period m to n.
X_j is the income in each period in activity X, requiring no training.
r is the rate of return on the total investment in training.
[5] For an analysis of the factors influencing the labour-force participation rates of women, see D.B.S., Special Labour Force Studies, *Women Who Work,* Series B, No. 2, December 1968.

The approach also helps in understanding why women are strikingly under-represented in most professional occupations and other high-status positions. Three occupational classes account for some 60 percent of the female work force: clerical workers, semi-skilled (assembly-line) workers, and service workers. Few of these generally require education beyond the high-school level. Two so-called female occupations are exceptions to this rule: teaching and nursing, which are firmly dominated by female workers. These two occupations account for an overwhelming proportion of the professional and technical classes shown in Table 2. It is significant that the ratio of women's earnings to men's earnings in teaching and nursing is higher than for other professional occupations (Table 3). Note also that of all occupations classified as professional, teaching and nursing have, or used to have, the shortest training period. This fact may explain why women and students from low-income families seem particularly attracted by these professions.

Training also has an important effect on the relation between earnings and age. Relative to persons with no training, trainees receive lower earnings when they are young (negative in numerous cases) and higher earnings once they have acquired their skill and start collecting returns. This means that the curve relating age and earnings of trained persons would be steeper than for persons with no training. The logic by which women are said to have less incentive to acquire skills applies to training on the job as well as to more formal training in schools. Actually, a good deal of what is usually referred to as experience is equivalent to training on the job. This may explain why wage differentials between men and women with given formal education widens with age. Women with equal formal education relative to men generally receive less training on the job.

While it does provide at least partial answers to some of the questions raised above, this discussion does not explain why women with given educational attainments obtain lower earnings than men and why young people experience unfavourable and volatile unemployment rates. To throw some light on these questions, it will prove useful to distinguish between two kinds of training acquired by people: specific and general. General training or education is useful in many firms, in the sense that it raises the productivity of the employee in these firms. Training acquired in schools and colleges is of this variety. By contrast, specific training is defined as increasing productivity more (or only) in firms providing it. Becker suggests training of astronauts, fighter pilots, and missile men as examples of training having little or no effect on the productivity of trainees in the civilian sectors.[6] In the more general case, much of the training provided on the job by firms is neither completely specific nor completely general. Expenditures incurred by employers to improve their knowledge of their employees' abilities are one form of specific training.

Firms would provide general training on the job only if they did not bear the cost, since trainees collect the returns. No rational firm would undertake an investment the returns of which are to be collected by others. On the other hand, wages paid to employees receiving specific

[6] G.S. Becker, "Investment in Human Capital: A Theoretical Analysis", p. 17.

training would be independent of the amount of training acquired; for, by assumption, employees would be unable to market such skills. Therefore firms would have to bear the cost of providing it, since no rational employee would accept carrying a burden which provides no benefits to himself.

Let us now apply this reasoning to the analysis of women's earnings and the employment patterns of the young. We have now established that firms provide specific training at their own expense and collect the returns therefrom. Furthermore, the level of these returns is dependent on the length of time the employee stays with the firm. In other words, the higher the employees' turnover rate, the lower the return to the firm's investment in its employees. Now, we know that, on the average, women spend less time in the labour force, and also less time in any one activity. Therefore not only do they have less incentive to invest in training themselves, but employers also find it less profitable to invest in specific training in their female work force — unless female wages are markedly lower.

This represents one reason why firms would be induced, on a mere productivity basis, to pay lower wages to women or, equivalently, to prefer male to female workers at the same wage rate in jobs requiring specific training, i.e., in most jobs. From their standpoint, women's marginal productivity is below men's, even though at a given time women may appear capable of accomplishing the same task with equal capacity. Notwithstanding the dictum "equal pay for equal work", the wage rate for women is likely to be below that for men because, in a very real sense, women's productivity over the whole period of time spent in a firm or in an activity is likely to be lower. This analysis goes a long way in explaining the persistent facts observed at the beginning of this section. It is obviously consistent with the fact that women's wages are generally lower than men's for apparently identical tasks.[7] Furthermore, there seems to be a high correlation between the amount invested in general training and the amount invested in specific training by individuals and firms. One should therefore find women over-represented in occupations requiring less general and specific training.

This is also consistent with the higher and more volatile unemployment rate of young people, for the following reasoning. Specific training entails that an employer invests capital in his employees, and this raises the latter's productivity inside the firm. To this extent, employers would be hurt by the departure of an employee who has received specific training; for quits prevent firms from capturing the full returns on costs incurred. They are therefore very much concerned with the turnover rate of their employees with specific training. They have less incentive to fire them, even in the face of a decline in the demand for their output, if the marginal product is only temporarily below wages. Laid-off employees could then find new jobs and thereby forever impose a loss on the investment undertaken by the firm. On the other hand, young workers have accumulated only limited experience and they have received little specific

---

[7] It should be mentioned that the earnings differential between men and women would be substantially lower if earnings were compared within detailed job classifications and within the same establishments.

training. Therefore employers are less reluctant to lay off young employees, since they incur less of a capital loss from the departure of their young work force. Wider variations in the unemployment rate of young workers and higher unemployment rates for this group are what this theory predicts.[8]

Note that lower wages for women may be observed even in industries and/or firms in which the turnover rate of men and women is the same, *provided the average life span spent by women in the labour force in the economy as a whole is shorter.* Competition in the female labour market would make it possible for firms in those conditions to hire female workers at lower wage rates, even though their marginal productivity is as high as men's. What this process would bring about is a tendency for firms experiencing low female quit rates to hire relatively more women. In graphical terms, the situation can be depicted by Figure 1.

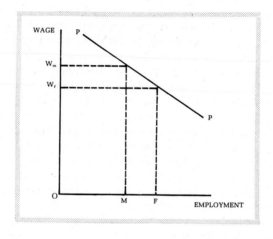

Figure 1

OW$_f$ and OW$_m$ represent, respectively, the average wage rate of women and men in the economy as a whole. OW$_m$ is higher than OW$_f$ for reasons analyzed above. Curve PP represents the marginal value productivity of both men's and women's labour in a given firm or industry, and at the same time the demand for labour on the part of that firm or industry. By drawing a single productivity curve, we make our assumption explicit that productivity of both men and women is the same, i.e., they have the same turnover rate in this particular sector. Should that firm or industry have to pay the men's wage rate, OM men would be hired. This will not take place, however. Since the women's rate is below the men's rate, the employer could hire OM women and obtain the same output with a lower payroll. The firm will ultimately settle at a level of employment of OF women, where the marginal value product

---

[8] In view of their higher quit rate, women should also receive less specific training on the job. As a consequence, both the variation and the level of unemployment in this group should be higher. However, this effect is offset for the group as a whole by the fact that women are concentrated in industries and occupations where employment is highly stable, namely, the services industry and clerical work.

is equal to the women's wage rate and output is larger than if men had been employed. Empirically, this process should result in women being concentrated in those firms and industries where, for some reason, women's quit rate is not significantly higher than men's.

One final consideration appears to be worth mentioning in this context. Minimum-wage legislation is designed to help those people possessing no, or minimum, marketable skills. But it may actually bring about opposite results by depriving the least-skilled workers of their best employment opportunities. To the extent that women and young people have invested less in training, they are more likely to suffer from unemployment as a result of minimum-wage laws. Table 1 shows that the unemployment differential in favour of adult workers (column 6) reached unprecedented levels by the early 1970s. Conversely, the differential between the unemployment rate of men and women (column 5) declined relative to the early 1960s. Substantial rises in minimum wages may have played a role in bringing about these results. By way of illustration, let us mention that the minimum wage rate was raised by 200 percent in Manitoba between 1957 and 1972. The corresponding rise for women in Newfoundland was 180 percent between 1965 and 1972. Between 1968 and 1972, Quebec raised its minimum wage rate by close to 75 percent outside the Montreal area.

III. Discrimination and Minorities

We have thus far identified two groups and developed an analytical framework to understand their origin as "minorities." G. S. Becker has suggested a second approach for the study of minorities, based on the economic concept of discrimination.[9] Let us define two groups, F and B, differentiated by some characteristic which could be colour, race, sex, or any other property. Let us further assume that group F is endowed with more labour and less capital relative to group B. We have established earlier that under "classical" conditions wage rates and rates of return on capital would not differ as between these two groups. Furthermore, the employment of factors would be distributed randomly between firms and industries, i.e., according to their relative supply. If B-labour is a perfect substitute for F-labour and B-capital is a perfect substitute for F-capital, every unit of each factor receives a remuneration equal to its marginal value product, irrespective of whether B-factors are combined with F-factors or B-factors.

Suppose now that members of group B develop what Becker calls a "taste for discrimination" against members of group F. In this concept, individuals in group B are thus assumed to be willing to pay something, directly or in the form of reduced income, not to be associated with persons in group F. Since members of group B have been assumed to be mainly owners of capital, it means in our institutional setting that they are the main employers of F-labour. B's taste for discrimination can be quantified by means of a discrimination coefficient. When faced with the

[9] G.S. Becker, *The Economics of Discrimination*, University of Chicago Press, Chicago, 1957.

money wage rate π_F for F-labour, employer-B is assumed to act as if $\pi(1 + d_F)$ were the net wage rate, with d_F measuring the intensity of his taste for discrimination against F-labour.

From here on, it has proved useful to study this question along lines suggested by the analysis of international exchange.[10] Groups B and F may be considered as two different societies with group B exporting capital, its relatively abundant factor, and group F exporting labour. Exporting capital on the part of society B means hiring F-labour, as, for instance, setting up an establishment in an F-geographical area and employing F-workers.

What would be the main effects of discrimination by B-capitalists against F-labour? Discrimination implies that they are ready to forfeit money income, i.e., to accept lower rates of return on capital, in order to avoid hiring F-workers. They will reduce the amount of capital exported to group F and thereby increase the supply of capital to be combined with B-labour. This reduces the money return that B-capital can receive by combining with B-labour. By the same process, the amount of F-labour exported to B will be lower, i.e., less F-labour will be demanded at given wage rates than would be the case without discrimination. The wage rate received by F-labour will consequently be lower. In equilibrium, too much capital is combined with B-labour, too little with F-labour. The marginal value productivity of both F-labour and B-capital is higher than their rate of remuneration (their money price). Indeed, B-capitalists hire F-labour only to the point where $MP_F = \pi_F(1 + d_F)$ instead of $MP_F = \pi_F$, where MP_F is the marginal value productivity of F-labour. In money terms, production factors are not combined in the most productive proportions. Net incomes of both societies are lower than they would otherwise be.

While the over-all net incomes of both societies are reduced by discrimination, all production factors are not equally affected. The return to B-capital and to F-labour is reduced when discrimination by employers occurs, while the return to B-labour and to F-capital is increased. This results from the fact that more than the optimal amount of capital is combined with B-labour and less with F-labour.

This is the essence of the argument by which Becker estimates that Negroes lose from discrimination in the United States. The relative endowment of capital and labour by whites and Negroes is estimated to be of the order of 150 to 1 in the case of capital and 9 to 1 in the case of labour. Becker then determines that, without discrimination, Negro per capita income would be about 66 percent of that of whites. Due to white capitalists employing fewer Negroes than dictated by marginal value productivity alone (capital "export" is lower by 40 percent), the actual per capita Negro income stands at only 57 percent of that of whites. Negro incomes would rise by 16 percent if market discrimination stopped. Incomes of whites would decline only by a negligible amount, since factor trading between Negroes and whites is substantially less important to whites.

[10] See ibid., pp. 11–16, and A. Raynauld and G. Marion, "Une analyse économique de la disparité inter-ethnique des revenus", Revue économique, XXIII, no 1, janv. 1972, pp. 1–19.

It is now easy to conceive that from the standpoint of society B as a whole, there exists an optimum amount of discrimination, such that the over-all income of group B is maximized. Defining groups B and F as two ethnic groups, differently endowed with capital (more in B) and labour, group B could raise its aggregate income by discriminating against F-labour, as long as gains to B-labour more than offset losses to B-capitalists. This is precisely the thesis developed by Raynauld–Marion to explain the *per capita* income disparity between the French-speaking and English-speaking groups in Quebec.[11] Their analysis is based on an application of the theory of optimum tariff in international trade, previously developed by Krueger.[12]

The argument runs as follows: If by some collective process the English-speaking group, which is richly endowed with capital, were brought to seek to maximize its over-all group income, less than the optimal amount of capital would be exported to the French-speaking group. Since the demand for the factors discriminated against would be reduced, the return to capital would be higher and the return to labour lower in the French sector than in the English sector. The results obtained by Raynauld–Marion are summarized in Table 4.

Table 4

Export of capital by B to F	Rate of return to Labour in F as percent of B	Capital in F as percent of B	Over-all income of Group B	Group F
0	35	1237	1933	2639
4.4 (maximum over-all income of group B)	69	132	2653	3308
7.0 (maximum income to B-capitalists)	100	100	2527	3633

Source: Raynauld–Marion, *op. cit.*, p. 12.

Let the relative endowment of the British (B) and French (F) sectors in labour (L) and capital (K) be:

$$L_B = 1, \quad L_F = 4, \quad K_B = 9, \quad K_F = 1.$$

These numbers were selected by Raynauld–Marion to reflect the true relative endowments in the Quebec economy. Given the specific production function adopted, it is shown that sector B should export 4.4 of its 9 units of capital to maximize the over-all income of group B. This would also imply a rate of return on capital 131.6 percent higher in F than in B. The return to labour in the F sector would be 69 percent of the return to labour in B. (Second row of Table 4.) On the other hand, assuming that B-capitalists seek to maximize not the over-all income of group B but their own-class income (the classical assumption), they would export 7.0

[11] Raynauld and Marion, *op. cit.*
[12] A. Krueger, "The Economics of Discrimination", *Journal of Political Economy*, XXI, No. 5, October 1963, pp. 481–486.

instead of 4.4 units of capital, or 60 percent more than under the first assumption. The rate of return to capital would decline in the F sector to the level in the B sector and the per unit income of labour would also be equalized in both sectors. (Third row of Table 4.) The aggregate income of the two groups taken together is then a maximum. Since the magnitudes of capital and labour, the inputs to the production function, are presented in relative terms, the significance of the over-all income figures is also in relative terms only.

Raynauld and Marion found that in the real world the return to labour (after standardized for age and education) in the French sector stands at some 79 percent of the return to labour in the British sector. This implies that while B-capitalists do not export as much capital as would maximize their class income (7 units), they nonetheless do not maximize the "national" income of group B. The level of capital export implied by the observed labour income stands at some 5.4 units. In other words, it looks as though an amount of discrimination is exercised by British capitalists against French labour. On the other hand, the intensity of this taste for discrimination does not appear to be strong enough to generate a maximum aggregate income for group B.

This is as should be expected. One can, of course, prove that an optimum amount of discrimination exists that would maximize the B-sector income. But this is only mathematical logic as long as the rationality leading to such an equilibrium point has not been shown to exist. What motives would indeed drive B-capitalists to sacrifice their own income in favour of the collective good of their fellow B-workers?[13] Unless some process of bribing emerged whereby B-workers could induce B-capitalists into discriminating against F-labour more than they would otherwise do, the level of discrimination and the resulting equilibrium levels of wages are determined only by the capitalists' taste for discrimination. Only by accident could the intensity of this taste correspond to the level that would maximize the over-all income of group B. No such process has so far been proposed by Raynauld–Marion or any other analysts.

Another important conclusion of this analysis, which might help in understanding the ethnic distribution of employment in Quebec, has to do with the concept of market segregation. It was shown above that discrimination by employers decreases "trade" of factors between groups B and F. But a decrease in trade also implies segregation. For instance, if B-employers discriminate against F-workers, the latter will seek employment from F-employers. If the number of F-employers is large enough, complete segregation might occur. F-employees would work with F-employers and B-employees with B-employers. While complete segregation does not appear to exist in Quebec, it does seem that members of each of the two groups, B and F, are employed with each other and with employers of the same ethnic group to a significantly greater extent than

[13] Note how Raynauld–Marion's result differs from George Grant's assumption in *Lament for a Nation*, McClelland & Stewart, Toronto, 1965. Grant's thesis states that Canadian capitalists' greed brought them to maximize their own-class income at the cost of Canada's economic independence.

would result from a random distribution of all members. That taste for discrimination and perhaps some other factors like cultural affinities do in fact result in segregation is suggested by studies sponsored by the Royal Commission on Bilingualism and Biculturalism.[14] These studies tend to show that in Quebec French-Canadian firms hire almost exclusively French employees whereas non-French-Canadian firms hire mostly French Canadians at the lower hierarchical levels but English Canadians at the higher administrative and technical levels.

It should be noted at this stage that not only employers' discrimination but also fellow-employees' discrimination can result in employment segregation. Let us assume that B-employees, who are perfect substitutes for F-employees, have a taste for discrimination against F-employees. Every employer must then pay a higher wage rate to members of B to induce them to work with F-labour rather than with other B. In these circumstances, a profit-maximizing employer would not hire a mixed work force. Market segregation would result. Only teams of B or teams of F workers would be employed by firms or establishments. In the real world, F and B employees are not perfect substitutes, but to some extent complements. In this situation, market discrimination and segregation can be shown still to occur, but on a smaller scale.

Some other empirically verifiable effects which can be derived from this analysis are worth mentioning: a) Rather than hiring a mixed labour force, employers may be induced to set up smaller establishments, with each one employing only members of a single group. b) Relatively more F-employees should be found in industries with small establishments, since the cost of employing them (in terms of higher wages to B-employees) would be smaller. In other words, segregation is more easily attained if small establishments are the rule. No systematic evidence is available to support or disprove these conclusions.

IV. Information Networks and Minorities

This framework of analysis could, of course, be used to study and explain the employment and income conditions of any minority group thought to be discriminated against, whether these minorities are composed of French Canadians, women, young workers, Negroes, Jews, etc. It shows that the market does reflect the values and the behavioral patterns of society. For instance, several persons hold that a large portion of the income differential and employment-pattern disparity between men and women results from discrimination by employers (and fellow employees) against women. While this opinion cannot be proved wrong, our approach in the first section has sought to concentrate on other factors thought to be more powerful in explaining such disparities.

The analysis presented above was based on the explicit assumption that labour suppliers (once standardized) of both groups B and F have the same marginal value productivity. The discriminating employer elects

[14] See, for example, R.N. Morrison, *Corporate Adaptability to Bilingualism and Biculturalism, A Study of Policies and Practices in Large Canadian Manufacturing Firms,* Queen's Printer, Ottawa, 1970.

to hire fewer members of the ethnic group to which he does not belong because he himself derives disutility from combining his capital with members of the other group. We will now propose an alternative explanation of the phenomena observed by resorting to another approach.[15] The basic assumption in this second approach is that when all the relevant elements are taken into account, the marginal value productivity of F-labour is permanently below that of B-labour.

For that purpose, we will attempt to describe a process which may be called the logic of information gathering. One must realize, to start with, that an economic agent, consumer, producer, or factor supplier, requires information to enter into an exchange with other agents. The information needed consists essentially of two types of knowledge: a) some knowledge about the outlets for the output he has available for trade (price, quality, and other market conditions) — his output may be labour services, capital goods, or consumption goods; b) some knowledge about the sources of the inputs he needs in terms of capital and labour services, know-how, technology.

Let us try to apply these general propositions to the labour market. All workers find it necessary to acquire some information on present and future working conditions in jobs offered by firms, on the nature of the job, wage rates, stability of employment, physical and social environment, advancement opportunities, etc. Should this information be freely available, every potential employee would become fully informed on all potential jobs. Such is not the case in the real world. Information gathering on job offers entails costs. These costs are represented by the numerous efforts required, including direct canvassing, personal contacts, visits to placement agencies, reading want-ads, attending social gatherings, and going over many other forms of information pooling. The returns to this investment in information take the form of improved monetary and working conditions resulting from search. The rational worker will carry his search to the point where the expected marginal benefit of search is equal to the expected marginal cost.

Employers also need information on the conditions in the labour market. They have to acquire knowledge about candidates available and wage rates. Information on the qualifications and talents of potential employees is as important as information on wage rates, in view of the lack of homogeneity of the workers. This is particularly true at the higher and administrative levels of the production organization. The greater the specialization needed (e.g., atomic engineer) and/or the smaller the number of employees desired (e.g., chief accountant), the tougher the requirements; thus the greater is the knowledge required by the employer. Direct resources allocated to gather information on the labour force and to process it through the organization measure only one part of the cost of information. Information requirements also include the amounts spent by

[15] The thesis developed here is worked out at greater length and along more formal lines in two papers by this writer: J.-L. Migué, "Le nationalisme, l'unité nationale et la théorie économique de l'information", Canadian Journal of Economics, III, No. 2, May 1970, pp. 183–198 and J.-L. Migué, "L'industrialisation et la participation des Québécois au progrès économique", in J.-L. Migué, ed., Le Québec d'aujourd'hui, Editions HMH Hurtubise, Montréal, 1971, pp. 227–251.

firms in familiarizing new employees with their organization, through testing, rotation, etc. Improved knowledge raises the marginal productivity of employees as it leads to more productive utilization. Here again, the search by firms will be carried out until prospective returns from acquiring new knowledge are equal to prospective costs.

The thesis to be developed at this stage is based on the assumption that there are scale economies in the process of gathering, filtering, and interpreting information in the labour market (and in other markets). Economies of scale refer to the process through which unit costs of production decline as the size of the production unit or of the industry increases. Actually, the presence of scale economies constitutes the very basis why production processes come to be divided into establishments, firms, and various industries. The ensuing specialization of production units reduces costs. For instance, automobile makers find it advantageous to obtain from separate departments, establishments, or firms a large variety and number of parts and accessories. Presumably this arrangement reduces prices and costs.

What concretely are those economy-generating processes whereby the cost of information-producing is lowered? It is the main proposition of this thesis that a large number of groupings and interrelations between groups are communication centres between individuals and organizations whose output is partly or wholly the production of information for members. Professional associations, employers and employees associations, social clubs, conventions, journals, magazines and papers, pressure groups, social, religious and friendship gatherings are some of the more visible expressions of these information-producing processes. But the concept of scale economies in information collecting goes even further and embraces most of a society's institutions. The primary role of these networks of institutions may cover a wide range of functions, but it can be presumed that they also generate a side product which consists in placing individuals and organizations in contact with other individuals and organizations. In that sense they provide information for members of the group. They produce information for the benefit of their members on ways to obtain inputs and dispose of outputs.

For illustration purposes, let us consider the educational system together with the interrelationships that are established between the various levels of the system and between the system and the rest of the community. Such institutions as schools, vocational training centres, universities, and research agencies turn out education and scientific knowledge as their main output. What is maintained here is that they also serve as important channels of identification for future and potential employers and employees. This side-product of the educational system is far from negligible. Vocational schools and colleges perform functions which were at one time carried out within the firm. The local primary school attended by a young child not only guides him through the next stages of his educational progress, but also determines to a large extent the probable length of his stay in the school system and also the type of employment and activities he will perform in society after he has completed his education.

Interrelationships between the various levels and sectors within the educational system are completed by the communication network between the system and the rest of the community. Of all the institutional interrelationships that are found in societies, those between the educational system and the firm (or the production organization in general) are obviously among the most important. Any one can observe the close association that is often found between employers and schools at the financing and administration levels, in devising curricula, research projects, and exchange arrangements, and in recruiting employees and students.

What this tends to show is that the relationships between individuals within groups, as well as between groups, generate scale economies in the acquisition of information on how to progress in life and in the labour market in particular. The nature and scope of the institutional network of a society is what distinguishes it from another society. Because I was born a French Canadian, I am not normally likely to be a member of the same groups or to move through the same institutional network as my English Canadian counterpart. I should therefore be expected to receive different guiding information on the orientation to take and the behaviour to adopt.

Moving on to the next step in the analysis, one finds that the structure of groups in a society is largely determined by the requirements of the production technology. Social grouping is organized by reference to the firm. Production requirements basically determine the contour of the institutional network. On the other hand, the production organization with which members of the French group are associated is imported. Technological innovations, capital, and know-how are brought in from outside the French-Canadian community. For some reason, "foreign" capital owners have not found it advantageous or necessary to set up in the French-Canadian community the institutional network through which communications are established between the firm and the individuals in the society. The result is that two main grouping networks have emerged in Canada and in Quebec. They have been referred to as the two "solitudes." And the French-Canadian network does not lead to the firm.

To this very extent, the cost to the potential employers and employees of recruiting and promoting French Canadians through the firm's employment and hierarchy structure is higher. No or few scale economies of information are realized by French Canadian employees and their employers, because the information industry is underdeveloped. Underinvestment in information-producing facilities constitutes one of the basic deficiencies of the French-Canadian society.

Since the need for information is most pressing at the higher ranges of the organizational structure, the consequences of information deficiencies should be more easily detectable at these levels. One can view the Quebec labour market as split into two sub-markets, differentiated by the level of information that members of each possess on prospective employers and also by the amount of information that employers possess about members of each group.

A number of empirically verifiable propositions can be derived from this statement of the question. For the average employer, the cost of recruiting a French-Canadian employee of given qualifications and talents is higher. This is equivalent to saying that French Canadians have a lower marginal productivity. The demand for French-Canadian labour is lower as a result. By virtue of the lower information available on prospective employees, greater dispersion in the qualifications obtained by hiring firms should be observed. Finally, the wages and salaries offered to French Canadians for given qualifications should be more widely distributed.

From the employee's standpoint, the cost of information being higher, he will not possess as much investment as his English-speaking counterpart in the knowledge of prospective employers, of the requirements of various jobs, of pay rates, of ways to get the jobs. Therefore the supply of French-Canadian candidates at the administrative and technical levels will be lower. Their qualifications will be unevenly adapted to the needs of the employer, i.e., more widely dispersed. Finally, their salaries and wages will show greater dispersion (variation).

How does the conclusion that demand and supply of French-Canadian employees are shifted downward fit with the facts observed? The lower *per capita* incomes of French Canadians already described for identical levels of education are quite consistent with the conclusions of this analysis. This outcome would result from the demand for French Canadians being depressed more than the supply in high-income occupations.

More important from an analytical point of view is the question whether salaries at the higher echelons of the employment structure are more widely distributed in the French-Canadian market than among English-speaking employees. If this is the case, it will tend to give greater support to this thesis relative to the discrimination hypothesis. Taste for discrimination by employers or employees would of itself give rise not to a greater dispersion in wages and salaries, but only to lower salaries for the discriminated factor.

No data on salary dispersion by ethnic groups for identical occupations are available. This difficulty can be overcome to some extent by comparing the distribution of salaries and wages in Quebec and Ontario for given occupations. From our point of view, Ontario can be viewed as a homogeneous labour market where only one information network exists. In contrast, in Quebec the two French- and English-speaking groups are represented and thus the two networks. Consequently, a higher salary dispersion should be noted, at least at the upper echelons of the hierarchical structure.

Table 5 confirms our prediction. Out of 23 known occupational classes of professionals and scientists (including technologists[16]), only 3 show a higher salary dispersion coefficient[17] in Ontario than in Quebec. In 14

[16] The Pay Research Bureau (source of Table 5) describes a technologist 1st grade as "a training and junior working level for graduates of a recognized institute of technology". The technologist level stands somewhere between the technician and the engineer.

[17] The coefficient calculated here is a measure of variability known as the "inter-quartile dispersion coefficient," defined as $(Q3-Q1)/Q2$, where $Q1$, $Q2$, and $Q3$ are the first, second, and third quartile, respectively. The first (second, third) quartile is the salary level below which 25 (50, 75) percent of the workers are paid. For more details, see J.-L. Migué, "Le nationalisme, l'unité nationale et la théorie économique de l'information," p. 196.

classes, the coefficient is more than 25 percent higher in Quebec. The spread reaches more than 50 percent in 4 cases. There is also evidence that the spread increases as the level of responsibility expected increases, i.e., as we move up the hierarchy. Below the technologist level, the difference between the dispersion coefficient of salaries in Quebec and Ontario is either small or randomly distributed between the two provinces.

Table 5: Differentials Between Dispersion Coefficients of Salaries,[a] Quebec and Ontario

	Differential between dispersion coefficients in Ontario and Quebec[b] (percent)		No. of times
Ontario > Quebec			3
Quebec > Ontario	$0 \leqq$ differential	15	3
Quebec > Ontario	$15 <$,, $\leqq 25$		3
Quebec > Ontario	$25 <$,, $\leqq 50$		10
Quebec > Ontario	$50 <$,, $\leqq 75$		1
Quebec > Ontario	$75 <$,, $\leqq 100$		3
Total No. of cases			23

[a] Occupations covered: technologists, professionals of various responsibility levels, scientists.
[b] Difference between the interquartile dispersion coefficient in Quebec and that in Ontario, divided by that in Ontario.

Source: Pay Research Bureau, Public Service Staff Relations Board: Rates of Pay, Technicians, Technologists and Draftsmen, Ottawa, July 1, 1967; Rates of Pay, Engineers, Ottawa, July 1, 1967; Taux de traitements des chercheurs scientifiques et gestion en recherche, Ottawa, 1er juillet 1967.

1. Canada's Income-Maintenance System And Proposals for Change

Christopher Green *

McGill University

One of the roles government should and does play is that of redistributor of income among the population. This paper is about the role that Canadian governments now play and could play in redistributing income *via* income transfers to households. In the fiscal year 1970, public income transfers amounted to $4.4 billion, absorbing about 15 percent of total government expenditures and 5.4 percent of GNP. In addition, Canadian governments, federal, provincial, and municipal, made transfers-"in-kind" through health, educational, and low-income-housing programs. Canada is not alone among the wealthier nations of the world in having developed a complex and expensive apparatus for maintaining and supplementing family incomes. In the last two or three decades, almost all of the richer countries of the world have experienced rapid increases in the amount of income transferred from one family to another through the mechanism of taxes and transfers. It would appear that as nations grow more affluent the importance of income transfers grows too, suggesting that the demand for social justice is income-elastic. There is also a "structural" reason for this relationship.

In no country in the world are income and wealth equally distributed. But suppose, for a moment, that *within* each country income and wealth were redistributed so as to make everyone equally well-off. Then in very poor countries everyone would be made poor, and redistributing income would have resulted in an increase rather than in a decrease in the incidence of poverty, i.e., an increase in the fraction of the population which is poor. In contrast, making incomes equal in rich countries would imply that no one need be poor, if poverty is measured in terms of income. In

* I wish to thank my colleagues Antal Deutsch and Eric Kierans for their useful comments.

fact, of course, incomes *within* rich *and* poor countries are generally quite unequally distributed, so that rich and poor people can be found in each. The difference between rich and poor countries is in the fraction of the population which is poor and the fact that income-transfer programs which attempt to reduce the inequality in the distribution of income and wealth will be more effective in reducing poverty and, because of a larger income pie, more easily afforded in richer than in poorer countries.

I. The Existence of Poverty

Between a sixth and a fourth of the Canadian population is poor, depending on how poverty is defined. The poverty lines or "thresholds" adopted by the Economic Council of Canada indicate that 18 percent of the Canadian population had incomes below the poverty thresholds in 1969. In contrast, the Report of the Special Senate Committee on Poverty,[1] utilizing higher poverty thresholds, estimated that about 25 percent of the Canadian population were poor in 1969. The differences in the poverty lines, and therefore in the numbers who are defined as poor, reflect differences in how poverty is defined. The Economic Council of Canada poverty lines, one for each family size, were developed by Statistics Canada using budget data to estimate the minimum income needed to cover basic needs adequately. The Senate Committee's poverty lines attempt to indicate relative income deprivation as well as minimum needs by relating the poverty thresholds to the growth in average family income. In any event, as Table 1 indicates, there is a wide dispersion of family incomes and there is a substantial low-income population in Canada. Table 1 also shows that transfer payments are a very important source of family income for many families in the lowest income brackets. An estimated 50–60 percent of transfer payments are received by families with a before-transfer income which would classify them as poor.

Why is income distributed so unequally? Why are there poor families in rich countries? The answers to these questions lie deep in the political, social, and economic fabric of a society and will not be searched for in this essay. Suffice it to say that there are a large number of factors affecting the distribution of income: some are historical and cultural, others economic, social, and demographic. For example, a region settled early in a country's history, such as the Canadian Maritimes, may fall behind other regions as time passes, the dwindling economic opportunities of the former contributing to a relatively high incidence of low incomes and poverty. Or, to take another factor, individuals vary in their ability to contribute to production of goods and services which other people want. These variations in economic contributions, or productivity, generally result in differences in economic rewards in the form of wages and salaries, and contribute importantly to differences in incomes. Some persons have low income because they are old or young, while some families are poor because there are a large number of persons dependent on a single earner's

---

[1] *Poverty in Canada, A Report of the Special Senate Committee on Poverty,* Information Canada, Ottawa, 1971.

Table 1: Distribution of Families and Transfer Payments by Income Class[a]: 1969

Income Class (dollars)	Number of Families (thousands)	Percentage Distribution of Families	Percentage of Income in the Form of Transfer Payments	Percentage Distribution of Transfer Payments
Under 2000	215	4.5	58.9	6.1
2000–2999	341	7.1	52.9	19.4
3000–3999	332	6.9	29.2	14.3
4000–4999	356	7.3	14.8	10.0
5000–5999	385	7.9	9.2	8.2
6000–6999	407	8.4	7.3	8.1
7000–7999	446	9.2	4.7	6.7
8000–8999	428	8.9	3.9	6.0
9000–9999	376	7.8	2.8	4.2
10,000–11,999	583	12.1	2.3	6.2
12,000–14,999	492	10.2	2.0	5.5
15,000–24,999	384	8.0	1.5	4.5
25,000 and over	86	1.8	.6	.8
Total	4,380	100.0	5.6	100.0

[a] Excludes individuals (persons not in families). In 1969, 42 percent of persons not in families had total incomes under $2000. These persons received 66 percent of all transfers received by persons not in families. Transfers comprised 12.5 percent of the income of persons not in families and 6.5 percent of the combined income of families and persons not in families.
Source: Statistics Canada, Family Incomes, 1969 (Ottawa, July 1972), Tables 10, 14. Reproduced by permission of Information Canada.

income. Whatever its cause, the problem of low incomes in an otherwise affluent society poses critical problems if for no other reason than that in North America, at least, poor and non-poor alike have rapidly advancing expectations of the "good life."

II. The Income-Maintenance System

One way most modern societies attempt to deal with low incomes and income loss is through income transfers. The totality of income-transfer programs comprises what may be called the "income-maintenance system". Transfer payments represent a transfer of income from one household to another *via* the public treasury. On the one hand, *most* households pay taxes and, on the other hand, *many* households are eligible to receive transfer payments financed out of taxes paid by themselves and by other households. One might expect that the chief rationale for income-transfer programs is to redistribute income from middle- and high-income taxpayers to low-income households. In fact, the objectives of income-maintenance systems of most Western countries are multi-faceted, and Canada's is no exception. There are more than a dozen money-income-transfer programs in operation in Canada, which vary in numerous respects, including design, eligible population, and contribution toward raising the incomes of poor members of the population. One can identify at least four different program designs. These include demogrants, social-insurance, income-conditioned, and needs-tested programs. It is important to understand the meanings of these terms, if one is to comprehend the implications and contributions of our income-maintenance system. Table 2 attempts to portray the structure of and the chief facts about Canada's income-transfer programs.

Demogrants are payments of a specified dollar amount to all members of specified population (demographic) groups. For example, all persons 65 years of age or over receive $100 a month under the Old Age Security (OAS) program. OAS recipients receive the $100 monthly payment — which is taxable — regardless of their income. Similarly, families with children under 16 years of age received, prior to 1974, family allowances (FA) of $6 or $8 per child, the amount depending only on the age of the child, not on the family's income. Youth allowances (YA) of $10 per person 16 or 17 years of age were paid solely on the basis of age and enrollment in school. In 1974, YA was eliminated and FA was raised to $20 per child under 18 except in the provinces of Quebec and Alberta, which vary the amount per child with respect to the number of children in the family. FA is now taxable. Canada's three demogrant programs (OAS, FA, and YA) expended $2.2 billion in fiscal year 1970. In 1974, this figure was approximately doubled because of the increases in OAS and FA enacted in 1973.

Some transfer programs relate benefits to prior contributions. These are the so-called social-insurance programs, which include the Canada Pension Plan (CPP), Unemployment Insurance (UI), Veterans' Pensions, and Workmen's Compensation. The word "insurance" is somewhat misleading, because contributions to and benefits from the programs are not

Table 2: Canada's Income-Maintenance System: 1972

	[1] Level of Government Involved	[2] Type of Program	[3] For Whom Program Is Intended	[4] Payment Schedule	[5] Number of Recipients (1969–70)	[6] Total Expenditure (1969–70) (millions of dollars)	[7] Estimated Percentage of Payments Received by Before-Transfer Poor	[8] Proposals Contained in Federal White Paper on Income Security
Old Age Security (OAS)	Federal	Demogrant	All aged persons	$100 a month	1,671,000	1,467	60–70	De-emphasize
Family Allowances (FA)	Federal, Quebec	Demogrant	Families with children under 16	$6 and $8 a month per child	2,977,556 for 6,865,302 children	657	15–20	Convert to FISP, an income-conditioned plan
Youth Allowances (YA)	Federal, Quebec	Demogrant	Youths aged 16 and 17 who are still in school	$10 a month	484,000	78	15–20	Same as FA
Canada Pension Plan (CPP)	Federal, Quebec	Social Insurance	Aged with a previous work history	Related to past earning history	145,000 (Jan. 1970)	48	10–20[e]	Strengthen
Unemployment Insurance (UI)	Federal	Social Insurance	Unemployed	2/3 of previous weekly wage. Max. payment of $107 a week in 1973	1,600,000[a]	695[a]	30–40[e]	Supported proposals of UI White Paper which were implemented in June 1971

Table 2 (cont'd)

	[1] Level of Government Involved	[2] Type of Program	[3] For Whom Program Is Intended	[4] Payment Schedule	[5] Number of Recipients (1969–70)	[6] Total Expenditure (1969–70) (millions of dollars)	[7] Estimated Percentage of Payments Received by Before-Transfer Poor	[8] Proposals Contained in Federal White Paper on Income Security
Veterans' Pensions	Federal	Social-Insurance Related	Disabled veterans, widows, and other dependents	Maximum pension as of April 1971 was $3,504 per annum for 100-percent disability	159,000b [March 1971]	218	60–70e	Consider integrating with CPP
Workmen's Compensation	Federal	Social Insurance	Persons or survivors of persons with work-related injuries	NA	300,000c	185	Unknown	Consider integrating with CPP
Guaranteed Income Supplement	Federal	Income Conditioned	Aged poor	Maximum payment: $70 a month for a single pensioner, $125 for a couple	813,000	263	100	Raise payments to present levels, see Column (4)

Table 2 (cont'd)

	(1)	(2)	(3)	(4)	(5)	(6)	(7)	(8)
Canada Assistance Plan	Federal–Provincial Cost Sharing	Needs-Tested	Qualified poor; provincial goverments and local administrators determine qualifications	Varies from province to province. In 1970, max. payments to a 4-person family ranged from about $2,200 in N.B. to $4,000 in Alta.	1,244,000 (Mar. 1970)	678	90–100	Make more universally available to the poor
Aid to Blind	Federal–Provincial	Means-Tested	Blind poor	$72^d	4,800	4	80–100	Phase out of federal financing
Aid to Disabled	Federal–Provincial	Means-Tested	Disabled poor	$74^d	25,000	24	80–100	Phase out of federal financing
Unemployment Assistance	Federal–Provincial	Needs-Tested	Unemployed poor	NA	NA	29	90–100	Phase out of federal financing
Indians and Eskimos	Federal	Means-Tested	Indians and Eskimos	NA	NA	18	90–100	—
Other	—	—	—	—	—	31	—	—

a Figures are for calendar year 1970.
b All pensions, disability and dependent.
c Excludes those who received medical aid only.
d Average monthly payment in 1970.
e "Guesstimates" based on very meager information.
NA: not available.

Sources: Department of Health and Welfare, *Income Security for Canadians*, Ottawa, 1970; *Canada Yearbook*, Ottawa, 1972. Reproduced by permission of Information Canada.

actuarially related. However, with the exception of Veterans' Pensions, employees and/or employers contribute to the financing of the social-insurance programs through special taxes on employee earnings and/or employer payrolls.[2] Veterans' Pensions are included in the social-insurance category because service in the Armed Forces leading to disability or death can be thought of as a contribution for which benefits are payable. To some extent, the amount of an individual's contribution to a social-insurance program is related to his earnings. Similarly, the amount of benefits an individual or his family ultimately are entitled to receive will, up to a point, be related positively to past earnings. The direct relationship between benefits and past earnings reflects the fact that the social-insurance programs are chiefly designed to protect against partial or total *income loss* on account of age, unemployment, or injury. The contribution of social-insurance programs to alleviating poverty is a secondary, but not an unimportant, goal, since many — although by no means all — social-insurance beneficiaries would be poor in the absence of social-insurance programs.

Nevertheless, the structure of social-insurance programs, with benefits directly related to previous earnings, limits their usefulness in further reducing poverty in Canada. For example, unemployment-insurance benefits are two-thirds of previous weekly wages up to a maximum weekly wage of $160, as of 1973. (For weekly wages below $50, the benefit-to-wage ratio is three-quarters.) Low earnings mean low unemployment-insurance beenfits; so that a family which is poor because earnings are low in relation to family size will remain poor after receiving UI. In 1969–70, payments made under social-insurance programs amounted to about $1 billion. This figure has increased rapidly and will continue to do so, in response to the increasing number of aged persons becoming eligible for CPP payments and the broadened coverage and increased benefits resulting from recent revisions in the UI Act.

A third type of income-transfer design is the income-conditioned program. Under income-conditioned programs, transfers are related inversely to an individual's or family's income, usually calculated on an annual basis. Currently the only example of an income-conditioned transfer program in Canada is the Guaranteed Income Supplement (GIS). The GIS is payable to aged persons whose sole or major source of income is their monthly OAS payment — which at annual rates amounts to $1200 per aged person. Since the poverty thresholds for single individuals and couples are approximately $1800 and $3000, respectively, it is clear that OAS payments alone do not allow an aged person or couple with no other means of support to escape poverty. The amount of GIS payment an aged person or couple may receive depends on how much other income he or they have, not including OAS payments. The maximum GIS payment is $70 a month for a single person and $125 a month for an aged couple. For each two dollars of non-OAS income, GIS payments are reduced by one dollar. Thus an aged individual with no other income receives a total of $170 a month in OAS-GIS payments, or $2040 a year. An aged couple

---

[2] The Unemployment Insurance program also receives general-revenue financing.

with no other income receives $325 a month, or $3900 a year. Thus OAS–GIS virtually eliminates income poverty among the aged. In the fiscal year 1971, when maximum GIS payments per person were lower, total GIS payments amounted to $280 million paid to 860,000 aged poor. (As an inflation adjustment, OAS and GIS payments were raised further by 5.3 percent as of October 1, 1973.)

If instead of utilizing the income-conditioned technique, OAS payments were raised from $100 to $170 a month, the additional cost of the OAS program in 1973 would have been approximately $1500 million.[3] In contrast, GIS payments amounted to about $600 million in 1973. From the viewpoint of reducing or eliminating poverty among the aged, the income-conditioned technique utilized in the GIS is cheaper by $900 million than is sole reliance on the demogrant alternative. Thus, the Department of National Health and Welfare in its White Paper on Income Security[4] proposed that the demogrant technique begin to give way to the income-conditioned technique in modeling future income-transfer programs. Specifically, the White Paper proposed eliminating family allowances in favour of a Family Income Security Program (FISP) whereby family-allowance payments would be conditioned by family income as well as size. Maximum payments of $16 a month per child would be received by families with incomes under $4500. Payments per child would decline as family income rose, with payments terminating entirely when family income reached $10,000. The proposal was subsequently modified to make the cut-off vary between $10,000 and $14,000, the level depending on the number of dependent children. Although in 1971 the government presented the FISP proposal in the House of Commons, it never received a third reading.

In April 1973, the government finally abandoned the idea of an income-conditioned approach to family allowances. Instead, the government opted for an increase in the family allowance to $20 a month per child effective January 1, 1974, and for making the allowances taxable. However, the Health and Welfare Minister's *Working Paper on Social Security in Canada*[5] also proposed that the income-conditioned technique be used to make supplements to the "working poor" — that is, to supplement the incomes of those workers whose earnings are "inadequate" when considered in relation to family size.

A fourth type of income-transfer program is the needs-tested one, generally identified with the term "social assistance." The major example is the Canada Assistance Plan (CAP), which is financed 50 percent by the federal government and 50 percent by provincial and/or municipal governments, but wholly administered at provincial and/or municipal levels. Eligibility for and levels of CAP payments vary from province to province. In general, the provinces define the conditions under which an individual

---

[3] 1.8 million aged persons receiving an extra $70 a month or $840 *per annum.*
[4] Department of National Health and Welfare, *Income Security for Canadians,* Ottawa, 1970. For a critique of this White Paper, see Antal Deutsch and Christopher Green, "Income Security for Canadians: A Review Article," *Canadian Tax Journal,* Jan.–Feb. 1971, pp. 8–16.
[5] *Working Paper on Social Security in Canada,* presented by Hon. Marc Lalonde, Minister of National Health and Welfare, April 18, 1973.

or family may be eligible to receive payments. Once eligible, the level of payment is based on a family's needs, which are budgetarily determined. That is, an estimate is made of the minimum costs of shelter, food, clothing, and other necessities that a family of a given size and circumstance must finance. If the family has any income or other resources of its own, some or all of these will be subtracted in calculating the family's monthly payment.

The essential difference between income-conditioned and needs-tested programs as they now operate in Canada is that the former is based only on annual income and age, while the latter limits eligibility and makes payments to individuals and families based on estimates of needs and resources at a given point in time. In addition to the CAP, there are a number of provincially administered "means-tested" programs, chiefly for the blind and disabled (see Table 2), the costs of which are shared with the federal government. The term "means test" signifies that eligibility to receive aid to the blind or aid to the disabled is limited to individuals or families with annual incomes below a specified level. Increasingly, provinces have been placing the blind and disabled under the CAP, so that in time the means-tested programs are likely to disappear or, at the very least, lose federal financing. In 1969–70, expenditures on needs- and means-tested social-assistance programs totaled $891 million. In 1971, social-assistance expenditures are estimated to have risen to $1,436 million.

III. Proposals for Change

In recent years, there have been several proposals for change in Canada's income-maintenance system. The White Paper's proposal to replace FA with FISP has already been mentioned. The Senate Committee on Poverty, in contrast, suggested replacing the demogrants (OAS, FA, YA) and most social-assistance expenditures with a guaranteed annual income of the negative-income-tax type. Quebec, too, has shown interest in re-modeling its own and the federal family-allowance systems into a form of guaranteed annual income called the General Plan for Social Allowances.[6] Manitoba is planning to experiment with a guaranteed annual income, with special attention given to its potential work-disincentive effects.[7] Most recently, the Working Paper on Social Security in Canada has proposed that the federal government together with the provinces discuss replacing the needs-tested social-assistance programs with a guaranteed annual income for "unemployables," and creating a new program of income supplements for the "working poor."

Reference to a guaranteed annual income (GAI) and negative income tax (NIT) requires some explanation.[8] Essentially, a GAI can take one of

[6] See Report of the Commission of Inquiry on Health and Social Welfare, Income Security, Vol. 5, Province of Quebec, 1971 (Castonguay—Nepveu Report).
[7] See Clarence Barber, Welfare Policy in Manitoba. A Report to the Planning and Priorities Committee of Cabinet Secretariat, Province of Manitoba, Winnipeg, December 1972.
[8] For further reading, see Christopher Green, Negative Taxes and the Poverty Problem, Brookings Institution, Washington, 1967. Earl R. Rolph, "The Case for a Negative Income Tax Device," Industrial Relations, February 1967, pp. 155–65; James Tobin, Joseph Pechman, and Peter Mieszkowski, "Is a Negative Income Tax Practical?" Yale Law Journal, November 1967, pp. 1–27.

two forms. One form, sometimes called a "social dividend," would pay out a specified amount to each person or family regardless of income. The large outlays would be financed by a special tax levied on income. This form of GAI is essentially a demogrant to the whole population, and has the same deficiency that all demogrants have: a high budgetary cost is incurred in order to redistribute some income to low-income groups. The other form of GAI, often called negative income taxation, would condition actual payments upon family income and size. The term "negative taxes" has long been used as another way of saying "transfer payments," and has suggested to some fiscal experts that in practice as well as in theory the income-tax system could be used to pay out income as well as collect it. While negative income-tax plans need not necessarily be tied to the tax system, I think there is much to be gained administratively by doing so. In the next section I will show that a simple device, the refundable tax credit, nearly integrates the tax and transfer systems, which should make it possible to reduce the administrative apparatus associated with the existing welfare system.

A negative income-tax plan has three basic variables: (1) a basic income allowance or guarantee, G, the level of which is related to family size; (2) a break-even level of income, B; and (3) an implicit tax rate, r, relating changes in NIT payments to changes in recipient or family income. Given the values of any two of the three basic variables, G, B, and r (the three variables are related to each other as $G=rB$), a recipient unit's eligibility to receive a negative income-tax payment depends only on its size and income, thereby attaining a certain universality lacking in existing transfer programs. Table 3 shows how NIT payments vary with family income under two different plans, assuming a family of four members. For plan A, column (2) indicates the relationship between family income and the size of the negative income-tax payment. (For different family sizes the basic guarantee, and therefore the amount of payment for any given level of income, would vary, but the principle remains the same.) The ratio in which family income and negative income-tax payments vary depends on the negative tax rate, r, which in column (2) is assumed to be 40 percent. In plan A, payments are reduced by $400 for each $1,000 increase in the family's pre-NIT income. The break-even level of income is the point at which payments decline to zero.

The negative income-tax payment is a percentage, equal to the negative tax rate, of the difference between the family's pre-NIT income (column 1) and the break-even level of income. When the family has no other income, it receives the income guarantee. For example, examine Plan B. The break-even level of income, again assuming a family of four for illustrative purposes, is set at $4,000. Given a negative tax rate of 50 percent, the income guarantee is determined, as are NIT payments for any given level of income.

The NIT plans in Table 3 differ in the magnitudes of the three basic variables. There is some "inevitable arithmetic" here, which is exceedingly uncomfortable for policy makers. It is desirable that the income guarantee be high enough to assure an adequate income for families with little or no other income. It is also desirable that the negative tax rate,

Table 3: How Negative Income-Tax Plans Work

(1)	Plan A G = 3000; r = .40; B = 7500		Plan B G = 2000; r = .50; B = 4000	
	(2)	(3)	(4)	(5)
Family Income Before NIT Payments	NIT Payment (family of four)	Total Income[a] (1) + (2)	NIT Payment (family of four)	Total Income[a] (1) + (4)
0	3,000	3,000	2,000	2,000
1,000	2,600	3,600	1,500	2,500
1,500	2,400	3,900	1,250	2,750
2,000	2,200	4,200	1,000	3,000
2,500	2,000	4,500	750	3,250
3,000	1,800	4,800	500	3,500
3,500	1,600	5,100	250	3,750
4,000	1,400	5,400	0	4,000
5,000	1,000	6,000	0	5,000
6,000	600	6,600	0	6,000
7,000	200	7,200	0	7,000
7,500	0	7,500	0	7,500

[a] Ignores (positive) income taxes.

r, be relatively low, so that the transfers do not undermine work incentives. Note that it is the negative tax rate, r, which governs how much an increase in pre-NIT income actually increases the family's total income. The higher r is, the more rapidly do NIT payments decline as pre-NIT income rises, thus reducing the monetary incentive to earn more income. If a relatively high income guarantee is combined with a relatively low negative tax rate, then the break-even level of income is pushed to relatively high levels, thereby substantially increasing the plan's cost and reducing the fraction of NIT payments going to the poorest members of the population. Something has to give, and in Plan B it is the income guarantee, which is kept low by constraining the break-even level of income to $4,000.

The dilemma presented by the relationship between the three basic variables is reflected in the GAI plan proposed in the Senate Committee's Poverty Report. The Senate Committee chose to set a high G ($3,500 for a family of four) and a break-even level of income constrained to the poverty lines utilized by the Committee ($5,000 for a family of four). The result is a negative tax rate of 70 percent ($3,500 ÷ .70 = $5,000), which critics feel could seriously impair work incentives and raise the cost of the plan. A GAI was rejected by the Department of National Health and Welfare in its White Paper. Nevertheless, the specifics of their FISP proposal, which would make family allowances income-conditioned, can be discussed in terms of the three basic variables. The maximum family allowances are analogous to the G, and the point at which families become ineligible to receive family-allowance payments is analogous to the B in negative income-tax plans. The FISP proposal employs a low G and a high B, with the result that the implicit tax rate is low and the work-disincentive problem is negligible.

If demogrants are to be replaced by income-conditioned programs, would we be better off adopting FISP or a NIT? The answer, of course, depends in large part on one's value judgments; but some light can be shed on the question by noting, first, that the programs listed in Table 2 do little for the "working poor." By "working poor" is meant those families headed by an employed person whose earnings are very low in relation to the family's basic needs. In 1967 about 9 percent of all families headed by a paid worker were poor on a total-income, including transfer, basis. Most of these families had dependent children and therefore received nominal amounts of transfer in the form of FA and/or YA. However, the working poor are usually ineligible to receive social assistance (SA), as is attested by the fact that of 662,000 SA recipients (not including dependents) in July 1970, only 20,000 were in the working-poor category. Moreover, in view of the manner in which SA is currently administered, it is probably desirable that the working poor are generally excluded, since the needs-tests provisions, under which a dollar increase in a family's resources (including earnings) may result in a dollar decrease in assistance, are potentially very damaging to work incentives.

What would FISP and NIT do for the working poor? To simplify the comparison, let us assume that the aged are excluded from the NIT on the grounds that (a) the OAS–GIS combination adequately handles the

Table 4: A NIT Plan

(1) Size of Family	(2) Guaranteed Income Level (when family has no other income)	(3) Negative Tax Rate %	(4) Break-even Level of Income	(5) Value of Exemptions and $100 Standard Deductions Allowed Under Income-Tax System[a]	(6) Guaranteed Income Level, r = .50
1	750	50	1,500	1,700	850
2	1,250	50	2,500	3,100	1,550
3	1,750	50	3,500	3,400	1,700
4	2,250	50	4,500	3,700	1,850
5	2,750	50	5,500	4,000	2,000
6	3,000	50	6,000	4,300	2,150
7	3,250	50	6,500	4,600	2,300
8 or more	3,500	50	7,000	4,900	2,450

[a] Assumes only one income-tax filer, declaring the remaining members of the family as dependents. The value of exemptions and deductions are those which apply in calculating income tax for 1973.

problem of income-poverty among the aged and (b) the growth of the CPP and private pension plans will increasingly cushion the income loss associated with retirement. Let us further assume, for the purposes of a valid comparison, that the basic variables of the NIT will be set so that the cost of the NIT equals the estimated cost of FISP plus an estimated 80 percent of social-assistance expenditures, which it is assumed can be replaced if a NIT were adopted. If FISP had been in effect in 1969–70, it would have cost $660 million. Eighty percent of a $891 million social-assistance bill for 1969–70 is $713 million. These total $1,373 million. Using 1967 census family-income data it is estimated that a GAI, NIT-type, with the dimensions indicated in the left-hand side of Table 4 would have cost $1,364 million, or approximately the amount that would not be spent on FISP and social assistance.

The basic difference between the NIT and the FISP–SA combination rests in the distribution of their respective transfer payments. This is so because NIT payments simply replace SA. However, an important fraction of FISP and NIT payments is received by different households. For example, low-income childless couples, or those whose children have grown up, are eligible for NIT but not for FISP payments. More important is the fact that over 50 percent of FISP payments would have been received by families with incomes between $5,000 and $10,000, whereas about 90 percent of NIT payments would be received by families with pre-NIT incomes under $5,000. Benefits are approximately equal under FISP and NIT when a four-person (two-children) family's pre-transfer income is $3,750. The comparable level of income for a six-person (four-children) family is $4,500. When family incomes are at half these levels ($1,875 and $2,250, respectively), NIT payments are approximately three times as great as FISP. Clearly, the NIT does much more for the very poor, while FISP, but not NIT, supplements the income of low-middle-income workers, many of whom see themselves as barely able to earn enough to cover the basics. As indicated earlier, the question of which approach is better ultimately turns on value judgments, but the analysis does help to make us better informed about the relative contributions of each proposal.

IV.   Integrating the Welfare and Income-Tax Systems

One of the problems with the NIT plan discussed above is that it does not relate well to the income-tax system. Columns (4) and (5) of Table 4 show that except for one- and two-person families, the break-even levels of income exceed the value of exemptions and $100 standard-deductions an income-tax filer may take in computing his income tax. This means that if the NIT plan shown in Table 4 were adopted, some families (those whose income fell between the levels given in columns (4) and (5)) would both be eligible to receive NIT payments and be required to pay income taxes. It does not seem reasonable to give NIT payments to an income-taxable household. There are a number of ways in which to eliminate the "overlap" between the positive and negative income-tax systems. One way is to set the break-even level of income equal to the value of exemptions and standard deductions. The resultant income guarantees, assuming a negative tax rate of 50 percent, are shown in column (6) of Table 4. This approach has some logic in terms of equity. It allows income-tax filers whose income is too low to make them taxable to become eligible to "get back" some percentage, equal to the negative tax rate, of their "unused" exemptions and deductions (i.e., the amount by which income falls below a tax filer's allowed exemptions and deductions).

Perhaps the simplest and, in my opinion, the most sensible way of tying negative and positive taxes together is to convert the present system of exemptions into "refundable" tax credits. Tax credits differ from exemptions in the following way. Whereas exemptions reduce the income against which tax rates are applied, tax credits are subtracted from "gross" tax liability in calculating the actual or "net" tax liability of the income-tax filer. Suppose, for example, that the present system of exemptions in the income-tax system were eliminated and replaced by *per capita* tax credits of $500 per person. A new income-tax schedule could then be designed to raise the revenues required to pay for the NIT plan as well as to finance other expenditures now financed from revenues raised by the income tax. We may suppose, for simplicity, that a proportional tax schedule is adopted with a 25-percent tax rate levied against total family income (less any deductions the family is still permitted to take). A four-person family with no other income would have refundable tax credits (NIT payments) equal to $2,000 (4 × $500). When the four-person-family's income is $2,000, it would have a gross tax liability of $500. (.25 × $2,000). The family's net tax liability is −$1,500 ($500 − $2,000), allowing it to receive a $1,500 "refund" check from the government after filing its tax return.

The scheme is pictured in Figure 1. The 25-percent tax rate is reflected in the slope of line ABC. The break-even level of income, where gross tax liability equals total tax credits, occurs at $8,000. Families of four with incomes below $8,000 would have negative tax liabilities and thus receive payments from the government. Four-person families with incomes above $8,000 would have a net tax liability. For example, a four-person, $12,000 family would pay $1,000 in income tax (.25 × $12,000 − $2,000). A four-person, $25,000 family would pay $4,250. The reader can do the arithmetic for different incomes and family sizes.

While a proportional tax schedule is not necessary to the scheme, the simplification it would contribute to administration and tax law commends it. From a redistributive viewpoint, a graduated (progressive) tax schedule over lower and middle ranges of income is unnecessary once refundable tax credits are adopted. However, in the high-income ranges it will be desirable to attach a surtax in order to stem partially the impact of high incomes on the accumulation of wealth and thus upon inequality in the distribution of income and wealth. Another advantage of a proportional income-tax schedule is that it would reduce the "fiscal drag" on the economy that a steeply graduated (over middle-income ranges) income tax, like the Canadian one, is liable to produce. Many income recipients now find that 40 or 50 cents of each *additional* dollar of income received is returned to the government as income tax. This means that when government increases spending or reduces taxes by a given dollar magnitude in order to stimulate the economy and reduce unemployment, a large fraction of the stimulus is lost in the form of income-induced increases in tax payments. Fiscal policy is thus made less effective. On the debit side, however, is the fact that a proportional income tax does not have the automatic stabilizing features of a progressive income tax.

Britain shows signs of becoming the first nation to attempt an integration of its welfare and income-tax systems utilizing the tax-credit device. The first step has already been taken, with the adoption of a simplified tax schedule consisting of a single 30-percent rate on the first £5,000 (about $12,000) of earnings.[9] Earnings in excess of £5,000 would be liable

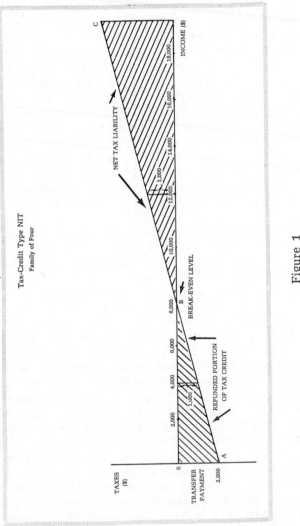

Figure 1

to a surtax in addition to the basic rate. The second step, the elimination of exemptions and their replacement by tax credits, is at the planning or testing stage. In October 1972, the British government published a "Green Paper" entitled *Proposals for a Tax Credit System*,[10] which details a workable plan with which the government proposes to experiment. A married couple would receive a weekly tax credit of £6 with an additional £2 per child. Taxes withheld from a worker's paycheck would be reduced by the amount of credits due him. Any negative remainder would be added to the worker's paycheck.

One aspect of the British proposal which is of particular interest is the timing of payments. Tax credits would be calculated on a weekly basis, in line with the usual timing of wage and salary payments and income-tax withholding in Britain. This would allow the credits to serve as a weekly supplement to low earnings, and in times of unemployment — whether involuntary or voluntary — as a partial replacement for the weekly pay-check. The proposal in a Canadian context might work as follows.[11] Tax credits could be set at, say, $20 a week per adult and $10 per child declared as a dependent on an adult's tax return. This means that a four-person family composed of two adults and two children would be guaranteed $60 a week ($3,120 a year) if the family had no other income in that period. The cost of the plan plus other expenditures financed by the personal income tax can potentially be financed with a proportional tax of one-third levied on total personal income, a base much broader than the current tax base. If a tax rate of 33 percent were utilized, a four-person family including two children would not become taxable in net terms until its income exceeded $180 a week ($60 ÷ .33) or $9,360 a year. The comparable figure for a six-person, four-child family is $12,480. The plan would allow for the elimination of GIS, FA, YA, and most SA without making any low-income family worse off. The weekly credit would also permit a reduction in outlays for UI benefits. But the plan would not replace OAS or the social insurances, which would continue to play important roles in the income-maintenance system. The cost to the Treasury from credits actually refunded would amount to about $4 billion, but the net cost to the Treasury after eliminating or reducing expenditures made under some existing programs would be between $2.5 and $3 billion.

A tax-credit type of NIT is a powerful and simple device for both establishing an income floor and providing a means for redistributing income more generally from households whose income is above average to households whose income is below average. There would, of course, be some technical problems in defining income and eligible recipients, but those occur in any welfare or tax system. One lesson, however, is that while a relatively simple redistributive mechanism can be designed, it is not cheap — before it is adopted society must evince a willingness to redistribute income more generally.

[10] *Proposals for a Tax-Credit System*, presented to Parliament by the Chancellor of the Exchequer and the Secretary of State for Social Services, London, Her Majesty's Stationary Office, October 1972.
[11] A similar proposal is made by Anthony Frayne, *Financial Post*, January 20, 1973, p. 7, and *Le Devoir*, February 13, 1973, p. 5.

V. Conclusion

The Canadian income-maintenance system clearly contributes to making life more livable for many Canadians whose means would otherwise be extremely limited. While a certain amount of transfer income is now "wasted" on high-income families who are not in need, it would be an error, I think, to attempt a complete replacement of the existing income-maintenance system with a single "master plan," no matter how ideal such a plan appears on paper. Nevertheless, there is room for change and reform. The major emphasis, I think, should be on doing more to supplement the incomes of low-income workers, and to do so in a way which maintains incentives to work and weakens the incentives of families to slide onto social assistance. Although free medical care and subsidized low-income housing and education programs make low incomes a little easier to bear, there is still a need to provide more cash income to low-income families and to do so in a way which more systematically reduces income inequality. In this regard I would give high marks to an NIT, especially one implemented through refundable tax credits.

The need for reform is stimulated by the liberalizations in the coverage and benefits of the UI program. In a period of two years, UI outlays jumped from about $700 million in 1970 to almost $2,000 million in 1972. Part of the growth is due to weaknesses in the economy, although these existed in 1970 as well as 1972. Combined with a liberal administration of UI claims, the system may also produce work disincentives, especially for persons whose labour-market alternative is a low-paying job.

Clearly, the liberalization of UI coverage and benefits is desirable where a family's sole earner loses his livelihood. His unemployment-insurance benefits now more closely approximate the income lost due to no fault of his own, helping him and his family maintain their standard of living. But it seems to me that the liberal benefits are somewhat more difficult to defend for second and third earners where the primary earner's income places the family in middle- or high-income brackets. In contrast to a NIT, the UI benefits are related to the earner's last weekly wage and not to family size or annual income. Thus, as a means of redistributing income, a NIT is more equitable than is the UI program. The NIT gives more weight to lowest incomes, is adjusted to family size, and provides income supplementation to the employed as well as unemployed. While there is an important role to be played by UI, with its chief emphasis on protecting against income loss, the large current outlay for UI benefits does pose the question whether a portion of those expenditures should not be used to finance a more universal, income-conditioned program. The Lalonde *Working Paper on Income Security* indicates that the government may be thinking along similar lines. Its most important proposals, in my opinion, are those which would restructure the income-maintenance system in order to maintain work incentives by creating a more equitable relationship between the incomes of low-wage workers, the income guarantees provided to unemployables, and payments to persons who are able to work but are unemployed.

2. The Analysis of Tax Reform

John Bossons *

University of Toronto

The tax system is important because of its size — $33.2 billion was collected in taxes and in social-insurance premiums from Canadian individuals and businesses in 1972, an amount equal to roughly 32 percent of Canadian gross national expenditure. It is also important because of its all-pervasive character. Few individuals are not directly influenced in their decisions by the effect of the tax system.

When taxes are changed as a tool of fiscal policy, it is customary in simple macroeconomic models to assume that all taxes are changed in the same proportion. In actual fact, this never happens. Macroeconomic fiscal changes take the form of a change in the tax structure (a "tax reform") which benefits particular groups and serves other objectives at the same time that it acts as a macroeconomic policy tool.

This paper describes a framework that can be used to analyze tax-reform proposals. This framework is then used to assess both the tax-reform proposals made by the Royal Commission on Taxation ("Carter Commission")[1] in 1967 and the Canadian tax-reform legislation in 1968–73 in response to the Carter Commission proposals.

I. Social Objectives and Tax Policy

1. Defining social objectives

The objectives of a tax system cannot be discussed separately from the basic objectives of any government. I shall distinguish among six basic classes of social objectives in order to facilitate subsequent discussion.

* The author is indebted to Richard M. Bird for a number of useful comments and suggestions.
[1] Report of the Royal Commission on Taxation (Ottawa: Queen's Printer, 1966).

The first and probably the oldest purpose of government consists of executing community tasks and providing "public goods" — things which cannot be financed or provided in amounts required by charging for them or by having people pay a price for them. These public goods include such things as irrigation canals, defence, education, anti-pollution measures, parks, and other community projects which cannot easily be provided by single individuals and have to be funded by a co-operative effort.

A second social objective providing purpose for government is to regulate how people deal with one another. This involves such activities as the administration of justice, the establishment of a criminal code, anti-fraud laws, regulation of consumer information provided to consumers, land-use controls, and so forth. Most of these activities are concerned with protecting individuals from undesirable "external effects" of other individuals' choices.

A third objective is the redistribution of the spending power of individuals in a society. Some part of the population will always need financial support; they may be chronically unemployed, ill, or aged. How much redistribution should take place is, of course, a question of values. It is fair to state that there is a general consensus among Canadians that spending power must be redistributed to needy individuals from the more affluent. Beyond this, most Canadians seem to be agreed upon the need for redistributive transfers among different regions of the country as well. In contrast to redistribution to the poor (which is aimed at providing a minimum availability of private consumption goods), redistribution among regions is largely aimed at ensuring the universal availability of a minimum level of public goods.

A fourth objective of government is fostering economic growth and maintaining economic stability. This objective is met by establishing institutions that facilitate such growth, re-allocating resources to enhance economic growth, and maintaining economic stability through the elimination of fluctuations in the economy that cause price inflation and unemployment.

A fifth objective of government is promoting national unity and reducing inter-regional discord. Why is the nation in itself so important? National unity is a separate goal reflecting a social consensus that it is valuable to belong to a country and to owe loyalties to the larger group which is the nation. A government can foster an increased sense of pride among its people, and by so doing make it easier to form a social consensus that the benefits of government are worth its cost. This fifth purpose of government can be of importance even in the designing of tax policy, both in the negative sense of trying to reduce interprovincial disagreement and in the positive sense of trying to ensure that the Canadian tax system is something of which Canadians can be proud.

A sixth social objective is concerned with the means of achieving the first five. Insofar as possible, a government implementing generally agreed-upon social objectives should do so in such a way that individuals' freedoms of choice are not unnecessarily restricted and in a way that is generally regarded as fair. It is, of course, always difficult to define what is fair and what restrictions are truly necessary. But it is nevertheless safe to say that this sixth general objective has two essential components: (1) Individuals in the same situation should be treated by government laws in the same way; and (2) the choices made by individuals should be as close as possible to what they would be if no government existed. The latter objective implies that government policies should be designed so as to minimize the extent to which individual choices have to be constrained in order to achieve the other objectives of government.

2. Conflicts among objectives

There are certain conflicts evident among these objectives. For example, redistribution of economic spending power may lead to a slower rate of economic growth. Consider unemployment insurance. The desire to ensure that no individual will be bereft of support while unemployed may lead a government to establish a system of unemployment insurance or benefits that will partially make up for lack of income. Such a scheme may fully reflect the social consensus regarding the way in which income should be distributed. But the effect of unemployment insurance is necessarily to reduce the rate of economic growth.

Suppose, as an example, that an unemployed individual is granted unemployment benefits equal to 100 percent of his previous salary as long as he remains unemployed. The effect of this benefit scale would be to increase the rate of unemployment in the country; for the unemployed would not actively re-enter the labour market as quickly. Removal of the benefit upon re-employment would act as a 100-percent tax on income obtained through becoming re-employed, and would reduce the speed with which many unemployed individuals would seek new employment. This disincentive could have profound consequences on the rate of economic growth. The redistribution objective thus, in this case, conflicts with the objective of fostering economic growth.

The problem of government policy making is to see how all objectives are affected by government decisions and to try to resolve conflicts among objectives in a way which meets the social consensus that is reflected in the ballot box. This is no mean task.

3. Social objectives and the goals of tax policy

Public services use resources. If the government must provide public goods, then it must raise funds to cover the costs of transferring such resources from the private sector without inflation. The funds have to be obtained by some type of tax, since (by definition) people will not pay on a voluntary basis. We may assume that the nature and effect of the public service is unaffected by the form of taxation. The same may be said with respect to the function of taxation in financing the expenditures of government agencies concerned with the protection of individual rights. The function of the tax system is simply to provide the necessary funds.

Generally speaking, most Canadians seem to regard redistribution as calling for a floor under the incomes of the needy, but not for a ceiling on the incomes of those better off. One qualification should be made: namely, that while most Canadians view redistribution as concerned only with transfers to the needy, some citizens would want, in addition, to impose surtaxes on wealth transferred across generations.

The redistribution of spending power thus involves only the question of deciding to what groups of people transfer payments are to be paid. In assessing a transfer-payment scheme, it must be decided what payments will be paid to different individuals, conditional on their circumstances. The answer to this question is obviously dependent upon the total to be raised through taxes, but is not dependent upon the form of these taxes. As with the first two categories of expenditure, the function of the tax system is simply to raise money.

It may well be asked at this point whether it is very profound to say that the function of taxes is to raise money. Why should this statement be significant? The important conclusion of what has been stated thus far is that, with respect to the first three social objectives underlying government goals, the form of the tax system is not a relevant factor. Because the purpose of taxes, given these three objectives, is merely to raise money, these objectives need not be considered in determining how the money is to be raised. This simplifies the problem of discussing how a tax system should be designed.

The fourth objective of government is in fact two-fold: the maintenance of economic stability and the stimulation of longer-term growth. The economic stability of a country can be in part regulated by changes in the levels of expenditures of government and of taxes raised by government. As an initial generalization, economic stability is affected primarily by the relative level of government taxes and expenditures (i.e., by the size of the government budgetary surplus or deficit) rather than by the forms of the taxes and expenditures.

This irrelevance of the form of taxes does not hold so strictly when we turn to the objective of fostering economic growth. To foster economic growth, the tax system must raise funds in such a way that the result will be the best allocation of resources to bring about that economic growth. Taxes necessarily change the allocation of resources. The form of taxation affects this allocation, and so alters the rate of economic growth. To a considerable extent, the effect of the form of a tax system upon economic growth is the result of hidden subsidies built into the tax system that distort the allocation of resources away from what it would be in the absence of the tax system.

From the viewpoint of deriving what a tax system should be, it makes sense to separate such subsidies from the tax system and to make them explicit. Such subsidies may be used to encourage certain types of investment which are of strategic value in economic development and so engender a greater return to society than they do to the private investors making the investments. However, there is a greater likelihood of subsidies being made efficient if they are made explicitly than if they are hidden within a complicated tax system — one reason why most special-interest groups prefer tax concessions to subsidies.

Because subsidies should be considered as separate expenditures and evaluated simply on the basis of whether their effect is worth their cost, subsidies to promote economic growth can be regarded — like the provision of public services — as having only one implication for a tax system: namely, that the tax system will have to provide sufficient revenue to pay for those subsidies which are considered desirable in spite of their out-of-pocket cost to the taxpayer.

The essential effect of the fifth objective of government — the maintenance of national pride — is to engender additional expenditures that have to be paid for, and so is the same as that of the first three objectives. For the most part, then, this objective may be ignored in defining the ideal tax system. There is one exception: most countries have tax systems similar to Canada's in their complexity and *ad hoc* nature; the accomplishment of implementing a more rational tax system would necessarily foster national prestige.

From the viewpoint of the first five objectives here discussed, the over-all function of the tax system is simply to pay for transfer payments, public services, and subsidies provided by the government in meeting these objectives. The sixth social objective — that of implementing government programs in as fair a way as possible and in such a way as to minimize interference with individual choice — thus becomes the paramount objective governing how a tax system should be designed.

The important questions in designing a tax system thus become: How can the tax burden be distributed equitably across individuals? How can the burden of financing government spending be distributed equitably across the country? What sort of tax system will interfere least with individual decision making? There should be few significant conflicts of objectives in defining the tax system; for the principal objective to be met in designing a tax system is to achieve a fair distribution of the tax burden.

II.   Defining an Ideal Tax System

The quality of fairness is one which must underlie the tax system if it is to reflect the social objectives which we have defined as the purposes of government. Fairness means that individuals in the same situation should be treated in the same way. In order to define fairness, it is necessary to divide government expenditure programs to be financed into two classes: (1) those for which the resultant benefits to individuals can be fairly easily defined and related to specific individuals, and (2) those which supply benefits that are of a sufficiently general nature to be difficult to apportion among individuals.

1.   The scope of benefit-related taxation

As an example of the first type of expenditure, consider spending on highways. A highway is clearly used by automobiles, trucks, and so forth, and furthermore is used to a greater extent by people who drive more than others. It would consequently seem sensible to apportion the costs of highways among individuals roughly in accordance with the amount of use they make of the highways. Naturally, it is diffcult to do this directly; for with very few exceptions it is impractical to levy tolls on the use of roads. However, the use of gasoline and diesel oil for fuel in cars and trucks is on the average fairly closely related to the use of highways, and so can serve as a fairly good proxy for the amount of such use. It consequently is reasonably equitable to finance highway construction and maintenance out of revenues raised from levying a tax on gasoline and diesel oil sold for this purpose — though only reasonably so, because fuel usage is not a completely accurate proxy for the benefit derived by individuals from highways. Thus in cases such as the provision of highway facilities, a tax can be designed that distributes the financial burden of these services over individuals roughly in relation to the benefits received by the individuals who pay the tax.

Where the benefits of a government service can be clearly identified, and where it is not the purpose of the government expenditure program to transfer resources to the individuals who are receiving the benefits (as is the case with the family-allowance program, for instance, which is a pure transfer program), it is equitable to finance these services out of tax revenues that are related to the benefits. As the example discussed above may suggest, the majority of expenditures which can be financed by benefit-related taxes are made by provincial and municipal governments, and wherever possible, government services should be paid for by levying user charges.[2]

While some government services, some public goods, and some expenditures can be financed through taxes that levy charges on the individuals who receive the benefits, a substantial number of government expenditures cannot be related to specific individuals in this way. Some government services provide benefits which are impossible to allocate to specific individuals. The provision of public defence is one example. The provision of mass education with its general benefit to society as well as the individuals affected, provides another, though very different, example. In both cases not only is it impossible to charge a price voluntarily paid by individuals for such services which would cover the full cost of services, but it is also impossible to impose a tax which is clearly related to the benefits provided by these services.

Transfer payments constitute another large category of normal governmental expenditures which cannot be financed out of taxes related to the benefits they provide. It is obviously nonsense even to consider the idea of trying to finance family-allowance payments or welfare payments

---

[2] Contrary to a statement in the *Report of the Royal Commission on Taxation* that: "A careful examination of the goods and services provided by government or government enterprises does not suggest that greater emphasis should be placed on the benefit approach in Canadian taxation" (Vol. 3, p. 3), the increasing strain on general taxation caused by expenditure growth at all levels of government necessitates a much closer examination of the feasibility of financing certain categories of expenditure through benefit-related taxation. Interurban expressways, university education, and health services constitute three principal areas where the potential role of user charges has been insufficiently examined. One proposal of a benefit-related tax for the financing of universities involves a special surtax on the income of university graduates. See M. Friedman, *Capitalism and Freedom* (Chicago: University of Chicago Press, 1962), ch. 6.

out of taxes levied only upon the recipients of these benefits. Consequently, there are a large number of government expenditures which have to be levied out of taxes on individuals in general. How can this be done?

It has come to be generally agreed that all expenditures which cannot be paid for by user charges or by taxes which are related to the benefits received from the expenditures should be based on ability to pay. We thus have a second class of taxes — general taxes, in that they are levied on all individuals — which should be based on ability to pay. All that remains is to define what constitutes ability to pay.

2. Defining ability to pay

While there are a number of ways in which different individuals might define "ability to pay," essentially all such definitions generally reduce to either what an individual has available to spend, or what an individual does spend. There are, in other words, two bases which are generally used as definitions of ability to pay — income and spending. In both cases, most individuals would define ability to pay as either one's income received in a year or as what one spends within a year.

It is worth immediately emphasizing that such definitions of ability to pay imply that there are only two taxes which can allocate fairly the burden of financing general expenditures which cannot be paid for by user charges: the income tax and a general sales tax. Other taxes, such as the property tax, may provide a means of allocating user charges to finance expenditures giving rise to specific, allocable benefits. However, such other taxes cannot allocate fairly the costs of general expenditures on education, welfare programs, or similar government activities. The current use of the property tax to finance education and welfare programs is indefensible from the viewpoint of equity.

A sales tax can be levied which is based on one definition of ability to pay. It is important, however, to point out that a sales tax can be based on ability to pay only if it is in fact a general sales tax, based on all expenditures on goods and services by an individual and not just on purchases of selected goods and services. In particular, a general sales tax must include services in the sales-tax base if it is to allocate taxes in accordance with ability to pay. The present federal manufacturers sales tax and provincial retail sales taxes are not general sales taxes.[3] A sales tax can be made progressive, with progressive rates, exemptions, and tax credits applied to total expenditures over an annual period.

More than anything else, income would be selected by most people as the thing which best measures ability to pay. Income, however, must for this purpose be defined to take in everything which an individual receives in a given period. The Carter Commission's *Report* stated this in words that have been widely quoted:

[3] The Carter Commission recommended that the existing sales and excise taxes be replaced by a general sales tax levied on retail sales and on services. (See the *Report of the Royal Commission on Taxation*, Vol. 5, Part A, especially ch. 27.) The Royal Commission excluded the special taxes on liquor and tobacco from this recommendation. It goes without saying that arguments for the equity and necessity of special taxes on liquor and tobacco must be analyzed more from a sociological viewpoint than from the viewpoint of the logic developed in this paper.

We are completely persuaded that taxes should be allocated according to the changes in the economic power of individuals and
families. If a man obtains increased command over goods and
services for his personal satisfaction we do not believe it matters,
from the point of view of taxation, whether he earned it through
working, gained it through operating a business, received it because
he held property, made it by selling property, or was given it by a
relative. Nor do we believe it matters whether the increased command over goods and services was in cash or kind. Nor do we believe it matters whether the increase in economic power was expected, whether it was a unique or recurrent event, whether the man
suffered to get the increase in economic power, or it fell into his lap
without effort.[4]

The tax system should not tax a man who has worked to get money
at a lower or higher rate than that applied to a man who has received the
same amount of money as a gift. The tax system should not differentiate
between an investor and a labourer. All individuals should be treated in
the same way, regardless of the source or nature of their income.[5] A tax
system based on ability to pay should thus be based on a comprehensive
definition of income that includes all sources of income: wages, salaries,
gifts from other people, capital gains, money won in gambling, dividends,
interest paid by others, money received from the federal government in
the form of transfer payments, unemployment-insurance benefits, family
allowances, or any other receipt of income which increases an individual's
economic power. For ability to pay to be the basis on which an income
tax is defined, the tax base must include all forms of income.[6]

A social consensus exists, I believe, that one's ability to pay is based
not on income as such, but on what is left over after non-discretionary
expenses are deducted from income. One has to live. One has to pay for
the expenses of one's family. All individuals have certain non-discretionary expenses, and it consequently makes sense to say that ability to pay
is related to what is left over after these non-discretionary expenses are
deducted. It is, of course, difficult to define what non-discretionary expenses are. However, the following can be said: (1) For everybody there is
some minimal amount of money which one needs to have in order to be
able to survive in Canada. An ideal tax should consequently levy tax only
on what remains after this amount has been subtracted from income.
(2) Non-discretionary expenses probably rise somewhat as income rises,
but become increasingly less important as a proportion of income as income rises. In other words, non-discretionary expenses are a smaller and

---

[4] *Ibid.*, Vol. 1, pp. 9–10.
[5] The only possible exception to this statement results from one qualification
made earlier with respect to the form of redistribution which is desirable. It may
be considered desirable to impose special taxes on transfers of wealth (other
than transfers between spouses), and so desirable to impose *heavier* taxes on
income received in the form of a gift, bequest, or unexpected gain. The present
tax system does exactly the opposite: lower rates of tax are imposed on all
categories of unearned income.
[6] For a detailed discussion of these matters, see J. Bossons "The Value of a Comprehensive Tax Base as a Tax Reform Goal," *Journal of Law and Economics*, 13
(October 1970), pp. 327–363.

smaller fraction of an individual's total income as total income increases. This proposition implies that an ideal tax system should levy an increasingly high rate of tax on individuals as income increases. An income tax based on ability to pay must thus be a progressive income tax — that is, the tax rate levied on an individual's income must increase as that individual's income increases.

3. Interference by a tax system in individual decision making

The second major consideration affecting the design of a tax system is that a government implementing social objectives should do so insofar as possible in such a way as to minimize the extent to which individual choices are restricted. The very fact of taxing means, of course, that resources are diverted from some individuals to other individuals, thus changing the choices that would have been made by the individuals in the absence of taxation. Moreover, the essence of the purpose of the government is, after all, to divert resources to achieve those social purposes for which there is general support and which cannot be achieved through the private sector alone. Government, by its very nature, therefore, involves a change in the choices that otherwise would collectively be made by individuals on their own.

Nevertheless, given the objectives which a government is pursuing, the goal of least unnecessary interference in decision making means that one prime objective to be kept in mind in designing a tax system should be that the taxing system should interfere as little as possible with individual decision making. To put this in different terms, a tax system should be as neutral as possible from an economic point of view — that is, it should not bias decision making. Such bias arises in a tax system when different types of income are taxed at different rates.

Fortunately, tax neutrality and tax fairness are achieved by the same tax system: namely, a tax system that treats all types of income or all types of sales in the same way. It is therefore possible to obtain a tax system which interferes with individual decision making as little as possible by obtaining a tax system which is fair.

III. The Carter Commission Proposals

The present tax system in Canada is an accumulation of the results of a number of historical accidents. It is really a misnomer, in fact, to call it a system; for it is anything but systematic. The Canadian income tax was hurriedly imposed in 1917 as an emergency income war tax. The complexities of our present Canadian system of taxation have been built in over the years, partly by judicial interpretation, partly by attempts to close loopholes, party by ad hoc subsidies added to the tax system, and partly as a result of other essentially accidental developments.[7] At no

---

[7] A brief but instructive summary of the way in which important loopholes were first introduced as "temporary" expedients is contained in an address by J. Harvey Perry to the November 1967 Tax Conference; see *Proceedings of the Twentieth Tax Conference* (Toronto: Canadian Tax Foundation, 1968), pp. 7–21.

time prior to the 1960s was there any comprehensive examination of the tax system.

The Royal Commission on Taxation, headed by K. LeM. Carter, attempted to provide the organized scrutiny of the tax system which Canada had previously lacked. The Commission attempted to define what an ideal tax system would be for Canada, and from this derived a number of recommendations which would bring about as ideal a tax system as the Commission believed could be implemented and at the same time be administratively feasible. It took more than four years to complete its task, during which time it undertook a massive program of research and analysis.

The Carter Commission's proposals were partly implemented in the tax-reform acts of 1968 and 1971, with some back-tracking in 1972 and 1973. What happened is described in section IV.

1. The Carter Commission recommendations

The essential recommendations of the Carter Commission were as follows:

(1) The personal income tax — the principal tax based on ability to pay in Canada — should be based on a comprehensive definition of income that would include all forms of receipts. (2) All other direct taxes on income (such as the corporation income tax and taxes on gifts and bequests) should be either eliminated or integrated with the personal income tax. (3) The tax unit whose income would be taxed should be defined as the family unit rather than the individual. (4) Sales taxation should be reformed by substituting a general sales tax on all retail sales and services for the present federal manufacturing sales tax and provincial retail sales taxes.

The recommendation to tax the family unit rather than the individual has some interesting implications. Any transfer between two individuals in the same family unit should not be taken into account for tax purposes. Moreover, the tax unit should be taken to survive as long as any member of it survives. If a husband dies and leaves money to his wife, that gift to his wife should not be taxable, since the family unit remains. A gift should be taxable only when it is a gift of money to somebody outside the family unit.

The taxation of gifts and bequests is substantially changed by the adoption of the family unit as the basis for taxation. The Carter Commission recommended that gifts made by a husband to his wife or to dependent children should not be taxed, since these would be transfers within a family unit. However, taxation should be applied to transfers, whether gift or inheritance, between parent and child, provided that the child is over twenty-one and so outside the family unit.

A number of specific recommendations flow from the Carter Commission's recommendations for the adoption of a comprehensive tax base and integration of all income taxes. These include specific recommendations for the taxation of capital gains at full rates, the taxation of gifts and bequests received from outside the tax unit, the abolition of the separate gift and estate taxes now collected, the integration of corporation income taxes and personal income taxes for Canadian residents, and the elimination of many loopholes in the definition of the personal income tax base. Integration of the corporation and personal income taxes for Canadian residents would be achieved by treating the corporation income tax as essentially a withholding device, under which corporate income taxes allocable to a resident shareholder would be refunded to the shareholder while the shareholder would pay personal income tax on his share of the corporation's taxable income.

2. Impact of the Carter Commission's proposals
    on different individuals

If a tax system is unfair, it will contain ways in which taxes can be avoided on certain types of income. Studies prepared for the Carter Commission estimated that almost $5 billion in income received by Canadian individuals and corporations in 1964 either escaped taxation or were taxed at unduly low rates.[8] While some of this untaxed income was offset by some expenses not deductible from income under the current tax law (a situation particularly frequent among certain types of employees), a substantial amount of income would be added to the tax base if the income tax were defined in accordance with true ability to pay. As a result, adoption of a fairer tax system would make possible a significant reduction in tax rates.

The extent to which an individual's taxes would be changed under the Carter proposals would depend upon the nature of the income received by the individual. Because wages and salaries are currently taxed at full rates and expenses of employment are currently non-deductible, many employees are currently over-taxed, regardless of income. Under the Carter Commission's recommendations, employment expenses would be deductible and tax rates would be reduced. Most dividend income is likewise over-taxed as a result of being subject to tax both when earned by corporations and when distributed to shareholders. Gifts, capital gains, and certain other types of income are presently either under-taxed or not taxed at all.

It has been estimated — referring to tax returns for the year 1964 — that adoption of the Carter Commission's proposals would have resulted in 3.8 million Canadians — more than one-half of all taxpayers — having direct taxes paid by or attributable to them reduced by more than 15 percent. At the same time, roughly 330,000 taxpayers would have had their taxes increased by over 15 percent.[9]

[8] Of this, $2.6 billion consisted of personal income which escaped taxes altogether, $1.2 billion consisted of gifts and bequests received from outside the family unit which was taxed in part through separate taxes on gifts and bequests, and $760 million consisted of corporate income not currently subject to corporation income tax. For details of these estimates, see J. Bossons, A General Income Tax Analyzer, Studies of the Royal Commission on Taxation, Number 25 (Ottawa: Queen's Printer, 1967), especially Table 7; and Vol. 6 of the Report of the Commission, especially Table 35–4.

[9] See Bossons, A General Income Tax Analyzer, p. 61. By "direct taxes" is meant the sum of personal income taxes, corporation income taxes, and taxes on gifts and bequests.

In addition to these changes in direct taxes levied on income, the burden of federal sales taxes would be reduced for all but high-income families by the Carter Commission's recommendations for changes in the sales tax. Combining the effects of the proposed changes in the sales and income taxes, implementation of the recommendations of the Carter Commission would have resulted in a fairly material redistribution of purchasing power from higher-income groups to lower-income families in spite of a large reduction in the top marginal rate of taxation.[10]

3. Evaluating the implicit subsidies of the tax system

In proposing that the tax base be widened to include all sources of income, the Carter Commission recommended the abolition of numerous subsidies hidden within the tax system. It should be immediately emphasized that it is not necessarily the case that subsidies are "bad;" for some subsidies may have beneficial economic or social effects that more than outweigh their costs. Nor is it necessarily the case that subsidies cannot be extended through the tax system; for it may prove administratively most efficient to extend certain subsidies in that manner.

From the point of view of designing an ideal tax system, the only important effect of subsidies is their cost. There are, of course, other questions that need to be answered in order to determine whether a subsidy is justifiable, such as the evaluation of (1) whether a given subsidy is more efficient than alternative means of achieving the desired objective, and (2) whether the benefit obtained through the subsidy program is worth its cost. But for a tax system, the chief implication of a new subsidy program which has to be financed out of general tax revenues is that tax rates will have to be higher than they would otherwise be.

The most important fact suggesting a need to re-evaluate many of the subsidies presently contained within the Canadian tax system is that before the research undertaken by the Carter Commission was made available, there were no accurate estimates of their cost. The sudden availability of facts must necessarily change the nature of any debate, and this has certainly been the case with respect to public evaluation of a number of subsidy programs.

The cost estimates provided by the Commission indicate that the total cost is the equivalent of 16 percent of the total revenue which would have been obtained in 1964 from the corporation and personal income taxes by both federal and provincial governments under the tax law in force in 1967, when the Carter Report was published. To put this in other terms, the rates of personal income tax recommended by the Carter Commission would have had to be raised by an average of roughly 18 percent had the Commission not recommended the abolition of these subsidies.[11]

It, of course, does not necessarily follow just because these subsidies

---

[10] For details, see *Ibid.*, Table 17.
[11] These calculations are based on data presented in *Ibid.*, Table 5 and Appendix L, Table L-2. The subsidies involved are subsidies to the mining industry, petroleum industry, life insurance industry, and other financial institutions, and the non-taxation of capital gains and employee benefits.

are expensive that they do not merit continuation. The Carter Commission recommended their abolition chiefly because (1) it concluded that these subsidies had to be justified on the grounds of their contribution to Canadian economic growth, and (2) it concluded, after taking into account the effect of these subsidies on general tax rates, that on balance these subsidies hindered rather than fostered national economic growth.

IV. The 1968-73 Tax Reforms

The Carter Commission proposals were the principal stimulus of the tax reforms that actually occurred in the years 1968-73, and the case for many of the proposals that were not implemented still remains strong.

1. The income-tax reforms of 1968 and 1971

Most of the Carter Commission's proposals regarding the tax treatment of insurance companies and financial institutions were implemented in tax changes made in 1968. The main reform bill, however, was introduced in June 1971. The 1971 Income Tax Act was massive both in size and substance, and involved a complete revision of the income-tax statute.

A rough score on the extent to which the subsidy-eliminating proposals of the Carter Commission were implemented is as follows:

Subsidies to mining industry	30%
Subsidies to petroleum industry	60%
Subsidies to life insurance industry	90%
Subsidies to other financial institutions	95%
Non-taxation of capital gains	50%
Non-taxation of employee benefits	95%

Given the magnitude of the political problems caused by implementing tax reforms, this is an impressive amount of reform. The long-term revenue gain resulting from the elimination of these subsidies (measured in terms of 1972 incomes and population) was approximately $760 million.[12] This enabled the government to reduce tax rates and to increase personal exemptions.

Other proposals made by the Carter Commission fared less well. The proposal to tax a family as a single tax unit was dropped early. The proposal to integrate corporation and personal income taxation for Canadian resident shareholders was, after long and acrimonious debate, dropped in March 1971.

The single most important reform included in the 1971 Income Tax Act was the introduction of a capital-gains tax with a deemed realization at death. A "deemed realization at death" is a technical feature of a capital-gains tax which ensures that capital gains accrued by an individual

---

[12] This estimate is calculated from the "post-transition impact" estimates reported in J. Bossons, "Economic Overview of the Tax Reform Legislation," in *Proceedings of the Twenty-Third Tax Conference* (Toronto: Canadian Tax Foundation, 1972), Tables 1 and 2. The figure shown is based on the pre-1971 federal corporate tax rate of 50 percent.

are taxed at least by the end of his lifetime; it represents a compromise between taxing capital gains on an accrual basis (like business income) and allowing accrued taxes on capital gains to be indefinitely postponed without limit as long as the asset is not sold. The deemed realization at death is not a minor technical feature; it has been estimated that the additional opportunities for tax postponement which would arise in the absence of a deemed realization at death would reduce the revenue yield of the capital-gains tax by one-third.[13] In this respect the new Canadian capital-gains tax is much stronger than the U.S. capital-gains tax, which it otherwise resembles. The new capital-gains tax is like the U.S. capital-gains tax in that it imposes tax on only half of realized capital gains; however, the U.S. tax does not include a provision for deeming accrued gains not realized before death to be realized for tax purposes at death.

2. The 1971-73 reductions in tax rates

The adoption of many Carter Commission recommendations to eliminate loopholes and *ad hoc* subsidies provided the basis for a substantial reduction in tax rates in the personal and corporation income taxes. This was used in the following ways: (1) to increase personal exemptions by an amount roughly equivalent to the increase in the price level since 1948, when the previous exemptions were defined, (2) to reduce the top marginal rate of personal income tax from 80 percent to approximately 60 percent, (3) to reduce the rate of corporation income tax from 50 percent to 40 percent, and (4) to introduce an automatic adjustment of personal income tax rate brackets and exemptions for the effect of future inflation in prices. The reduction in the top marginal tax rate to 60 percent reflected the introduction of the capital-gains tax, which substantially reduced the previous opportunities for avoiding the top marginal rate.

The introduction of an automatic adjustment of personal income tax rates for price inflation is an exceptionally important change, for two reasons: (1) It makes the tax system more equitable by eliminating the tax increases that otherwise are caused by inflation for individuals whose real incomes do not change. It preserves the relationship between real discretionary income and real earned income, which should underlie the rate schedule of the personal income tax. (2) It eliminates a powerful incentive for the government to pursue inflationary policies. Without the inflation adjustment, government personal income tax revenues are increased by approximately 2 percent for every 1-percent increase in prices. To put this in other terms, 1971 government revenues were approximately $1.8 billion greater than they otherwise would have been as a result of the price inflation that occurred between 1964 and 1971.[14]

3. The estate-tax battle

The major casualty of the 1971 reforms was the federal estate tax,

[13] This estimate is based on an analysis of U.S. data reported in Bossons, "Economic Overview of the Tax Reform Legislation," Statistical Appendix, pp. 65–66.
[14] See J. Bossons and T.A. Wilson, "Adjusting Tax Rates for Inflation," *Canadian Tax Journal*, 31 (May–June 1973), pp. 185–199.

which was abandoned in order to make a deemed realization of capital gains at death more palatable politically. The estate tax is a tax on wealth — indeed, the only comprehensive wealth tax in Canada — which is levied only once during a person's life (namely, when he or she dies). By its very nature, an income tax taxes only income; it does not tax the wealth from which the income is obtained. Consequently, the estate tax is the only fiscal instrument which can have any appreciable effect on accumulations of wealth.

The federal estate tax was in part a casualty of federal-provincial fiscal arrangements. While the federal government receives approximately 76 percent of the revenue from the personal income tax, it received only 25 percent of the revenues from the estate tax (the remaining 75 percent being collected for or abated to the provinces). Consequently, the substitution of 76 percent of capital-gains tax revenues for 25 percent of estate-tax revenues represented a substantial revenue gain for the federal government.

Removal of the federal estate tax has resulted in substantial pressure on provincial governments to follow suit. (Some — notably Alberta and the Maritime Provinces — already have.) Eliminating provincial succession duties as well as the federal estate tax is the equivalent of a lump-sum transfer of $4.5 billion to owners of large amounts of wealth accumulated prior to 1972 and so not taxed through the capital-gains tax.[15] Such elimination is obviously attractive to the individuals who would benefit.

The partial elimination of estate taxes and succession duties is a substantial aberration in the tax reforms of the early 1970s. It is particularly striking when contrasted with the Carter Commission recommendation that gifts and bequests simply be taxed as ordinary income of the recipient, which would have meant a substantial increase in taxes on gifts and bequests.

V. Concluding Comments

In examining the basis for designing a better tax system, the various objectives of the government have been evaluated. While all government expenditures have to be financed (directly or indirectly) by tax dollars, only two objectives are of critical importance for the form of the tax system: that the tax system be fair, and that it interfere with individual freedom of choice as little as possible.

The goals of fairness and neutrality fortunately coincide to a very great extent. At the risk of some over-simplification, it is consequently possible to say — taking all the varied objectives of government into account — that an ideal tax system is one which distributes the burdens of taxation as fairly as possible.

The Royal Commission on Taxation attempted to design a general sales tax and a general income tax that would be both as fair and as

---

[15] Bossons, "Economic Overview of the Tax Reform Legislation," pp. 54–57. The current provincial succession duties and alternative potential ways of making them more viable are discussed in J. Bossons, "The Effect of Income Tax Reform on Estate Taxes in Canada," *Proceedings of the 1973 Tax Conference* (National Tax Association).

neutral in their effects on decision making as is feasible. The *Report* of this Commission has justly been called a landmark in the annals of taxation.

A number of the Carter Commission's proposals were implemented in the income-tax-reform laws of 1968–73. Many proposals were rejected. In the case of taxes on transfers of wealth, what was implemented ended up being the opposite of what would be desirable on grounds of fairness and equity.

No important reforms have even been adopted immediately upon being proposed, and it would be wild optimism to predict that the remaining Carter Commission recommendations will become quickly accepted. Nevertheless, it is safe to say that the proposals of the Royal Commission on Taxation have become the standard against which future government tax-reform programs will be compared.

3. Economic Issues in Canadian Education

David A.A. Stager

University of Toronto

I. Education and Personal Income Distribution

There are numerous economic issues in Canadian education: How much should be spent on each level and type of education? Who should pay how much directly, or indirectly through taxes? How should the student's share be financed? Who should decide what, where, and how education will be provided? Underlying most of these questions is the concern that education has a substantial impact on an individual's income and the relative distribution of incomes among individuals. The purpose of this essay is to consider some of the reasons for the variation in income associated with different levels of education and to examine some of the public-policy actions which can modify the differences in income arising from these factors.

Table 1 presents data on how income rises with education level. It shows, for example, that male university graduates receive about 82 percent more income than do male high-school graduates. Why do such differences exist? More importantly, why do such differences persist for long periods of time? It is not sufficient to say that income differences by education level are simply the outcome of the operation of a free-market system which rewards the higher levels of productivity associated with higher levels of education and training. Although it is sometimes suggested that such income differentials are due to the high cost of further education, this is but a partial explanation. One must also consider imperfections in the operation of two related markets, the education market and the labour market.

Section II outlines the investment aspects of education; section III compares the benefits and costs of investment in education; sections IV

311

Table 1: *Average Annual Income by Education Level, Males, Canada, 1971*

Education	Average Annual Income (dollars)
Elementary school	
0 to 4 years	3,663
5 to 8 years	5,716
Secondary school	
Some	6,303
Completed	7,815
Post-secondary, non-university	
Some	6,747
Completed	8,663
University	
Some	7,653
Completed	14,227

Source: Statistics Canada, *Income Distributions By Size In Canada, 1971.*

and V investigate the relevant characteristics of the education and labour markets; and finally, section VI explores some policies — current and proposed — relating to the operation of these markets.

II. Investment Aspects of Education

The economics of education has attracted much attention in the past fifteen years. Initially, this interest was stimulated by attempts to measure the relative contributions of various factors to the rate of economic growth in the postwar period. When economists estimated the growth that was due to the traditional factors of production — land, labour, and capital — they found that these accounted for only part of the increased productivity of the economy. The unexplained part was said to be due to residual factors, which included technological change, research and development, and education.[1] This last factor, education, was given the special term of "human capital."

Capital is defined as any man-made, or reproducible, means for producing other goods and services. For example, grain harvesters and printing presses are produced because they in turn can be used to produce other goods (grain and newspapers) at lower cost than if these goods were produced by using manual labour. The physical capital in these examples consists of the machines themselves. They are used in producing grain and newspapers, but they are not used up. Rather, the machines provide a service over their lifetimes. It is this *stock* of future or potential services embodied in the machines which constitutes physical capital.

Similarly, human capital consists of the stock of potential labour services which may be provided by a person in the future. Human capital is increased by those things which increase the quantity or improve the

[1] See, for example, Gordon W. Bertram, *The Contribution of Education to Economic Growth* (Ottawa: Queen's Printer, 1966).

type of services a person may offer. Hence, human capital is increased not only by further education and training, but also by improved health, and migration to areas where one's skills may be better utilized. Each of these increases in human capital has costs associated with attaining it. The comparison with physical capital can therefore be extended further. Just as one must ask whether the cost of a new machine will be justified by the extra revenue it yields through improved productivity, so too one must ask whether the cost of adding to human capital will be at least offset by its increased productivity. Human capital may seem to differ from physical capital at this point; for there may be some immediate enjoyment (consumption) associated with learning, and there usually are future non-monetary benefits associated with further education. These apparent differences, however, can be accounted for within the technique that is used to compare the benefits and costs of both types of capital, namely, benefit-cost analysis.

III. Benefit–Cost Analysis of Education

The usual purpose of benefit–cost analysis is to determine whether an investment project should be undertaken, or which of various projects should be given priority.[2] However, this technique can also indicate some of the areas where market imperfections may be the cause of a particular distribution of personal income. Problems with benefit–cost analysis are related to the limitations of the available data rather than to the conceptual basis of the technique. For example, some of the benefits and costs of education are of a non-monetary nature. Society benefits in many undefined ways from the education of its population, and an individual forgoes various other opportunities when he enrolls in an educational program. Until effects such as these can be measured, and in a common unit, only those items for which data are available in dollar terms can be included.

Benefits and costs can be calculated from the perspective either of the individual or of the entire economy. In the latter case, the costs of post-secondary education would include the direct or institutional expenditures for salaries, books, supplies, and equipment; the indirect costs of depreciation and imputed interest forgone on the physical plant and equipment; tax exemptions; students' expenditures for books, supplies, and travel; and the value of the output forgone because students are not in the labour force. For the individual, the costs of education include tuition fees; expenditures for academic supplies, books, and travel; and forgone earnings.

Not all educational costs necessarily represent investment: some part of the cost may be incurred for the current enjoyment of the educational experience. (It might also be argued that the costs are underestimated to the extent that there is disutility associated with some aspects of education). By assuming that all costs are investment, however, one can

---

[2] For a full discussion of benefit–cost analysis in public policy-making, see Economic Council of Canada, *Eighth Annual Review: Design for Decision-Making* (Ottawa: Information Canada, 1971).

err on the side of underestimating the net return and thereby avoid possible misallocation or wastage of resources into education.

The benefits of education are much more difficult to define and measure. At a minimum, these are the direct, monetary returns the individual enjoys in the form of increased earnings. The counterpart for the economy is the increased output of the more highly trained individual. From the individual's perspective, additional earnings are an appropriate measure of one expected benefit of education, provided that these are adjusted for the probabilities of death before retirement, unemployment, participation in the labour force, and the additional personal income tax. An individual should also consider how his earnings would differ from the average for all individuals because of differences in his own ability, motivation, and the likelihood of succeeding in his chosen occupation.

Benefits and costs typically are compared by at least one of three common calculation techniques: net present value, benefit–cost ratio, and internal rate of return. The *net present value* is the sum of the benefits minus the sum of the costs, both discounted at an appropriate discount rate to the present. This is given by the formula:

$$V = \sum_{t=1}^{n} \frac{B_t}{(1+i)^t} - \sum_{t=1}^{m} \frac{C_t}{(1+i)^t}$$

where V is the net present value, B_t is the benefit (adjusted earnings differential) in year t, C_t is the cost in year t, n is the working lifetime in years, m is the length of the educational program, and i is the discount rate.

The *benefit–cost ratio* is the sum of the discounted benefits divided by the sum of the discounted costs, each defined as above. The *internal rate of return* is the discount rate in the preceding formula which will cause the net present value to be equal to zero.

Various studies have found wide differences in the internal rates of return to different types of post-secondary education. For example, one study estimated the private returns for male university graduates as ranging from 24 percent in dentistry, to 15 percent in medicine, 12 percent in law and engineering, and negative returns in theology. Similar studies estimated the private returns to be 13 percent for technology diploma graduates, and about zero for graduates of some master's and doctorate programs.[3] Although these studies refer to specific times and places and are based on special assumptions, the results are illustrative of those reported for many studies based on other sets of data. Part of the difference in rates of return to different programs is due to differences in the non-monetary aspects of the occupations of graduates: persons with M.A. and Ph.D. degrees generally enjoy more challenging work, have

[3] See David A. Dodge and David A.A. Stager, "Economic Returns to Graduate Study in Science, Engineering and Business," *Canadian Journal of Economics*, V, No. 2 (May 1972), pp. 182–198; and Systems Research Group, *Cost and Benefit Study of Post-Secondary Education in the Province of Ontario* (Toronto: Commission on Post-Secondary Education in Ontario, 1972).

more independence in their work, and thus are prepared to accept the lower rate of return that one finds when only monetary benefits are taken into account. But not all of the difference can be explained in this way. It will be shown in the following sections that part of the variation in rates of return to education is due to restrictions on the operation of the education and labour markets.

IV. The Market for Education

Some of the factors contributing to the pattern of income distribution by education levels can be found in the education market itself. The product on which this market is based is taken to be instructional services; that is, a student who enrolls in an educational institution is considered as buying one year (or one term or semester) of "education." This approach excludes the years of schooling during which school attendance is compulsory.

Consider first the demand side of the market. Studies of private demand for post-secondary education have examined the effect of price changes and factors causing changes in demand (that is, shifts in the demand curve). The quantity is usually measured in terms of enrollments, as representing the number of student-years of instructional services. The price of instruction should be defined in terms of the total private cost, including forgone earnings; but some studies have used only tuition fees to measure price.[4] Even the "total-cost" definition of price is unsatisfactory for some purposes, since the individual buyer of education who regards education primarily as an investment will also want to take expected returns into account when deciding how much education to buy. In this case, the net present value or internal rate of return is the appropriate price measure to which individuals respond in making decisions about education.

The analysis of empirical data is further complicated by the possibility of market disequilibrium. Demand may increase with rising incomes; but if educational institutions fix both the number of admissions and the tuition fee, the result may be excess demand. Enrollments are then rationed by raising admission standards instead of the tuition fee.

Only a few studies of the demand for post-secondary education have been undertaken in Canada and the United States. These generally indicate that the demand for university education is elastic with respect both to price (whether only tuition fee or other costs are included) and to family income levels. (In other words, a one-percent decrease in price, or a one-percent increase in income, will lead to more than a one-percent increase in the demand for university education.) A survey of such studies concluded, however, that the results have not been "refined suffi-

---

[4] For public secondary education, where fees are zero, forgone earnings represent the total private cost. For a study of the demand for secondary education using this approach, see John F. Crean, "Forgone Earnings and the Demand for Education: Some Empirical Evidence," *Canadian Journal of Economics*, VI, No. 1 (February 1973), pp. 23–42.

ciently, in a quantitative sense, to provide the basis for educational policy-making."[5]

Stronger conclusions have emerged from studies of socio-economic factors influencing the probability of a high-school student continuing to higher education. The levels of the parents' education are found to be among the most important influences, suggesting that the "taste for education" may shift the demand curve more than does the level of family income.[6] This taste or preference factor is reinforced by the attitudes of peer-groups and teachers. Moreover, it is not clear whether the level of family income is a factor which operates directly on demand for education as a consumption good or whether it acts indirectly on the demand for it is an investment good, since many students rely on parents or relatives for loans to continue their education.

Availability of financing may not be as important as the reluctance of students to incur a large debt for their education. This may be due to lack of information about the monetary return that can be expected on their investment in professional education, a lack of confidence by potential students that they can succeed in these professions, and a lack of understanding or appreciation of the non-monetary rewards that accrue to these professions. It is in this sense at least that socio-economic background is an important factor in determining how many and which students select specific occupations such as medicine and law.

The supply side of the education market cannot readily be described in terms of conventional supply theory, because so little of the Canadian education system lies in the private sector. Rather, the quantity of instructional services supplied (or student places provided) is determined by public decisions based on either, or a combination, of two approaches to educational planning: social demand and manpower requirements.

The social-demand approach may be based on projections of the number of students who could be expected to enroll in different levels and types of education on the basis of past experience. By starting with the total number of persons in the elementary schools and making assumptions about the percentages who would continue to each higher level, the number of places to be provided can be determined. Serious errors in estimation can occur, however, because the actual number of enrollments will depend on several factors not taken into account in this approach: changes in the real private cost of education, in expectations about future employment opportunities, in students' relative preferences for education and other activities, and in the propensity for persons to return to education either full-time or part-time after an interruption in their schooling.

Alternatively, the social-demand approach may be based on the political view that every qualified student should have the opportunity to continue his or her education. Projections based on this approach encounter the same difficulties just described, but also require judgments

[5] M.L. Handa and M.L. Skolnik, "Empirical Analysis of the Demand for Education in Canada," in Sylvia Ostry, ed., Canadian Higher Education in the Seventies, Economic Council of Canada (Ottawa: Information Canada, 1972), p. 37.
[6] Robert M. Pike, Who Doesn't Get to University — And Why? (Ottawa: Association of Universities and Colleges of Canada, 1970).

about the percentage of students at each level who are "qualified" to continue. This approach requires more political decisions than the other approaches described here, and hence is susceptible to greater discrimination with respect to the location and type of education offered and the age, sex, and other personal characteristics of students for whom provision will be made.

The manpower-requirements approach consists of first estimating the number of persons who will be required in the various occupations to meet specific economic-growth targets. The next step is to estimate the number of persons who will be in each occupation at the specific future time by projecting the current labour force, together with deaths, retirements, migration, and graduation. If the result shows the number required to differ from the number anticipated, the student places would be varied in accordance with the estimates.

This approach can encounter many problems. It is difficult to forecast changes in the socio-economic factors that influence both interprovincial and international flows of persons in each occupation and the labour-force participation rates (the percentage of people in each age–sex–marital-status class who are in the labour force), especially of married women. As noted previously, the decisions of high-school graduates to continue into specific institutions or courses can also change in unpredictable ways. The manpower-requirements approach also raises the serious question of whether students should be directed into particular fields on the basis of employment considerations. Finally, forecasts of manpower requirements require the assumption that there are specific education requirements for particular occupations. This assumption is not supported by the evidence, which shows a wide range in the level of schooling for persons within each occupation — except in professions such as law, dentistry, and medicine.[7]

V. Education and the Labour Market

Labour markets probably exhibit more imperfections than any other type of market in the economy. This section outlines some of the imperfections which are directly related to different levels of education. Consider first the demand side of the market for educated persons. One of the major problems an employer faces in determining the number of such people to hire at the prevailing wage, or the wage to be paid a specific employee, is how to measure the productivity of an individual. This is especially true for more educated persons who tend to have "white-collar" jobs where their efforts cannot be related directly to measurable output. Employers therefore are inclined to rely on the educational institutions as screening or sorting mechanisms, and to use various diplomas and degrees as objective criteria on which to base pay differentials.

Next, consider the supply side of the labour market. First, collective power is one of the most important causes of an imperfect labour market, especially for graduates of post-secondary institutions. Professional as-

---

[7] David Sewell, "Education Planning Models and the Relationship Between Education and Occupation", in Ostry, *op. cit.*, pp. 45–74.

sociations, such as those for engineers, lawyers, doctors, teachers, and government employees, cover a large portion of the post-secondary graduates. To the extent that such associations can control the supply of their labour services by imposing certification requirements, the earnings of their members are higher than they would be if determined in a free market.

Second, some professions associated with higher levels of education have a large proportion of members who are self-employed, and higher incomes tend to be associated with self-employment for several reasons. The reported income may include a return to physical capital used in one's practice; this return is difficult to separate from payments for labour services. The self-employed person may also work longer hours than the employed person who is regulated by the standard work week of the firm. Even if the latter works longer hours, he is less likely to be compensated proportionately than is the self-employed person. In many cases, however, an individual would find it difficult to offer his professional services as a self-employed person, because the particular field is dominated by a few large firms. Such a situation tends to prevail in architecture, engineering, accountancy, and management consulting.

Third, the more educated persons usually have better knowledge about alternative job opportunities in other occupations, industries, and geographical areas, because they have learned how to acquire information, and also because their work often exposes them to a wide range of other persons who know of employment openings.

VI.   Public Policies — And Some Implications

One of the basic economic goals of Canadian society, as expressed by the Economic Council of Canada, is "an equitable distribution of rising incomes." Although there is no consensus on the precise definition of an equitable distribution, numerous government programs have been implemented to reduce income differentials. Some of these are designed to redistribute income, in an effort to reduce the differences produced by the market system, while other programs are designed to reduce the imperfections in the operation of markets which accentuate the income differences. Both types of public programs are used to reduce the income differentials relating to different levels of education. This section looks first at the redistributive effects of the public subsidies for education, and then turns to various policies for removing imperfections in the education and labour markets.

One of the several objectives in public financial assistance for post-secondary education is to provide a subsidy to parents who might not otherwise be able to contribute to the costs of further education for their children. A substantial part of this subsidy is provided indirectly, by government grants to educational institutions to offset a large portion of the capital and operating costs and thus to maintain tuition fees at a much lower level than would be charged in the absence of the grants. A somewhat smaller part of the subsidy is provided directly through income-tax exemption for tuition fees and through government bursaries awarded to students whose parents are in the lower-income levels. These subsidies can be treated as if they were a supplement to the income of the parents concerned. Conversely, taxes paid to finance these subsidies decrease the disposable incomes of parents and other taxpayers. The net effect of this program can be estimated in terms of the redistribution of income from one income class to another. Such a study by the Economic Council of Canada found that for post-secondary education in Canada in 1968–69 these income transfers were "essentially 'progressive' — that is, the lower-income groups receive greater amounts in subsidies than they pay in taxes for post-secondary education, while the opposite is true for the higher-income groups."[8] Note, however, that this conclusion refers only to *groups* of families or taxpayers. The redistribution in favour of lower-income groups is actually enjoyed only by those parents with children in post-secondary institutions. Note also that the progressivity of income redistribution is based on the total of all types of institutions and programs. Another study has found regressive income redistribution for some fields — such as law and medicine — at the university level.[9]

There have also been several policies designed to reduce the imperfections in the education and related markets. Until 1964, many students were unable to borrow funds to continue their education, if only because they legally were minors and could not borrow from chartered banks without adult endorsement. This had the effect of restricting the demand for higher education. This imperfection in the capital market was partly overcome by the Canada Student Loan Plan, under which the federal government guarantees loans made by chartered banks directly to students. The Plan, however, has been criticized on two basic points. Loans are not available to students whose parents have incomes higher than a given level — even though these parents might not assist their children to the amounts assumed in the means test; and until recently, loans were not available to part-time students.

Inadequate and erroneous information has been a long-standing problem influencing the demand for further education. Many high-school students are unsure of the costs of post-secondary education, the financial assistance available to them, and the various opportunities for further study.[10] Although high-school guidance programs can provide some such information, students whose parents and other relatives have some post-secondary education have a more complete picture of the diverse costs and benefits. Guidance programs and information provided through various media may gradually reduce this problem, but the same kind of information must also be directed increasingly toward the parents, especially in the lower-income groups.

The most important public policy on the supply side has been the creation of alternatives to university in the form of community colleges, although these have different names in the various provinces. In

---

[8] Economic Council of Canada, *op. cit.*, p. 221. This study did not include government grants to post-secondary institutions for capital construction.
[9] Systems Research Group, *op. cit.*
[10] See D.A. Dodge and N.M. Swan, "Factors Influencing Career Choices of Students," Discussion Paper No. 48 (Kingston: Queen's University, 1971).

many cases, notably in the technological fields, community-college graduates compete closely with university graduates for jobs, hence reducing the income gap that existed previously between university and high-school graduates. Similarly, the rapid expansion of university places in the 1960s reduced the proportion of high-school graduates and increased the proportion of university graduates in the labour force, further decreasing their income differential. However, the university expansion appears to have been greater in the arts and sciences than in the professional fields, which *ceteris paribus* will increase the income differential between these two broad groups.

The major need for policy action in labour markets, relating to different education levels, is to restrict the power of professional associations to regulate the fee schedule and/or the supply of labour services. Some associations, such as those for physicians and lawyers, have been granted this power so that they might act "in the public interest" to prevent incompetent persons from practising the profession. However, in some professions, the power to regulate standards and specify the kind of work that can be done by no one other than an authorized professional has restricted entry into the profession and curtailed the emergence of para-professionals — persons with less training than the professional who act as auxiliaries to the professional — far beyond what is in the public interest.

VIII. Economic Growth

1. Government Policy, Resource Allocation, and Economic Growth

Philip A. Neher

University of British Columbia

I. Measures of Growth

Economic growth is widely regarded as a "good thing." Growth ranks along with full employment, price stability, and an equitable distribution of income as a major goal of government policy.[1] But what is meant by "growth?" Growth of what?

One measure can be discarded right away as inappropriate for any purpose: gross national expenditure (or product) computed at currently prevailing market prices. By this measure, Canadian incomes rose from $13.5 billion of goods and services in 1947 to $103 billion in 1972 — an eight-fold increase in twenty-five years.[2] But some of that increase has been due to price increases alone. People are not better off if incomes and prices simply rise concomitantly. Allowing for inflation, Canadian income in 1972 was only 3.3 times its 1947 value. Any appropriate measure must allow for inflation.

But during the same period, the Canadian population increased from nearly 13 million to almost 22 million, with the consequence that gross per capita income only doubled, from $1,657 to $3,213 (measured in constant [1961] dollars to correct for inflation).

What is to choose between these two measures? If per capita incomes

---

[1] Indeed, the Economic Council of Canada was established to study and advise on the growth of the Canadian economy in relation to these other goals of policy. Various publications of the Council are a good source of information on the problems, performance, and prospects of economic growth in Canada. See especially its Annual Reviews and the underlying Staff Studies. For general discussion of growth as a policy objective, see Edmund S. Phelps, ed., The Goal of Economic Growth, revised edition (New York: W.W. Norton & Company, 1969), Part One, pp. 10–89.

[2] Unless otherwise noted, statistics are taken from Information Canada, Economic Review (Ottawa, April 1973).

increase, then there is *intensive growth*. To the extent that individuals alone count, then intensive-growth measures are the appropriate ones. But suppose that numbers of persons count too. Then the appropriate measure might be the *per capita* figure multiplied by the number of persons — or, the original gross-national-expenditure figure. If this measure grows, then there is *extensive growth*.

One might distinguish between intensive and extensive-growth measures by asking oneself the following question. Suppose the Canadian economy doubles in population but *per capita* incomes halve in the next twenty-five years; will the economy have grown, declined, or stayed even? The answer will depend on how one values a change in individual incomes as against a change in the number of people. The values may be conditioned by the effects of these changes on the attainment of other goals. Has military potential been enhanced? Have empty lands been filled? Has national identity been strengthened?

The analysis in section II will emphasize *intensive* growth. The reader who believes that numbers of persons count also can multiply up the intensive-growth measure by the population.

But is it growth of income that counts, or of something else? A measure of income includes spending on investment goods (lathes, factory buildings, homes, and the like) which are desired not for their own sakes, but for future productive services they are expected to render. If public and private investment are subtracted from income, then public and private consumption remains. Many people would argue that it is the growth of *consumption* that really counts. It so happens that consumption and income have increased apace due to a trendless saving ratio[3] since 1947. But that need not have been the case.

For some purposes, it is *labour productivity* that matters. Incomes cannot rise over long periods of time unless output per hour of labour input is increasing.

A number of factors stand between productivity measures and income or consumption measures. For any economy, the labour-force participation rate (the proportion of people who can work who actually offer themselves for employment), the unemployment rate, demographic structure, and the like must be taken into account in order to convert labour productivity into *per capita* income. A declining participation rate, for example, can cause *per capita* income to rise less rapidly than labour productivity. However, for simplicity, it will be assumed that these factors do not change over time, so that labour productivity in Canada is assumed proportional to per worker domestic product in Canada. Growth in one is taken to be matched by growth in the other.

However, not all the *domestic* product (the output produced in Canada) remains at home as Canadian income. Some of it is exported to pay foreigners for the use of the capital which they have invested in the Canadian economy. These payments to non-residents must be subtracted from the domestic product produced in Canada to arrive at *national* expenditure, product, or income figures. Thus, labour productivity and *per*

---

[3] The ratio of saving to national income, both measured net of depreciation.

capita domestic product could be rising together, but if profits made by foreigners in Canada and interest payments to foreigners are rising faster, then national income is rising more slowly.

It is impossible to know for sure how important this wedge between domestic product and national income really is. The national accounts show interest and dividend payments *actually made* to non-residents. These amounted to $337 million in 1947 as compared with a (current-dollar) gross domestic product of $13,746 million in that year. At the same time, Canadians received $64 million from their investments abroad, so that net payments of $273 million were made abroad in that year. This was 1.9 percent of gross domestic product. The corresponding figure for 1972 was 0.9 percent. It appears that Canadian *national* expenditure has risen more rapidly than its *domestic* product.

However, foreigners *reinvest* some of their profits. Since these profits are not recorded as dividends paid to foreigners, they were not counted in the above calculation. If foreigners reinvested more of their profits in 1972 than in 1947, the picture could be reversed. If it were, Canadian national income and expenditure would have risen less rapidly than its domestic product.

All the measures of growth discussed so far are quantitative (dollar) indicators. They can only *suggest* whether Canadians have become "better off" over the years, for three reasons. First, "better-offness" includes non-economic as well as economic welfare. Second, the numbers do not tell us how growth benefits (or hurts) some people as compared with others. Third, the numbers read out of the national accounts were designed to reflect market transactions. There is now impressive evidence of *market failure*, a failure of markets to capture economic effects that bear on economic welfare. No "market," for example, "charged" firms for the right to pollute Lake St. Clair. If it had, it may not have been necessary to close the lake to commercial fishing. Some suggestions for redesigning the national accounts are included in section III.

II. Sources of Growth

1. Introduction

Economists have identified, and in some cases measured, sources of economic growth in Canada and elsewhere.[4] The major ones will be examined from the point of view of developing a conceptual framework for understanding the process of growth. Related policies, which governments could or should pursue, will be suggested.

Since "everything depends on everything else" and since virtually every policy measure has *some* impact on the growth process, it is impossible to be complete. Consequently, policy areas discussed elsewhere in this volume will be skirted. Stabilization policy, for example, bears upon

---

[4] For a general discussion, see Phelps, *op. cit.*, Part Two, pp. 90–171. In the Canadian context, one may consult T.N. Brewis, ed., *Growth and the Canadian Economy* (Toronto: McClelland and Stewart Limited, 1968). For an advanced treatment, see N.H. Lithwick, *Economic Growth in Canada: A Quantitative Analysis*, second edition (Toronto: University of Toronto Press, 1970).

the process of growth, but it is examined in detail elsewhere.

The main conceptual device will be the "guns-and-butter" or "production-possibilities" curve. It shows the maximum combinations of economic goods which an economy can produce (during a period of time) *if* all its resources are fully and efficiently employed. For analytical purposes, it will be assumed that only two products are produced: a consumption good, and a "capital good" called "machines." It will be assumed that only two resources or "inputs" are used to produce the outputs: labour, and "machines" which have been accumulated in the past.

This very simplified framework seems to expose the core of the growth process. But it concentrates on quantities, numbers, rates of change, and the like. It is a highly quantitative device which is only partially capable of pronouncing on such qualitative questions as whether or not economic growth improves the quality of people's lives. This deficiency is partially remedied in section III.

2. Saving and investing

More machines per worker mean more output per worker. By "machines" are meant all kinds of man-made factors of production (inputs): turret lathes, punch presses, factory buildings, proven natural-resource reserves, office furniture, typewriters, computers, arc-welders, reclaimed land, goods-in-process, and even knowledge and skill embodied in human beings. The enlargement, through net (of depreciation) saving and investing, of the capital-resource base (which has itself been produced) is a source of economic growth.

How does capital formation occur and how can government policy be used to influence it? The answers depend on the nature of the economy in question. Our understanding of capital formation in an essentially "closed" economy, as the United States or the Soviet Union, is the more complete, and we shall look first at that case. The Canadian case is more complex because Canada is "open" in the sense that foreigners, as well as Canadians, can make large-scale investments in Canada (that is, large-scale relative to our economic size [GNP]) and thereby influence our rate of capital accumulation and growth.

●*The closed economy:* A source of intensive growth is an increase of capital per worker (or per man-hour or per head of the population). This increase occurs when saving is sufficient for the total output of machines to be more than enough to replace the machines that have worn out and been scrapped, plus providing required maintenance on existing equipment, plus providing new workers in a growing labour force with the same amount of capital equipment that older workers have been working with. As a crude numerical example, suppose each of 100 workers has been working with 5 "machines" and one of those wears out and is scrapped during the year. Imagine at the same time that the labour force grows by 2 percent from 100 to 102. Then the economy must produce one machine per old worker (100 machines) to allow for depreciation *plus* 10 more to equip the new workers, just to hold constant the number of machines per man. These investments are sometimes lumped together and collectively called "maintenance" investment. In this case, maintenance investment is 102 machines. If the economy produces, say, an *additional* 102 machines during the year, then the number of machines rises from 5 to 6 per worker. This is called "capital deepening." When this occurs, output per worker rises and intensive growth occurs.

The production-possibilities frontier in Figure 1 can be used to illustrate the process. The output of consumption goods (C-goods) is shown along the horizontal axis, and the output of machines (M-goods) is indicated on the vertical axis. Both outputs assume full and efficient use of resources, and they are computed on a *per-worker* basis.[5] Machines and men work together to produce the maximum possible combinations of C and M-goods indicated by the curve. At point P on the solid-line production-possibilities curve the output of M-goods is just sufficient to hold constant the number of M-goods per worker in the face of depreciation and labour-force growth. So long as production remains at point P, the production-possibilities curve is stationary over time.[6] There is extensive growth due to labour-force growth and corresponding maintenance investment, but intensive growth is nil.

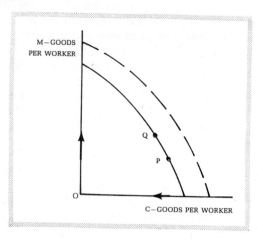

Figure 1

If, however, the economy were to save and invest more, it could produce at point Q (more M-goods and less C-goods, as indicated by the arrows on the axis); then machines per man will rise, production possibilities per man will be enlarged, and the economy can move from the solid-line production-possibilities curve to the enlarged, broken-line one. The outward movement of the curve illustrates intensive economic growth.

Which point should society choose, P or Q? The answer is not easy,

[5] It should be noted that the usual production-possibilities curve is constructed with outputs measured in *absolute*, not per-worker, amounts.
[6] If outputs were measured in absolute rather than per-worker amounts, then point P would be moving outward on a ray (straight line) passing through the origin, denoting balanced (or proportional) growth of both inputs and both outputs.

but one point deserves emphasis. Enlarged production possibilities in the *future* means giving up consumption (saving more) *now*. There is a real trade-off, a real choice to be made. Do we want jam now or jam in the future? Some countries — the Soviet Union and Japan are examples — have chosen relatively high rates of saving and investment: points like Q rather than P. Less jam today but more tomorrow. Other countries — the United States and Haiti are examples — have chosen rather lower saving and investment rates. They have grown more slowly in per worker terms. More jam today but less (than otherwise) tomorrow.

In planned economies, such as the Soviet Union and some countries in Eastern Europe, the investment rate, once chosen, is enforced by the economic-planning mechanism. In a "mixed" economy, such as the United States, the government can influence the investment rate but, for the most part, only by indirect means. It can, to be sure, direct resources from C-goods production to M-goods production by raising taxes (reducing the ability of people to spend on C-goods — forcing them to save) and making direct investments in the economy (increasing spending on M-goods). However, except during wartime, the investment channels controlled directly by the state are limited by ideology and tradition to "social-overhead-capital" expenditures: highways, schools, and the like.

But the chief instruments of control over the investment rate are the traditional ones of monetary and fiscal policy. "Tight" fiscal policy in the form of relatively high rates of personal taxation can be used to reduce the demand for consumption goods, thereby suppressing their rate of output and releasing men and machines to produce more machines. "Easy" monetary policy can then be used to ensure that the men and machines released from C-goods industries are absorbed into M-goods production. This occurs by making money more easily available at lower interest rates to businesses contemplating investment projects. Other investment incentives can be contrived. Lower rates of corporation taxation and investment tax credits[7] are examples. The introduction in the United States of the investment tax credit in the early 1960s may well have been a major factor underlying the relatively rapid growth of that country in that decade.

●*The Canadian case:* Canada is one of the most open economies in the world. Not only does trade in goods and services with the outside world dominate a large proportion of economic activity in Canada, but also a large proportion of investment in Canada is made by foreign corporations or financed in capital markets abroad. In fact, the financial markets in Toronto and Montreal are so closely linked with those in New York and London that it is geographic, not economic, remoteness which distinguishes Bay Street from Wall Street and Lombard Street. With relatively minor exceptions, securities of all kinds — stocks, bonds, commercial-credit instruments — trade freely between these financial centres. Edmonton municipal bonds sold in New York could be bought by an English-

---

[7] An investment tax credit involves a reduction in the tax paid by a firm. The reduction is greater, the greater has been the value of the firm's investment in new equipment and structures during the tax year .

man who, in turn, borrowed the funds in the Euro-dollar market in London.[8] The growth of the large international corporation has strengthened these international links. A pharmaceutical company with headquarters in Zurich may use profits earned in the United Kingdom to expand its Canadian operations.

A major implication of this high level of integration of Canadian financial markets with those elsewhere is that the rate of return on investments in Canada cannot significantly differ from comparable investments elsewhere. No American, and few Canadians, would buy a share in a Canadian corporation expected to yield 7 percent *per annum* if a comparable share in an American corporation is expected to yield 10 percent *per annum*.

This means that capital accumulation *in Canada* is not as easily controlled as it is in a closed economy. Recall that "easy" monetary policy could be used in a closed economy to make funds available at lower interest rates in order to stimulate investment spending. That policy just will not work in Canada. Our interest rate is effectively the "world" interest rate; and that, unless our capital markets are artificially sealed off from the rest of the world, is that.

Isolating our capital markets has some appeal, especially to economic nationalists who view with alarm foreign (especially American) domination of certain industries, notably secondary manufacturing and natural-resource exploitation. It is natural to ask, therefore, what role has been played by foreign investment in Canada, how it has shaped our economic development, and how Canada might develop in the future if it were to finance its own investments. These are tough questions. There are no easy answers, but economists do have some insights.

Why has Canada been splashed with so much foreign capital? Foreign investment makes up the difference between investment which actually occurs in Canada and saving by Canadians. One can think of the Canadian economy as a gigantic sausage machine turning out a given number of internationally saleable sausages per year. If Canadians do not buy them, foreigners will. Now read "investment opportunities" for "sausages" and return to the numerical example in the preceding section on the closed economy. Take the following as data. The "world" interest rate dominates the economy and it is determined in New York and London. The interest rate is, say, 10 percent. At that rate it pays to employ 5 machines per man in Canada.[9] Imagine that machines do not depreciate, that there are no new resource discoveries, and that techniques of production are not changing. Imagine that the *only* change going on in Canada is expansion of the labour force (due to natural increase plus immigration) at the rate of 2 percent *per annum*. Then to hold the machine-man ratio constant, machines must expand at the rate of 2 percent *per annum* as well. At a "world" interest rate of 10 percent, 100 workers require 500 machines. With labour-force growth, 102 workers require 510 machines. Labour-force growth alone has created investment opportunities equal to 10 machines. Who will take up these opportunities? Canadians will, at least in part. If Canadian corporations, households, and governments have saved enough to buy, say, 8 machines and if they invest entirely at home, then Canadians get 8 and foreigners snap up the other 2. Typically, however, Canadians invest some of their savings abroad. This increases the scope for foreign investment in Canada.

Of course, the Canadian sausage machine generates investment opportunities beyond those created by labour-force growth alone. General improvements in the education and skill of the labour force, improved techniques of production, and natural-resource discoveries have all helped to create investment opportunities in excess of the capacity of Canadian saving to capture them.

If this view of foreign investment is correct, then sealing off the Canadian capital market would mean fewer machines per man in Canada, and lower labour productivity. Income, of course, would not fall as much because Canadian *income* is what is produced in Canada *minus* interest and dividend payments made to foreigners for the use of their capital. No foreign capital means no cost of foreign-debt service. But taken together (lower productivity, but keeping more of what is produced), income would fall. By how much, we do not know. However, it is a safe guess that no Canadian government would interfere in a substantial way with the international capital market. Canada will have to accept the "world" rate of interest and all that it implies for the development of its economy.

But while Canada will probably not, as a matter of policy, exercise substantial control over the interest rate, control can be exercised over the amount we save and invest at that interest rate. The world capital market, including Canada's, is like an enormous bank in which national saving can be invested. The option is open for Canadians to consume less of their incomes *now,* in order to have enlarged consumption opportunities in the *future.* Just as in the closed economy, less jam today means more jam tomorrow.

The fiscal power of the state could be turned toward promoting growth in this sense. For example, higher taxes (including Canada Pension Plan contributions) could be used to reduce consumption now. The proceeds could then be invested, in Canada or elsewhere, in order to produce more income in the future. This income could be used to reduce future taxes. More taxes today mean less taxes tomorrow.

The mechanism for making these enlarged investments is already in place. Capital projects of various kinds are undertaken by all levels of government and crown corporations. Roads, schools, dams, thermal-power stations, harbour improvements, bridges, park development, and the like, are traditional modes of government investment. More recently, the establishment of the Canada Development Corporation has provided a versatile mechanism for making a variety of investments.[10] Truly imaginative, less

---

[10] The Canada Development Corporation is a creature of the federal government. It was set up to facilitate the flow of Canadian saving into equity investments in Canada. It is structured along the lines of a trust or mutual fund, but its directors presumably have a special responsibility to promote the national interest.

traditional, investments could be made. Why not, for example, buy up controlling interest in American *parent* corporations which operate Canadian branch plants? The mind boggles.

3. Employment

Industrial, market-oriented economies like Canada do not automatically achieve full employment of men and machines. If resources are unemployed, the economy can be thought of as operating *inside* the production-possibilities frontier.

Sometimes spectacular, but relatively short-lived, periods of growth occur if, by good luck or through implementation of wise stabilization policy, the economy moves toward the frontier.

The process is illustrated in Figure 2. Recall that the frontier represents combinations of consumption goods (C-goods) and capital goods (machines or M-goods) which the economy could produce if all its resources were fully and efficiently employed. The point P represents one possible combination of C- and M-goods that could be produced. Since it is on the frontier, it is an *atemporally* efficient production point (where "atemporally" means "at a point in time"). If, however, some resources are unemployed, then some goods are not being produced which could have been. The economy is operating at some point like P', inside the frontier, if there is unemployment.

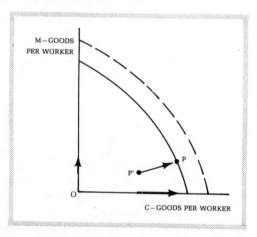

Figure 2

The movement from P' to P represents an absorption of unemployed resources and a consequent rise in both C-good and M-good production. There is economic growth between P' and P.

But there are subsequent effects as well which take rather longer in historical time to work themselves out. The long-term effects are somewhat different for closed economies, such as the United States, and for open ones, such as Canada, which are integrated through international capital markets with other, and much larger, economies.

•*The closed economy:* Suppose at P' the economy is producing just enough M-goods to replace the M-goods that are wearing out, that the labour force is not growing, and that production methods are not improving. Then P' is a *sustainable* point: the production of the economy could be characterized by P' for year after year after year.

However, the movement from P' to P involves an increase in C-goods output (which disappears as current consumption) *and* an increase in M-goods output, which constitutes a *net* increase in the stock of M-goods. These enlarge the productive capacity of the economy. This is shown by the outward movement of the frontier from the solid line to the broken one. The elimination of unemployment has a double-barrelled effect: not only is there a temporary growth due to a move *on to* the old frontier, but also there is a consequent *shift* of the frontier. Both effects give rise to recorded economic growth.

•*The Canadian case:* The movement from P' to P illustrates recovery from a slump (at P') to full employment (at P). The "cause" of the recovery has not been specified, but typically increased spending of all kinds is associated with the rise of employment. It must be stressed, however, that whatever the "cause" of the recovery, the rise of employment is accompanied by an increase in the rate at which investment opportunities are being created. There are incentives to equip the newly employed with new machines, and these incentives are strengthened by the spirit of optimism which prevails during such recoveries.

As unemployment falls, Canadian income rises. Saving increases along with consumption. But typically, increased investment opportunities during the recovery run ahead of the increased savings required to capture them all. Foreigners fill the gap and capital is imported.

Hence, an economic recovery in Canada is also associated with an increase in domestic production possibilities. But foreign investment in Canada will likely have increased as well, with the consequence that interest and dividend payments to foreigners will have risen also. Canadian national income will not have risen as much as Canadian domestic production.

4. Atemporal resource allocation

Just as in the case of unemployment, the economy can be thought of as operating inside the production-possibilities frontier if resources of all kinds are not efficiently allocated throughout the economy. An economy is *atemporally* inefficient at a point in time if it is possible to reallocate resources and get more output of at least one good without reducing the output of other goods. It is possible to get "something for nothing" if resources are originally misallocated among occupations and industries.

Canadian governments at all levels are deeply involved in the resource-allocation business. They participate directly as suppliers of goods and services: community centres, roads, the postal service, national defence, education. They administer crown lands: forests in British Columbia, oil pools in Alberta. The federal government regulates industry: anti-combines policy, public-utility rates. It subsidizes others: gold mining, shipbuilding. Above all, taxes collected throughout the economy by all levels of government have pervasive resource-allocation effects. One can go on and on. The point is that governments do affect atemporal resource allocations, and often profoundly so. Specific resource-allocation problems are discussed elsewhere in this volume.

The point must be made, however, that improvements in resource allocation have *intertemporal* effects (that is, effects over time) as well as atemporal effects. This is because improved allocation means more output, some of which is saved and invested to enlarge the resource base in future periods. The general analysis and the distinction between a closed economy and that of Canada (which was developed in the previous section) applies to this case as well.

5. Terms of trade

The terms of trade is the ratio of the price index of exported products to the price index of imported products. Since these prices are largely determined in world markets in which Canada is a "small" buyer and seller, the terms of trade should be thought of as *given* from the Canadian point of view. An "improvement" in the terms of trade means that the ratio rises and Canadians can import more goods and services for any given volume of exports. A "once-and-for-all" improvement permits a "once-and-for-all" rise in Canadian income. But sustained growth of income due to terms-of-trade effects requires a continuous improvement in those terms.

The Canadian terms of trade have changed very little in the post-World-War-II period. Between 1947 and 1972, the terms of trade reached a maximum of 110.3 (in 1950) and a minimum of 97.2 (in 1951). The period began with the ratio standing at 104.1 and ended at 98.8. One must conclude that the terms of trade have had little effect on Canadian growth during this period.

6. Technological improvement

Capital accumulation, reduced unemployment rates, and improved atemporal resource allocation have been cited as sources of intensive economic growth. Yet there are good practical and theoretical reasons to believe that none of these factors has had a large impact on Canada's long-run rate of growth. The level of unemployment has had its ups and downs, between 3.5 percent and 7 percent or so during successive business fluctuations, but the unemployment rate shows no noticeable trend since 1947. With the exception of a gradual movement of people from low-paid agricultural jobs to high-paid urban occupations, there has probably been little change in the degree of resource misallocation in the Canadian economy over the years.

Even capital accumulation, through higher saving rates, seems to be a short-lived source of growth. In a closed economy, a higher rate of saving and investment *will* result in more mechanization and a growth of labour productivity. But as machines build up relative to the people who man them, they begin to lose their productivity and thus their power to generate the even-higher incomes required to sustain the higher rate of growth. The "productivity" of *Canadian* saving and investment, in contrast, cannot fall as more *Canadian-owned* capital builds up as a consequence of higher saving and investing rates. Even so, as shown in the Appendix, capital deepening through higher saving rates cannot be counted upon as a source of intensive growth over long periods of time. In any case, the Canadian saving and investing rate is nearly trendless.

Nevertheless the Canadian economy *has* experienced intensive growth. No matter how one measures growth (per *capita*, per worker, per man-hour), the upward trend since Confederation is unmistakable.

It seems that constantly improving levels of applied technology, the efficiency with which inputs can be transformed into outputs, must account for sustained growth. One observer[11] suggests that just under half the intensive growth of the Canadian economy (in terms of output per man-hour) between 1937 and 1961 has been due *directly* to improvements in applied technology. Most of the rest has been due to capital deepening brought about *indirectly* by technological change which has made profitable the installation of more machines per man. The remainder is due to other causes, which cannot be explored here.

Technological improvement can also be visualized in terms of the production-possibilities frontier. In Figure 3, the direct impact of technological improvement is shown by the outward shift of the production-possibilities frontier, from the one indicated by the solid line to the one indicated by the broken one. With improved means of production, more output can be had with the *same* quantity of inputs. The productivity of all inputs will generally rise, some more than others. In Figure 3 the productivity of workers has risen in both the C- and M-goods industries. But the productivity of machines will also have risen. At a given "world" rate of interest there is now an incentive to invest in Canada which did not exist before. Some of the new machines will be made in Canada and,

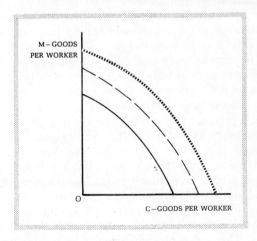

Figure 3

11 Lithwick, *op. cit.*

typically, some will be imported. Some of the investment will be financed by Canadians and, typically, some will be financed abroad.

The discovery that a natural-gas field is larger than expected might be thought of as a technological improvement, since it means that more output can now be had with the same inputs (higher pressure at the well-head, lower drilling costs, and the like). But the discovery means higher productivity of both men and capital equipment. Some of the equipment will be produced by Canadians (laying down additional transmission lines) while some (the pipe) may be imported. The additional investment could be financed by a joint Canadian-foreign venture. No matter how it is financed, the new investment enlarges the productive capacity of the economy still further. This indirect impact of a technological improvement is illustrated by the dotted frontier in Figure 3.

Such fortuitous events are relatively unimportant as compared with the relentless advance of applied technological knowledge. This advance is in turn based on fundamental scientific research which advances frontiers of knowledge year by year. Technological knowledge is a kind of capital (or resource) in that it contributes, along with other inputs (or resources), to produce output. But it differs profoundly from conventional inputs in that technological knowledge is a *public good*: the use of it by one person does not deprive others of it. This property, together with the accumulative nature of knowledge, gives technological improvement special stature as a source of intensive growth.

It is commonly understood that a free market will produce less technological knowledge than is socially desirable. While research and development cost something, the benefits are only partially protected by patents, industrial secrecy, and the like.

Governments recognize that individuals and firms cannot capture the full rewards for their research and development efforts. As a consequence, it is common that governments subsidize these efforts through research-and-development grants, aid to universities, support of government laboratories, and so on. But, in view of the tendency of technology to diffuse, even internationally, is it appropriate for the *Canadian* government to support research and development? Should not Canadians help themselves to a "free ride" on a given world rate of technological growth?

That is another tough question, but one point deserves emphasis. The more fundamental is knowledge, the more rapidly and cheaply it diffuses. A theorem on differential equations can be of great significance to systems designers, control engineers, and even economists. But, once proved and published, it becomes common knowledge throughout the world.

At the other extreme, specific, goal-oriented, applied research leads to technology that is less easy to get "for free." Canada must either pay for patent rights, invite foreign firms holding those rights to use them in Canada, or invest in producing duplicate technology. The last course should be chosen if it is the least-costly alternative.

By world standards, however, Canadians are an educated and inventive people who can do their share in adding to the world's stock of knowledge. That stock of knowledge is of greater benefit to Canada if it is richer in applied techniques of particular use in the Canadian economy.

Consequently, research efforts in natural-resource exploration and exploitation, construction methods for arctic cities, the ecology of northern places, transportation technology, and so on, are particularly appropriate activities for Canadian scientists and engineers.

7. Consumption possibilities

It is clearly the role of governments to pursue policies which keep the Canadian economy on the production-possibilities frontier. That is, they should devise effective stabilization policies to ensure full employment. They should, in addition, ensure that employed resources are efficiently employed.

The production-possibilities frontier itself moves outward over time as applied technology improves. To a large extent, Canada shares that technology with other advanced, industrial economies, so that the Canadian rate of technological improvement is largely independent of Canadian research-and-development activity. (Exception: research and development on technological problems specific to Canada may have large payoffs.)

Once on the frontier, the problem is to choose the best single point. This is a problem of *intertemporal* efficiency, the problem of allocating resources over time. It can be visualized in terms of the consumption-possibilities frontier.

•*The closed economy:* For any given technology and rate of labour-force growth, there is a maximum rate of consumption per worker which can be produced in a period (call it period one) by devoting all resources to C-goods output and none whatsoever to M-goods production. This quantity is denoted by $\bar{C}_1$ in both diagrams in Figure 4. On the other hand, if all resources were thrown into M-good production, then C_1 would be zero and machine production would be its maximum in period one ($\bar{M}_1$).

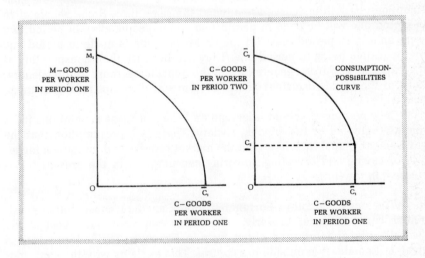

Figure 4

What happens in the next period, period two? If $\overline{C}_1$ ($M_1 = O$) were chosen in the first period, then second-period consumption could be not more than $\underline{C}_2$. It is less than $\overline{C}_1$ because some machines will have worn out and not have been replaced. In addition, the labour force will have grown. On the other hand, if $\overline{M}_1$ ($C_1 = 0$) were chosen in the first period, then maximum second-period consumption is possible at $\overline{C}_2$. It is greater than $\overline{C}_1$ because net additions beyond depreciation would have been made to the stock of machines per worker, notwithstanding labour-force growth in the meantime.

Points along the line connecting $\overline{C}_1$ and $\overline{C}_2$ correspond to different levels of M-goods production in the first period. Higher levels of saving and investing in period one (greater M_1) correspond to lower C_1 and higher C_2. The curve bows outward because of diminishing returns to machines as more of them are combined with the workers who man them.

The consumption-possibilities curve illustrates the choice which must be made: more jam today means less jam tomorrow; less jam today means more jam tomorrow.

The choice is similar to ones made by consumers every day in allocating their limited incomes among consumption goods: more socks means fewer shirts, and vice versa. Does not the consumption-possibilities curve present the same kind of problem that is presented by the consumer's budget constraint? Should not governments allow the C_1–C_2 problem to be solved the same way as the consumer's socks–shirts problem: through the free market?

No! The free market does not work unless *all persons* concerned with a transaction (buyers and sellers, consumers and producers) are represented. There is a *market failure* if they are not. Example: Citizens of Vancouver cannot "transact" with citizens of New Westminster who happily dump municipal wastes into the Fraser river and, ultimately, onto Vancouver's beaches.

In a similar way, not all the people who "transact" along the consumption-possibilities curve are alive at the same time. Some people alive in period one will be dead in period two. Some people alive in period two were unborn in period one. Yet the C_1–M_1 decision is made in period one by the people living in period one. They can increase their consumption at the expense of future generations. Who represents those future generations in the C_1–M_1 decision? If the government does not represent them, who will?

The government should intervene on behalf of these generations in its role as custodian of the ongoing society. There is a presumption that the government should interfere with the market process and promote a higher rate of saving and investing, lowering consumption in the present to increase it in the future.

•*The open economy:* Fortunately, the Canadian consumption-possibilities curve is easier to derive. Canadians can save and invest at the "world" rate of interest, denoted by r in Figure 5. This interest rate is given to Canada. It is outside her control. This explains why the consumption-possibilities curve for Canada is a straight line.

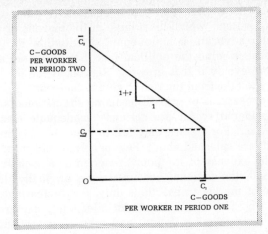

Figure 5

Canadians can always trade off a unit of consumption today for $1 + r$ units of consumption tomorrow. A sacrifice of 100 bottles of beer today yields 105 bottles tomorrow if r is 5 percent.

The representation of future generations in the C_1–C_2 decision is a problem in the Canadian economy as well as in a closed economy. It can be thought of as a problem of determining the size of "bequests" of income-earning assets which are handed down from generation to generation. Again, there is a presumption that these "bequests" are too small: that there is too much C_1 at the expense of C_2. Again, it is clear that Canadian governments can influence the rate of saving and investing (the size of "bequests") through their ability to tax and spend and through their powers to regulate the rate at which natural resources are exploited.

But goals often conflict and very thorny policy questions arise as a consequence. Example: Stabilization policy might call for a large federal budget deficit (dissaving), while at the same time there is growth policy which calls for more saving. Another example: Growth policy might call for more saving, and the reduction of estate duties and death taxes could promote saving; but income-distribution policies call for more equal distribution of income among persons alive at the same time.

III. Shaping the Future

Economic growth has to do with the allocation of resources over time. It has been suggested that the government should intervene in the saving and investment process to allocate more resources to the future, depressing the level of present consumption, so that more can be had in the years to come. Yet, why more consumption? Do we not consume much too much already?

Most people think not, and for good reason. Even if we include only the consumption goods recorded in the national accounts, nearly everyone would prefer more of these goods to less of them. This is particularly true of people in the lower-income categories, who already view with suspicion the efforts of "environmentalists" and others who propose measures that would raise prices of food, housing, clothing, and transportation — items which loom large in the budgets of the poor. Moreover, those who advocate a more equal distribution of the world's goodies should bear in mind the political fact that it is more acceptable to divide a pie more evenly if it is growing. Reason: if the pie is growing, it is not necessary to take from the rich to give to the poor.

Yet the measures of growth based on the national accounts which have been considered so far are certainly inadequate measures of increasing "welloffness." For a start, they fail to take into account how the blessings of growth are splashed about. Few people would regard a "growth for the rich at the expense of the poor" program as a socially desirable one.

Second, the national accounts were originally designed to measure the value of market transactions *only*. But increasingly the quality of life is shaped by forces which are not adequately captured by markets. The costs of congestion, pollution, and other forms of environmental decay, for example, are not captured, on the whole, in the national accounts. New accounts are required which can more adequately reflect Canadian "welloffness" and how it changes over time.

The question is not "to grow or not to grow?" but "how to grow?" Canadians have traditionally relied on market mechanisms for that determination. But markets seem less and less up to the task as market failures become more frequent and important. The role of governments is clear. Political processes must replace market processes where the latter fail.

Appendix

A simple model of capital accumulation in Canada is suggested here. One implication of it is that higher saving and investment ratios should not be regarded as a permanent source of intensive growth. Canadian income (Y) has two principal components:

1. Labour income, which equals the average wage rate (w) multiplied by the number of people employed (L)
2. Property income, which equals the average rate of return (r) on capital of all kinds multiplied by the amount of Canadian-owned capital (M)

Thus $Y = wL + rM$

Canadian-owned capital builds up ($\triangle M$) as a consequence of saving a portion (s) of net income.

Thus $\triangle M = sY$

Taken together,

$$\triangle M = s(wL + rM)$$

Dividing by the quantity of Canadian-owned capital (M),

$$\frac{\triangle M}{M} = sw \cdot \frac{L}{M} + sr$$

This expression shows the *proportional* growth of Canadian-owned capital.

For example:

$s = 0.05$ (5 percent of income is saved)

$w = \$10,000$ (the average wage)

$\dfrac{M}{L} = \$20,000$ (value of capital per worker)

$r = 0.10$ (the average rate of return on capital is 10 percent)

$$\dfrac{\Delta M}{M} = (0.05) \cdot (\$10,000) \cdot \dfrac{1}{\$20,000} + (0.05) \cdot (0.10)$$

$$= 0.025 + 0.005$$

$$\dfrac{\Delta M}{M} = 0.030 = 3 \text{ percent}$$

The formula is illustrated in Figure 6 by the rising solid line, with intercept sr and slope sw. There is capital deepening if the growth rate of capital $(\Delta M/M)$ exceeds the growth rate of labour $(\Delta L/L)$. The latter rate is shown by the horizontal line in Figure 6. It is assumed insensitive to the average number of men per machine (L/M). Canadian immigration, however, appears sensitive to wages and job opportunities. Thus, more machines per man (lower L/M) could be associated with higher labour-force growth rates $(\Delta L/L)$. In that case, the $\Delta L/L$ curve would slope downward.

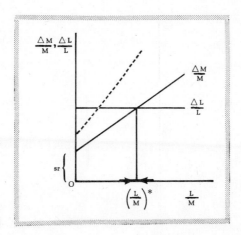

Figure 6

In either event, the economy gradually converges to an equilibrium $L/M = (L/M)^*$, as shown by the arrows on the horizontal axis. Why? Suppose the prevailing L/M lay to the right of $(L/M)^*$. Then the figure shows that $\Delta M/M$ exceeds $\Delta L/L$. Capital is growing at a faster rate (say, 4 percent) than the labour force (say, 2 percent). The ratio of L to M is therefore falling, An analogous argument can obviously be made for values of L/M which lie to the left of $(L/M)^*$.

If Canadians decided to save more (an increase in s), then the $\Delta M/M$

line would shift up and become more steeply inclined, as both the intercept (sr) and slope (sw) would increase. This is indicated by the dotted line in Figure 6. The new equilibrium would lie to the left of (L/M).* Capital deepening and growth would occur during the transition and incomes would rise. But the growth of income comes to a halt as the new equilibrium is reached.

2. The Allocation
Of Research-and-Development Resources

G. Bruce Doern

Carleton University

Concern about the allocation of the scientific and technological resources of a society is largely a post-World-War-II phenomenon. In the case of Canada, explicit concern about the problems of resource allocation seems to have begun only in the 1960s. The purpose of this paper is to describe some of the basic concepts and issues in resource allocation and to relate them to recent Canadian developments.

I. Basic Concepts and Issues

The difficulties of resource allocation in the scientific and technological fields are ultimately related to the problems of defining and understanding the nature of, and interrelationships between, the main elements of the spectrum of scientific and technological activity. The recent Senate Report on Science Policy defined science as "the rational and systematic understanding of man and nature," and technology as "the organization of knowledge for the achievement of practical purposes."[1] These two definitions reflect the two ends of the spectrum of activity and are often equated with the categories of "basic" or "pure" research and "applied" and "developmental" activity respectively. The concept of developmental activity has recently been extended to become a third category in the spectrum. This concept now applies not only to the application of research in the technical sense of the development of prototypes of products or services but also to the eventual manufacture and marketing of such goods and services. Hence it lengthens the spectrum to cover the full cycle of industrial innovation.

---

[1] Senate Special Committee on Science Policy, *A Science Policy For Canada*, Vol. I (Ottawa: Information Canada, 1970), pp. 3–4.

Each of these kinds of scientific and technological activity is often difficult to classify, particularly in the borderline areas of applied and developmental activity and innovation. Each of the types of activity implies different types of possible economic benefit and cost, and hence the allocation of research-and-development (R & D) resources is inextricably linked to these main categories.

The following quotation illustrates one approach regarding a rationale for allocating resources to basic research.

Science is a continuum that goes from the most basic (such as high energy physics) to the heavily applied (such as nuclear reactor engineering). The basic parts of science support the applied parts in several important ways: first, from basic research come the completely new break-throughs, like the laser or nuclear fission, which rejuvenate old technology; second, basic research, when conducted in either actual or intellectual proximity to technology, establishes a tone and standard that keep technology at a high level of sophistication; and third, basic research provides a training ground for young scientists, many of whom eventually become technologists. For all these reasons I view basic research as a justified "overhead" on the entire scientific–technological enterprise, an expense which must often be borne by society as a whole since it is not always clear which part of basic research is the most relevant to which part of technology or, for that matter, to the rest of science.[2]

Hence, it is suggested by this "pure science as overhead" concept that some fixed percentage figure be utilized (such as 10 percent of total R & D resources) to guide resource allocation to basic research, the assumption being that most of such research would be located in universities.[3] These figures or percentages, given the absence of more rational criteria, are usually drawn from simple comparisons with other states or societies.

The more one moves away from the basic end of the spectrum, the more complicated the trade-offs in costs and benefits become. It has been in the applied and developmental part of the spectrum that the recent so-called "science-policy" debate has really been centred, particularly in Canada.

Science policy consists of both policies *for* science and science *in* policy. Policies *for* science refer broadly to the government's support for the development and management of scientific skills, and hence includes aspects of "education" or at least the support of research scientists in educational institutions. Science *in* policy refers broadly to those policies for utilizing and organizing science and technology as a *technique* or *means* for understanding and solving other policy problems, such as economic growth and industrial competitiveness, pollution, urban problems, etc.

[2] Alvin M. Weinberg, "Scientific Choice and the Scientific Muckrakers", *Minerva*, VII, Nos. 1–2 (Autumn–Winter 1968–69), p. 60.
[3] See, for example, Organization for Economic Co-operation and Development, *Fundamental Research and the Policies of Governments* (Paris: OECD, 1966).

The two dimensions of policy are, of course, closely linked. This is particularly true with respect to the increasing incidence and appearance of so-called "big-science" and "major-program" facilities and concepts.[4] These are programs which are increasingly funded by government with a view to helping serve some social mission (science in policy) but which also will require and will help train more scientists (policies for science). This is to be contrasted with the formerly dominant pattern of so-called "little science," in which government grants are awarded to individual pure and applied scientists of merit who have applied for grants.

The allocation of R & D resources in the "science-in-policy" dimension involves a determination of which social and economic priorities are to be pursued and what costs and benefits, in the short run and in the long run, are to be incurred or tolerated. While methods have been suggested to determine economically the best allocation of resources, the ultimate decisions in this aspect of science policy are usually arrived at through regular political processes involving politicians, scientists, and civil servants.[5] There are numerous competing claims on the limited R & D resources, and these claims are made by and through numerous decision-making centres in both government and industry.

Until recently, the principal centres of influence in the allocation of R & D resources in Canada have been the three main granting bodies, the National Research Council (NRC), the Medical Research Council (MRC), and the Canada Council, with NRC clearly the dominant influence. In addition, virtually all government departments, including the NRC, are engaged in granting R & D resources and in operating their own in-house (intramural) research activity. In the late 1960s and early 1970s, these traditional centres of influence were challenged by the Science Council of Canada, an external advisory body, and by the Ministry of State for Science and Technology (and its predecessor, the Science Secretariat), an internal co-ordinative policy "ministry" headed by a cabinet minister.[6] These two bodies have no operating responsibilities, but are intended to help co-ordinate and develop policies regarding science and technology.

II. The Allocation of R & D Resources in Canada

To understand the allocation of R & D resources in Canada, one must look first not at the objectives to which such resources are directed, but rather at the location where the R & D is performed (in government labs, universities, and industry). The questions of "objectives" and "location" are, of course, related, but recently the major political issue in the allocation of R & D has been an attempt to reverse the historical "location" pattern of R & D activity, a pattern in which "in-house" government re-

[4] See G. Bruce Doern, "Science Policy Making: the Transformation of Power in the Canadian Scientific Community", *Journal of Canadian Studies,* Vol. 5, No. 4 (November 1970), pp. 23–25.
[5] For an economic analysis of R & D policy in Canada, see N.H. Lithwick, *Canada's Science Policy and the Economy* (Toronto: Methuen Co., 1969).
[6] For an analysis of these organizations, see G. Bruce Doern, *Science and Politics in Canada* (Montreal: McGill-Queens University Press, 1972) and G. Bruce Doern and Peter Aucoin, eds., *The Structures of Policy Making in Canada* (Toronto: Macmillan Company of Canada, 1971), chs. II, VII, and IX.

search has been predominant in Canada. This part of the essay will describe and analyze very briefly the most recent effort to change the R & D expenditure pattern, an effort centred on the so-called "Make-or-Buy" Contracting-Out policy developed by the Ministry of State for Science and Technology (hereafter referred to as MOSST). MOSST was established in 1971 to provide a cabinet-level focus on science-policy issues and to improve the co-ordination of the government's activities and programs in this field. The "Make-or-Buy" policy quickly became the focus of MOSST's early efforts.

The "Make-or-Buy" policy reflects a consensus of the 1960s and early 1970s which required a decade to build and which was revealed in a succession of science-policy studies and reports by the Glassco Commission, the Science Council, and the Lamontagne Senate Committee Reports on Science Policy.[7] In comparison with other states such as the United States, Japan, and the United Kingdom, for example, Canada performs relatively little of its R & D activity in industry, where it would presumably be closer to market incentives and hence would result in new marketable (and exportable) products and services with their accompanying employment and other economic benefits. In 1969, for example, Canada performed about 35 percent of its total R & D activity in government, 35 percent in industry, and 30 percent in higher education and private non-profit institutions. The comparable figures for the United States were about 14 percent in government, 68 percent in industry, and 17 percent in higher education. In Japan 12 percent of R & D is performed in government, 68 percent in industry, and 20 percent in higher education. In the United Kingdom 25 percent of R & D is performed in government, 65 percent in industry, and 10 percent in education and private non-profit institutions.[8]

Thus, the greatest part of our R & D was performed in government and tended to be of a more basic or applied, rather than developmental, nature. The incentive structure of government bureaucracies, it was felt, would not be conducive to developmental activity. Hence a change in location was essential if market incentives were to become more important.

Each of the previously mentioned studies or reports cited expenditure patterns similar to those quoted above. Following each report, there was usually some expression at the cabinet level of the need to reverse the expenditure trend and to contract out more to industry.[9] Despite these statements of intent, the patterns of allocation did not change appreciably. The "Make-or-Buy" policy of MOSST, adopted as government policy by the cabinet, was the most extensive effort to *make* the pattern change. The policy sought to outline the criteria and circumstances under which government would "make" or do its own research and development and

[7] See *Royal Commission on Government Organization*, Vol. 4, Report no. 23 (Ottawa: Queen's Printer, 1963); Senate Special Committee on Science Policy, *A Science Policy For Canada*, Vols. 1 and 2 (Ottawa: Information Canada, 1970 and 1972); and OECD, *Reviews of National Science Policy: Canada* (Paris: OECD, 1969).
[8] These percentages are extrapolated from Ministry of State for Science and Technology, *Scientific Activities, Federal Government Costs and Expenditures 1963–64 to 1972–73* (Ottawa: Information Canada, 1972), chart 10, p. 14.
[9] See Doern, *Science and Politics in Canada*, pp. 213–214.

under which it would "buy" research by contracting it out to industry or other suppliers of research.

In announcing the "Make-or-Buy" policy, Alastair Gillespie, then the Minister of State for Science and Technology, enunciated the consensus referred to above:

> The traditional policy of having government facilities perform by far the largest share of R & D work for government has served its purpose but cannot meet Canada's future needs. In the light of this country's experience in recent years and the experience of other nations it has become clear that when little of a nation's research and development takes place in industry the results are less likely to be transferred in the market place.[10]

The objective of the "Make-or-Buy" policy was to insure that "a progressively larger portion of government funded research and development is done by industry," and R & D results are "translated more effectively into additional Canadian industrial capability." The first target would be to secure a more even balance between governmental and industrial performance of R & D. It was stressed, however, that this would take "at least five years to bring about" and that because of the need to keep the government's own R & D facilities strong, "there would be no firings or layoffs of government employees engaged in R & D work." At least five years would be needed also because the policy would apply only to new or additional mission-oriented research, rather than to the total existing intramural R & D budget.[11]

The policy announcement specifically noted several agencies "whose contracting-out ratios [the percentages of total research expenditure performed outside the agency] could increase markedly." These included the National Research Council, and the Departments of National Defence, Agriculture, Environment, Communications, and Energy, Mines and Resources. For these departments, the percentages of R & D contracted out to industry varied anywhere from less than 1 percent to about 25 percent.[12]

As a result of the policy, "the onus is now on the government departments to place their research and development contracts with private industry rather than do it themselves."[13] The policy statement declared further that

> Criteria for having research done in government facilities are based on the exceptional situations in which the best interests of the country would appear to be served if the R & D were done 'in-house'. In all other instances new mission-oriented R & D will be contracted out.[14]

[10] Office of the Minister of State for Science and Technology, "New Contracting Out Policy," News Release, August 1972, p. 5.
[11] Ibid., pp. 5–8.
[12] See ibid., Table on Total Costs of Research and Development by Department or Agency by Performer.
[13] Ibid., p. 3. For other official presentations of the MOSST position, see Hon. Jeanne Sauve, "Incentive for Innovation in Canadian Industry", Speech to the Canadian Club, Toronto, February 19, 1973; and Dr. Aurele Beaulnes, Speech to Technical Section of the Canadian Pulp and Paper Association, Montreal, January 25, 1973.
[14] "New Contracting Out Policy", pp. 10–11.

The criteria are:

1. Where questions of national security prohibit industrial involvement;
2. Where no suitable industrial capability exists and it would not be of optimum benefit to Canada to create it;
3. Where R & D is essential to provide direct support to a regulatory function, such as that associated with protection of the public from unsafe drugs, or the certification of food additives, and where a potential conflict of interest might arise in a commercial establishment;
4. Where the R & D is essential to the development of national primary standards involving weights, length, and time, etc., and, in some cases, secondary and consumer standards, including their relationship to international standards;
5. Where the conduct of R & D is essential to departments in order to establish and maintain a limited in-house competence sufficient to assess opportunities represented by the current state of the art, to enable the operating department to perform its mission and manage contract research in industry;
6. Where it would be wasteful to duplicate capital facilities owned by the government and servicing industry.

Henceforth, when a department of the federal government requires R & D work in support of its departmental mission, it must identify the nature of the R & D project and make an initial judgement, based on the foregoing criteria, as to whether the project should be done in government facilities or contracted out. The R & D needs will be publicized to industry through the Department of Supply and Services and a request for proposals made. Then a decision to do the R & D "in-house" or to contract out will be reached. Assuming that most projects will increasingly go to industry, the actual procurement of the R & D and the management of the subsequent contract will be carried out by the Department of Supply and Services.

It is, of course, not expected that every R & D contract let to industry in the above manner will miraculously "spin off" some new product or service with instant export and employment potential. It is hoped that a percentage of the projects might do this indirectly, but the immediate strategy seems to be that if industry increasingly is engaged in servicing the government's R & D needs, it will increasingly develop the skills and even the critical mass of R & D personnel in its own establishments to enable it to perform and compete more effectively in the medium- and longer-run time frame.

It should be noted, of course, that the "Make-or-Buy" policy represents the aggregate strategy in that there are other somewhat separate efforts to encourage the same objective under such programs as the Industrial Research and Development Incentives Act (IRDIA) and the Program for Advanced Industrial Technology (PAIT).[15]

---

[15] See Pierre L. Bourgault, *Innovation and the Structure of Canadian Industry*, Background Study for the Science Council of Canada (Ottawa: Information Canada, 1972) and Science Council of Canada, *Innovation in the Cold Climate* (Ottawa: Information Canada, 1971).

III. "Make or Buy" and the Politics of R & D Resource Allocation

Presumably, over time, one ought to be able to see a definite change in the location or performance of R & D in Canada, with the percentage done by industry eventually equalling or perhaps even exceeding that performed by government departments, agencies, and universities. There are two kinds of analytical questions to raise with regard to the anticipated change. First, assuming that one agrees with the objectives and assumptions of the "Make-or-Buy" policy, how does one actually alter the basic resource-allocation mechanisms and incentives of the federal government? What potential constraints might arise? The second kind of question, of course, challenges the basic assumptions of the "Make-or-Buy" policy. The future politics of R & D resource allocation will naturally involve both of these dimensions, and hence the remaining parts of this essay will examine both, albeit briefly.

The basic target of the policy is the intramural, and hence intra-bureaucratic, resource-allocation processes. The basic feature of intra-bureaucratic R & D resource allocation is that it is characterized primarily by "little-science" relationships. "Little science" is the phrase usually used to characterize the kind of science allocation that takes place within the main granting bodies, such as the National Research Council, Medical Research Council, and Canada Council, in their dealings with the academic science community. It implies the allocation of relatively small amounts of money on an individualized "one-to-one" relationship between the applicant and the granting body or committee.[16]

It is important to stress, however, that the little-science pattern is also fairly characteristic of the intra-bureaucratic process, in that the process consists of many hundreds of decisions and proposals each of which individually involves relatively modest amounts of money. The process involves small clusters of R & D personnel in a continuing relationship with budgetary officials and organization heads. This is not to suggest that large R & D projects do not arise. It merely suggests that in terms of numbers and volume of decision-making occasions, the "little-science" pattern tends to prevail.

The crux of the political dilemma is that the "Make-or-Buy" policy must attack a myriad of decision-making fronts. The policy must operate in a highly distributive political arena where individual agencies and departments will frequently perceive their R & D needs, and who should perform them, in ways that are quite different from those of central "control" agencies such as the Treasury Board, or from other "monitoring" agencies such as MOSST.

Some of these constraints are already implicitly acknowledged in the "Make-or-Buy" policy and in the current operation of MOSST. Other constraints are not acknowledged. For example, the fact that the "Make-or-Buy" policy applies only to future marginal increases in R & D expenditure rather than to total expenditure clearly acknowledges the practical impossibility of challenging existing R & D establishments in departments.

---

[16] See Doern, *Science and Politics in Canada*, chs. 5 and 7.

MOSST, moreover, does not possess any direct control over the R & D budget. It can only maintain a watching brief over the expenditures which occur.

One of the major constraints to which the policy does not adequately address itself is the basic incentive structure of the bureaucracy. The policy assumes that R & D managers and departmental managers can be persuaded to have others rather than their own staff do the research. The promotion, salary, and classification structure of the bureaucracy, however, still disproportionately rewards managers on the basis of how large a permanent shop they have. The "Make-or-Buy" policy implies that in the future "thou shalt divest thyself of permanent personnel" (or at least, not add on new permanent personnel), whereas the reward system of the bureaucracy still suggests that "thou shalt collect as many personnel and subordinates as possible"! Perhaps the "Make-or-Buy" policy will assist in altering these features of the bureaucracy; but at the moment, and in the foreseeable future, they remain an important influence.

It would be quite misleading to view such constraints as only bureaucratic inertia or bureaucratic pathology. They may well reflect a genuine view by some departments that some of the assumptions of the "Make-or-Buy" consensus of the 1960s are not self-evidently true for the 1970s. For example, the policy statement identified a number of criteria (listed above) under which R & D could justifiably be done in-house. At the same time, the statement identified these criteria (such as national security, regulatory activity, standards, conflict of interest, R & D contract management needs, etc.) as representing "exceptional situations" in government.

But these elements of government activity are hardly "exceptional," particularly those related to the pervasive and growing regulatory functions of government. The 1960s science-policy debate was overwhelmingly concentrated on the *expenditure* side of government activity. But regulatory activity has always represented at least the "other half" of the reality of government, and hence is hardly exceptional; nor is it likely to be less exceptional in the future, given the greater demands for social regulation of private activity.

A further issue of no small importance is the practical definition of research-and-development activity as distinguished from policy analysis and planning activity inside government departments. Activity which departments might have called R & D ten years ago may now be called policy analysis or planning activity. Not only might such expenditures escape the "Make-or-Buy" net altogether; they might reflect an area where contracting out is inappropriate on strictly democratic grounds. After all, the American R & D "contract" state, which we are now trying to emulate and encourage *via* the "Make-or-Buy" policy, has been frequently criticized as to its implications for public control and for questions of conflict of interest.[17]

Most of the potential problems ultimately involve questions of political control over a decentralized scientific industrial complex. Should

---

[17] See Bruce L.R. Smith and D.C. Hague, eds., *The Dilemma of Accountability in Modern Government* (London: Macmillan, 1970), pp. 3–69.

the next decade see the development of expenditure patterns somewhat as MOSST envisages, it is likely that there will be an increased blurring of the distinction between the public and private sectors in Canada. As this author has suggested earlier, it is by no means too early to paraphrase the questions asked by one American observer about the contemporary American scene, and direct them to the Canadian scene:

> When several of the country's largest firms are entirely dependent on Government business for their existence, when Government must look to outside firms or individuals to define the choices before it, or when individuals divide their time between Government and private positions, the distinctions between public and private become difficult to make. And then where does public responsibility lie? Who is accountable? Who, in fact, makes policy decisions, and with what political authority?[18]

The present emphasis has been on criticizing the degree of public-sector dominance and the difficulty of evaluating and auditing its performance. But the industrial and university sectors are also composed of complex bureaucracies which are equally susceptible, over the long haul, to the sins of goal displacement and to the tendency to act as interest groups. How can the government effectively monitor and evaluate highly advanced projects in industry if the technical competence tends to rest more and more in industry? We have had very little experience with problems of this kind, but they are problems of science policy and organization which, one can fairly safely predict, will occur.

Election issues such as the corporate "rip-off" suggest that the relationship between private and corporate gain and public expenditure will receive increasing scrutiny. This fact will not escape the attention of departments, especially new-frontier departments such as the Department of the Environment, for example.

A further issue concerns the empirical validity of the assumption that more R & D spending located in industry will lead to more industrial innovation and its related benefits. It is argued that variables other than the location of R & D activity are more important causal variables.[19] These other variables include competition policy and the structure of Canadian industry, tariff policy, and general fiscal policy. The importance of these other variables is recognized by agencies such as MOSST, but each of these areas of activity has its primary policy "home" in departments other than MOSST. Moreover, departments such as Finance, Industry, Trade and Commerce, and Consumer and Corporate Affairs have large on-going missions and responsibilities and hence have more political and bureaucratic clout than a strictly "co-ordinative" ministry such as MOSST.

Issues of political and public control of the R & D "contract" state lead to even more fundamental challenges to the "Make-or-Buy" policy. It is unlikely that this challenge will prevail in the immediate future, if

---

[18] Eugene B. Skolnikoff, "The Difficult Political Choice of Science", *World Politics* (April 1968), XX, No. 2 (April 1968), p. 543.
[19] See Bourgault, *op. cit.*, passim.

for no other reason than that it would take almost a decade to build up a political consensus different from the one which seems to be the basis of the "Make-or-Buy" policy and which itself took a decade to establish.

Those who do challenge the assumptions, however, do so in at least two broad ways. Some feel that if the private sector requires so much R & D incentive from the state (and indeed, other incentives as well), then the state ought to reap the profits in the form of direct state enterprise or shared enterprise. This has been a recurring criticism by the New Democratic Party. Others suggest that the "Make-or-Buy" policy reflects the desire to develop, on the American model, industrial and high-technology industries when Canada ought to be devoting its primary R & D effort to so-called tertiary, service, and socially related employment opportunities and hence avoid some of the pitfalls of the classic industrial state.

As one writer has observed when commenting on the somewhat similar assumptions of the Senate Committee on Science Policy reports, "we are urged to tie our future to the same mechanisms that are driving the U.S. economy and have contributed in no small way to the serious social ailments of that country."[20]

The Science Council of Canada stressed the same point in its critique of the recommendations of the Senate Committee on Science Policy. The council felt that the Senators' view "has implicit within it the danger that science and technology may come to be regarded as goals in themselves".[21] Hence it felt that the Senators' relative emphasis on high-technology manufacturing industries was misplaced in at least two respects. First, it feared that by concentrating too much on the level of funding and the location of R & D, the Senators' strategy would ignore more important elements of the total process of industrial innovation. As the Council stated:

Industrial innovation comprises a whole range of activities from original conception of new goods or services to their acceptance in use by the consumer. R & D is frequently the least expensive link in this chain. A policy of increasing industrial R & D five-fold in the next eight years — without considering the adequacy, funding and managerial aspects of all other links — would fail to meet the objective . . . of increasing the total innovative capability of our industries. Pushing on the innovative chain from the R & D end is not nearly as practical or rewarding as pulling on it from the market end.[22]

The Science Council's second criticism was that the Senators' emphasis on secondary-manufacturing industry gave inadequate weight to the factors which were shaping Canada's economy. In particular, the Council

[20] N.H. Lithwick, "Technology and Progress: a Lesson the Senators Have Not Learned", *Science Forum*, Vol. 5, no. 2 (April 1972), p. 10.
[21] Science Council of Canada, *Annual Report 1971–72* (Ottawa: Information Canada, 1972), p. 29. Extracts from this report reproduced by permission of Information Canada.
[22] *Ibid.*, p. 30.

challenged the Senators' interpretation of the role of the service sector of the economy:

The Senators state that 'the country cannot expect to base its long-term growth strategy on service as prime movers'; we could ask why not? . . . This sector already employs more Canadians than manufacturing (all services, public and private, employ about 60 per cent of the labour force) and its rate of growth is far larger. Its record of productivity gains is extremely disappointing, however; this derives in very large measure from its slow rate of technological change. It is, in short, a field for which innovation is even more important than for manufacturing.[23]

The Council felt, and this writer largely concurs, that the time was appropriate to take a new look at what the service sector of the economy does and how it is related to the production and manufacturing sectors. In short,

how valid is our traditional concept which regards services as a component of economic activity that comes *after* production and is ancillary to production. We must ask if production *per se* is a primary goal. On such a conceptual base, it is hard to reconcile the fact that manufacturing, in an advanced economy, is a dwindling proportion of GNP and the labour force. However, our whole concept of the relationship of services to production could be reversed, and the provision of services, or *servicing of needs*, could be taken as the primary objective, with material production as the necessary but ancillary activity. In such a framework, the goals of technology and of science policy might be seen in a new light, and the conventional attitudes, developed under conditions of low technology and widespread material scarcities might greatly change.[24]

The 1960s' assumptions and setting for the *development* of the "Make-or-Buy" policy were generally related more to the model in which secondary-manufacturing economy is paramount. Its *implementation*, however, will occur when a different set of value assumptions is presented. One set of assumptions does not totally replace the other, of course; but the competing assumptions can and likely will influence the criteria used to allocate Canadian R & D resources in the 1970s.

It is important to note, therefore, that the implementation of the "Make-or-Buy" policy will encounter both the behavioral constraints of the bureaucracy as well as several often-legitimate challenges to the interpretation of the policy in individual cases, and even more fundamental challenges to its value assumptions. It is likely that some shift in resources in favour of the private sector will occur, but perhaps not as quickly as the "Make-or-Buy" policy envisages, or to the extent that current policy deems desirable.

[23] *Ibid.*, pp. 38–39.
[24] *Ibid.*, p. 39.

IX. Regional and Urban Issues

1. Regional Economic Disparities

Alan G. Green

Queen's University

Regional income inequality is an integral part of all nation states whether they be highly developed or backward. Canada is no exception. Given the wide geographic spread and the attendant differences among regions in natural endowments (e.g., fertility of the soil, existence of economically valuable minerals, etc.), it is little wonder that disparities in average income levels have formed a central feature of this country's development over most of its history. Indeed, at times questions have been raised as to whether Canada is in fact a *single* country or whether it is really a series of regional units — the Maritimes, the Central Provinces, and the West. It is the contention here that the problem of regions in Canada can best be studied by considering their economic performance not as separate entities but rather as subnational units where the observed rate of national growth is affected critically by the regional units' performance (i.e., those factors which tend to enhance regional efficiency in production automatically improve the performance of the country as a whole) and vice versa.

I. Free Markets and Regional Disparities

One of the factors which makes regional disparities easier to study than international income inequality is the absence of any explicit barriers to the movements of commodities and factors. The existence of such freedom might also explain why, in most developed countries at least, inequality in average income between the richest and poorest regions rarely runs much more than 2 or 3 to 1, while it is not unusual for international differences to exhibit disparities of 15 to 1 or greater. Within a country, goods, men, and capital are generally allowed to move unhindered (save for the usual "natural" impediments of distance, etc.) between regions and so, theoretically, are able to attain their own highest reward.

Given that a free market exists between regional units of a national state (i.e., that people in Canada, for example, are able to migrate from Nova Scotia to British Columbia without having to secure an immigrant visa from the latter), how does a model which relies solely on the response of differential economic opportunity for capital and labour operate to reduce regional income disparities?[1] Before directly answering this question, it might be best to outline some reasons why inequalities in factor payments may exist between regions (i.e., why workers doing the same job receive a lower money wage in one region than in another). It will then be possible to examine, under free market conditions, how (theoretically) these discrepancies may be eliminated.

Assume that we are dealing with a country which has only two regions and that each region produces only one commodity. Conditions of competitive industrial structure, full employment, and similar technologies are assumed to prevail. Initially the only difference between the two regions is in their factor supplies, and only capital and labour are inputs in production. Assume, then, that due to a high rate of past population growth, one region (Region A) has a larger labour force relative to other factors than does another region (Region B). As a result of these differential rates of growth, wages paid to workers in the former region will be less than those paid to workers in the latter. Also assume that the converse set of conditions holds between regions with regard to relative capital supplies; i.e., due to higher savings, Region B has a larger supply of capital relative to other factors in its region than does Region A, and consequently the price of capital (borrowing charges) is relatively lower in B than in A. With more capital per worker (a higher capital/labour ratio) and therefore a higher labour productivity and higher wage rate, B is the high-income region, while A is the low-income, poorer, or less developed region.

The regional production results which emerge from such differential relative factor supplies are as follows. For a given level of output, Region B will use proportionately more capital per unit of labour (since it is relatively less expensive) than does Region A. Briefly, all this says is that an entrepreneur given a choice between two different ways of producing the same product will, if he resides in Region B, opt for a technique which uses more of the less expensive factor (here capital), while an entrepreneur in Region A will adopt a technique which uses relatively more labour per unit of capital. Under these conditions, labour in Region A will earn less than similarly placed labour in Region B, and capital the reverse. It would "pay," then, for some labour to migrate from Region A to Region B and for some capital to move in the reverse direction. If indeed sufficient movement of this nature took place, the supply differentials postulated above would be eliminated and, assuming demand remained constant, wages and the cost of capital would be the same in

---

[1] The basis of this discussion owes much to the work of G.H. Borts and J.L. Stern and can be found in their book, *Economic Growth in a Free Market* (New York: Columbia University Press, 1964).

Regions A and B. At this point no further factor movement would occur, since nothing is to be gained in terms of higher returns by shifting between regions; i.e., differential economic opportunity has been eliminated, and with it, the initial regional income inequality.

An implicit assumption in this model is that capital and labour move with equal facility between regions. Personal knowledge plus casual observation show that in practice this is not the case. The barriers to human migration are generally greater than for capital migration; for the former often involves higher pecuniary (dollar) costs of relocation as well as higher non-pecuniary costs (i.e., the unmeasurable cost of separation from friends and relatives) than the latter; and so capital is more likely to move than labour. This difference provides us with the first step toward bringing our model closer to reality; for it implies that capital expansion, and so output growth, is likely to be more rapid in the low- than in the high-income region. Thus part of the reason for income convergence among regions in this framework results from an increase in the capital/labour ratio in the poorer region. This comes about partly by reducing the supply of labour in this region through emigration and partly by increasing the amount of machinery, tools, etc., through capital inflow, which the remaining labour has at its disposal. The result is to increase labour productivity in the low-income region, thus permitting wages to rise. The basic free-market model (adjusted for reality by differential mobility between factors) predicts, then, that disparities will be reduced *via* higher growth in the poorer (labour-surplus) region than in the richer region. Conversely, as labour flows into the higher-income region and some capital leaves, labour productivity will decline relative to what it was in the past, thus causing incomes here to converge toward those in the poor region — just as the latter's incomes, for reasons set out above, are rising.

Even with the adjustment of labour mobility, it is obvious that this simple model is not capable of entirely explaining the course of regional income growth. In the real world, income disparities still exist: in Canada the range between the highest and lowest average provincial income is slightly better than 2 to 1, and similar disparities exist in the United States. It is necessary, then, to examine one or two of the basic assumptions underlying this model to see why inequalities should *persist*. The most severe restriction imposed by the model (the element which takes us furthest from the real world) is the assumption that each region produces only one product — i.e., we have been dealing with a one-sector model.

As a first step toward reality, consider a *two-sector* model where output is divided between agricultural and non-agricultural output. This change allows us to introduce more explicitly than before the concept of inefficiency. Inefficiency is defined as the case where factor returns are not equalized. Under these conditions, gains in real *per capita* income can be realized by shifting factors from low to high return. In the single-sector model outlined above, these gains could be obtained only by shifting factors between regions. If we assume that productivity in agriculture is less than in the non-agricultural sector, then one region may experience a lower average money wage than another simply because it has more resources (manpower) working in the low-productivity sector (agriculture) than has the other region. Convergence in regional average income may require, then, a shift of labour between sectors, as well as from the low-wage to the high-wage region (as specified earlier). An incomplete adjustment in either of these two migrations means that resources are inefficiently allocated either *between* regions or *within* regions (i.e., between sectors). The critical feature in regional income convergence is the movement of factors (especially labour) from lower-productivity to higher-productive employment (i.e., the movement toward an efficient allocation of resources). This shift will simultaneously raise the relative rate of growth in the low-income region (so causing convergence) *and* raise the rate of output growth for the country as returns are equalized. In a free-market situation as postulated here (where factors are "free" to seek their highest rewards), we would expect, *over time,* that both of these types of factor migration would occur.

II. Regional Income Trends

In a free market for factors (and commodities), such as we assume exists between sub-national units, time is a critical variable in reducing income inequalities (and if the country is large and diverse with respect to resource endowments, as is Canada, perfect equality may not be attainable at all). To see if our simple theoretical explanations have validity, then, will require a look at long-term regional income growth. Fortunately, two studies — one for the United States and the other for Canada — are available. The evidence on *per capita* regional income (and output) is shown in Table 1.

Table 1: Long-Term Trends in the Weighted Mean Deviation[a]
of State Personal Income[b] Per Capita (United States)
and Gross Value Added[c] Per Capita (Canada),
from Their Respective National Levels

	United States (1)			Canada (2)
1)	1880	47	1890	14
2)	1900	34	1910	19
3)	1919–21	28	1929	23
4)	1953–57	18	1956	17

[a] Weighted mean deviation is the absolute deviation of state (or provincial) income (or output) *per capita* from the national average for the given date weighted by the particular state's (or province's) share in total population. These weighted deviations are then totalled, disregarding signs, and the result divided by the average income (or output) for the country as a whole.

[b] Income received by persons before deducting income tax.

[c] Value of output before deducting depreciation of capital.

Sources: Col. (1): Weighted mean deviation of state personal income *per capita* from the national level. R.A. Easterlin, "Interregional Differences in Per Capita

Income, Population, and Total Income, 1840–1950," in National Bureau of Economic Research, *Trends in the American Economy in the Nineteenth Century* (Princeton: Princeton University Press, 1960), p. 94.

Col. (2): Weighted mean deviation, by province, from Canadian average output *per capita*. A.G. Green, *Regional Aspects of Canada's Economic Growth* (Toronto: University of Toronto Press, 1971), p. 48.

The procedure used to measure income inequality between regions (i.e., states or provinces) follows very closely the simple statistical techniques for measuring the amount of dispersion (deviation or variation) from a central value. Here the central value is the *per capita* income for the country as a whole. We are asking: what is the extent of the variation in provincial (or state) *per capita* income about the national average, and is there a trend through time for *per capita* income in the regions where average income is below the national average to grow more rapidly than in the country as a whole and so converge toward the latter; and conversely, is there a tendency for regions which initially enjoy average income positions above the national average to grow slower than the national average and so move toward the latter? If this convergence does occur, then the "index of dispersion," or measure of differences between regions relative to the national average income, would decline through time, so signifying a reduction in regional inequality.

The measure used by Easterlin (see col. (1) of Table 1) for the United States is the *weighted sum* of the deviations of state average income from the national average income (the sum over all states), divided by the *per capita* national income for the particular year. The weights used are the populations for the various states. For Canada the same basic technique was used, with the provinces weighted by the size of their respective populations at the given date. This weighting scheme was used since, in Canada as in the United States, the sub-national units are of such unequal size with respect to population (compare Ontario and Prince Edward Island) that some scheme had to be adopted to give the proper weight of each such unit to the measure of inequality.

Finally, the reader should be warned that a direct comparison of levels of regional income inequality between Canada and the United States is impossible. Not only do the methods of measuring regional incomes differ significantly (personal income is used for the United States, while output estimates are used for Canada), but in addition the number of units (48 for the United States versus 9 for Canada) preclude a meaningful comparison of the absolute level of regional income inequality between the two countries. Our central interest is with the trends in these two series: do regional incomes tend, over time, to converge toward or diverge from the national average?

The trend of *per capita* income (output) in both countries shows a movement toward their respective countrywide averages, although for Canada the shift toward convergence comes only after a substantial increase in regional disparity (1890–1929), which is followed in the last period by a subsequent narrowing. The latter, however, is less pronounced for Canada than for the United States.[2] In both countries, convergence

---

[2] For further details, see A.G. Green, *Regional Aspects of Canada's Economic Growth* (Toronto: University of Toronto Press, 1970), esp. ch. II.

toward the national average is a joint result of the shift of high average-income regions toward the countrywide average (in the United States this involves a relative deterioration in such regions as New England and the Mountain and Pacific states, while for Canada it embraces a downward shift in the relative positions of Ontario and British Columbia) and a rise in the relative position of low-wage regions (e.g., the Southern States in the United States and the Maritime Provinces in Canada). As explained above, these results imply that high-income regions tended to exhibit slower growth rates than did the country as a whole and so converged from above toward the latter, while the low-income regions did the opposite. This, in broad outline, is approximately what our model would predict: relatively faster growth in the low-income regions, due to labour exodus and capital inflow, and slightly slower growth for the initially high-income regions, due to large labour inflows and slower relative capital expansion.

A puzzling question remains, however: why should the regional adjustment process be stronger in the United States than in Canada? Our model provides us with two lines of attack on this question (although it must be admitted, at the start, that no definite answer to this question is as yet at hand). First, interregional factor migration may have been less "complete" in Canada than in the United States. This contention is difficult to quantify, although the volume of internal migration in the United States has been very large, e.g., black migration out of the South (beginning in the mid-1920s) to the North and to the West Coast and the westward migration both from the East Coast states and from the Midwest has gone on at a high rate over most decades of this century. In Canada, 20th-century migration patterns have been fairly simple: first (up to World War I), large inflows into the Prairies and Ontario and British Columbia, and since the interwar period, and especially since 1946, large inflows from the Maritimes to the Central Provinces and from the Prairies to British Columbia and Ontario. A statistical study of this problem suggests that these flows have not been large enough to effect a significant convergence in average income.[3] The question, for Canada at least, remains open.

The second point derives from our two-sector model — the convergence among regions in the structure of production, i.e. the decline in the less developed regions of the labour force attached to agriculture. In terms of the over-all model, we might conceive of this occurring through the migration of capital to such regions, to capture the higher returns available there. The result of such a flow would be to expand demand for unemployed or underemployed labour in the region, i.e., "pull workers off the farm." The statistical measure to see if incomplete intraregion migration causes slower convergence among regions is the share of each region's (province's) labour force devoted to non-agricultural production. The less complete is the convergence in structure (the shift toward a

---

[3] After a careful statistical examination of the relationship between regional income difference and the internal allocation of labour, Courchene proposed the tentative hypothesis that "interprovincial flows are not adequate for purposes of regional economic adjustment." See T.J. Courchene, "Interprovincial Migration and Economic Adjustment," *Canadian Journal of Economics*, III, No. 4 (Nov. 1970), p. 575.

similar distribution of labour among the major sectors — agriculture, manufacturing, etc.), the greater theoretically might be *per capita* income inequality among regions.

The evidence of regional structural convergence in the United States and Canada seems to provide some basis for the view that structural differences form an important element in the slower and less complete adjustment in the latter than in the former country. U.S. measures of structural differences among states (such information is available only from 1919) show strong convergence in the share of workers in the different sectors toward the national average over the last 40 years.[4] Casual observation supports this conclusion. Most notable in this regard is the flow of capital toward the American South. The investment induced by this flow covers a wide range of economic activity, from leisure-time construction in Florida to petrochemical and space investment in Texas. These are largely post-World-War-II phenomena and were led by a shift of the New England textile industry to the deep South in the mid-1920s — a shift induced by a search for low-wage labour, not surprisingly given our theoretical expectations. The more recent movement (since 1946) has been due largely to specific locational advantages for space and petrochemical industries provided in the Southern States plus the desire for more people to seek a "permanent place in the sun."

In Canada, on the other hand, little such structural convergence has taken place.[5] In fact, regional concentration of manufacturing activity (potentially the sector most able to migrate in response to better labour opportunities, as compared to the resource sectors or service sectors, which are "rooted" to their own localities) has become, at least up to the late 1950s, even more concentrated in a few provinces (mainly Ontario and Quebec) than it was at the turn of the century and, apparently, only slight modification in this concentration has occurred during the last decade and a half.[6] As a result, Canada is a country of highly specialized regions — the Prairies and British Columbia specializing largely in resource production (with the Atlantic Provinces following a somewhat similar pattern of resource concentration); Ontario and Quebec, on the other hand, containing the majority of secondary manufacturing in the country. Given the potentially different returns to labour in these two activities (agriculture versus non-agriculture), one cannot discard these different regional patterns of development in Canada as an important element in the slower and possibly less complete adjustment of regional incomes to the national average. As will be discussed later, part of the solution to continued regional income disparity may be to adopt policies which will improve production efficiency in both sectors.

III. An Opposing View

The evidence on long-run trends in regional income inequality showed

---

[4] See Simon Kuznets, "Industrial Distribution of Income and Labour Force by States, United States, 1919–21 to 1955", *Economic Development and Cultural Change*, VI, No. 4, Part II (July 1958).
[5] See Green, *op. cit.*, p. 57.
[6] See S.E. Chernick, *Interregional Disparities in Income*, Economic Council of Canada (Ottawa: Queen's Printer, 1966), ch. II.

that the process of convergence was incomplete, and that this was especially the case for Canada. What explanations, then, might be offered to account for this failure to achieve equality? Although one might not have expected complete equality among regions, given the stringent assumptions built into the free-market model; nevertheless, the absence of a steady movement towards convergence, and even at times observed divergence (e.g., Canada, 1890–1929), requires some explanation. An opposing hypothesis, using the basic market mechanism but coming to quite different conclusions regarding the "inevitability" of regional income equality, has been proposed by Gunnar Myrdal.[7] His hypothesis states that regional divergence rather than convergence is the more likely outcome of the operation of market forces.

The argument runs as follows. Suppose that a region experiences an accidental change in its economic fortunes; for example, a fire sweeps away its natural forest cover, or international competition makes its major export unsalable in world markets. In addition, suppose that these changes are so serious that the people residing in the region see little hope for recovery in the near future. What is the result? First, of course, incomes will drop as workers become unemployed and plant and equipment lie idle. With excess capacity and little hope for the future, businessmen will cease investing in the community; so incomes will be further depressed. Rather than suffer such losses, the mobile factors (capital and labour) will begin to leave the region for another area where the economic climate is the reverse, i.e., where exports are expanding, investment is booming, and incomes are rising.

Myrdal partitions the consequences of such a change in fortune into three parts: the emigration effect, the capital-exodus effect, and the trade effect. The emigration effect strikes particularly hard at the disadvantaged region, since it is generally the youngest and most able members of the labour force who are the first to leave (the human-migration process is highly selective with respect to age and talent). The result of such emigration is to limit severely the supply of just that talent which might find alternative solutions to the region's problems and which would have the energy to carry them through to completion. Instead, the region becomes increasingly dominated by older workers and the very young (dependents). The outcome of this loss is, as suggested, to depress incomes further in the sending region, while at the same time providing an unexpected gain in talent to the already expanding region, thus driving incomes between the two even further apart.

In a similar manner, the other two effects tend to increase income divergence. The case of capital exodus parallels that of labour. With investment opportunities declining in the contracting region, savings begin to move out to the expanding region, thus bolstering demand in the latter. This results in the expansion of job opportunities and attendant higher incomes, which encourages even more emigration from the declining region to take advantage of this expansion. Finally, as the expanding region grows in size, it is able to enjoy economies of large-scale manu-

[7] Gunnar Myrdal, *Economic Theory and Underdeveloped Regions* (London: Gerald Duckworth Co., 1957), chs. 2 and 3.

facturing production and, as a consequence, competes successfully with the disadvantaged region's industries (the trade effect). The net result of all these forces is to widen the income gap between the two regions.

Myrdal calls this a model of circular causation with cumulative effects. Once conditions begin to deteriorate in one region (or conversely, if one region gains a competitive advantage on another), the system works to widen (move away from equilibrium) rather than narrow the initial gap. To reinforce the economic argument (movements of labour and capital and the trade effects), Myrdal also adds the influence of non-economic forces. For example, a backward (or disadvantaged) region often finds itself with increasingly inferior medical and education services and eventually becomes trapped in rigid social, political, and religious institutions, all of which inhibit its attempts to close the income gap. The total result Myrdal calls the "backsetting effects" of regional interaction.

Even in Myrdal's world of ever-increasing divergence among regions, there is some hope. As the advantaged region grows in size, it is less and less able to supply all of its own needs, especially food but also some types of raw materials. The result is that export demand in the disadvantaged region increases, and the forces which, up to this point, were leading to regional retardation begin to reverse themselves (capital begins to flow back into the region, less of the young leave, etc.), and further income divergence is halted and it may even be reversed. Myrdal calls this process the "spread effects" of economic development. However, he is very pessimistic about how effective such forces will be in closing the income gap, and he points to Western Europe's experience which shows that the poor regions only in the high-income countries have experienced such a gain through the spreading of demand from the advantaged to the disadvantaged area. Poor regions in low-income countries in Western Europe have witnessed few gains and, in fact, have tended to diverge even more from the high-income areas within their own boundaries.

The main policy implication which emerges from Myrdal's argument is that, for most countries, strong government intervention in regional development is essential if the cumulative effects (ever-widening regional income differences) are to be reversed. Market forces alone will not bring convergence in income. The central government must intervene to improve the "climate" for investment in the disadvantaged region and therefore stimulate development, so reversing the process embodied in the "backsetting-effects" argument.

With this alternative view of the relationship between market forces and regional income inequality at hand, it might be worthwhile to review the Canadian postwar experience in regional disparity and compare this with the two analytical explanations (the equilibrium versus disequilibrium approaches). To do this, new estimates of provincial per capita personal-income dispersion were calculated at two periods of time, where personal income is defined basically as wage income, earnings of unincorporated businesses, interest and rental income, plus government transfer payments.

The index constructed is a weighted measure of per capita personal income, where the weights are the recorded populations of the different provinces. Two points of time were chosen — the mid-1950s and the later 1960s. In constructing dispersion measures at these two points of time, a three-year average centred at 1955 and 1966 was used; i.e., the dispersion statistics are the simple averages of the years 1954, 1955, and 1956 for the first time period and 1965, 1966, and 1967 for the second. Three-year averages were used in order to eliminate some of the short-run (cyclical) influences on the statistic and so to allow one to obtain an indication of pure trend change in regional income inequality over the intervening decade.

It should be mentioned in connection with these postwar dispersion statistics, as was done in the discussion of the United States–Canada comparison, that a comparison of *levels* of dispersion (here between the earlier and later period) should be avoided. For example, the postwar statistic for Canada is measured in personal-income terms, whereas the longer-run series is in output (gross-value-added) terms. In addition, the more recent period includes Newfoundland, whereas the earlier estimates do not, since that province did not join Canada until 1949.

With these caveats in mind, it is possible to turn to the statistics of regional personal-income dispersion shown in Table 2. The point which comes out clearly from these two statistics is that the slight trend toward regional convergence in *per capita* output observed between 1929 and 1956 (Table 1 — lines 3 and 4) has continued in the postwar period and, if anything, has strengthened. This latter conclusion parallels the findings

Table 2: Weighted Mean Deviation of Canadian Provincial Personal Income Per Capita from the National Level, $\overline{1955}$ and $\overline{1966}$[a]

	Year (1)	Measure of Dispersion[b] (2)
1)	$\overline{1955}$	24
2)	$\overline{1966}$	13

[a] The "bar" over the two dates indicates that the statistics (col. 2) are three-year averages centred on the years shown (col. 1).
[b] For an outline of the method of computation, see note a, Table 1.
Source: All data are drawn from Dominion Bureau of Statistics, *National Accounts, Income and Expenditure, 1958*, p. 34 for line 1 and *1967*, p. 36 for line 2.

of Chernick, who shows, also using weighted mean deviations of personal income *per capita*, a shift toward regional income equality beginning in the early 1950s and continuing into the early 1960s.[8] Although it is impossible to say whether this new trend will continue into the future (we simply cannot predict with any accuracy what types of external shocks may inhibit regional development, especially in the low-income regions), nevertheless the impression here is that gradually some easing of income differentials has occurred over the last two or three decades.

[8] Chernick, *op. cit.*, p. 15.

These data, unfortunately, do not permit us to test for the last quarter century whether along with some income convergence there has occurred a parallel shift toward regional similarity in output structure (whether the provinces are beginning to look more alike with respect to their shares of agricultural, manufacturing, and service output). However, even without these latter figures, the recent trend poses some interesting questions, especially here, where we have two hypotheses regarding the relationship between market forces and regional income growth. Do these recent trends, then, demonstrate the operation of the free-market model, i.e., labour moving from low- to high-income regions while capital moves in the reverse direction, or are we observing the "spread effects" outlined by Myrdal, which supposedly are a mark of a highly developed (high-income) country? There is no answer yet to this question, but it is worth noting that in examining the actual provincial changes over this decade, the share of population in the provinces whose average income was below that of the leaders (i.e., below Ontario, Alberta, and British Columbia) fell (e.g., between 1955 and 1966 the share of total population in the Atlantic Provinces — Newfoundland, Prince Edward Island, Nova Scotia, and New Brunswick — declined from 11.1 to 9.8 percent, while the leading three provinces' share rose from 49.2 to 51.2 percent).

Thus population redistribution has moved, over this period, in the direction predicted by the free-market theory (and, of course, by the circulation-causation thesis). Whether, however, compensating capital movements (capital flows from high- to low-income regions) are also taking place, and at a significant magnitude to exert some positive effect on productivity in the latter regions, is still an open question. It is obvious in this regard that whether or not capital is moving toward the low-income regions, large amounts are still being invested in the Central Provinces, Alberta, and British Columbia — the "have" provinces — and are providing added impetus to their growth. This is precisely what Myrdal predicted would happen, since these are the areas where investors can expect high returns (just as labour does) on their invested dollar. Yet some segments of government regional policy are designed to counter this "cumulative process" by investing in the disadvantaged regions. In addition, private capital may be finding such regions increasingly attractive, either as potential suppliers of raw materials or as a source of relatively low-wage labour. It is the delicate balance between population and capital movements which will determine much of the future course of differential regional income growth and, as yet, the outcome is not clear.

IV. Regional Development Policies

Despite the recent movement toward regional income equality, the relative ranking (between high and low *per capita* income provinces) remains today much like it was at the end of the 19th century. The Atlantic Provinces' average income is still about one-third less than the national average, and some sub-provincial areas undoubtedly have greater income disparities than are recorded in these provincial aggregates. It is little wonder, then, that federal and provincial governments are, and have been, concerned about this problem of the uneven spread of economic welfare (average income) among the country's ten provinces. This concern has taken the form of two basic types of government policies. The first to evolve were those which dealt with the impact that national development policies had on regional development. Initially they were designed to promote countrywide growth but, as became painfully obvious to the government in Ottawa, the "national policies" created certain undesirable side effects on regional growth. Tariff, transportation, and monetary policies are the three major areas most often referred to in this connection.

Tariffs, for example, were originally designed to promote industrialization in Canada. As we discussed above though, such output is largely in Ontario and Quebec, and continues to be concentrated there. The Western Provinces objected strongly to this policy; for they claimed, quite rightly, that tariffs reduced their international competitive position (for wheat) by forcing them to buy higher-priced producers' goods (tractors, reapers, etc.) from Canadian makers when they could have bought equally good equipment at lower prices from foreign producers, while simultaneously they were forced to face international price competition for their products. The result was to lower, relatively, their real income vis-à-vis the Ontario manufacturer. (As a side note, it is interesting to speculate how much of the resulting intergovernmental income transfers — unemployment insurance benefits, family allowances, old age security payments, etc. — are really an attempt to compensate the "losers," e.g., the new provinces in the West, for adopting such a policy.)

In the same vein, the Maritimes for years have claimed that Canadian railway transportation rate differentials operated against them and in favour of the Ontario manufacturer by allowing the latter to compete more easily in markets in the East than the Maritimes can in the Central or Western Provinces. Finally, monetary policy, when designed to curb inflation by raising interest rates, can seriously affect low-wage areas. The latter are often attempting to raise their standard of living by undertaking large-scale investment projects in social overhead capital (roads, electrical plants, etc.). The result of a tighter credit position is to push up the cost of such projects and, given the marginal nature of some, threaten their very progress.[9]

Partly to offset some of the adverse side effects of national policies, but also to respond to the demand for assistance from the slower-growing parts of the country, the federal government has been required to include in its arsenal of policy tools specific programs designed to accelerate the growth of the "have-not" provinces, i.e., to hasten the convergence process. Under this second approach, three major programs have been developed to cope with this problem.[10] They are the Agricultural and Rural

[9] For a more complete discussion of the effects of national policies on regional growth, see W.A. Mackintosh, *The Economic Background of Dominion–Provincial Relations*, reprinted in the Carleton Library Series (Toronto: McClelland and Stewart, 1964).

[10] Much of the basic information on regional development policies presented in this section is drawn from the excellent study by T.N. Brewis, *Regional Economic Policies in Canada* (Toronto: Macmillan, 1969), especially chs. 6–8.

Development Act (ARDA), the Area Development Agency (ADA), and the Atlantic Development Board (ADB) — now reconstituted as the Atlantic Development Council. All of these programs plus others were drawn together into the newly created Department of Regional Economic Expansion (DREE) in 1969.

It might be well to start this discussion on regional development policies by stating the goals of DREE (i.e., those goals set out in the legislation which brought this Department into existence). According to the Act, DREE's main function is "to ensure that economic growth is dispersed widely enough across Canada to bring employment and earnings opportunities in the slow-growth regions as close as possible to those in the other parts of the country, without interfering with a high overall rate of national growth."[11] These lofty goals, at least on the surface, conform closely to our earlier discussion; i.e., factors should be so directed as to remove any inefficiencies in their use and by so doing promote maximum regional *and* national rates of growth.

Is this, in fact, how regional development policies have been enacted? Optimal policies in this area, by way of a benchmark, should be aimed at reinforcing market tendencies, e.g., giving encouragement to private capital to seek investment opportunities in low-wage regions and assisting in the exodus of low-paid workers from backward sectors (e.g., low-productivity agriculture) and low-wage regions toward sectors/regions where their productivity is greater. It might be suggested that these policies will be most successful when they are moving *with*, not against, the economic tide.

It is fair to say that such an ideal set of policies has not always been achieved either by the new Department or by earlier government agencies charged with this responsibility. For example, the initial programs under ARDA were designed largely to preserve the family farm and to do so by methods designed to raise the income level of these farmers. The principal methods used were to encourage farmers to improve the use they made of their land. Such a policy, then, designed to perpetuate the *status quo*, tends to run against, not with, the economic tide; even though it was apparently aimed at improving this sector's efficiency, it froze factors in a relatively low-productivity sector. Only recently has this policy come under some change. It is now designed, through improved rural education for the young and retraining programs for the older workers (plus help in relocating off the farm), to encourage the exodus, especially of the young, from low-productivity agriculture to higher-paying job opportunities in distant urban areas or in nearby towns. The emphasis now is on improving the efficiency of labour utilization.

The Atlantic Development Board, on the other hand, was aimed, as is obvious from its title, at improving conditions in a specific region rather than in a given sector (like ARDA). The ADB, at least until it was absorbed by DREE, concentrated its efforts in building social overhead capital in the Maritime Provinces (e.g., roads, power projects, etc.). The

---

[11] A full outline of the legislation which created DREE can be found in any *Canada Year Book* from 1969 onward. This particular quote came from the *Canada Year Book, 1969* (Ottawa: Queen's Printer, 1969), p. 1133.

object, at least as revealed by the projects it undertook, was to build up the infrastructure (roads, harbours, etc.) of this region, thus generating a demand for local employment. With these new facilities in place, it was hoped that private capital would be attracted to the region and so further absorb the surplus labour. It was *not* aimed at relieving unemployment by encouraging widespread emigration (although some such relocation schemes do exist).

According to Professor Brewis, the main criticism of the Board's actions has been that it focused largely on specific development projects rather than on an investment scheme which would encompass the whole region.[12] The effect has been to create a series of fragmented local projects, with the result that total expenditure of money under this scheme has had only minimal "employment-multiplier" effects (the number of new jobs created per dollar of investment) for the region as a whole. Also, the attempt to provide short-term employment (while the projects were being built) may have retarded the rate of out-migration that would have occurred under normal market conditions, and so left a local labour force of inefficient size. The joint result, then, may have been to perpetuate a low-level equilibrium position for the region, i.e., a labour force (population) too small to enjoy the benefits of scale economies (the increased productivity gains made by spreading fixed production costs over a larger volume of output) but too large to be supported at the national wage level, given the supply (and quality) of local natural resources, capital, etc.

The last major program, and the one where specific reference is made in the legislation establishing DREE, is aid to "designated areas." Designated areas are usually defined by their high level of unemployment. If an area becomes "designated," then it is in line for special aid in the form of development funds (low-interest loans, etc.) designed to entice businessmen into the region by subsidizing their investment projects. The aim of such subsidization is to generate sufficient local investment so that intolerably high levels of unemployment can be reduced. The basic question, not too often asked under ADA, is why capital decided to leave the region in the first place. The failure to investigate adequately other options (e.g., assist emigration) means that such action stands the high chance of freezing labour in areas where its full productive potential cannot be realized. Such policies, for obvious reasons, are often politically motivated, and they are at times essential to give immediate relief to sustain minimum consumption levels. However, if adopted as long-term policies, they run the grave risk of leading to an inefficient solution to these problems. In fact, in an open economy such as Canada, which must remain internationally competitive, policies which purposely freeze resources in low-productivity areas can potentially place the economy *as a whole* in jeopardy. The end result of such tendencies would be higher unemployment levels for all Canadians and a slower rise in the country's standard of living.

[12] Brewis, *op. cit.*, p. 183.

V. An Alternative Approach to Regional Policy

The major conclusion which emerges from this brief review of regional-policy programs of the federal government is that they are mainly, although not exclusively, aimed at moving capital into low-income regions or areas and less committed to promoting labour emigration. Given the political implications of the latter (smaller populations exert less political pressure in Ottawa), this posture of industrialization (capital inflow) is not unreasonable. Nevertheless, it raises the question about whether such an approach is consistent with the government's stated view that government intervention should seek not only to spread regional economic growth more widely across Canada but to do so "without interfering with a high overall rate of national growth." The government's approach, then, seems more in line with Gunnar Myrdal's thesis (and its implications) of circular causation and cumulative process; i.e., if a disadvantaged region receives a positive external shock, through the infusion, say, of new money invested there by the federal authorities, then the existing situation will be reversed and a shift toward equality will have begun.

This approach to regional policy contains, it seems to this writer, two basic flaws. First, despite DREE's pronouncements that national growth is a prime concern in the formulation of its policies, proposals to reduce regional inequality start nevertheless with specific local problems rather than by asking the alternative question: given the nature of the Canadian economy (a small, export-oriented economy) and given its particular regional makeup, how can federal intervention maximize the growth of the whole country while at the same time reducing regional disparities? This puts the whole problem in a different light from the quote stated earlier, which implies that regional problems will be considered first and then a check made to see if they have any adverse effects on national growth. Second, it appears that the federal government has not yet fully and systematically explored the implications of the theory of comparative advantage in formulating regional development policy.

If these approaches were adopted, they might involve the following actions. First, the government should increase, not decrease (as is apparently part of the government's plan), the concentration of industry in Quebec and Ontario, i.e., reinforce the tendencies, in this regard, shaped largely by market forces. A national population of 21 million people competing in the production of manufactured products with giants like Japan (over 100 million people) or the United States (over 200 million) needs to concentrate its industrial activities in such a way as to secure for itself all of the economies of large-scale production encompassed in modern technology.

Second, the government should adopt a policy which would make the other provinces the most efficient raw-material producers, for their respective products, in the world. For example, besides the obvious advantage of oil production in Alberta, the Prairie Provinces are uniquely suited to agricultural production both in terms of soil and climate. Given the world food requirements over the foreseeable future, concentration in wheat and other grain production, using the most efficient production techniques available, would bring prosperity to "Westerners," and rebound to the balance of the country in terms of capital and consumption expenditures between the resource-oriented regions and the manufacturing-oriented provinces. The Atlantic Provinces, on the other hand, should be aided in exploiting their own unique comparative advantage in such areas as sea products, port services, recreation facilities, etc. Improved productivity in these latter industries, which could involve not only new investment but also reduction in excess labour supplies, would in time substantially raise wages and income in the Maritimes and thus bring about the desired goal of more equal standards of living. Basing such decisions on the known comparative advantage of each region simply uses the power of government intervention to stimulate market forces toward the ends desired.

The implications of building a policy on regional comparative advantage (each region concentrating on the production of goods and services for which it is best suited by location, resource supplies, etc.) are obviously far reaching and in some cases potentially very disruptive. For example, the full adoption of such a policy may mean encouraging additional population exodus, say, from the Atlantic Provinces and the Prairies. Intervention of this nature would involve the federal government in a massive plan to assist the relocation and retraining of the prospective movers in order that the cost of such adjustment (in monetary and non-monetary terms) might be minimized. In addition, the concentration of manufacturing activity in the Central Provinces (Ontario and Quebec) might also involve the complete revamping of the country's transportation rate structure. Such a realignment would have to ensure that the residents in the resource-oriented provinces could obtain consumer products and producer durable equipment at a "laid-down" cost (the cost at their residence or place of business) identical to that available to consumers and producers in the Central Provinces. This type of rate structure plus a favourable rate on their export products could, given favourable international markets, provide the residents of these provinces with a *per capita* income closer to the national average.

Moreover, it should be mentioned that such a policy based first on regional productivity considerations (i.e., concentrating economic activity by region on the basis of local comparative advantage) does not imply the depopulation of the resource-oriented region. An economically strong region of this type requires a wide variety of services (e.g., barber shops, drug stores, schools, etc.), all of which create employment opportunities for local residents. In addition, the possibility of processing the raw materials at the site before they are exported provides numerous opportunities for jobs in the region. For example, in the case of the Atlantic Provinces, the promotion of this area as a recreation region opens up a large number of "industries" — hotels, resorts, etc., most of which are by their nature labour intensive. The main point here is that by starting from a national perspective based on regional structural differences evolved over the decades largely through the operation of the market mechanism, the government stands a higher chance of significantly reducing regional income disparity than by trying to stimulate artificially production activity in areas where it is not suited, i.e., by encouraging the emigration of secondary manufacturing from the Central Provinces to the Maritimes and the Prairies.

Finally, the promotion of such a policy would require the presence of a strong federal government, since the short-run dislocations involved in concentrating regional activity on the basis of comparative advantage would not be without its "costs." In most cases, local authorities would be reluctant to promote such a change, since some of the benefits to be derived from this new approach would unquestionably evolve not only to the particular region but, as suggested, would also accrue, through improved national productivity, to the country as a whole. All of the increased productivity could not be "captured" by any one region, and so a given region might be a reluctant participant. Strong federal intervention is therefore an essential feature in such a scheme. In addition, the federal government is in a prime position to allocate aid to the various regions during the transition and so ease the problems of adjustment. On the basis of the proposal set out here, then, any move toward decentralizing regional policy would be harmful to the long-run position of the country and ultimately to the low-income regions themselves.

2. Economics of Urban Areas

N. H. Lithwick

Carleton University

Urban areas, and particularly large, diverse, intense, interactive, rapidly changing urban areas, have become the habitat for the majority of Canadians. Perhaps because of the scale and complexity of these units, they have defied attempts to understand their functioning and hence their problems and potentials. This is evident not only in the sad record of public policy in dealing with the city, but in the generally inadequate analytical frameworks being used to study urban areas.[1] In consequence, the urban populace approaches its cities with exaggerated expectations and simplistic prescriptions for the good urban life, and ends up with mounting frustrations instead. The dream-house in the suburbs becomes less and less affordable, access to the many attractive things and places that exist in cities gets increasingly difficult, the environment steadily deteriorates, recreational activities become harder and more costly to reach, the security of persons and property is steadily eroded, large-scale breakdowns or shutdowns of public services — from garbage collection to postal service to electricity supplies — become more frequent, and so forth.

Faced with this apparent deterioration in our urban areas, but unable to perceive its causes, urbanites have called for an unending list of superficially obvious solutions — law and order, decent housing, improved quality of life, etc. Unfortunately, slogans are not explanations, and sloganeering offers few solutions to deeply embedded, corrosive problems. More productive of long-term solutions would appear to be a clarification of the issues involved.

In the context of this rather modest goal, what role can economics

---

[1] See N.H. Lithwick and G. Paquet, eds., *Urban Studies: A Canadian Perspective*, Methuen, Agincourt, Ont., 1968.

play in helping to clarify the nature of urban areas and their difficulties?

There are two central features of urban areas that lend themselves to the analytical approaches of economics. The first is the predominant internal feature of cities, namely, their interconnectedness. Economics has a long history of dealing with interdependencies, ranging from the concept of "derived demand," to the full elegance of "general-equilibrium theory" and its practical applications in "input-output analysis." Our first section, then, will include the application of some of these concepts to the internal workings of urban areas.

The second feature of cities that might be somewhat better understood using the tools of economic analysis is the pattern of their growth and development; for the forces which shape the "progress" of a city are closely linked to the determinants of the nation's economic development. Our second section will apply some concepts from the theory of economic development to the issues surrounding the growth of urban areas.

In section three, we shall see how far these economic ideas help explain the problems of urban areas, the simultaneous occurrence of which appears to constitute what is generally regarded as an urban crisis. Some of the problems reflect the failures of urban marketplaces, but, as we shall see, many of these failures are man-made, and are not inherent in the economic structure or processes of cities. The latter consideration leads us into the fourth section, which is a discussion of some of the policy issues that follow from this review.

I. Urban Areas as Closely-Linked Sectors

While it is now a commonplace to talk about the complexity and interdependence of urban areas, making effective use of this knowledge is less simple. As a result, the typical reaction to matters urban is to throw one's hands up in despair over the complexity, and to treat each issue as if it did not affect, or was not affected by, other issues. This partial approach to urban issues reached its apex in the era of expressway construction, where wider, faster, and more limited-access roads were proposed and built to relieve existing congestion. The fact that such expressways had massive impacts on residential location, firm location, inter-city transport, and scores of related phenomena was rarely if ever considered. In another field, housing, no wider perspective can be observed. Houses have been built with significant public assistance, but without adequate regard to the consequent impact on transportation, local tax rates and expenditures, jobs, the environment, and so forth.

In part, of course, this myopia reflects the organizational structure of governments, both within and between levels, which for administrative ease leads to a partitioning of problems into the hermetically sealed areas of departmental responsibilities. But the difficulty of having to deal with problems that transcend these boundaries is not new. It typifies most of the areas of modern public concern, such as regional development, social policy, industrial policy, human-resources development, etc. What is required — and remains lacking — in these areas is an understanding of the central mechanism(s) that explains much if not all of the interdependencies, and which, as a result, can provide the organizing principle around which administrative and political reorganization can take place.

In urban areas, is it possible to discover an organizing concept that does explain much of the connectedness between the key marketplaces? Merely stating that markets are interrelated and can be understood in terms of a general-equilibrium framework is, of course, a first step. But general equilibrium remains more a way of thinking about economic interdependence than dealing with it, and the same would appear to be true for urban interdependencies. Recognition of the difficulties in economics led to the development of input–output analysis as an operational way of capturing the most significant economic interdependencies. These occur principally in the production sector of the economy, and input–output tables provide detailed information on industrial interdependencies.[2]

In urban areas, the centre of the stage is not really occupied by inter-industry flows. Though important, they are no more important than interactions between consumers, between workers, within families between "workers" and "consumers," and between each of these and firms In addition, the role of the public sector in shaping these interactions, through its taxing authority and the provision of services, is of paramount importance.

In the absence of an economic sector of obvious centrality, it might be useful to try to identify a key commodity which enters into the production and consumption functions of urbanites, and helps explain, as a result, their interdependence. In economic theory, such an approach has been followed with significant analytical insights resulting in several areas. The nature of money as a commodity, for example, has helped explain (not without controversy) key aspects of our macro-economy. More recently, the nature of public goods has been explored, once again with significant gains in our understanding of the behaviour of the public economy.

In urban areas, the key commodity can be identified as land. Its chief attribute is its inelasticity of supply — the quantity of land at any point is fixed. Substitutes do exist, particularly for the services that land provides. Land further away can be developed through extending services, particularly sewer, water, and transportation lines. Furthermore, land at a specific location can be more intensively developed, by replacing single-family homes with high-rise, for example. Or land formerly restricted from some kinds of uses can be rezoned to serve those uses. All these substitutes tend to be costly and time-consuming, however, so that while in the very long run the supply curve of all land will be more elastic, in the short and even the intermediate run the supply curve will retain its highly inelastic properties.

As for the demand, it is clear that land enters into the demand function of all urbanites, simply because in urban areas it matters very

[2] The 1961 input–output table for Canada, for example, provides detailed information on inter-industry flows by commodities as well as by industries. See Dominion Bureau of Statistics, *The Input–Output Structure of the Canadian Economy, 1961*, 2 vols. Queen's Printer, Ottawa, 1969.

much where one locates. This is in contrast to other areas of conventional economic analysis, where all markets are assumed to occur at a point. Thus, an input–output table provides no information as to "where" inputs or outputs are located.

Why is location so important in urban areas? The explanation has to do with why activities become urbanized in the first place, which we shall discuss more fully in the next section. For the moment it is sufficient to note that economies of scale and the changing tastes of consumers have favoured the production and sale of those commodities and services that require large pools of labour on the one hand, and large accessible markets on the other. Further, the growing inter-industry linkages, which are seen in input–output tables, are made more economical if flows between industries have minimal transport costs. In addition, the provision of increasingly important public services, such as education and health care, is less costly if economies of scale and large markets co-exist, as they do in urban areas.

As a result, there are strong economic reasons to explain why activities and persons wish to locate in urban areas, and most of these reasons relate to the advantages of being near other activities and persons. One label assigned to this explanation is the existence of "co-locational economies."[3]

The existence of these economies means that a large and growing number of persons and firms will want to realize them. They will attempt to do so by bidding for the optimally located site or sites. Such sites are "nodes" (points of concentration) in the city which have particularly advantageous locational attributes. The primary one is referred to as the Central Business District (CBD), but other nodes at major junctions, etc., can be readily identified.

Because of widespread competition for these sites, the price of these sites will be bid up. As the price gets bid up, the substitutes begin to be considered, and we witness the universal two-dimensional spread of cities, upward and outward. The behaviour of any urban decision-maker in the face of these objective alternatives can thus be predicted, given his utility or production function.[4]

From this starting point, the city emerges as a series of connected marketplaces, the major connection being the land market. Any decision which influences that market yields a new spectrum of land prices which, in turn, calls for further adjustments in all related markets.

One single example will perhaps make this point clearer. Consider the implantation of a new expressway. By reducing the cost of travel, persons and firms will tend to move out along that expressway and away from the high-priced core land. This in turn will begin raising the price of land along the expressway, particularly at optimal access points near ramps. At the same time, the lower cost of private transportation will induce relatively more automobile usage, which will add to the demand

[3] M. Edel & J. Rothenberg, eds., *Readings in Urban Economics*, Macmillan Company of Canada, Toronto, 1972, Introduction.
[4] More formal analyses of these hypotheses are contained in Edel & Rothenberg, *op. cit.*

for roads and parking areas in the core. The latter will bid up core-land prices, and might well induce further moves by households. Retail stores, observing markets moving farther away, respond by locating in shopping plazas in the new areas, where lower land costs can better accommodate automobile-using customers. Availability of these suburban markets further induces residential relocation, and so on.

What emerges is a very powerful force – the land market — responding in reasonably predictable ways to the pressures of demand and supply. As a result, a general-equilibrium perspective on urban areas is necessary if the ramifications of any particular change are to be comprehended. Our first conclusion, then, is that a micro-economic perspective is useful in establishing one of the key properties of urban areas, its interdependence, and its rootedness in the urban land market.

II. Urban Areas and Economic Development

The second aspect of urban areas that might be more easily understood using the tools of the economist is their macro-dynamics. What determines the growth and changing structure of cities? It would appear that the development of cities is both a cause and consequence of the development of the nation. The economics of development suggest that capital, labour, resources, and technology will determine the growth of real output. Further, the composition of that growth will shift over time, from essentially primary activities (agriculture, forestry, fishing, etc.) to secondary (manufacturing) and then tertiary activities (services), as a result of changing tastes and technology. But these changes both cause and are influenced by the spatial requirements of the various economic sectors. Primary activities are diffused in space — people follow economic potential — whereas the latter activities are increasingly concentrated in space. This is due to their technology, which typically features economies of scale. Transportation costs prevent all activity from congregating at one point, and a series of relatively large, rapidly growing centres results.

These emerging centres in turn accelerate the pace of over-all economic development. By providing large pools of labour and capital, easily accessible markets, pools of innovative potential, increasingly refined input–output linkages, and a variety of related "external economies" (cases in which expansion of output in one firm or industry results in a fall of costs for other firms or industries), they render industrial and tertiary activity increasingly productive. The result is a mutually reinforcing process that leads, in the end, to the polarization of economic growth, and hence population, in urban areas.

Thus our summary of the economics of growth suggests a second conclusion, which is that the determinants of city growth are closely interwoven with developments in the national economy, and can best be understood in the context of those larger developments.

This finding suggests a further attribute of urban areas that relates back to their general-equilibrium features. If some of the most powerful influences on our cities are the secular trends in the national economy, at any point in time the city will be in the process of adjusting to these pressures. In other words, the various parameters that one typically looks at — such as housing prices, family incomes, the demand for public goods — will be on a series of paths headed toward some long-term general-equilibrium result. Because movement along these paths often appears to be slow, due to the dominance of capital-intensive stocks (housing, service infrastructure, etc.), it is easy to lose sight of these paths entirely. The cost of doing so, unfortunately, can be to destabilize further the process of urban development. Although the importance of lags in the adjustment process of economic systems has long been recognized — as have the serious consequences of ignoring them — such an understanding has yet to penetrate thinking about urban areas.

One particularly important problem area that illustrates these ideas is the so-called "housing crisis," and in particular the rapid increase in housing prices in the late 1960s and early 1970s. For the economist, the central analytical question is: do these price increases reflect primarily a shift in demand (due to increased income, population growth, etc.) or a shift in supply (due to increases in the price of materials, land, or credit)? The weight of public opinion — and public policy — would appear to favour the latter explanation, perhaps because it is easier to find culprits with that explanation — construction unions, landlords, bankers, speculators, and developers. While the evidence in part supports that explanation, it is clearly inadequate, largely because of the behaviour of the second important economic variable, quantities. Supply shifts would tend to reduce the relative number of new units being constructed, while in fact there was an increase in new units built to record levels of over 250,000 per year. Such a situation suggests that demand shifts have been an important source of price increase and that the problem on the supply side might be as much the short-run inelasticity of the curve as its shifting.

From this diagnosis of the housing problem, the solutions would appear to lie in policies designed to restrain demand and to impart greater elasticity to the supply curve. The former would entail a rather wider set of policies regarding migration patterns (manpower and regional-development policies as well as immigration targets) together with a cutback in efforts to expand the demand for land inherent in most zoning by-laws, for example. Increased supply elasticity could be achieved by means of transportation improvements (particularly those that are land-saving), extending services, and better use of existing areas.

Because all these policies ultimately required to deal with our urban housing problems go beyond housing, because of the dynamics of housing demand and the interdependencies on the supply side, they are rarely considered and are almost never pursued. On the contrary, primarily "housing" solutions are still being attempted — augmenting the demand for housing and restraining the supply, through down-zoning and the curtailment of suburban development. The inflation of housing costs is therefore being fuelled rather than restrained by public policy. This is occurring at a time when demand will continue to be high as a lagged consequence of the postwar baby boom, so that we are unlikely to experience any significant relief from housing inflation in this decade.

III. The Urban Crisis and the Urban Economy

Our previous sections used some elementary tools of micro and macro economics to identify more precisely two essential features of urban areas — their dynamics and their interconnectedness. At this point, we shall try to see to what extent the economist's perspective on these matters can help explain what is generally felt to be the emerging urban crisis in Canada.

Since 1945, Canada has undergone a very rapid rate of economic development. This was due to the very rapid expansion of its labour force, its ability to draw on substantial volumes of capital from abroad, rapid productivity advances, and significant structural changes, particularly industrialization.[5] As our analysis in the previous section suggests, this led to very rapid urban growth. Indeed, our largest urban centres expanded their populations by 28 percent from 1941 to 1951 and by over 45 percent from 1951 to 1961.[6]

This rapid urbanization of economic activity and population has had substantial impacts on those urban areas (as well as on non-urban areas, of course) that can be explained in large part by our concept of intra-urban sectors linked by means of the land market.

The primary impact has been a significant and sustained increase in the demand for urban land. In consequence, urban land prices have risen sharply and the predicted pattern of increased densities at the centre, with increased dispersion at the periphery, has been observed. With suburban drift came a dramatic increase in the use of private automobiles and a resulting general decline in mass transit. This in turn led to a very large expressway-building period in the fifties and sixties, which in turn encouraged further CBD congestion and suburban dispersion. As servicing costs for new lots rose, municipalities tried to adjust to this rapid-growth phase by curtailing outlays or delaying them significantly. These policies reduced the rate of expansion of new serviced lots, creating significant scarcity and, therefore, even higher land costs in large, rapidly growing cities like Toronto.

An additional policy that further increased land costs was the imposition of servicing costs on the developers, who in turn passed them on to home purchasers. The cost increase came about not, as is commonly believed, by the imposition of a new levy on home buyers. They ultimately had to pay for the services by means of local improvement charges when the municipalities installed the services. The real cost difference is due to the higher cost of capital to the home buyer, who must pay for the services at the first- or second-mortgage rate of interest, as opposed to the developer, who can get a loan at prime rates, and the municipality, which can borrow even cheaper.

These land-cost increases in turn encouraged a shift toward higher-density units, particularly in the core areas. This lucrative use of valuable

[5] See my *Economic Growth in Canada*, 2nd ed., University of Toronto Press, Toronto, 1970.
[6] L.O. Stone, *Urban Development in Canada*, Dominion Bureau of Statistics, 1961 Census Monograph, Ottawa, 1967.

land began to displace less profitable uses, particularly in older areas. At the same time, continual expansion of facilities to move and store cars in the CBD led to further pressure on these areas. This "invasion" of poor residential areas has led to increasing tension and resistance by the inhabitants. Many are tenants unable to afford their own homes, or even better-quality (and therefore more expensive) apartments. The result has been an attempt to arrest further encroachment. The joint impact of retarded expansion in the core as well as in the suburbs has necessarily reduced the supply of urban space, which, as could be expected, has further fuelled the increase in land prices. So rapid have these been in the past decade that the average price of houses in Toronto, for example, increased by 135 percent from 1965 to 1972,[7] and most of that increase appears to be due to the inflation in the price of serviced land.

It would appear, therefore, that the urban land market has responded in reasonably predictable ways to increased urbanization, and that a cluster of problems related to these responses is producing a sense of urban crisis. This is not to deny that other key factors are also operative. There are negative as well as positive externalities related to urbanization and many of these become important in larger urban areas. These include many of our environmental problems of dirty water and air, noise, and perhaps violence. These are in part the result of an inability to develop institutions such as property rights to price urban public goods as well as nuisances appropriately.[8] In addition, there may be a cultural lag by Canadians in adapting their behaviour to the rapid metamorphosis of our urban areas. The desire for a single-family home on a large lot, with two cars, and the serenity of village life may well be incompatible with scarce land, the high social costs of automobile usage, and the interpersonal frictions of an urban society. In most cases, however, these phenomena aggravate urban problems precisely because they have an impact on urban land markets. They tend to increase the demand for land and produce the expected adjustments which appear to be the most problematical in urban areas. Thus, these explanations enrich our understanding of the forces at play on urban land markets and do not appear to be inconsistent with our central hypothesis about the fundamental role of urban land.

IV. Public Policy and the Urban Economy

Our analysis suggests that an important market mechanism has played a central if not exclusive role in determining a variety of our urban problems. If such a straightforward result emerges, the question that immediately comes to mind is: why have we failed to deal effectively with these problems?

There are, of course, political, organizational, and ideological factors that explain the not insignificant policy failures. Our contention here,

---

[7] Toronto Real Estate Board, Oct. 1972.
[8] See John H. Dales, *Pollution, Property and Prices*, University of Toronto Press, Toronto, 1968.

however, is that even an ideal political system would be inadequate in the face of a lack of conceptual clarity. And in no area does clarity of thought appear to be a more rare commodity than in urban affairs. Why this is so we leave to philosophers and other social scientists to find out. That it is so can be readily discerned by examining several areas of outstanding policy failure.

Consider first the policy of urban renewal. Designed to assist in the upgrading of urban facilities (removing blight), it proceeded to destroy low-quality housing. This amounted to a reduction in the supply of housing affordable to low-income households. Even with compensation at market prices, the need to purchase from the more expensive remaining stock of housing in fact made those displaced worse off. At the very least, compensation ought to have been sufficient to permit them to acquire replacement housing with no loss in real income. The confusion of objectives in this area has been, at best, embarrassing. It is arithmetically correct that the average quality can be improved by eliminating the lowest-quality units. But the meaningfulness of such simplistic targets in the realm of public policy defies comprehension.

A second policy issue has to do with the financing of services. Faced with large and increasing costs and inadequate revenues, how better to react than to shift the "burden" from the municipality to developers? But these costly services must be paid for in cash in advance; thus only large developers can acquire adequate lines of credit. Not surprisingly, concentration in the industry has increased dramatically, and the potential consequences of industrial concentration are familiar to all students of economics — greater market power and greater control over prices.

One offshoot of this development that is also plagued with conceptual confusion has to do with the land-speculation question. Observing the necessarily large land inventories in the hands of large planning-conscious developers, it has become fashionable to label them speculators and to blame them for the inflation in land costs.

Three theoretically suspect assumptions underlie this argument. First, an orderly inventory-management policy may actually provide lower-cost serviced land, through economies in acquisition as well as servicing contiguous parcels. Second, there are no theoretical grounds for believing that speculative behaviour per se raises prices. Third, the high profits of some firms in the development industry might more accurately reflect their market power rather than the so-called speculative profit.

Empirically, there is little direct evidence to show that the profits of developers are attributable primarily to speculative activities as opposed to their construction, sale and/or rental activities. In other words, the existence of high profits and large land holdings on the part of developers does not establish that speculation is the cause of land inflation. Further, the solutions that are offered based on that assumption — such as public land acquisition — can conceivably lead to either higher land prices or to public subsidization of land below its marginal social cost, augmenting even further the demand for scarce urban land.

What is most distressing in all this is the general belief that policy failure has been the result of failure of urban markets and particularly urban land markets. In fact, it would appear that many of our urban problems have been caused not by market failure but by the market behaving in a reasonably normal way. That problems emerge proves not market failure but that the basic determinants of market outcomes, such as rapidly increasing demand and limited supply, are operative. No market can be expected to produce other than rising prices in such a situation.

Failure to understand this rather obvious truism has plagued urban policy making for decades. Unhappiness with urban problems and inability to understand at least the economic mechanisms that helped produce them has led to the development of extra-market, indeed anti-market, mechanisms of land-use control. The favoured tool among these is zoning. The purpose of zoning is to allocate urban space in some optimal way. In most cases, optimality is defined by a master plan that gives a visual picture of the spatial goals at some point in the future. Because of its future concern, this approach is presumed to be "forward looking." In fact, the reverse is true. Stressing a situation at one point in time rather than the process by which we get to that point, the technique is static in the extreme. In addition, the situation at the target date is rarely derived from analyses which take into consideration changes in tastes, changes in technology, and the impact of each on the other. Rather, they are a compendium of usually highly personal, largely aesthetic desiderata — interesting perhaps as an art form, but of damaging consequence to our cities.

The reason is that zoning creates new "rules of the game" that may be inconsistent with the changes in tastes and technology — in demand and supply — that are proceeding apace. As a result, lands designated for low-density construction in areas where there are powerful reasons to have high-density activity provide an enormous challenge to individuals to break the rules. The profits on rezoning the land are so enormous that entrepreneurs will be induced to try to share them with obliging politicians and bureaucrats. Not surprisingly, spot rezoning has been a highly successful urban activity in North America.[9] On the other hand, over-zoned lands — i.e., lands which are zoned in excessive quantities for uses that traditionally pay the highest rents — lead owners to have excessive price expectations, with the result that the land tends to remain unused for long periods of time. As a result, most cities contain a paradoxical mixture of genuine land scarcity with high prices, while substantial amounts of prime land are underused and are often vacant.

Few would argue that no controls over land use should exist;[10] for there are problems of relying on the market where such things as externalities exist. But the total rejection by policy-makers of the relevance of the market and hence the need to understand it — despite the

---

[9] See B. Siegan, "Non-Zoning in Houston," *Journal of Law & Economics*, 1970, p. 133.
[10] However, see *ibid.*, for an examination of land use in the city of Houston, where zoning does not exist.

fact that it does operate in critical ways — has been the most costly conceptual confusion of all. It has led to short-term, ineffectual solutions to pressing problems, because policy-makers have identified the wrong culprits on the urban scene and have trivialized very difficult issues. The general policy failure has, in turn, been in large part responsible for the growing feeling by urbanites that, as the pressures of urbanization intensify — and there is evidence to suggest that these pressures will be particularly severe throughout the 1970s[11] — the quality of urban life will necessarily deteriorate. Needless to say, this expectation is already leading to predictable outcomes — even greater resort to legal–political practices to isolate persons and groups from these changes, and an incessant stream of *ad hoc,* ill-considered, and probably counter-productive policies.

One might conceivably adopt the line of argument that says the market will, in the end, produce appropriate results. By permitting our cities to deteriorate, it is argued, urbanites will respond by "voting with their feet," and go to more desirable places. This, however, is to mistake an understanding of the market with the ideological position that the market produces optimal results. Our analysis was designed to demonstrate some of the costs of failing to understand how urban land markets operate. The alternative is not necessarily to stand back and let it go its own way, but rather to influence the market to yield more desirable outcomes.

V. Conclusion

Economic analysis does not provide us with easy solutions to the troubling problems of our urban areas. Indeed, it cautions us against attempts to offer simplistic answers. However, it does suggest that greater clarity about the central processes of urbanization and urban land use can help us begin to understand the complexity of those problems and the reasons for our seeming inability to solve them.

This brief review has explored a number of urban problems that to date have been plagued by conceptual confusion and inadequate policy responses. Most common to these has been a misunderstanding of the role of markets, and a widespread readiness to disregard urban market-places entirely. Because of the centrality of the urban land market, this attitude has led to a general worsening of most of our urban problems. Transportation has become a steadily deteriorating problem, the "housing crisis" is deepening, the problems of the urban poor are not being solved, and the fiscal and therefore political position of local governments is being rapidly eroded.

This failure to understand but one key aspect of our urban places is symptomatic of a larger problem — a general unwillingness to take our cities seriously. We seem unprepared as individuals as well as groups to devote the effort to understand better the nature of our urban prob-

[11] See *Urban Canada: Problems and Prospects,* a report I prepared for the Government of Canada in 1970 (published by Central Mortgage and Housing Corporation), Part III.

lems. Instead, we are excessively willing to pronounce vociferously, if superficially, on all matters urban. Perhaps this is due to the enormous individual costs of a serious effort to learn and to alter our behaviour, and to the very small private (as opposed to collective) benefits; for improvement will be slow in coming and far in the future. Clearly, there is a strong case here for public action, a case that appeared to underlie the tentative first steps taken by the federal government in 1970.[12] Regrettably, the initiative appears to have been lost. "Ad hocery" is still being resorted to, and the institutional reforms essential to learning about and coping with this new kind of policy issue have not come about.

Our emerging urban crisis is more a result of inadequate policy making than it is inherent in our urban development. In other words, our urban future need not be a dismal one. Preventing it from becoming dismal, however, will take much greater clarity of thought about the problem, thought that can and must inform about the development of appropriate policies. Because of the pervasive forces determining that future in Canada, and the long lags involved, the longer we delay in addressing ourselves to the task of policy reform, the less likely will we be able to provide ourselves with alternatives to what so many have already accepted as our inevitable urban future.

---

[12] A Ministry Responsible for Housing was established and it sponsored a research effort culminating in the report *Urban Canada: Problems and Prospects* (*op. cit.*) and six underlying research monographs, all published by the Central Mortgage and Housing Corporation.

3. Housing Issues and Housing Policy

Lawrence B. Smith

University of Toronto

Residential construction plays an important role in the Canadian economy because it is the means by which the nation's housing standards are improved, because it accounts for a significant proportion of the nation's output,[1] and because it is the sector most highly responsive to monetary influences and policy. As a result of this diversity, considerable controversy exists over the proper function and objectives of federal housing policy. At one extreme is the contention that the primary if not sole function of federal housing policy should be the provision of a decent home for every Canadian as quickly as possible, while at the other extreme is the contention that federal housing policy should enhance the stabilizing influence that residential construction typically exerts on the economy. Underlying these positions are different views of the nature of the housing problem and the responsiveness of residential construction to market pressures. One group sees a poorly functioning market with pervasive and major housing problems, while the other group sees a reasonably well functioning market with only selected problem areas.[2]

The purpose of this paper is to describe the operation of the Canadian housing market and to develop a framework for analyzing federal housing objectives and policies. Section I describes the structure and operation of the housing market. Section II discusses the objectives of federal housing programs and policies introduced prior to the 1970s.

---

[1] It directly accounts for about 5 percent of GNP and considerably more indirectly through induced service investment and consumer-durables expenditure.

[2] See M. Dennis and S. Fish, *Programs in Search of a Policy: Low Income Housing in Canada* (Toronto: A.M. Hakkert, 1972), for the former view and L.B. Smith, *The Postwar Canadian Housing and Residential Mortgage Market and the Role of Government* (Toronto: University of Toronto Press, 1974), for the latter view.

Section III considers the appropriateness of a housing-start target as the objective for recent federal housing policy. Section IV reviews recent housing performance and analyzes a number of current proposals for housing policy.

I. Structure and Operation of the Housing Market

The housing market functions like most markets, except that it has a number of unique characteristics. First, shelter space is not a homogeneous commodity and the housing market is not really a single market in the classical sense that there are a large number of identical units. Rather, there is a series of overlapping submarkets consisting of owner-occupied dwellings and rental dwellings, new dwellings and old dwellings, dwellings in the urban core and dwellings on the periphery of an urban market. Yet each of these dwellings provides housing services which are substitutes for one another, and there is a market for housing services. Second, the price of housing services determined in this market is somewhat vague. In the case of rental dwellings, the price for housing services is observable and is the rent paid for the use of these dwellings. In the case of owner-occupied dwellings, the price is not directly observable, as it is that rent that would have been paid if the dwelling were occupied by someone other than the owner, and it is called imputed rent.[3] Third, the market is complicated by the existence of three sets of participants: the demanders of housing services, the suppliers of housing services, and the developers whose construction activity increases the stock of dwellings and thereby the supply of housing services. This complication is increased by the fact that many participants play more than one role in the market — the most important dual role being that of owner-occupiers, who are both the suppliers and demanders of the same housing services. Thus there are owner-occupiers who supply housing services to themselves, landlords who supply housing services to others, and tenants who rent housing services from the landlords.[4] Fourth, and perhaps most important, there is a large virtually permanent stock of housing units and supply of housing services. Unlike other markets, new construction adds only 2.5–3 percent a year to the existing housing stock and supply of housing services, so that for most purposes the supply of dwellings and housing services can be viewed as fixed in the short run.[5]

The existence of a large existing stock of dwelling units means that the housing market can be viewed in a "stock-adjustment" framework. At any given time, there is a *demand for housing services* which

---

[3] There is a direct relationship between the price for housing services and the price of the housing unit. The price of the housing unit is the present value of the future stream of the actual net rent or imputed net rent, i.e., the sum of all future rents (net of owning or operating expenses) discounted to the present by applying a rate of discount.

[4] An important implication of this is the distinction between the demand for housing services and the demand for the ownership of housing stock.

[5] Strictly speaking, the supply of housing stock and housing services do not vary in proportion; since existing dwellings depreciate, reducing the services they supply while remaining part of the stock. The services supplied by a dwelling depend upon its quality.

depends upon a variety of factors including the price of housing services, the cost of mortgage credit, the *per capita* income of the population, and the size and age composition of the population.[6] This demand interacts with the *supply of housing services* available from the existing housing stock to determine the price for housing services. When the price for housing services is so high that some developers expect a satisfactory profit from building and selling dwellings for owner-occupancy, or building and leasing rental dwellings, new residential construction occurs and new dwelling units are produced. Similarly, at some price it pays owners of the existing stock to upgrade their dwellings; so that the price mechanism leads to an increase in the supply of housing services primarily from the construction of new residential dwellings and also from improvements in the existing stock. The volume of residential construction activity depends upon the expected profitability of this construction and, other things being equal, will be higher the higher is the price of housing services. Finally, the larger the volume of residential construction, the larger will be the future supply of housing services and hence, the lower will be the price of these services.

In addition to depending on the price of housing services, the profitability and volume of residential construction activity depend upon the cost of producing and supplying housing services and the cost and availability of mortgage credit. For any given price of housing services, the higher the cost of land, interim financing, building materials, and labour, the less profitable will be construction and the smaller will be the volume of residential construction activity. Similarly, the higher the cost of mortgage credit the less profitable will be construction activity, because higher mortgage costs reduce the price that can profitably be paid for the ownership of dwelling units. In the case of owner-occupied homes, higher mortgage costs increase the owning or operating costs of a home, thus reducing the demand for home-ownership and reducing the price.[7] In the case of rental dwellings, higher mortgage costs increase the operating costs, reducing the net rent and the value of rental dwellings.

The cost of mortgage credit is very important in the housing market, and especially in determining the volume of new residential construction, because over 80 percent of the funds for new construction are obtained by way of mortgage credit.[8] Higher borrowing costs therefore have a very significant impact upon the affordability of home ownership and profitability of rental dwellings, and this makes the volume of new residential construction and the supply of additional housing services highly sensitive to the cost and availability of mortgage credit.

This analysis has a number of implications for government policy. It indicates that government can stimulate the supply of housing services

[6] There is some question whether the cost of mortgage credit belongs in the demand function for housing services, or in the demand function for the ownership of housing stock, or in both.
[7] Price can be thought of as falling because increased mortgage costs reduce the net imputed rent and hence their present value with a constant discount rate, or because the discount rate rises.
[8] Calculated from Central Mortgage and Housing Corporation, *Canadian Housing Statistics, 1969*, pp. 13 and 16.

by policies which increase the demand for housing services, such as the provision of income or rent subsidies; by policies which facilitate the production of new dwellings, such as the servicing of additional land and the stimulation of research into systems building; by policies which encourage the upgrading of existing dwellings, such as appropriate revisions to the tax regulations; by policies which increase the efficiency of the capital market; and by monetary policy. Policies which increase the demand for housing services operate by increasing the price of these services, while policies which facilitate the construction of new dwellings generally reduce the price of housing services (although they may increase the price of other items). Policies which reduce the cost of mortgage credit tend to increase the nominal price of housing services (by increasing demand), but reduce the financial costs, on balance usually reducing the over-all cost of housing services.

Because of its sensitivity to the cost and availability of mortgage credit, residential construction activity tends to vary in an anti-cyclical manner. When general economic activity expands, the over-all demand for investable funds exerts upward pressures on interest rates. This has the effect (1) of reducing the availability of mortgage credit, as investment flows are directed to relatively higher-yielding securities, and (2) with a lag, of increasing the cost of mortgage credit. Both of these forces act to reduce residential construction. Since these anti-cyclical monetary forces usually outweigh the pro-cyclical income forces (when increasing incomes increase the demand for housing services), residential construction has a tendency to fluctuate anti-cyclically: contracting in an economic expansion, and increasing in an economic recession.[9] This tendency may be either reinforced or ameliorated by short-run housing policies.

II. Federal Housing Programs and Policies

Prior to the 1970s, federal housing policies had two main thrusts: to improve the nation's housing standards by increasing the efficiency of the capital market, and to stabilize the general economy without permitting excessive fluctuations in the housing sector.[10]

In an attempt to improve the nation's living standards, the National Housing Act (NHA) was introduced. This created a new form of mortgage, the NHA mortgage, which has the advantage that the federal government insures lenders against losses on funds advanced on NHA mortgages. Because this insurance reduces the risks associated with mortgage lending and the charge for this insurance is less than lenders would impute for self-insurance, more funds are available for mortgage lending and the interest rate on NHA mortgages is lower than the mortgage rate would otherwise be. Lowering the costs and increasing the supply of

---

[9] For an elaboration of this behaviour, see Smith, *op. cit.*, chs. 2–4, and J. Guttentag, "The Short Cycle in Residential Construction," *American Economic Review*, 51 (June 1961), pp. 275–98.

[10] For a discussion and analysis of these policies, see Smith *op. cit.*, chs. 8–9, and J.V. Poapst, *The Residential Mortgage Market*, working paper prepared for the Royal Commission on Banking and Finance (Ottawa: Queen's Printer, 1962).

mortgage credit increase the volume of residential construction and the supply of housing services.[11]

Housing standards have also been improved by a direct lending program of the Central Mortgage and Housing Corporation (CMHC), the government housing corporation. CMHC makes funds available for residential construction when private funds are not forthcoming. Between 1946 and 1971, 15 percent of all housing starts were financed by government funds, although only 6.1 percent of total housing starts were specifically earmarked as low-income housing.[12] By increasing the total supply of mortgage credit, this direct government lending increased the volume of residential construction and improved housing standards.[13]

The federal tax system also has encouraged residential construction and home-ownership by not taxing imputed rents. By supplying housing services to himself, the owner of an owner-occupied dwelling is receiving income in the form of housing services without there being a market transaction. The value of these services is the imputed rent the home-owner is receiving from his home-ownership. Since this imputed rent is not considered income for income-tax purposes, the home-owner obtains a benefit equivalent to allowing his payment for housing services to be tax deductible. Because an equivalent treatment is not provided for other consumption goods and services, this tax treatment gives a preference to the consumption of housing services and shifts resources into the housing sector.[14]

Federal housing policy, defined here to include monetary policy in a restricted sense, has also been used for stabilization purposes. Monetary policy has a pronounced effect on residential construction activity by altering the cost and availability of mortgage credit. A tight monetary policy increases interest rates and reduces the availability of funds, thereby reducing residential construction; while an easy monetary policy stimulates residential construction. As a result of the reliance placed on monetary policy for stabilization purposes, residential construction plays a major role in economic stabilization.

Because the government provides the insurance for NHA mortgages, it establishes the terms that qualify for this insurance. Some of these terms include the maximum loan permitted, the maximum ratio of the loan to the value of dwelling, the term of the mortgage, and the maximum ratio of the mortgage payments and property taxes to the borrower's income. By changing the terms that qualify for insurance, the government can increase or reduce the number of borrowers that qualify for this

[11] Between 1946 and 1971, almost 30 percent of all privately financed housing starts and 25 percent of total housing starts were financed by government-insured mortgages. However, because of offsets in the conventional (non-government-insured) sector of the mortgage market, the net increase in the supply of mortgage credit and housing starts was considerably less. A "housing start" is the commencement of production on one new dwelling unit.

[12] There was a considerable change in the nature of CMHC lending after 1969. In 1970–71 this lending led to low-income housing starts accounting for 21 percent of total housing starts.

[13] Because of offsets in the private sector, CMHC direct lending increased housing starts by approximately 11 percent in 1946–71. See Smith, op. cit., for the derivation of this figure.

[14] Because this benefit accrues only to owner-occupiers, it provides a stimulus to home-ownership as opposed to rental housing.

lower-cost credit and thereby change the costs of housing for these borrowers. If these requirements are tightened, the demand for housing and volume of residential construction activity can be reduced; while if these requirements are eased, demand and construction activity can be stimulated. NHA lending terms can therefore be varied to exert a stabilizing influence upon the economy.

CMHC direct lending can also be used for stabilization purposes, if this lending is co-ordinated with monetary and fiscal policy. However, what is meant by co-ordination is not always clear. Usually, co-ordination means reduced CMHC lending during periods of monetary and fiscal restraint and increased lending during periods of monetary and fiscal expansion. But there are situations when the converse is appropriate. Since monetary policy enhances general market tendencies, it accentuates fluctuations in residential construction. In particular, tight monetary policy increases the possibility of an excessive contraction in the residential construction industry in the sense that there is a reduction in long-run productive capacity. To avert such an excessive contraction in the residential construction sector when severe monetary contraction is required, CMHC direct lending could be increased, softening the impact of monetary restraint on the housing sector and avoiding a possible premature curtailment of monetary restraint. Such a situation could arise, for example, if monetary restraint were required for balance-of-payments purposes under fixed exchange rates, since an increase in Canadian relative to foreign interest rates rather than a reduction in domestic economic activity would be desired. CMHC direct lending, therefore, may be part of a co-ordinated stabilization policy both when it reinforces and when it ameliorates monetary policy in the residential construction sector.

III. The Housing-Start Target and Policy Objectives

Although housing policies have two primary objectives, these objectives need not conflict. During general economic slowdowns, policies that stimulate residential construction are appropriate from both a stabilization and housing-standard viewpoint. During economic expansions, however, these objectives appear to conflict, because stabilization calls for reduced residential construction. But with an intermediate time horizon of a business cycle, or a five- or six-year period, the stabilizing aspect of housing policy need not reduce housing standards; for housing demand is not eliminated permanently but merely postponed, so that the volume of residential construction activity should balance out.[15]

Despite the possibility of co-ordination between these objectives, many researchers have advocated the dominance of the housing-standard objective. The Federal Task Force on Housing and Urban Development in its *Report* stated as the objective of housing policy that "every Canadian

[15] A similar view has been expressed by L. Grebler, "Criteria for Appraising Governmental Housing Programs," *American Economic Review*, 50 (May 1960), p. 321–32, and S. Maisel, "The Relationship of Residential Financing and Expenditures on Residential Construction," in *Conference on Savings and Residential Financing, 1965 Proceedings* (Chicago: U.S. Savings and Loan League, 1965), p. 132.

should be entitled to clean, warm housing," and to effect this, it set as an intermediate target the production of one million housing units during the five years from 1969 to 1973.[16] This objective was very quickly translated into an annual target, and the production of 200,000 units a year became the objective of government policy.

The provision of "clean, warm shelter for every Canadian" is a meritorious objective for the housing industry, but one that is empirically very elusive and ambiguous.[17] The translation of this into an annual target unfortunately does little to ensure that the primary objective is attained, but does much to reduce the co-ordination between housing policy and general macro-economic stabilization. The weakening of the stabilization function is obvious, since the faithful pursuit of an annual housing target implies that residential construction is to be insulated from market fluctuations and is to be independent of the state of the economy. Since residential construction tends to fluctuate anti-cyclically and thus dampens fluctuations in the rest of the economy, and since monetary policy exerts its major impact on residential construction, the adherence to an annual target increases instability in the rest of the economy.

A second implication of an annual target is that the pricing system does not efficiently allocate resources between sectors; for if it did, then no target would be necessary. The correct amount of resources would automatically be devoted to housing. Thus if a target is required, there is a presumption that the market allocates fewer resources to the housing sector than is optimal and more to other sectors. On the other hand, if there are few impediments to the proper allocation of resources and an annual target increases the resources flowing to the housing sector, then it creates a misallocation of resources by shifting resources away from the other sectors in the economy. The housing-start target assumes that housing has relatively larger positive externalities than other sectors, but there is no evidence that this is the case.

A third theoretical difficulty with housing-start targets is the tendency for these targets to focus attention on housing *starts* as the means of upgrading housing standards, to the exclusion of improving the existing housing *stock*. Since new construction increases the housing stock by a relatively small proportion each year, policies that ignore the existing stock are seriously deficient.

In addition to these theoretical problems, housing-start targets suffer from a variety of specification difficulties which make the targets very imprecise estimates and guides for policies.[18] Housing targets are usually defined quantitatively as the number of housing starts required to satisfy the demand for housing from net family formation and net non-family

---

[16] *Report of the Federal Task Force on Housing and Urban Development* (Ottawa: Queen's Printer, 1969), p. 22. This target was also stated by the Economic Council of Canada, *Fourth Annual Review: The Canadian Economy from the 1960's to the 1970's* (Ottawa: Queen's Printer, 1967), p. 166.

[17] For a discussion of difficulties with policy objectives, see L.B. Smith, "Evaluating National Housing Policy Criteria in Canada," *American Real Estate and Urban Economics Association Journal*, 1 (Sept. 1973).

[18] See A. Downs, "Moving Toward Realistic Housing Goals," in K. Gordon, ed., *Agenda for the Nation* (Washington, D.C.: The Brookings Institution, 1968), pp. 141–178.

household formation, and to eliminate the use of substandard dwellings and the "doubling-up" of families in shared accommodation over a reasonable period of time, after allowing for demolitions and conversions. However, there are serious conceptual and empirical difficulties in determining the components of the target. This can be illustrated by examining two of these components, the provision of shelter for non-family households and the elimination of substandard dwellings.

Since net non-family household formation accounted for 27 percent of the realized net increase in housing demand between 1961 and 1971,[19] the provision of housing space for non-family households is an important element in the target calculation. However, there is little consensus as to the amount of housing that should be provided for non-family households. Non-family households refer to households of one or more unrelated persons, and hence the question arises as to the entitlement to separate housing in a social-objective sense. Should all non-family persons over the age of 21 be entitled to their own dwelling? Should they share a dwelling? Should the age be 25? or 18? The answer is purely a value judgment and is usually avoided by incorporating in the total housing target the number of housing units demanded by these households. But since the supply of new housing ultimately affects the price and hence demand, the problem remains, albeit well hidden.

More difficult is the problem of substandard housing, since what is substandard housing in an economic sense? Policy makers and architects have some notion of substandard housing in a physical sense, based upon the need for major repairs and lack of basic facilities, but this does not always coincide with substandard in an economic sense. In 1961, data on substandard dwellings using a physical definition[20] indicated that 15.7 percent of non-farm owner-occupied substandard dwellings were occupied by households whose incomes were in the top 40 percent of non-farm family incomes and 5.2 percent were occupied by households with incomes in the top 20 percent. For tenant-occupied dwellings, these percentages were 15.7 percent and 4.7 percent respectively.[21] Thus, many households that could afford to live in "decent" accommodations lived in socially defined substandard dwellings. One explanation for this is that many households have a low preference for housing services and prefer to live in inferior housing in order to afford a greater consumption of other goods and services. A second explanation is that these households do not feel they are living in substandard dwellings. In both cases, substandard in a physical sense does not imply substandard in an economic sense. The elimination of the substandard housing occupied by these persons would force them to devote a greater proportion of their budget to housing services and would reduce their over-all satisfaction.

On the other hand, the absence of substandard dwellings would not necessarily indicate that households do not have housing difficulties. In 1969, 31 percent of all families with incomes in the lowest 20 percent of

[19] Derived from Central Mortgage and Housing Corporation, *Canadian Housing Statistics, 1971*, pp. 1, 90.
[20] Dwellings in need of major repair or lacking such basic facilities as piped water and installed flush or chemical toilets.
[21] Dennis and Fish, *op. cit.*, p. 48.

non-farm family incomes spent over 40 percent of their income for shelter, and 58 percent spent over 25 percent of their income for shelter. Since only 11 to 14 percent of urban households with incomes in the lowest 20 percent in 1967 lived in substandard dwellings,[22] even if all those living in substandard dwellings devoted a disproportionate proportion of their income to shelter, there would still have been a highly significant proportion of low-income families living in socially acceptable housing only by spending a disproportionate proportion of their income for shelter. These families can be thought of as experiencing difficulties with housing as much as families living in substandard dwellings; yet they are not reflected in any components of the housing target.

The preceding analysis suggests that many households experiencing difficulties in the housing sector experience these difficulties because of low incomes. In this case, policy action in the housing sector alone is not the most appropriate nor most efficient way of alleviating these problems. Rather, housing policies should be combined with income-distribution policies to provide low-income households with sufficient income to afford socially acceptable housing and also socially acceptable amounts of other necessities. Where the housing market would respond to the demand generated by income-distribution policies, rent or income supplements are appropriate methods of upgrading housing standards. Where market imperfections prevent the housing industry from meeting this demand, possibly in the case of housing for the elderly, disabled, native peoples, and large low-income families, direct government intervention to build or encourage the construction of this housing would also be necessary. Housing-start targets are usually little help where the basic problem is insufficient income or the lack of housing for some special group with little market power.[23]

IV. Recent Housing Performance and Policy Proposals

During the last few years, politicians and journalists have regularly proclaimed deficiencies in Canadian housing performance. These proclamations have persisted despite the claim of a Federal Task Force in 1969 that Canadian housing standards were tied for first place in the Western world in terms of the lowest occupation density per room and were first in terms of average rooms per dwelling;[24] despite the fact that by mid-1973 housing starts had already surpassed the one-million-start target established for the full 5-year period 1969–1973; and despite the fact that government housing policy had drastically shifted its emphasis and was responsible, through its lending policies, for low-income housing starts accounting for 21 percent of total starts in 1970 and 1971.

In view of these standards and performance, how do we explain the persistent criticism of housing performance? One answer is that housing critics and commentators have recently been concerned primarily with

[22] *Ibid.*, pp. 49, 60.
[23] Housing targets are sometimes specified separately for special groups, in which case the distributional deficiencies are reduced.
[24] *Report of the Federal Task Force on Housing and Urban Development*, p. 6.

the price of housing services rather than the physical condition of the housing stock.

In recent years, the cost of home-ownership has risen considerably faster than the consumer price index and the rate of increase in personal disposable income. The cost of rental housing services has risen more quickly than the consumer price index but not as quickly as personal disposable income.[25] A variety of factors combined to cause this situation. These factors include a sharp increase in the demand for owner-occupied dwellings as the population bulged in the twenties as a lagged consequence of the postwar "baby boom," a sharp increase in the cost of mortgage credit as a consequence of rising world interest rates, and often a shortage of available land as a consequence of inappropriate zoning or lack of services.[26]

As a result of the high inflation rate in the cost of housing services and especially home-ownership, a number of policy proposals have been suggested. These proposals range from rent controls to mortgage interest subsidies, from the creation of land banks to the deductibility of mortgage interest and property taxes for income-tax purposes. In order to demonstrate the importance of understanding the market mechanism in formulating housing policies, three such housing proposals are analyzed below.

1. Rent controls

Despite the fact that the rental housing sector has experienced a considerably lower rate of inflation than the home-ownership sector and has had an inflation rate below the rate of increase in personal disposable income, rent controls have been seriously advocated by many policy makers. These controls are often suggested because they have an immediate effect on the price of rental housing services without appreciably affecting the supply of these services for a lengthy time period. This follows from the existence of a large housing stock, which is increased by only 2.5–3 percent each year by new construction, and from the long construction period, which means that the abandonment of projects upon the introduction of rent controls will not cause a significant reduction in the volume of housing completions for at least a year and probably even longer. Hence, rent control is a policy with an immediate price gain and a very delayed cost.

However, the cost of price controls is likely to be considerable if introduced as more than a short-run expedient to alleviate a temporary

---

[25] As an illustration of these price variations, the selling price of the average new single-family dwelling in Toronto was estimated to have risen by 235 percent and monthly carrying costs (mortgage payments and taxes) by 223 percent between 1961 and 1972. During this same period in Toronto rents rose between 44 and 65 percent and average weekly earnings rose 92 percent (*The Globe and Mail,* Toronto, May 11, 1973, p. 21). The consumer price index for Canada rose 40 percent during this period.

[26] Developers are usually responsible for the installation of basic services such as sewers and water in their projects, but they require local and provincial governments to provide the trunk lines and disposal units for them to connect with. It is the provision of trunk lines and disposal units that is referred to when services are said to be unavailable.

crisis. By artificially restraining the price of housing services below the market price, the profitability of new construction of rental dwellings is reduced and the volume of this construction will correspondingly decline. Unless policies are simultaneously introduced to reduce construction costs and restore the profitability of construction at the controlled price, a reduced volume of construction will result in a lower long-run housing stock and ultimately in rationing and queues for housing services.[27] If the controls are removed, rents will rise to a level higher than they would otherwise have been.

2. Imposition of a ceiling on mortgage interest rates

The imposition of a ceiling on mortgage interest rates has been suggested to reduce the cost of home-ownership. In its simplest form this proposal would lead to a disastrous decline in housing starts, since financial institutions, which provide the vast majority of the mortgage credit for new residential construction, and private investors would seek non-controlled investments and virtually eliminate the supply of mortgage credit.

A more elaborate version of this proposal couples the interest ceiling with the requirement that financial institutions be forced to devote a fixed percentage of their investment portfolios to mortgage investments. This refinement would temporarily mitigate some of the reduction in mortgage credit but ultimately would be ineffective, because financial institutions obtain the bulk of their investment funds from the public. If institutions are compelled to invest in artificially low-yielding mortgages, the interest rate they would be able to pay for funds would necessarily decline and they would obtain fewer funds to invest, as private investors seek more profitable investment outlets. The supply of mortgage credit would thus be substantially reduced, reducing the volume of residential construction. This would exacerbate rather than alleviate rising housing prices.

3. Supply policies

Supply policies such as the provision of additional sewer, hydro, and water services to increase the supply of usable land have often been suggested to restrain rising housing prices. If rising prices are a manifestation of an increased demand for housing services and if residential construction is limited by short-run industrial capacity and not artificially constrained by shortages of serviced land or oligopolistic producers acting in concert,[28] then increasing the available land will affect neither residential construction activity nor housing prices. If, on the other hand, construction is below potential industrial capacity because of the unavail-

---

[27] Reduced private construction could be offset by increased government construction. However, this not only subverts the market system more completely but is unlikely to result in lower-cost housing.

[28] An indication of the concentration of market power can be seen from the fact that in 1970 24 percent of NHA housing starts were by builders producing less than 26 NHA units each, while 48 percent were by builders producing more than 100 NHA units each (Central Mortgage and Housing Corporation, *Canadian Housing Statistics, 1970*, p. 84).

ability of serviced land, policies that increase the supply of serviced land will have a considerable impact upon the volume of residential construction and ultimately the price of housing services.

V. Conclusion

The preceding analysis suggests that policy makers must be cognizant of the market mechanism and operate in conjunction with it if their policies are to have the desired results. Policies that ignore the private sector or the existing state of the market are likely to encounter considerable offsets in the private sector, and thereby prolong the difficulties they seek to remedy. On the other hand, if policies (including direct intervention in the provision of mortgage credit or housing services) are formulated to minimize offsets in the private sector and to alleviate imperfections and distortions in the market, federal housing policy can play a vital and positive role in the housing market.

X. Economics of Federalism

1. Some Economic Problems Of a Federal System *

R. Ian McAllister

Dalhousie University

A federal system of government can stem from one of two origins — either it can represent the loosening of a unitary state, presumably because the components seek greater autonomy, or it can represent a merger of previously independent units.

Either way, periodic tensions appear inevitable regarding the division of powers, the direction — and sense of direction — of the whole, and the trade-offs between some blend of efficiency goals, on the one hand, and some blend of equity goals, on the other.

Either way, also, the acceptance of a federal system presumably is an expression of a prevalent view that the whole, politically and perhaps — but less certainly — economically as well, would be able to be greater in some measurable manner than the sum of its parts. The logic for and against holding such a view, however, appears somewhat sterile outside the context of a particular time, place, people, and set of ambitions. While arguments supporting larger-scale operations for business and government activities, whether on the basis of securing greater international political and trade influence, or on some mix of economies of scale, or on internal market size, or on hedging one's bets (e.g., not all areas of a large country are likely to be flooded, have a poor harvest, produce a single product for a single foreign market, or be burned in a forest fire, etc., at the same time), can be quite convincing in the abstract, so too can be arguments based on the logic of diminishing marginal returns of scale; at some point too many cooks presumably really can spoil the broth.

Just as history has many examples of "successful" large countries, so also it appears to have many examples of apparently effectively managed small ones. Size and "effectiveness" are not necessarily synonymous.

Embarking on a federal system of government, like embarking on a

*While some comments have relevance to the federal systems of a number of countries, the observations are drawn from aspects of Canadian experience.

unitary form of government or entering a customs union such as the European Common Market, represents something of a gamble. Rapid and unforeseen changes in individual-state or national circumstances are likely to occur, whether because of the decision (e.g., former trading partners may form counter-blocs of some kind), or independently of it (e.g., technological discoveries might suddenly ring the death knell for a particular form of production, remove some previously critical locational advantages, etc.). Any system of government, to be regarded as successful, must obviously enable those responsible to be as pace-setting as the electorate requires, and responsive to internal and external opportunity and change.

The opportunity cost of opting for a federal system can be speculated on only in a particular-country situation — and, similarly, any discussion of "the economic problems of federalism" cannot ignore the possibility that equal or greater economic problems might very well have been encountered by the same country or state, if some other form of government had prevailed. Moreover, as cannot be stressed too often, competent and well-motivated people have frequently made the strangest of systems perform well (whether at the single-project or government-system level), while no system can compensate for lack of competence and motivation on the part of the people. The positive experience of the Marshall Aid program after the Second World War in Europe and the disappointing record of a range of international-aid programs in many of the less developed countries reinforce this point.

I. Some General "Economic" Indicators of the
   Canadian Experience

Canada did not embark on a federal system of government without misgivings. John A. Macdonald and A. T. Galt, for example, appear to have viewed a unitary form of government as a more satisfactory mechanism, whereas Joseph Howe and the Nova Scotian anti-confederationists wanted no confederation at all. Quebec's concern for cultural identity, together with the virtual absence of municipal government in the Maritimes, suggested some form of federal system would be the most practical outcome, if a political union was to be attempted at that time.[1]

The broad economic success of the venture would seem, in the Canadian case, to be evident from aggregate data.

In 1871, four years after the original union of the Dominion of Canada, the census indicated a population of 3,486,000. One hundred years later, the 1971 census recorded a population of 21,568,000 for the territorially larger Canada. By 1971, Canada had built up an economic system that enabled her to generate a gross national product of some $93 billion, exports of goods and services accounting for some 22.7 percent of GNP

[1] For a discussion of the background to Confederation, see the *Report of the Royal Commission on Dominion–Provincial Relations*, King's Printer, Ottawa, 1940; W.A. Mackintosh, *The Economic Background of Dominion–Provincial Relations*, King's Printer, Ottawa, 1939; and D.G. Creighton, *Canada's First Century*, Macmillan of Canada, Toronto, 1970.

(1964-71 average). As Table 1 suggests, the Canadian over-all record — particularly bearing in mind the relative newness of the country — compares favourably with that of most other industrial countries.[2]

Table 1: GNP Per Capita: 1970

(in U.S. dollars)[a]

Australia	2,830
Belgium	2,670
Canada	3,550
France	2,920
Italy	1,700
Japan	1,910
Norway	2,940
Spain	960
Sweden	3,840
Switzerland	3,240
United Kingdom	2,170
United States	4,870

[a] At current prices and exchange rates.
Compiled from appendix "Basic Statistics", O.E.C.D. Economic Surveys, Canada, Paris, 1973.

II.   Canadian Economic Goals and Some Regional Implications

In the early years of Confederation, attention had focused heavily on means of linking Canada more closely together. Thus the construction of the intercolonial railway, the improvement of the Canadian canals, and the opening up of the Northwest Territories loomed as priorities. At the same time, the Western provinces wanted to monopolize the Maritime markets for flour and grain, and the Maritimes sought to sell coal out west.

As the economy became more complex, as government grew proportionate to the private sector, and as Keynesian arguments became accepted to some considerable degree at the federal level of government, so macro socio-economic goals began to be articulated for the country as a whole — even if they were not fully subscribed to by governments, particularly at the provincial and municipal levels.

In 1964 the new Economic Council of Canada expressed such goals, perhaps most formally to that date, in terms of:

(1) A relatively high and stable rate of growth;

(2) A viable balance of payments;

(3) An equitable distribution of rising incomes;

(4) A high level of employment, defined as a situation with a maximum of 3 percent unemployment;

(5) Reasonable price stability, defined as a maximum of 2 percent per year in the GNP price deflator.[3]

[2] International comparisons of economic growth, using measures such as GNP, do raise numerous statistical difficulties. For a clear discussion of some of these, see S. Kuznets, Six Lectures on Economic Growth, The Free Press of Glencoe, Inc., New York, 1959, especially Lecture 1.

[3] Economic Council of Canada, First Annual Review, Queen's Printer, Ottawa, 1964, pp. 31f. The GNP price deflator divides GNP in current prices to yield GNP in constant prices (prices of a base year).

Looking back on these targets, the Economic Council in 1972 noted that such goals for employment and price stability proved ambitious. Not once during the last fifteen years had the Canadian economy approached both simultaneously; indeed the 1960-70 average unemployment rate was 5.2 percent, and the annual average rate of price increase was 3.2 percent.[4]

Some form of trade-off relationship thus appeared to exist between such macro-economic goals,[5] the regional implications of which are particularly pertinent to inter-governmental economic relations. Thus, for example, the Organization for Economic Co-operation and Development in 1973, drawing on the Canadian experience over the preceding eighteen

Table 2: Trends in Income and Employment,
Each Region Compared to Canada, 1950–1971

Averages for periods shown, Canada = 100

Region	Period	Earned income per head[a]	Unemployment rate
Atlantic	1950–59	63	176
	1960–69	66	167
	1970–71	69	132
Quebec	1950–59	86	131
	1960–69	89	134
	1970–71	88	131
Ontario	1950–59	120	74
	1960–69	119	71
	1970–71	120	77
Prairie	1950–59	99	61
	1960–69	95	63
	1970–71	92	73
British Columbia	1950–59	118	116
	1960–69	110	117
	1970–71	108	119
Canada (actual levels)[b]	1950–59	1,169	4.2
	1960–69	1,177	5.1
	1970–71	2,653	6.2

a Earned income: Personal income *minus* government transfer payments (excluding interest) *minus* interest, dividends, and miscellaneous investment income of persons.
b Dollars in column 3, percentage of labour force in column 4.

Source: O.E.C.D. Economic Surveys, *Canada,* Paris, 1973, p. 15; based on Statistics Canada information.

4 Economic Council of Canada, *Ninth Annual Review,* Queen's Printer, Ottawa, 1972, p. 91.
5 A useful discussion of national trade-off relationships, including a comparison of the Canadian experience with that of twelve other industrial nations, can be found in Daniel B. Suits, *Principles of Economics,* Harper and Row, New York, 1970, in a section on the Phillips curve, pp. 153f.

years, suggested that over the 1972–77 period even a seasonally strong time of activity in Ontario and the Prairies (with unemployment falling below 3 percent in some summer months) would imply an annual average unemployment rate in the Atlantic region of 8.8 percent, and an annual average unemployment rate in Quebec of 7.9 percent.[6]

It is, of course, hardly surprising that, as indicated in Table 2, a country as enormous as Canada has considerable differences between regions in such yardsticks of economic performance as output or earned income *per capita*. Moreover, such has been the case since Confederation.[7] Indeed even today, despite substantial transfer payments, average *per capita* income in Newfoundland is only about half of that in Ontario (to take the extremes).

Such measures of regional disparities, however imperfect they might be when scrutinized in "real-income and wealth" terms and in terms of disguising intra-regional differences, do raise essentially two of the main undercurrents that run through inter-governmental relations in the Canadian (or, to varying degrees, any) federal system:

(a) What is really meant by economic-development and stabilization goals?

(b) What is a "reasonable" distribution policy — whether in terms of population, earned income, or income including transfers from richer to poorer? How far should a process of equalization be pursued?

III. Economic-Development and Stabilization Goals

Recent years have seen increased concern to link stabilization goals with economic growth. Inflation and unemployment are viewed more and more, in the Canadian setting, as needing to be seen in a dynamic context.[8] Increased productivity of labour and a growing labour force imply an additional employment requirement — unless society is very radically to change its orientation and develop a substantially different outlook on work, leisure, and income distribution.

It can be seen, from the data in the previous section, that the provincial governments of Newfoundland, Prince Edward Island, or Quebec, for example, are unlikely to be sympathetic to a federal policy of curbing national demand on the grounds of inflationary pressures (largely stemming from Ontario or regions of the Western provinces) when the unemployment rates in their provinces might be registering 8 percent or more. Moreover, it can also be recognized that (because of the close inter-relationship of the parts of the Canadian economy) in times when inflationary pressures may be severe in Ontario, the federal government will be apprehensive that substantially easier monetary and fiscal policies for the "poorer" regions will spill over into increased demand for goods and services from Ontario.

[6] This is discussed further in O.E.C.D. Economic Surveys, *Canada*, Paris, 1973, pp. 19–21.

[7] For additional statistical documentation, see Alan G. Green, *Regional Aspects of Canada's Economic Growth*, University of Toronto Press, Toronto, 1971.

[8] This is elaborated on by Ian M. Drummond, *The Canadian Economy — Structure and Development*, revised ed., Irwin-Dorsey Ltd., Georgetown, Ont., 1972, especially ch. 3.

For stabilization measures thus to be more uniformly effective, structural changes would appear to be necessary — particularly in the slower-growth parts of the country. These regions tend to contain a more than proportionate share of slower-growth industries and smaller family businesses — while they have the dual manpower problem of finding it hard to retain the younger, better-educated people and, at the same time, they contain a larger than proportionate share, when compared with the wealthier provinces, of unskilled and semi-skilled labour.

Stabilization policies cannot usefully be viewed outside the context of national and international economic growth, and national economic growth cannot be viewed without a consideration of what is really meant by economic development. Clearly there is a qualitative element to the concept; GNP growth rates do not tell the whole story. It is precisely at this point that federal, richer and poorer provincial, and municipal views tend to diverge most fundamentally. Economic development, in the eyes of a municipality, tends to be viewed in terms of employment and municipal tax revenues generating activity within the geographic borders of its own jurisdiction. The concept of economic development to a richer province, such as Ontario, tends to include some cost–benefit weighting of the nature, extent, and future implications of foreign ownership of Ontario-based industry, as well as of the impact of industrialization on the environment. Economic development to a poorer province, such as Nova Scotia or New Brunswick, tends to be viewed almost exclusively in terms of job generation — the environment and foreign ownership being generally regarded as "non-issues." Concepts such as comparative advantage and their expression in some form of national industrial strategy — when viewed from these vantage points — tend to be relegated for use by the more esoteric federal speech writers, to be dutifully read at international conferences.

The federal government, largely because of such regional differences of view, has been far from incisive in articulating national commercial and industrial policies. There has been a reluctance to produce paper plans, when so much depends on other levels of government, on the private sector, and on international forces, if they indeed are to be made to work. As a consequence, such Canadian regional policies as can be said to have an economic-growth orientation have themselves tended to be somewhat obscure as to any over-all national direction. They have tended to be responsive to problems that are generally recognized as acute, for example, the Cape Breton coal situation, rather than new-opportunity oriented, for example, linking government purchasing to the kind of multi-industry complex venture that Saint John, New Brunswick, is attempting to launch. While there are strong signs that the new federal Department of Regional Economic Expansion is attempting to be rather more growth-opportunity oriented,[9] there appears little reason for optimism that its efforts will meet with substantial success — unless the federal government and provinces are prepared to establish, and support politically, a rather

---

[9] This change in attitude by the Department of Regional Economic Expansion was indicated by its Minister in a speech to the Standing Committee on Regional Development of the House of Commons, April 10, 1973.

more comprehensive economic-planning machinery than has appeared to date.

An additional dimension to the situation has been the rapid growth of a relatively few cities. Recent forecasts suggest that Toronto, Montreal, and Vancouver might contain some 45 percent of the Canadian population by the end of this century, that almost 75 percent will be living in 12 major centres, that 94 percent will be living in urban communities. The Atlantic provinces are forecast to account for 6 percent of the Canadian population by the same period; in 1900 they contained 20 percent of the Canadian population.[10] Such forecasts obviously tell nothing about the kind of economic development that is appropriate for Canada over the next few decades, but they do serve to raise questions as to what kind of balance should be sought, and who should be taking the lead. At present the respective levels of government have tended to skirt these longer-term questions; the kinds of economic concerns at the outset of Confederation appear pleasantly clear with the benefit of hindsight, the current economic concerns appear to be disconcertingly out of focus. The over-all economic-growth indicators do not appear unsatisfactory, but a sense of direction in terms of longer-run government economic policy seems far from apparent. The trade-off between economic efficiency and equity, while obviously a fact of life, is not surfacing noticeably in the present inter-governmental dialogue.

IV. Distribution and Equity Goals

Among the recommendations of the Special Joint Committee of the Senate and the House of Commons on the Constitution of Canada (1972), it was stated:

> The equitable distribution of incomes should be recognized in the preamble of the Constitution as a dynamic and humane objective of our social policy . . . the preamble of the Constitution should provide that every Canadian should have access to adequate Federal, Provincial and Municipal services without having to bear a disproportionate tax burden because of the region in which he lives. This recommendation follows logically from our acceptance of the principle of equality of opportunity for all Canadians. . . . We completely accept the following [objective] . . . The promotion of economic development to reduce disparities in the social and economic opportunities for all individuals wherever they may live. . . .[11]

Three elements, for the purpose of this discussion, might be disentangled from this somewhat woolly recommendation.

First, there is the social-justice element. Obviously, any humanitarian

---

[10] For a discussion of such forecasts, see N.H. Lithwick, *Urban Canada, Problems and Prospects*, Queen's Printer, Ottawa, 1970; and J.W. MacNeill, *Environmental Management*, a report prepared for the Privy Council Office, Government of Canada, Ottawa, 1971.
[11] Special Joint Committee of the Senate and the House of Commons on the Constitution of Canada, *First Report*, Queen's Printer, Ottawa, 1972, p. 26.

system of government will accord such concerns high priority and, in practice, the question is one of defining what really is meant by social justice, and what weight is given to such a concept. Two main program strands might be isolated in this regard: programs dealing directly with individuals, and programs involving inter-governmental transfer payments so that lower levels of government can finance enriched programs. In the case of programs to individuals directly, such as family allowances or unemployment insurance, arguments of three general varieties abound. First, there is the question of their influence on the incentive to work of the "able-bodied"; second, there is the issue of their adequacy for those who are unable to take gainful employment; third, there is the question of regional as opposed to federal interpretations of social priorities — and with this question, the problem, if provinces opt out of federal programs, of ill-fitting social-security programs across the country.

Such issues are relevant to the entire social health and welfare fields, both on the expenditure-allocation and tax-arrangement side of the picture. The degree of progressivity of the over-all tax structure, which varies somewhat between provinces, given the mix of local property and sales taxes, etc., is as important an expression of social-justice concerns as the manner in which expenditures are allocated.[12]

In the case of transfers between levels of government, the basic case is well argued in a Working Paper on the Constitution:

> It is . . . true that in the ideal state provincial governments ought to have access to enough tax fields that they themselves can discharge their responsibilities. But in fact the tax-raising potential of Canada's provinces differs very markedly across Canada, because of the differing levels of income and economic activity in the country. One percentage point of personal income tax, for example, yields about $3.14 per capita in Ontario . . . $2.21 in Quebec . . . and 91 cents in Prince Edward Island (1968–69 figures). Similarly one point of corporation income tax yields $3.40 per capita in Ontario, . . . $2.39 in Quebec . . . and $1.00 in Prince Edward Island. It is evident from these figures that federal grants to the lower income provinces are essential if these provinces are to provide adequate levels of public services at levels of taxation which are not too far out of line with those in the higher income provinces.[13]

What, however, is far from evident is how far such an equalizing process should be taken — viewed in terms of the "social-justice" argument. The federal government obviously faces this question when considering its relationship with provincial governments, and provincial governments similarly wrestle with this question when considering their relationships with the municipalities. The extent to which transfers should

---

[12] For a discussion of the tax incidence of the over-all Canadian system, see Allan M. Maslove, *The Pattern of Taxation in Canada*, Economic Council of Canada, Information Canada, Ottawa, 1973.

[13] Working Paper on the Constitution, prepared by the Continuing Committee of Officials as a result of the Constitutional Conference in February 1969, entitled *Federal-Provincial Grants and the Spending Power of Parliament*, Queen's Printer, Ottawa, 1969, p. 30.

be siphoned from the economically more productive areas of the country to the more depressed areas, and the extent to which they should be siphoned from the economically more productive individuals in the community to the economically less productive (granted problems of adequate measurement), is a complex political question, carrying with it obviously a number of fundamental economic implications.

A second element that might be disentangled can be summarized in broad terms as "spill-over."[14] From a national social benefit-cost point of view, it can be argued that costs incurred in one region often spill over benefits into other regions, as well as vice versa. Education is an obvious case in point; for example, if there is a net movement of educated people from, say, Prince Edward Island to Ontario. The same kind of case can be made for transport links that run through regions, for example, the Trans-Canada Highway or the St. Lawrence Seaway. Such kinds of examples obviously merit some form of inter-governmental transfer payments, and hence, both an element of the fiscal-equalization program can be justified on this ground, as well as a variety of the joint-ventures, cost-sharing programs, etc., that the federal government has with the provinces, and the provinces have with municipalities. The main difficulty here, of course, becomes particularly apparent in the case of explicit cost-sharing programs, when the federal government, for example, might have somewhat different views on priorities and objectives from those of a provincial government. Economic considerations will almost inevitably be well-mixed with socio-political ones, and the respective weights are frequently hard to reconcile. For example, in the A.R.D.A.[15] program in some provinces, the federal Department of Agriculture appeared to be primarily concerned with increasing the productivity of labour (with a consequent effect of accelerating the reduction of the employed labour force in some regions), while some provinces (e.g., Manitoba, New Brunswick) were primarily concerned with holding onto and generating more jobs in that sector, for want of apparent alternatives within the borders of their particular provinces. Agreements, consequently, have periodically been signed between levels of government, couched in language of "broad intent," without basic agreement among respective politicians and officials as to the weights between such factors as economic efficiency regionally, and employment support or generation regionally. This obviously has often had serious implications when the implementation of such programs is underway, e.g., the experience of the development plans in the Interlake of Manitoba and the Gaspé of Quebec, in both of which cases the federal and provincial governments lagged far behind agreed rates of expenditure, because of difficulties in coming to grips with concrete projects that were mutually acceptable.

A third element is the issue of whether focus should be on jobs where people presently live, or on encouraging people to move to areas where the marginal social benefits of labour can be higher. To take an extreme case, just because people might be living — and be choosing to live — in a desert, should programs be developed at great public cost in order

14 A systematic treatment of many of these points can be found in Richard A. Musgrave, *Fiscal Systems*, Yale University Press, New Haven, Connecticut, 1969.
15 Agricultural and Rural Development Act, established in 1961.

to bribe industry of some kind to locate there, so that these people can be employed? And if not, what is to be done for their children? While the Canadian federal government and some provincial governments would appear, at times, to have become involved with programs pursuing an implicit policy of "jobs at almost any price in almost any place," in general there has tended to be an uneasy vagueness about what is being attempted in many of the poorer regions of the country. There are obvious reasons for this. For example, there is the political reaction to consider when spokesmen for one level of government suggest that the economic prospects of any area are bleak. Then there is the problem of being sure of one's facts: how poor, for example, are the economic prospects really for the northeast of New Brunswick or the coast of Labrador? The world is full of examples of areas where a determined people have generated viable development out of apparently poor areas. It is far more full, of course, of examples of poor areas that have stayed poor! Moreover, there is the strong distaste apparent for any talk of "planned migration," and recollections of earlier Soviet programs come quickly to the fore; thus manpower-mobility policies have tended to be somewhat soft-peddled, particularly when they involve crossing provincial borders. Added to this, there is considerable unease as to whether the urban Canada that is so rapidly transforming the country is necessarily providing a richer way of life than that to be had in many of the poorer regions. The outcome of an amalgam of such reasons has tended, therefore, to be a mix of *ad hoc* programs — federal, provincial, and municipal — that attempt "to be all things for all men."

V. Increasing and Changing the Role of Government

Total government spending in Canada, at all levels and for all purposes, amounted to some 35 percent of GNP in 1970; in 1950 it had amounted to some 23 percent, in 1960 to some 30 percent. The increasing relative importance of the public sector is apparent in most industrial countries over the 1960s in terms of expenditures, as well as in the less-easily-assessed regulatory and other non-expenditure roles of government.[16] Economic Council forecasts suggest that by 1980 "close to 40 per cent of the nation's total income and output would be passing through the government sector" — either in terms of direct expenditures on goods and services, or as a redistribution of income."[17] A number of functions have increasingly been transferred from the private to the public domain, health services being a major example. Since the Second-World-War years, the federal government has been accounting for proportionately smaller percentages of government expenditures, whereas provincial governments (and, to a lesser degree, municipal governments) have been accounting for an increasing share.

As the government role has grown in size, so it has increased in complexity, so the over-lapping between the various levels of government has

[16] For further discussion of the growth and distribution of government spending in Canada, see Economic Council of Canada, *Eighth Annual Review,* Queen's Printer, Ottawa, 1971, p. 10.

[17] Economic Council of Canada, *Ninth Annual Review,* Queen's Printer, Ottawa, 1972, p. 47.

become substantially greater. We seem, in fact, to have strayed a long way from K.C. Wheare's traditional definition of federalism: "By the federal principle I mean the method of dividing powers so that the general and regional governments are each, within a sphere, coordinate and independent."[18]

Increased over-lapping of government functions, while it can lead to closer inter-governmental co-ordination that spills over into areas where the jurisdictional responsibility is relatively clear-cut, can also lead to a great deal of friction. While in any system the competence and motivation of the people involved is of critical importance, good working relations "cannot stand as an answer alone and without a basis of constitutional support."[19]

The breakdown in the federal–provincial discussions on constitutional reform and the drastic modifications of the Carter Commission proposals on tax reform serve as reminders of the difficulty in the Canadian system of government of designing any systematic package of changes, and therefore of the reason that so much of the government operation as a whole, when closely inspected, appears piecemeal and *ad hoc*. To some extent, consolation can be sought in the view that an *"ad hoc"* approach implies government responsiveness to change, and to local and individual points of view. But this obviously has to be balanced by a concern that the government machine, growing larger and less clear as to over-all direction by the year, could become ponderously a greater threat to the individual social concerns than the very shortcomings of the market system which it is government's partial role to compensate for.

Phrased another way, the question is whether the Canadian federal system of government has reached already a point where substantial dismantling might be in order — and that far greater emphasis might be placed on closer and more systematic planning with, and delegation to, the private sector. At least, the Economic Council's forecasts that the public sector is likely to account for an increasing proportion of GNP should not merely be accepted as if this is an automatic and necessarily desirable process.

Moreover, the federal and provincial governments, in particular, do need to develop a clearer public understanding of the regional economic frameworks as they view them, so that a greater awareness of the implications of projects and programs can be generated both inside and outside government. A clearer public understanding and agreement, for example, of the costs and benefits of greater population concentration in a very few cities across the country does appear to be needed, if indeed policies are to emerge deliberately to reinforce or counteract such an apparent trend. Without such a perspective, often narrowly conceived regional interests could easily serve to balkanize Canada further, rather than to contribute in a reasonably harmonious manner to ensure that the whole really is larger than the sum of the parts.

[18] K.C. Wheare, *Federal Government*, 4th ed., Oxford University Press, London, 1963, p. 10.
[19] R.M. Burns, *Report on Intergovernmental Liaison on Fiscal and Economic Matters* (prepared for the Minister of Finance as a background paper), Queen's Printer, Ottawa, 1969, p. 11.

2. The Political Economy of Québec Libre

Antal Deutsch *

McGill University

For some years now there has been in existence a political party which in its platform advocates the conversion of Quebec Province to a sovereign state. That term, in itself, is not free of ambiguity: the United States of America, the People's Republic of Outer Mongolia, and Texas each regard themselves, though not necessarily each other, as sovereign. To complicate matters, it is not entirely clear that all those within the separatist camp favour the same ends; nor is it self-evident that such sentiment is confined to the group marching behind the separatist banner, or to residents of Quebec. There is no generally accepted scenario to describe how Quebec or any other province could cease to be a part of Canada, or what would happen to the rest. Consequently, on these very basic grounds alone, it is impossible to translate this uncertain picture of what many continue to regard as a remote possibility into a unique list of probable economic consequences. What remains as a reasonable approach is to postulate some circumstances and to apply these to the pattern of existing economic interrelationships among the various parts of Canada.[1] This essay concludes that little can be said with much authority about what would happen to income and wealth if a part of Canada were to secede. The intent here is to challenge those who make claims to the contrary.

The main lines of inquiry pursued here concern trade, the distribution

* This article was written when the author was, with the support of the Canada Council, Honorary Research Fellow at Harvard University. Written comments on a previous draft of this paper by Glenn P. Jenkins are gratefully acknowledged.

[1] I first discussed the economics of separation in an essay entitled "Quebec Libre and the Economics of Disintegration", *Journal of Canadian Studies*, February 1968, pp. 29–34; reprinted in Norman Sheffe, ed., *Canadian/Canadien*, McGraw-Hill Ryerson, Toronto, 1971, pp. 87–94. This essay draws freely on that earlier work.

of the burden of taxes, and the benefits from government expenditures and the flow of private investment. To simplify matters, I shall initially assume that the now prevailing patterns of internal migration will not change substantially no matter what, and that there will be no civil war involving major destruction. I also assume, for the moment, that if secession should take place, the remaining parts of Canada shall constitute one country, to be referred to as rump-Canada. In the final section of this paper, I discuss alternative possibilities.[2]

I. Trade

The framework of this section is provided by what economists call the theory of economic integration: to analyze disintegration, some things have to be reversed.[3] To make that theory work in this instance, we have to assume no more than the general tendency of rational persons to buy a given good from the seller who offers it at the lowest price. The mechanics of the theory are generally valid, whether the break-away province is called British Columbia or Newfoundland. In the following paragraphs we shall call it Quebec.

In line with our assumption about lowest-cost suppliers, in Confederation residents of Quebec buy some goods from their home province, others from producers elsewhere in Canada, and still others from exporters abroad. Some of the goods bought within Canada would not be competitive if the Canadian tariff barrier did not keep out potentially cheaper foreign suppliers. Where tariff "protection" diverts Quebec consumer dollars to Quebec producers, the consumers lose and some producers gain higher profits, some workers gain higher wages and possibly employment opportunities, on account of the "extra" added to both the Canadian and to the foreign price by the tariff. But by no means all tariff-diverted purchases go to producers who happen to reside in the province where the buyer lives. In Confederation, Quebec consumers lose to producers in Ontario and Alberta, and vice versa. (Economic literature does show that the losses by consumers through the tariff are greater than the gains realized by the producers, but that is not the issue here.) Transfers through the tariff criss-cross Canada, but our statistics do not really tell us who gains and loses how much, chiefly because we do not know how much the "extra" is, and who really gets it. It must be remembered that this transfer is the consequence of a unified Canadian tariff structure.

Hauling down one flag and raising another in any part of Canada would do nothing to alter the distribution of trade or of tariff transfers. If Quebec separates but continues all the existing trade and tariff arrangements, it and rump-Canada will form what is known as a customs union.

[2] The economic implications of separation are also explored by André Raynauld, "Economic Analysis of Separatism," in Canadian Perspectives in Economics, Collier—Macmillan, Toronto, 1972. In addition, numerous pamphlets have been written in support of causes related to the future of Quebec. The current crop should be available, typically in French only, from the offices of the political parties operating on the provincial level in Quebec.

[3] Readers interested in a full exposition of the theory of economic integration might consult Bela Balassa, "The Theory of Economic Integration," Irwin, Homewood, Illinois, 1961.

(A customs union is an arrangement between two or more trading partners with mutual free access to each other's markets behind a common wall of tariffs shielding these markets from non-partner competition.) But this is only one of the possible trade arrangements open to the two successor states, and there is no reason to assume that both would fail to engage in a full exploration of all alternatives: this is one element of economic sovereignty.

The political climate of separation might possibly result in bitterness sufficient to make any rational attempt at co-operation difficult. Once more, let me assume, however, that rationality would prevail. An objective examination of the alternatives may lead the government of each successor state to one of the following conclusions:

1. Both partners potentially benefit most by continuing in the customs union.
2. One partner is better off within the customs union, the other is not.
3. Both partners are worse off within the customs union than with some other alternative.
4. The continuation of the customs union is of little importance to either partner.

Suppose, for the moment, that both parties find themselves in agreement that they both potentially benefit by the continuation of the customs union. Their next step is to agree on the size of the potential gains to each; the difficulties involved in producing and agreeing on these numbers should not be underestimated. Once that has been settled, negotiations must take place to decide whether the potential gains agreed upon should be divided as they may naturally fall, or in some other way. On this last question, textbooks of economics have no guidance to offer. Whether the customs union survives depends on the willingness of the two parties to compromise in the face of conflicting internal pressures in both cases.

Assume now that the two parties agree on outcome 2; there is a potential gainer and a potential loser, and there is agreement on the amounts involved. Clearly, the potential loser will continue with the customs-union arrangement only if the potential gainer can and will offer sufficient compensation. The potential gainer, in turn, is unlikely to surrender all that it could gain.

If the two parties agree on result 3, nothing can save the customs union; if they agree on 4, non-trade factors are likely to determine the outcome.

In all cases treated so far, I assumed that the experts advising the governments of the two successor states are able to agree on a set of facts regarding the potential consequences of continuing with the customs union. Should there be disagreement, an explicit undertaking on future policy becomes difficult.

Suppose now that the two parties explore the alternatives to maintaining their customs union; the following are likely to emerge as the major options:

1. the establishment of a free-trade area between Quebec and rump-Canada

2. the creation of two independent trading units
3. the association of either party (or both parties) with another country or trading group in some form of economic integration

Let me now turn to a brief discussion of each option. Option 1 involves an arrangement whereby goods produced either in rump-Canada or Quebec have duty-free access to both markets, but goods originating outside the area are subject to tariff rates which need not be equal in Quebec and rump-Canada. In principle, such an arrangement permits one partner to transfer some income to selected industries within its particular territory, via the tariff, beyond the level provided in the partner country. The drawback of the arrangement is the consequent disparity in the prices of the affected goods, the natural attempts to deflect trade to flow into the area through the lower tariff barrier, and the cost of the elaborate policing required to meet this problem. Under this arrangement, the appearance of customs posts on the border between rump-Canada and Quebec becomes inevitable. Once more there would be a pattern of income transfers through the tariff between the trading partners. Again, I cannot tell what that pattern would be in the absence of the relevant numbers.

One of the difficulties with the free-trade-area solution is that each partner has to accept unrestricted competition from the other. For example, Quebec might wish to expand its refrigerator output, but this objective might be frustrated by the inflow of relatively low-priced fridges from Ontario. No tariffs or quotas on partner goods are usually acceptable within a free-trade area. The remaining instrument to promote the goal of more made-in-Quebec refrigerators would be the granting of subsidies to the industry. That might also be considered a trade violation, and even if not, the money would have to be appropriated in public session as part of the government's budget. (Politicians seem to have a preference for using less direct, less scrutable methods for transferring income to private hands. This is the reason tariffs have generally not been replaced by subsidies even though economists have long argued that such a step would be highly desirable.) Similarly, allowing industries in rump-Canada, or anywhere else, unfettered access to Quebec markets would place serious constraints on the growth of those Quebec industries which cannot be developed on the basis of market needs, but might be desired for prestige or as providers of privileged employment opportunities. If either partner perceives this to be too high a price to pay, the free-trade-area solution may prove unworkable.

As yet another alternative, both Quebec and rump-Canada might become independent trading units, with their own tariff walls facing the rest of the world, including their former partners. This would involve a radical change in the present trade streams, and would completely eliminate income transfers via the tariff between Quebec and rump-Canada. Quebec goods would sell in rump-Canada only if they could compete in quality and price with all other exporters around the globe, and rump-Canadian output would have to compete with the rest of the world for sales in Quebec. Further, each former partner would have to meet the terms of the home industry protected behind a new tariff wall in the other trading unit. The initial impact would probably be a loss of markets. For example, Quebec consumers would soon discover that it would be cheaper to buy TV sets from Japan than from Ontario if both sets were subject to the same rate of duty. As the next step, I would expect to see attempts to regain lost markets: rationalization, belt-tightening, real-wage cuts, and devaluation. To the extent that such measures would prove unsuccessful, the resources formerly used to cater to partner markets would become unemployed.

At this point, both rump-Canada and Quebec would be tempted to re-direct their unemployed resources by raising tariffs to displace imports with new domestic production. Such a policy might work to soak up some of the unemployment, but only at the cost of a permanent increase in consumer prices and a consequent lowering of the standard of living. If import displacement is at least partially successful, the former suppliers lose business; this in turn leads to more unemployment in the economy of the former partner and elsewhere. With this scenario, increasing protection results in a lower volume of trade, higher prices, and lower living standards.

Now let us turn this picture around by visualizing a situation where both former partners establish separate tariff walls but use their newly gained sovereignty to lower barriers to trade. The initial steps may be easy, as each former partner drops those inherited tariffs which protected special interests no longer included within its territorial limits.

(For an illustration, assume that the bulk of the rubber-footwear industry in Canada is located in Quebec. After separation, rump-Canada could, at little cost to itself, drop the tariff protecting that industry. As a result, Torontonians would be able to slosh through the snow in rubber boots sold at Hong Kong prices plus transport costs, even if the actual footwear was manufactured in Montreal. Note that the Montreal supplier has to meet the Hong Kong price no matter what the level of rump-Canada's uniform tariff, but the Toronto consumer receives the full benefit only if that tariff rate is zero. If the tariff is more than zero, there is a danger of new, inefficient capacity springing up in rump-Canada. That, in turn, would place obstacles in the way of rump-Canadian consumer benefits through lower prices.)

Let us return to considering the possibility of each trading unit separately moving in the direction of no tariffs and quantitative restrictions, otherwise known as free trade. This is the situation permitting the maximum benefits from the international division of labour through the lowest possible consumer prices. Note that free trade provides the highest level of real income to a country *even if other countries continue to levy tariffs*, because benefits accrue through being able to buy at the lowest cost. (In the economists' never-never land there exists one still higher level of bliss, where a tariff is imposed to be borne by foreigners. The proposition has little practical relevance to small countries such as Canada.)

Two problems arise in connection with free trade. The first one is transitional: firms producing output formerly sheltered by a tariff, along with their employees and suppliers, will have to absorb either a reduction of earnings or a loss of employment and sales. To deal with this in a free-trade context, the government may be expected to use some of the gains accruing to society as a whole from the abolition of tariffs to support where necessary the transfer of resources to other uses. The second problem, not nearly as weighty as the first, involves the loss of tariffs as an instrument of industrial development. Whether or not either successor state could take advantage of the potential benefits of free trade hinges on its ability to cope internally with both of these problems. That, in turn, depends on the stability of the surviving political institutions to resist "solutions" proffered by extremists and demagogues.

One more class of alternative trade arrangements merits attention. Either Quebec, or rump-Canada, or both, could enter some form of economic integration with some existing trading unit, such as the United States or the European Economic Community (E.E.C.). A sine qua non of such an arrangement would be the perceptible existence of a potential gain for the major partner, as well as for each of the Canadian successor states.

A study by Wonnacott and Wonnacott,[4] based on 1961 information, concludes that the disappearance of tariffs between the United States and Canada would add about ten percent to the Canadian gross national product. The potential gain to the United States is much less. (These gains would not accrue evenly to all. Some portion would have to be appropriated in the transitional period to compensate those who lose out through the free-trade arrangements.) Wonnacott and Wonnacott do not tell us what would happen if only part of what is now Canada would join in some form of integration with the United States. But it is clear from their work that manufacturing wages were generally higher in the United States, and in Ontario, than in Quebec. Interregional wage differentials tend to be eroded by the movement of industry to low-wage areas and by the migration of labour in the direction of higher potential earnings. To what advantage could Quebec turn its relatively low wages? How long would the advantage last? Is it really an advantage that could or should last?

I have not been able to find any serious study of the potential consequences of trade integration either between Canada and the European Economic Community, or between any part of Canada and the E.E.C. About all that can be said here with certainty is that either combination is bound to lead to a major realignment of present trade patterns. I know of no public expression of interest by the Europeans for any form of integration with Canada or parts thereof. There is little that can be said now of the outcome of such an unlikely union in terms of the welfare of the participants.

II.   Investment

Investment is defined, for purposes of this discussion, as the addition to the stock of productive resources of society. In being able to generate, with the co-operation of other inputs such as labour, land, and entrepreneurship, successful investment today, society enables itself to enjoy higher real income tomorrow. Investment is financed by the savings of residents

---

[4] Ronald J. Wonnacott and Paul Wonnacott, *Free Trade Between the United States and Canada,* Harvard University Press, Cambridge, Mass., 1967.

and non-residents; if it is the latter, we speak of foreign investment. If the savings are marshalled through the government sector, the resulting addition to resources is referred to as public investment.

The act of investment creates employment, and simultaneously gives rise to property rights in the newly created resources. The possibility of a political breakdown of Confederation is thought to affect the volume of investment, and through it the current rate of economic activity. If we assume that private investment is undertaken in the expectation of returns no lower than obtainable elsewhere at comparable risk, and that for investment in manufacturing businessmen prefer to build plants of the optimum size consistent with the size of the market to be served, we can easily see how uncertainty may prove to be discouraging. In the preceding section of this paper, the reader was asked to consider the prospects of free-trade areas ranging in market size from Quebec to North America. If businessmen perceive the same range of prospects, with uncertain probabilities attached to each, the risk as seen by the investor increases, and the volume of investment will fall below what it would otherwise be. For it can hardly be a matter of indifference for a manufacturer looking at the prospects of locating a plant in Quebec whether the plant is to be designed to serve a market of 6 million persons (Quebec), 22 million (Canada), or 240 million (the United States plus Canada). The comparable numbers for a businessman looking at a location elsewhere in Canada are 16 million, 22 million, or 240 million.

Note that the increased risk is applicable to investors both in Quebec and in rump-Canada: if the prospect of secession is treated as a significant one by businessmen, investment should be lower than otherwise in all of Canada. There may be a difference in impact between Quebec on the one hand and the English-speaking provinces on the other. Industries where the minimum efficient plant size is small enough to cater to the Quebec market alone should be least affected. Where the minimum efficient size is too large for Quebec alone, but small enough for a market of rump-Canada's size, we should expect to observe continued investment in the English-speaking provinces. For those industries whose optimum scale requires a market larger than rump-Canada, we should expect to see a decline in new investment in all of Canada. These statements should hold unless (a) the prospect of secession is not taken very seriously, and/or (b) less-than-optimal-scale plants are built, in the anticipation of continued tariff protection, and/or (c) government subsidies and tax concessions are made available in sufficient volume to mitigate the effects of the disintegration risks. If (c) is the case, the cost to Canadians is obvious and has been, albeit from a different viewpoint, widely discussed. The cost of the permanent consequences of less-than-efficient-scale plant construction has somehow not received the same popular attention.[5]

---

[5] Government subsidies to corporations (the so-called "corporate rip-off" enjoyed by "corporate welfare bums") have been a Canadian election issue in the 1970s and thus are much in the public consciousness. In comparison, the inefficiencies associated with small-scale plant size in Canada are not well known to Canadians, although this topic has been discussed in the economic literature. See, for example, Stefan Stykolt, *Efficiency in the Open Economy*, Oxford University Press, Toronto, 1969.

Separatists have been heard to argue that if continued uncertainty imposes costs on the Canadian community, we could minimize that cost by breaking up the country now. There are two obviously weak points associated with this argument. First, it ignores the wishes of the electorate: to date, in all elections in which it has been an issue, separatism has been rejected by more than two-thirds of the Quebec voters. Second, the argument assumes that the declaration of an independent Quebec would end uncertainty now. Not only can we point to recent experience in Africa where attempts at secession (Katanga, Biafra) ended in failure, but also to reasonable evidence that the survival of the United States was viewed as doubtful by many for a long period after the Declaration of Independence. It is reasonable to argue that even if an independent Quebec did come about, it might take a long time before people believed that it is here to stay. If the separatists are genuinely concerned with their effect on investors, they might improve matters by ceasing to talk about separation, right now.

Over and above the trade risks concerning prospective tariff walls, businessmen may perceive risks through political instability, discrimination, excessive taxation, and threats to property rights. Some years ago, shrill voices threatening such things were audible in Quebec but rarely elsewhere in Canada. The early seventies brought about a change. While in Quebec the extremists have apparently been contained, their type of rhetoric can now be heard in all major urban areas across Canada. The limited electoral prospects of extremists in Canada imply that investment should not be impaired significantly.

III.   Tax and Expenditure Transfers

The government of Canada collects taxes in all parts of Canada and spends them from coast to coast. If the geographic point of collection could be regarded as the place where the burden of the tax rests with local residents, and if the location of the disbursement would also be the point where benefits are received, tracing the transfer of benefits between the various parts of Canada would be a simple matter. Unfortunately, it is not.

Governments tax legal entities on the basis of legally defined transactions or property. A corporation resident in Montreal pays tax on profits earned anywhere and everywhere, between Vancouver and Halifax. The casual reader of tax statistics may think that a separate Quebec may be able to collect the same amount of money — but this is wrong. If rump-Canada becomes a separate legal entity, it will most likely insist on a legal head office there for corporations operating within its territory. The ultimate consequence for the Quebec tax collector would be a shrinkage of the base on which to levy taxes. Here again we encounter an offsetting factor; corporations now doing business in Quebec with head offices elsewhere would have to separate their bookkeeping to show profits earned in Quebec. On the basis of existing statistics, there is no way to tell who would benefit.[6]

(Another question is of interest to the economist, though not to the tax collector. Who bears the final burden of the tax levied on corporate profits? Is it the shareholder? Is it the consumer who pays it through higher prices? Is it the worker who receives lower wages? The answer may be very important whenever one or more of these groups reside outside the tax jurisdiction.)

Roughly the same discussion may be duplicated with respect to federal manufacturers sales taxes, excise taxes, and customs revenues. The one major tax source where it seems reasonable to pinpoint the geographic location of the burden is the personal income tax. (To the extent that the personal income tax reflects collections from unincorporated businesses, the same considerations as to corporations may apply. Even where income from employment is taxed, it is possible to argue that where people can move between jurisdictions it is not necessarily the person designated by the law who bears the burden of the income tax.) The problem is that the distribution of income underlying the tax calculations is heavily influenced by the pattern of industrial and trade activity. If secession changes the trade flows, the past pattern of income-tax collections becomes an uncertain guide to the future.

The preceding paragraphs sketch the reasons for the inapplicability of the current tax statistics to the revenue picture of the successor states. The next, very important, point to make is that the expenditure side of the federal-government accounts also fails to lend itself to easy regional disaggregation.

How much do residents of Quebec benefit through federal spending? In arriving at the answer, a dangerous pitfall must be avoided. The layman is tempted to say that by counting the number of dollars Ottawa spends in Quebec, we also obtain the sum Ottawa spends on Quebec. This, of course, is wrong.

The federal government pays certain sums to the provincial government in Quebec. This is spent in Quebec for the presumed benefit of residents of that province. Similarly, there are transfer payments paid to some residents of La Belle Province, and presumably these payments are enjoyed chiefly by the recipients. Only these two elements of federal fiscal activity lend themselves to ready assignment.

Much of the federal-government expenditure is undertaken to purchase goods and services. These are then transformed into benefits radiating across the country. Defence expenditure is the obvious example. A soldier hired and perhaps stationed in New Brunswick contributes to the defence of the entire country by being available to be shipped anywhere.

---

[6] It is worth noting that a separate Quebec would find itself with surprisingly little freedom to set its tax rates. Because of close links among firms in Quebec, rump-Canada, and the United States, profits as well as industrial activity would be subject to sufficient mobility to make rates that are *too high* in relation to those of the neighbours costly in terms of tax yield. Because, under the international tax agreements on the pattern of the present Canada–U.S. Tax Treaty, those engaged in investment abroad pay, effectively, the higher tax rate as between the two countries, setting rates *too low* does not attract foreign investment, but merely transfers taxes to treasuries abroad.

A federal Department of Health official engaged in checking arriving passengers at Toronto International Airport for signs of disease protects not only Ontario but all of Canada (perhaps all of North America?) from epidemics. The common characteristic of this type of expenditure is the practical geographic indivisibility of the benefits.

(Quebec's share could conceivably be measured by asking what would be the reduction in defence and public-health expenditure requirements by Ottawa in case of Quebec's secession. But there is no evidence that these requirements would necessarily be reduced, because these are "public goods.")

Economic analysis does not provide us with useful tools to attribute to Quebec an over-all contribution to or benefit from federal finances. Any politician who appears with a set of figures is suspect.

IV. The Political Economy of Nationalism

Professor Albert Breton, in an article that is now a classic,[7] concluded that nationalism in the economic sphere tends to concentrate energies on discouraging "foreign" investors so as to increase the returns to "national" owners of capital, and to rearrange the distribution of personal income by creating prestige jobs for the elect. In the process, income is redistributed from the broad group of taxpayers, including working-class persons, to members of the indigenous middle-class and elite. For this process to take place, there is no need for the over-all income of the community to grow.

An illustration of nationalist sentiment in the Breton spirit is provided in a summary of the "Main Recommendations of the Gendron Commission."[8]

(4) Steps should be taken, over the next 10 years, to give French Quebecers greater access to middle and upper management positions in private enterprise. The report urges the following increases over 10 years in the proportion of Francophones at various income levels: in the $10,000 to $15,000 category, there should be a 10 per cent increase; in the $15,000 to $20,000 bracket, 20 per cent; and in the $20,000 and over group, 10 per cent . . .[9]

The government of Canada seeks to meet some aspects of Francophone nationalist sentiment by broadening the use of the French language in the English-speaking areas of the country and in parts of the federal civil service. Because bilingualism has now become an important criterion for success in the civil service, and because many bilingual persons in Canada happen to be French-Canadian, the effect is a greater degree of participation by French-speaking Canadians in the senior ranks. This has not gone unobserved by the other civil servants.

Implicit in Ottawa's policy is an effort to make French-Canadians more mobile across Canada. This policy could be greatly aided if the

[7] Albert Breton, "The Economics of Nationalism", *Journal of Political Economy*, August 1964, pp. 376–386.
[8] The Gendron Commission was appointed by a Union Nationale government and reported to a Liberal one on linguistic problems in Quebec.
[9] *The Gazette*, Montreal, February 14, 1973, p. 1.

provincial governments could be persuaded to add enough to school resources to give Canadians sufficient knowledge of both official languages
to get by from coast to coast. The reader will have noted that the policy
of the federal government, and nationalist aspirations as stipulated by
Breton, are not fully congruent. The difference lies not in the analysis, but
in the underlying definition of what constitutes the relevant community.
Ottawa seeks to find an outlet for nationalist sentiments by promoting
Canadianization of the economy through restricting investment from
abroad and by encouraging certain types of posts to be occupied by citizens of Canada, with the understanding that French-Canadians will collect
a proportion of the spoils. By contrast, Quebec separatists would reject
this view and argue that what matters to them is the transfer of economic
leadership and benefits to persons who speak French in the Francophone
environment of Quebec. The only useful test of what definition of the
community is to prevail must lie with the electorate.

V. Concluding Comments

I do not propose a "Save Canada" plan. If Ottawa's objective is to
keep Quebec in Confederation, the obvious (economic) policy involves
putting as high a price tag on separation as possible. The obverse of this
position is to make continued participation in Confederation profitable.

The first thing is to spread information dealing with some false issues.
For example, consider the question of the national debt. It should be
impressed upon Canadians that this country's debt is generally internally
held. A repudiation of the debt will merely confiscate the wealth of
Canadian bond-holders in favour of Canadian taxpayers. If an independent
Quebec were to refuse contributions to the jointly incurred federal debt,
in retaliation rump-Canada might cancel the direct and indirect bond-
holdings of Quebec residents. Quebecers might well lose on balance. As
a side issue, probably both Quebec and rump-Canada would find it rather
difficult to borrow thereafter.

Another false issue to be dismissed from the discussion is the dream
of maintaining a joint central bank between Quebec and rump-Canada.
One of the persistent regional complaints in Canada is the need for
easier money in the depressed Maritimes and eastern Quebec. A central
bank receiving conflicting orders from its two sovereign masters cannot
operate for long. Monetary separation would be an inevitable consequence
of Quebec's secession. Whether the costs of the probable loss of monetary
stability would be compensated for by the gains from the increased flexibility of monetary policy, I cannot say. I do not believe that anyone can.[10]

---

[10] There is little doubt that with fixed rates of exchange both Quebec and rump-
Canada would find their respective monetary policies captured by the need to
equilibrate the balance of payments; therefore the central banks would be of
little use in dealing with domestic employment and price-level problems. Even if
exchange rates are floating, there exist dangers of imported inflation and unemployment. On these matters, see Richard E. Caves, *Looking at Inflation in the
Open Economy*, Discussion Paper 286, Harvard Institute of Economic Research,
Cambridge, Mass., March 1973. It should be noted that the problems arising from
open economies in the successor states would differ only in degree, but not in
kind, from the quandries facing a united Canada.

Many of the real issues follow from the preceding discussion of trade flows, investment, and fiscal transfers. As I point out in the section on trade flows, an independent Quebec could probably push its real-income level above the present one by following free-trade policies. An alert federal government could cut tariffs unilaterally to approximate Quebec's potential gains from free trade now. Such action would not only reduce Quebec's pay-off from independence but also fight inflation.

On the fiscal front, Ottawa can buy favour only with dollars. How much of this is necessary depends on how much is done to lower consumer prices, to keep full employment, and to restore the confidence of private investors.

This essay is intended to show that forecasts of the economic consequences of Canada's disintegration are based on a great deal of guesswork, and cannot be taken seriously enough for policy formulation. The discussion has assumed (a) no substantial departure from normal internal migration patterns in what is now Canada, (b) no civil war involving major destruction, and (c) that the nine English-speaking provinces would form a single country. It is appropriate now to speculate on the possibilities excluded above.

An announcement of sovereignty in Quebec might trigger an exodus. Not only part of the non-Francophone minority of a million might leave, but also those mobile French-speaking Canadians who do not trust the politicians who happen to be in charge. Whether the mass departures take place under mutually organized government auspices, like that of the non-Moslems from Algeria, or by unilaterally imposed expulsion, like that of the Asians from Uganda, the result is not only human tragedy but also the loss of human and physical capital. That can be prevented in the case of secession only if the successor government inspires the confidence of the minority by meaningful guarantees and by a demonstrated ability to stand by these in the face of strong internal pressures. This holds, of course, with respect to the Francophone minority in the English-speaking provinces as well as for the Anglophones in Quebec.

The most awkward assumption in this essay is the continued existence of a unitary state consisting of two sets of English-speaking provinces, separated by a sovereign Quebec. If nothing else, the prevailing climate of the acceptability of realignments should bring about a surfacing of regional demands for stronger North–South links, at least in the field of trade. These would be particularly strong in the West and in the Atlantic provinces. Washington would welcome closer access to secure energy and other resource supplies. If every Canadian province is placed in a position where it can elect its economic and political affiliation in an atmosphere of disintegration, one might speculate on which units will follow Alberta and British Columbia into the American orbit, and at what speed: it seems reasonable to expect that no English-speaking province could hold out. If that should happen, Quebec's choices would be severely circumscribed. There would be an element of tragic irony in the submersion of French Canada into an insignificant minority in a unified English-speaking North America as the outcome of a flight from an almost equal partnership in a potentially almost bilingual Canada.